ISSUES FOR DEBATE IN
AMERICAN PUBLIC POLICY

SAGE was founded in 1965 by Sara Miller McCune to support the dissemination of usable knowledge by publishing innovative and high-quality research and teaching content. Today, we publish more than 750 journals, including those of more than 300 learned societies, more than 800 new books per year, and a growing range of library products including archives, data, case studies, reports, conference highlights, and video. SAGE remains majority-owned by our founder, and after Sara's lifetime will become owned by a charitable trust that secures our continued independence.

Los Angeles | London | Washington DC | New Delhi | Singapore | Boston

ISSUES FOR DEBATE IN AMERICAN PUBLIC POLICY

SELECTIONS FROM CQ RESEARCHER

16TH EDITION

$SAGE | CQPRESS

Los Angeles | London | New Delhi
Singapore | Washington DC | Boston

Los Angeles | London | New Delhi
Singapore | Washington DC | Boston

FOR INFORMATION:

CQ Press

An Imprint of SAGE Publications, Inc.

2455 Teller Road

Thousand Oaks, California 91320

E-mail: order@sagepub.com

SAGE Publications Ltd.

1 Oliver's Yard

55 City Road

London EC1Y 1SP

United Kingdom

SAGE Publications India Pvt. Ltd.

B 1/I 1 Mohan Cooperative Industrial Area

Mathura Road, New Delhi 110 044

India

SAGE Publications Asia-Pacific Pte. Ltd.

3 Church Street

#10-04 Samsung Hub

Singapore 049483

Printed in the United States of America

ISBN: 978-1-4833-8396-5

Library of Congress Control Number: 2015935708

Acquisitions Editor: Sarah Calabi

Senior Development Editor: Nancy Matuszak

Editorial Assistant: Katie Lowry

Production Editor: Kelly DeRosa

Typesetter: C&M Digitals (P) Ltd.

Cover Designer: Candice Harman

Marketing Manager: Amy Whitaker

15 16 17 18 19 10 9 8 7 6 5 4 3 2 1

Contents

Annotated Contents

ENVIRONMENT

Food Policy Debates

Inspired by a movement that touts healthy eating and warns of danger from an industrialized food supply, millions of Americans are cutting back on processed and fast foods and sugary soda. Many are turning to fresh, lean and "clean" foods out of fear that sugar, salt, fat and additives can lead to heart disease, obesity, diabetes and other problems. Other Americans, however, continue to eat unhealthily, contributing to record levels of diet-related illnesses and rising health care costs. Healthy-eating activists want the government to tax sugary sodas, mandate expanded nutrition labels and restrict portion sizes. The food industry is fighting such proposals, contending that changing the nation's eating habits lies more with the free market than with legislation. Meanwhile, nutritionists and medical professionals are debating the value of gluten-free diets, with proponents claiming that wheat products lead to a wide range of illnesses and critics arguing that the diets lack scientific merit.

Regulating Toxic Chemicals

After a leak from a chemical storage tank contaminated the Charleston, W. Va., water supply in 2014, many experts contended that U.S. chemical plants and refineries need stricter regulation. But industry representatives assert that chemical companies have an excellent safety record and that government should focus on helping all companies comply with existing regulations. The West Virginia incident revealed lax state enforcement of federal laws designed to protect the nation's waterways from chemical contamination. Current law assumes that the thousands of chemicals widely used in commerce are safe unless the government shows otherwise. The approach puts the burden of proof on regulators, who have banned only five toxic chemicals in nearly 40 years. Health and environmental advocates want a more precautionary approach, similar to Europe's policy, in which manufacturers must show that chemicals introduced to the market can be used safely. Meanwhile, scientists are finding new evidence that some potentially harmful industrial chemicals are more widespread throughout the environment than previously thought.

BUSINESS AND ECONOMY

Future of Cars

Cars that drive themselves, long a staple of science fiction, could be in auto showrooms in the next few years. Automakers and researchers around the world are testing and refining technologies that allow a car to know where it is going and to communicate with other vehicles. Special sensors and software make the breakthroughs possible. Already, cars are selling with automated features designed to keep them in the correct lane, brake to avoid collisions and park themselves. Technology giant Google, which has tested vehicles with self-driving features on a half-million miles of roads, recently demonstrated a car with no steering wheel, accelerator or brake pedal. It remains unclear, however, how safe super-smart cars would be, how they would affect traffic congestion, how consumers and the nation would pay for the cars and the supporting infrastructure they would need and whether Americans will accept such a radical change in their relationship with automobiles. Google's driverless electric car has no steering wheel, accelerator or brake pedal and reaches a top speed of 25 mph. Although the prototype, unveiled on May 27, 2014, is far from ready for consumers, self-driving cars could begin appearing in auto showrooms within a few years.

Wealth and Inequality

The very richest now claim a share of the world's wealth not seen since the Gilded Age of the late 1800s and early 1900s. The world's top 1 percent owns about half of global wealth and the bottom half less than 5 percent, according to French economist Thomas Piketty. President Obama is calling for a variety of steps to help struggling middle-class and poor Americans climb the income ladder and to provide more government revenue for programs benefiting the poor. Among his proposals are a hike in the minimum wage and an end to tax loopholes favoring the wealthiest Americans. Likewise, New York City Mayor Bill de Blasio swept to victory with a proposal to help pay for preschool programs for poor children by taxing the rich. But conservative economists say such measures would punish entrepreneurialism and stifle economic growth, arguing that wealth at the top translates into investment that creates jobs at the bottom.

Women and Work

In the 50 years since author Betty Friedan's The Feminine Mystique helped spark the feminist movement, American women have made phenomenal gains. Women now comprise more than half of the U.S. workforce, earn half of college degrees and hold half of management and professional jobs. Yet relatively few have gained top executive and political leadership positions, and women still earn less than men for comparable work. Moreover, flexible work arrangements, paid family leave and other accommodations designed to relieve domestic pressures shouldered largely by women remain elusive. Some argue that women have limited their own progress in the quest for full equality — the controversial argument of a recent book by Facebook executive Sheryl Sandberg. But others say persistent cultural and economic barriers are the main reasons the feminist movement remains a work in progress a half-century after it began.

Youth Unemployment

Nearly 6 million Americans ages 16 to 24 are not working and not in school, keeping the youth unemployment rate at nearly 15 percent. Young people are always twice as likely to be unemployed as the population as a whole, but many economists worry that young Americans are having a more difficult time since the recent recession in getting a start in the adult world. The effects of high youth unemployment are staggering: delayed marriages, depressed rates of home ownership and, for a growing percentage of young adults, the inability to move out of parental homes into a more independent lifestyle. The number of college graduates working in minimum wage jobs has more than doubled over the past five years, while the situation is even grimmer for young people with less education — particularly minorities. Meanwhile, working Americans are paying more in taxes to support social welfare expenses for young people without jobs.

RIGHTS AND LIBERTIES

Abortion Debates

Anti-abortion activists have been lobbying heavily in recent years in the nation's state legislatures, which since 2010 have passed more than 200 laws imposing new regulations on abortion. Supporters of the procedure are challenging many of the new state laws in court, contending they are unreasonable and prevent women — especially poor women — from accessing safe, legal abortions. Proponents of the laws say one of their primary goals is to test the limits of the Supreme Court's 1973 Roe v. Wade decision legalizing abortion. Meanwhile, the federal government is implementing its sweeping health-care reform law, which requires health insurance plans to cover contraception, leading two companies whose owners oppose birth control on religious grounds to sue the government — a case the Supreme Court will hear this month. Anti-abortion activists say they'll bring their arguments to a receptive electorate in 2014, while their opponents say polls show a majority of voters continue to support abortion rights.

Big Data and Privacy

Big data — the collection and analysis of enormous amounts of information by supercomputers — is leading to huge advances in such fields as astrophysics, medicine, social science, business and crime fighting. And big data is growing exponentially: According to IBM, 90 percent of the world's data has been generated within just the past two years. But the use of big data — including Tweets, Facebook images and email addresses — is controversial because of its potential to erode individual privacy, especially by governments conducting surveillance operations and companies marketing products. Some civil liberties advocates want to control the use of big data, and others think

companies should pay to use people's online information. But some proponents of big data say the benefits outweigh the risks and that privacy is an outdated concept.

Domestic Drones

Drones, or unmanned remote-controlled aircraft, are well known for their deadly role in warfare. But in the past few years they have emerged on the domestic front in a variety of civilian applications, from firefighting and police surveillance to scientific research and aerial photography. The growth of domestic drones has sparked excitement over their commercial potential. But drones have also prompted concern that they could violate personal privacy or pose safety hazards for other aircraft and for people on the ground. The Federal Aviation Administration is required to develop regulations to integrate unmanned aircraft into U.S. airspace by 2015. Meanwhile, drone advocates forecast that the industry's development could have a total nationwide economic impact of $82 billion from 2015-2025, with California, Washington state, Texas, Florida and Arizona benefiting the most

Voting Controversies

Election laws and voting procedures have been a major source of controversy in the United States ever since the stunted recount in Florida that determined the outcome of the 2000 presidential contest. Republicans and Democrats have clashed fiercely in state after state over GOP-backed proposals to require government-approved photo IDs for voters to cast ballots. Republicans say the laws prevent fraud; Democrats say the laws are aimed at vote suppression. Court rulings on the laws are mixed. The Supreme Court added to the controversies with a decision in June 2014 to disable a major provision of the federal Voting Rights Act that required some states and localities with a history of discrimination to obtain permission from the government before instituting any change in voting procedures. A bill to restore the provision has been introduced in Congress, but no hearings have been scheduled yet. Election officials are also looking at recommendations from a presidential commission for online registration, more early voting and costly replacement of technologically obsolescent voting machinery.

SOCIAL POLICY

Housing the Homeless

Although homelessness has fallen almost continuously since 2007, about 1.5 million Americans use a shelter in a given year — and advocates for the homeless say that figure badly understates the problem. Unemployment, cuts in funding for mental health care and the psychological effects of war on veterans all have helped fuel the homeless crisis. The Obama administration vows to end homelessness among veterans and individuals by the end of 2015 and to eliminate it among families by 2020. But experts are divided on whether "rapid rehousing" programs that provide short-term rental aid will keep individuals and families from becoming homeless again. Meanwhile, many cities are trying to banish the homeless from their downtowns by enacting anti-vagrancy laws — an approach opposed by those who say living on the street should not be treated as a crime.

Paying College Athletes

The multibillion-dollar industry that college sports has become has richly rewarded the National Collegiate Athletic Association (NCAA), university athletic programs and top football and basketball coaches. Athletes, however, continue to play under a decades-old system in which scholarships pay for tuition and room and board but fall short of covering the full cost of attending school. In return, players are expected to maintain a rigorous training and playing schedule while keeping up their studies. A recent ruling that Northwestern University football players are school employees and thus have the right to unionize, along with class-action lawsuits demanding more compensation and better treatment for college athletes, has amplified debate over whether they should be paid. Supporters of the system say the education and training athletes receive are adequate compensation; critics say college athletes are being exploited. Observers also differ over whether colleges could afford salaries for players, and whether schools should pay more attention to athletes' academic experience.

Regulating Lobbying

Lobbying is undergoing a transformation. Once seen mainly as glad-handing influence peddlers buttonholing lawmakers in Capitol corridors, federal government lobbyists today face multiple challenges: A gridlocked Congress, an end to special-interest funding provisions known as earmarks that once created big business for lobbyists and an Obama administration that has taken steps to curtail their access and influence. Increasing numbers of lobbyists are calling themselves "strategic advisers" effectively to skirt a 2007 law enacted in response to the Jack Abramoff lobbying scandal. Since then, Congress has shown little interest in closing loopholes in lobbying laws, and many observers predict it will take another major scandal for any action to occur. Meanwhile, lobbyists are forming closer alliances with public relations firms and other entities while trying to better explain the breadth of their services. Yet the industry continues to fight an image problem: In a 2013 poll, lobbying scored lowest among 22 professions on honesty and ethics.

School Discipline

Two decades after the nation's schools began adopting zero-tolerance discipline policies to curb violence, drug use and gun threats, reform efforts are underway. New data on high rates of suspensions and expulsions are leading school officials to question whether zero-tolerance policies are being overused, especially when applied to minor infractions. Critics say get-tough discipline has disproportionately targeted minority and disabled students and created a "school-to-prison-pipeline." Encouraged by the Obama administration, many school districts are trying new approaches, such as behavior counseling. Advocates of zero tolerance acknowledge that some school districts have been overzealous but say schools are safer today largely because of strict discipline policies. Schools also are grappling with whether hiring armed security officers improves school safety or encourages higher student arrest rates. Meanwhile, civil liberties advocates question whether school officials can regulate off-campus misbehavior, such as cyberbullying, without infringing on free speech.

HEALTH

Assisted Suicide

Decisions about sustaining life, allowing it to end or even hastening death are among the most difficult choices terminally ill patients and their families can face. Such decisions also are at the heart of a debate about what is commonly called "physician-assisted suicide" — or "aid-in-dying" by supporters. Oregon and Washington — and now likely Vermont — allow physicians to write a prescription for lethal drugs if requested by someone who is terminally ill and mentally competent. A Montana court also has allowed the procedure. Supporters of assisted suicide say it allows the terminally ill to avoid unnecessary suffering and meet death on their own terms, and they say safeguards in the laws prevent abuse of the procedure. But opponents say assisted suicide devalues life, opens patients to exploitation by relatives or others and could lead to widespread euthanasia of the sick and vulnerable. Meanwhile, insurers and patient advocates struggle to interpret federal laws requiring equal treatment of mental and physical illnesses.

NATIONAL SECURITY
Police Tactics

The killing in August 2014 of an unarmed, black 18-year-old by police in Ferguson, Mo., has intensified a long-simmering debate over how police do their jobs. The shooting of Michael Brown by white officer Darren Wilson has led to angry and sometimes violent protests, initially heightened when police in military-style gear and armored vehicles responded to the unrest. The tactics highlighted what some criticize as the "militarization" of America's police forces, fueled by a Pentagon program that supplies local police with surplus weapons and vehicles. Others say police overuse SWAT teams to serve warrants and enforce drug laws. The Ferguson shooting and other recent high-profile police killings of unarmed African-Americans also has ignited a national outcry against what many say is disproportionate police action against black males. Police respond that low-income communities of all races have the highest crime rates and that they need military-style equipment to defend themselves in a heavily armed society.

Preface

S hould the use of personal information be restricted? Has
U.S. law enforcement become militarized? Will good jobs
continue to elude young adults? These questions—and
many more—are at the heart of American public policy. How can
instructors best engage students with these crucial issues? We feel
that students need objective, yet provocative examinations of these
issues to understand how they affect citizens today and will for
years to come. This annual collection aims to promote in-depth
discussion, facilitate further research and help readers formulate
their own positions on crucial issues. Get your students talking
both inside and outside the classroom about *Issues for Debate in
American Public Policy*.

This sixteenth edition includes sixteen up-to-date reports by *CQ
Researcher*, an award-winning weekly policy brief that brings complicated issues down to earth. Each report chronicles and analyzes
executive, legislative, and judicial activities at all levels of government. This collection is divided into six diverse policy areas: environment; business and economy; rights and liberties; social policy;
health; and national security and foreign policy—to cover a range of
issues found in most American government and public policy
courses.

CQ RESEARCHER

CQ Researcher was founded in 1923 as *Editorial Research Reports* and
was sold primarily to newspapers as a research tool. The magazine

was renamed and redesigned in 1991 as *CQ Researcher*. Today, students are its primary audience. While still used by hundreds of journalists and newspapers, many of which reprint portions of the reports, the *Researcher's* main subscribers are now high school, college and public libraries. In 2002, *Researcher* won the American Bar Association's coveted Silver Gavel award for magazine excellence for a series of nine reports on civil liberties and other legal issues.

Researcher staff writers—all highly experienced journalists—sometimes compare the experience of writing a Researcher report to drafting a college term paper. Indeed, there are many similarities. Each report is as long as many term papers—about 11,000 words—and is written by one person without any significant outside help. One of the key differences is that writers interview leading experts, scholars and government officials for each issue.

Like students, staff writers begin the creative process by choosing a topic. Working with the *Researcher's* editors, the writer identifies a controversial subject that has important public policy implications. After a topic is selected, the writer embarks on one to two weeks of intense research. Newspaper and magazine articles are clipped or downloaded, books are ordered and information is gathered from a wide variety of sources, including interest groups, universities and the government. Once the writers are well informed, they develop a detailed outline, and begin the interview process. Each report requires a minimum of ten to fifteen interviews with academics, officials, lobbyists and people working in the field. Only after all interviews are completed does the writing begin.

CHAPTER FORMAT

Each issue of *CQ Researcher*, and therefore each selection in this book, is structured in the same way. Each begins with an overview, which briefly summarizes the areas that will be explored in greater detail in the rest of the chapter. The next section chronicles important and current debates on the topic under discussion and is structured around a number of key questions, such as "Should

government regulate unhealthy foods?" and "Are U.S. schools becoming resegregated?" These questions are usually the subject of much debate among practitioners and scholars in the field. Hence, the answers presented are never conclusive but detail the range of opinion on the topic.

Next, the "Background" section provides a history of the issue being examined. This retrospective covers important legislative measures, executive actions and court decisions that illustrate how current policy has evolved. Then the "Current Situation" section examines contemporary policy issues, legislation under consideration and legal action being taken. Each selection concludes with an "Outlook" section, which addresses possible regulation, court rulings, and initiatives from Capitol Hill and the White House over the next five to ten years.

Each report contains features that augment the main text: two to three sidebars that examine issues related to the topic at hand, a pro versus con debate between two experts, a chronology of key dates and events and an annotated bibliography detailing major sources used by the writer.

CUSTOM OPTIONS

Interested in building your ideal CQ Press Issues book, customized to your personal teaching needs and interests? Browse by course or date, or search for specific topics or issues from our online catalog of over 150 *CQ Researcher* issues at http://custom.cqpress.com.

ACKNOWLEDGMENTS

We wish to thank many people for helping to make this collection a reality. Thomas J. Billitteri, managing editor of *CQ Researcher*, gave us his enthusiastic support and cooperation as we developed this fifteenth edition. He and his talented staff of editors and writers have amassed a first-class library of *Researcher* reports, and we are fortunate to have access to that rich cache. We also thankfully acknowledge the advice and feedback from current readers and are gratified by their satisfaction with the book.

Some readers may be learning about *CQ Researcher* for the first time. We expect that many readers will want regular access to this excellent weekly research tool. For subscription information or a no-obligation free trial of *Researcher*, please contact CQ Press at www.cqpress.com or toll-free at 1-866-4CQ-PRESS (1-866-427-7737).

We hope that you will be pleased by the sixteenth edition of *Issues for Debate in American Public Policy.* We welcome your feedback and suggestions for future editions. Please direct comments to Sarah Calabi, Acquisitions Editor for Political Science, CQ Press, an imprint of SAGE, 2600 Virginia Avenue, NW, Suite 600, Washington, DC 20037; or send e-mail to *Sarah.Calabi@sagepub.com*

—The Editors of CQ Press

Contributors

Sarah Glazer contributes regularly to *CQ Researcher*. Her articles on health, education and social-policy issues also have appeared in *The New York Times* and *The Washington Post*. Her recent *CQ Researcher* reports include "Plagiarism and Cheating" and "Telecommuting." She graduated from the University of Chicago with a B.A. in American history.

Alan Greenblatt covers politics and government for NPR. He was previously a staff writer at *Governing* magazine and *CQ Weekly*, where he won the National Press Club's Sandy Hume Award for political journalism. He graduated from San Francisco State University in 1986 and received a master's degree in English literature from the University of Virginia in 1988. His *CQ Researcher* reports include "Confronting Warming," "Future of the GOP," "Immigration Debate," "Media Bias" and "Aging Polulation."

David Hosansky is a freelance writer in the Denver area who specializes in environmental issues. He previously was a senior writer at *CQ Weekly* and the *Florida Times-Union* in Jacksonville, where he was twice nominated for a Pulitzer Prize. His previous *CQ Researcher* reports include "Wind Power" and "Distracted Driving."

Michelle Johnson is a writer and digital media editor based in Winston-Salem, N.C., with more than 20 years' experience covering higher education, local government and cultural issues for print, online and broadcast media. She holds a bachelor's degree in English from Augustana College in Rock Island, Ill., and a master's degree in English language and literature from the University of Minnesota. She also earned a graduate certificate in communication and technology at the University of North Carolina at Chapel Hill.

Kenneth Jost has written more than 160 reports for *CQ Researcher* since 1991 on topics ranging from legal affairs and social policy to national security and international relations. He is the author of *The Supreme Court Yearbook* and *Supreme Court From A to Z* (both CQ Press). He is an honors graduate of Harvard College and Georgetown Law School, where he teaches media law as an adjunct professor. He also writes the blog Jost on Justice (http://jostonjustice.blogspot.com). His previous reports include "Police Misconduct" (2012) and "Policing the Police" (2000).

Reed Karaim, a freelance writer in Tucson, Ariz., has written for *The Washington Post, U.S. News & World Report, Smithsonian, American Scholar, USA Weekend* and other publications. He is the author of the novel, *If Men Were Angels*, which was selected for the Barnes & Noble Discover Great New Writers series. He is also the winner of the Robin Goldstein Award for Outstanding Regional Reporting and other journalism honors. Karaim is a graduate of North Dakota State University in Fargo.

Peter Katel is a *CQ Researcher* contributing writer who previously reported on Haiti and Latin America for *Time* and *Newsweek* and covered the Southwest for newspapers in New Mexico. He has received several journalism awards, including the Bartolomé Mitre Award for coverage of drug trafficking, from the Inter-American Press Association. He holds an A.B. in university studies from the University of New Mexico. His recent reports include "Mexico's Future" and "3D Printing."

Robert Kiener is a freelance writer based in Vermont whose work has appeared in *The London Sunday Times, The Christian Science Monitor, The Washington Post, Reader's Digest,* Time Life Books and other publications. For more than two decades he worked as an editor and correspondent in Guam, Hong Kong, Canada and England. He holds an M.A. in Asian studies from Hong Kong University and an M.Phil. in international relations from England's Cambridge University.

Chuck McCutcheon is a freelance writer in Washington, D.C. He has been a reporter and editor for Congressional Quarterly and Newhouse News Service and is co-author of the 2012 and 2014 editions of *The Almanac of American Politics.* He also has written books on climate change and nuclear waste.

Daniel McGlynn is a California-based independent journalist who covers science and the environment. His work has appeared in *The New York Times Magazine, Earth Island Journal, Bay Citizen,* and other publications. He has a master's degree in journalism from the University of California, Berkeley. His last report for *CQ Researcher* was "Whale Hunting."

Tom Price, a Washington-based freelance journalist and a contributing writer for *CQ Researcher*, focuses on politics, government, science, technology, education and business. Previously, Price was a correspondent in the Cox Newspapers Washington Bureau and chief politics writer for the *Dayton Daily News* and *The* (Dayton) *Journal Herald.* He is author or coauthor of five books, including *Changing The Face of Hunger* and, most recently, *Washington, DC, Free & Dirt Cheap* with his wife Susan Crites Price.

Anne Farris Rosen is a freelance journalist in Washington, D.C., with more than 30 years of experience covering government and social policy issues for newspapers and documentary television. She is the co-author of the 2001 book *Stanley H. Kaplan: Test Pilot: How I broke testing barriers for millions of students and caused a sonic boom in the business of education.* She has won numerous awards, including the Associated Press Managing Editor's Award and the Best of Gannett award. She is an adjunct professor of journalism at the Philip Merrill College of Journalism at the University of Maryland. She holds a BA in English from Rhodes College and a masters degree in Urban Affairs from St. Louis University.

Bill Wanlund is a freelance writer in the Washington, D.C., area. He is a former Foreign Service officer, with service in Europe, Asia, Africa and South America. He holds a journalism degree from The George Washington University and has written for *CQ Researcher* on drone warfare and downtown development.

Jennifer Weeks is a Massachusetts freelance writer who specializes in energy, the environment and science. She has written for *The Washington Post, Audubon, Popular Mechanics* and other magazines and previously was a policy analyst, congressional staffer and lobbyist. She has an A.B. degree from Williams College and master's degrees from the University of North Carolina and Harvard. Her recent *CQ Researcher* reports include "Coastal Development" and "Managing Wildfires."

Issues for Debate in American Public Policy

1

Food Policy Debates

Robert Kiener

First lady Michelle Obama helps students from Washington prepare a meal on June 12, 2014, using vegetables from the White House Kitchen Garden. As part of her "Let's Move!" fitness campaign, Mrs. Obama championed the Healthy, Hunger-Free Kids Act of 2010, which authorized new nutrition standards for the nation's more than 97,000 school cafeterias.

From *CQ Researcher*, October 3, 2014.

A s the closing credits rolled in a packed theater at this year's Sundance Film Festival, the audience rose to its feet and gave the new movie a standing ovation.

The surprise hit, which received an enthusiastic 85 percent approval rating on the popular viewer-review website *Rotten Tomatoes*, featured "the greatest villain to appear on movie screens this summer," said CBS News.[1] But it had no super heroes or giant battling alien monsters.

Instead, the documentary "Fed Up" largely features talking heads, flip charts and four obese teenagers. It portrays the sugar industry and large food companies as the prime culprits behind America's obesity and diabetes epidemics. Sugar is the new tobacco, the movie proclaims.[2]

The film joins other recent food-related documentaries, such as "Food, Inc.," "Supersize Me," "Fast Food Nation," "Fat, Sick & Nearly Dead," and big-selling books such as *Grain Brain, Wheat Belly, Food Politics* and *The Omnivore's Dilemma*. They all reinforce the same message: that America has what food industry critic and *Omnivore's Dilemma* author Michael Pollan calls a "national eating disorder."[3]

Some critics — such as Michael Moss, author of *Salt Sugar Fat: How the Food Giants Hooked Us* — say much of that eating disorder is orchestrated by the nation's food industry. Companies add high levels of sugar, salt and fat to processed foods in "a conscious effort — taking place in labs and marketing meetings and grocery-store aisles — to get people hooked on foods that are convenient and inexpensive," he writes.[4]

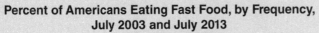

Americans Eating Fast Food Less Frequently

The percentage of Americans who eat regularly in fast-food restaurants has declined over the past decade, while the percentage of those who eat fast food once a month or "a few times a year" has risen.

Percent of Americans Eating Fast Food, by Frequency, July 2003 and July 2013

Source: Niall McCarthy, "1 in 5 Americans Eat Fast Food Several Times a Week," Statistica, Aug. 9, 2013

The books, articles and documentaries touch a nerve among consumers trying to eat "clean" food — organic,* grass-fed or gluten-free items with minimal additives, processing and antibiotics — and those trying to follow healthy-eating advice by limiting their sugar, salt and fat.

Americans are paying more attention to what they consume than ever before, according to a new U.S. Department of Agriculture (USDA) study, assiduously reading nutrition labels.[5] Some want the government to address the nation's obesity and diet-related health problems, improve its oversight of food additives and require labels on genetically modified foods (GMOs) — those made from organisms whose DNA has been altered through genetic engineering.

"People are finally waking up and asking how their food is produced and marketed," says Marion Nestle, a nutrition professor in the Department of Nutrition, Food Studies, and Public Health at New York University and author of *Food Politics: How the Food Industry Influences Nutrition and Health.*

To help promote healthy eating, government agencies have moved to limit sugary sodas, eliminate dangerous trans fats from the food supply and issued new, healthier, federal school lunch dietary guidelines. While unhealthy eating is not the sole cause of obesity and related diseases — a sedentary lifestyle is another culprit — most experts consider it the leading factor.[6]

The food industry — responding to consumer demands for healthier foods, especially those marketed to children — has begun offering hundreds of organic products as well as new processed foods with less fat, sugar, salt and additives. At the same time, however, some food and beverage trade groups have resisted restrictions on trans fats and sugary sodas and tried to water down the new federal school lunch dietary guidelines.

As some Americans replace Twinkies with healthier goji berries and egg-white chips, restaurants are cashing in on the healthy-eating trend. Chefs are creating dishes made with quinoa and kale and serving smaller portions.[7] So-called "fast-casual" food chains like Chipotle, Panera, Freshii and sweetgreen — which feature low-fat salads, vegetarian wraps or organic ingredients — are gaining in popularity. Despite healthy additions to their menus, fast-food stalwarts like McDonald's and Burger King are seeing flat or falling sales. There are now more than 21,000 fast-casual restaurants, up from 9,000 a decade ago.[8]

"We want to eliminate the excuse that people don't eat healthy because they either can't afford to or it's not convenient," said Matthew Corrin, CEO of the Freshii restaurant chain.[9]

However, as waistlines and statistics show, much of America is still overeating and eating unhealthily. More than 30 percent of U.S. adults and 17 percent of adolescents are obese. And while the rates of increase have slowed in the past decade, if current trends continue, half of all adults will be obese by 2030, according to a 2012 study in the *American Journal of Preventive Medicine.**[10]

---

* Food can be labeled "organic" if it is grown and processed using no synthetic fertilizers or pesticides.

* An adult with a body mass index of 30 or more is considered obese; for example an adult who is 5 feet 9 inches tall weighing 203 pounds or more is obese.

Beef, Dairy Consumption on the Decline

Over the past four decades, Americans gradually have consumed fewer dairy products and eggs and less red meat while eating more fish, chicken and turkey. Consumption of fruits, vegetables and grain products* rose until 2000 but has declined since.

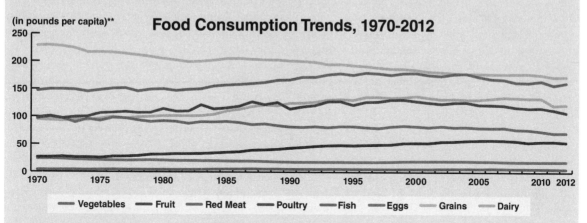

Food Consumption Trends, 1970-2012

(in pounds per capita)**

Legend: Vegetables — Fruit — Red Meat — Poultry — Fish — Eggs — Grains — Dairy

* Rice not included 2011-12.

** The chart uses a "Loss-Adjusted Food Availability" index devised by the U.S. Department of Agriculture's Economic Research Service. While the index does not directly measure consumption, the USDA says it is a reliable reflection of consumption trends.

Source: Jean Buzby and Jeanine Bentley, "Food Availability (Per Capita) Data System," Economic Research Service, U.S. Department of Agriculture, http://tinyurl.com/pk42bcg

On the positive side, obesity rates among young children, ages 2 to 5, fell from 13.9 percent to 8 percent from 2003 to 2012, the Centers for Disease Control and Prevention (CDC) found. And a study in the journal *Pediatrics* in 2013 found that American teenagers in 2009 and 2010 exercised more, watched less TV, ate more fruits and vegetables and drank fewer sugar-sweetened beverages than children the same age did in 2001 and 2002.[11]

Meanwhile, the percentage of Americans regularly eating in fast-food restaurants has declined over the past decade, while the percentages eating fast food once a month or "a few times a year" have risen.[12]

Americans are following nutritionists' advice and eating more turkey and chicken while cutting down on red meat, but the oft-repeated recommendation that they eat more fruits and vegetables is not being heeded, according to U.S. Department of Agriculture (USDA) statistics. Consumption of both is down over the past decade. Some believe the decline is due to lower incomes and

perceived price increases along with the allure of processed and convenience foods.

"The challenge for the fruit and vegetable industries is to close the gap between what consumers say they want and what they actually do," said Cindy van Rijswick, an analyst with Rabobank, a Dutch bank that completed a study on the drop in fruit and vegetable consumption in the United States. "Surveys have shown that, in principle, consumers are positive-minded about healthy eating, but in practice they are easily swayed by creative marketing of processed food and beverages and exhibit a strong bias for convenience products."[13]

However, some new statistics indicate that America's eating habits are beginning to change for the better, such as:

• Working-age adults consumed an average of 118 fewer calories a day in 2009-10 than four years earlier, according to the USDA, which attributed the decline in part to more consumers than ever reading nutrition labels.[14]

- More than 80 percent of Americans reported buying organic food in 2012, and domestic organic food production rose 240 percent from 2002-11, compared to 3 percent for nonorganic food.[15]
- Wal-Mart, the nation's biggest food seller, expects to sell more organic food than any other retailer.
- A "locavore" movement promoting locally grown food bought at farmers markets and eating in so-called farm-to-fork restaurants is gaining popularity. Between 1994 and 2014 the number of farmers markets in the United Stated jumped nearly fivefold, from 1,755 to 8,268.[16]

Locavores prefer buying local produce because fruits and vegetables can lose a good portion of their nutritional value before landing on a grocery shelf.[17]

"This is not a passing fad," B. Hudson Riehle, research director for the National Restaurant Association, said of the farm-to-fork movement, adding that locally grown food and sustainability were top customer priorities in the group's annual poll of American chefs this year. "It's only going to get stronger."[18]

However, for some Americans, when it comes to food, bigger is better. Some restaurants proudly tout their supersized dishes loaded with fat, sugar, salt and calories. Hillbilly Hot Dogs, in Lesage, W.Va., serves its signature "Home Wrecker," a 15-inch hot dog smothered with 12 towering toppings.[19] The Ben & Jerry's ice cream chain offers the "Vermonster" sundae. Its 20 scoops of ice cream, four bananas, four ladles of hot fudge, 10 scoops of walnuts, three chocolate chip cookies, one fudge brownie, two scoops of topping and whipped cream provide a whopping 14,000 calories and 500 grams of fat.[20]

And B-52 Burgers and Brew in Inver Grove Heights, Minn., challenges customers to try its M.O.A.B. The Mother of All Burgers contains two pounds of burger patties, two eggs, BBQ pork, cheddar and pepper jack cheese and fried onion "tanglers" served on a 15-inch French loaf. Mark Reese, B-52's owner, says he doesn't promote overeating, and "few people ever finish one of our M.O.A.B.s. But no one should tell someone what they can or can't eat."

Some nutritionists and healthy-eating activists want the government to adopt higher taxes on sugary sodas, expanded nutrition labels and restrictions on portion sizes; they also want better regulation of additives as well as the antibiotics and synthetic chemicals used in agriculture. Such proposals have triggered push-back from some food companies and consumers, particularly those who are political libertarians. When former New York City Mayor Michael Bloomberg proposed banning sugary soft drinks larger than 16 ounces in May 2012, some consumers and the beverage industry attacked the proposal. Eventually the New York Supreme Court ruled that the city health board lacked authority to impose the ban.[21]

"The food police won't be happy until they tell the rest of the country what they can and can't eat," says Jayson Lusk, a professor of agricultural economics at Oklahoma State University and author of *The Food Police.* "They want to regulate us into submission."

Such views trigger resentment among those advocating healthier eating habits. "Obesity is not just a matter of personal responsibility, says Nestle. "It also incurs costs to society that must be paid by the population at large" through higher health insurance and health care costs.

The heated battle over food shows no sign of cooling. "There may be no hotter topic in law schools right now than food law and policy," said a recent *Harvard Law Today* article.[22]

As nutritionists, dieticians, politicians and consumer advocates debate food policy and trends, here are some of the questions under discussion:

Are concerns about food quality warranted?

In recent years Americans have seen repeated outbreaks of food-borne diseases such as salmonella, *E. coli*, Listeria and botulism. According to the CDC, roughly one in six Americans — or 48 million people — are sickened, 128,000 are hospitalized and 3,000 die each year from such illnesses.[23]

Some outbreaks are limited to a region, while others have been more severe and widespread, such as a 2008-09 salmonella outbreak from tainted peanut butter that killed nine people and sickened at least 714 others nationwide. The peanut company's owner was convicted of conspiracy, fraud and other federal charges. No sentencing date has been set; he faces up to 20 years in prison.[24]

Despite such outbreaks, agricultural economist Lusk contends that America's food system "is among the safest in the world and is getting safer. For example, since 1996 *E. coli* incidents are down 30 percent, and Listeria incidents down 42 percent. Unfortunately there is a 'fear market' created by some food activists who often unfairly target the food industry."

Fred Yiannis, vice president of food safety for Wal-Mart, said America's "food supply is safer than it's ever been," and "food safety awareness is at an all-time high."[25]

But critics complain weaknesses exist in the regulation of the food supply. "Part of the problem is that U.S. food-safety laws are quite old," said Caroline Smith Dewaal, food safety director at the Center for Science in the Public Interest (CSPI), a food-safety group that advocates science-based government policies. "Most were drafted a century ago."[26] In addition, she continued, the nation's food supply is monitored by both the Food and Drug Administration (FDA) and the USDA, which "allows things to fall through the cracks."

"Experts say the FDA and the USDA often work in a piecemeal fashion, reacting to the outbreak of the day, rather than taking steps to prevent safety problems," said a report on food safety from the Robert Wood Johnson Foundation.[27] The report recommended, among other things, that the two agencies jointly coordinate federal efforts to fight salmonella. "The lack of a unified strategy has impaired the government's ability to appreciably reduce salmonella risks," the report said.[28]

The FDA Food Safety Modernization Act, the biggest overhaul of food safety regulations in decades, was an attempt to address such concerns. It stressed prevention over criminal punishment after food-borne disease outbreaks and authorized new regulations designed to increase food safety. Among those were stronger controls on imported foods, new procedures to prevent produce contamination and more inspections and tougher regulation of facilities that produce packaged foods and animal feed.

However, implementation of the new law has been slow. The FDA is currently accepting public comments on proposed regulations to implement the law.

Public worries about the increasing number of additives in America's food supply were exacerbated in April, when the Natural Resources Defense Council (NRDC),

AFP/Getty Images/Saul Loeb

Demonstrators near the White House protest on Jan. 10, 2013, that the Food and Drug Administration does not adequately protect farmers who prefer not to grow genetically modified crops (GMOs). Some farmers and consumers think such crops are unsafe, but GMO seed developers dispute that and say GMO crops enable farmers to use fewer chemicals on their land.

a Washington-based environmental group, released a report that cast doubt on the agency's oversight of food additives. At least 1,000 of the 10,000 food additives used today were approved as safe, the report said, based on industry safety data never disclosed to the FDA.[29]

Under FDA procedures revised in 1997 during the Clinton administration to reduce years-long delays in obtaining approval of new additives, the report said, manufacturers can now bring their additives to market without FDA review if they certify that the additives are "generally recognized as safe (GRAS)," based on internal corporate research. That research, however, is not required to be independently reviewed by the FDA.[30]

As a result of the new fast-track procedures, according to a *Washington Post* investigation, in hundreds of cases "the FDA doesn't even know of the existence of new additives, which can include chemical preservatives, flavorings and thickening agents." FDA Deputy Commissioner for Food Michael Traylor told *The Post*, "We simply do not have the information to vouch for the safety of many of these chemicals."[31]

The FDA says on its website that food and color additives today "are more strictly studied, regulated and monitored than at any other time in history." And the agency carefully reviews company safety data — when companies provide it, the NRDC says.

Farmers Market Total Rises Fivefold

The number of farmers markets in the United States jumped from 1,755 in 1994 to 8,268 in 2014. As of 2013, Vermont had the most markets per capita: 15 per 100,000 residents.

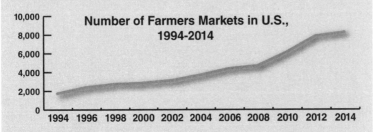

Number of Farmers Markets in U.S., 1994-2014

Sources: "National Count of Farmers Market Directory Listing Graph: 1994-2014," Agricultural Marketing Service, U.S. Department of Agriculture, updated Aug. 14, 2014, http://tinyurl.com/nyrp6v9; farmers' market density figure from "State Indicator Report on Fruits and Vegetables 2013," Centers for Disease Control and Prevention, 2013, http://tinyurl.com/mkqtj93

Since the NRDC report came out, the nation's largest food industry trade group, the Grocery Manufacturers Association (GMA), has announced it is creating a database containing information on all industry assessments of food additives. It will be made available to the FDA in 2015, but it is unclear how much, if any, of that information will be made public.

Leon Bruner, chief science officer for the GMA, said in August that the grocery industry "is committed to providing consumers with safe, quality, affordable and innovative products." The GMA's database initiative will "strengthen the food safety programs used by the entire food industry and thereby provide consumers more assurance that food products produced by U.S. manufacturers are, and will remain, the safest available in the world."[32]

Should foods linked to diet-related diseases be regulated?

As America has gotten fatter, calls to regulate what people eat and drink and how that food is marketed have grown increasingly louder.

"We live in a food swamp, and there is food everywhere," says Deborah Cohen, a physician and researcher at the Rand Corp., a global policy think tank, and author of *A Big Fat Crisis: The Hidden Forces Behind the Obesity Epidemic and How We Can End It.* "We are hard-wired to notice food, and because there is so much food marketing and advertising trying to convince us to eat — especially junk food and other high-calorie food — we need to address the problem."

Citing government regulation of alcohol and tobacco, she says foods linked to diet-related diseases should be similarly regulated. "The harms associated with overeating are at least as great as the harms from drinking," says Cohen.

Food activists are promoting measures such as attaching warning labels to junk food, restricting portion sizes and removing candy bars from checkout lines, moves that Cohen says food companies have resisted. "We needed policies to protect people from having alcohol pushed at them almost wherever they went, and we need policies that protect people from triggers designed to make them eat when they are not hungry," Cohen contends.

Robert Lustig, a pediatric endocrinologist and professor of clinical pediatrics at the University of California, San Francisco, calls the nation's high sugar consumption a public health crisis. "When taken in high doses, sugar can be as toxic as high doses of alcohol," he says. When sugar is metabolized it can start a process that generates fat that can lead to diabetes, heart diseases and stroke.[33] "Because it is a public health crisis, you have to do big things, and you have to do them across the board," Lustig says.

With tobacco and alcohol, he says, "we made a conscious choice that we're not going to get rid of them, but we are going to limit their consumption. I think we need to treat sugar the same way."

Many advocates of regulation say governments must act because the food industry cannot — or will not — regulate itself. "The food, beverage and restaurant industries collectively spend roughly $16 billion a year to promote sales through advertising agencies, and perhaps $2 billion of that is targeted at children," says Nestle of New York University, who sees government intervention with regard to marketing to children as essential. "To expect these companies, whose sole purpose is to increase sales and report growth in sales every quarter, to voluntarily stop marketing junk food to children makes no sense."

Food industry advocates, however, say the industry already is heavily regulated. "If we start regulating in ways that outlaw various foods, what we are really doing is denying consumers choice," said John Bode, a lobbyist for the industry.[34]

Many critics of regulation echo the view that "the less government regulation, the better" and that consumers should take more responsibility for what they eat.

Elaine Kolish, vice president of the Children's Food and Beverage Advertising Initiative (CFBAI), a voluntary industry program to advertise healthier dietary choices to children, calls food advertising to children a "perfect example of a topic that is wholly inappropriate for government regulation." Such protection is "a role for a nanny, not the government," she contends, and points out that the products being sold to children "are perfectly legal to sell, and in most instances the advertised products are being purchased by adults."

Michael D. Tanner, a senior fellow at the libertarian Cato Institute think tank, calls food restrictions and taxes bad ideas. "Food bans or taxes are, in effect, anti-responsibility. Because they assume that the government will protect me against any adverse consequences from my lifestyle choices, they grant the government the right to make those choices for me. Effectively, it treats us all as children who can neither be trusted to make our own choices or be held responsible for those choices."[35]

Taxing, restricting or regulating foods is "insulting and elitist," says Lusk of Oklahoma State University. "The 'food police' advocate a 'fat tax' partly because they claim they know what's good for us, and that individuals won't take personal responsibility."

Moreover, he says, food taxes would be hardest on the poor, because they cost low-income people a greater percentage of their income than that of wealthier consumers. Also, Lusk says, many studies show taxes on food aren't effective. "Because we spend a relatively small portion of our income on food," he says, "taxes don't affect our bottom line enough for us to change our food choices."[36]

Lusk advocates letting the free market determine what foods are produced. "There is a viable alternative to paternalism. It is the market," he says. "We should have enough faith in consumers to let them make their own choices."

But others bristle at such views, arguing that the direct medical costs of treating obesity alone are estimated to be $150 billion-$210 billion annually, costs that boost everyone's insurance premiums as well as taxes to pay for ever-increasing Medicare and Medicaid bills.[37]

Should the federal government require healthier school lunches?

Four years ago school cafeterias became center stage in efforts to improve what children eat. The Healthy, Hunger-Free Kids Act of 2010, famously championed by first lady Michelle Obama as part of her "Let's Move!" fitness campaign, passed unanimously in the Democratic-controlled Senate and by a wide margin in the then Democratic-controlled House.[38]

Supporters hoped it would help reduce childhood obesity and improve kids' overall health by offering them healthy foods during the school day. "We've seen the connection between what our kids eat and how well they perform in school," President Obama said when he signed the bill into law.[39]

The legislation authorized the USDA to create nutrition standards for the nation's more than 97,000 public school cafeterias, which serve about 30 million students.[40] Schools began replacing foods high in fat, sodium and "empty calories" (lacking nutritional value) with healthier fare. White bread and salt-covered fries, for example, were replaced by whole grains, more fruits and vegetables and low- or nonfat milk.

Many applauded the new standards, which were drawn up by the federal Institute of Medicine after input from an expert panel of nutrition scientists and educators.

But since then, some politicians, food industry representatives and school lunch officials have complained that parts of the law are too costly and that menus have proved unpopular with students.

A January 2014 Government Accountability Office (GAO) report on the new standards found that 321 local school food officials in 42 states decided in 2012-2013 to leave the National School Lunch Program. And student participation in the program declined by 1.2 million students — or 3.7 percent — between the 2010-2011 and 2012-2013 school years, after having increased steadily for many years.

The report said school cafeteria managers had problems with "plate waste — or foods thrown away rather than consumed by students — and managing food costs, as well as planning menus and obtaining foods that complied with portion size and calorie requirements."[41]

For example, the Fort Thomas Independent School District in northern Kentucky sold 30,000 fewer school meals last year than the year before. Students who don't like the new offerings are "just skipping lunch and stopping by the minimart on the way home," said Superintendent Gene Kirchner. "And when they do buy a lunch, they . . . throw half of it away."[42]

Some who previously supported the new standards are reconsidering, including the School Nutrition Association (SNA), representing 55,000 cafeteria professionals and representatives of the food industry. "Our members are very frustrated with some of the requirements of the bill, and we are asking for more flexibility," says SNA spokesperson Diane Pratt-Heavner. For example, the requirement that students be given a fruit or vegetable is too costly for some schools, the group says.

Critics of the SNA's reversal note that nearly half of the group's $10 million operating budget comes from food industry members such as Minnesota-based Schwan Food, which sells pizzas to more than 75 percent of the country's 96,000 K-12 schools.[43] Plus, 19 of the SNA's past presidents disagree with the organization's new position.[44]

The National School Board Association has called the nutrition requirements "federal overreach on school meals."[45] And a Republican-led effort steered the House Appropriations Committee to vote to let school districts receive waivers to temporarily opt out of the new dietary requirements.[46]

Daren Bakst, a research fellow in agricultural policy at the conservative Heritage Foundation, says the 2010 bill is based on "the underlying assumption that federal technocrats and people like Michelle Obama need to act on everyone else's behalf to meet the best needs of their children. It's arrogance. And the lunch program isn't working."

The first lady hit back at the law's opponents in a May *New York Times* op-ed piece. "Remember a few years ago when Congress declared that the sauce on a slice of pizza should count as a vegetable in school lunches? . . . We're seeing the same thing happening again with these new efforts to lower nutrition standards in our schools," she wrote. The new guidelines, she said, were "evidence-based" and relied on "the most current science" showing that kids needed less sugar, salt and fat in their diets.[47]

Some critics of the House waiver proposal say it is the result of pressure from food companies worried that the new requirements will hurt their food sales to schools. "I am astonished," says New York University's Nestle. "This is simply politics as usual in Washington. The food industry couldn't get its way so it did an end run and got Congress to overturn the work of countless committees and experts."

The White House has threatened to veto any bill that contains the waiver, and House Republicans repeatedly have delayed a vote on the measure by the full House.

Nancy Brown, CEO of the American Heart Association, said, "By giving special interests a seat at the school lunch table, some members of Congress are putting politics before the health of our children."[48]

"The House waiver proposal is an attack on kids' health dressed up as a favor to schools, when in fact 90 percent of schools are already meeting the new healthy lunch standards, helping kids eat more fruits, vegetables and whole grains," said Margo Wootan, nutrition policy director at the Center for Science in the Public Interest, a consumer advocacy organization. A USDA fact sheet on the new nutrition standards reports that more than 90 percent of schools are successfully meeting them, food waste has not increased and children are eating more fruits and vegetables.[49]

Wootan says of the House measure: "Perhaps it's more a favor to the pizza companies, french fry makers, steel can manufacturers and any number of corporate special interests that think the school lunch program is their own ATM."[50]

Donna Martin, school nutrition director of Georgia's Burke County School District, takes the long view. "Whenever you change something, the kids complain, 'We're not eating this,' " she said. "But they get over it. You just have to give them time."[51]

Elizabeth Pivonka, president of the Delaware-based, produce-industry-backed Produce for Better Health Foundation, says, "Some children just don't like being told what they must do, and it takes time for some to change their eating habits.

"We have also seen that when they have some control over what they are served, say via a salad bar or where they have helped design a menu, they are often more eager to eat fruits and vegetables," she says.

BACKGROUND

Rise of Industrial Farming

The nation's food culture has evolved over the centuries due to a unique combination of factors, including, "The food gathering and cultivation methods of native peoples; America's successive waves of immigration in the colonial and antebellum periods; and 20th century revolutions in agricultural and cooking technologies," according to a 2002 exhibition on America's culinary heritage at Cornell University.[52]

Between 1860 and 1910 the number of farms in the United States more than tripled, to about 6.4 million, and total farm acreage in production quadrupled.[53]

The invention of synthetic fertilizers in the early 1900s led to a dramatic increase in crop harvests, more than doubling the number of people that could be fed from a hectare of land (2.47 acres).[54] American farmers, who produced 173 million bushels of wheat in 1859, were producing 945 million bushels by 1919.[55]

Fertilizer helped usher in the industrialization of the U.S. food system in the 20th century, as farms became more mechanized, specialized and efficient. But with growing industrialization came calls for legislation to regulate the food industry.

In 1889 the first pure food and drug bill was proposed to control the sale of patent medicines, but was defeated, as were several others that followed.

The food industry fought any attempt to regulate foods as government interference. In 1902 an official from a large food distributor said, "Make us leave preservatives and coloring matters out of our food, and [make us] call our products by their right name and you will bankrupt every food industry in the country."[56]

It was muckraking journalist Upton Sinclair's popular 1906 book, *The Jungle*, that helped convince the public and legislators that the food industry needed to be regulated. The novel was based on Sinclair's research at meat-packing plants and included nauseating scenes of spoiled meat being sold, unsanitary processing and even workers falling into rendering tanks and being ground along with animal parts. "I aimed at the public's heart and by accident I hit it in the stomach," said Sinclair.

Within months of *The Jungle*'s publication, Congress passed the Federal Meat Inspection Act, establishing inspection standards for meat processing plants. The same day that President Theodore Roosevelt signed the meat inspection law he signed the Pure Food and Drug Act of 1906, which banned adulterated or mislabeled food and drug products from interstate commerce. It also established a Bureau of Chemistry within the Department of Agriculture to inspect products, which in 1930 became the Food and Drug Administration.

The early 1900s also saw the introduction of ready-to-eat foods. Chemicals, such as preservatives and colorings, were added to foods during processing to extend life and make food more attractive to consumers. Oreos went on sale in 1912, Kraft processed cheese in 1915 and Hostess CupCakes in 1919. In the 1920s Clarence Birdseye, a New York taxidermist, perfected a system for flash-freezing vegetables, and the first quick-frozen vegetables, fruits, seafoods and meat were sold in 1930.

Kraft's cheese, popular with consumers for its long-lasting qualities, is an excellent example of how processed foods would change the food marketplace. Kraft's innovation "tapped into a changing food ethos among American housewives and served as a model for processed food to come — products that were attractively packaged, nationally advertised, longer lasting, more convenient and of inferior nutritional value," noted Melanie Warner, author of *Pandora's Lunchbox: How Processed Food Took Over the American Meal*.[57]

After World War II, domestic and international demand for crops soared, pushing American agriculture to become more industrialized. Diversified farms, where farmers raised a variety of crops and animals, began to be replaced by highly specialized, monoculture operations that produced single crops across vast acreages. Improved fertilizers, pesticides and mechanization changed the face of farming, creating so-called "mega-farms" or "factory farms" that specialized in a single crop, such as corn or soybeans. The average farm size rose from around 205 acres in 1950 to almost 400 acres in 1969.[58]

The big farms often supplied food to support the nation's growing fast- and frozen-food industries — which demanded standardized and quality-controlled products. McDonald's quickly became the nation's biggest buyer of potatoes, apples and beef.

By the 1970s, another boom in domestic and international demand helped American farmers prosper, and the government began rewarding production instead of limiting it.[59]

A European-inspired movement to eat locally sourced, organically grown foods from smaller farms began to take hold in the 1970s.

CHRONOLOGY

1900s-1950s *Federal agencies begin regulating food; processed and frozen food goes on sale; farms become increasingly mechanized.*

1906 Congress passes Pure Food and Drug and Meat Inspection Acts.

1912 Oreos go on sale, followed in a few years by Kraft processed cheese and Hostess CupCakes.

1917 U.S. Department of Agriculture (USDA) issues standards for grading potatoes and meat.

1926 Clarence Birdseye pioneers quick-freezing and frozen food.

1933 Congress approves the first farm bill to support the prices of commodity crops like corn.

1939 USDA issues standards for a frozen product — peas — and publishes the first daily nutrition guide.

1948 McDonald brothers apply assembly-line techniques to cooking hamburgers. . . . A doughnut shop opens that will become Dunkin' Donuts.

1958 Worried about the burgeoning use of additives, Congress passes the Food Additives Amendment, which establishes the "generally recognized as safe" (GRAS) standard.

1960s-1970s *Environmental movement begins.*

1962 Rachel Carson publishes *Silent Spring*, revealing the dangers of pesticides on the environment.

1966 Child Nutrition Act requires federal regulations for school meals.

1969 USDA's Food and Nutrition Service begins operations.

1971 Chef Alice Waters opens Chez Panisse in Berkeley, Calif., using locally sourced organic produce.

1972 Congress establishes Environmental Protection Agency.

1980s-1990s *Genetically engineered crops appear; Congress sets up an organic-certification process.*

1983 Researchers develop first genetically engineered plant.

1990 Congress passes Organic Food Production Act, establishing nationwide standards for organic food.

1994 Studies show nearly 23 percent of American adults are obese.

1997 Revised GRAS program allows food additive industry to self-regulate.

2000s-Present *Federal oversight of food production increases; processed food comes under closer scrutiny.*

2002 A genetically engineered tomato is the first food to be nutritionally improved with the help of biotechnology.

2004 Morgan Spurlock's "Super Size Me" documentary triggers a debate about fast food.

2009 First lady Michelle Obama plants an organic garden at the White House.

2010 Congress passes Healthy, Hunger-Free Kids Act of 2010, setting nutritional guidelines for federally funded school lunches.

2012 Food sales reach $81.3 billion, up 13.5 percent from 2011.

2013 In response to changing tastes, McDonald's adds fruit and vegetables to its menu.

2014 The documentary "Fed Up," attacking the amount of sugar in American processed foods and beverages, opens nationwide. . . . The number of farmers markets in the United States has risen five-fold since 1994, from 1,755 to 8,268. . . . Rep. Rosa DeLauro proposes the Sugar-Sweetened Beverages Tax Act (SWEET Act), which would impose a tax on sugary soft drinks. . . . Consumer groups sue the U.S. Food and Drug Administration, claiming its revised GRAS procedures do not adequately protect the public.

Back to the Land

Organic farming has been practiced in the United States since the 1940s, but a growing demand for pesticide-free food in the 1960s and '70s — during the birth of the U.S. environmental movement — spawned the modern organic food industry.

Many consumers were alarmed by books criticizing modern farming methods and the dangers of excessive pesticide use, such as Rachel Carson's 1962 classic *Silent Spring*. They began demanding foods grown without man-made pesticides and other chemicals and sought out farmers who used non-chemical pesticides and herbicides and other environmentally friendly, or "sustainable," farming methods. The movement also attracted growing numbers of people interested in a "back to the land" alternative lifestyle that reconnected them with nature.

Although there was general agreement about what constituted organic farming, there were no national standards for organic food and animal production until 1990, when Congress passed the Organic Foods Production Act (OFPA). Only foods that meet those federal guidelines can be labeled "organic" and must be from farms certified as organic by a USDA-accredited entity.

Organic food producers and sales have grown steadily. In 2012, 12,771 organic-certified farms existed in the United States, according to the USDA, up 14 percent since 2008, and organic food sales reached $32.3 billion in 2013.[60]

The rise in demand for organic foods has been driven in part by consumers wanting to avoid foods containing genetically modified organisms, which were introduced on a large scale in U.S. commodity crops such as corn and soybeans in the late 1990s. Under USDA regulations, foods certified as organic cannot contain GMOs.

Some consumers oppose GMO foods on the grounds that they have not yet been proved to be safe for consumption, a claim most scientists dispute. GMO critics have been pushing, so far unsuccessfully, for labels to be required on GMO foods.[61]

Also in the 1990s, consumers became concerned about the amount of sugar in American food products. In 1998 the Center for Science in the Public Interest published a report, "Liquid Candy: How Soft Drinks are Harming Americans' Health," which criticized sugary soft drinks and suggested they may be linked to a rise in obesity, diabetes and tooth decay.

With the increased industrialization of agriculture and food production, consumer groups had long complained about what they felt were excessive amounts of additives in processed foods and antibiotics in meat, chicken and dairy products. Adding to some consumers' fears about food safety, news headlines reported outbreaks of diseases such as *E. coli* infections and other food-borne illnesses and so-called mad cow disease in Europe.[62]

In 1996, after television host Oprah Winfrey aired a show about mad cow disease and declared that she would never eat another hamburger, beef prices plunged. In response, a group of Texas cattle ranchers claimed she had defamed the entire industry and sued her in 1998 under a Texas law that prohibits "knowingly making false statements" about a perishable food business. The ranchers lost the $10.3 million suit.[63]

In 1997, under pressure from the food industry and Congress to speed up its additive certification program, the FDA began allowing manufacturers to certify that their food additives were generally recognized as safe (GRAS) — based on their own research — and the companies were not required to share that research data with the FDA.[64] As a result, industry critics say, many food companies began using new additives without sending their research findings to the agency or even notifying the agency that they were using new additives.

In 2001 Eric Schlosser's book, *Fast Food Nation*, followed in 2003 by Nestle's *Safe Food: The Politics of Food Safety* and Pollan's *The Omnivore's Dilemma*, helped jump-start what some have called the "good food" movement, a diverse collection of groups concerned about the shortcomings of industrial food production. The books and films "succeeded in making clear and telling connections between the methods of industrial food production, agricultural policy, food-borne illness, childhood obesity, [and] the decline of the family meal as an institution," Pollan said.[65]

However, most Americans were eating more processed and fast foods than ever before and were cooking at home less and less. As women took jobs outside the home, families increasingly depended on restaurant take-out meals. Between 1970 and 2008 Americans' food purchases for meals prepared outside the home rose from 34 percent to 49 percent, according to the Institute of Medicine.[66]

Dueling Food Studies Confuse Consumers

Conflicts of interest often plague nutrition studies.

Butter is bad for you. Butter is good for you. Salt is harmful. Salt is healthy. Saturated fats are a no-no. Saturated fats are not so bad. It's no wonder consumers are confused about nutrition and healthy eating.

A recent study showed that conflicting news stories about nutrition and health confound readers and make them likely to ignore the contradictory information as well as widely accepted nutritional advice, such as the importance of eating fruits and vegetables and exercising regularly, said the study's author, Rebekah Nagler, an assistant professor at the University of Minnesota School of Journalism & Mass Communication in Minneapolis.[1]

Analysts cite three causes for the problem: Reporters may be too quick to sensationalize a story, critics say, or simply get the facts wrong. Others say scientists might disagree about their conclusions, or vested interests on opposite sides of a debate may be skewing the results of studies without clearly revealing their conflicts of interest.

Robert Lustig, a pediatric endocrinologist and a University of California professor of clinical pediatrics, criticizes the media. "Nutrition is a complex subject and requires knowledge and expertise that many journalists just don't have," he says. "We need more reporting based on solid science."

Examples are not hard to find. A 2013 Australian study found that mice fed a high-fat diet and given a large dose of chlorogenic acid (a naturally occurring acid in coffee beans) and one of the primary plant compounds in coffee developed more fat than other mice. The mice, of course, had drunk no coffee, but the headlines said: "Drinking 5 cups of coffee will lead to obesity" and "Wrong amount of coffee could kill you."[2]

When *The New England Journal of Medicine* published the results of a recent study examining the health effects of sodium, different publications emphasized different aspects of the findings. *The Wall Street Journal* headline stressed that using too little salt could be dangerous: "Low-salt diets may pose health risks, study finds."[3] *Science Daily* began its article on the same study with a different slant: "More than 1.6 million cardiovascular-related deaths per year can be attributed to sodium consumption above the World Health Organization's recommendation of 2.0 g per day."[4]

The second problem involves conflicts of interest that plague many nutrition studies. "It's important to find out if a person conducting a study was funded and who funded them," says nutrition professor Marion Nestle of New York University. That's the first thing she checks when evaluating a study, she says. (Many journals require authors to report any potential conflicts of interest when they publish their work.)

Even studies that appear to be "scientific" should be examined closely for bias, experts say. When researchers recently examined studies investigating a link between sugary sodas and obesity, they found that all the studies that had been supported by the beverage industry found no link. But 10 of the 12 studies with no conflict of interest found a link.[5]

In a 2013 paper "Myths, Presumptions, and Facts About Obesity" in *The New England Journal of Medicine*, the authors claimed, among other things, that there is no proof that "snacking contributes to weight gain and obesity."[6] Some nutritionists who questioned the article's findings noted that the authors had received funding, grants or

Between 1970 and 2001 the number of fast food restaurants jumped from 30,000 to 222,000.[67]

This growing dependence on processed and fast food represented a massive nutritional shift toward added fat, sodium and sugar. As author Warner noted, "As a population, we ingest double the amount of added fats, half the fiber, 60 percent more added sugars, three-and-a-half times more sodium and infinitely greater quantities of corn and soybean ingredients than we did in 1909."[68]

Government, Industry Respond

Over the last two decades, the good-food movement has become more visible and powerful. University programs in nutrition studies have proliferated, and researchers have begun linking diseases such as diabetes to the national diet.

Locavore advocates have stressed the benefits of buying food locally, and food-safety proponents — along with animal-welfare groups and farm reformers — extoll

support from scores of food and beverage companies, including Coca-Cola, McDonald's, Kraft Foods, General Mills, PepsiCo, Red Bull and the World Sugar Research Organization. Their conflict-of-interest disclosures took up nearly half a page in the journal. [7]

Others, such as Jayson Lusk, a professor of agricultural economics at Oklahoma State University and author of *The Food Police*, say the public is often misled by "fear mongering" activists who paint a bleak picture of the nation's food quality. "The data just doesn't support the belief that everything is terrible, and it's the worst it's ever been," he says.

Adding to the confusion, the food and beverage industries fund numerous nonprofit organizations whose purpose is to rebut food activists' claims. For example, the nonprofit Center for Consumer Freedom, financed by food companies and restaurants, regularly attacks activists whose views it disagrees with. The group calls Nestle a "food fascist" and the Center for Science in the Public Interest (a Washington-based research group that examines nutrition, health and food safety issues) "the joyless eating club."[8]

Like many nutrition experts, Nestle advises consumers to closely check the conflict of interest notes in each scientific study for potential conflicts and bias. Others recommend respected nutrition sites, such as the Harvard School of Public Health's "The Nutrition Source."[9]

— *Robert Kiener*

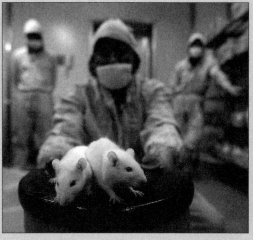

Getty Images/China Photos

Media reports are often blamed for sensationalizing science stories, or just getting the facts wrong. Reports on a 2013 study about mice erroneously concluded that drinking five cups of coffee could lead to obesity.

[1] Rebekah Nagler, "Contradictory nutrition news creates consumer confusion," *Science Daily*, Jan. 28, 2014, http://tinyurl.com/mvznqpr.

[2] Julie Flaherty, "Debunk the Junk," *Tufts Nutrition Magazine*, Summer 2014, http://tinyurl.com/l8ttwnc.

[3] Ron Winslow, "Low-salt diets may pose health risks, study finds," *The Wall Street Journal*, Aug. 13, 2014, http://tinyurl.com/lqzo5cx.

[4] Tufts University, "Estimated 1.65 million global cardiovascular deaths each year linked to high sodium consumption," *Science Daily*, Aug. 14, 2014, http://tinyurl.com/kgc9zfg.

[5] Maira Bes-Rostrollo, *et al.*, "Financial Conflicts of Interest and Reporting Bias Regarding the Association between Sugar-Sweetened Beverages and Weight Gain: A Systematic Review of Systematic Reviews," *PLOS Medicine*, Dec. 31, 2013, http://tinyurl.com/nhfv58h.

[6] Christa Cassaza, *et al.*, "Myths, Presumptions and Facts About Obesity," *The New England Journal of Medicine*, Jan. 31, 2013, http://tinyurl.com/k8kon3o.

[7] *Ibid.*; also see Gary Schwitzer, "The list of potential conflicts of interest in authors of the NEJM obesity myths paper," *Health News Review*, Jan. 31, 2013, http://tinyurl.com/a39y2a8.

[8] "What is the Center for Consumer Freedom?" Center for Consumer Freedom, http://tinyurl.com/7e2ypqm.

[9] "Knowledge for Health Eating," *The Nutrition Source*, Harvard School of Public Health, http://tinyurl.com/o64tllb/.

the benefits of smaller, more sustainable farming. Others have pressed government to better regulate additives, antibiotics and synthetic agricultural chemicals.

Retailers have listened. Organic food sales rose, as did the number of farmers markets. Supermarkets, led by chains like Whole Foods, catered to a growing demand for healthy foods. The chain's sales rose from $8 billion in 2009 to $12.9 billion in 2013, and profits more than tripled.[69] Wal-Mart expanded its Wild

Oats Marketplace organic foods brand and offered it nationwide — soon becoming the nation's largest seller of organic foods.[70]

In response to changing tastes and to compete for health-conscious customers, McDonald's announced in 2013 that it was adding more fruit and vegetables to its menu.[71]

Washington also got involved. First lady Michelle Obama oversaw the planting of a vegetable garden at the

Going Gluten Free: Fact or Fashion?

Some experts warn that the popular diet may be harmful.

Until recently, the only consumers who scoured grocery shelves for foods without gluten — a protein found in barley, rye and wheat — were those suffering from celiac disease, an autoimmune disorder. For them, consuming gluten can lead to iron deficiency, abdominal pain, diarrhea and other problems.

But only about 1 percent of the population suffers from celiac disease. To help them avoid gluten, the Food and Drug Administration in August implemented new labeling rules defining what the "gluten free" label on packaged foods means: The products must contain fewer than 20 parts per million of gluten.[1]

Despite the small percentage of celiac sufferers who avoid gluten for medical reasons, millions of Americans without the disease are opting for gluten-free diets. In a 2012 survey, nearly one-third of respondents said they were trying to eliminate or reduce gluten.[2]

The growing popularity of gluten-free diets has sparked a spirited debate among scientists and others. "There's no scientific evidence that [a gluten-free diet is] better for you if you don't have celiac disease," said Carol M. Shilson, executive director of the University of Chicago Celiac Disease Center.[3]

Seeing a profitable new market to exploit, the food industry has responded to the increased demand for gluten-free products: Items ranging from bacon to chicken nuggets to cereals and pancake mix now feature gluten-free labels. Even foods that never contained gluten, such as Chobani Greek Yogurt or Green Giant vegetables, are being marketed as gluten free.

Sales of such products have doubled in the past four years, to $23 billion.[4] Since General Mills began selling gluten-free Rice Chex in 2008, sales of the cereal have risen by double digits annually. The company now labels more than 600 products as gluten free.[5]

Facebook has more than 1,000 groups with gluten free in their name, including a dating group called "gluten-free singles."[6] There's even a magazine called *Gluten-Free Living*. A typical article, "Gluten-Free Wedding Bliss," details how the author "planned a completely gluten-free reception, and you can too."[7]

Some of the demand is driven by the popularity of best-selling diet books such as *Grain Brain*, *Wheat Belly* and the *Paleo Diet*, which shun wheat and other grains and link modern wheat varieties to obesity, diabetes, heart disease and even autism and Alzheimer's Disease.

According to David Perlmutter, a neurologist and the author of *Grain Brain*, in the last 40 years people have become addicted to gluten, which he calls "a modern poison."[8] New wheat hybrids have greatly increased the amount of gluten in wheat-derived products, Perlmutter contends, drastically increasing gluten sensitivity and overwhelming the immune system's ability to respond normally to gluten. (People are considered gluten sensitive if their bodies react badly to gluten but they do not have celiac disease.)

Perlmutter estimates that up to 30 percent of the population could be gluten sensitive today. He attributes that to the overuse of antibiotics, anti-inflammatory drugs and other medications, which, he says, when coupled with modern wheat varieties, have disturbed the bacterial balance in the gut. "This leads to inappropriate and excessive reactions to what might otherwise have represented a nonthreatening protein like gluten," says Perlmutter.[9]

William Davis, a cardiologist and author of *Wheat Belly*, says modern wheat varieties "raise blood sugar higher than nearly all other foods, including table sugar and many candy bars," leading to weight gain, diabetes, arthritis, cancer and heart disease.

Some consumers avoid gluten because of a study, published last April in *Rheumatology International*, indicating that a gluten-free diet can help alleviate fibromyalgia, a disorder characterized by widespread musculoskeletal pain and fatigue, often accompanied by irritable bowel syndrome, anxiety and depression.[10]

But skeptics abound. *Time* magazine's science and technology editor, Jeffrey Kluger, calls the gluten-free trend "a whole lot of . . . hooey, a result of trendiness, smart marketing, Internet gossip and too many people who know too little about nutrition saying too many silly things."[11]

"There are a lot of people who think that if they see something with a gluten-free label, it's healthier," said Tricia Thompson, a registered dietician who specializes in gluten-free diets. "And that's simply not true."[12]

David Katz, director of the Yale-Griffin Prevention Research Center, said that while a gluten-free diet is beneficial to people who react badly to gluten, "for everyone else, going gluten free is at best a fashion statement . . . and at worst an unnecessary dietary restriction that results in folly."[13]

Perlmutter has his scientific supporters, however. Gerard E. Mullin, associate professor of medicine at The Johns Hopkins School of Medicine in Baltimore and author of *The Inside Tract: Your Good Gut Guide to Great Digestive Health*, has called Perlmutter's book a "scientific account of how diet profoundly influences nerve health and brain function" and of "how the American diet rich in gluten and inflammatory foods is linked to neurological conditions."[14]

Some health experts warn that a self-administered gluten-free diet can make it harder to diagnose celiac disease and that if dieters have the disease and don't follow the gluten-free program properly they can harm their bodies.[15] And some nutritionists warn that a gluten-free diet could lead to a drop in needed nutrients and fiber.[16]

Davis warns against eating processed gluten-free foods, which usually contain rice flour, cornstarch, tapioca starch and potato flour. Such flours "are packed with highly digestible, high-glycemic index carbohydrates [that] send blood sugar through the roof," he said.[17]

And going gluten free can be expensive. According to one study, gluten-free foods are 242 percent costlier than their gluten-containing counterparts.[18]

— *Robert Kiener*

Getty Images/Bloomberg/Daniel Acker

Bisquick pancake mix is aimed at the millions of Americans turning to gluten-free diets. Scientists intensely debate whether they make sense for people without celiac disease.

[1]Michelle Healy, "Gluten-free food labels must now comply with FDA rules," *USA Today*, Aug. 5, 2014, http://tinyurl.com/nqjlumt.

[2]Julie Jargon, "The gluten-free craze: Is it healthy?" *The Wall Street Journal*, June 22, 2014, http://tinyurl.com/m6yvxk2.

[3]Nancy Stohs, "Gluten intolerance rising in developed countries," [Milwaukee] *Journal Sentinel*, April 27, 2010, http://tinyurl.com/2b85yfm.

[4]Jargon, *op. cit.*

[5]*Ibid.*

[6]*Ibid.*

[7]Jules Shepard, "Gluten-free wedding bliss," *Gluten-Free Living*, Aug. 27, 2014, http://tinyurl.com/ocel2b6.

[8]James Hamblin, "This is your brain on gluten," *The Atlantic*, Dec. 20, 2013, http://tinyurl.com/oph4xkw.

[9]See the FAQs on Perlmutter's website at http://tinyurl.com/pjopwgd.

[10]Carlos Isasi, *et. al.*, "Fibromyalgia and non-celiac gluten sensitivity: a description with remission of fibromyalgia," *Rheumatology International*, April 12, 2014, http://tinyurl.com/n8tuwgg.

[11]Jeffrey Kluger, "Eat more gluten: The diet fad must die," *Time*, June 23, 2014, http://tinyurl.com/nznz6fj.

[12]Helene Ragovin, "Gluten free-for-all," *Tufts Nutrition Magazine*, Summer 2013, http://tinyurl.com/podkwzm.

[13]David Katz, "Is gluten-free just a fad," *The Huffington Post*, Sept. 24, 2011, http://tinyurl.com/3wqsduy.

[14]"Grain Brain: The Surprising Truth about Wheat, Carbs, and Sugar — Your Brain's Silent Killers," *Integrative Practitioner*, www.integrativepractitioner.com/article.aspx?id=19834.

[15]Ragovin, *op. cit.*

[16]Holly Strawbridge, "Going gluten free just because? Here's what you need to know," *Harvard Health Blog*, Feb. 20, 2013, http://tinyurl.com/m8kkjlz.

[17]See William Davis, "Wheat Belly FAQs," The Wheat Belly Lifestyle Institute, http://tinyurl.com/nohft86.

[18]Ragovin, *op. cit.*

White House and later urged the food industry to "entirely rethink the products that you're offering, the information that you provide about these products and how you market those products to poor children."

Her "Let's Move!" campaign focused attention on the need for a balanced diet to combat obesity and helped spur Congress to pass the 2010 Healthy, Hunger-Free Kids Act, which authorized new nutritional standards for federally funded school lunches.

But there was also pushback. After animal rights activists began exposing poor conditions and abuses at farms and slaughterhouses across the country, the food industry backed restrictive state bills that made it illegal to take pictures or videos on a farm without the farmer's consent. These so-called "ag-gag" laws were passed in Iowa, Missouri and Utah in 2011 and 2012, and submitted for consideration in 10 state legislatures — Arkansas, California, Indiana, Nebraska, New Hampshire, New Mexico, Pennsylvania, Tennessee, Wyoming, and Vermont — last year. Some are being challenged as unconstitutional.

The food industry complained that food choice was a personal responsibility, and denied links between diet and obesity or other health conditions. Industry-backed groups lobbied successfully against proposed soda taxes and federal standards for marketing foods to children. Other groups fought proposed changes to nutrition labeling, such as making serving sizes larger to more realistically show how much sugar, sodium and calories are contained in a typical serving.

Consumer activists and others accused some food industry supporters of using tactics similar to those tobacco companies once used to defend their products, including disputing links between their products and illness, marketing to juveniles, using front groups to spread their message and insisting on self-regulation.

The food and beverage industries have backed up their lobbying efforts with big spending. In 2009 the American Beverage Association, Coca-Cola and PepsiCo spent more than $40 million lobbing Congress to help defeat a proposed soda tax, and between 2009 and 2012 food industries more than doubled their spending in Washington.[72] In contrast, the Center for Science in the Public Interest, the lead lobbying force for healthier food, spent about $70,000 lobbying in 2011 — about what the food industry spent every 13 hours, according to an analysis by Reuters in 2012.

"At every level of government, the food and beverage industries won fight after fight during the last decade," Reuters reported. "They have never lost a significant political battle in the United States. . . . In the process, they largely dominated policymaking — pledging voluntary action while defeating government proposals aimed at changing the nation's diet. . . ."[73]

After a rash of outbreaks of food borne illnesses, such as *E. coli* and salmonella, shook consumer confidence in the 2000s, in 2011 President Obama signed into law the FDA Food Safety Modernization Act. The first major piece of federal legislation addressing food safety since 1938, the law gave the FDA new powers to regulate how foods are grown, harvested and processed as well as the authority to recall foods.[74]

CURRENT SITUATION
Scrutinizing the FDA

In response to growing consumer concerns over whether the Food and Drug Administration is sufficiently vetting food additives, the Center for Food Safety (CFS), a consumer advocacy group, is suing the agency to force it to vacate its new fast-track additive-review process and return to procedures used before they were revised in 1997.

"For more than 15 years, FDA has allowed food manufacturers to decide whether a food additive requires FDA review," according to a suit filed by the center. "Under the proposed rule, which has never been finalized, FDA created a fast-track for manufacturers who believe a substance should be 'generally recognized as safe' (GRAS)."[75]

Previously, the FDA had to approve an additive before it could be used and was required to notify the public about the additive and provide opportunity for comment.

In its lawsuit, the CFS identifies several substances allowed under the fast-track process that may pose health risks and asks the court to order the FDA to fulfill its responsibility to protect public health. "FDA has an obligation to provide the regulatory scrutiny the public deserves," the suit said.

Some researchers say several additives certified as safe under the new rules may be linked to medical conditions. For instance, according to *The Washington Post*'s investigation, some scientists think the seaweed-derived texturizer and

Should the government tax sugary soda?

YES
Michael F. Jacobson
*Executive Director, Center
for Science in the Public Interest*

Written for *CQ Researcher*, September 2014

"big soda" has big denial issues. Whether it's the mounting scientific evidence of the diseases related to soda or the meaningful policy reforms needed to address those health effects, "big soda" responds with denial.

That's why the industry's response to Rep. Rosa DeLauro's Sugar-Sweetened Beverages Tax Act (SWEET Act) is so predictable. The bill is a bold, common-sense initiative to tax the sugar or other caloric sweeteners in sugary drinks at a rate of 1 cent per teaspoon, potentially raising $10 billion for the prevention and treatment of tooth decay and other soda-related diseases.

The measure also would direct prevention and treatment funds to populations that disproportionately bear the burden of soda-related diseases. According to the Department of Health and Human Services, Hispanic-Americans are 20 percent more likely to be obese than white Americans and 50 percent more likely to die from diabetes, while African-Americans are 50 percent more likely to be obese than white Americans and more than twice as likely to die from diabetes. Capturing the real social costs of sugary drinks and directing resources to critical public health needs is sound public policy.

By taxing the sugar and other caloric sweeteners in sugary sodas, the SWEET Act could spur the soda industry to produce healthier beverages. Instead, we have seen the industry respond to the decline in soda consumption by moving into high-sugar "energy drinks," as evidenced by Coca-Cola's recent purchase of a stake in the Monster Energy Drink franchise.

As for the legislation itself, "big soda" came out with its usual potted talking point: Obesity is complex, and you can't tax your way to health. Obesity and the other soda-related diseases are indeed complex, but the math on the health impact of sugar drinks is pretty simple. A 12-ounce cola contains a little more than nine teaspoons of sugar, according to the U.S. Department of Agriculture. The American Heart Association recommends that an average woman limit her daily consumption of added sugars to six teaspoons, and a man to nine.

Sugar drinks are nutritionally worthless, adding totally unnecessary calories to our diet. The overwhelming scientific evidence concludes that soft drinks are the only food or beverage that increases the risk of obesity and diabetes, cardiovascular disease and many other health problems.

The federal excise tax proposed in the SWEET Act charts a path toward improved health in the United States.

NO
Jayson L. Lusk
*Regents Professor and Willard Sparks Endowed
Chair of Agricultural Economics, Oklahoma State
University*

Written for *CQ Researcher*, September 2014

Should the government tax sugared soda? It already does. Farm policies make U.S. sugar prices two to three times higher than elsewhere. Moreover, ethanol policies have led to a more than doubling of the price of high fructose corn syrup since 2005. It's no wonder that per capita sugar consumption has fallen precipitously over the last decade.

Yet sugar tax advocates, either failing to understand the complex effects of existing policies or simply wanting more taxes, call for higher prices still. Increasing the price of sugared sodas will no doubt lower soda consumption, but by how much? And at what cost?

Numerous studies show that sugar tax policies have very small effects on a person's intake and weight. When sodas are taxed, consumers substitute other caloric foods or drinks, such as fruit juice or alcohol. That is one reason why some analysts argue that only across-the-board food taxes will significantly affect weight. The problem with food taxes, however, is that they are regressive, meaning the burden is disproportionately borne by the poor, who spend a larger share of their income on food than the rich.

Fundamentally, what philosophical basis motivates the view that soda taxes will increase consumers' well-being? Taxing soda is analogous to reducing consumers' real income. Few people look forward to a pay cut. It is true that excess soda consumption will to lead to health problems, but we also care about consuming tasty, satisfying food and beverages. Life is full of difficult trade-offs, and it is problematic, and paternalistic, for a third party to deem another person's choices "wrong," given that different people have different preferences and incomes. If people do not understand the risks of sugar consumption, then the appropriate policy response is information, not a tax.

Even if tax revenues could be directed toward education programs, one would need to show how the benefits of extra information offset the loss of that tax revenue, since there is scant evidence that nutritional education works. There are already several public and private health information campaigns, and it is unclear what effect yet another would have.

Obesity is a complicated issue. Soda taxes often appear to be a simple (if partial) solution for a big problem. But as witnessed by Denmark's recent decision to rescind its version of the "fat tax," the consequences and impact of such taxes are anything but simple.

Catering to the healthy food movement, restaurant chains like Chipotle, Panera, Freshii and sweetgreen feature low-fat salads and vegetarian wraps. The nation has more than 21,000 "fast-casual" restaurants, up from 9,000 a decade ago. Above, diners patronize a Chipotle Mexican Grill outlet in Hollywood, Calif.

stabilizer carrageenan, used in products ranging from ice cream to toothpaste, may cause diabetes or irritable bowel disease.[76]

But the FDA has refused to re-examine carrageenan's GRAS classification and continues to rely on industry-funded studies. It denied a petition for a review of the additive's safety filed by Joanne Tobacman, a University of Chicago physician and professor who submitted studies linking the additive to diseases.[77]

The Grocery Manufacturers Association insists that its proposed database will confirm the accuracy of industry assessments of the safety of food additives. Bruner, at the GMA, said the initiative is "a big step forward for the industry" and that it's important that the GMA "communicate to the world that we're taking the lead on this."

This is the right time for the food industry to rethink how it approaches food chemicals, he added, "in part because the entire food safety system is being redesigned under the Food Safety Modernization Act."[78]

Pandora's Lunchbox author Warner says the FDA has been unable to keep up with the food industry's push for new additives. "The food industry's blistering pace of innovation and the force of its lobbying efforts have always overwhelmed those charged with reining it in," she wrote.[79]

"In the five decades since Congress gave the FDA responsibility for ensuring the safety of additives in the food supply, the number has spiked from 800 to more than 9,000, ranging from common substances such as salt to new green-tea extracts," reported *The Washington Post*.[80]

The FDA has asked the food industry to voluntarily disclose its GRAS determinations and notify the agency before using new additives. "We are supportive of any initiative that promotes scientific rigor and transparency to independent GRAS determinations," FDA said in a statement.[81]

But such FDA declarations do not convince Laura MacCleery, chief regulatory affairs attorney for the Center for Science in the Public Interest. "That this [database] is seen as a step forward neatly illustrates the dysfunction built into the current system," she said. "It is outrageous that FDA doesn't already have the identity, much less the safety data, of all the substances added to the nation's food supply."[82]

Soda Tax Battle

On Sept. 23, three of the nation's biggest soft drink manufacturers — Coca-Cola, PepsiCo and Dr Pepper Snapple Group — vowed to cut by 20 percent the number of calories Americans consume from sugary sodas by 2025. They plan to accomplish this by selling more zero- and low-calorie drinks, reducing the size of their beverage containers and sponsoring educational campaigns to encourage consumers to reduce their calorie consumption.[83]

In announcing the initiative, an industry spokesperson seemed to acknowledge the role sugary sodas play in the country's obesity crisis and the escalating rates of diabetes and heart disease. "This is the single-largest voluntary effort by an industry to help fight obesity," said Susan K. Neely, chief executive of the American Beverage Association, the industry trade group.[84]

However, the soft drink industry has long questioned claims that health issues such as obesity are linked to the consumption of soft drinks, often noting that while soft drink consumption has declined recently, obesity rates have continued to rise. "There is no scientific evidence that connects sugary beverages to obesity," Coca-Cola's president of North America Brands, Katie Bayne, said in 2012.[85]

But Marlene B. Schwartz, director of the Yale Rudd Center for Food Policy and Obesity, says emphatically, "There are dozens of research studies documenting that sugary drinks significantly increase the risk of obesity, as well as Type 2 diabetes and metabolic syndrome," which is a group of risk factors that occur together and increase the risk for coronary artery disease, stroke and Type 2 diabetes. "There is absolutely no question that Americans will be healthier if they reduce their consumption of sugary drinks."

The new initiative by the soda industry builds on the companies' earlier initiatives to reduce the calories in soft drinks sold on school campuses and in vending machines in public buildings. "The focus really will be on transforming the beverage landscape in the U.S. over the next 10 years," said Neely.

But critics of the industry scoffed at the initiative, noting that consumption of high-calorie beverages has been declining in recent years. "What better way to get a public relations boost than to promise to do what's happening anyway?" said Kelly Brownell, an expert on obesity and dean of the Sanford School of Public Policy at Duke University.[86]

Nestle, of New York University, pointed out that the soda companies have been vigorously fighting a slew of state and local proposals to regulate sugary soft drinks, ranging from New York's failed effort to limit the size of soda containers to a proposed California bill that would require warning labels on such drinks. "While they're making this pledge, they are totally dug in, fighting soda tax initiatives in places like Berkeley and San Francisco that have exactly the same goal," said Nestle.[87]

A proposal for a federal tax on sugary drinks has been introduced by U.S. Rep. Rosa L. DeLauro, D-Conn., and three Democratic co-sponsors. Dubbed the SWEET Act, the Sugar-Sweetened Beverages Tax Act would impose a 1-cent tax on each teaspoon of sugar in soft drinks, or about 15 cents on a 20-ounce bottle of Coca-Cola.[88]

"The United States is facing a health crisis and the SWEET Act will help correct the path we are currently on," says DeLauro. The estimated $10 billion a year that would be generated by DeLauro's proposal would fund prevention, treatment and research for diet-related health conditions. The measure is pending in the House Energy and Commerce Subcommittee on Health.

"The soda tax is an old idea that voters have rejected time and time again," says Christopher Gindlesperger, spokesperson for the American Beverage Association. "People don't support taxing of grocery items such as soft drinks."

Although DeLauro's bill has almost no chance of passing in the Republican-dominated House, she insists, "We cannot rely on industry to deal with this problem voluntarily. If I have to introduce the bill in another session I will."

In California soda tax bills will be voted on in San Francisco and Berkeley in November.

OUTLOOK

Slow Change

Advocates of the good-food movement predict that over the next decade the availability of organic food, farmers markets, farm-to-table programs and interest in food issues will continue to grow.

"There should be good news in the future," says Center for Science in the Public Interest Executive Director Michael Jacobson. "The prices of organic foods are dropping and may continue to fall. Availability should rise. The drive to get locally sourced food, via farm-to-table and other movements will continue to expand."

"There's a vibrant interest in eating healthier," says New York University's Nestle. "And this movement will get stronger in the future. Schoolchildren are eating healthier, more young people are going into farming and there's more interest than ever in producing local, sustainable food."

The recent growth in university nutrition studies indicates that more people "are thinking critically about all aspects of food and nutrition," she says. In 1996, when New York University established its food studies program, she points out, it was, "virtually alone. Today scores of universities offer food studies programs."

Meanwhile, some unhealthy food trends likely will continue. Shannon King, whose family owns Hillbilly Hot Dogs in West Virginia, predicts "more and more people will be attracted by the fun and novelty of eating the latest, the biggest, the best new thing. Eating doesn't always have to be serious."

While few doubt that the interest in small, local farms will grow, experts point out that small farms alone can't feed the world, which is expected to reach a population of 11 billion by 2100.[89] "Farm-to-table is a great idea but it is not scalable nationwide," says Lusk, of Oklahoma State University. "There's no way we can rely on small farms to feed the nation or as much of the world as we are feeding now."

Many good-food activists are optimistic about the future of the movement, citing past successes in food nutrition labeling, banning many harmful additives and trans fats and regulating organic foods. But, they say, change comes slowly. "Forty years ago you had a hard time finding yogurt, brown bread or brown rice in supermarkets, and few people talked about nutrition," says Jacobson. "We've made real progress spreading the message about eating healthily, and we will make more."

Although the food and beverage industries have often resisted change, many experts think market forces will eventually force manufacturers to respond to a growing consumer demand for more nutritious, safer foods.

"For example, science is behind us on the dangers of consuming too much sugar," says Lustig, of the University of California, San Francisco. "We just need to spread the message and educate the public, then the industry will react."

NOTES

1. David Morgan, "Documentary: "Fed Up" with rising childhood obesity," CBS News, May 8, 2014, http://tinyurl.com/l6bo6zc.

2. *Ibid.*; also see Mark Bittman, "An Inconvenient Truth About our Food," *The New York Times*, May 13, 2014, http://tinyurl.com/mv4xr5y. See http://tinyurl.com/mr53bxu.

3. Michael Pollan, "Our National Eating Disorder," *The New York Times*, Oct. 17, 2004, http://tinyurl.com/ppbwshg.

4. Michael Moss, "The Extraordinary Science of Addictive Junk Food," *The New York Times*, Feb. 20, 2013, http://tinyurl.com/bzvvg6a.

5. "American adults are choosing healthier foods, consuming healthier diets," U.S. Department of Agriculture, Jan. 16, 2014, http://tinyurl.com/pm3qxc2.

6. For background, see Barbara Mantel, "Preventing Obesity," *CQ Researcher*, Oct. 1, 2010, pp. 797-820.

7. Tracy Saelinger, "Meet the BrusselKale, the Brangelina of Vegetables," *USA Today*, March 12, 2014, http://tinyurl.com/p2df7p5.

8. Julie Jargon, "McDonald's faces 'millennial' challenge," *The Wall Street Journal*, April 24, 2014, http://tinyurl.com/qhxkp99.

9. Megan Durisin, "Here's why healthy dining will be the next big thing in fast food," *Business Insider*, May 1, 2013, http://tinyurl.com/ct76rom.

10. See Cheryl D. Fryar, Margaret D. Carroll and Cynthia L. Ogden, "Age-Adjusted Prevalence of Overweight, Obesity, and Extreme Obesity Among Adults: United States, 1960–1962 Through 2011-2012," National Center for Health Statistics, Centers for Disease Control and Prevention, September 2014, p. 4, http://tinyurl.com/kbd9z8b. Also see Erik E. Finkelstein, *et al.*, "Obesity and severe obesity forecasts through 2030," *American Journal of Preventive Medicine*, June 2012, http://tinyurl.com/ov8see3. For statistics on obesity, see "Overweight and obesity: Facts," Centers for Disease Control and Prevention, Sept. 13, 2014, http://tinyurl.com/pg9ngan.

11. Melissa Healy, "Some good news about teen obesity rates," *Los Angeles Times*, Sept. 16, 2013, http://tinyurl.com/p23322l.

12. Gallup Poll, "Nutrition and Food," "How often, if ever, do you eat at fast food restaurants, including drive-thru, take-out, and sitting down in the restaurant — every day, several times a week, about once a week, once or twice a month, a few times a year, or never?" http://tinyurl.com/qh87m82.

13. "Rabobank: Fruit and vegetable consumption falls despite government efforts to promote health," *Rabobank*, July 4, 2013, http://tinyurl.com/mvtemv5.

14. Melinda Beck and Amy Schatz, "Americans' eating habits take a healthier turn, study finds," *The Wall Street Journal*, Jan. 16, 2014, http://tinyurl.com/qgas58l; also see "American adults are choosing healthier food, consuming healthier diets," U.S. Department of Agriculture, Jan 16, 2014, http://tinyurl.com/pm3qxc2.

15. Stephen Daniells, "U.S. organic food market to grow 14% from 2013-2018," *Food Navigator*, Jan. 3, 2014, http://tinyurl.com/mrb9zaj.

16. "National count of farmers market directory listing graph 1994-2014," U.S. Department of Agriculture, Aug. 14, 2014, http://tinyurl.com/nyrp6v9.

17. "Local food time ticker," The Land Connection, http://tinyurl.com/ms7a9ex.

18. Julia Moskin, "Hold the Regret? Fast Food Seeks Virtuous Side," *The New York Times*, July 25, 2014, http://tinyurl.com/m8nkzwv.

19. See "Food Paradise: Hot Dog Paradise," Travel Channel, undated, http://tinyurl.com/md5d5xw.

20. Erica Walsh, "Best Places to Pig Out: Meals That Will Blow Your Mind and Tip the Scale," Travel Channel, undated, http://tinyurl.com/m5stmoo.

21. Chris Dolmetsch, "New York soda ban rejected by state's highest court," Bloomberg.com, June 26, 2014, http://tinyurl.com/nvwh5fn.

22. "For clinical students interested in food law and policy, a cornucopia of opportunities," *Harvard Law Today*, June 1, 2013, http://tinyurl.com/oy9f2y6.

23 "2011 Estimates of food borne illnesses in the United States," Center for Disease Control and Prevention, Jan. 28, 2014, http://tinyurl.com/b28kn8l.

24. Moni Basu, "Unprecedented verdict: peanut executive guilty in deadly salmonella outbreak," CNN, Sept. 20, 2014, http://tinyurl.com/n57zawr.

25. Jenni Spinner, "Wal-Mart: food safety awareness at an all time high," *Food Production Daily*, Feb. 17, 2014, http://tinyurl.com/mcd6zvk.

26. Caroline Smith Dewaal, "Is America's Food Supply safe?" *Upfront*, May 1, 2014, http://tinyurl.com/kcjkwd6.

27. "Keeping America's Food Supply safe," Robert Wood Johnson Foundation, 2013, http://tinyurl.com/mkay4fz.

28. *Ibid.*

29. Lydia Zuraw, "Report identifies chemicals 'quietly added' to food under GRAS," *Food Safety News*, April 9, 2014, http://tinyurl.com/kaexz4o.

30. "NRDC Report: Potentially Unsafe Chemicals in Food Threaten Public Health," Natural Resources Defense Council, April 7, 2014, http://tinyurl.com/ngd8krf.

31. Kimberly Kindy, "Food additives on the rise as FDA scrutiny wanes," *The Washington Post*, Aug. 17, 2014, http://tinyurl.com/ouejrk4.

32. Lydia Zuraw, "Food Industry Association Plans to Make GRAS More Transparent," *Food Safety News*, Aug. 29, 2014, http://tinyurl.com/ph5wj4k.

33. For background, see Marcia Clemmitt, "Sugar Controversies," *CQ Researcher*, Nov. 30, 2012, pp. 1013-1036.

34. Kimberley Halkett, "US food industry battles against regulation," Al-Jazeera, Feb. 10, 2013, http://tinyurl.com/bsquqoa.

35. Betsy McKay, "What role should government play in combating obesity," *The Wall Street Journal*, Sept. 18, 2012, http://tinyurl.com/mvddroo.

36. For examples, see Jayson Lusk, *The Food Police* (2013), pp. 147-148.

37. "F as in fat; how obesity threatens America's future," Trust for America's Health, Sept. 2012, http://tinyurl.com/b85yp92.

38. "School Meals," Food and Nutrition Service, U.S. Department of Agriculture, http://tinyurl.com/lnjekm3.

39. "Remarks by the President and First Lady at the Signing of the Healthy, Hunger-Free Kids Act," The White House, Dec. 13, 2010, http://tinyurl.com/2gxzl4u.

40. Katrina Heron, "When did school lunch become a political issue?" *Politico*, May 26, 2014, http://tinyurl.com/kxnoh42.

41. "School Lunch: Implementing Nutrition Changes Was Challenging and Clarification of Oversight Requirements Is Needed," Government Accountability Office, January 2014, http://tinyurl.com/qyzr729.

42. Claire Suddath, "Tossing the First Lady's lunch," *Bloomberg Businessweek*, Aug. 21, 2014, http://tinyurl.com/koykrpl.

43. Tom Hamburger, "Michelle Obama's school lunch agenda faces backlash from some school nutrition officials," *The Washington Post*, May 30, 2014, http://tinyurl.com/lj72bf7.

44. Helena Bottenmiller Evich, "Behind the school lunch fight," *Politico*, June 4, 2014, http://tinyurl.com/oj7eb7x.

45. Allison Aubrey, "School nutrition fight widens as school board members join in," NPR, June 23, 2014, http://tinyurl.com/ktfqv4l.

46. Tom Hamburger, "House panel votes to allow school districts to temporarily opt out of dietary rules," *The Washington Post*, May 29, 2014, http://tinyurl.com/onnz56f.

47. Michelle Obama, "The campaign for junk food," *The New York Times*, May 28, 2014, http://tinyurl.com/o5d6qau.

48. "American Heart Association presses Congress to keep special interests off school menus," American Heart Association, May 29, 2014, http://tinyurl.com/nml5gel.

49. "Fact Sheet: Healthy, Hunger-Free Kids Act School Meals Implementation," U.S. Department of Agriculture, June 13, 2014, http://tinyurl.com/ner3py5. Wootan quote comes from: "House Continues Partisan Attack on Children's Health," Center for Science in the Public Interest, May 29, 2014, http://tinyurl.com/ledvvln.

50. *Ibid.*

51. Suddath, *op. cit.*

52. "America's culinary heritage: Not by bread alone," Cornell University, 2002, http://tinyurl.com/k6funfd.

53. Peter A. Coclanis, "Changes in American Agriculture in the Late 19th Century and the Early 20th Century," http://tinyurl.com/ob49cvv.

54. Gaia Vince, "Fertilisers: enriching the world's soil," BBC, Aug. 29, 2012, http://tinyurl.com/mkovh26.

55. Coclanis, *op. cit.*

56. Quoted in Melanie Warner, *Pandora's Lunchbox* (2013), p. 26.

57. *Ibid.*, p. 38.

58. Bill Ganzel, "Shrinking farm numbers," in Living History Farm, 2007, http://tinyurl.com/6oavjuq.

59. Bill Ganzel, "Farm boom of the 1970s," in Living History Farm, 2009, http://tinyurl.com/lvw3lsz.

60. Jane Sooby, "2012 Ag census reveals organic farming growth," California Certified Organic Farmers, June 30, 2014, http://tinyurl.com/n3u3vhf.

61. For background, see Kathy Koch, "Food Safety Battle: Organic vs. Biotech," *CQ Researcher*, Sept. 4, 1998, pp. 761-784; and Jason McLure, "Genetically Modified Food," *CQ Researcher*, Aug. 31, 2012, pp. 717-740.

62. For background, see Hoyt Gimlin and Marc Leepson, "Food Additives," *Editorial Research Reports*, 1969 (Vol. II); and Hoyt Gimlin and Marc Leepson, "Food Additives," *Editorial Research Reports*, 1978 (Vol. I); and David Hosansky, "Food Safety," *CQ Researcher*, Nov. 1, 2002, pp. 897-920; Mary H. Cooper, "Mad Cow Disease," *CQ Researcher*, March 2, 2001, pp. 161-184.

63. For background, see "Texas Cattlemen vs. Howard Lyman & Oprah Winfrey," Aug. 27, 2002, http://tinyurl.com/msssgkc.

64. For background, see Richard L. Worsnop, "Reforming the FDA," *CQ Researcher*, June 6, 1997, pp. 481-504.

65. Michael Pollan, "The food movement, rising," *The New York Review of Books*, May 20, 2010, http://tinyurl.com/2fm7fo8.

66. McLure, *op. cit.*

67. Sahasporn Paeratakul, *et al.*, "Fast-food consumption among US adults and children: Dietary and nutrient intake profile," *Journal of the American Dietetic Association*, October 2003, http://tinyurl.com/kdj7uje.

68. Warner, *op. cit.*, p. xvi.

69. David Aaker, "How Whole Foods market created the ultimate successful subcategory," Linked In, May 5, 2014, http://tinyurl.com/qzwwkag.

70. Lusk, *op. cit.*, p. 85.

71. Stephanie Strom, "With tastes growing healthier, McDonald's aims to adapt its menu," *The New York Times*, Sept. 27, 2013, http://tinyurl.com/psy8ycp.

72. Duff Wilson and Janet Roberts, "Special Report: How Washington went soft on childhood obesity," Reuters, April 20, 2012, http://tinyurl.com/7ww8zqb.

73. *Ibid.*

74. "FDA Food Safety Modernization Act (FSMA)," U.S. Food and Drug Administration, Sept. 25, 2014, http://tinyurl.com/m4x3shg.

75. "Center for Food Safety sues FDA over food additives," Center for Food Safety, March 13, 2014, http://tinyurl.com/kr9ns96. Also see http://tinyurl.com/mdqo2gj.

76. Kindy, *op. cit.*

77. *Ibid.*

78. Helena Bottemiller Evich, "Big food to divulge chemical info," *Politico*, Aug. 28, 2014, http://tinyurl.com/khwxs4l.

79. Melanie Warner, *Pandora's Lunchbox* (2013), pp. 104-105.

80. Kindy, *op. cit.*

81. Helena Bottemiller Evich, "Big food to divulge chemical info," *Politico*, Aug. 28, 2014, http://tinyurl.com/khwxs4l.

82. Maggie Hennessy, "Food manufacturers divulge chemical use; shouldn't be the last word, CSPI says," *Food Navigator*, Aug. 29, 2014, http://tinyurl.com/l6keqv4.

83. See Stephanie Strom, "Big Soda Makers Agree on Efforts to Cut Americans' Drink Calories," *The New York Times*, Sept. 24, 2014, p. B2, http://tinyurl.com/ma5cagf.

84. Bruce Horovitz, "Soda giants to cut calories 20% by 2025," *USA Today*, Sept. 23, 2014, http://tinyurl.com/letxe66.

85. Bruce Horovitz, "Coke says obesity grew as sugary drink consumption fell," *USA Today*, June 7, 2012, http://tinyurl.com/m5g68bm.

86. Strom, *op. cit.*

87. *Ibid.*

88. Chris Prentice, "U.S. lawmaker takes soda tax battle to Capitol Hill," *Reuters*, July 30, 2014, http://tinyurl.com/me96mtk.

89. Hannah Hickey, "World population to keep growing this century, hit 11 billion by 2100," *UW Today*, Sept. 18, 2014, http://tinyurl.com/kvwtkmx.

BIBLIOGRAPHY

Selected Sources

Books

Cohen, Deborah A., *A Big Fat Crisis: The Hidden Forces Behind the Obesity Epidemic — and How We Can End It*, Nation Books, 2013.

A senior natural scientist at the RAND Corp. think tank argues that the modern food environment — featuring larger portions, lower prices and intensive advertising — is to blame for America's obesity epidemic.

Lusk, Jayson, The Food Police: A *Well-Fed Manifesto About the Politics of Your Plate*, Crown Forum, 2013.

A professor of agricultural economics at Oklahoma State University criticizes food activists for not backing up their attacks on Big Food with scientific research.

Moss, Michael, *Salt Sugar Fat: How the Food Giants Hooked Us*, Random House, 2014.

A Pulitzer Prize-winning reporter investigates how food and beverage companies use sugar, salt and fat to entice consumers to overindulge in unhealthy foods and drinks.

Nestle, Marion, *Food Politics: How the Food Industry Influences Nutrition and Health*, University of California Press, 2013.

Blaming Americans' nutrition problems on the food industry's drive for consumers to eat more, a New York University nutrition professor explores the politics and economics of food.

Pollan, Michael, *Cooked: A Natural History of Transformation*, Penguin Books, 2014.

A leading activist in the food movement offers his view on how food moves from farm to table.

Pritchard, Forrest, *Gaining Ground: A Story of Farmers' Markets, Local Food, and Saving the Family Farm*, Globe Pequot Press, 2013.

A seventh-generation farmer chronicles his struggles to save his family's farm in an era of industrial farming.

Warner, Melanie, *Pandora's Lunchbox: How Processed Food Took Over the American Meal*, Scribner, 2013.

A freelance writer details the health implications of eating heavily processed food.

Articles

Beck, Melinda, and Amy Schatz, "Americans' Eating Habits Take a Healthier Turn, Study Finds," *The Wall Street Journal*, Jan. 16, 2014, http://tinyurl.com/qgas58l.

After years of pressure by activists and the government to eat healthier, Americans are cutting calories, fat, cholesterol and fast food.

Fleming, Amy, "Food trends in 2014: from digital dining to healthy junk food," _The Guardian_, Jan. 5, 2014, http://tinyurl.com/kg3p668.
Food's future may include innovations as varied as holographic chefs, "healthy" chocolate, frozen kale treats, edible soil and protein bars made from insects.

Heron, Katrina, "When Did School Lunch Become a Political Issue?" _Politico_, May 26, 2014, http://tinyurl.com/kxnoh42.
Some Republican lawmakers are working to scale back the revamped school lunch program, the executive director of the Edible Schoolyard Project writes.

Jargon, Julie, "The Gluten-Free Craze: Is It Healthy?" _The Wall Street Journal_, June 22, 2014, http://tinyurl.com/m6yvxk2.
Although only a small percentage of Americans have medical reasons for removing gluten from their diet, millions of others have decided to become "gluten free." How safe is their decision?

Kindy, Kimberly, "Food additives on the rise as FDA scrutiny wanes," _The Washington Post_, Aug. 17, 2014, http://tinyurl.com/ouejrk4.
This deeply reported exposé reveals that companies have succeeded in weakening government oversight over the additives used in food processing and production.

Patton, Leslie, "Have we reached peak burger?" _Bloomberg Businessweek_, Sept. 4, 2014, http://tinyurl.com/lop22wx.
After years of expansion and increasing sales, fast-food operations are beginning to slow, and some experts believe the industry has reached saturation levels.

Tanner, Lindsey, "Eating habits improve a bit, except among poor," The Associated Press, _USA Today_, Sept. 1, 2014, http://tinyurl.com/kzxc2y5.
A recent study shows a widening rich-poor diet gap, exacerbated during recent financial downturns.

Reports and Studies

"Access to Healthy Food: Challenges and Opportunities," Public Health Law Center, June 2012, http://tinyurl.com/pcfgkr7.
A well-researched overview by policy specialists covers key strategies to reduce or prevent obesity.

"Food Pyramids and Plates: What Should You Really Eat?" Harvard School of Public Health, www.hsph.harvard.edu/nutritionsource/pyramid-full-story/.
Harvard University nutritionists critique the Department of Agriculture's latest dietary guidelines for Americans and suggest changes.

For More Information

American Beverage Association, 1101 16th St., N.W., Washington, DC 20036; 202-463-6732; www.ameribev.org. Trade group representing companies producing nonalcoholic beverages.

Center for Science in the Public Interest, 1220 L St., N.W., Suite 300, Washington, DC 20005; 202-332-9110; www.cspinet.org. Food-safety group that advocates science-based government policies.

Grocery Manufacturers Association, 1350 I St., N.W., Washington, DC 20005; 202-639-5900; www.gmaonline.org. Represents large food and beverage companies.

Organic Trade Association, 28 Vernon St., Suite 413, Brattleboro, VT 05301; 802-275-3800; www.ota.com/index.html. Represents businesses in the organic supply chain, including those that produce food, fiber/textiles and personal care products.

Rudd Center for Food Policy & Obesity, Yale University, P.O. Box 208369, New Haven, CT 06520-8369; 203-432-6700; www.yaleruddcenter.org. Studies and advocates for policies aimed at preventing obesity, improving diets and decreasing stigmatization of obesity.

School Nutrition Association, 120 Waterfront St., Suite 300, National Harbor, MD 20745; 301-686-3100; www.schoolnutrition.org. Represents more than 55,000 school cafeteria and food workers.

U.S. Food and Drug Administration, 10903 New Hampshire Ave., Silver Spring, MD 20903; 888-463-6332; www.fda.gov/Food. Responsible for the safety of 80 percent of the food supply (not including meat and poultry) and the safety of food additives.

2

Regulating Toxic Chemicals

Jennifer Weeks

A shopper loads her cart with water in St. Albans, W. Va., on Jan. 10, 2014, a day after a chemical spill at Freedom Industries in nearby Charleston contaminated drinking water supplies for 300,000 West Virginians. The spill from a 40,000-gallon storage tank showed the vulnerability of the nation's water supplies as well as the flaws in federal and state laws designed to protect the public from hazardous chemicals.

Getty Images/Tom Hindman

O n Jan. 9, Charleston, W. Va., residents be-gan complaining of a strong licorice-like smell in the air. Inspectors soon found a 40,000-gallon tank at a Freedom Industries chemical storage facility leaking an oily substance into the Elk River, just upstream from the intake for the drinking water supply for 300,000 people.

The odorous substance was 4-Methylcyclohexanemethanol, or MCHM, a chemical used in washing mined coal. At 6 p.m., after residents had been using their tap water all day, Gov. Earl Ray Tomblin declared a state of emergency, ordering people in nine counties not to drink, cook with or bathe in the contaminated water.[1] Bottled water stocks quickly disappeared from store shelves.

But federal and state officials were unable to clearly explain the risks posed by the leak. On Jan. 11 local water samples contained less than one part per million of MCHM — a level federal officials considered safe to consume.[2] The state began lifting the water ban, even as doctors and hospitals continued to receive numerous complaints of skin rashes, nausea and other symptoms.

On Jan. 15, officials at the Centers for Disease Control and Prevention (CDC) in Atlanta advised pregnant women not to drink the water. By Jan. 20, Tomblin said, "I'm not going to say absolutely, 100 percent that everything is safe," and "if you do not feel comfortable, don't use it."[3]

Two days later, Freedom Industries executives said smaller amounts of another chemical, a blend of polyglycol ethers known as PPH, had also leaked into the river. However, the company refused to provide the specific chemical formula of the blend, which it called "proprietary."[4]

From *CQ Researcher*,
July 18, 2014.

25

Mining, Chemical Plants Are Key Toxic Sources

About 70 percent of toxic chemical disposals and releases in 2012 originated from metal mining, chemical manufacturing and electrical utilities.

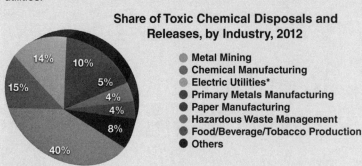

Share of Toxic Chemical Disposals and Releases, by Industry, 2012

- Metal Mining
- Chemical Manufacturing
- Electric Utilities*
- Primary Metals Manufacturing
- Paper Manufacturing
- Hazardous Waste Management
- Food/Beverage/Tobacco Production
- Others

* Includes coal combustion and natural gas production.

Source: "2012 Toxics Release Inventory National Analysis Overview," U.S. Environmental Protection Agency, Toxics Release Inventory, February 2014, p. 17, http://tinyurl.com/qajwd86

Tomblin finally lifted the emergency ban on Feb. 28, but many skeptical residents continued to use bottled water for months.[5] During the first two weeks of the spill, according to a review by the CDC and state regulators, hundreds of emergency room patients who had been exposed to tainted water had complained of symptoms such as nausea, rashes and vomiting.[6]

The spill revealed multiple flaws in federal and state laws designed to protect the public from hazardous chemicals. It also showed that public water supplies are vulnerable to chemical spills. Unlike U.S. laws regulating drugs and pesticides, the Toxic Substances Control Act (TSCA), which regulates commercial chemicals in the United States, does not require manufacturers to prove their products do not harm human health or the environment when used as directed. Instead, TSCA requires the U.S. Environmental Protection Agency (EPA) to prove that a chemical poses an "unreasonable" risk to health or the environment before it can order a manufacturer to test it. Because the agency has to meet such a high standard to prove the need for testing, in the nearly 40 years since TSCA was enacted the EPA has required manufacturers to test only about 200 of the 84,000 chemicals in use today — and has banned only five.[7]

Thus, regulators, emergency responders and the public have little health and safety information about many widely used chemicals. For example, the Safety Data Sheet (a standard summary that manufacturers must publish about a potentially hazardous chemical) for MCHM says there is "no data available" on its flammability, explosive properties, carcinogenicity or potential for hazardous reactions.[8] Similarly, the CDC said information was "very limited" about the potential health effects of PPH.[9]

Such incidents highlight the "utter failure" of the Toxic Substances Control Act, said Erik Olson, senior director for health and food at the Natural Resources Defense Council, an environmental advocacy group. "[W]e simply don't know much if anything about the toxicity of these and thousands of other chemicals used in commerce, including many that are in widespread use. And there are virtually no rules applicable to ensure safe use of most of these chemicals."[10]

Chemical industry representatives reject that view. "The notion that there are 84,000 substances in commerce that have never been tested is wrong," says Michael Walls, vice president for regulatory and technical affairs at the Washington, D.C.-based American Chemistry Council (ACC), the largest U.S. trade association for the chemical industry. "The TSCA inventory [of chemicals in commerce] is updated every four years, and recent updates have found that there are only about 8,000 substances in commerce that are in active use. EPA has [at least some] information on the vast majority of them."

The Freedom Industries spill also revealed lax state enforcement of federal laws designed to protect drinking water.[11] West Virginia regulators, for instance, had not inspected the Freedom site since 2001 to verify whether it had been meeting the conditions in its permit under the Clean Water Act (CWA). West Virginia's agreement with the EPA on CWA enforcement left inspection schedules up to the state.[12] And the state's Bureau of Public Health had not assessed the Charleston water system for possible threats since 2002, as the federal Safe Drinking Water Act (SDWA) requires periodically.[13] Without a current assessment, state agencies had no plan to protect the city's drinking water, which the SDWA recommends — but does not require.[14]

Many experts are also worried about accidents at chemical manufacturing plants and petrochemical refineries, which use large quantities of industrial chemicals. Serious accidents in the past several years include:

- An April 17, 2013, explosion at a fertilizer plant in West, Texas, that killed 14 people and injured hundreds more;
- A fire and release of flammable vapor and fire particles at a petrochemical refinery in Richmond, Calif., on Aug. 6, 2012, that forced neighboring communities to shelter indoors and caused more than 15,000 people to seek medical treatment for respiratory problems; and
- An April 2, 2010, explosion and fire at a petrochemical refinery in Anacortes, Wash., that killed seven workers.[15]

The United States "is facing an industrial chemical safety crisis," Rafael Moure-Eraso, chairman of the U.S. Chemical Safety Board (CSB) — an independent federal agency that investigates industrial chemical accidents — told a congressional committee in March. And many recent accidents could have been prevented if companies had used available technologies to make their plants safer, he added.

"[S]tate and federal regulators are not able to ensure safety at refineries," Moure-Eraso stated. "They are under-resourced [and] outgunned by a powerful industry that seeks to blunt and sometimes even roll back the already inadequate regulatory system in the U.S." [16]

Industry trade groups strongly disagree. "Data from the Bureau of Labor Statistics consistently show that chemical manufacturing is one of the safest industries in the United States," says William Allmond, vice president for government relations with the Society of Chemical Manufacturers and Affiliates (SOCMA) in Washington, D.C., which represents makers of specialized chemicals. "We have some of the most stringent regulations in the world."

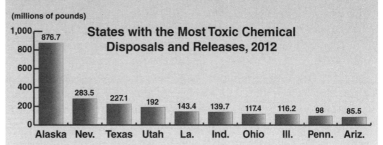

Alaska Leads in Toxic Chemical Disposals

Facilities in Alaska released or disposed of more toxic chemicals than in any other state in 2012. Most of those chemicals came from waste rock and other materials related to metal mining.

(millions of pounds)

States with the Most Toxic Chemical Disposals and Releases, 2012

State	Millions of pounds
Alaska	876.7
Nev.	283.5
Texas	227.1
Utah	192
La.	143.4
Ind.	139.7
Ohio	117.4
Ill.	116.2
Penn.	98
Ariz.	85.5

Source: TRI Explorer, U.S. Environmental Protection Agency, Toxics Release Inventory, data released March 2014, http://tinyurl.com/nq8dlup; "A Guide to Toxics Release Inventory for Alaska," Division of Spill Prevention and Response, Alaska Department of Environmental Conservation, 2011, http://tinyurl.com/o746ltn

But Moure-Eraso wants U.S. chemical facilities to be required to use "inherently safer" designs and equipment in order to reduce the possibility of accidents.[17] Inherently safer strategies can range from simplifying complicated industrial processes to using smaller quantities of hazardous chemicals or replacing hazardous chemicals with more benign ones.

Health, environment and labor advocates as well as homeland security specialists have urged Congress to require chemical companies to consider inherently safe design for more than a decade, but have failed, in part due to opposition from the chemical industry. "[T]here are very powerful influences, and in politics you always sort of trace that back to the money," said Christine Todd Whitman, who proposed legislation to promote inherently safe technology when she headed the EPA from 2001-2003.[18]

Chemical industry representatives say inherent safety is complex and could end up shifting risks rather than reducing them. For example, storing smaller quantities of hazardous chemicals at factories could require more frequent shipments of those substances, increasing the risk of accidents in transit. In their view, the chemical industry is already highly regulated, and federal agencies should help companies comply with existing health and safety standards.

"Inherently safe technology is not a one-size-fits-all solution," says Walls of the ACC. Companies might use different processes to create the same product, he explains, so regulations mandating certain steps at one plant might not make sense at another.

Besides workplace accidents and spills or leaks of toxic chemicals, Americans are also exposed to many potentially hazardous chemicals in household and consumer products. For instance, some flame-retardant chemicals widely used in furniture, carpet and electronics have been banned for certain uses because they cause cancer or nerve damage. But many still show up in products made before the bans or in nonrestricted uses, resulting in the chemicals being widely dispersed into the environment.[19]

Health and environmental advocates also worry about endocrine disruptors — chemicals used in many consumer products that mimic the natural hormones that regulate growth and other processes in the body. Such chemicals can harm growth, reproduction and neurological and immune systems in humans and animals, according the National Institute of Environmental Health Sciences.[20]

As Congress, advocacy groups and regulators debate how to protect Americans from chemical hazards, here are some issues they are considering:

Do chemical plants need stronger safety regulations?

Recent accidents at chemical plants and refineries have spurred calls for stricter regulation of such sites, but manufacturers' trade groups say the industry is highly regulated and has a better safety record than other major industries.

Last August, after the fertilizer plant explosion in West, Texas, President Obama appointed an interagency working group to find ways to improve safety at chemical plants and protect communities from industrial chemical accidents.[21] The group has identified key areas for action, including:

- Strengthening community-level planning and preparation for chemical accidents;
- Improving coordination among federal and state regulators;
- Improving interagency management of data on hazardous chemicals, and

- Modernizing policies and regulations governing the management of hazardous chemicals and prevention of chemical spills.[22]

Manufacturers' representatives say that the industry has greatly improved safety through voluntary initiatives. The American Chemistry Council (ACC) began a Responsible Care program in 1988, which is required for all council members. It sets out broad leadership and management principles for members, including making "continual progress toward a goal of no accidents, injuries or harm to human health and the environment." More than 240 U.S. companies participate in the program, including major corporations such as Dow, DuPont and 3M.

"The chemical sector has an injury rate 45 to 50 percent lower than overall manufacturing in the United States, and ACC member companies' records are better than the chemical industry overall," says ACC vice president Walls. If Freedom Industries had been an ACC member, Walls contends, it would have been required to address problems with the storage tank that leaked MCHM into the Elk River.

"Voluntary systems are helpful when facilities adopt them, and when they're comprehensive, but they don't take the place of regulations," says Anna Fendley, legislative representative for the United Steelworkers, which represents the majority of unionized chemical workers. "Not every facility adopts voluntary initiatives." As for the industry's safety record, she says, her union's members "see small releases and near-misses at their facilities all the time."

Workplace chemicals are regulated by multiple agencies under various laws. For example, ammonium nitrate, an ingredient in some types of fertilizer, fueled the 2013 fertilizer plant explosion in Texas. By itself, ammonium nitrate does not burn, but when it comes in contact with combustible materials, the risk of fire increases. It also can explode if stored in a confined space and heated to a high temperature. Anti-government extremist Timothy McVeigh used an ammonium nitrate bomb to destroy a federal office building in Oklahoma City in 1995, killing 168 people and injuring 680 others.[23]

After the West, Texas, explosion, the U.S. Government Accountability Office (GAO) reported that no one knows the total number of U.S. facilities that store ammonium nitrate, although more than 1,300 facilities in 47 states reported to the Department of Homeland Security (DHS) in 2013 that they had the chemical on-site. The DHS tracks some explosive chemicals, but some types and quantities fall below its reporting thresholds.

The GAO also found that the Occupational Safety and Health Administration (OSHA) (which regulates ammonium nitrate storage in workplaces) rarely inspects fertilizer plants, and that EPA regulations requiring risk-management plans for facilities storing certain hazardous chemicals did not cover ammonium nitrate.[24]

After the Texas disaster, two trade organizations, the Fertilizer Institute and the Agricultural Retailers Association, began a voluntary initiative called ResponsibleAg. Fertilizer distributors and retailers were invited to join the program, which aims to educate members about federal regulations for storing and handling ammonium nitrate and anhydrous ammonia, another chemical component of fertilizer that can burn the eyes, skin and lungs. Under the program, members' facilities will be audited every three years to demonstrate that they are complying with federal requirements.[25]

The United Steelworkers has called for major changes in the use of another toxic chemical, hydrofluoric acid (HF), which the union says is used by 50 U.S. refineries to boost gasoline octane. When accidentally released, HF can produce a dense vapor cloud that can travel up to 25 miles before the cloud disperses.[26] Contact with the chemical can cause burns and harm eyes, skin, throat and lungs. High exposures can be deadly.[27]

According to a 2013 union survey of workers, during the three years before the report was published 131 accidents and near-misses involving hydrofluoric acid occurred at the 23 refineries covered by the study. It also found gaps in HF safety systems and accident readiness at many of the refineries, putting at risk an estimated 26 million people living nearby.[28]

The union wants oil companies to phase out the use of HF. "There are safer processes and chemicals" available, says Findley. "But the industry has not been receptive to the idea of switching because changing out equipment could be costly."

In response to the report, a spokesperson for the American Petroleum Institute said refineries use HF to meet government requirements for cleaner-burning fuels, and asserted, "Our safety record is strong and we are committed to keeping it that way."[29]

Should manufacturers be required to prove their chemicals are safe before marketing them?

Environment, health and labor advocates say TSCA's central flaw is that — unlike federal laws regulating drugs and pesticides and chemical regulations adopted in 2006 by the European Union — American chemical manufacturers do not have to prove new chemicals are safe before they put them on the market.

"People think that when they buy products in a store and use them, they can assume they're safe, but that's not the case," says Lynn Goldman, dean of the Milken Institute School of Public Health at George Washington University. Goldman served as assistant administrator for toxic substances at the EPA from 1993-1998.

Under TSCA, before the EPA can order a manufacturer to test a new chemical, the agency must show that the substance either poses an "unreasonable" risk to human health or the environment or will be produced in large enough quantities that it could result in substantial exposure for humans or the environment. The EPA also must show that testing is needed to predict how the chemical will affect health or the environment.[30]

"Even when we know a lot about a chemical and it's clearly toxic, EPA can't do anything about it because of the way the law is written and the legal hurdles," says Andy Igrejas, national campaign director for Safer Chemicals, Healthy Families, an alliance of more than 450 environment and health advocacy groups. Moreover, he argues, manufacturers have no incentive to generate health and safety data on their products. "If you have it, you are required to disclose it to the EPA, so their incentive is not to do testing," he says.

EPA leaders want Congress to amend TSCA and give the agency more power to require manufacturers to test chemicals. In 2009 the agency published six principles for updating the law. One stated that manufacturers should provide the EPA with "the necessary information to conclude that new and existing chemicals are safe and do not endanger public health or the environment."[31] The agency also began using its limited powers under TSCA to obtain more information from manufacturers, instead of asking them to volunteer it.

Fourteen people died and hundreds were injured in a fertilizer plant explosion in West, Texas, on April 17, 2013. An apartment building, above, was among the many neighboring structures destroyed or damaged. More than 1,300 facilities in 47 states reported to the Department of Homeland Security that as of August 2013 they stored ammonium nitrate, a fertilizer component that caused the Texas explosion. In August, President Obama appointed a task force to find ways to protect communities from industrial chemical accidents.

In a 2013 report the GAO said the EPA's new approach was an improvement, but the agency could do more. Notably, the EPA was not requiring chemical companies to share toxicity and exposure data that they now must provide to European Union (EU) regulators in order to market their products in Europe.

Europe's toxic chemicals law — the Registration, Evaluation, Authorisation and Restriction of Chemicals act (REACH) — is based on the precautionary principle, which contends that if something could potentially harm human health or the environment, it should be regulated even if a full scientific case has not yet been made to support controls.[32]

Under REACH, companies that manufacture or sell chemicals in the EU are required to register information about the properties of their products in a central database at the European Chemicals Agency (ECHA) in Helsinki, Finland. The law also requires them to identify substitutes for the most dangerous chemicals currently in commerce (known as Substances of Very High Concern, or SVHCs), a group that includes chemicals that cause cancer or birth defects, harm reproductive systems, or persist in the environment. Companies must obtain permission from the chemicals agency to import these

chemicals into the EU, and over time will be required to find substitutes for them.[33] REACH is being enacted in phases and is scheduled to be fully in force by 2018. The EU is evaluating chemicals to determine whether they will be listed as SVHCs: currently 155 chemicals are on the candidate list.[34]

U.S. companies that were selling chemicals in the EU had to register in 2008, and have been submitting safety and exposure data on their products. The burden is heaviest on smaller companies. SOCMA's Allmond called REACH a serious trade barrier in testimony before the International Trade Commission last November.[35] But larger companies appear less burdened. For example, multinational giant Dow states on its website that it has fully complied with recent REACH deadlines, and that its customers "will be able to purchase products from Dow as easily as they have done in the past."[36]

By not requiring U.S. chemical companies to share the same toxicity and exposure data that they now provide the EU, the GAO report said, the "EPA is missing an opportunity to collect data that it has identified as an essential part of assessing chemical risk and future chemical regulation."[37]

In response, EPA Acting Assistant Administrator James Jones wrote, "as EPA identifies needs for REACH-generated data . . . the Agency intends to pursue obtaining these data from U.S. companies using voluntary or regulatory means as necessary." However, Jones also stated, unless Congress gives the agency more authority to obtain information from manufacturers and regulate chemicals, the EPA "will not be able to successfully meet the goal of ensuring chemical safety now and into the future."[38]

Some U.S. chemical companies have told the EPA that they cannot give the agency toxicity data submitted to the EU under REACH because the information is protected by legal agreements between the companies and the ECHA.[39] Currently, the EPA is asking European regulators to let companies share their REACH data with the agency. The EPA could also use subpoena power under TSCA to obtain the data.[40]

Industry representatives also say requiring all chemicals to be tested before they enter the market would be impractical and expensive. "[T]he sheer number of new chemicals that are submitted to EPA each year (roughly 20 per week) and the constantly evolving universe of new uses means that the detailed scrutiny and use-by-use approval that makes sense for food additives, drugs and pesticides will never work for industrial chemicals more generally," Beth Bosley, president of the Boron Specialties chemical company, told Congress in February.[41]

Chemical trade groups are willing to provide some information about chemicals already on the market but say the EPA should focus on chemicals produced in large quantities and used in ways likely to pose risks. The EPA, in fact, is moving in that direction. In 2012 it identified 83 high-risk chemicals known to be hazardous and that meet one of four conditions: They build up in the tissue of living organisms, are used in consumer or children's products, are widely dispersed or have been detected in humans or the environment.

The agency is performing risk assessments for those chemicals but has not estimated how long the work will take. (Risk assessments are studies that review health and exposure information to decide which threats are the most dangerous and which groups are most vulnerable.) It is seeking data from government databases and medical research libraries on thousands of other chemicals to determine whether they should also be assessed.[42]

"EPA should look at the chemicals that are in commerce, prioritize the ones that need additional review, do a timely assessment of those substances, and take whatever actions are required," says ACC's Walls. "We've worked with them to prioritize chemicals for further review, and we want to help EPA speed up those assessments."

Chemical manufacturers also say many of the 84,000 chemicals on the EPA's TSCA inventory of chemicals in commercial use are no longer being produced or sold, so it would be pointless to test them. "EPA should be required to reset the inventory," says Allmond of SOCMA. "The public deserves to know how many chemicals are really in commerce." The true figure is probably somewhere between about 10,000 and 25,000, according to SOCMA.[43] In 2012, companies reported to EPA that they produced or imported 7,690 chemicals in

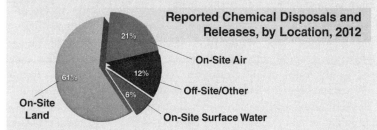

Most Toxic Chemical Disposals Occur on Land

In 2012, 21,024 facilities reported total on- and off-site disposal or other releases of 3.6 billion pounds of toxic chemicals. Most were disposed of or released on-site to land (including landfills, other land disposal and underground injection).

Reported Chemical Disposals and Releases, by Location, 2012

21%
12% — On-Site Air
6% — Off-Site/Other
61% — On-Site Surface Water
On-Site Land

Source: "2012 Toxics Release Inventory National Analysis Overview," Toxics Release Inventory, U.S. Environmental Protection Agency, February 2014, p. 2, http://tinyurl.com/qajwd86

what the agency considers significant quantities (25,000 pounds or more).[44]

But little public information is available about the health and safety effects of many chemicals in use today. As a result, when a risky chemical is banned or becomes controversial, manufacturers might substitute others that also could pose health risks. For example, many companies have removed the plasticizer BPA from food and beverage containers because of concerns that it may affect human health at very low doses.[45] However, some scientists have found that certain BPA substitutes may also have similar affects.

And after the Consumer Product Safety Commission banned a widely used but carcinogenic flame retardant called TRIS from children's clothing in 1977, manufacturers substituted other flame retardants thought to be safer.[46] But evidence is growing that the substitute chemicals are also risky and that they are released into the environment when the clothing is discarded. Other recent studies show that commonly used brominated flame retardants can mimic estrogen hormones and may be endocrine disruptors — chemicals that mimic hormones responsible for regulating biological processes, such as brain growth.[47]

"We call it the toxic treadmill," says Laurie Valeriano, executive director of the Washington Toxics Coalition, a state-level advocacy group based in Seattle. "Manufacturers keep switching from one toxic chemical to another. That's why we need national regulation that would require chemicals to be tested. If manufacturers had to put information about their products out before they could sell them, we could solve this problem."

Should companies have to disclose information about hazardous chemicals?

Under TSCA, when companies submit data to the EPA from health and safety studies of chemicals, they can designate it as confidential business information (CBI) if it would reveal manufacturing processes or other commercially sensitive information. The data is available to EPA staff with clearances but is not released to the public.

Many critics argue that manufacturers have abused this policy. "A tremendous amount of information is claimed as CBI," says former EPA assistant administrator Goldman. "To challenge those claims, you need a staffer to read them and write responses, which takes resources. For companies, it's easier to stamp information confidential than to determine whether it really is sensitive, because they know EPA doesn't have the staff to challenge them."

Chemical producers say if they disclose sensitive information about the composition of chemicals or production processes, competitors can use the information to undercut them. "Companies may spend 10 years or more developing and testing a specialty chemical," says Allmond of SOCMA. "Innovation is what keeps our members in business. If they publicly disclose everything about their products, their competitors will immediately mine their data." SOCMA has recommended allowing companies to use generic names when they submit information to the EPA instead of specific chemical names.

In 2010, the EPA began tightening its policy on CBI claims, reviewing past claims that shielded the identity of chemicals in health and safety studies and then declassifying information found to have been inappropriately classified. It also provided for the first time free web access to the TSCA inventory of the chemicals currently on the market.[48]

Health and environmental advocates worry that TSCA reform proposals being considered in Congress would reverse that progress. A draft bill circulated by Illinois Republican Rep. John Shimkus, chairman of the Energy and Commerce Committee's Environment

and Economy Subcommittee, "would effectively require EPA to hide the identity of a chemical in the context of a health and safety study if the manufacturer has claimed it as confidential," Igrejas of Safer Chemicals, Healthy Families testified in April. "Thus, the public would be able to see that there is a chemical on the inventory that causes cancer, birth defects, infertility or brain damage, but they would not be allowed to know the name of that chemical."[49]

In fact, retailers are responding to public protests and requests from consumer advocates for stores to disclose the chemical ingredients in the products they sell. For instance, late last year Target began asking vendors to complete assessments of 7,500 household, personal care and baby products. The national retailer developed a system to rank products based on the sustainability of their ingredients, overall environmental impacts and ingredient transparency (whether the product gives customers a complete ingredient list.)[50] Walmart and Whole Foods also have developed product rating systems that require suppliers to disclose information about chemicals in their products.[51]

Some states have passed laws and regulations — including disclosure requirements — to control chemicals more stringently than TSCA. In 1989 Massachusetts enacted the Toxics Use Reduction Act, which requires companies that use large quantities of hazardous and toxic substances to tell the state how much of each chemical they use. Companies also must develop plans for addressing chemical spills and leaks and for reducing their use of toxic chemicals.

"When you carefully look at chemical usage and where waste occurs, there always are places where you can make improvements and either find substitutes or use less," says Liz Harriman, deputy director of the Toxics Use Reduction Institute (TURI) at the University of Massachusetts-Lowell. TURI works with companies and communities in Massachusetts to reduce the use of toxic chemicals. Between 1990 and 2005, facilities subject to the law reduced their use of toxic chemicals by 40 percent and onsite spills by 91 percent. "Usually those changes save money" as well, Harriman says.[52]

For example, TURI has shown Massachusetts dry cleaners how to clean clothes using water and detergent — instead of the solvent perchloroethylene (PERC) — and then shape the garments with special equipment to prevent shrinkage. "PERC is a neurotoxin and suspected carcinogen. There are a number of alternatives on the market for it now, and regulators are starting to clamp down on PERC use," says Harriman.

"That eliminates a very toxic substance. But left to their own devices or their vendors' recommendations, dry cleaners probably would have changed to replacement chemicals that might only be slightly better than PERC," Harriman states.

Last fall California began requiring manufacturers to seek safer alternatives to harmful chemicals in some widely used products.[53] As a first step, the state proposed three categories of consumer products for scrutiny: children's sleeping products that contain foam padding, spray polyurethane foams and paint and varnish strippers.[54] Companies that make or sell these products in California must report what their products contain and options for substituting more benign chemicals. The state can then limit, restrict or ban use of those chemicals in those products.[55]

However, SOCMA's Allmond predicts that California's regulations will harm the state's economy. "There's a lot of industry concern about the direction California is taking," he says. "Manufacturing is already fleeing the state because companies can't afford to give up that information."

BACKGROUND

Modern Hazards

Humans have long recognized that chemicals can be both hazardous and useful. Ancient Greeks knew that exposure to asbestos fibers caused "sickness of the lungs," but nonetheless used them in cloth and candle wicks.[56] Lye — a caustic compound extracted from wood ashes that can burn eyes and skin — has been used for centuries to make soap and cure foods.

But as Europe and the United States industrialized in the late 1800s, factory workers were exposed to large quantities of acids, solvents, dyes and other toxic substances. Industries buried wastes or dumped them into rivers and harbors, and consumers did not know whether products they purchased contained dangerous substances.

From the 1890s through the 1920s muckraking U.S. journalists publicized many dangers, including unsafe workplaces and threats to public health. Upton Sinclair's 1906 novel *The Jungle* described filthy and dangerous conditions in Chicago's meatpacking industry. And *Collier's* magazine spotlighted false claims and unsafe ingredients in so-called patent (nonprescription) medicines.

Describing one concoction, "Dr. King's New Discovery for Consumption" [tuberculosis], which contained chloroform and opium, journalist Samuel Hopkins Adams observed: "The chloroform temporarily allays the cough, thereby checking Nature's effort to throw off the dead matter from the lungs. The opium drugs the patient into a deceived cheerfulness. The combination is admirably designed to shorten the life of any consumptive who takes it steadily." [57]

In response Congress in 1906 passed the Meat Inspection Act and the Pure Food and Drug Act, empowering government regulators to inspect meat processing plants and seize products that were mislabeled or contained harmful or spoiled ingredients. But while manufacturers could be punished for making false claims, they did not have to obtain government permission before marketing new products.

That changed in 1937, after 107 people in 15 states (including 34 children) died after taking elixir of sulfanilamide, a new medicine for strep infections. A chemist

A bulldozer exposes one of the tanks used to hold toxic waste in the Love Canal neighborhood in Niagara Falls, N.Y. In the late 1970s, state agencies began relocating residents from the community, which had been built atop a former chemical dump site, after tests showed high rates of cancer among residents. The disaster sparked passage of the Comprehensive Environmental Response, Compensation and Liability Act (the Superfund law) and prompted grassroots groups across the nation to organize against toxic threats.

Getty Images/Liason/Joe Traver

had dissolved the powdered medication in diethylene glycol, normally used as antifreeze, which he failed to realize was poisonous.[58] In response Congress passed the Federal Food, Drug, and Cosmetic Act, which required new drugs to be tested for safety before marketing.

By then the fast-growing chemical industry was inventing thousands of new materials, including polychlorinated biphenyls (PCBs), used as coolants and lubricants; synthetic estrogens (female hormones); pesticides such as DDT, a potent mosquito-killer; and many types of plastic. The Haber-Bosch process, invented in 1909, made it possible to convert nitrogen from the air into a form used during World War II to manufacture explosives, and later to make synthetic fertilizer.

In the 1930s and '40s thousands of U.S. workers joined unions, which pressed businesses to reduce the risk of workplace accidents and exposure to toxic substances. By the 1930s scientists had shown that inhaling silica dust and asbestos caused lung disease. Unions pressed for workplace safety standards, but reforms through the 1940s and '50s focused mainly on traumatic injuries, such as machine accidents, rather than on exposure to toxic substances.

Abundance and Risks

After World War II the chemical industry generated a plethora of new products, including vaccines, food additives, pesticides and herbicides. New materials, particularly plastics, found their way into consumer goods. For most Americans these advances were signs of progress. DuPont's advertising campaign for years used the motto "better things for living . . . through chemistry."

But some products proved to be unsafe. In the 1950s regulators banned more than a dozen food additives because they caused cancer, organ damage or other toxic effects in animals.[59] In 1958 Congress adopted the Delaney Clause, which banned any food additive that caused cancer in laboratory animals. Rachel Carson's 1962 bestseller *Silent Spring* warned that some long-lasting pesticides, such as DDT, were accumulating in the environment, harming fish and birds and contaminating food supplies.

In the late 1960s, as Americans became increasingly concerned about pollution, waste and overuse of natural resources, a national environmental movement emerged, marked by celebration of the nation's first Earth Day on April 22, 1970.[60] More than 20 million Americans attended rallies and teach-ins designed to force environmental issues onto the national agenda.

In response, Congress created new agencies to protect workers and the public from toxic chemicals and pollutants, including the U.S. Environmental Protection Agency (EPA) in 1970, the Occupational Safety and Health Administration (OSHA) in 1971 and the Consumer Product Safety Commission (CPSC) in 1972.

Congress also enacted landmark environmental laws, including the Clean Water Act (1972), the Safe Drinking Water Act (1974) and the Toxic Substances Control Act (1976).[61] TSCA required companies to give the EPA 90 days' notice before marketing new chemicals, and authorized the agency to require a manufacturer to do safety testing if a chemical presented "unreasonable" risk of injury.

Environmentalists said this "long, slow, cumbersome process" put the burden of proof on the EPA to first show that chemicals were harmful instead of requiring manufacturers to demonstrate that they were safe before they went on the market.[62] In 1980 the U.S. General Accounting Office [later renamed the Government Accountability Office] chastised the EPA for moving too slowly to test chemicals, asserting that "neither the public nor the environment are much better protected" than they were before TSCA was enacted.[63]

In the mid-1970s, frightened residents of the Love Canal neighborhood in Niagara Falls, N.Y., discovered toxic substances leaking into their basements and reported a high incidence of cancer. Their homes had been built on a former chemical waste dump, where thousands of tons of industrial chemicals had been buried between 1947 and 1952. In 1978 New York state and the federal government declared emergencies at the site and relocated more than 200 families.[64]

Health studies ultimately failed to show conclusive links between chemical exposures and cancer risks at the site, but the disaster led to the passage of the Comprehensive Environmental Response, Compensation and Liability Act (CERCLA, better known as the Superfund law), which created a trust fund to pay for cleanup of abandoned toxic waste sites.[65] Love Canal also underlined how little was known about the health effects of many commercial chemicals. And it launched an environmental health movement as grassroots groups started organizing against toxic threats across the nation.

C H R O N O L O G Y

1906-1958 *U.S. begins regulating consumer goods to protect buyers from unsafe products, but has little control over workplace safety.*

1906 Congress passes Pure Food and Drug Act after journalists expose filthy conditions in meatpacking houses and widespread use of dangerous ingredients in patent medicines.

1924 Five employees at a Standard Oil refinery die and 32 are hospitalized after exposure to tetraethyl lead, a gasoline additive.

1930 Congress creates Food and Drug Administration (FDA) to regulate food and pharmaceuticals.

1938 After tainted medicine kills 105 people, Congress passes the Food, Drug and Cosmetic Act, which requires food additives and drugs to be proven safe before they can be marketed to the public.

1947 A ship carrying ammonium nitrate catches fire and explodes while docked in Texas City, Texas, killing 586 people and injuring thousands.

1958 Congress adopts the Delaney Clause to the Food, Drug and Cosmetic Act, banning food additives that cause cancer in animals.

1970-1978 *Congress creates new agencies to protect consumers and workers from hazardous substances.*

1970 Congress creates U.S. Environmental Protection Agency (EPA).

1971 Congress creates Occupational Safety and Health Administration (OSHA) to regulate conditions in the workplace.

1972 Consumer Product Safety Commission (CPSC) is established. . . . EPA bans pesticide DDT due to its harmful impact on environment and human health, as Rachel Carson's 1962 bestseller *Silent Spring* warned.

1976 Congress passes the Toxic Substances Control Act (TSCA), authorizing the EPA to regulate new commercial chemicals but exempting the 62,000 already in use at the time.

1978 New York state agencies start moving residents out of Love Canal, a Niagara Falls community built on top of a former chemical dump site, after tests suggest a connection between chemical exposures and cancer among residents.

1980-2000 *New concerns emerge about chemicals, including special risks to children.*

1983 OSHA requires employers to show workers how to safely handle toxic chemicals.

1986 California requires warning labels on products that are carcinogenic or cause birth defects

1990 Congress orders leaded gasoline to be phased out by 1996.

1996 Congress tightens standard for pesticide residues in food and requires special protection for infants and children.

2005-2014 *Health and environmental advocates lobby for tighter regulations.*

2005 Explosion at BP refinery in Texas City, Texas, kills 15 workers, and injures more than 170; BP receives record fines for safety violations.

2007 European Union's REACH chemical regulation law, which requires manufacturers to prove chemicals are safe before they enter the market, enters into force. . . . Department of Homeland Security publishes anti-terrorism standards for chemical facilities.

2013 Ammonium nitrate at a fertilizer plant in West, Texas, explodes, killing 14 people, injuring more than 160. . . . President Obama directs federal agencies to improve safety and security at chemical facilities.

2014 An estimated 10,000 gallons of industrial chemicals leak from storage tanks into West Virginia's Elk River, leaving 300,000 residents without clean drinking water. . . . Chemical industry supports congressional proposals to reform Toxic Substances Control Act, but health and environmental advocates call draft laws too weak.

Debate Continues Over Widely Used BPA

Scientists are studying whether the chemical is safe at very low levels.

Bisphenol A (BPA) is an industrial chemical used in plastic resins and many consumer products, particularly in food and beverage containers such as bottles and cups. Researchers have known for years that BPA causes negative health effects when humans are exposed to it at high levels, but the federal government is now studying whether very low doses of BPA can also be harmful.

Researchers discovered in the 1930s that BPA is an endocrine disruptor, meaning that when it enters mammals' bodies it mimics estrogen, the natural hormone that regulates female sexual development and reproductive cycles. For many years, experts believed BPA was harmful only at high doses, but in the late 1990s studies began to detect harmful effects — such as cancer, genital defects in males, malformed eggs and obesity — in lab animals exposed to levels as low as a few parts per billion.[1]

Other scientists said the low-dose results could not be replicated or that tests using other methods produced conflicting results.[2] But as confusing reports accumulated, consumers became alarmed that BPA might leach from containers into food and drinks. In response, many retailers offered water bottles and cups made from other plastic resins, prominently labeling the containers "BPA-Free."

In 2008 the National Toxicology Program, a federal interagency program that studies toxic effects of chemicals in the environment, reported "some concern" that BPA could harm the brain and prostate gland and cause behavioral problems in fetuses, infants and young children; "minimal concern" that it could harm breast development or cause early puberty in girls; and "negligible concern" that it could have reproductive effects in adults.[3]

Two years later the Food and Drug Administration (FDA), which regulates the use of chemicals in food and medicines, announced that it shared the toxicology program's concern about BPA's impact on the brain, prostate gland and behavior in fetuses, infants and young children. However, the agency did not ban the use of BPA in food containers. Instead, it sought more input on BPA science while supporting the chemical industry's voluntary steps to stop using BPA in baby bottles, infant feeding cups and food and formula packaging for infants.[4]

Today the FDA says other uses of BPA in food packaging are safe and that the levels of BPA that can migrate from containers into food or beverages are very low.[5] But scientists are continuing to study the impact of BPA at very low doses.

"The data increasingly suggests that BPA exposure has very subtle effects," says Linda Birnbaum, director of the National Institute of Environmental Health Sciences (NIEHS) and the National Toxicology Program. "It also is starting to suggest that standard studies that are done on rats and mice to test for endocrine disrupting effects are not asking the right questions. Things may happen at low doses that don't happen at higher doses."

Anti-Regulatory Backlash

In the 1980s political momentum swung against government regulation, which many business advocates and conservative politicians argued was slowing economic growth and stifling innovation. President Ronald Reagan (1981-89) slashed budgets at the EPA, OSHA, and CPSC and appointed officials opposed to what they viewed as overregulation. Reagan also required that proposed regulations undergo a cost-benefit analysis so that no regulation could be implemented unless its potential benefits to society were greater than its costs — a policy continued by all of his successors.[66]

In response, health and safety advocates focused on other measures, such as so-called right-to-know policies that required companies to notify federal and state officials about significant quantities of hazardous chemicals used in their plants, and to tell emergency responders about any accidents or leaks involving those substances. Right-to-know measures were in part a response to the deadly 1984 chemical gas leak at a plant owned by a Union Carbide subsidiary in Bhopal, India. The leaking methyl isocyanate killed at least 3,800 people and injured thousands more.[67] Less than a year later, a chemical leak at a Union Carbide plant in West

For most toxic substances, scientists assume that "the dose makes the poison" — in other words, that harm increases as subjects are exposed to larger doses. But some recent studies have found that even low doses of BPA and other hormone-disrupting chemicals have negative effects — results that would not be found by studies involving higher doses.[6] The idea that some chemicals may be harmful at levels well below those that have been tested and determined to be safe has become known as the "low-dose hypothesis."

Scientists are divided on this idea. In one recent study, 12 FDA researchers found that high doses of BPA in the womb affected rats' body weight, reproductive development and hormone levels after birth, but low doses (at levels that humans routinely are exposed to) did not produce those effects, thus contradicting the low-dose hypothesis. Scientists who had found effects at low doses of BPA in other studies argued that the experiment's methods were flawed. Nevertheless, the FDA reiterated its position that BPA exposures "at the very low levels that occur in some foods" were safe.[7]

As scientists debate how to design studies and measure BPA's effects at low doses, researchers are starting to question whether some BPA substitutes are safe. In May, scientists at a Texas company that specializes in testing chemicals for their effects on the endocrine system published a study in which they heated 50 BPA-free baby bottles, cups, water bottles and other products made from hard, clear plastic. Many of the products leached other chemicals, which also had estrogenic effects.[8]

The researchers emphasized that their findings showed only a possible hazard, not a confirmed risk to human health, which would require much more information to prove. The study also found that some products containing BPA substitutes did not leach estrogenic chemicals, indicating that it is possible to make safe BPA-free products.[9]

— Jennifer Weeks

[1] Adam Hinterthuer, "Just How Harmful Are Bisphenol A Plastics?" *Scientific American*, Aug. 18, 2008, http://tinyurl.com/k9gwroz.

[2] Denise Grady, "In Feast of Data on BPA Plastic, No Final Answer," *The New York Times*, Sept. 6, 2010, http://tinyurl.com/kqevu8h.

[3] "Bisphenol A (BPA)," National Toxicology Program, August 2010, http://tinyurl.com/ngsgfrl. The program's scale has five levels of adverse effects: serious concern, concern, some concern, minimal concern and negligible concern.

[4] "Update on Bisphenol A for Use in Food Contact Applications," U.S. Food and Drug Administration, January 2010, http://tinyurl.com/modh73s.

[5] "Questions and Answers on Bisphenol A (BPA) Use in Food Contact Applications," U.S. Food and Drug Administration, May 13, 2014, http://tinyurl.com/mytavno.

[6] Laura N. Vandenberg, *et al.*, "Hormones and Endocrine-Disrupting Chemicals: Low-Dose Effects and Nonmonotonic Dose Responses," *Endocrine Reviews*, vol. 33 (June 2012), pp. 378-455, http://tinyurl.com/q5ae7gs; Elizabeth Grossman, "Scientists Warn of Low-Dose Risks of Chemical Exposure," *Yale Environment 360*, March 19, 2012, http://tinyurl.com/6pcmp6a.

[7] Brian Bienkowski, "New BPA Experiment Finds No Low-Dose Effects," *Scientific American*, Feb. 13, 2014, http://tinyurl.com/msjzwun.

[8] George D. Bittner, Chun Z. Yang and Matthew A. Stoner, "Estrogenic Chemicals Often Leach from BPA-Free Plastic Products That Are Replacements for BPA-Containing Polycarbonate Products," *Environmental Health*, vol. 13, no. 1, May 28, 2014, http://tinyurl.com/n2yp82l; Mariah Blake, "These Popular Plastic Bottles May Be Messing With Your Hormones," *Mother Jones*, June 16, 2014, http://tinyurl.com/lbjtjsj.

[9] Bittner, *et al.*, *op. cit.*

Virginia caused at least 135 people to seek medical treatment for eye, throat and lung irritation.[68]

In 1986 Congress passed the Emergency Planning and Community Right to Know Act, which required companies to tell the EPA and state officials about hazardous chemicals used at their plants, and to notify emergency responders about any chemical leaks or accidents. The same year California required state regulators to list chemicals used by companies in the state that were known to cause cancer, birth defects or other reproductive damage. Businesses had to put warning labels on products containing the listed chemicals and warning signs in workplaces where the substances were used.[69]

During President Bill Clinton's administration (1993-2001), Congress passed the Food Quality Protection Act, tightening standards for pesticide residues in foods. The law was one of the first to require regulators to consider children's greater sensitivity when establishing human tolerance levels for chemicals.[70]

In 1998 the EPA teamed with chemical and oil industry trade groups and the advocacy group Environmental Defense to launch an initiative called the High Production Volume (HPV) Challenge. It called on

Water Supplies Vulnerable to Chemical Spills

"State agencies usually don't have enough resources."

Experts warn that many public water supplies could be contaminated by chemical spills like the MCHM that this year leaked into the river that provides drinking water for Charleston, W. Va. Even though federal laws set standards for drinking water quality and require states and communities to analyze their water sources for possible threats, those laws often are poorly enforced.

"It's always a challenge for state environmental agencies to inspect all of the permitted facilities they regulate," says Evan Hansen, president of Downstream Strategies, a private environmental consulting firm in West Virginia. "Agencies usually don't have enough resources, so they have to set priorities and decide which sites to inspect."

The U.S. Environmental Protection Agency (EPA) implements the Clean Water Act, which forbids industrial companies from discharging pollutants into rivers and lakes without a permit. In addition, under the Safe Drinking Water Act, the EPA sets maximum allowable levels of chemical, biological, radiological and physical contaminants in drinking water supplied by public water systems, which provide water to 86 percent of Americans.[1]*

In nearly all states, the EPA has delegated authority to state environmental agencies to enforce the two laws. The EPA is responsible for monitoring how well states apply the laws but retains authority to enforce them if states don't.[2] Every state except Wyoming implements the Safe Drinking

---

* Fourteen percent of Americans, mostly in rural areas, get their water from private wells, which are not regulated by the EPA.

Water Act, and all but Idaho, Massachusetts, New Hampshire and New Mexico implement Clean Water Act programs within their states.[3]

In 1996 Congress amended the Safe Drinking Water Act to require states to determine which public water supplies were vulnerable to pollution; the law provided federal funding for the studies. The law encouraged — but did not require — states to then develop plans for protecting water supplies found to be vulnerable to pollution.

"We have reviewed many of these documents from water systems all over the United States," said Erik Olson, senior director for health and food with the Natural Resources Defense Council, an environmental advocacy group. "Most of those for surface water systems highlight known or potential industrial, commercial or other sources of pollution upstream of their facility."[4] Surface water systems include lakes, rivers and wetlands.

For example, West Virginia's assessment for the Elk River found 53 possible contamination sources in the Charleston area's watershed, including seven industrial sites in the "Zones of Critical Concern" — areas where a spill or leak would quickly affect drinking water supplies. But the Natural Resources Defense Council found little evidence that either the state or Charleston's private water utility had done anything to address those threats.[5]

As occurred in West Virginia, many state agencies also do not frequently inspect sites that have permits to discharge pollutants into rivers and lakes. The EPA has called for inspections of large facilities every two years and smaller ones every five, but the agency does not track state inspections of specific facilities from year to year.[6]

---

companies to make data available on hazardous chemicals produced or used in the United States in large quantities (greater than 1 million pounds per year). During the ensuing decade the EPA collected information on more than 2,200 chemicals.[71]

During the 1990s scientists also began focusing on so-called endocrine disruptors. A controversial 1996 book by two scientists with doctorates in zoology, Theo Colborn

and John Peterson Myers, and journalist Diane Dumanoski, *Our Stolen Future*, warned that endocrine-disrupting chemicals were widespread in the environment and could be linked to birth defects, lower sperm counts in men and certain types of cancer.[72] But some scientists said the case was not proved yet.

Pressure to regulate endocrine-disrupting chemicals was "a political movement, and it's based on lousy science,"

After the Freedom Industries disaster, Democratic U.S. Sens. Joe Manchin and Jay Rockefeller of West Virginia and Barbara Boxer of California introduced a measure that would require states to inspect chemical storage facilities every five years, and every three years for those near public water supplies. The bill also would set minimum federal standards for chemical tank construction and leak detection and require companies to inform the states, the EPA and local water systems about which chemicals they store.[7]

The Senate Environment and Public Works Committee approved S. 1961 by voice vote in April, but the measure has not been scheduled for floor action. U.S. Rep. Shelley Moore Capito, R-W.Va., has introduced a companion version in the House, but it had not been discussed or voted on as of mid-July.

Water utilities say companies need to immediately inform them of spills and provide detailed information on the leaked substance, including human health risks and any available guidance for treating and removing it from drinking water.[8]

But for many chemicals, including the MCHM that spilled in West Virginia, little information is available on toxicity. The safety information sheet produced by the MCHM manufacturer says there is "no data available" on the chemical's flammability, its explosive or hazardous properties or its potential for causing cancer.[9]

After the spill, the West Virginia legislature passed a bill requiring better planning and enforcement to protect drinking water from chemical leaks. The legislation also created a program to monitor above-ground chemical storage sites and required the state public health bureau to study long-term health effects from the Elk River spill. It also required all water utilities in the state to have written plans for protecting their water sources from chemical spills.[10]

But as the state Department of Environmental Protection — widely viewed by environmentalists as deferential to the industries it regulates — writes regulations implementing the new law, observers predict that it may weaken those reforms. "A bill this strong never would have passed in a normal year here," says Hansen. "Now there's lots of pressure from industries that want to minimize its impact."

— Jennifer Weeks

[1]"National Primary Drinking Water Regulations," U.S. Environmental Protection Agency, http://tinyurl.com/7adas3b.

[2]For background on delegation see Robert Esworthy, "Federal Pollution Control Laws: How Are They Enforced?" Congressional Research Service, May 23, 2014, pp. 10-13, http://tinyurl.com/m62znet.

[3]"Delegation by Environmental Act," Summary data (December 2007, updated November 2010), Environmental Council of the States, http://tinyurl.com/oc6qbkf.

[4]Erik Olson, testimony before the Committee on Environment and Public Works, U.S. Senate, Feb. 4, 2014, p. 5, http://tinyurl.com/pzoytf2.

[5]*Ibid.*

[6]"What Are Expectations Related to Compliance Monitoring Within States?" U.S. Environmental Protection Agency, last updated June 19, 2014, http://tinyurl.com/ouk7ow9.

[7]"S. 1961, Chemical Safety and Drinking Water Protection Act of 2014," http://tinyurl.com/ngrk4z6.

[8]Letter to Senate Environment and Public Works Committee, Subcommittee on Water and Wildlife, American Water Works Association and Association of Metropolitan Water Agencies, Feb. 3, 2014, http://tinyurl.com/q2wzc8g.

[9]"Material Safety Data Sheet for Crude MCHM," Eastman Chemical Co., http://tinyurl.com/pt5tcht.

[10]Ken Ward, "What Now For West Virginia, Its Water and Its Future?" *Coal Tattoo, The Charleston Gazette,* March 9, 2014, http://tinyurl.com/n8m53jc.

said Bruce Ames, a professor of biochemistry and molecular biology at the University of California at Berkeley.[73]

But the authors responded that their book presented "a profoundly new way to examine the impacts of chemical contamination," and that critics who questioned whether chemicals with hormonal effects could harm humans were ignoring extensive research showing that these chemicals had harmful effects on animals.[74]

Reach

After Clinton-era efforts to control chemicals, political momentum during President George W. Bush's administration (2001-08) again swung away from strong regulation of industries, including the chemical sector. The pace of federal regulation fell sharply after pro-business officials were put in change at many regulatory agencies and budgets were cut. Rulemaking fell by more than 50 percent at the FDA and 57 percent at the EPA between 2001 and 2008 compared to during the Clinton administration. OSHA withdrew more than a dozen regulations that had been proposed under Clinton and delayed acting on silica dust, which had been identified as a workplace health threat.[75]

Meanwhile, the European Union — an important market for U.S. companies — was moving toward tighter regulation of chemicals. After five years of debate, the EU in 2006 adopted the REACH law, based on the precautionary principle.[76] The approach was the reverse of the Toxic Substances Control Act (TSCA), which allowed chemicals to be marketed unless the government could show conclusively that they would be harmful. REACH also required European manufacturers to provide more information about their products' health and environmental effects than TSCA.[77]

Europe's alternative model helped to build political support for reforming chemical regulations in the United States. In 2009 President Obama's first EPA administrator, Lisa Jackson, outlined principles for TSCA reform, which included faster EPA and manufacturer review of high-priority chemicals and requiring manufacturers to provide information showing that new and existing chemicals are safe.[78]

CURRENT SITUATION

Congress and TSCA

Chemical manufacturers, regulators and advocacy groups all agree the Toxic Substances Control Act (TSCA) needs updating, but they have different ideas on how it should be revamped.

Chemical trade groups say the law should require the EPA to update its list of commercial chemicals, focus its screening efforts on a few key, high-volume chemicals and expedite risk assessments. Health and environmental advocates want TSCA to shift the burden of proof for safety to the chemical industry and allow the EPA to regulate chemicals based on health effects, without requiring it to minimize burdens on industry.

Both houses of Congress have held hearings on TSCA reform proposals in the past year. A bipartisan group of 13 Republicans and 12 Democrats is cosponsoring a Senate bill, the Chemical Safety Improvement Act, but

it has yet to move out of the Environment and Public Works Committee.[79] In the House, the Energy and Commerce Committee has held hearings on Republican Shimkus' draft proposal — the Chemicals in Commerce Act — but Shimkus has not introduced a formal bill.[80]

But with time running out before the fall midterm elections, experts say there is virtually no chance Congress will pass TSCA reform this year. Politics is partly to blame. The 113th Congress, deeply divided along party lines, has struggled to pass even essential measures, leading many critics, liberal and conservative, to call it a "do-nothing Congress."[81]

"To call the 113th Congress bad is like calling water wet," *USA Today* scolded in a May editorial. "It is harming the economy in the short term while running from serious long-term problems."[82]

Chemical manufacturers and trade groups generally support both the Senate and House drafts. The House and Senate proposals would make chemical regulation "both more effective and more efficient" by requiring the EPA to prioritize its reviews of existing chemicals and set deadlines for acting on those reviews, American Chemical Council President Cal Dooley testified in April. Dooley also endorsed limiting states' ability to regulate chemicals more stringently than the EPA, asserting that such steps would "help restore the public's confidence" in federal regulation of chemicals.[83]

Health, environment and labor advocates are much more critical of both bills, which they say fail to shift the burden of proof about a chemical's safety to the manufacturers and could even make the public less safe. For example, both bills direct the EPA to focus reviews on "high priority" chemicals, but then would limit states' power to regulate chemicals the EPA lists as low-priority.

"Thousands of untested or poorly tested chemicals like MCHM . . . are likely to be declared 'low priority' under both bills," said Michael Belliveau, president of the Environmental Health Strategy Center in Portland, Maine, testifying before Congress in March. "Once EPA sets aside low-priority chemicals, they can't take a second look unless new information appears. But where will those new data come from? Not from EPA-required testing. And states could never act."[84]

Safety Board Controversy

As the Chemical Safety Board investigates recent disasters like the Freedom Industries spill in West Virginia and the

Should "inherent safety" be required for chemical plants?

YES

Rafael Moure-Eraso
*Chairman, U.S. Chemical
Safety Board*

Excerpted from testimony, Senate Committee on Environment and Public Works,
March 6, 2014

The most effective accident prevention measures typically involve what is called inherent safety. I realize this is a term that has drawn some controversy, but it is really just a well-established industry-developed concept that focuses on prioritizing the elimination of a hazard or minimizing it. And, it looks to inherently safer chemical processing and equipment design. For chemical storage tanks like [the tank that leaked in West Virginia], the first question that should always be asked is, do they need to be near the water supply for some reason? Unfortunately in the case of Freedom Industries, the answer would have been "no." The facility was simply a truck terminal, and its position alongside the Elk River just upstream of the water intake had tragic consequences. The facility just did not need to be where it was. And although relocating it would have had some costs, those pale beside the costs that hundreds of thousands of West Virginia residents and businesses are now paying for this disaster.

Another form of inherent safety, or safety in design, is using corrosion-resistant materials for tank construction. That is something we will need to explore further as we determine the failure mode for this particular tank.

Moving down the hierarchy are engineering solutions that don't eliminate the risk of an accident but make it far less likely. These may include double-walled tank designs, leak detection systems and secondary containment structures like dikes and liners. A large segment of the industry has moved in this direction over the many decades since the Freedom Industries tanks were constructed.

Finally, near the bottom of the hierarchy are measures such as inspections for corrosion or other potential failure mechanisms. Now, inspections are absolutely essential in any sort of hazardous process operation or storage site. But I would caution that, according to the hierarchy of controls, they are among the least effective of safeguards. Hazards can be missed in inspections — we see that frequently at the Chemical Safety Board. The effectiveness of inspections totally depends on the skill and thoroughness of the inspector. And of course, there can be significant intervals between inspections, and bad things can happen during those periods. So inspections are essential, but they are not a complete solution by any means. What is needed — and what I hope the proposed Chemical Safety and Drinking Water Protection Act of 2014 leads to — is a holistic approach to preventing these accidents.

NO

Lawrence D. Sloan
*President and CEO, Society of Chemical
Manufacturers and Affiliates*

Written for *CQ Researcher*, July 2014

On the surface, "inherent safety" is a well-intentioned idea. Dig a little deeper, however, and the complex truth is apparent: A regulatory mandate on alternative chemistry and chemical processes would produce a litany of unintended consequences that would severely impact the operations of businesses of all sizes, local economies and consumers.

Economic impacts aside, from a purely practical standpoint, a government mandate simply isn't workable. Quite simply, inherently safer technology (IST) is a process-related engineering concept, not a regulatory panacea. It rests on the premise that, if a particular chemical process hazard can be reduced, the overall risk associated with that process will also be reduced. A reduction in hazard will reduce overall risk if, and only if, that hazard is not displaced to another time or location or does not creates some new hazard. Some companies have substituted one chemical for a "safer" alternative, only to shift the "risks" of the substituted chemical to elsewhere in the supply chain.

In addition, there is no agreed-upon methodology to measure whether one process is inherently safer than another. That is why the world's foremost IST experts consistently recommend against regulating inherent safety. Sam Mannan, director of the Mary Kay O'Connor Process Safety Center at Texas A&M University, testified to Congress that, "In developing inherently safer technologies, there are significant technical challenges that require research and development efforts. These challenges make regulation of inherent safety very difficult. . . . Facilities should be allowed the flexibility of achieving a manageable level of risk using a combination of safety and security options."

At a more basic level, no one knows how to compare the "inherent safety" of two processes. Neal Langerman, a process safety expert with Advanced Chemical Safety Inc., told Congress, "While scientists and engineers have made great strides in understanding the impacts of industrial processes and products over the past several decades, there is still no guaranteed formula for developing inherently safer production processes." Experts at the National Research Council have concluded, "Inherently safer chemistry . . . offers the potential for improved safety at chemical facilities. While applications show promise and have found use within the chemical industry, these applications at present are still quite limited in scope."

Safety experts agree that regulating inherent safety is not feasible. Before government considers mandating IST, methodologies must exist to compare inherent safety alternatives, but doing so must not just shift a risk to elsewhere down the road.

Texas fertilizer explosion, Congress is looking critically at the board's internal workings. In June the House Committee on Oversight and Government Reform held a hearing to examine charges that board leaders were not cooperating with other agencies and that a "toxic" work environment was driving experienced investigators away.[85]

Chairman Moure-Eraso defended his leadership, citing a long list of CSB investigations that have led to reforms and new safety policies. The board, he said, was "a very small agency charged with a huge mission of investigating far more accidents than we have the resources to tackle."[86]

But Beth Rosenberg, a Tufts University environmental health expert who resigned from the board this spring after serving for 17 months, spoke of a "chilled atmosphere," ineffective and unaccountable management and a lack of transparency in CSB actions. "The staff of the CSB, and the American people, deserve better," she said.[87]

On July 7 six House Republicans wrote to President Obama calling for Moure-Eraso to resign. "Immediate change in CSB leadership is necessary to allow this besieged agency to heal and regain focus on its public safety mission," they argued.[88]

Some observers point out that the CSB is understaffed and underfunded. With a $10 million yearly budget and a staff of 34, the board currently is managing 12 investigations into major chemical accidents.[89] By comparison, the National Transportation Safety Board, which investigates plane crashes and major rail, highway, pipeline and marine accidents, is managing nearly twice as many investigations (22) but has 10 times the budget — more than $100 million a year — and more than 400 staffers.[90]

New Questions

Scientific understanding of environmental exposure has made great progress in recent decades, and health experts say attention should be focused on protecting society's most vulnerable groups, particularly pregnant women, their unborn fetuses and young children.

"Vulnerability to chemicals starts well before a child is born," says Goldman, the former EPA assistant administrator. "The placental barrier guards the fetus from fairly large things like microbes, but it's not good at blocking the passage of lead or certain organic chemicals that dissolve right into fat, which the fetus needs to develop."

Infancy and early childhood are also critical times because children's brains are growing very quickly. "Young children are far more sensitive than adults to lead and other chemicals, such as dioxins and certain pesticides," says Goldman. "And changes occur at lower dosage levels than they do for adults."[91]

Scientific progress also raises additional questions. "We need more focus on biological pathways for exposure," says Julia Brody, executive director of the Silent Spring Institute, a Massachusetts research group that studies links between chemical exposures and breast cancer. "Pathways" are the routes by which people are exposed to chemicals, such as through contaminated drinking water or by breathing emissions from an industrial facility. An institute study launched in 1994 has shown that elevated breast cancer rates on Cape Cod were caused by hormone-disrupting substances in household and consumer products.[92]

Another potential pathway receiving extra attention today is hydraulic fracturing — the process of injecting water and chemicals into underground shale to free trapped oil and natural gas.[93] Millions of gallons of chemical-laced water flow back to the surface along with the oil and gas. The U.S. Environmental Protection Agency is reviewing assertions from many homeowners and communities that so-called fracking operations have contaminated their drinking water.[94]

No federal law requires energy companies to disclose what chemicals they inject underground to help dissolve rock and make oil and gas flow, although some states have imposed laws requiring disclosure. Several recent studies have found that widely used fracking chemicals have endocrine-disrupting effects.[95] The EPA has proposed requiring companies to reveal ingredients in their fracking fluids, using its authority under TSCA.[96]

Most oil and gas companies and trade associations strongly oppose disclosure of fracking chemicals, which they say are trade secrets. Disclosing the chemicals could threaten drilling companies' profitability, they say.

"We are in a competitive business," Steve Leifer, an attorney for the oil services company Halliburton, said during a legal proceeding on fracking fluid disclosure in Wyoming last year. "Halliburton prides itself on having the most effective and efficient frack fluids."[97]

But last April Baker Hughes, another major oilfield services company, announced that it would reveal the chemicals used in its hydraulic fracturing fluids. Some observers say this step could pressure other companies to do the same. Formulas (which could still remain confidential) are more important than specific ingredients, these experts said.

"It's like the secret formula for Coca-Cola," said Larry Nettles, an energy attorney with the Houston-based law firm Vinson & Elkins. "When you buy a can of Coke, you can look on the label and it will tell you what the ingredients are, but you can't go make Coca-Cola."[98]

OUTLOOK

Better Protection?

While prospects for TSCA reform this year appear slim, industry, environmental advocates, labor unions and health experts all agree the law needs to be updated in the next several years, and some are optimistic that current divisions can be bridged.

"Industry and advocacy groups have some very clear mutual interests," says Allmond of the Society of Chemical Manufacturers and Affiliates. "Everyone wants EPA to make quicker decisions on risk assessments of chemicals. We can't afford to let TSCA reform sit on the shelf for decades longer."

Fendley of the United Steelworkers sees another reason for businesses to support TSCA reform: access to markets such as the 28-member European Union, where laws require manufacturers to show that chemicals are safe before they can enter commerce. "The United States is quickly falling behind the rest of the world with respect to protecting people against hazardous releases," Fendley says. "This issue is a major topic in U.S. trade negotiations with the European Union. They're looking at nontariff barriers to trade, which include inconsistent laws. The chemical sector could see great benefits from reconciling the U.S. and European systems. But the European Union doesn't want to weaken its regulations."[99]

Brody of the Silent Spring Institute believes scientific research is leading toward new ways of protecting people from harmful chemical exposures. "When people actually look at the research, they see a lot of evidence that environmental chemicals are linked to breast cancer and a lot of opportunities for prevention. We have to move that knowledge into the mainstream," she says. "We're spending too much money on treatment, so we need to get doctors on board" to advocate for steps that reduce risk.

Advances in medical research, especially genomics, will also lead to new solutions, predicts George Washington University's Goldman. "The environmental burden of cancer has been underestimated, because earlier efforts focused only on cancers where the sole cause was a single environmental agent, such as asbestos. But now we know that almost all cancers have both environmental and genetic components. Genes are involved, but they are triggered by environmental exposures," she says. "It's been hard to unravel the influence of different types of exposures and figure out their strengths, but genome analysis is helping a lot."

Meanwhile, Linda Birnbaum, director of the National Institute of Environmental Health Sciences (NIEHS), which studies the impacts of environmental factors on human health, says debates about chemicals and health are producing information that consumers can use to reduce their own risks from chemical exposure.

"Americans should make practical changes," she says. "I stopped microwaving foods in plastic 20 years ago, not because of any specific substance but because there was evidence that when you heat foods in plastic, chemicals may move into the food. And it may make sense to take extra precautions during the times in our lives when we're most susceptible to environmental impacts, including in utero, early life, puberty and pregnancy."

Birnbaum also says it may be time to rethink the use of some chemicals. "Humans are living longer today than we used to, but low-level exposure to chemicals may affect the quality of our lives," she says. "We need to start making choices about risks and benefits from these substances, and deciding which ones we really need."

NOTES

1. "Trouble on the Elk: A Chronology of the West Virginia Water Crisis," The Associated Press, Jan. 9, 2014, http://tinyurl.com/pjmecd9.

2. *Ibid.*

3. *Ibid.*

4. Ken Ward Jr., "Information on Leak's 2nd Chemical 'Very Limited,' " *The Charleston Gazette*, Jan. 22, 2014, http://tinyurl.com/k4o9a54.

5. Molly M. Ginty, "Up the River," *In These Times*, May 26, 2014, http://tinyurl.com/plldw2x; Kimber Ray,

"Doubts Follow Elk River Contamination," *Appalachian Voices*, June 3, 2014, http://tinyurl.com/nh6tzab.

6. "Findings of Emergency Department Record Review from Elk River Chemical Spill," West Virginia Department of Health and Human Resources, April 23, 2014, http://tinyurl.com/pedqpbw.

7. "Toxic Substances: EPA Has Increased Efforts to Assess and Control Chemicals but Could Strengthen Its Approach," Government Accountability Office, March 2013, pp. 10-12, http://tinyurl.com/clxyubk. The five banned chemicals are PCBs, chlorofluorocarbons, dioxin, asbestos and hexavalent chromium for use in water treatment. EPA's decision banning asbestos was reversed in *Corrosion Proof Fittings v. EPA*, 947 F. 2d 1201 (1991).

8. "Safety Data Sheet for Crude MCHM," Eastman Chemical Company, http://tinyurl.com/pt5tcht.

9. Ward, *op. cit.*

10. Erik Olson, testimony before the Committee on Environment and Public Works, U.S. Senate, Feb. 4, 2014, p. 8, http://tinyurl.com/pzoytf2.

11. For background, see Mary H. Cooper, "Water Quality," *CQ Researcher*, Nov. 24, 2000, pp. 953-976.

12. "The Freedom Industries Spill: Lessons Learned and Needed Reforms," *Downstream Strategies*, Jan. 20, 2014, pp. 6-7, http://tinyurl.com/nqvooqo.

13. The Safe Drinking Water Act does not specify how often source water assessments should be updated, but the EPA says the assessments are "a snapshot in time" that "will need to be updated, enhanced, and refined at the local level." See "Frequent Questions about Source Water Assessments," U.S. Environmental Protection Agency, March 6, 2012, http://tinyurl.com/q8s3ll7. For background, see J. Hamer, "Drinking Water Safety," *Editorial Research Reports*, 1974, available at *CQ Researcher Plus Archive*.

14. *Downstream Strategies, op. cit.*, pp. 8-10.

15. U.S. Chemical Safety Board, summaries of current investigations (West, TX and Richmond, CA) and completed investigations (Anacortes), http://tinyurl.com/p8h6x9h.

16. Rafael Moure-Eraso, testimony before the Committee on Environment and Public Works,

U.S. Senate, March 6, 2014, pp. 1, 3, http://tinyurl.com/pqto7pa.

17. Glenn Hess and Jeff Johnson, "Deconstructing Inherently Safer Technology," *Chemical & Engineering News*, March 10, 2014, http://tinyurl.com/nrmno5m; "Debate Over Inherently Safer Technology (IST) at Chemical Plants Intensifies," *Homeland Security News Wire*, March 19, 2014, http://tinyurl.com/muf8269.

18. Daniel Zwerdling, "After Deadly Chemical Plant Disasters, There's Little Action," NPR, May 17, 2013, http://tinyurl.com/b4t9bzd.

19. Robin E. Dodson, *et al.*, "After the PBDE Phase-Out: A Broad Suite of Flame Retardants in Repeat House Dust Samples from California," *Environmental Science & Technology*, Vol. 46, No. 24, Nov. 28, 2012, http://tinyurl.com/p6vf2r8; Deborah Blum, "Flame Retardants Are Everywhere," *The New York Times*, July 1, 2014, http://tinyurl.com/qbpulwy.

20. "Endocrine Disruptors," National Institute of Environmental Health Sciences, June 13, 2014, http://tinyurl.com/o55p9vd.

21. "Improving Chemical Facility Safety and Security," White House, Aug. 1, 2013, http://tinyurl.com/nahvaxd.

22. "Actions to Improve Chemical Facility Safety and Security — A Shared Commitment," Report for the President, Occupational Safety and Health Administration, May 2014, http://tinyurl.com/q3xtt7k.

23. For background, see Peter Katel, "Hate Groups," *CQ Researcher*, May 8, 2009, pp. 421-448.

24. "Chemical Safety: Actions Needed to Improve Federal Oversight of Facilities with Ammonium Nitrate," Government Accountability Office, May 19, 2014, pp. 14, 23, http://tinyurl.com/n7ktsng. For background, see T. R. Goldman, "Worker Safety," *CQ Researcher*, Oct. 4, 2013, pp. 837-860.

25. "ResponsibleAg," http://tinyurl.com/o6ooy4v.

26. Octane rating is a standard measurement of the performance of motor and jet fuel. Higher-octane fuels burn more smoothly and in a more controlled manner than lower-octane fuels.

27. "A Risk Too Great: Hydrofluoric Acid at U.S. Refineries," United Steelworkers, 2013, p. vi, http://tinyurl.com/ofxyu39.

28. *Ibid.*, pp. vi-vii.

29. "U.S. Refinery Workers See Risk from Hydrofluoric Acid," Reuters, April 16, 2013, http://tinyurl.com/coesfd5.

30. "Toxic Substances: EPA Has Increased Efforts to Assess and Control Chemicals," GAO, *op. cit.*, p. 8.

31. "Essential Principles for Reform of Chemicals Management Legislation," U.S. Environmental Protection Agency, Dec. 20, 2012, http://tinyurl.com/yds9mnw.

32. For background see "Wingspread Conference on the Precautionary Principle," Jan. 26, 1998, http://tinyurl.com/keqn39t, and Jennifer Weeks, "Regulating Toxic Chemicals," *CQ Researcher*, Jan. 23, 2009, pp. 49-72.

33. "What is REACH?" European Commission, March 6, 2014, http://tinyurl.com/klkjcpt.

34. "ECHA Updates Candidate List, "REACH Ready News, June 16, 2014, http://tinyurl.com/moegsvb.

35. Rebecca Trager, "REACH is a Big Trade Barrier, Say U.S. Manufacturers," *Chemistry World*, Nov. 27, 2013, http://tinyurl.com/ktm7hh4.

36. "Dow and Reach," http://tinyurl.com/czpazx3.

37. "Toxic Substances," GAO, *op. cit.*, p. 17, http://tinyurl.com/ksljxbf.

38. *Ibid.*, pp. 38-39, http://tinyurl.com/ksljxbf.

39. Cheryl Hogue, "Data Snarl," *Chemical & Engineering News*, May 28, 2012, http://tinyurl.com/n95rrad.

40. "U.S. EPA Weighing Legal Action To Get REACH Data," *Chemical Watch*, March 5, 2014, http://tinyurl.com/loxumvz; "U.S. EPA Seeking Data Sharing With Europe on EDCs," *Chemical Watch*, May 8, 2014, http://tinyurl.com/kvrq7y2.

41. Beth Bosley, testimony before the U.S. House of Representatives, Energy and commerce Committee, Subcommittee on Energy and the Environment, Feb. 4, 2014, p. 2, http://tinyurl.com/l2lbgvc.

42. "Existing Chemicals Program: Strategy," U.S. Environmental Protection Agency, February 2012, http://tinyurl.com/kh3g76d.

43. "Myth Versus Fact About Chemicals in Commerce," Society of Chemical Manufacturers and Affiliates, undated, http://tinyurl.com/m9lt3q4.

44. "2012 Chemical Data Reporting Results," U.S. Environmental Protection Agency, June 11, 2014, http://tinyurl.com/nyoft6g.

45. For background, see Jennifer Weeks, "Regulating Toxic Chemicals," *CQ Researcher*, Jan. 23, 2009, pp. 49-72.

46. "CPSC Bans Tris-Treated Children's Garments," U.S. Consumer Product Safety Commission, April 7, 1977, http://tinyurl.com/mr9mbl2.

47. Robin Mackar, "3-D Images Show Flame Retardants Can Mimic Estrogens," Environmental Factor, National Institute of Environmental Health Sciences, September 2013, http://tinyurl.com/m8vtfub; Sarah Mishamandani, "Lecture Highlights Flame Retardants," Environmental Factor, April 2014, http://tinyurl.com/q5q24zy.

48. For information on the TSCA inventory, see http://tinyurl.com/7gdxn4j. On EPA's management of CBI, see http://tinyurl.com/psflhsc.

49. Andy Igrejas, testimony before the U.S. House of Representatives, Environment and Economy Subcommittee, Energy and Commerce Committee, April 29, 2014, http://tinyurl.com/pyh59st.

50. "Introducing the Target Sustainable Product Standard," Target Corporation, Oct. 14, 2013, http://tinyurl.com/l2zu9yy. Details at "Target Sustainable Product Standard," http://tinyurl.com/kj4xste.

51. Mark Rossi, "Target, Wal-Mart, Whole Foods Lead Retail Race To Safer Chemicals," *GreenBiz.com*, Nov. 18, 2013, http://tinyurl.com/ljz3eaf.

52. Rachel I. Massey, "Program Assessment at the 20 Year Mark: Experiences of Massachusetts Companies and Communities with the Toxics Use Reduction Act (TURA) Program," *Journal of Cleaner Production*, Vol. 19 (2010), p. 506.

53. "Safer Consumer Products Regulation," California Department of Toxic Substances Control, http://tinyurl.com/oszlesd.

54. "DTSC's Initial Proposed Priority Products List for the Safer Consumer Products Program," California Department of Toxic Substances Regulation, March 13, 2014, http://tinyurl.com/l4kwwpc.

55. "Safer Consumer Products Regulation," *op. cit.*

56. "History of Asbestos," Asbestos Resource Center, undated, http://tinyurl.com/yw2b3d.

57. Samuel Hopkins Adams, "The Great American Fraud: Articles on the Nostrum Evil and Quacks," Reprinted from *Collier's Weekly* (1905), p. 45, http://tinyurl.com/ojej9aj.

58. Carol Ballentine, "Taste of Raspberries, Taste of Death: The 1937 Elixir Sulfanilamide Incident," *FDA Consumer Magazine*, U.S. Food and Drug Administration, June 1981, http://tinyurl.com/omfgr4u.

59. "Chemical Cuisine: Learn About Food Additives," Center for Science in the Public Interest, http://tinyurl.com/nhluxf8.

60. For background, see Mary H. Cooper, "Environmental Movement at 25," *CQ Researcher*, March 31, 1995, pp. 273-296.

61. For background, see J. Hamer, "Drinking Water Safety," *Editorial Research Reports*, Feb. 15, 1974, available at *CQ Researcher Plus Archive.*

62. Philip Shabecoff, "President Signs Measure Curbing the Marketing of New Chemicals," *The New York Times*, Oct. 13, 1976, http://tinyurl.com/nv2x3ad.

63. Philip Shabecoff, "E.P.A. Faulted For Its Tardiness on Toxin Curbs," *The New York Times*, Nov. 6, 1980, http://tinyurl.com/mr9xffq.

64. For background, see R. K. Landers, "Living with Hazardous Wastes," *Editorial Research Reports*, 1988, available at *CQ Researcher Plus Archive.*

65. Andrew C. Revkin, "Love Canal and Its Mixed Legacy," *The New York Times*, Nov. 25, 2013, http://tinyurl.com/prdgncu.

66. Philip Shabecoff, "Reagan Order on Cost-Benefit Analysis Stirs Economic and Political Debate," *The New York Times*, Nov. 7, 1981.

67. Edward Broughton, "The Bhopal Disaster and its Aftermath: A Review," *Environmental Health*, May 10, 2005, http://tinyurl.com/37sdwhz.

68. Ben A. Franklin, "Toxic Cloud Leaks at Carbide Plant in West Virginia," *The New York Times*, Aug. 21, 1985, http://tinyurl.com/qyxxhqc.

69. "Proposition 65 in Plain Language," California Office of Environmental health Hazard Assessment, February 2013, http://tinyurl.com/m5bontx.

70. For background, see David Hosansky, "Regulating Pesticides," *CQ Researcher*, Aug. 6, 1999, pp. 665-688.

71. "High Production Volume (HPV) Challenge: Basic Information," U.S. Environmental Protection Agency, June 6, 2012, www.epa.gov/hpv/pubs/general/basicinfo.htm#success.

72. Theo Colborn, Dianne Dumanoski and John Peterson Myers, *Our Stolen Future: Are We Threatening Our Fertility, Intelligence, and Survival?* (1996).

73. Gina Kolata, "Chemicals that Mimic Hormones Spark Alarm and Debate," *The New York Times*, March 19, 1996, http://tinyurl.com/n4zj8dt.

74. "Why is *Our Stolen Future* Controversial?" *Our Stolen Future*, undated, www.ourstolenfuture.org/Basics/controv.htm.

75. Stephen Labaton, "OSHA Leaves Worker Safety in Hands of Industry," *The New York Times*, April 25, 2007.

76. For background see "Wingspread Conference on the Precautionary Principle," Jan. 26, 1998, http://tinyurl.com/keqn39t.

77. For details see "Chemical Regulation: Comparison of U.S. and Recently Enacted European Union Approaches to Protect Against the Risk of Toxic Chemicals," Government Accountability Office, GAO-07-825, August 2007, http://tinyurl.com/mlddqvk.

78. "EPA Administrator Jackson Unveils New Administration Framework for Chemical Management Reform in the United States," U.S. Environmental Protection Agency, Sept. 29, 2009, http://tinyurl.com/mjo55w7.

79. S.1009, Chemical Safety Improvement Act, bill summary and status at http://tinyurl.com/kpcvusw.

80. For the most recent draft, see http://tinyurl.com/ombzftr.

81. For examples, see Eric Bolling, "Time Running Out on Do Nothing Congress?" Fox News, July 5, 2014, http://tinyurl.com/qb22a8n; and "Obama Carries Weight of Do-Nothing Congress," The Rachel Maddow Show, MSNBC, June 30, 2014, http://tinyurl.com/okc49qj.

82. "Do-Nothing Congress Takes a Breather: Our View," *USA Today*, May 22, 2014, http://tinyurl.com/outdxqo.

83. Cal Dooley, testimony before the Subcommittee on Environment and the Economy, House Committee on Energy and Commerce, House of Representatives, April 29, 2014, pp. 3-4, 12-13, http://tinyurl.com/meeykw3.

84. Michael Belliveau, testimony before the U.S. House of Representatives, Committee on Energy and Commerce, Subcommittee on Environment and the Economy, March 12, 2014, pp. 12-13, http://tinyurl.com/ozwqu79.

85. "Whistleblower Reprisal and Management Failures at the U.S. Chemical Safety Board," Staff Report, U.S. House of Representatives, Committee on Oversight and Government Reform, June 19, 2014, p. 5, http://tinyurl.com/omc7c23.

86. Rafael Moure-Eraso, testimony before the U.S. House of Representatives, Committee on Oversight and Government Reform, June 19, 2014, p. 3, http://tinyurl.com/o8rncqq.

87. Beth Rosenberg, testimony before the U.S. House of Representatives, Committee on Oversight and Government Reform, June 19, 2014, p. 3, http://tinyurl.com/po2839b.

88. Online at http://tinyurl.com/p7m4ytq. Also see "Members Call on White House for Leadership Change at Chemical Safety Board," House Committee on Oversight and Government Reform, July 7, 2014, http://tinyurl.com/og9guc7.

89. Brian Naylor, "Undermanned and Limited, Chemical Safety Board Confronts a Crisis," NPR, Feb. 3, 2014, http://tinyurl.com/nomcpbt; CSB Staff List at http://tinyurl.com/oeusdv6.

90. Biography of Chairman Deborah Hersman, National Transportation Safety Board, undated, http://tinyurl.com/plhmp4w.

91. For background, see Mary H. Cooper, "Lead Poisoning," *CQ Researcher*, June 19, 1992, pp. 529-552.

92. "Findings of the Cape Cod Breast Cancer and Environment Study," Silent Spring Institute, 2006, http://tinyurl.com/q5w9orn.

93. For background see Daniel McGlynn, "Fracking Controversy," *CQ Researcher*, Dec. 16, 2011, pp. 1049-1072.

94. "EPA's Study of Hydraulic Fracturing for Oil and Gas and Its Potential Impact on Drinking Water Resources," U.S. Environmental Protection Agency, May 29, 2014, http://tinyurl.com/lza6h9y. See also "Fracking: Gas Drilling's Environmental Threat," *ProPublica*, http://tinyurl.com/79ukmc8.

95. "Hormone-disrupting activity of fracking chemicals worse than initially found," *Science Daily*, June 23, 2014, http://tinyurl.com/mqgzpjk; Christopher D. Kassotis, *et al.*, "Estrogen and Androgen Receptor Activities of Hydraulic Fracturing Chemicals and Surface and Ground Water in a Drilling-Dense Region," *Endocrinology* Dec. 16, 2013, http://tinyurl.com/qzc4xbb; Eddy Ball, "Scientists Begin to Fill In the Gaps in Understanding About Fracking," *Environmental Factor*, February 2014, http://tinyurl.com/q7x7fbg.

96. Mark Drajem, "EPA Takes First Step Toward Regulating Fracking Chemicals," Bloomberg.com, May 9, 2014, http://tinyurl.com/mxndnhx; notice of proposed rulemaking online at http://tinyurl.com/ln6etf6.

97. Adam Voge, "Fracking Trade Secrets Arguments Heard by Casper Judge," *Billings Gazette*, Jan. 22, 2013, http://tinyurl.com/jw9eevr.

98. Keith Goldberg, "New Fracking Fluid Disclosures Weaken Trade Secret Claims," *Law360.com*, April 30, 2014, http://tinyurl.com/lma9xe6.

99. For background, see Brian Beary, "U.S. Trade Policy," *CQ Researcher*, Sept. 13, 2013, pp. 765-788.

BIBLIOGRAPHY

Selected Sources
Books

Davies, Kate, *The Rise of the U.S. Environmental Health Movement, Rowman & Littlefield*, 2013.
A public health expert with experience in government and advocacy organizations traces the growth of a movement to fight chemical pollution.

Fagin, Dan, *Toms River: A Story of Science and Salvation,* **Bantam, 2013.**
Journalism professor and former Newsday reporter Fagin won a Pulitzer Prize for this investigation of childhood cancers caused by decades of chemical dumping in a New Jersey seaside town.

Vogel, Sarah A., *Is It Safe? BPA and the Struggle to Define the Safety of Chemicals,* **University of California Press, 2012.**
The managing director of the health program at the Environmental Defense Fund examines the scientific debate over BPA and its estrogen-like effects at low doses.

Articles

Brown, Valerie J., "Why Is It So Difficult to Choose Safer Alternatives for Hazardous Chemicals?" *Environmental Health Perspectives,* **July 2, 2012, http://tinyurl.com/p3dd4ss.**
The U.S. Environmental Protection Agency promotes safer alternatives to chemicals that may be health risks, but the program has no authority or budget to do new chemical testing.

Hess, Glenn, and Jeff Johnson, "Deconstructing Inherently Safer Technology," *Chemical & Engineering News,* **March 10, 2013, http://tinyurl.com/nrmno5m.**
Proponents say requiring chemical manufacturers to design facilities and equipment that reduce the possibility of accidents would reduce the risk of accidents at chemical plants. Industry says this approach is already in place and working.

Lifsher, Marc, "California Picks First Products for 'Green Chemistry' Screening," Los Angeles Times, March 13, 2014, http://tinyurl.com/lbu5va6.
To reduce toxic ingredients in consumer products, California is requiring manufacturers to analyze products that might contain hazardous chemicals and try to find alternatives. The law requires that they first analyze fire retardants, spray insulation and paint and varnish strippers.

Moore-Eraso, Rafael, *"The Next Accident Awaits,"* **The New York Times, Jan. 28, 2014, http://tinyurl.com/la4r686.**

The chair of the U.S. Chemical Safety Board warns of a national "industrial safety crisis" at chemical plants and calls for adoption of safer technology.

Morris, Jim, and Chris Hamby, "As Critics Press for Action, Chemical Safety Board Investigations Languish," Center for Public Integrity, April 17, 2013, http://tinyurl.com/bu7s3t3.
A special report by a nonprofit investigative journalism organization finds that the Chemical Safety Board is overstretched and struggling to complete investigations of major accidents, with critics charging mismanagement.

Osnos, Evan, "Chemical Valley: The Coal Industry, the Politicians, and the Big Spill," The New Yorker, April 7, 2014, http://tinyurl.com/mmuy863.
The Freedom Industries chemical spill in West Virginia spotlighted the state's pro-business culture and weak enforcement of environmental laws.

Urbina, Ian, "As OSHA Emphasizes Safety, Long-Term Health Risks Fester," The New York Times, March 30, 2013, http://tinyurl.com/krgkuro.
More than 40,000 Americans die prematurely each year from exposure to toxic substances at work. The federal Occupational Safety and Health Administration does not have enough inspectors or enforcement power to effectively police on-the-job health risks.

Reports and Studies

"Chemical Safety: Actions Needed to Improve Federal Oversight of Facilities with Ammonium Nitrate," U.S. Government Accountability Office, GAO-14-274, May 19, 2014, http://tinyurl.com/n7ktsng.
U.S. companies produce millions of tons yearly of ammonium nitrate, the chemical that caused an explosion in West, Texas, in 2013 that killed 14 and injured at least 200. But no one knows how many facilities store ammonium nitrate across the nation, or where all of them are located.

Pool, Robert, and Erin Rusch, "Identifying and Reducing Environmental Health Risks of Chemicals in Our Society," Institute of Medicine of the National Academies, 2014, http://tinyurl.com/luz4c4p.
An expert workshop convened by the congressionally chartered Institute of Medicine examines ways to improve industrial chemical safety, set priorities for chemical testing and promote safer alternatives.

Bullard, Robert D., *et al.*, "Environmental Justice: Milestones and Accomplishments: 1964-2014," Texas Southern University, February 2014, http://tinyurl .com/ona2smv.

Four scholars trace the growth and achievements of the environmental justice movement, and propose further steps to reduce disproportionate negative effects of pollution on poor and minority communities.

For More Information

American Chemistry Council, 700 Second St., N.E., Washington, DC 20002; 202-249-7000; www.ameri canchemistry.com. The largest trade organization for the U.S. chemical industry.

Downstream Strategies, 295 High St., Suite 3, Morgantown, WV 26505; 304-292-2450; www.downstreamstrategies.com. A private environmental consulting firm active on water, energy and land issues in West Virginia.

National Institute of Environmental Health Sciences, 111 T.W. Alexander Dr., Research Triangle Park, NC 27709; 919-541-3345; www.niehs.nih.gov. One of 27 institutes and research centers that make up the National Institutes of Health.

Safer Chemicals, Healthy Families, 1050 30th St., N.W., Washington DC 20007; 202-503-8581; www.saferchemicals .org. A national coalition of more than 450 environmental,

health and labor organizations and businesses working to reform toxic chemical laws, phase out use of hazardous chemicals, and educate the public.

Toxics Use Reduction Institute, 600 Suffolk St., Wannalancit Mills, Lowell, MA 01854; 978-934-3275; www.turi.org. Non-profit that works with businesses, communities and government agencies to reduce use of toxic chemicals in Massachusetts.

United Steelworkers, Five Gateway Center, Pittsburgh, PA 15222; 412-562-2400; www.usw.org. Largest industrial union in North America, representing workers in industries that manufacture chemicals or use and store chemicals in large quantities.

U.S. Chemical Safety Board, 2175 K St., N.W., Washington DC 20037; 202-261-7600; www.csb.gov. An independent federal agency that investigates root causes of industrial chemical accidents and recommends ways to improve safety.

3

Future of Cars

David Hosansky

Motorists leaving Chicago for the Memorial Day weekend jam the Kennedy Expressway on May 23, 2014. Traffic problems – along with collisions and pollution – could be reduced by self-driving cars, according to boosters of automated auto technology. But some experts warn of possible downsides of autonomous cars, including technological failure or deliberate sabotage. Others say such cars could actually increase pollution and congestion.

From *CQ Researcher*,
July 25, 2014.

T he car that Google unveiled on May 27 is like no other.

Never mind its odd appearance, which observers liken to a cross between a golf cart and a Volkswagen Beetle. Or the limited performance of its electric engine — a 25 mph top speed and a range of about 100 miles.

The really noteworthy feature of the latest Google prototype car is its controls. Or, rather, the lack of them.

The vehicle has no steering wheel, accelerator or brake pedal. Even though Google and automobile manufacturers have been working on technologies that allow vehicles, at least under certain circumstances, to drive themselves, the Google car startled observers because it would permit no human control except pressing a button to start or stop it. Destinations could be chosen with a smartphone app.

"They won't have a steering wheel, accelerator pedal or brake pedal because they don't need them," said a Google blog post. "Our software and sensors do all the work."[1]

The prototype, which is far from ready for consumer use, is just the latest innovation in the suddenly fast-moving field of vehicle technology. After decades in which engineering improvements were, for the most part, rolled out incrementally, dramatic advances could soon change not only the vehicles themselves, but also society's approach to personal transportation. Other gee-whiz transportation technologies — flying cars and personal jet packs — have remained fantasies, but many experts say this time the promises could become reality.

51

Self-Driving Cars Allowed in Four States, D.C.

Four states and the District of Columbia have laws permitting the driving or testing of self-driving cars, and seven rejected such laws. Eleven other states have recently considered similar legislation.

Laws Allowing Testing or Driving of Autonomous Vehicles, by State

* Bills did not move past committee or were voted down

Source: Gabriel Weiner and Bryant Walker Smith, "Automated Driving: Legislative and Regulatory Action," The Center for Internet and Society, Stanford Law School, http://tinyurl.com/8l23jrl

Yet, it remains unclear how safe super-smart cars would be, how they would affect traffic congestion, how individuals and the nation would pay for them and whether Americans are ready to accept such a radical change in their century-plus relationship with automobiles. Legislators, regulators and the public have just begun to consider these issues.

Enabling the breakthroughs are a combination of specially designed sensors and sophisticated software systems that interpret data about the road environment and relay it to the driver or directly to the car.

"It's a golden age for innovation in automobiles," says Gary Silberg, an automobile industry specialist at the consulting firm KPMG. "It can be an absolute sea change."

In addition to self-driving cars, related technologies already in use include:

- **Crash-avoidance.** Equipped with radars, cameras and other tools, cars can detect when a front-end collision is about to occur. A number of higher-end models now include systems to alert the driver that something is wrong or even to automatically take action, such as applying the brakes if the vehicle is at risk of rear-ending the car in front.

- **Assisted driving.** Vehicle manufacturers are providing options that can be activated to control cars in certain situations with the use of advanced sensors and software. These include adaptive cruise control, which monitors distances to other vehicles; lane assist, which warns the driver if the vehicle is veering from its lane or even corrects the course of the car; and parking assist, which automatically parallel parks the car.

- **Vehicle-to-vehicle communications.** Motor vehicles in the next few years are expected to begin using wireless technology to communicate their position, speed and direction to each other as well as to certain road infrastructure, such as traffic lights. Officials at the National Highway Traffic Safety Administration (NHTSA), who are working to facilitate the technology, believe it will dramatically improve road safety by alerting drivers if a nearby vehicle is about to run a red light or is otherwise operating unsafely.

While self-driving cars may seem futuristic, they are expected to begin appearing in showrooms within a few years. Some cars already include so many advanced features that they provide a preview of the technology. A *New York Times* reviewer of Nissan's 2014 Infiniti Q50, for example, talked about letting the car manage its own speed and adjust its course, even on highways with curves.

"I found myself driving the Infiniti on surprisingly long highway stretches without touching the accelerator, brake pedal or steering wheel," the reviewer wrote. "Girded with digital-, camera- and radar-based co-pilots, the Q50 charts a course toward the self-driving cars of tomorrow."[2]

Although Nissan, perhaps the most aggressive car manufacturers in this area, pledges to begin bringing

Traffic Fatalities Hit Five-Decade Low

Motor vehicle deaths fell to 32,479 in 2011, the fewest in nearly five decades, before rising slightly in 2012. Fatalities peaked at 54,589 in 1972. The number of deaths per 100 million miles traveled declined from six to 1.1 from 1954 to 2012 thanks to improved automobile safety, better road designs and heightened awareness of drunken driving.

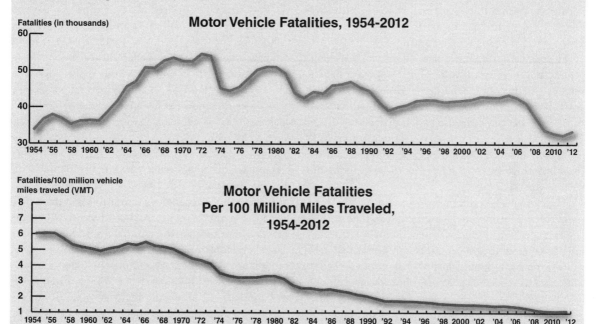

Source: 2011-12 data from "Traffic Safety Facts, 2012 Data," National Highway Traffic Safety Administration (NHTSA), U.S. Department of Transportation, May 2014, http://tinyurl.com/km6pmvc; 1975-2010 data from NHTSA, Fatality Analysis Reporting System; 1954-74 data from National Center for Health Statistics, U.S. Department of Health and Human Services and state accident summaries

self-driving cars to market by the end of the decade, other carmakers are keeping pace. The 2014 Mercedes S-Class, for example, offers several optional autonomous driving features, including steering, lane-maintenance and acceleration/braking at both city and highway speeds. Volvo is readying an adaptive cruise control for sale later this year that includes steering assist, enabling the car to follow the vehicle ahead of it. General Motors and Ford are also advancing automated technologies with the goal of offering self-driving cars within a few years. The GM Cadillac SRX test vehicle can be taken for a spin on test tracks without the driver touching the steering wheel or brakes, while Ford unveiled a prototype self-driving car last year. And Google since 2010 has tested a fleet of conventional cars equipped with self-driving features on more than 500,000 miles of roads.

Boosters envision a future in which the road experience is entirely transformed. If technology reliably enables vehicles to communicate with each other and use sensors to maintain safe distances, most collisions could be avoided. Congestion could be reduced (along with excessive pollution associated with cars inching forward in traffic jams) if cars could safely follow each other much more closely while traveling at high speeds. Platoons of trucks could ship goods more efficiently and safely. A fleet of automated cars could even reshape the transportation system, as people might choose to summon self-driving taxis for commutes or errands rather than purchasing their own car.

When Google announced widespread testing of self-driving vehicles in 2010, the company explained its motivation in terms of sweeping benefits to society: "Our goal is to help prevent traffic accidents, free up people's time and reduce carbon emissions by fundamentally changing car use."[3] The company's plans for marketing the technology remain unknown, although executives at traditional carmakers are nervously wondering if it may emerge as a competitor.[4]

The company has stressed that self-driving cars would benefit some of the most vulnerable members of society, such as elderly people who can no longer drive. In a YouTube video, a Google engineer chatted with a blind man, Steve Mahan, as he used a self-driving car to run errands. "I love it," said Mahan. "Where this would change my life is to give me the independence and the flexibility to go [to] the places I both want to go and need to go."[5]

The potential of automated cars, however, can go only so far in meeting the nation's transportation challenges. Even if such vehicles achieve their potential, they are not expected to compensate for an overloaded aviation system and lack of high-speed rail, or put an end to motor vehicle emissions that contribute to air pollution and climate change.

In fact, some experts warn that this technological leap, like any other advance, comes with potential downsides. Automated cars and vehicle-to-vehicle communications could make traffic dangerously susceptible to technological failure or to deliberate sabotage, and they wouldn't do away with some motorists speeding or otherwise maneuvering their cars aggressively. While the new technologies could potentially reduce the annual death toll of about 33,000 people on U.S. roads, experts worry that a major accident or a death caused by a self-driving car could have much different ramifications than one caused by a negligent driver.

Even if autonomous cars save thousands of lives, "One headline, 'Machine Kills a Child,' trumps 30,000 obituaries," said Bryant Walker Smith, a fellow at the Center for Automotive Research at Stanford University.[6]

Others caution that automated cars, far from making transportation less stressful, could further clog roads, cause more air pollution, or lead to more sprawling development if they are so convenient people don't mind sitting in them for long commutes.

"If the transition isn't managed appropriately, there could be unanticipated negative consequences as a result of behavior changes and land-use changes," says University of Texas computer science professor Peter Stone, who is researching future approaches to traffic management.

"Personally, I'm excited about it. But you have to adopt a little bit of cautious optimism with any new technology," he says. "I think it would be naïve to say it will have an entirely positive effect on society."

The future price of automated cars is also uncertain. The light-detection and ranging system atop a Google self-driving car, known as lidar, costs about $70,000 and enables the vehicle to scan its surroundings and determine its location. Additional sensors, software and technology can add another $30,000. But, as with other technology, observers expect the costs to plunge with mass production.[7]

Even once the technology is available and prices fall, it may be many years before self-driving cars become widespread. Americans are not as quick to buy new cars as in the past because cars are engineered to last longer, and it is not clear whether consumers will soon warm up to the concept of robotic vehicles. A mix of traditional and automated cars on the highways may place new strains on infrastructure, as engineers have begun looking into the possibility of designating lanes for each and redesigning intersections and traffic lights to accommodate the different types of vehicles.

Automotive experts say self-driving features will be phased in slowly, as vehicles transition from being partially to more fully autonomous. "You have to introduce the technology on a gradual basis," says Brad Stertz, a spokesman for Audi of America. "It's not like in two years we're all going be in the back seat watching movies."

Rapid automotive technological progress has caught the attention of policy makers. Four states and the District of Columbia have passed laws to regulate automated vehicles, and about a dozen others have begun debating legislation, spurred in part by NHTSA recommendations urging states to begin looking into the legal and safety ramifications. For instance, who is liable when an autonomous vehicle gets into an accident?

Other countries, especially those with large automakers, are moving ahead on regulations to permit self-driving cars. Last year, for example, Japanese Prime Minister

Shinzo Abe took a ride in a self-driving car and pledged to support the technology as part of his economic program.[8]

This comes as other technological advances are increasing the financial strain on the U.S. system for building and maintaining roads and bridges. More fuel-efficient cars, particularly electric ones, mean drivers buy less gasoline. That translates into less revenue for highway trust funds, which finance roads with money from gasoline taxes. Declining gas receipts are sparking battles in Washington and state capitals around the country, as policy makers scramble to make up the difference.

As emerging automotive technologies promise to reshape the transportation system, here are some of the key questions being debated:

Will new technologies improve safety?

Although automobile accident rates have dropped significantly in recent decades, about 33,000 people still die annually on American roads and more than 3 million are injured, according to NHTSA. Annual cost to the economy: $277 billion, according to the agency.[9]

Many experts say new technologies, including vehicle-to-vehicle communications and self-driving cars, will make roads safer, because at least 90 percent of accidents are caused at least in part by human error. As safety systems become more automated, human error will become a less important factor, they say.[10]

"We think there's a great potential here to improve the safety of transportation," says David Zuby, vice president and chief research officer of the Insurance Institute for Highway Safety, an Arlington, Va., group funded by auto insurers.

Over the past several decades, carmakers have incorporated such safety technologies as air bags, antilock brakes, electronic stability controls and, more recently, rearview cameras and adaptive headlights, which automatically adjust as the car changes direction and speed. These innovations, coupled with improvements in road design and heightened public awareness of the dangers of drunken driving, have reduced motor vehicle deaths about 40 percent from a peak of 54,589 in 1972.[11]

Some new higher-end models now offer front-crash prevention systems that use sensors, such as cameras, radar or lidar, to detect when a car is getting dangerously close to the vehicle in front of it. These systems generally are designed to alert the driver and pre-charge the brakes to maximize their effect. In some cases, the system brakes the car if the driver doesn't respond.

Carmakers are also beginning to offer vehicles with lane departure warning systems, which detect how close the car is to lane markings and alert the driver if the car is about to drift across the line while the turn signal is off. A more advanced variant, known as lane keeping assist, automatically keeps the car centered in its lane.

As much as these technologies are designed to improve safety, experts see far bigger gains in the future. Part of the reason: NHTSA is working on regulations to foster vehicle-to-vehicle and vehicle-to-infrastructure communication systems, which will alert vehicles to fast-developing dangerous situations nearby.

For example, if highway traffic suddenly comes to a halt, the drivers of approaching cars will be notified so they will have ample time to brake—even if the backup is around a curve and not yet visible. Or, if a driver is speeding toward an intersection where the light is about to turn red, the light in the other direction may remain red for a few additional seconds to prevent other cars from being struck.

Such connected vehicle technology would address about 80 percent of crash scenarios that involve nonimpaired drivers, according to NHTSA. "This technology could help prevent the majority of types of crashes that typically occur in the real world, such as crashes at intersections or while changing lanes," the agency said.[12]

The technology could not greatly improve safety until it has been installed in a large number of vehicles that can communicate. Although it can take some time for such vehicles to become common — the average American owns a car for about five years, and used cars remain on the road for many years — some experts predict there will be aftermarket products that will enable even an older car to communicate with other vehicles and infrastructure.

"I think you'll see a full-court press, with aftermarket products and even apps on smartphones, to get to the critical threshold as soon as possible," says Leo McCloskey, senior vice president for technical programs at the Washington-based Intelligent Transportation Society of America.

A report last year by the Eno Center for Transportation, a Washington think tank, concluded that traffic deaths could drop by 21,700 per year if 90

Japanese Prime Minister Shinzo Abe gets the feel of Toyota's autonomous vehicle in Tokyo on Nov. 9, 2013. Abe also tried out driverless Hondas and Nissans. He has pledged to support driverless technology as part of his economic program.

percent of vehicles were self-driving. Automated vehicles "can be programmed to not break traffic laws. They do not drink and drive. Their reaction times are quicker," the report stated.[13]

Safety experts, however, say much will depend on the safety standards the government sets for the vehicles and on how the technologies work in practice. Otherwise, said Clarence Ditlow, executive director of the Washington-based consumer advocacy group Center for Auto Safety, "you could be substituting computer errors for human errors."[14]

Safety also could become compromised as vehicles with different levels of technology share the same roads, whether because drivers are reluctant to accept the technology or because they can't afford to do so. Automated cars, for example, could be closely following each other and maintaining a constant speed while human-controlled cars zip around them. "Even if tomorrow the Google car went on sale and was guaranteed never to crash, it would take 20 to 30 years before everyone had one in their driveway," Zuby says. "There's definitely a concern for any intermediate period."

There also are worries about drivers abusing the technology. An internal FBI report speculates that autonomous cars could become "lethal weapons," with criminals using them as self-driving getaway cars, according to the website of the British newspaper *The Guardian*, which said it obtained a copy of the report.[15]

Underscoring both the benefits and limits of new technologies, a series of studies by the Insurance Institute for Highway Safety found that recently installed automotive safety systems are generating uneven results. The institute found that cars with forward collision-avoidance systems that warned the driver of upcoming dangers had a 7 percent reduction in accidents with other vehicles, with the accident reduction rate increasing to 10 to 15 percent with more advanced systems that automatically applied the brakes, Zuby says.

But lane departure warning systems have an inconsistent effect on safety. Some of the institute's research has suggested no benefits, although the group's most recent analysis of one model found that a lane departure warning system combined with forward collision warning reduced crashes with other vehicles by 14 percent.

Experts wonder whether drivers could become so reliant on automated cars that they stopped paying attention to the road — and were unable to respond quickly if the technology failed. There may be an analog with the aviation industry, where some pilots appear to become so dependent on technology that their flying skills get rusty. Last month, for example, a National Transportation Safety Board panel blamed pilot error for the July 6, 2013, crash of Asiana Airlines Flight 214 at San Francisco International Airport, saying the crew mismanaged the landing after relying too much on automated flight controls that they did not entirely understand.

Zuby says it will be a major challenge to design technologies that improve safety without allowing drivers to pay even less attention than they do now.

"If your car is nearly all the way automated, drivers are going to be tempted to take advantage of that and engage in things that are not related to monitoring what is going on around them," he says. "You could have a problem if the system depends on them knowing when to take over. That's something that people who are designing these systems are struggling with."

Will new technologies reduce congestion?

On the congested streets of New York City, vehicles have barely picked up speed since horse-and-buggy days.

A recent study, using GPS devices in taxicabs, found the average pace in Manhattan on weekdays is 9.5 miles per hour. That's "about the speed of a farmyard chicken at full gallop." On a busy day, when speeds drop to 7.5 miles per hour, cars would barely be able to keep pace with a horse and cart or a Central Park jogger.[16]

Such driving speeds are not unusual for major cities — and that's assuming favorable conditions. Accidents or relatively minor snowstorms can spawn seemingly interminable gridlock. Many Atlanta drivers spent six hours or more to travel a few miles on Jan. 28, when a couple inches of snow brought traffic to a standstill. "This was, hands down, the worst day of my life," said Evan McLean of Canton, Ga., who spent two and a half hours without any forward progress.[17]

Traffic congestion is estimated to cost the United States more than $100 billion a year in wasted time and fuel, not to mention air pollution caused by idling cars.[18] The effect on quality of life in the United States and overseas — where heavy traffic in growing megacities can be even worse — is incalculable.

Those who say new automotive technologies could reduce traffic delays cite several reasons:

- Accidents should become less frequent, especially as anticollision systems and vehicle-to-vehicle communication become common. This would result in far fewer accident-related backups.
- Vehicles that can communicate with each other and with roadside infrastructure may be able to safely proceed through intersections with stop signs without stopping when no other vehicles are present or by alternating with each other more efficiently when traffic exists. In time, emerging technologies may even eliminate the need for traffic signals and stop signs.
- Traffic flows are expected to become more efficient. There would be fewer incidents of human drivers trying to save time with maneuvers such as cutting in and out of lanes, which may gain a few moments for an individual car but slow down traffic overall.

Fewer Teens, Young Adults Are Driving

Only 41 percent of American teenagers had a driver's license in 2012, down from 56 percent in 1982. Young adults in their 20s and 30s also are driving less, with the number of licensed 20- to 24-year-olds falling 12 percentage points, 25- to 29-year-olds nine points and 30- to 39-year-olds eight points.

Percentage of Licensed Drivers by Age Group, 1982 and 2012

Source: "Table DL-20, Distribution of Licensed Drivers — 2012, by Sex and Percentage in Each Age Group and Relation to Population," Federal Highway Administration, U.S. Department of Transportation, January 2014, http://tinyurl.com/lprscyo; "Table DL-20 — Highway Statistics 1982," Federal Highway Administration, U.S. Department of Transportation, September 1983, p. 32, http://tinyurl.com/maq8ofy

- Automated vehicles will be able to follow each other much more closely and at higher speeds because they will have information about what the cars around them are planning to do. Thus, highways could safely accommodate substantially more cars and trucks.

"You can pack a lot more vehicles on the highways, they can run optimally to reduce traffic jams, and you don't have all the lane changing that slows traffic down," says John O'Dell, senior editor of Edmunds, the car-shopping website, and a longtime observer of the automobile industry. "Cars will be able to form platoons and increase the speed at which they can safely travel."

"It's not going to eliminate congestion, but I think we're going to see a dramatic reduction," says McCloskey of the Intelligent Transportation Society of America.

A 2011 study by Columbia University indicated that fully automated vehicles could eventually increase highway capacity to nearly four times current levels because the cars will be able to safely travel more closely together. At present, vehicles take up just 5 percent of highway capacity (about 2,200 vehicles per lane per hour) because human drivers require considerable space around their cars to ensure safety. But if all cars were automated, the spacing between vehicles would drop from about 150 feet to 20, the researchers estimated.[19]

Other analysts, however, doubt the new technologies will end traffic jams. "It can help around the margins," says Richard Wallace, director of transportation systems analysis at the Center for Automotive Research, in Ann Arbor, Mich., which studies trends and changes related to the automotive industry. (The center is not related to the similarly named center at Stanford University.) "But there really are no solutions for too many vehicles in the same place at the same time. To the extent that we're car dependent, there's only so much capacity out there. New York City rush hour is not going to be aided."

Some even worry that autonomous vehicles, far from easing gridlock, may make it worse. The reason: Motorists may be more willing to sit in traffic if they can work or read while their car is driving. If the technology advances to the point that people can send their cars on errands, such as picking up groceries or even their children, that could further clog roads with empty vehicles.

"I know that people are already careless in their car use," says Robin Chase, an entrepreneur and cofounder of car-sharing services Buzzcar and Zipcar. "When they don't have to be in their cars, they will be more profligate. The attitude can be, 'Even if my car sits in traffic for two hours, what do I care?' "

Will consumers buy automated cars?

The love affair between Americans and cars runs deep.

From an Oldsmobile Rocket 88 to a sporty red Corvette, automobiles have been the passkeys to freedom and self-reliance. As heralded by the earliest rock n' roll songs and hit movies such as "American Graffiti" and "Thelma and Louise," Americans, it seems, are destined to be behind the wheel.

So why would motorists voluntarily give up driving and hand over the controls to self-driving cars?

Some who follow the automotive market say consumers may be receptive because driving has lost some of its appeal. "Do you want to drive in your car when in reality you're stuck in traffic, you're frustrated, you can't find a place to park?" asks entrepreneur Chase. "In daily commuting to work and running errands with your kids, I don't think

ELECTRICITY MAY BE THE DRIVER. One day your car may speed along an electric super-highway, its speed and steering automatically controlled by electronic devices embedded in the road. Highways will be made safe— by electricity! No traffic jams . . . no collisions . . . no driver fatigue.

Power Companies Build for Your New Electric Living

Your air conditioner, television and other appliances are just the beginning of a new electric age.

Your food will cook in seconds instead of hours. Electricity will close your windows at the first drop of rain. Lamps will cut on and off automatically to fit the lighting needs in your rooms. Television "screens" will hang on the walls. An electric heat pump will use outside air to cool your house in summer, heat it in winter.

You will need and have much more electricity than you have today. Right now America's more than 300 independent electric light and power companies are planning and building to have twice as much electricity

for you by 1967. These companies can have this power ready when you need it because they don't have to wait for an act of Congress—or for a cent of tax money—to build the plants.

The same experience, imagination and enterprise that electrified the nation in a single lifetime are at work shaping your electric future. That's why in the years to come, as in the past, you will benefit most when you are served by independent companies like the ones bringing you this message— America's Independent Electric Light and Power Companies".

—Company names on request through this magazine

A futuristic ad from the mid-1950s shows a family playing dominoes in their self-driving car. Sponsored by "America's Independent Electric Light and Power Companies," or by individual local utilities, the ad appeared in newspapers and magazines and reads in part, "Electricity may be the driver. One day your car may speed along an electric superhighway, its speed and steering automatically controlled by electronic devices embedded in the road. . . . No traffic jams . . . no collisions . . . no driver fatigue."

many people say, 'I love driving.' I feel like every time I drive, I'm shortening my life through frustration."

O'Dell of Edmunds, who lives in the congested Los Angeles area, feels much the same. "I'm like a great many people of my generation who grew up thinking of driving as an escape and as a fun thing to do because the roads weren't as crowded when we were 16 or 17 years old," says O'Dell, who got his first driver's license in 1963. "Now it's no longer fun. I'd be happy if I could push a button and lean back and let the car do the driving."

But polls indicate it may take some time before the public warms up to the new technology.

In April, a survey by the Pew Research Center concluded that Americans were roughly split over whether they would be willing to ride in an automated car. Forty-eight percent of respondents said they would, while 50 percent said they would not.[20]

A survey last year commissioned by the Chubb Group of Insurance Companies found that two-thirds of respondents would not feel comfortable in a self-piloted car, and only 18 percent said they would buy one.[21]

An aversion to self-driving cars is understandable, according to Stanford's Smith. "It's the fear of robots," he said. "We saw that in the Toyota unintended acceleration cases, when people would describe their horror at feeling like they could lose control of their car."[22] In those sometimes-fatal cases, cars sped up uncontrollably, seemingly on their own. At first Toyota blamed driver error, but it eventually recalled millions of cars for design defects. In March, the company agreed to a $1.2 billion U.S. criminal penalty and admitted it had lied about the causes.[23]

But the Chubb survey also revealed some ambivalence, especially about some of the features that enable cars to drive themselves. For example, 88 percent of respondents said they would pay extra for a system that alerts a driver if the vehicle inadvertently drifts out of its lane, 77 percent want a car to automatically apply the brakes to avoid or minimize a crash, and 70 percent were open to an adaptive cruise control system that would maintain both a set speed and a safe distance from other traffic.

In a recent study of the issue, the consulting company KPMG concluded that consumers would warm up to the idea of self-driving cars as they become more aware of the potential advantages. They would even be willing to pay a premium of 15 percent if it meant a better experience on the road.

The KPMG team conducted a series of focus groups. At the beginning of each two-hour discussion, the groups were roughly split, with about six in 10 people saying they would be willing to ride in an autonomous car. But that number climbed to nine in 10 or even reached unanimity after the groups were asked how they would feel if the drive time could be more predictable and shorter and if the vehicle was certified by an organization such as NHTSA.[24]

"A vast majority moved to wanting it and even be willing to pay a premium for it," says KPMG's Silberg.

Automotive experts see potential generational differences in attitudes. Elderly people whose reflexes have slowed and younger people who may be more focused on texting and Internet connectivity tend to be the most accepting of the idea of turning over the wheel.

"A lot of people who are in the 40s and 50s and enjoy driving have no interest in the self-driving cars," says Michigan state Sen. Mike Kowall, a Republican who is vice-chairman of the Senate Transportation Committee, who won approval of a bill last year regulating self-driving cars. "But you talk to some of the older folks, who have trouble seeing at night or have trouble driving, they're excited. And a lot of younger people don't want to be bothered driving — they say just give me mass transit or a car that can get me from point A to point B."

Automated cars may prove to be especially appealing to people with disabilities as well as to the elderly — an increasingly important demographic as baby boomers age. Self-driving cars will "make people more independent," said Maarten Sierhuis, director of Nissan's Research Center in Silicon Valley.[25]

One way to ease consumer fears may be to provide an option to take over the controls. "I would long for the day when I can push a button and the car will do all my work on my miserable commute," says O'Dell. "But on a nice weekend drive, I'd want to turn off that autonomous function."

BACKGROUND

8,000 Cars to 8 Million

In the mid-1880s, after decades in which inventors worked on various approaches to self-propelled road vehicles. In 1885, German engineer Karl Benz created the first gasoline-powered motor vehicle, which had three bicycle-style wire wheels and a four-stroke engine. In the same year, another German engineer — Gottlieb Daimler — attached a four-stroke gas engine to a bicycle, creating the first motorcycle.

When the 20th century began, there were an estimated 8,000 automobiles in the United States. The technology, which promised to transform long-distance travel, initially evoked mixed reactions.

As long as automobiles were beyond the easy reach of all but the wealthy, they spurred resentment as playthings of the rich that posed a public safety threat and frightened livestock. A letter writer to *The New York Times* referred to car owners as the "idle and vicious rich."[26]

CHRONOLOGY

Early 1900s *Car manufacturers introduce major innovations such as electric starter, hydraulic brakes, automatic transmission and independent suspension.*

1908 Henry Ford's Ford Motor Co. builds first production Model T. As Model T prices fall, millions of Americans will become car owners.

1913 Revolutionizing American manufacturing, Ford installs first conveyer belt assembly line, reducing costs.

1921 Federal Highway Act provides matching funds to states to create national highway system.

1925 American inventor Francis P. Houdina demonstrates radio-controlled, driverless car in New York City traffic.

1939 General Motors (GM) exhibit at New York World's Fair depicts radio-controlled, driverless electric cars powered by circuits embedded in the roadway.

1950s-60s *America's love affair with cars heats up after World War II, as consumers flock to muscle cars and United States builds more highways.*

1956 President Dwight D. Eisenhower signs Federal-Aid Highway Act of 1956, authorizing construction of Interstate Highway System.

1965 Consumer advocate Ralph Nader assails car industry's approach to safety in his exposé, *Unsafe at Any Speed*, which accuses car manufacturers of resisting safety features such as seat belts, and ushers in era of greater attention to automotive safety.

1970s-1990s *Concerns about traffic, air pollution and gas shortages grow; consumers begin focusing on fuel efficiency and reliability.*

1970 President Richard M. Nixon signs Clean Air Act, regulating motor vehicle emissions.

1973 Oil embargo imposed by members of the Organization of Petroleum Exporting Countries (OPEC) leads to gas shortages.

1975 Congress requires corporate average fuel economy (CAFE) standards.

1979 With the Big Three U.S. automakers facing increasing competition from overseas competitors, Congress authorizes $1.5 billion loan to foundering Chrysler Corp., keeping the company in business.

1999 Japanese carmaker Honda releases the Insight, the first hybrid car to be mass-marketed in the United States. Environmental Protection Agency (EPA) says it gets 61 mpg in city driving, 70 mpg on the highway.

2000s *Development of more advanced vehicles, including automated cars, speeds up.*

2005 Five no-driver vehicles successfully navigate a 132-mile course in Nevada in a competition sponsored by U.S. Defense Advanced Research Projects Agency (DARPA).

2010 Google announces its self-driving cars have logged more than 140,000 miles.

2011 Nevada becomes first state to establish regulations governing testing self-driving cars.

2013 National Highway Traffic Safety Administration (NHTSA) releases guidelines to states on regulating testing of self-driving vehicles. . . . Google invests $258 million in Uber Technologies, whose mobile apps run car services.

2014 NHTSA announces it will take steps to enable vehicle-to-vehicle communication (Feb. 3). . . . Google unveils automated car without a steering wheel or gas or brake pedals (May 27). . . . GM recalls 8 million more cars for safety reasons following previous recall of more than 20 million earlier this year (June 30). . . . Congressional Budget Office warns that a shortage of federal highway funds will force delays in federal payments to states. . . . Sens. Bob Corker, R-Tenn., and Chris Murphy, D-Conn., propose raising gas tax by 12 centers per gallon, indexed to inflation, to provide more highway funds.

But that view began to change when industrialist Henry Ford made cars widely affordable. After introducing the iconic Model T in 1908, Ford revolutionized automobiles — and American manufacturing — by installing the first conveyer belt-based assembly line in his Highland Park, Mich., car factory in 1913. Thanks to modern assembly line techniques that reduced manufacturing costs, the Ford Motor Co. built more than 15 million Model T's in the United States by 1927, becoming the world's largest car manufacturer. The cars were plain to look at — each was black because that paint color dried quickly — but they were affordable, selling for as little as about $260, or about $3,500 in 2014 dollars.

Ford's innovations marked the beginning of America's car culture, transforming the automobile from a luxury item for the wealthy to essential transportation. By 1920, U.S. vehicle ownership had increased to 8 million.

America Transformed

Few inventions have changed the nation as much as the automobile. Dirt roads that worked well for horses would trap early cars in mud. Gas stations and road maps were non-existent. When Horatio Nelson Jackson and a co-driver became the first to drive across the country in 1903, their countless breakdowns highlighted the need for more durable automobiles and better roads. Alice Huyler Ramsey, a 22-year-old housewife and mother from Hackensack, N.J., chronicled her misadventures when she became the first woman to make the cross-country drive in 1909:

"At Fort Steele, Wyoming, we pulled up short at a dead-end in the road where the bridge over the swollen North Platte had been washed out. I sent my passengers ahead on foot across a paralleling Union Pacific railroad trestle and then bumped the Maxwell for three-quarters of a mile on the ties to the opposite side. Across Wyoming the roads threaded through privately owned cattle ranches. My companions were obliged to take turns opening and closing the gates of the fences which surrounded them as we drove through. If we got lost we'd take to the high ground and search the horizon for the nearest telephone poles with the most wires. It was a sure way of locating the transcontinental railroad which we knew would lead us back to civilization. In Utah we hit a prairie dog hole in the road with such force that a tie bolt came out of the tie rod connecting the front wheels."[27]

Automobilists banded together to form associations in major cities, some of which joined forces in 1902 to form the American Automobile Association (AAA). These associations lobbied for pro-automobile legislation and for appropriations to build and improve highways. The federal government stepped in after World War I with the Federal Highway Act of 1921, which provided federal matching funds to states to create a national highway system.

As the number of registered drivers nearly tripled during the 1920s to 23 million, the landscape and the economy were transformed. Gas stations and motels sprang up alongside new highways. Roadside diners began offering quickly prepared food, such as hamburgers, french fries and milk shakes, so drivers in a hurry could get on their way. Demand for steel, vulcanized rubber and oil skyrocketed. Road construction created tens of thousands of jobs. The American love affair with the car endured the Depression and World War II, then reached new heights after President Dwight D. Eisenhower signed the Federal-Aid Highway Act of 1956, authorizing construction of the interstate highway system.

But even as Americans enjoyed the freedom offered by cars, they confronted an increasingly apparent downside. As car ownership rose, with many families owning two vehicles, traffic congestion worsened. To provide easy access to urban areas, highways were built through cities, often dividing neighborhoods and destroying historic districts. By the mid-1960s, the annual death toll from auto accidents began to exceed 50,000. Mounting concerns about air pollution spurred the 1970 Clean Air Act, which regulated emissions from motor vehicles as well as other sources. The 1973 oil embargo led to limited supplies of gasoline and seemingly endless lines at the pump. The Big Three automakers began facing increasing competition as consumers bought foreign cars — especially reliable and energy-efficient models from Japan.[28]

Improved Technology

In the early years of automobiles, manufacturers had rolled out a series of important innovations: the electric starter, four-wheel hydraulic brakes, windshield wipers, automatic transmission, power steering, front-wheel drive, independent suspension and more. But by the 1930s and '40s, as cars began taking modern form and the number of

Laser Is Key to Self-Driving Cars

Combination of technologies lets vehicle study its environment.

Although self-driving vehicles may seem futuristic, most cars already come equipped with some automated features. Cruise control keeps a car's speed steady on highways, antilock brakes prevent brakes from locking up and newer stability and traction control systems deter skidding or rollovers.

Some higher-end models offer advanced systems to keep the vehicles within their lane, adjust the speed while in cruise control to maintain a safe distance from other cars and sound a warning or apply the brakes to avoid a forward collision. These features rely on sensors, such as radar or cameras, that scan the environment and relay the information to onboard software systems.

To move beyond computerized control of key steering, acceleration and braking systems and build a vehicle that can drive itself, three additional features are required: sensors to detect what is happening around the vehicle, a mapping system so the vehicle can follow a route and software to pull all the information together.[1]

With Google's self-driving cars, the primary sensor is a laser range finder, or lidar, mounted on the roof. It generates a three-dimensional map of the environment as the car moves along. Because it can see in all directions, it may gather more information than a human driver.

Additional information comes from other sensors. These include four radar devices — two each on the front and rear bumpers — that enable the car to detect other traffic; a camera to detect traffic lights; GPS; an inertial measurement unit (which incorporates gyroscopes and accelerometers); and wheel encoders that work together to determine the car's location and speed and to track its movements.

The car's software combines those measurements with high-resolution maps of roads and terrain, producing various data models so it can avoid obstacles and comply with traffic laws. Even though these maps are very detailed and supplement GPS measurements (which can be off by several yards), Google engineers also drive along the planned route to gather more information about the environment. That way, when the car drives itself, it can compare current observations with previous ones, enabling it to differentiate between pedestrians and fixed objects such as light poles.[2]

Because the autonomous car has to contend with human drivers in other traditional vehicles, engineers have added programming to keep it from being too passive. When approaching a four-way intersection, for example, it stops and yields. But if other cars do not yield as expected, the autonomous car will advance a little to demonstrate to other drivers where it is trying to go.

Without such programming, Google engineers have discovered, an autonomous car has trouble functioning in an environment where other cars are driven by humans.

As sophisticated as the cars are, there are certain things they cannot do. For example, Google has found that a car cannot decipher the hand gestures of a traffic police officer.

manufacturers dwindled, companies focused on cosmetic changes and increasingly powerful engines. Major advances, such as the emergence of modern electric and hybrid engines at the beginning of the 21st century, were few.

But automotive engineers never stopped thinking about radical changes. One of the most visionary notions, often dismissed as science fiction, was that cars could one day drive themselves. The concept dates back at least as far as 1925, when American inventor Francis P. Houdina demonstrated a radio-controlled, driverless car in New York City that navigated traffic on Broadway and Fifth Avenue. The vehicle, equipped with a special antenna, was operated by a second car that followed closely and sent out radio impulses, controlling small electric motors that directed every movement. At the 1939 New York World's Fair, General Motors sponsored an exhibit depicting electric cars powered by circuits embedded in the road and controlled by radio.

After World War II, interest in autonomous cars increased, with a focus on using specialized devices in roads to guide the vehicles. Nebraska worked with General Motors and RCA Labs in the 1950s to demonstrate a self-driving car that was guided on a strip of highway outside Lincoln by a series of experimental detector circuits in the pavement. Further testing in the 1960s and '70s demonstrated that cars could be controlled with buried magnetic cables.

An image from an April 28 testing video by Google shows how the company's self-driving car perceives nearby moving traffic, stopped cars and traffic signals. Inset at lower left shows how the road would look to a human inside the car. The light-detection and ranging system atop the self-driving car, a type of technology known as lidar, allows the vehicle to scan its surroundings and determine its location.

Instead, it will detect "there's a person standing in the middle of the road waving their hands in a funny way," said Google software lead Dmitri Dolgov. At that point, he said, the car will act conservatively — or it will ask the human behind the wheel to take control.[3]

— *David Hosansky*

[1]"How does a self-driving car work?" *The Economist*, April 29, 2013, http://tinyurl.com/cu95hqs.

[2]Erico Guizzo, "How Google's self-driving car works," *IEEE Spectrum*, Oct. 18, 2011, http://tinyurl.com/3l4bvnz.

[3]Alex Davies, "Avoiding squirrels and other things that Google's robot car can't do," *Wired*, May 27, 2014, http://tinyurl.com/qcso8kk.

But as radar, lidar and other technologies advanced during the second half of the 20th century, attention turned to equipping vehicles so they could drive themselves without special roadway devices. Mercedes-Benz in the 1980s developed a self-driving van that navigated quiet city streets at speeds up to 39 mph, while a consortium of U.S. research institutes developed an autonomous land vehicle.

In 1991, Congress passed legislation instructing the U.S. Department of Transportation to demonstrate an automated vehicle and highway system. The subsequent research and engineering work culminated in a 1997 demonstration on Interstate 15 in San Diego in which about 20 automated vehicles, including cars, buses and trucks, engaged in platooning and other maneuvers, attracting considerable media coverage.

A subsequent initiative by the U.S. Defense Advanced Research Projects Agency (DARPA) fostered another round of research. In a 2005 DARPA "grand challenge" competition, five autonomous vehicles successfully navigated a 132-mile course in southern Nevada. Two years later, six teams navigated a staged city environment in a DARPA urban challenge competition.

"That first competition created a community of innovators, engineers, students, programmers, off-road racers, backyard mechanics, inventors and dreamers who came

When Cars Are Smarter, Roads Can Be Smarter, Too

"Everything's changed but our highways"

A world with smart cars may not need traditional traffic signals, streetlights or other fixtures of today's road system.

Experts say, for instance, that if cars can communicate, red lights won't need to stay red when no traffic is coming. One model, developed by researchers at the University of Texas, foresees vehicles approaching an intersection and making "reservations" with a virtual traffic coordinator that will rapidly assign them time slots so they can proceed through the intersection without coming to a full stop or possibly even slowing down very much.

"They can almost go through it at full speed," says University of Texas computer science professor Peter Stone, who is studying how such a system could be implemented safely. "The vehicles have to slow down a little bit so they can be finely interweaved, but they accelerate and decelerate much less."

The phasing out of traffic lights, while still many years away, is just one potential change to highways and intersections. Designing lanes that can provide charges to passing electric vehicles is one of the most active areas of research among engineers and visionaries around the world. Last year, the city of Gumi, South Korea, turned on a system that powers electric buses on a 15-mile urban route. The charge comes from subsurface electrical cables that create magnetic fields. A receiving device installed on the underbody of the bus converts these magnetic fields into electricity.[1]

In Germany, the electrical engineering company Siemens is taking a different approach: outfitting stretches of the autobahn with overhead electric cables. This would enable hybrid trucks with diesel-electric engines to use these designated lanes for long-distance, zero-carbon transport. Operating somewhat like San Francisco street cars, the trucks would automatically switch to electric mode when they physically attach to the overhead cables.[2]

A more audacious vision for charging electric vehicles comes from an Idaho startup company, Solar Roadways. It wants to resurface U.S. roads with solar panels, which theoretically could generate more than triple the electricity the nation uses while providing other benefits such as warming wintertime roads to prevent ice buildup. Although the cost may ultimately be prohibitive, Solar Roadways has received two rounds of funding from the Federal Highway Administration and has built a prototype parking lot made of solar panels, microprocessors and LED lights — energy-efficient light-emitting diodes — encased in textured glass that it says can support a 250,000-pound truck.[3]

But charging electric vehicles is just one part of the picture. Daan Roosegaarde, a Dutch artist who specializes in interactive works, has emerged as an unlikely visionary for rethinking pavement design.

Roosegaarde has teamed up with Heijmans, a traditional infrastructure developer in Holland, to create glow-in-the-dark roads that use specially formulated, luminescent green markings. The goal is to eliminate the need for street lights

together to make history by trying to solve a tough technical problem," said Lt. Col. Scott Wadle, DARPA liaison to the U.S. Marine Corps. "The fresh thinking they brought was the spark that has triggered major advances in the development of autonomous robotic ground vehicle technology in the years since."[29]

As car manufacturers neared commercialization of semi-automated technologies such as front-end collision avoidance systems, Google quietly developed fully automated vehicles. In a 2010 blog post, the company disclosed that its self-driving cars had by then traveled more than 140,000 miles, always with a person behind the wheel who could take control if necessary. The cars used video cameras, radar and lidar to detect other vehicles, as well as detailed maps to enable them to navigate. "While this project is very much in the experimental stage, it provides a glimpse of what transportation might look like in the future thanks to advanced

and save electricity in busier areas, while illuminating more remote stretches of roads that previously did not have lights.

The team also is studying the feasibility of affixing symbols to road surfaces that can alert drivers or specially equipped cars under certain conditions. One approach is to design giant snowflakes on roads with a type of paint that appears when temperatures drop below freezing and roads become slick.

Roosegaarde said he is motivated by a concern that the pace of technological innovation has left roads behind. "Everything's changed but our highways," he said. "I wondered why we're sinking millions into these obsolete and ugly monstrosities instead of creating something new and better."[4]

It remains to be seen, however, whether any of these approaches wins widespread adoption. The technological challenges aside, upgrading thousands of miles of roads may prove prohibitively expensive. In the United States, for instance, policy makers are scrambling to find money just to maintain the current system of roads and bridges.

"These kinds of ideas always sound great," said Ferdinand Duddenhöffer, a German mobility expert at the University of Duisburg-Essen. "But the question is how much do they cost, and the answer is usually quite vague."[5]

Stone and his Texas team have won considerable attention for their work on intersections, partly because it could point the way to more efficient, safer traffic flow. Intersections are inherently dangerous places because cars cross them from different directions — and most accidents that occur there could be eliminated by so-called smart intersections, he says.

Now Stone is studying dynamic lane changes. In a future of self-driving cars that communicate with each other, why have four-lane highways on which two lanes always move one way? Depending on traffic flows, it may

Special luminescent paint lights up a highway near Oss, The Netherlands. Glow-in-the-dark roads could eliminate the need for street lights while illuminating remote, unlighted roads.

be more efficient to have three lanes of vehicles traffic in one direction and one lane in the other — with the potential to switch at any time, depending on traffic patterns.

"With autonomous cars," Stone says, "you could potentially have a system for changing the direction of traffic in a lane on a minute-by-minute basis."

— *David Hosansky*

---

[1] Bill Chappell, "The Road that Gives Electric Vehicles a Charge," NPR (blog), Aug. 7, 2013, http://tinyurl.com/mxsbslq.

[2] Paul Hockenos, "Street Smarts: From Holland, Bright Ideas for Highways," *The New York Times*, April 26, 2013, http://tinyurl.com/kmnfyqp.

[3] Adrianne Jeffries, "Crazy plan to cover the nation's roads with solar panels raises $1 million," *The Verge*, May 26, 2014, http://tinyurl.com/m3h78w9.

[4] Hockenos, *op. cit.*

[5] *Ibid.*

---

computer science," the post stated.[30] Since then, Google's cars have been involved in two accidents, although the company says the technology was not at fault. One accident occurred while a human was operating the car, and the other when an automated car that was stopped at a red light was rear-ended by a conventional car.[31]

The reality that autonomous cars could enter the market within a few years jolted policy makers into action. Nevada in 2011 became the first state to pass legislation

to regulate and license autonomous vehicles. Florida, California, Michigan and Washington, D.C., followed. The U.S. Department of Transportation in 2013 issued policy guidance on self-driving vehicles, including recommendations for states related to testing, licensing and regulation. "Whether we're talking about automated features in cars today or fully automated vehicles of the future, our top priority is to ensure these vehicles — and their occupants — are safe," said then-Transportation Secretary Ray LaHood.[32]

President Obama rides in a high-tech smart car simulator at the Turner-Fairbank Highway Research Center in McLean, Va., on July 15, 2014, before speaking on the economy. Congress is deadlocked over how to pump more money into the federal Highway Trust Fund, which helps pay for bridge and road maintenance. The Congressional Budget Office is warning that highway funds will dwindle to $2 billion by Sept. 30, requiring the Transportation Department to begin delaying payments to states to keep the balance above zero, as required by law.

CURRENT SITUATION

Regulatory Action

State and federal policy makers are just beginning to come to grips with what new auto technology may mean.

"Michigan is the home of automotive technology, so we're trying to stay ahead of the curve," says Kowall, the Michigan state senator, who sponsored the regulatory legislation his state adopted in December. "As of last count, we have more than 300 companies in Michigan currently working on some type of autonomous or connected vehicle technology. We're just making sure that there are no encumbrances on companies that want to do this testing."

About a dozen more states are looking into the issue, prodded by companies that want legal clarity when putting a self-driving car on the road. Automated cars generally are neither explicitly permitted nor banned because legislators have not had to confront the issue.

"States have assumed in all the laws they have written that there is a driver in the car," says Anne Teigen, a transportation expert with the National Conference of State Legislatures.

Now that such an assumption is becoming outdated, policy makers face questions including:

- Should operators of automated cars get special training, ensuring that they understand the technology and can take over controls when necessary?
- If an automated vehicle is involved in an accident, where does liability fall? On the owner or operator? The manufacturer? Or the company that designed a piece of software?
- If a state bans drivers from texting or using a cellphone, should it make an exception for drivers who are behind the wheel of a self-driving vehicle?
- Should intoxicated people be allowed to operate a self-driving vehicle?
- If an automated car exceeds the speed limit or violates other traffic laws, can the operator be ticketed just like the driver of a conventional car?

What makes these issues particularly challenging is the fast-changing technology: Entire new capabilities may emerge as a bill is being written. For example, policy makers have debated how to determine liability when a self-driving car gets into an accident vs. instances when the driver takes back control of the automated car and then gets into an accident. But in the case of the prototype Google car unveiled in May, a driver cannot take control in a traditional sense because the vehicle lacks a steering wheel or brake.

"It's difficult to regulate something when legislators don't know how it will work because maybe even the manufacturers don't know how it will work," Teigen says.

In California, officials at the Department of Motor Vehicles announced several requirements for testing autonomous vehicles, including that self-driving vehicles be registered, test drivers complete a training program, and drivers be capable of immediately taking control of the vehicle.

"Because of what is potentially out there soon, we need to make sure that the regulations are in place that would keep the public safe but would not impede progress," said DMV Deputy Director Bernard Soriano.[33]

Because California requires that a driver be able to take over if necessary, Google may have to modify its design. "Google is going to have to manufacture those vehicles with steering wheels and pedals," Soriano said.[34]

The National Highway Traffic Safety Administration (NHTSA) last year issued guidance to the states, advising them to require special training for operators who are

Should state replace the gas tax with a tax on miles traveled?

YES

Rep. Earl Blumenauer, D-Ore.
*Sponsor, Road Usage Fee Pilot
Program Act*

Written for *CQ Researcher*, July 2014

Last December I introduced a bill to raise the gas tax by 15 cents per gallon over three years and index it to inflation, restoring its lost purchasing power and providing the revenue necessary to keep the Highway Trust Fund solvent. A gas tax increase offers an immediate fix to our short-term problem, but it is not the solution for the future.

It is critical that policy makers at the local, state and federal levels prepare for a transition away from the gas tax. Due to government-mandated fuel efficiency standards, the rising popularity of electric and hybrid vehicles and declining driving, all of which are good things that lead to a cleaner environment and more livable communities, the gas tax soon will no longer be the best way to fund transportation.

That's why I've introduced H.R. 3638, the Road Usage Fee Pilot Program Act, which would provide funding for states to run pilot projects to explore a transition to a vehicle-miles-traveled (VMT) fee instead of a gas tax.

Oregon, which led the nation in 1919 with the first gas tax to fund road construction, has been developing a VMT fee alternative and has operated two pilot projects over the last decade.

A VMT fee preserves the user-fee model that our transportation funding system has relied on since 1956, and is actually fairer. Right now, the road use of the Toyota Prius driver is partially subsidized by the driver of the less fuel-efficient Ford F-150 pick-up.

The technology to implement a VMT is becoming standard in many new cars and provides opportunities to create a uniform payment platform for a host of transportation needs: parking, transit, Amtrak, bike share and car share. It can explain how to avoid the accident ahead, when the next bus or ferry leaves and where to find the nearest vacant parking space. This would make the entire transportation experience seamless and more efficient.

While we must extend the gas tax for a few more years, it's clear that one form or another of VMT is the future. The Oregon VMT pilot projects have shown that an alternative to the gas tax is possible, practical and private. States are moving forward with their own pilot projects, and I urge Congress to encourage this progress by passing my legislation and laying the groundwork for a transportation funding system that is ready for the future, not rooted in the past.

NO

Phil Byrd
*Chairman, American Trucking
Associations; President, Bulldog Hiway Express*

Written for *CQ Researcher*, July 2014

There is no more crucial role for government than maintaining our nation's roads and bridges. The American economy, and a good part of the American experience, depend on freedom to move safely and efficiently from place to place.

While it is certainly important for states to do their part to fund maintenance and repair work on our roads and bridges, we believe it is first and foremost the federal government's responsibility to fund these projects for the betterment of our nation's infrastructure and economy.

With the Highway Trust Fund strained due to lack of revenue, some misguidedly believe we should scrap the fuel tax altogether in favor of more radical approaches such as tolling or a vehicle-miles-traveled tax (VMT). This would be a catastrophic mistake for our economy and for the transportation industry.

Both tolling and a VMT are wildly inefficient, which requires the tax to be much higher than it ordinarily would be. Looking overseas to Germany, where trucks are subject to a VMT — the most sophisticated tax of its kind at the moment — the administrative overhead is 23 percent. That means for every dollar collected, 23 cents goes not into asphalt and concrete but into bureaucracy.

The fuel tax, however, puts 99 cents of every dollar into construction. That's a real value. And those dollars generate economic growth. We know every $1 spent on infrastructure generates nearly $2 in economic output in the first two years.

There's no way to have a VMT without a massive new bureaucracy. Today there are about 254 million registered vehicles — all of which would have to have a tax collected from them. For reference, the Internal Revenue Service processes fewer than 150 million tax returns annually.

Beyond the efficiency issues, the VMT presents several technical challenges — officials in Oregon concluded it would take at least 20 years to implement statewide. The Oregon pilot study also found the technology involved was unreliable, inaccurate and expensive to maintain.

Many states have already raised their fuel tax — and there's been a bold proposal in Congress to raise the federal fuel tax and index it to inflation to pay for our infrastructure needs. The tax is not, as some say, a Democratic idea. Republican icon Ronald Reagan raised the fuel tax. Leaders at all levels of government should embrace the fuel tax as the best way to fund infrastructure investment.

The I-495 bridge over the Christina River in Wilmington, Del., was closed indefinitely in June after four support columns were discovered to be tilting. Transportation experts say that because gasoline is taxed by the gallon, not price, the growing popularity of more fuel-efficient cars makes it more difficult to collect enough in gas taxes to maintain the nation's roads and bridges. A mix of traditional and automated cars on highways may further strain highway infrastructure, as intersections and traffic light systems are redesigned to accommodate the different types of vehicles.

testing autonomous vehicles as well as to require manufacturers to share information about all incidents or crashes. The agency also warned that the vehicles were not yet ready for public use.

"NHTSA does not recommend that states authorize the operation of self-driving vehicles for purposes other than testing at this time," the agency stated. "We believe there are a number of technological issues as well as human performance issues that must be addressed before self-driving vehicles can be made widely available."[35]

Some in Congress also are flashing a yellow light. "It's hard for me to fathom a car in New York City being without a driver," Rep. Albio Sires, D-N.J., said at a hearing last year on autonomous vehicles. "I mean, it's hard enough with a driver."[36]

Automotive industry leaders, however, are urging policy makers not to slow down the technology with burdensome regulations. "Let the market work," Mike Robinson, General Motors vice president of sustainability and global regulatory affairs, said at the same hearing. "Let manufacturers, like GM, do what we do best and compete for customers with features that add real value to the drive today and to the future generations of vehicles tomorrow."[37]

But the manufacturers' position may be weakened by widespread criticism of how slowly they have moved in handling recent safety problems, including GM's recalls this year of tens of millions of vehicles, many because of faulty ignition switches that sometimes prevented airbags from inflating, causing at least 13 deaths.[38]

U.S. policymakers also are under pressure to help American companies compete in the global marketplace. Other countries are forging ahead with self-driving vehicle technologies. Germany, Italy and France in May won agreement to a little-noticed amendment to the United Nations Convention on Road Traffic that would allow self-driving vehicles, thereby helping their high-end carmakers that are planning to bring autonomous vehicles to market within a few years.

"The problem isn't technology, it's legislation, and the whole question of responsibility that goes with these cars moving around . . . and especially who is responsible once there is no longer anyone inside," said Carlos Ghosn, head of the Renault-Nissan Alliance.[39]

NHTSA is also addressing another frontier in automotive technology: vehicle-to-vehicle communication, known as V2V. In February, the agency announced it would begin to enable the technology that allows vehicles to communicate with each other, exchanging basic safety data such as speed and position in order to avoid accidents.

V2V technology is designed, at least initially, to alert drivers to hazardous conditions. But NHTSA is also considering links to automated technologies on board a vehicle, enabling it to brake or swerve without the driver taking action. The technology eventually could also link to infrastructure, such as traffic lights.

"This is just the beginning of a revolution in roadway safety," said U.S. Transportation Secretary Anthony Foxx.[40]

Highway Funding

Even as vehicles are improving, the roads they are traveling over are deteriorating, in part because of evolving vehicle design.

The growing popularity of more fuel-efficient cars, especially those that use hybrid or electric technology, makes it more difficult for states to collect enough in gas taxes to maintain roads and bridges. Two other factors are contributing to the funding crisis, according to analysts: People are driving less and therefore buying less gasoline, and gas is taxed by the gallon instead of the price — meaning that gas tax revenue does not keep pace with inflation. The federal gas tax, which is 18.4 cents per gallon, has not been raised since 1993.[41]

"It's fair to say that we are in a well-documented and worsening transportation funding crisis nationwide," says Jaime Rall, transportation program manager with the National Conference of State Legislatures.

Congress is deadlocked over how to pump more money into the federal Highway Trust Fund. The Congressional Budget Office is warning that highway funds will dwindle to $2 billion by Sept. 30, requiring the Transportation Department to begin delaying payments to states as early as next month to keep the balance above zero, as required by law.

Various stopgap measures have been proposed in the House and Senate as well as by the Obama administration. Congress continued to consider options as its month-long August recess approached.[42]

A few on Capitol Hill maintain that a gas tax increase makes the most sense. Last month, Sens. Bob Corker, R-Tenn., and Chris Murphy, D-Conn., proposed raising the gas tax by 12 cents per gallon and indexing it to inflation.

"Congress should be embarrassed that it has played chicken with the Highway Trust Fund and allowed it to become one of the largest budgeting failures in the federal government," Corker said.[43]

Even as officials at the state level brace for the possible cutoff of money from the federal Highway Trust Fund, they have explored options to increase revenue from state gas taxes. Several states, including Colorado, Nebraska, North Carolina Virginia, and Washington, have imposed fees on electric vehicles. Other states have authorized studies of alternatives to the gas tax, and the Oregon legislature last year approved a pilot program under which 5,000 volunteer motorists will be able to choose to pay a fee based on miles driven instead of a tax on gasoline used.

These policies face opposition. Owners of fuel-efficient cars say it's unfair to penalize them for cutting their gas use, and privacy advocates worry about driving habits being tracked if they are taxed on mileage.

In February, Democratic Virginia Gov. Terry McAuliffe signed legislation repealing that state's $64 annual tax on hybrid vehicles. "The way to improve our environment is not to tax vehicle owners who are doing the right thing," said Democratic state Sen. Adam P. Ebbin, who introduced the legislation.[44]

Nissan's autonomous concept car is shown by Executive Vice President Andy Palmer in Irvine, Calif., on Aug. 27, 2013. Nissan plans to offer self-driving cars by 2020. Other car companies are keeping pace with automated car technology, including General Motors, Ford, Toyota, Volvo and Mercedes.

OUTLOOK

Ubiquitous Taxis

Automotive experts foresee a time when an automated car will show up at the doorstep, transport a person to the office and then head off to drive someone else. Instead of individually owned cars sitting in parking lots or garages most of the day, automated cars could be in almost continual motion, reserved by one user after another. In theory, fewer cars would be needed.

"It's exactly like a taxi service except the expectation is that it should be cheaper," says entrepreneur Chase. "You don't have to maintain it, you don't have to park it, you don't have to deal with it."

"Although demand can go up in terms of usage, the utilization of vehicles will be completely different," says KPMG's Silberg.

Google, in a potential signal that it is anticipating a new model of car use, surprised many observers by investing some $258 million last year in Uber Technologies, a company whose mobile apps run car services.[45] It marked Google's biggest-ever venture capital investment and fed speculation that the search engine giant is working not just on new vehicle technology but rather on a whole new approach to how people get around.

Experts note that transforming how vehicles are rented and used will have implications for existing industries. Already, traditional taxi services and online alternatives such as Uber and Lyft are squaring off over regulations in several cities and states. If society were to need fewer cars, the future of the automotive industry could be threatened.

"What scares the auto industry a lot is that demand is going to go down," Silberg says.

A transition to greatly reduced car ownership would have other profound impacts on society. When cars are not needed, they could be parked in peripheral parking lots miles from stores or businesses, enabling developers to convert parking areas around shopping centers and in downtown areas for other purposes.

"The real potential is for something quite different: ubiquitous taxis — summoned via smartphone or weird glasses — that are so cheap they make car ownership obsolete," economics journalist Matthew Yglesias wrote last year. "It explains why the same company [Google] that's invested in the technology to drive the cars is now investing in the technology to hail them. . . . Cities based on cheap autonomous cabs would be much greener than today's cities. Without the parking, they'd also be denser and more productive, but people wouldn't have to sacrifice their large homes. It would be a true economic game-changer."[46]

Some experts, however, say the attachment of Americans to their cars will not easily go away. After all, vehicles are intensely personal for many drivers, who express themselves by purchasing, say, a European sedan or heavy-duty pick-up truck, and using it as a mobile den and storage area. "Automation may enable a shift from car ownership," says Wallace at the Center for Automotive Research, "but it remains to be seen if people want that."

NOTES

1. Chris Urmson, "Just press go: designing a self-driving vehicle," Google Official Blog, May 27, 2014, http://tinyurl.com/n6d53dj.

2. Lawrence Ulrich, "Feeling a Bit Obsolete in the Driver's Seat," *The New York Times*, Dec. 13, 2013, http://tinyurl.com/km35wvp.

3. Sebastian Thrun, "What We're Driving At," Google Official Blog, Oct. 9, 2010, http://tinyurl.com/38jnhnk.

4. Jason Mick, "Google's Self-Driving Cars Are a 'Threat,' Says GM," *Daily Tech*, May 30, 2014, http://tinyurl.com/mo6pu5q.

5. "Self-Driving Car Test: Steve Mahan," Google, March 28, 2012, http://tinyurl.com/7xcsg56.

6. "The Road to Self-Driving Cars," *Consumer Reports*, April 2014, http://tinyurl.com/jwoaqrw.

7. Daniel J. Fagnant and Kara M. Kockelman, "Preparing a Nation for Autonomous Vehicles," Eno Center for Transportation, October 2013, http://tinyurl.com/lzrjmzl.

8. "Japanese Prime Minister Shinzo Abe Tests Out Self-Driving Cars in Tokyo," Agence France-Presse, Nov. 9, 2013, http://tinyurl.com/kpcganw.

9. Lawrence Blincoe, *et al.*, "The Economic and Societal Impact of Motor Vehicle Crashes, 2010," National Highway Traffic Safety Administration, May 2014, http://tinyurl.com/n69u5pg.

10. Bryant Walker Smith, "Human Error as a Cause of Vehicle Crashes," Stanford University Center for Internet and Society, Dec. 18, 2013, http://tinyurl.com/phobdqm.

11. "An Analysis of the Significant Decline in Motor Vehicle Traffic Fatalities in 2008," NHTSA, June 2010, p. 11, www-nrd.nhtsa.dot.gov/Pubs/811346.pdf.

12. "Vehicle-to-Vehicle (V2V) Communications for Safety," National Highway Traffic Safety Administration, undated, http://tinyurl.com/q8o4fja.

13. Fagnant and Kockelman, *op. cit.*

14. Joan Lowy, "Leaving the Driving to a Computer Has Big Benefits," The Associated Press, Oct. 23, 2013, http://tinyurl.com/pc2b7op.

15. Mark Harris, "FBI warns driverless cars could be used as 'lethal weapons,' " *theguardian.com*, July 16, 2014, http://tinyurl.com/olx2z36.

16. Michael M. Grynbaum, "Gridlock May Not Be Constant, But Slow Going Is Here to Stay," *The New York Times*, March 23, 2010, http://tinyurl.com/pywlv8k.

17. Alexis Stevens, "Atlanta Snow Jam 2014: Metro commuters recount their hours-long trip home,"

The Atlanta Journal-Constitution, Jan. 29, 2014, http://tinyurl.com/q2b38su.

18. 2012 Annual Urban Mobility Report, Texas A&M Transportation Institute, 2013, http://tinyurl.com/6scas.

19. Evan Ackerman, "Study: Intelligent Cars Could Boost Highway Capacity by 273%," *IEEE Spectrum*, Sept. 4, 2012, http://tinyurl.com/bs25a3u.

20. Aaron Smith, "U.S. Views of Technology and the Future," Pew Research Internet Project, April 17, 2014, http://tinyurl.com/mmpyf67.

21. Jim Gorzelany, "Most Consumers Say They'll Steer Clear of Self-Driving Cars, Survey Says," *Forbes*, Sept. 23, 2013, http://tinyurl.com/pndf87f.

22. Claire Cain Miller, "When Driverless Cars Break the Law," *The New York Times*, May 13, 2014, http://tinyurl.com/q2zt4k7.

23. Danielle Douglas and Michael A. Fletcher, "Toyota reaches $1.2 billion settlement to end probe of accelerator problems," *The Washington Post*, March 19, 2014, http://tinyurl.com/ko592ww.

24. "Self-Driving Cars: Are We Ready?" KPMG, 2013, http://tinyurl.com/ovezqkv.

25. Alex Davies, "Self-driving cars will be a huge deal for the elderly and handicapped," *Business Insider*, Aug. 29, 1013, http://tinyurl.com/pqqosva.

26. James Barron, "Cars and the City, Imperfect Together," *The New York Times*, March 19, 2010, http://tinyurl.com/pfr32x2.

27. "Early Adventures with the Automobile," *EyeWitness to History*, 1997, http://tinyurl.com/rofv3.

28. For background, see Thomas J. Billitteri, "Auto Industry's Future," *CQ Researcher*, Feb. 6, 2009, pp. 105-128.

29. "The DARPA Grand Challenge: Ten Years Later," Defense Advanced Research Projects Agency press release, March 13, 2014, http://tinyurl.com/o2th4o6.

30. Sebastian Thrun, "What We're Driving At," Google Official Blog, Oct. 9, 2010, http://tinyurl.com/38jnhnk.

31. Jay Yarow, "Human driver crashes Google's self-driving car," *Business Insider*, Aug. 5, 2011, http://tinyurl.com/3lz9zpn; and John Markoff, "Google cars drive themselves, in traffic," *The New York Times*, Oct. 9, 2010, http://tinyurl.com/krbrzy2.

32. "Provides guidance to states permitting testing of emerging vehicle technology," National Highway Traffic Safety Administration press release, May 30, 2013, http://tinyurl.com/q8r9drs.

33. Justin Pritchard, "Google: We're Building Car With No Steering Wheel," The Associated Press, May 28, 2014, http://tinyurl.com/l3hcve8.

34. Paul A. Eisenstein, "Self-driving cars rewriting rules of the road," CNBC, May 30, 2014, http://tinyurl.com/lzpgawg.

35. Peter Valdes-Dapena, "Gov't proposes rules for self-driving cars," CNN Money, May 31, 2013, http://tinyurl.com/oaoorxt.

36. Keith Laing, "Driverless cars approach the starting line," *The Hill*, June 24, 2014, http://tinyurl.com/ml45uow.

37. *Ibid.*

38. Matthew Rocco, "GM's top lawyer takes heat over ignition-switch recall," Fox Business, July 17, 2014, http://tinyurl.com/nbrmk9q; and Nathan Bomey, "GM recalls another 8.4 million vehicles, most for ignition switch defect," *Detroit Free Press*, June 30, 2014, http://tinyurl.com/ohyzaem.

39. "Self-driving cars may hit roads in 2018: Renault-Nissan CEO," Reuters, June 3, 2014, http://tinyurl.com/nydozw3.

40. Jerry Hirsch, "U.S. regulators plan car-to-car communications to prevent accidents," *Los Angeles Times*, Feb. 3, 2014, http://tinyurl.com/njcywvs.

41. "Highway History," U.S. Department of Transportation Federal Highway Administration, Oct. 17, 2013, http://tinyurl.com/23gt3vw.

42. Jonathan Weisman and Peter Baker, "House Passes Interim Fix for Highway Trust Fund," *The New York Times*, July 15, 2014, http://tinyurl.com/qdpl2sn.

43. Brett Logiurato, "Two Senators Have a Very Simple and Very Unpopular Idea for Saving the Highway Trust Fund," *Business Insider*, June 18, 2014, http://tinyurl.com/nqmokcb.

44. Patricia Sullivan, "Virginia legislators seek to repeal hybrid tax," *The Washington Post*, July 1, 2013, http://tinyurl.com/ngv7n7v.

45. Ryan Lawler, "Uber Confirms That It Raised $258M From Google Ventures And TPG," *TechCrunch*, Aug. 23, 2013, http://tinyurl.com/nqx2uj6.

46. Matthew Yglesias, "Google and Uber Could Transform America," *Slate*, Aug. 29, 2013, http://tinyurl.com/ph825pm.

BIBLIOGRAPHY

Selected Sources

Books

Parissien, Steven, *The Life of the Automobile*, St. Martin's Press, 2014.
A British cultural expert carefully documents the history of automobiles, dating back to the first cars in the late 19th century. Parissien mixes compelling profiles of leading industry figures, descriptions of major U.S. and overseas car models and a look ahead to the potential of alternative fuel sources.

Articles

"The Future of Transportation," Citylab, 2014, http://tinyurl.com/mbfzqqs.
With content sponsored by The Rockefeller Foundation, Citylab presents a series of thought-provoking articles and essays by reporters and analysts about the future of urban transportation. They include pieces about electric cars, Google self-driving cars, connected vehicles and potential changes in society's approach to car ownership. The articles, intermixed with others about mass transit, transportation apps and highways, provide an in-depth view of the complex transportation system.

Fisher, Adam, "Inside Google's Quest to Popularize Self-Driving Cars," *Popular Science*, Sept. 18, 2013, http://tinyurl.com/lka692w.
A technology writer takes a detailed look at Google's work on self-driving cars. The article examines the potential benefits of autonomous cars, some of the key technical and legal challenges and the uneasy relationship between Google and carmakers.

Guizzo, Erico, "How Google's Self-Driving Car Works," *IEEE Spectrum*, Oct. 8, 2011, http://tinyurl.com/3l4bvnz.
A short but detailed article explains the technology that enables a Google car to drive itself.

Hirsch, Jerry, "U.S. regulators plan car-to-car communications to prevent accidents," *Los Angeles Times*, Feb. 3, 2014, http://tinyurl.com/njcywvs.
Transportation Secretary Anthony Foxx discusses the potential benefits and challenges of vehicle-to-vehicle communications, as seen by the National Highway Traffic Safety Administration.

Hockenos, Paul, "Smart Streets: From Holland, Bright Ideas for Highways," *The New York Times*, April 26, 2013, http://tinyurl.com/ngmosz7.
Dutch inventors and others have proposed many innovations for creating so-called smart highways that could better charge electric vehicles, improve visibility and otherwise serve the needs of motorists.

Miller, Claire Cain, "When Driverless Cars Break the Law," *The Upshot, The New York Times*, May 13, 2014, http://tinyurl.com/q84598m.
A technology writer analyzes one of the biggest barriers to the mass marketing of autonomous vehicles: Who will be held responsible when one of them gets into an accident? The article looks at the legal ramifications.

Yglesias, Matthew, "Google and Uber Could Transform America," *Slate*, Aug. 29, 2013, http://tinyurl.com/ph825pm.
An economics writer contends that car-sharing with autonomous vehicles can reshape consumer attitudes toward vehicles and also the urban landscape.

Reports and Studies

"2012 Annual Urban Mobility Report," Texas A&M Transportation Institute, 2013, http://tinyurl.com/6scas.
The latest in a series of annual reports on urban congestion provides detailed statistics on traffic in 498 U.S. urban areas, with five large metropolitan areas — Washington, D.C., Los Angeles, San Francisco-Oakland, New York-Newark and Boston — experiencing the worst traffic. The report also measures the degree to which certain trip times are unpredictable due to delays and

includes an estimate of the additional carbon dioxide emissions that can be attributed to traffic delays.

"Self-Driving Cars: Are We Ready?," KPMG, 2013, http://tinyurl.com/ovezqkv.
KPMG, a global auditing and professional-services company, conducted a series of focus groups to determine why some people resist the notion of self-driving cars and what could sway them to accept the technology. The key finding: Consumers will be more receptive if autonomous cars can safely deliver a more efficient and predictable driving experience. This report summarizes those focus groups and provides background about self-driving cars.

Fagnant, Daniel J., and Kara M. Kockelman, "Preparing a Nation for Autonomous Vehicles," Eno Center for Transportation, October 2013, http://tinyurl.com/lzrjmzl.
The Eno Center, a think tank focusing on the transportation industry, analyzes the prospects for autonomous vehicles. The report looks at potential benefits of the vehicles, such as improved safety and reduced congestion, as well as potential barriers to their adoption, such as cost and questions about liability. It concludes with a series of policy recommendations, including expanding federal funding for autonomous vehicle research; developing federal guidelines for autonomous vehicle licensing and determining appropriate standards for liability, security and data privacy. The Eno Center was founded in 1921 by William Phelps Eno, who pioneered the field of traffic management in the United States and Europe.

For More Information

Center for Automotive Research, 3005 Boardwalk, Suite 200, Ann Arbor, MI 48108; 734-662-1287; www.cargroup.org/. Studies the global automotive industry; formerly associated with the University of Michigan.

Center for Auto Safety, 1825 Connecticut Ave., N.W., Suite 330, Washington, DC 20009; 202-328-7700; www.autosafety.org. Consumer advocacy group that concentrates on auto safety and defective automobiles.

Eno Center for Transportation, 1710 Rhode Island Ave., N.W., Washington, DC 20036; 202-879-4700; www.enotrans.org. Think tank that studies transportation issues; funded by a foundation endowed by an early 20th-century traffic control pioneer.

Intelligent Transportation Society of America, 1100 New Jersey Ave., S.E., Washington, DC 20003; 800-374-3472; www.itsa.org. Advocates research, development and deployment of intelligent transportation systems.

National Highway Traffic Safety Administration, 1200 New Jersey Ave., S.E., West Building, Washington, DC 20590; 888-327-4236; www.nhtsa.gov. Federal agency that regulates vehicles and funds highway safety programs.

4

Wealth and Inequality

Sarah Glazer

An Occupy Wall Street demonstrator protests against economic inequality at a rally in New York City on May 1, 2012. The top 1 percent of the world's richest people own about half of all global wealth, and the bottom half less than 5 percent. President Obama is proposing steps to help struggling Americans climb the income ladder, including raising the minimum wage and ending tax loopholes for the richest Americans. But conservative economists say such measures would punish entrepreneurship and stifle economic growth.

From *CQ Researcher*, April 18, 2014.

The excavation machines are busy these days in London's most fashionable neighborhoods, digging several stories under historic mansions to create the swimming pools, wine cellars and bowling alleys demanded by their wealthy owners.[1]

Yet many of these houses will remain empty most of the year, as their owners divide their time among other homes in Europe, Asia or the Middle East, according to real estate agents. London's prime homes are becoming a "global reserve currency" where the world's richest people can park their money, London journalist Michael Goldfarb recently wrote. He mourned the loss of neighbors joining the exodus of middle-class families no longer able to afford the city.[2]

In Miami, an apartment in a new luxury building designed by world-renowned architect Zaha Hadid gets the buyer a roof-top helipad and a private vault for storing precious jewelry and artwork. Prices start at $5 million and go up to $45 million for the duplex six-bedroom penthouse, whose 15,207 square feet include an indoor pool, media room, library, gym, staff quarters and more than 1,000 square feet of terrace.

These are just some of the more ostentatious signals that the very rich in the United States and around the world have been doing very well since the recession, even though many middle-class households still struggle. The astounding rise in wealth of the very few continues to make international headlines, such as the recent report by the anti-poverty charity Oxfam that the wealth of the world's 85 richest billionaires now equals that of the poorest half of the world's population.[3]

Once the backwater of economics and the concern of a few public-interest groups, the issue of income inequality — the term used for

Wealthiest Americans Control Record Share of U.S. Income

The wealthiest 10 percent of Americans controlled half of the nation's income in 2012, the largest share since just before the Great Depression.

Share of income (including capital gains)

Income Share of Top 10 Percent of Americans, 1917-2012

Source: Emmanuel Saez, "Striking it Richer: The Evolution of Top Incomes in the United States (Updated with 2012 preliminary estimates)," University of California-Berkeley, Sept. 3, 2013, http://elsa.berkeley.edu/~saez/saez-UStopincomes-2012.pdf; data from http://elsa.berkeley.edu/~saez/TabFig2012prel.xls

the growing disparity between the incomes of society's poorest and wealthiest sectors — is getting new attention on the national and international scene. The World Economic Forum, which sponsors the annual Davos gathering of the world's economic glitterati, recently declared the worsening wealth gap the problem most likely to pose a risk on a global scale, based on its survey of 700 experts.[4] The concern raised at Davos that increasing inequality threatens the political and financial stability of nations has also become a new focus of the 188-nation International Monetary Fund, which lends money to countries in trouble.[5]

"The reason we worry about inequality is [that] it's not a good thing to be a plutocracy," says liberal University of Texas-Austin economist James K. Galbraith.

Scott Winship, a senior fellow at the conservative Manhattan Institute think tank, suggests the current preoccupation with equality is related to economic anxiety during and following the recession. "I do believe if the economy picks up and unemployment goes back down to 5 percent, the interest in income inequality will go away again," he says.

In a widely discussed new book, Thomas Piketty, a professor at the Paris School of Economics, warns that rising inequality could threaten the very fabric of democracy and proposes confiscatory taxes on the rich. But those and other tax-increase proposals are strongly opposed by conservatives, who say high taxes stifle growth. Those critics argue that rising wealth at the top

doesn't hurt those at the bottom, because as long as the economy is growing overall, all will benefit.

Liberal economist Paul Krugman, a *New York Times* columnist and Nobel Prize winner, is among those referring to the current era as a new Gilded Age, harking back to the 19th century, when so-called "robber barons" such as J. P. Morgan and John D. Rockefeller were accused of accumulating enormous wealth at the expense of the new industrial working class.[6]

In the United States, research shows growing inequality, with the richest 10 percent of families now capturing half of all personal income, a level not seen since 1917 and even greater than the Roaring '20s, according to University of California-Berkeley economist Emmanuel Saez.[7]

Even starker is how far the richest households in America have pulled ahead of everyone else since the 2007-2009 recession. The top 1 percent — those with annual incomes of more than $394,000 — saw their incomes grow by 31 percent in the three years following the end of the recession, compared with a less than 1 percent gain for the other 99 percent. As a result, that upper stratum captured 95 percent of the nation's income gains during the recovery, Saez calculates.[8]

The United States reflects a global trend toward concentration of wealth, according to *Capital in the Twenty-First Century*, Piketty's new book. Worldwide, inequality now appears comparable to stratified Europe in 1900-1910, with the top 1 percent holding about half of global wealth, and the rest of the population owning less than 5 percent, according to Piketty.[9]

President Obama has contrasted today's stagnating middle class incomes with the post-World War II years, when wages rose along with the nation's economy. "[F]or some, that meant following in your old man's footsteps at the local plant, and you knew that a blue-collar job would let you buy a home, and a car, maybe a vacation once in a while, health care, a reliable pension," Obama said.[10]

Conservative economists and some liberals say that rosy period of middle-income growth in the 1950s-1970s was unique — before American manufacturing faced global competition and before a high-tech economy required more than a high school education to support a family.

Those factors drove down wages for the less educated: "This is part of globalization and all these changing things about society you can't put back in the bottle," says Salim Furth, senior policy analyst in macroeconomics at the Heritage Foundation, a conservative think tank in Washington. "If [employers] are going to compete, they have to pay global wages," Furth says.

Writing in the op-ed pages of *The Wall Street Journal*, commentator Mickey Kaus, author of *The End of Equality*, suggested Americans are more concerned about social inequality than income inequality. "Do we remember the 1950s as a halcyon egalitarian era because the rich weren't rich — or because rich and poor had served together in World War II?" he asked. He questioned the growing preoccupation with income differences: "If the poor and middle class were getting steadily richer, would it matter that the rich are getting richer much faster?"[11]

Like Kaus, others on the more conservative end of the spectrum who have studied recent trends, tend to agree that income inequality has increased, though some experts say it has increased less drastically than Piketty claims.

Winship of the Manhattan Institute says Piketty has "overstated" the differences between growth in wealth

U.S. Has Highest Share of Millionaires

Of the world's millionaires, 42 percent are from the United States, by far the largest share. Canada, France, Germany, Italy, Japan and the U.K. account for a combined 33 percent share of the global total.

Share of Millionaires by Country of Residence

- Rest of world 12%
- Japan 8%
- France 7%
- Germany 5%
- United Kingdom 5%
- Italy 5%
- China 4%
- Australia 4%
- Canada 3%
- Switzerland 2%
- Sweden 2%
- Spain 1%
- Taiwan 1%
- United States 42%

Note: Percentages do not add to 100 because of rounding.

Source: "Global Wealth Report 2013," Credit Suisse, p. 23, https://publications.credit-suisse.com/tasks/render/file/?fileID=BCDB1364-A105-0560-1332EC9100FF5C83

among the richest and poorest because he failed to include safety net programs such as food stamps for the poor. Winship points to a calculation by the Congressional Budget Office that finds — after taxes and employer fringe benefits are accounted for — that the top 1 percent increased their share of national income between 1979 and 2007 from 7 to 17 percent, less than Piketty's 10 to 24 percent.[12]

Even when conservatives accept the general direction of Piketty's findings, they tend to disagree with the implication — that a growing share at the top means less wealth for those below. In testimony before the congressional Joint Economic Committee in January, Winship said living standards have improved for the middle class even as income inequality has grown. "Inequality was high and rising during the late 1990s," he noted, "but because the growing economy was largely benefiting everyone, few people were worried about income concentration at the top."[13]

Liberals such as Yale political science professor Jacob S. Hacker argue that middle-class incomes have stalled mainly because of government policies supported by the

French economist Thomas Piketty warns in a widely discussed new book that rising inequality could threaten the very fabric of democracy and proposes high taxes on the rich. The book, Capital in the Twenty-First Century, argues that the United States reflects a global trend toward concentration of wealth and that inequality worldwide now appears comparable to stratified Europe in the early 20th century.

rich: "Government rewrote the rules," in three areas, leading to weakening of unions, weakening of oversight of financial markets and looking the other way on exploding executive pay, he says.

However, Winship points out that economic growth has slowed not only in the United States but also in Japan and Europe. "We are talking about global economic trends that are not specific to the U.S.," he says, citing global competition and a freer labor market. "It's not that we crushed unions and that's the whole story," he says, or that pro-union European countries have done a lot better.

"We are the 99 percent," the 2011 slogan of the protest movement Occupy Wall Street, called attention to the advantages of the wealthiest 1 percent, and recently some politicians have taken up the cry. New York City Mayor Bill de Blasio, elected after promising to reduce the gap between rich and poor, advocated increased taxes on the wealthy to fund universal pre-kindergarten. On the federal level, Obama has also proposed increasing taxes on the wealthiest Americans.

Yet conservatives warn that raising taxes on the rich will hurt the entire economy because the wealthy will have less money to invest in job-producing activities that benefit the rest of the population. "There is a large literature that high tax rates clearly hurt growth," says the Heritage Foundation's Furth.

Experts and the public remain deeply divided about growing wealth at the top and its implications for everyone else. Here are some of the questions being debated in the press, academia and the political arena:

Does income inequality hamper economic growth?

Middle-class stores like Sears and JCPenney are closing down in malls and downtowns across America, and mid-priced restaurants like Olive Garden and Red Lobster are struggling.[14] Meanwhile upscale dining chains like Capital Grille are thriving as the rich account for a bigger slice of U.S. consumption, *The New York Times* recently reported.[15]

Some economists say the shrinking of middle-class consumption could seriously hurt economic growth — and that a sluggish recovery may already reflect reduced consumer demand.

The top 5 percent of U.S. earners were responsible for 38 percent of domestic consumption in 2012, up from 28 percent in 1995, according to a recent study by two economists from the Weidenbaum Center at Washington University in St. Louis.[16] Since 2009, spending by those top earners rose 17 percent, compared with 1 percent among the bottom 95 percent.[17]

Some economists and activists blame this phenomenon on stagnating middle-class wages since 1980. A middle-income family would have had $18,897 more to spend in 2007, the year before the recession, if there "had been no growth in income disparities since 1979," according to the Economic Policy Institute, a liberal think tank in Washington that focuses on working Americans.[18] More spending from those families would have helped stimulate the economy, argues Princeton economist Alan Krueger, who was a top economic adviser to Obama from 2009 to 2013.

If the shift in income to top earners in recent years had been more evenly distributed, Krueger calculates that annual consumption would be $400 billion to $500 billion higher today, equal to 3.5 percent of gross domestic product (GDP).[19]

Conservatives counter that investment is just as important as consumption to a growing economy and that more wealth at the top means more investment, with benefits trickling down in the form of new jobs. "The combination of more investment, innovation and risk taking at the top that's been facilitated by rising income" has contributed to continued economic growth, says the Manhattan Institute's Winship.

Winship estimates that the increase in the top 1 percent's share of national income between 1979 and 2007 raised GDP during that period and therefore increased household income for the middle class.[20]

"If the top 1 percent continues to get a bigger share of a pie that grows fast enough, then the middle class and poor may receive pretty big gains themselves," he says. The rising share of national income going to the wealthiest — the statistic cited by Piketty that has attracted so much recent attention — "may be the wrong indicator to focus on," Winship says.

One reason the United States may have more inequality than other rich countries is that "we honor entrepreneurs more," says Heritage's Furth. When a young unknown like Bill Gates suddenly becomes a millionaire, he pulls far ahead of everyone else.

"I don't think there's any evidence that inequality hurts growth," says Furth. "The United States has remained at the top of GDP per capita charts for large countries for 60 to 80 years," he says, pointing out that the median household in the United States earns more than its counterparts in countries including Great Britain, France, Italy and Spain.

But others say the pie is being divided unfairly even amid growth. "As long as productivity is growing, someone's getting the money; it just ain't America's middle class," says Heather Boushey, executive director of the Washington Center for Equitable Progress, a project studying inequality at the Center for American Progress, a liberal think tank in Washington.

Economists generally agree that some amount of inequality is inevitable once a country shifts from a mainly agrarian economy, where most people are living at a more or less equal subsistence level, to an industrialized economy.[21]

That theory was first advanced by the influential American economist Simon Kuznets in the 1950s and 1960s. As Piketty explains, Kuznets theorized that as countries shifted to industrialized economies the disparities between those living off the land and those in factory jobs would increase inequality "because only a minority of people would be prepared to benefit from the new wealth." In later stages of a country's development, Kuznets believed, inequality would automatically

decrease as a larger and larger fraction of the population shared in economic growth.[22]

"For any kind of functioning economy, you wouldn't want inequality to be zero," says UT-Austin's Galbraith. However, he adds, "It's like blood pressure. . . . When inequality is going up rapidly, it's a sign you have trouble."

A recent international comparison by the International Monetary Fund (IMF) finds countries that have lower inequality, after taking into account taxes and welfare benefits, tend to have "faster and more durable growth."[23]

An earlier study from the IMF, one of the most frequently cited in this debate, found slower recovery from downturns in countries with high inequality. But "its boosters generally fail to note that only developing nations are examined," says Winship.[24]

"To generalize from that to industrialized countries and the U.S. is egregious," Winship says. Instead, he cites another study supporting his view that "economic growth has benefited from rising inequality" by leaving poor and middle-class households "with a smaller share of a bigger economic pie and no worse off for it."[25]

With so many studies on both sides of the debate, and with conclusions that vary depending on which countries and periods of time they examine, there probably isn't a one-for-one relationship between inequality and growth, concludes Hacker, the Yale political scientist. "The more relevant question is, 'Does income inequality hamper middle-class income growth?' " he says. "In the U.S. you had a big increase in average incomes, but most of that's driven by the rise at the very top."

Increasingly, experts on both right and left have been pointing to America's highly unequal educational system, in which affluent suburbs provide far better public schools than struggling inner cities, as a root cause of inequality. However, they disagree on the solutions — school choice for Republicans, universal pre-kindergarten for Democrats.

That educational gap between rich and poor hurts the economy because the nation doesn't make the most of all its talented citizens, most experts agree. A recent report shows that the gap between low-income and upper-income children in obtaining a college education is large and widening.[26]

A roving bus in New York City in December 2013 offers British-style tea and biscuits to promote season four of the hit period drama "Downton Abbey." In the United States, unlike in the early-20th-century England portrayed in the popular PBS series, the very wealthy tend to be the "working rich," rather than aristocrats who inherited their fortunes.

In a recent *New York Times* column, liberal economist Krugman said the educational divide "represents a huge and growing waste of human potential — a waste that surely acts as a powerful if invisible drag on economic growth."[27]

Are parental background and inheritance becoming more important for success?

In his book, economist Piketty finds a trend echoing the aristocratic class system described in the 19th-century novels of British writer Jane Austen and French writer Honore de Balzac: Inherited wealth in some European countries is becoming as important for individual financial success as it was in the 19th century, he writes. Inherited wealth accounts for nearly half of the total amount of the largest fortunes worldwide, he estimates.[28]

Even in the United States, where inheritance has historically been less important than in Europe, wealth is providing an ever-more cumulative advantage, Piketty argues, because wealth begets more wealth once invested.

According to *Forbes'* global billionaires list, the top wealth holders have seen their wealth rise at 6 to 7 percent per year from 1987-2013, a rate more than three times faster than the growth in income and output at the global level.[29] That means rich people can accumulate wealth at far higher rates than the majority of workers, whose wages grow no faster than the economy or their own productivity, Piketty argues.

In an interview, Piketty explained, "If wealth is rising three times as fast as the economy and this goes on for several decades, it means the middle class is vanishing and a rising fraction of national wealth will be taken by a small fraction" of people at the very top.

"It's not sustainable unless you are able to accept an oligarchic concentration of wealth, which is not fully compatible with the democratic idea," says Piketty, whose solution is a global tax on wealth combined with higher income taxes on the richest in the United States.

"Growing income and wealth inequality is skewing our democracy: We're supposed to have a system where every vote counts but where increasingly money counts," says Lawrence Mishel, president of the Economic Policy Institute, a liberal think tank in Washington.

In his January State of the Union speech, Obama declared that "upward mobility has stalled" and stressed the need to build "ladders of opportunity into the middle class."[30] Conservative Republicans Rep. Paul Ryan of Wisconsin and Florida Sen. Marco Rubio have given speeches in recent months bewailing social immobility and saying there should be more reward for people who work hard.[31]

But a recent study finds upward mobility in the United States is at a level similar to a generation ago.[32] Yet, many don't see that as good news because it still means most families at the bottom never make it to the top. According to a study led by Harvard economist Raj Chetty, the probability that a child born in 1971 in the bottom fifth of incomes would make it to the top fifth was 8 percent, compared with 9 percent for children born in 1986.[33]

And mobility in the U.S. is about half that in some Scandinavian countries. In Denmark, a poor child has twice the chance of making it to the top fifth as in America.[34]

A new study by University of California-Davis economist Gregory Clark finds the elite status of aristocratic families is amazingly resilient over generations even in a country like Sweden, famous for its income equality.[35] His finding runs counter to most previous studies, which find more upward mobility in Europe and Scandinavia than in the United States.

The American dream of upward mobility for all "is clearly a myth," he recently told a London audience, based on his study of the persistence of elite families in professions like medicine and law.

Clark uses an unconventional method — tracking elite surnames over centuries — and comes to an unconventional conclusion: "We can't find any society that is achieving high rates of social mobility," he says, concluding, "It's not going to be worthwhile making massive social investments in trying to improve social mobility." But he does favor Scandinavian-style welfare to produce more income equality.

There's no question that Sweden's system of welfare benefits evens out differences in income, making that nation one of the most equal of rich countries. Sweden starts out similar to the United States in inequality if just incomes paid by employers before taxes and welfare benefits are counted. In the United States, "The really big story is [that] we redistribute much less," says Janet Gornick director of the Luxembourg Income Study Center, of Luxembourg and New York.

Many policymakers maintain there are ways to boost social mobility in America without recreating a Swedish welfare state. Ron Haskins helped design 1996 welfare reform legislation as a Republican congressional staffer, later serving as a White House adviser to Republican President George W. Bush, and currently serving as a senior fellow in economic studies at the centrist Brookings Institution think tank. He says that with a college diploma, young people born into low-income families can quadruple their chance of making it to the top of the income ladder — from 5 percent to 20 percent.

However, Haskins stresses the role of personal responsibility. In 2009, he analyzed census data to see how adult Americans were doing if they followed three norms of modern society: finish high school, get a full-time job, and wait until age 21 to get married before having children. Young adults who followed all three had only a 2 percent chance of winding up in poverty and a 74 percent chance of reaching the middle class, he found.[36]

"Liberals are very reluctant to talk about personal responsibility because it's blaming the victim," Haskins says.

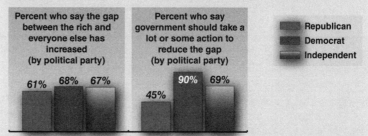

Americans Divided on Action to Curb Inequality

A majority of Americans belonging to both political parties agree that economic inequality has worsened over the past decade, according to a recent survey. However, 90 percent of Democrats interviewed say the government should take "a lot" or "some" action to reduce the gap, compared with 69 percent of independents and 45 percent of Republicans.

Percent who say the gap between the rich and everyone else has increased (by political party)

61% 68% 67%

Percent who say government should take a lot or some action to reduce the gap (by political party)

45% 90% 69%

Republican
Democrat
Independent

Source: "Most See Inequality Growing, but Partisans Differ over Solutions," Pew Research Center, Jan. 23, 2014, www.people-ress.org/2014/01/23/most-see-inequality-growing-but-partisans-differ-over-solutions/

In the United States, unlike in 19th-century Europe or even in the early 20th-century England portrayed on the PBS series "Downton Abbey," the very wealthy tend to be the "working rich," and there hasn't been a big increase in inherited wealth since the 1980s. In fact, wealth transfers as a proportion of net worth have fallen from 29 percent to 19 percent between 1989 and 2007.[37]

That's a big contrast to Europe, where French economist Piketty finds inheritance is reaching levels not seen since the 19th century as a share of national income.[38]

However, when Piketty looks more broadly at accumulated wealth globally, not just inheritance, he finds it comparable to the levels in Europe in 1900-1910, during France's so-called Belle Époque, when industrialists were accumulating wealth and there was a large underclass. Today the top 1 percent owns about half of all global wealth and the bottom half less than 5 percent.[39]

Wealth, inherited or not, is a huge advantage in becoming even wealthier, Piketty says, because the wealthy have financial advisers and can afford high-risk, high-return investments, compared with the small saver, who can't afford to risk any part of a nest egg.

Yet Americans still believe in the rags-to-riches American dream, polls by the Pew Charitable Trusts find.[40] That may be because most families (84 percent)

President Theodore Roosevelt addresses a crowd from the back of a train, circa 1907. President from 1901 to 1909, Roosevelt championed an estate tax in 1910 to prevent extreme accumulation of wealth. "The absence of effective state . . . restraint upon unfair money-getting has tended to create a small class of enormously wealthy and economically powerful men, whose chief object is to hold and increase their power," he charged.

are making more than their parents, notes Erin Currier, director of economic mobility research for Pew. But the glass is only half-full. "For families at the bottom, yes, they have more money than their parents, but often the increase is so small that it's not enough to move them out of the bottom," she says. Seventy percent of children born into families in the bottom 20 percent never even make it to the middle class as working adults, according to Pew.[41]

Should the wealthy be taxed more?

Increasing taxes on the rich has received new attention as Obama and New York Mayor de Blasio have called on the wealthy to share more of the burden.

A controversial proposal by French economist Piketty to impose a global tax on "wealth" — including all assets such as trusts, partnerships and stocks — has also stimulated debate. To keep the rich from evading the tax by moving their money abroad, such a tax should be global, Piketty argues. While conceding that it is probably utopian to think all governments would agree to that measure, he suggests it would "realistic" for Europe.

For Piketty, his brash proposal is a way to draw attention to his central concern: Accumulating capital is conferring unfair advantages on the rich in a cycle that could eventually see the disappearance of the middle class. "The point is not just to raise taxation — it's to help the diffusion of wealth and make sure the wealth of the middle class expands rather than continues to shrink," he says.

And he thinks this is a more effective way to tax the rich than solely through income tax. "If some people are taxed on the basis of declared incomes that are only 1 percent of actual incomes, then nothing is accomplished by raising income tax rates to 50 or even 98 percent," he writes.[42]

Heritage Foundation conservative Furth objects that taxing capital is like penalizing the modest Swedish millionaire who invests to create jobs and drives a beat-up Saab while favoring the decadent consumption of a "Wolf of Wall Street"-style millionaire.[43] "Investment helps everyone else, consumption only helps you. If you want to help labor, tax capital at zero," he says.

In a recent critique of Piketty's book published in *The Wall Street Journal*, Christopher DeMuth, Republican President Ronald Reagan's deregulation czar in the 1980s and now a distinguished fellow at the conservative Hudson Institute, argued that in practice income redistributed by government often ends up in the hands of the powerful rather than the needy. The pro-government "intellectual imagines redistributing capital profits while leaving owners with the losses, but the opposite — profits for owners and managers, losses for taxpayers — has been frequently observed in the wild," he wrote.[44]

Some concerned about inequality in the United States have proposed raising income tax rates on the rich — now at 39.6 percent on the highest income bracket. Political scientist Hacker says that rate kicks in well below the richest of the rich. He has proposed raising the top rate on the truly rich — to 45 percent for those with annual incomes between $1 million and $10 million and to 49 percent for those with income of $1 billion or more.[45]

Hacker argues that the prospect of such high taxation would stem extremely high corporate pay packages — which have skyrocketed in recent years — because so much would get taxed away. He predicts "companies would pay slightly smaller packages and plow some of that into firm investment or salaries for the rank and file. But the main reason to do it is to raise money and assure the tax code is progressive all the way up the income distribution." (A progressive income tax is one in which the tax rate increases as the payer's income increases.)

Arguments for taxing the rich often stem from "a misguided belief that the economy is a zero-sum game and that reducing the position of the top 1 percent automatically improves everyone else's," Sendhil Mullainathan, a professor of economics at Harvard, cautioned in *The New York Times*.[46]

In a recent public debate, conservative supply-side economist Arthur Laffer argued that the rich already pay enough — more of the nation's income tax than anyone else. He also argued, "You aren't going to get the money from these guys. They can hire lawyers, they can hire accountants. . . . they can hire congressmen, . . . senators."[47]

Former Labor Secretary Robert Reich, who served in the administration of Democratic President Bill Clinton, countered that the country's budget deficits require tax increases and that those ought to come mostly from people at the top because "people at the top have never had it so good."[48]

Conservatives like Furth cite findings that high taxes on the rich remove incentives to continue working and thus ultimately hurt growth. "I'd argue incentive effects matter. Even if the rich have a Learjet, they want more money and are willing to work for it and create more businesses," he says.

That was the argument of Reagan, under whose administration top rates were lowered, as recommended by Laffer. But, says the University of Texas' Galbraith, "We taxed the rich a lot less 34 years ago and got no more investment."

Rather than a high income tax, Galbraith favors a high estate tax to "actively discourage dynasty building." Piketty does not: "Life is very long these days," he says. "If you wait until people die to regulate the consumption of wealth it will be too long; you need a lifetime wealth tax."

Ultimately, the argument comes back to whether the income of the wealthy should be redistributed through the tax system to counter inequality. Haskins of Brookings argues that on that score the "government is already fighting inequality dramatically." Households at the bottom of the ladder earning $8,100 a year received almost $23,000 in government benefits in 2010, including Social Security and Medicare, according to the Congressional Budget Office.[49]

However, those transfers still leave the United States far behind Scandinavia and some European countries on equality measures, because those countries have far more generous welfare benefits.

Yet a self-described budget hawk like Haskins questions how much more the government can afford to do. "After all, we're spending $1 trillion between the federal government and the states on benefit programs, and our tax system is hugely progressive: The upper 20 percent pay over 90 percent of federal income taxes," he says.[50] "You want the rich to pay 96 percent of federal income taxes?"

Even some liberal activists who are calling attention to growing inequality say they're more interested in seeing changes that create more opportunity — like a higher minimum wage, more jobs and more bargaining power for workers. "I think we need to have more taxes on the best-off, but I think what matters for me is what happens in the marketplace," says the Economic Policy Institute's Mishel.

Pointing to trends such as the growing competitiveness of foreign workers and the education gap between rich and poor, Urban Institute tax expert Eugene Steuerle, who served in four White House administrations, both Republican and Democratic, cautions, "The forces in society that are leading to inequality are much larger" than the solutions currently proposed such as "nipping at the taxes the rich pay or bumping up the transfers that low-income people receive."

BACKGROUND

'Fatal Ailment'

Ancient philosophers and their Enlightenment heirs believed that democracy required not a utopian form of equality but rather laws that would limit the excesses

CHRONOLOGY

1870s-1900s *Gilded Age sees rising inequality; progressives call for taxes on the rich.*

1913 States ratify 16th Amendment to U.S. Constitution, allowing Congress to institute income tax.

1916 U.S. Congress incorporates estate tax into tax code.

1920s-1930s *FDR's Depression-era New Deal creates social programs; increases taxes on the rich.*

1929-1933 Great Depression; U.S. unemployment nears 25 percent.

1933 Under President Franklin D. Roosevelt, top U.S. tax rate increases to 63 percent.

1940s-1970s *World War II brings highest U.S. tax rates on the rich.*

1941 U.S. enters World War II.

1942 Congress raises top tax rate to 88 percent to pay for war effort. . . . Nation's wealthiest 10 percent see their share of U.S. income drop from about 45 percent to 33 percent, where it stays into the 1970s.

1944 Congress raises top rate again to 94 percent on income over $200,000 — $27 million in current dollars.

1954 Union membership peaks at more than one in three workers.

1974 Union membership drops to less than one in four workers — plummeting to 11 percent in 2013.

Late 1970s-1990s *Conservatives support tax cuts as key to growth; middle-class income growth falls behind productivity growth.*

1979-1980 Supply-side economics advocates Margaret Thatcher and Ronald Reagan elected to top positions in Britain and the United States.

1981 Economic Recovery Tax Act reduces top U.S. tax rates.

1986 Tax Reform Act of 1986 reduces top income tax rate from 50 percent to 28 percent.

1992-2000 *Average income grows 32 percent as economy expands, income of bottom 99 percent grows 20 percent, income of wealthiest 1 percent grows 99 percent.*

1992 After 1990-91 recession, President Bill Clinton elected.

2000 Unemployment drops to 20-year low of 4 percent from peak of 7.5 percent in 1992.

2000s *Financial collapse leads to new financial regulation; average family income drops during Great Recession (2007-2009).*

2001 Under President George W. Bush, tax cuts adopted despite budget deficit; taxes cut again in 2003.

2008 Global financial crisis follows subprime mortgage collapse.

2010 Dodd-Frank Wall Street reform law increases financial regulation as well as reporting of executive pay.

2012 Top 10 percent capture more than 50 percent of U.S. income — highest share since 1917, according to Berkeley economists.

2013 Berkeley researchers say top 1 percent of earners captured 95 percent of income gains since 2009 recovery. . . . Bill de Blasio elected New York City mayor promising to tax rich to pay for pre-kindergarten. . . . Bush tax cut expires; top tax rates raised from 35 percent to 39.6 percent.

2014 Senate hearings find thousands of U.S. taxpayers hiding money in offshore havens (February). . . . President Obama sends budget to Congress urging taxes on rich, expanded preschool (March).

of the wealthy. "An imbalance between rich and poor is the oldest and most fatal ailment of all republics," the Greek philosopher Plutarch (A.D. 45-120) declared.[51]

The French Enlightenment philosopher Montesquieu (1689-1755) identified "real equality" as the soul of democracy, but acknowledged that in practice republics could only "fix the differences to a certain point."[52]

Similarly, the architects of American democracy shared a concern that political factions arising from deep class divisions and "unequal distribution of property," in the words of Founding Father James Madison, could undermine democracy. Madison stressed that the new American republic would derive its powers from the people, not from aristocratic or hereditary privileges as in England.[53]

Fear of coming to resemble old Europe was part of American interest in imposing progressive taxes. Throughout the 19th century the United States had no income tax. But the industrial revolution, which created a small class of American plutocrats, changed that.

During that era, some of the rich flaunted their wealth: At an 1897 costume ball in New York, the mother of millionaire John Jacob Astor came as Marie Antoinette in a dress adorned with $250,000 in jewels.[54]

Between 1870 and 1914, an era known as the Gilded Age, the increasing concentration of wealth at the top created extreme inequality. As late as 1919, Irving Fisher, president of the American Economic Association, expressed alarm that the top 2 percent owned more than 50 percent of the wealth while two-thirds of the population "owns almost nothing."[55]

Politicians calling themselves "Progressives," including Republican Theodore Roosevelt, railed against monopolies for stifling competition and for treating workers badly. "The absence of effective state . . . restraint upon unfair money-getting has tended to create a small class of enormously wealthy and economically powerful men, whose chief object is to hold and increase their power," charged Roosevelt in 1910.[56]

Roosevelt, president from 1901 to 1909, championed an estate tax in 1910 to prevent extreme accumulation of wealth, which, along with a graduated income tax, became a key plank of the Republican Party.

In 1913, the states ratified the 16th Amendment to the Constitution, giving Congress the power to collect income taxes; in October of that year, Congress passed a law creating the first permanent U.S. income tax.[57] In 1916, seven years after Roosevelt left office, Congress incorporated an estate tax into the federal code.[58]

Between World War I and World War II, the United States was the first country to try very high tax rates — 70 percent on the top tier of income in 1919-22 and 70 percent on estates in 1937. The purpose was to put an end to such large incomes and estates — not to raise revenue, writes Piketty.[59]

After World War I, many countries adopted a progressive income tax, including Britain (1909), France (1914), India (1922) and Argentina (1932).

During the Roaring '20s, an era of rising fortunes, the top income tax rate was cut to 25 percent and again to 24 percent in 1929.

Coming to power during the Great Depression, President Franklin D. Roosevelt immediately moved to raise the top tax rate — and succeeded in raising rates on the wealthiest, first to 63 percent in 1933, then to 79 percent in 1937, surpassing the 1919 record.

As FDR expressed it in 1936, "For too many of us the political equality we once had was meaningless in the face of economic inequality. A small group had concentrated . . . an almost complete control over other people's property, money . . . labor . . . lives."[60]

As part of FDR's program to make sure the excesses that led to the Depression were not repeated, banks were regulated and deposits insured. The securities industry was placed under new tight restrictions; higher taxes were levied on the rich.[61]

Roosevelt's economic officials also supported measures that gave labor unions greater power to organize. Old-age and unemployment insurance provided workers economic protection.

Top U.S. income tax rates reached their highest points during World War II: The 1942 Victory Tax Act raised the top rate to 88 percent; in 1944, Congress raised the rate again to 94 percent on annual income over $200,000 — $27 million in current dollars.[62]

Postwar Prosperity

Following World War II, all developed countries including the United States enjoyed high economic-growth rates. Americans' income grew at roughly the same rate no matter how much money they made.

The traditional economic view promoted by American economist Kuznets in the 1950s held that the post-WWII period represented an inevitable trend toward increasing equality and greater upward mobility, which would continue indefinitely.[63]

Tax Havens Shelter Trillions

"The current estimates of inequality are massively understated."

An estimated $21 trillion to $31 trillion is squirreled away in offshore bank accounts, largely untaxed, by the world's 10 million richest people, estimates the British advocacy group Tax Justice Network.[1]

"The current estimates of inequality are massively understated because they exclude offshore wealth," says John Christensen, executive director of the network. Most people with assets of more than $4 million "hold much if not the majority of their wealth offshore — and therefore outside the national statistics."

Offshore tax havens are loosely defined as places that permit individuals and companies to escape their home jurisdiction's laws and regulations — especially those involving taxes —"using secrecy as a prime tool," according to the Tax Justice Network.

The U.S. Foreign Account Tax Compliance Act (FATCA), passed in 2010 and scheduled to be phased in during 2014 and 2015, requires all foreign banks to inform the U.S. Treasury Department about bank accounts held abroad by U.S. taxpayers. The penalty for noncompliant banks is a 30 percent surtax on the banks' U.S. income, which Christensen describes as the "big American stick."

The law is far stricter than a 2003 European Union directive that called for information exchange to ensure proper taxation of interest-bearing accounts, which French economist Thomas Piketty calls "timid . . . meaningless . . . not enforced." (A directive is a legal action that tells European member nations what goal they must achieve, but does not dictate the means.)[2] But even FATCA is not sufficient in his view. It's not comprehensive enough to cover all taxpayers, such as certain trust funds and foundations, he writes, and the penalties against banks may not be enough of a deterrent.[3]

Last year, the leaders of eight of the world's major industrialized economies, known as the G8, called for tax authorities around the world, including those in smaller countries, to share information automatically to crack down on tax evasion.[4]

Following that action, and catalyzed by America's new law, famed tax havens such as the Cayman Islands, Luxembourg and Jersey were among more than 40 jurisdictions that agreed in February to pioneer a system of automatic information exchange for offshore bank accounts. Tax Justice Network hailed the move as "the first big step in putting together the nuts and bolts of real change."[5]

Forty-four countries have set a deadline of September 2017 to report investors' tax details to their home governments under plans announced by the Paris-based Organisation for Economic Co-operation and Development (OECD).[6]

More recently, conservatives have argued that there's no returning to a time when an unskilled worker with only a high school education could support a family. In 1992, economists John Bound and George Johnson pointed to "skill-based technological change" and globalization as the main reasons wages stopped growing at the same rate after the 1970s.[64]

That argument has been debated by liberal economists such as Hacker, Galbraith and Mishel, who say government policies after 1978 were more important in retarding wage growth. They point to the declining power of U.S. unions — from a peak of one in three workers after World War II, union membership has declined to one in nine — a decline they say was abetted by anti-union government policies.[65]

By breaking the air-traffic-controllers strike in 1981 and appointing a National Labor Relations Board heavily in favor of management, Yale political science professor Hacker charges, Reagan contributed to the increasingly aggressive posture of business against unions and helped create a political vacuum that unions once filled by arguing for middle-class concerns.[66]

The Great Switch

Much of the increase in the very highest incomes in the United States and the United Kingdom came after 1980, following the elections of conservatives Reagan and British Prime Minister Thatcher.

In the United States, the highest tax brackets had averaged 83 percent from 1932-80, according to Piketty, in

"If we were able to put into place effective information-exchange cooperation among countries, the ability to evade taxes would be massively diminished," says Christensen.

Sen. Carl Levin, D-Mich., chairman of the Senate Permanent Subcommittee on Investigations, along with ranking minority member Sen. John McCain, R-Ariz., released a report at a Feb. 26 hearing accusing Swiss banks and the Swiss government of helping to hide billions of U.S. taxpayer dollars in offshore accounts. Zurich-based Credit Suisse is one of 14 Swiss banks under investigation by the U.S. government for helping Americans evade taxes.[7]

The subcommittee reported that Credit Suisse had more than 22,000 U.S. customers with accounts containing the equivalent of $10 billion to $12 billion at the height of its efforts to recruit foreign clients. The committee described how bank employees traveled to the United States to recruit wealthy customers and engaged in secret-agent style transactions — even handing over a customer's bank statements hidden in a *Sports Illustrated* magazine.[8]

But Levin said the effort to collect the taxes and bring the bankers to justice appeared "stalled." Although seven Credit Suisse bankers were indicted by U.S. prosecutors in 2011, none has stood trial. "Less than a handful" of U.S. taxpayers with Credit Suisse accounts have been indicted, he said. "The reason for this near total failure to date is continued Swiss insistence on bank secrecy, and the United States letting them get away with it," Levin said.

In early April, Credit Suisse set aside the equivalent of $477 million to deal with the possible costs of the U.S.

Department of Justice probe, leading to speculation that the case was close to a final settlement.[9]

Right now it's so easy for kleptocrats from Eastern Europe or Asia to shift billions out of their home countries, says Christensen, that "this has created a criminogenic global financial market, where it is more profitable for lawyers, bankers and accountants to engage in criminal activity on behalf of clients than to do their job properly."

— *Sarah Glazer*

[1]"Inequality and Tax Havens," Tax Justice Network, no date, http://tinyurl.com/n49w879.

[2]European Commission, "What are EU directives?," no date, http://tinyurl.com/m4wlc9o.

[3]Thomas Piketty, *Capital in the Twenty-First Century* (2014), p. 522.

[4]George Parker and Vanessa Houlder, "G8 Seeks Rewrite of Global Tax Rules," *Financial Times*, June 18, 2013, http://tinyurl.com/lk3xblg.

[5]Vanessa Houlder, "Global Tax Standard Attracts 42 Countries," *Financial Times*, Feb. 13, 2014, http://tinyurl.com/k6y2etk.

[6]Vanessa Houlder, "Havens Set Deadlines for Reporting Investors' Tax Details," *Financial Times*, March 20, 2014, http://tinyurl.com/mtj3l4q.

[7]Gina Chon, Kara Scannell and James Shotter, "Credit Suisse 'Helped U.S. Tax Evaders,' " *Financial Times*, Feb. 25, 2014, http://tinyurl.com/jvnpzx8.

[8]"Opening Statement of Sen. Carl Levin," Senate Permanent Subcommittee on Investigations Hearing: Offshore Tax Evasion, Feb. 26, 2014, http://tinyurl.com/lnn782o.

[9]James Shotter, "Credit Suisse takes $477m Charge for Tax Inquiry," *Financial Times*, April 3, 2014, http://tinyurl.com/lnvwtg4.

contrast with continental Europe. In France and Germany, for instance, the top rate in those years never exceeded 30 to 40 percent. Rates in the United Kingdom were closer to those in the United States. In the 1980s, both the United States and United Kingdom cut rates sharply — U.S. top rates fell to 28 percent after the Reagan tax reform in 1986.[67]

According to Piketty, the "spectacular decrease" in the progressivity of income tax rates during those years probably explains much of the increasing fortunes at the top that followed.

However, in his book *Winner-Take-All Politics*, Hacker chooses 1978, when Democrat Jimmy Carter was still president, as "the great switch point."

In 1978, Congress passed a bill with deep cuts in the capital gains tax, mainly benefiting the wealthy, which

was signed by Democratic President Jimmy Carter. Congress also sharply raised payroll taxes, a levy that hits workers' pockets hardest, marking the beginning of a pronounced reversal in federal tax policy, Hacker argues.[68]

By 1981, under the Reagan administration, the tax debate had degenerated into a "frenzied bidding war" between Republicans and Democrats to shower benefits on business, writes Hacker.[69] As Reagan budget director Dave Stockman recalled, "the hogs were really feeding."[70]

Under the 1981 Economic Recovery Tax Act, top income tax rates came down sharply, and the tax on multimillion-dollar estates was cut from 70 percent to 50 percent.[71] Hacker's book argues that in the ensuing years, the wealthy have had an outsized influence on government policies and politicians of both parties, noting that in the

Luxury Homes Are Hot in London — and Controversial

The world's wealthy spend millions, while locals are priced out.

What do you get for $45 million in London's fashionable Mayfair neighborhood? That was the asking price in March for a narrow four-story house tucked into a mews, one of many cobblestone alleys that once served as the rear quarters for the servants and horses of grand townhouses, but are now enjoying a revival for their charm and proximity to luxury shopping.

Newly built to mimic the 18th-century style of the original house that stood on the 1,500-square-foot lot, this home packs six bedrooms plus a servant's room into 6,500 square feet. And it comes with all the amenities one might expect from the price tag: gym, screening room, separate his-and-hers bathrooms and dressing rooms and walk-in closets for each of the main guest rooms.

But increasingly the foreign buyers who dominate London's high-end market also are looking for Versailles-quality workmanship and prepackaged British taste right down to the candlesticks, according to a real estate agent and developer specializing in the luxury market who led this reporter on a recent walk-through.

Included in the price tag are the bespoke furniture and the carefully displayed *objets*, from the signed Picasso ceramics to an antique volume of the *Encyclopedia Britannica*. A chandelier specially designed for the soaring stairwell required two weeks of assembly by a team of eight working with 800 crystal pieces.

For most prospective buyers, this is their third or fourth home, so they're not interested in furnishing and decorating yet another house, explains Sanjay Sharma, a former investment banker. He cofounded luxury developer Fenton Whelan in 2010 with another London banker to build and renovate luxury homes and to provide investors with "record prices and exceptional returns on capital," according to the company's website.

The antiques and old-fashioned ceiling moldings like those that Fenton Whelan supplies fulfill the "zeitgeist of the moment — the desire to feel they're buying something British rather than generic," says Richard Cutt, an agent specializing in the city's luxury market for London-based international real estate firm Knight Frank.

Growth in the number of super-rich individuals around the world, particularly in emerging markets such as China, is driving London's hot luxury housing market, where prices have soared 65 percent since March 2009, according to Knight Frank.[1] Globally, the number of individuals with net assets of at least $30 million ballooned by 59 percent from 2003 to 2013; in aggregate, their assets total $20 trillion, according to the firm.

Skyrocketing housing prices for low- and middle-income Londoners and a supply shortage have intensified hostility toward new luxury homes. In April, Prince Charles said climbing prices would drive young people away from the city, noting the average London house price is now 10 times an elementary school teacher's salary. His Foundation for Building Community released a report criticizing the tendency for the majority of new housing to serve those in the highest income bracket. The report urged more building of affordable five- to eight-story apartment buildings rather than luxury residential towers.[2]

Several recent newspaper investigations finding mansions left empty by wealthy overseas owners have intensified criticism. Central London "is fast becoming a ghost-town where absentee investors park their wealth" while creative

1980s and '90s senators voted with the interests of the wealthiest upper third of their constituents.[72]

Continuing into the presidency of Bill Clinton, politicians from both parties increasingly accepted the view that excessive regulation impedes economic growth. During the 1990s, financial deregulation swept across national borders, and by 2001, Piketty writes, the owners of capital were prospering as they hadn't since 1913.

Under President George W. Bush in 2001, a huge tax cut bill was supported by Republicans advocating tax cuts even in the face of big deficits in order to stimulate the

types are pushed to the periphery, London club owner Alex Proud recently wrote in *The Telegraph*. "Tax empty houses? Why no. We wouldn't want to upset some ex-KGB thug who looted the Kazakh treasury in the mid-1990s."[3]

An investigation by the *Evening Standard* found more than 700 expensive homes standing empty throughout London. Many of the owners were offshore investors parking their wealth in mansions and hiding behind anonymous overseas post office boxes, the newspaper reported. Expressing shock, London Mayor Boris Johnson called on local city councils, which govern London's neighborhoods and have authority over local taxes, to impose punitive levies on owners of homes standing empty more than two years.[4]

On "Billionaires' Row," the latest moniker of The Bishops Avenue near fashionable Hampstead Heath, once known as Millionaires' Row, mansions owned by Saudi royals and oil magnates are valued at up to 65 million British pounds ($109 million). In a separate investigation, *The Guardian* found one-third standing derelict and empty.[5]

The Guardian expressed indignation at the avenue's 120 vacant bedrooms at a time when more than 6,000 Londoners are homeless and more than 300,000 families are on waiting lists for public housing. The cost of rising house prices is "borne by those lower down on the chain," wrote *Guardian* columnist Aditya Chakrabortty.[6]

In response, liberals have called for a "mansion" tax.[7] In its latest budget, the British government, which is a liberal-conservative coalition, compromised by expanding taxes on luxury homes bought through a corporate structure, citing concerns that rich individuals were using this avenue to avoid taxes.[8]

But some real estate agents say such moves are a xenophobic reaction to the fact that the city is becoming more cosmopolitan. "An Italian banker who is living here five years renting and then buys a house — is he a foreign buyer?" asks Liam Bailey, global head of residential research at Knight Frank.

And, indeed many of the elegant 19th-century houses that made the Belgravia and Mayfair neighborhoods posh were originally built as second homes for English aristocrats

Fenton Whelan Ltd.

The table is set with crystal service for 10 and fresh flowers at a house in London's fashionable Mayfair district being offered for sale for $45 million — tableware included.

who spent much of the year at country estates, Bailey points out. "It's not exactly a new phenomenon."

— *Sarah Glazer*

[1]Knight Frank, "The Wealth Report," March 2014, http://tinyurl.com/ntseto9.

[2]Prince's Foundation for Building Community, "Housing London: A Mid-Rise Solution," March 2014, http://tinyurl.com/p3zokr7. Also see, *op. cit.*, "Prince Charles: We Need More Homes for Londoners."

[3]Alex Proud, "'Cool London' is Dead, and the Rich Kids are to Blame," *The Telegraph*, April 7, 2014, http://tinyurl.com/nlqneju.

[4]Jonathan Prynn, *et al.*, "London's £3 bn Ghost Mansions," *Evening Standard*, Feb. 14, 2014, http://tinyurl.com/q5e2eal.

[5]Robert Booth, "Inside 'Billionaires' Row,' " *The Guardian*, Jan. 31, 2014, http://tinyurl.com/qhugbjl.

[6]Aditya Chakrabortty, "How to Handle the Hoarding of Houses on 'Billionaires' Row,' " *The Guardian*, Feb. 3, 2014, http://tinyurl.com/pl4u82z.

[7]James Kirkup, "Liberal Democrats would Tax the Rich to Clear Deficits, says Nick Clegg," *The Telegraph*, Feb. 10, 2014, http://tinyurl.com/paz2hwk.

[8]"Budget 2014: Upmarket Property Ripe for Raiding," *Financial Times*, March 19, 2014, http://tinyurl.com/pw2vq8w.

economy; more cuts followed in 2003, bringing down top tax rates further.[73]

In March 2008, the investment bank Bear Stearns collapsed, the start of a worldwide financial crisis and recession. While volumes have been written on the causes of the crisis, liberal economists like Boushey and Hacker

blame income inequality for driving excessive borrowing by those who couldn't afford it, abetted by lax oversight of the financial industry.

The tax legislation passed at the start of 2013, under Obama, permanently extended the Bush-era tax cuts for most people, but also added a top marginal tax rate of

President Obama calls for a hike in the minimum wage to $10.10 during an address at a Costco store in Lanham, Md., on Jan. 29, 2014. In his State of the Union address, Obama said upward mobility had stalled and stressed the need to build "ladders of opportunity" to the middle class. Conservative lawmakers have also been making speeches about social mobility, saying there should be more reward for people who work hard.

39.6 percent for those at higher incomes — $400,000 for single filers, $450,000 for married couples filing jointly and $425,000 for heads of household. For tax years 2012 and earlier the highest tax bracket was 35 percent.[74]

However, some critics say the very rich rarely pay that 39.6 percent because of numerous loopholes, including a provision that lets hedge fund and equity fund managers count some income as capital gains, which is taxed at a lower rate. According to analysts, the Bush tax cuts mainly benefited the wealthy and increased inequality but also cut taxes for the middle class.[75]

CURRENT SITUATION

Proposed Fixes

The budget that Obama sent to Congress March 4 echoes many of the solutions to inequality proposed by liberals — from more taxes on the rich to funding pre-school for the less advantaged.

"As a country, we've got to make a decision if we're going to protect tax breaks for the wealthiest Americans, or if we're going to make smart investments necessary to create jobs and grow our economy, and expand opportunity for every American," the president said that day.[76]

But noting the increasing emphasis on raising taxes and redistributing wealth coming from Obama and international organizations such as the International Monetary Fund (IMF), Dan Henninger, deputy editorial page director of *The Wall Street Journal*, wrote, "What's unacceptable about the income-inequality agenda of the Obama Democrats, the United Nations and the IMF is that all assume that the U.S.'s historic century of strong, capital-driven growth is over, and that it must reorder its priorities to admit the reality of reduced long-term economic performance. In short, it's time to slow down and divide up what pie we've got." That's what Europe and Russia did, he added. "That's what the United States would be nuts to do."[77]

Even supporters of Obama's proposals to expand pre-kindergarten and tax credits for low-income workers predicted that Republicans would resist "every dollar" of the $651 billion the president asked for over the next decade, said a *New York Times* editorial, which labeled the administration's budget the "What Might Have Been" budget.[78]

Indeed, the conservative Heritage Foundation instantly pronounced the budget "dead on arrival."[79] It called a cap on deductions for high earners "troubling" because it would apply to retirement savings, health insurance and municipal bond income.

And it singled out Obama's proposal to implement the so-called "Buffet rule" originally put forward by billionaire businessman Warren Buffet — to insure that wealthy millionaires pay no less than 30 percent of their income in taxes after charitable contributions.[80] Heritage said most top earners already meet that bar.[81]

Nevertheless, Obama's proposal shares a bit of common ground with a tax proposal made a week earlier by Rep. Dave Camp, R-Mich., the House Ways and Means chairman, to simplify the tax code. Both proposals would raise taxes on hedge fund managers and both would cap the value of tax deductions for high-income families, according to the Tax Policy Center, a joint project of the Urban Institute and Brookings Institution.[82]

Do the rich pay enough in taxes?

YES Curtis Dubay
*Research Fellow, Tax and
Economic Policy, Heritage Foundation*

Written for *CQ Researcher*, April 2014

when it comes to the rich paying taxes, how much is enough? Because everyone defines "enough" differently, for the debate to move forward, we need to ask better questions.

One "better" question: Do taxes overall need to rise at all? According to the Congressional Budget Office (CBO), tax receipts, as a share of the economy, will hover around 18 percent for the next 10 years — the historical average. Because tax revenues are running at the standard, operational level, it's difficult to argue that there's a crying need to extract more money from current taxpayers, be they rich or otherwise.

The next logical question is: Do the rich pay their fair share of the current tax burden? This, of course, is a more subjective question, but looking at the data can provide some guidance. Again, according to the most recent analysis by CBO, the top 1 percent of households earned just under 15 percent of all income in 2010. Yet they paid 39 percent of all federal income taxes—and more than 24 percent of all federal taxes that year.

These taxpayers paid an average tax rate of 29.4 percent. In other words, President Obama's Buffett Rule, which calls for a minimum tax rate of 30 percent on those who make more than $1 million a year, is essentially already in effect.

What if we broaden the definition of "rich" to the top 10 percent of U.S. households? They paid more than three-quarters of all federal income taxes — or more than half of all federal taxes in 2010.

Any way you slice it, the rich pay the lion's share of the taxes. Still, some may want to gouge the rich more, simply to satisfy their unique sense of fairness. So what would happen if we jacked up taxes on the rich, just to be "fair"? The rich would pay more, certainly. But the non-rich would feel the pain. High-earners also happen to be business owners, investors and entrepreneurs — the people who take risks that create opportunities for the rest of us. Raising their taxes reduces the resources they have to invest and their incentive to do so. Restricted capital means fewer jobs and lower wages.

Do the rich pay enough in taxes? If you think there is too much economic opportunity in America, the answer is "no." Otherwise, you'd have to agree that they already pay more than enough.

NO Peter Diamond
*Professor of Economics, Emeritus, Massachusetts
Institute of Technology*

Written for *CQ Researcher*, April 2014

whatever level of federal government spending comes from the political process, that spending must be covered by taxes. In paying for that spending, the more tax revenue that comes from those with the highest incomes, the less needs to come from everyone else.

In choosing how much to collect from the richest, we need to consider the impact on the economy and the differences in abilities to pay between those at the top and those with less, often much less. While views differ on what makes a tax fair, there should be a greater willingness for higher taxes on the highest incomes since income distribution has become dramatically more unequal over recent decades.

To consider the impact on the economy, we need to recognize that throughout the income distribution, taxes affect behavior — through changes in work and saving, changes in (legal) tax avoidance, and changes in (illegal) tax evasion. These responses affect the efficiency of the economy and affect the level of revenue collected with a given tax structure. Tax avoidance and tax evasion can be reduced by changes in tax rules and changes in tax enforcement, enhancing the ability to collect taxes more fairly and efficiently. And this approach permits more of tax collection to come from those with the greatest ability to pay.

We cannot run controlled experiments on the economy to estimate the additional revenues from tax changes, but we do have many studies of the effects from past tax changes.

While studies differ in their findings, overall, they shed considerable light on the revenue and efficiency implications of tax changes. The evidence supports the view that we can considerably increase the revenues currently being collected by taxes on the highest incomes, while having limited impacts on the functioning of the economy.

In light of this empirical evidence, I favor a federal tax rate on the highest incomes within the historical range from 50 percent (the 1982-86 level under President Reagan) to 70 percent (the level from 1965 to 1981, under Presidents Johnson, Nixon, Ford and Carter).

Collecting these extra revenues can help finance more public investments to enhance our country's future and can help limit the need for higher taxes on those with lower incomes as we deal with our sizable public debt.

New York City Mayor Bill de Blasio visits with a pre-kindergarten student studying worms at P.S. 1 on April 3. Democrat de Blasio was elected after promising to reduce the gap between rich and poor. He has advocated raising taxes on the wealthy to help pay for pre-K programs for all the city's children.

However, the chances for congressional action on Camp's proposal looked slim as the Republican leadership in Congress quickly distanced itself from the document. The House GOP budget unveiled earlier this month did not endorse Camp's tax reform plan.[83]

Steuerle, the Urban Institute fellow who coordinated the tax study in Reagan's Treasury that led to the 1986 Tax Reform Act, holds out hope for eventual action: "The more good things you can put in the hopper, especially if they get bipartisan support, the greater chance that down the road they could become part of something bigger," he predicts.

Obama's proposed budget got lower marks for its efforts to help low-income citizens move up the ladder, according to Steuerle, who conducted a study for the Pew Charitable Trusts of how government spending affects mobility. While expanding preschool education and the tax credit for low-income workers, the amount of help would be small, he stressed.

Haskins of Brookings cautions that most preschool programs aren't good enough to get the sterling results touted by advocates citing studies of high-quality early education. "If we really think preschool is going to bring these kids to the starting line of public schools roughly equal to their more advantaged peers, we need much better teachers, which means we have to pay a lot more money," he says.

Obama's proposal to double the earned income tax credit for low-income workers to $1,000 and expand it to childless adults won praise from liberals as well as from conservative Haskins, who said the credit, while not large enough, addresses what may be the country's No. 1 problem: the low labor force participation rate — 66 percent — among young black men ages 20-24.[84]

Obama has proposed an increase in the minimum wage — from $7.25 to $10.10 an hour — but even strong supporters of that measure don't expect it to get past Washington's political gridlock. "I don't think anything is going to pass Congress this year," says Mishel of the Economic Policy Institute, whose wish list also includes to "create lots of jobs, firm up the safety net and retirement, and restore the ability for workers to have collective bargaining."

In recognition of that political reality, Obama has addressed some equality issues by executive order — directing the Labor Department on March 13 to expand overtime to millions of workers, including fast food managers, previously classified as "executive or professional" to avoid paying overtime.

New York's de Blasio swept into office on a platform that vowed to fix the gap between the city's haves and have-nots. He proposed to tax the rich to fund universal pre-K education, which he dubbed a crucial weapon against inequality.

De Blasio's proposed tax became a lightning rod for conservative criticism and a stand-in for the larger debate about whether the rich should be taxed further to cure inequality.

At the end of March, Democratic New York Gov. Andrew Cuomo announced a budget agreement that rejected the mayor's proposed tax on high earners but provided most of the money de Blasio said he needed to create pre-kindergarten for every child in the city.[85]

While conservatives tend to agree with liberals that unequal education is a root cause of inequality, their solutions differ: Conservatives such as Furth back approaches that give parents more choice in picking schools, like vouchers and charter schools.

Executive Pay

Wall Street's 2008 financial meltdown and the accompanying recession focused new scrutiny on executive salaries. The pay for top executives has grown to 300 times that of the rank and file worker in recent years.[86]

As part of the 2010 Dodd-Frank Wall Street reform law that grew out of the crisis, regulators at the Securities and Exchange Commission (SEC) are considering a rule that would require public companies to disclose the ratio of an executive's earnings to a rank-and-file worker's pay.[87] The SEC rule, originally proposed last September, ran into opposition from businesses, which objected that it imposed a heavy logistical burden on companies with employees around the globe. Since then, the commission has been accused of foot-dragging. "Timing is uncertain" for issuance of the final rule, according to an SEC spokesperson.

Another measure, the so-called "say on pay" rule already issued by the SEC, allows shareholders a nonbinding vote on executive pay packages: Since the passage of Dodd Frank, say-on-pay may have given some investors new fortitude to question executive pay: Citigroup shareholders rejected a $15 million pay package in 2012 for the bank's chief executive, Vikram Pandit.[88]

Limiting executive pay could allow more of a firm's profits to go to its workers or be plowed back into the company, advocates hope. Yet some, like Yale's Hacker, are skeptical that the current rules go far enough, calling the say-on-pay rule's nonbinding vote a "weak" weapon.

"I wouldn't put too much faith in the information alone, but if you get some organized actors to shame companies to adopt more rational pay packages, I think that would be helpful," he says. So far, however, the rule is having a minimal effect, he says. "It seems executive pay has been skyrocketing back."

OUTLOOK

'Oligarchic Evolution'

While some advocates and politicians continue pushing for policies they say would help middle-class incomes grow again as they did pre-1980, others say rapid growth is unlikely to reappear in developed economies as population growth slows.

For French economist Piketty, who predicts a slow-growth future, that presents a potentially apocalyptic scenario if the richest continue claiming a growing share of income. "This risk of oligarchic evolution is something of concern — not just in Russia and China, but also in America and Europe. There is no natural economic mechanism that prevents such an extreme thing from happening," he says.

Conservatives tend to be more optimistic that the economy will pick up again and that workers will share in the benefits. James Sherk, a senior labor policy analyst at the Heritage Foundation, says worker pay has tracked productivity growth closely and will start to grow robustly once the economy picks up again. Policymakers, he says, "should look for ways to make less-skilled workers more productive, such as reducing the cost of higher education. Market forces will then force employers to increase compensation."[89]

Until recently, higher population growth in the United States reduced the relative importance of inherited wealth compared with a more static Europe. But that could soon change. The aging of baby boomers should bring a sudden boom in inheritances and potentially a "flood of princelings," as an article in *The New York Times* put it, peaking in 2031. Economists such as Piketty are predicting that this trend will contribute even further to growing wealth inequality in the United States.[89]

"We have more income inequality, and that means that down the road, we are bound to have more wealth inequality and more inequality of inherited wealth," predicted Piketty.[91]

Since the 1980s, the value of inheritance has drifted upward only slightly, and wealth transfers in the United States as a share of net worth have fallen. But experts say that trend could reverse drastically as baby boomers hand on their wealth to the next generation.

A lot of multimillionaires are men of age 60 or 70, said David Friedman of Wealth-X, an international research firm that studies habits of the wealthy. "They're sensing their mortality now. And there's a growing wave of liquidity that's going to fuel luxury and fuel philanthropy in a way that the market's never seen."[92]

NOTES

1. Eoghan Macguire, "Swimming Pools and Golf Ranges in London's Insane Luxury Basements," CNN, Jan. 24, 2014, http://tinyurl.com/kqx4m7d.

2. Michael Goldfarb, "London's Great Exodus," *International New York Times*, Oct. 12, 2013, http://tinyurl.com/l33hjbq.

3. "Working for the Few," Oxfam, Jan. 20, 2014, http://tinyurl.com/omp8zml.

4. "Worsening Wealth Gap Seen Biggest Risk Facing the World," press release, World Economic Forum, 2014, http://tinyurl.com/n8mpa8c.

5. Eduardo Porter, "In New Tack, I.M.F. Aims at Income Inequality," *The New York Times*, April 8, 2014, http://tinyurl.com/mqdjpjx.

6. Paul Krugman, "Liberty, Equality, Efficiency," *The New York Times*, March 9, 2014, http://tinyurl.com/q8y2grc.

7. Emmanuel Saez, "Striking it Richer: The Evolution of Top Incomes in the United States," University of California, Berkeley, Sept. 3, 2013, p. 3, http://tinyurl.com/o7zo3mm.

8. *Ibid.*, p. 3.

9. Thomas Piketty, *Capital in the Twenty-First Century* (2014), p. 438.

10. "Remarks by the President on Economic Mobility," White House, Dec. 4, 2013, http://tinyurl.com/mk4qe7n.

11. Mickey Kaus, "The Other Kind of Inequality," *The Wall Street Journal*, Jan. 26, 2014, http://tinyurl.com/ms2op6h.

12. Scott Winship, "Inequality Testimony before the Joint Economic Committee," E21: Economic Policies for the 21st Century, Manhattan Institute, Jan. 15, 2014, http://tinyurl.com/lwy9kjm.

13. *Ibid.*

14. Sears has closed about 300 stores since 2010; it closed its flagship store in Chicago in February. JC Penney announced in February it would close 33 stores, http://tinyurl.com/mpzlxgm.

15. Nelson D. Schwartz, "The Middle Class is Steadily Eroding," *The New York Times*, Feb. 2, 2014, http://tinyurl.com/l7fwj86.

16. Barry Z. Cynamon and Steven M. Fazzari, "Inequality, the Great Recession, and Slow Recovery," Washington University, Jan. 23, 2014, http://tinyurl.com/k4zvcup.

17. Schwartz, *op. cit.*

18. "The State of Working America, 12th Edition," Economic Policy Institute, March 17, 2014, http://tinyurl.com/4vb2ct.

19. Nelson D. Schwartz, "How Eroding the Middle Class Hits Economic Growth," *Economix* blog, *The New York Times*, Feb. 5, 2014, http://tinyurl.com/mlo6hnb.

20. Winship, *op. cit.*

21. See for example, Andrew G. Berg and Jonathan D. Ostry, "Inequality and Unsustainable Growth: Two Sides of the Same Coin?" International Monetary Fund, April 8, 2011, http://tinyurl.com/445a8t6.

22. Piketty, *op. cit.*, p. 13.

23. Jonathan D. Ostry, *et al.*, "Redistribution, Inequality and Growth," February 2014, International Monetary Fund, http://tinyurl.com/q5qz6l6.

24. Berg and Ostry, *op. cit.* Also see Winship, *op. cit.*

25. Winship, *op. cit.*

26. College completion rates increased only 4 percentage points from the generation of low-income children born in the early 1960s to those born in the 1980s. For high-income children the increase was 18 percentage points. "Gains and Gaps: Changing Inequality in U.S. College Entry and Completion, NBER Working Paper No. 17633, National Bureau of Economic Research, March 10, 2014, http://tinyurl.com/kp49o9y.

27. Krugman, *op. cit.*

28. Piketty, *op. cit.*, pp. 438-440.

29. Eduardo Porter, "Economix: Q&A on the Wealth Divide: Thomas Piketty," *The New York Times*, March 11, 2014, http://tinyurl.com/myxvxkz.

30. "President Barack Obama's State of the Union Address," White House, Jan. 28, 2014, http://tinyurl.com/kemgt7x.

31. Sean McElwee, "Republicans Suddenly Can't Stop Talking about 'Mobility,'" *The New Republic*, Feb. 19, 2014, http://tinyurl.com/lfwxxg8.

32. "Class in America: Mobility Measured," *The Economist*, Feb. 1, 2014, http://tinyurl.com/n9t3ar7.

33. Raj Chetty, *et al.*, "Is the United States still a Land of Opportunity?" National Bureau of Economic Research, January 2014, http://tinyurl.com/lphlkz2.

34. "Class in America," *op. cit.*

35. Gregory Clark, *The Son Also Rises: Surnames and the History of Social Mobility* (2014).

36. Cited in Ron Haskins, "Mobility Is a Problem: Now What?" Dec. 23, 2011, http://tinyurl.com/mnuuezj. The data was published in a book written by Haskins and Isabel Sawhill, *Creating an Opportunity Society* (2009).

37. Annie Lowrey, "What Comes after Rich Baby Boomers?" *New York Times Magazine*, March 11, 2014, http://tinyurl.com/l2xa7lv.

38. Inheritance as a share of national income in France was 20 percent from 1840 to 1914, declined to a low of 5 percent in the 1950s and rose to 15 percent in 2010. See Piketty, *op. cit.*, pp. 380-381.

39. Piketty, *op. cit.*, p. 438.

40. Pew Charitable Trusts, "Economic Mobility and the American Dream," May 2011, http://tinyurl.com/l5l4rc2.

41. "Pursuing the American Dream: Economic Mobility Across Generations," Pew Charitable Trusts, July 9, 2012, http://tinyurl.com/872oy5z.

42. Piketty, *op. cit.*, p. 525.

43. The Oscar-nominated film "Wolf of Wall Street" is based on the story of Jordan Belfort, who served 22 months in prison for security fraud between 2004 and 2006. See, "Real-life Wolf of Wall Street says his life of debauchery 'even worse' than in film," *The Guardian*, Feb. 28, 2014, http://tinyurl.com/o6oo3vs.

44. Christopher DeMuth, "Capital for the Masses," *The Wall Street Journal*, April 7, 2014, http://tinyurl.com/keenuwn.

45. Jacob S. Hacker and Nate Loewenthal, *Prosperity Economics* (2012), p. 48.

46. Sendhil Mullainathan, "A Top-Heavy Focus on Income Inequality," *The New York Times*, March 8, 2014, http://tinyurl.com/qdqkddd.

47. "The Rich are Taxed Enough," Intelligence Squared U.S., Oct. 24, 2012, p. 16, http://tinyurl.com/lb9q58c.

48. *Ibid.*

49. "The Distribution of Household Income and Federal Taxes," Congressional Budget Office, December 2013, p. 7, http://tinyurl.com/pxzutsz.

50. Households in the highest quintile paid 93 percent of federal income taxes in 2010. *Ibid.*, p. 13.

51. Jacob C. Hacker and Paul Pierson, *Winner-Take-All Politics* (2010), p. 75.

52. *Ibid.*

53. *Ibid.*, p. 76.

54. Chrystia Freeland, *Plutocrats: The Rise of the New Global Rich and the Fall of Everyone Else* (2012), p. 6.

55. Piketty, *op. cit.*, p. 506.

56. President Teddy Roosevelt's New Nationalism Speech, www.whitehouse.gov/blog/2011/12/06/archives-president-teddy-roosevelts-new-nationalism-speech.

57. "History of Income Tax in the U.S.," about.com, http://tinyurl.com/n2wep8k.

58. Tim Rutten, "And the Rich Get Richer," *Los Angeles Times*, Dec. 18, 2010, http://tinyurl.com/37ku7aq.

59. Piketty, *op. cit.*, p. 507.

60. Hacker, *op. cit.*, p. 87.

61. *Ibid.*, p. 88.

62. "History of Federal Individual Income Bottom and Top Bracket Rates," National Taxpayers Union, undated, http://tinyurl.com/2f3c277. Calculation of current dollars: http://tinyurl.com/lcywoao.

63. Eduardo Porter, "Free Market is no Remedy for Disparity," *International New York Times*, March 13, 2014, p. 15.

64. *American Economic Review*, cited in James K. Galbraith, *Inequality and Instability* (2012), p. 125.

65. Hacker, *op. cit.*, pp. 56-57.

66. *Ibid.* Also see Andrew Glass, "Reagan fires 11,000 striking air traffic controllers August 5, 1981," *Politico*, Aug. 5, 2008, http://tinyurl.com/yg8c9gq.

67. Piketty, *op. cit.*, pp. 507-509.

68. Hacker, *op. cit.*, pp. 99-100 and pp. 133-134. The capital gains tax, which taxes profits such as those from the sale of stock or business assets, was cut from 48 percent to 28 percent.

69. *Ibid.*, p. 134.

70. William Greider, "The Education of David Stockman," *The Atlantic*, December 1981, http://tinyurl.com/d43yal3.

71. "General Explanation of the Economic Recovery Tax Act of 1981," Joint Committee on Taxation, Dec. 29, 1981, p. 229, http://tinyurl.com/lf9w9pd.

72. Hacker, *op. cit.*, p. 111. The research cited is by political scientist Larry Bartels.

73. Hacker, *op. cit.*, p. 217.

74. "Federal Income Tax Table," http://tinyurl.com/cnrhnns. Also see, "New 39.6 Percent Tax Bracket," *Politico*, Jan. 22, 2014, http://tinyurl.com/kb3nwob.

75. "The Legacy of the Bush Tax Cuts in Four Charts," *The Washington Post*, Jan. 2, 2013, http://tinyurl.com/b9l5vca.

76. "Remarks by the President Announcing the FY 2015 Budget," White House, March 4, 2014, http://tinyurl.com/kapxcj6.

77. Dan Henninger, "The Income Inequality Love Train," *The Wall Street Journal*, April 2, 2014, http://tinyurl.com/l4xgwmt.

78. Editorial, "The What Might Have Been Budget," *The New York Times*, March 4, 2014, http://tinyurl.com/ktgyugc.

79. Stephen Moore, "Why Obama's Budget Should Be Dead on Arrival," The Foundry, Heritage Foundation, March 4, 2014, http://tinyurl.com/mfa2grw.

80. "FY 2015 Budget," White House, http://tinyurl.com/oo6gsdd.

81. Heritage Foundation on Obama Budget: "Live Analysis," Heritage Foundation, March 4, 2014, http://tinyurl.com/n3poqup.

82. Howard Gleckman, "A Tale of Three Agendas," Tax Vox, March 4, 2014, http://tinyurl.com/k6nyta3.

83. John D. McKinnon, "New House Budget Doesn't Back Rep Camp's Tax Reform Plan," *The Wall Street Journal*, April 1, 2014, http://tinyurl.com/mg8fb2z.

84. "Barack Obama says Fewer Black, Latino Young Men Participate in the Labor Force than Young White Men," *Tampa Bay Times, Politifact.com*, Feb. 28, 2014, www.politifact.com/truth-o-meter/statements/2014/feb/28/barack-obama/barack-obama-says-fewer-black-latino-young-men-par/. The labor force participation rate includes those employed and searching for work.

85. Thomas Kaplan and Javier C. Hernandez, "State Budget Deal Reached," *The New York Times*, March 29, 2014, http://tinyurl.com/mofuy4s.

86. "Exposing the Pay Gap," *The New York Times*, Sept. 25, 2013, http://tinyurl.com/kdfovsp.

87. Dave Michaels, "CEO-to-Worker Pay-Ratio Disclosure Proposed by Divided SEC," Bloomberg, Sept. 18, 2013, http://tinyurl.com/kjma4z7.

88. Editorial, "The Boss and Everyone Else," *The New York Times*, May 2, 2012, http://tinyurl.com/74dxau6.

89. James Sherk, "Productivity and Compensation; Growing Together," Heritage Foundation, July 17, 2013, http://tinyurl.com/mv2rh9g.

90. Lowrey, *op. cit.*, http://tinyurl.com/ku9fkhd.

91. *Ibid.*

92. *Ibid.*

BIBLIOGRAPHY

Selected Sources

Books

Clark, Gregory, *The Son Also Rises: Surnames and the History of Social Mobility*, Princeton University Press, 2014.
A University of California-Davis economist finds movement up the social ladder has changed little over eight centuries, even in highly equal countries such as Sweden.

Freeland, Chrystia, *Plutocrats: The Rise of the New Global Rich and the Fall of Everyone Else*, Penguin Books, 2012.
While a Reuters economics reporter, Freeland, now a member of the Canadian Parliament, wrote this book describing the world of today's global super-rich and their historic rise.

Galbraith, James K., *Inequality and Instability: A Study of the World Economy Just Before the Great Crisis*, Oxford University Press, 2012.
A University of Texas-Austin economist argues that the rise of inequality mirrors the rise of finance and free-market policies.

Hacker, Jacob S., and Paul Pierson, *Winner-Take-All Politics: How Washington Made the Rich Richer — and*

Turned its Back on the Middle Class, **Simon and Schuster, 2010.**
A Yale political scientist (Hacker) and a University of California-Berkeley political scientist argue that the American political system has been hijacked by the very rich, leading to government policies favoring the wealthy.

Piketty, Thomas, *Capital in the Twenty-First Century*, **Belknap Press, 2014.**
In this much-discussed study of 20 countries over 300 years, a professor at the Paris School of Economics argues that wealth is becoming too concentrated at the top and advocates a global wealth tax.

Articles

DeMuth, Christopher, "Capital for the Masses," *The Wall Street Journal*, **April 7, 2014, http://tinyurl.com/keenuwn.**
A conservative critique of Thomas Piketty's *Capital in the Twenty-First Century* says the book bolsters arguments for privatizing retirement systems such as Social Security.

Krugman, Paul, "Liberty, Equality, Efficiency," *The New York Times*, **March 9, 2014, http://tinyurl.com/q8y2grc.**
A liberal economist asks whether redistribution of economic wealth hurts growth — and answers in the negative.

Lowrey, Annie, "What Comes after Rich Baby Boomers?" *The New York Times Magazine*, **March 11, 2014, http://tinyurl.com/l2xa7lv.**
An economics reporter forecasts a new wave of well-to-do "princelings" will inherit wealth from the aging baby boomers.

Mullainathan, Sendhil, "A Top-Heavy Focus on Income Inequality," *The New York Times*, **March 8, 2014, http://tinyurl.com/qdqkddd.**
A Harvard economist argues that reducing income for the wealthy through higher taxes does not necessarily mean more for everyone else.

Saez, Emmanuel, "Striking it Richer: The Evolution of Top Incomes in the United States," Sept. 3, 2013, p. 3, http://tinyurl.com/o7zo3mm.
This unpublished paper by a University of California-Berkeley economist has been widely cited for its chart showing that the upper 10 percent now command an even greater share of national income than in the 1920s.

Reports and Studies

"Moving on Up," Pew Charitable Trusts, November 2013, http://tinyurl.com/jvw2egz.
The research group examines why some Americans move up the social ladder and others do not, finding that college education greatly increases one's chances.

"Offshore Tax Evasion: The Effort to Collect Unpaid Taxes on Billions in Hidden Offshore Accounts," U.S. Senate Permanent Subcommittee on Investigations, Feb. 26, 2014, http://tinyurl.com/lnn782o.
The Senate subcommittee, which found thousands of U.S. taxpayers hiding billions of dollars in offshore tax accounts, criticizes the Swiss government and Credit Suisse for secrecy, and says the U.S. Justice Department acts too slowly against possible wrongdoers.

"The Distribution of Household Income and Federal Taxes," Congressional Budget Office, December 2013, http://tinyurl.com/pxzutsz.
The nonpartisan agency looks at the incomes of a range groups in the United States both before and after taxes.

"The State of Working America, 12th Edition," Economic Policy Institute, March 17, 2014, http://tinyurl.com/4vb2ct.
A book-length report analyzes data on income, mobility, wages, jobs, wealth and poverty.

"The Wealth Report," Knight Frank, March 2014, http://tinyurl.com/ntseto9.
In its annual report, a London-based real estate firm examines recent trends of the global rich — where they live, where they're buying property and how they're consuming.

"Working for the Few," Oxfam, Jan. 20, 2014, http://tinyurl.com/omp8zml.
An anti-poverty charity finds the world's 85 richest billionaires have combined fortunes equal to those of the world's poorest half.

For More Information

Brookings Institution, 1775 Massachusetts Ave., N.W., Washington, DC 20036; 202-797-6000; www.brookings.edu. Think tank that covers a wide range of topics, with scholars who are generally moderate to liberal.

Economic Mobility Project, Pew Charitable Trusts, 901 E St., N.W., Washington, DC 20004; 202-552-2000; www.pewtrusts.org/our_work_detail.aspx?id=596. Research project investigating U.S. economic mobility.

Economic Policy Institute, 1333 H St., N.W., Suite 300, East Tower, Washington, DC 20005; 202-775-8810; www.epi.org. Think tank that studies low- and middle-income workers.

Heritage Foundation, 214 Massachusetts Ave., N.E., Washington, DC 20002; 202-546-4400; www.heritage.org. Think tank that promotes conservative policies based on free enterprise.

Oxfam, 226 Causeway St., Boston, MA 02114; 800-776-9326; www.oxfamamerica.org. Antipoverty charity that recently released a report on the global rich.

Tax Policy Center, Urban Institute, 2100 M St., N.W., Washington, DC 20037; 202-833-7200; www.taxpolicycenter.org. Joint project with the Brookings Institution that provides nonpartisan analyses of tax legislation.

Urban Institute, 2100 M St. N.W., Washington, DC 20037, 202-833-7200; www.urban.org. Think tank that focuses on U.S. social and economic issues.

Washington Center on Equitable Growth, 1333 H St., N.W., Washington, DC 20005; 202-682-1611; http://equitablegrowth.org. Project housed at the liberal Center for American Progress that investigates the effect of inequality on economic growth.

5

Women and Work

Michelle Johnson

Sheryl Sandberg, Facebook chief operating officer, argues in her new book that women, in their quest for full workplace equality with men, have limited their own advancement by not being forceful enough. Others blame persistent cultural and economic barriers for women's lack of greater progress.

From *CQ Researcher*,
July 26, 2013.

Laura Leigh Oyler decided in seventh grade that education was her ticket to a good life.

"My parents got divorced when I was pretty young," says Oyler, who grew up in Fayetteville, Ark. "And I remember watching the women in my mom's social circle, one by one, go through a divorce. They lost their big, pretty houses. They had to go back to work. A lot of them, and my mom was no exception, started cleaning houses. She did that while going to school and raising three children, and I thought, 'I'm not doing that.'"

Oyler attended law school at the University of Arkansas, where she met her husband. Four years ago she was offered a job in employment law at Reynolds American, the nation's second-largest tobacco company, with a huge pay jump from her salary as a juvenile prosecutor in Arkansas. Although she had no direct experience in employment law, her fiancé (now her husband) encouraged her to make the leap to the Winston-Salem, N.C., firm.

He is now an associate at a local law firm and Oyler — 32, pregnant with the couple's first child — just accepted a promotion to lead Reynolds' youth smoking-prevention efforts.

Having a supportive spouse has been essential for her career says Oyler, the family's primary breadwinner. "He was the first one to say 'you can do anything. I've got your back. Go for it,'" she says.

Although Oyler is reluctant to call herself a feminist, she realizes her generation benefited from the women's movement led by her mother's generation. "I live in a very different America than women even 30 years ago did," she says. "A lot of social change happened in the '60s

Women Now Earn Most College Degrees

Women are expected to earn more than half of all college degrees in the 2012-13 academic year, a significant increase from four decades earlier. The number of doctoral degrees increased sharply: Women earned 9,553 doctorates in 1972-73 compared with 90,100 in 2012-13 — an 800 percent increase. In 1972-73, women earned fewer than half of all degrees.

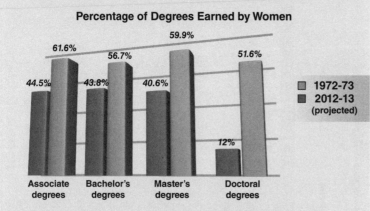

Percentage of Degrees Earned by Women

61.6% 44.5% — Associate degrees
56.7% 43.8% — Bachelor's degrees
59.9% 40.6% — Master's degrees
51.6% 12% — Doctoral degrees

- 1972-73
- 2012-13 (projected)

Source: "Degrees conferred by degree-granting institutions, by level of degree and sex of students: Selected years, 1869-70 through 2021-22," National Center for Education Statistics, U.S. Department of Education, http://nces.ed.gov/programs/digest/d12/tables/dt12_310.asp

the book was published. Women now make up half the workforce, earn more than half of almost all college degrees and hold half of all professional and management jobs in the United States.[2] They also have risen to the some of the highest levels in politics — including secretary of State and House majority leader — and have run some of the nation's biggest corporations, including Yahoo and Hewlett-Packard.

But despite such gains, women continue to face formidable barriers, from both within and without the movement: Ever since Friedan published her book half a century ago, sharp differences have arisen between those who have seen male oppression as women's primary obstacle and those who rejected sexual politics and pursued their goals within the traditional male-dominated economic and political system. The movement also has fought a tide of external social, cultural, political and economic barriers that continue to make it hard for many women to achieve full equality. American women still earn less than men for similar work, hold far fewer political and corporate leadership positions, shoulder more of family caregiving burdens and benefit from far fewer family-friendly corporate and government policies than women in other industrialized countries.[3]

What's more, some obstacles women face are self-imposed, according to Facebook chief operating officer Sheryl Sandberg, whose 2013 best-seller, *Lean In: Women, Work and the Will to Lead*, laments the dearth of females in leadership positions and urges women to be more assertive in their professional ambitions.

"It is time for us to face the fact that our revolution has stalled," she wrote. "The promise of equality is not the same as true equality. A truly equal world would be one where women ran half our countries and men ran half our homes."[4]

Sandberg's book has drawn both praise and criticism and established her as a new kind of feminist leader — one who acknowledges the social and cultural barriers

and the '70s, so I think that I benefit every day from that. And it's not just women who changed — it's men, too."

After women won the right to vote in 1920, feminism waned in the mid-20th century, overshadowed by concerns over the need to reintegrate returning veterans into the national economy after World War II. By the early 1960s, however, the "second wave" of the women's movement was quietly gaining momentum. Then, in 1963, labor journalist Betty Friedan's *The Feminine Mystique* landed as a bombshell in the lives of millions of American women.

"The feminine mystique," Friedan said in a 1964 interview, defined "woman solely in terms of her sexual relation to men, as man's sex object, as wife, mother, homemaker and never as a human being herself . . . and has not been good for their marriages, good for women, or good for love or good for men or even good for children."[1]

The feminist movement, which Friedan helped lead for decades before her death in 2006, has led to substantial gains in women's lives over the 50 years since

women face but challenges them to confront certain behaviors that she says keep them from achieving their full potential.

Christina Hoff Sommers, a resident scholar at the conservative American Enterprise Institute (AEI), calls the progress of women in the workplace and economy "a great American success story," since women "are represented in virtually every economic sector and at every level."

However, she would like to see a women's movement "that catches up with where women are," she says. "About 20 percent of women are high-powered careerists. They're just as committed and high octane [as men], and I'm very glad that we have a society that now permits them to flourish. However, they are not the majority of women. There are just about as many who would prefer to stay home and be full-time mothers, and there's a huge group in between. They're adapters, who want to work part time once they have children. It would be nice if we had a women's lobby that understood that and made it possible."

When large numbers of women began entering the workforce in the mid-1970s, nearly half of the country's families with children had stay-at-home moms and breadwinner dads. Today that is true for only one family in five.[5] Women increasingly are choosing nontraditional fields, ranging from natural resources conservation to homeland security and law enforcement. They now earn half of all business administration degrees and more than half of degrees in the biological sciences and health.[6]

Nearly three-quarters of Americans say having more women in the

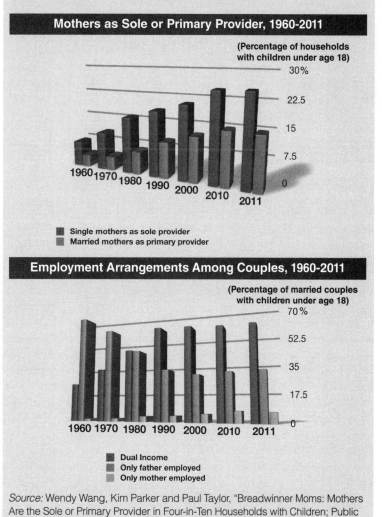

Families More Dependent on Mothers' Income

Mothers — married or single — were the sole or main breadwinner in a record 40 percent of households with children under age 18 in 2011, compared with only 11 percent in 1960 (top). Single mothers were the sole provider in a fourth of households with children, up sharply from five decades earlier. Meanwhile, the percentage of dual-income married couples with children rose sharply over the past five decades, reaching 59 percent in 1990 before hitting a plateau (bottom). The share of households in which only fathers were employed plunged from 70 percent in 1960 to 31 percent in 2011.

Mothers as Sole or Primary Provider, 1960-2011

(Percentage of households with children under age 18)

30%
22.5
15
7.5
0

1960 1970 1980 1990 2000 2010 2011

■ Single mothers as sole provider
■ Married mothers as primary provider

Employment Arrangements Among Couples, 1960-2011

(Percentage of married couples with children under age 18)

70%
52.5
35
17.5
0

1960 1970 1980 1990 2000 2010 2011

■ Dual Income
■ Only father employed
■ Only mother employed

Source: Wendy Wang, Kim Parker and Paul Taylor, "Breadwinner Moms: Mothers Are the Sole or Primary Provider in Four-in-Ten Households with Children; Public Conflicted about the Growing Trend," Pew Research Center, May 29, 2013, pp. 1, 20, www.pewsocialtrends.org/files/2013/05/Breadwinner_moms_final.pdf

workforce has been a change for the better in society and that marriages are more satisfying when men and women share responsibilities of work and children.[7] But workplaces and laws have yet to catch up with the realities of family life, says Joan C. Williams, director of the Center for WorkLife Law at the University of California's Hastings College of the Law. The American workplace is "still perfectly designed for the workplace of the 1960s," Williams says. "It assumes that you have someone else taking care of all your other family obligations, and that just isn't true anymore."

Feminist groups lobbying for family-friendly workplace policies have run into stiff opposition from organized business groups such as the U.S. Chamber of Commerce, which argues that they are overly burdensome for businesses. Conservative groups such as the Eagle Forum, based in Alton, Ill., also oppose federally subsidized daycare.[8]

Women have been a major force in American economic expansion. In the 1980s and '90s, their earnings grew relatively well, says economist Heidi Shierholz of the Economic Policy Institute, a liberal think tank. That growth helped to narrow the gender wage gap, though not entirely. Women's wages continued to rise in the early 2000s, despite forces such as the offshoring of manufacturing jobs and the decline in the power of labor unions. But the severe recession of the last few years has "wreaked havoc on wage growth," for both men and women, she says.

"The key thing driving women's wages is the same thing that's driving everyone's wages — persistent high unemployment," Shierholz says.

Besides fighting to get equal pay for equal work, women face the challenge of finding the kind of support necessary to succeed in the workplace, says Chanelle Hardy, senior vice president for policy at the National Urban League, a national civil rights organization based in New York City.

"From minimum wage to workers' compensation to family leave, are all critical," she says.

As women, their spouses, women's rights advocates and policymakers discuss the progress of women since publication 50 years ago of *The Feminine Mystique*, here are some of the questions being debated:

Are women better off today than they were 50 years ago?

The idea that women's equality benefits everyone is at the heart of feminism.

The modern women's movement challenged discriminatory laws in education and employment and advocated for stronger laws on spousal rape, domestic violence and reproductive freedom.

The women's movement has worked at the local, state and federal level to change laws, says Eleanor Smeal, president of the Fund for the Feminist Majority and a former president of the National Organization for Women (NOW). "We raised consciousness, but without the change in laws, we could not have influenced public opinion," she says.

Many social and cultural changes brought about by the feminist movement are deeply integrated into American life, but the debate about feminism is far from settled. "For the most part, women are vastly better off on almost every measure than they were 50 years ago," says Hanna Rosin, author of *The End of Men And the Rise of Women*.

For example, in 1960, women earned 35.3 percent of undergraduate degrees and only 10 percent of doctoral degrees in the United States. Since 1968, the percentage of women with at least a college degree has tripled.[9] In the 2012-13 academic year, women earned slightly more than half of all doctorates.[10]

Women now comprise 57 percent of U.S. college enrollment.[11] In fact, women are attending college — and graduating — in such great numbers that some schools have quietly begun practicing affirmative action for men.[12]

The wage gap between men and women is closing, slowly, in part because of women's educational attainment. Women, on average, earn 77 cents for every dollar a white male makes, up from about 61 cents in 1960.[13] At the present rate, women's earnings won't catch up to those of men until 2056. The wage gap is even greater for women of color — black women earn, on average, 68 cents for every dollar a white male makes, Hispanic women, 59 cents.[14]

In the last five years or so, most of the progress made on the wage gap is not because women have done better — it's because men have done worse, Shierholz says. "That is not the kind of equity we want to see," she says. "We want women to see real, rising wages without men seeing declines."

The recession hit men especially hard. Women, Shierholz says, did better as a group because so many of them work in jobs that are less cyclical than more male-dominated fields such as construction and manufacturing.[15]

But for all their progress, women in general today say they are less happy than women were 40 years ago, Rosin says. "That's probably a natural consequence of [having] lots of choices," she says. "Often when you are supposed to compete in many different realms, and when your role is less defined, there are just more opportunities to find yourself wanting."

Economists Betsey Stevenson and Justin Wolfers, both at the University of Michigan, termed the phenomenon "the paradox of declining happiness." Their findings were consistent among women, regardless of their marital status, age, education or income level. The trend also held true for European women.[16]

But, Stevenson says, the decline in reported happiness is not tied to women's participation in the labor force. Perhaps it's due to women's higher expectations, she suggests. "One of the possibilities is that the women's movement changed how people think about and answer these questions," she says.

Stevenson and Wolfers also theorized that declines in family life or social cohesion have hurt women more than men. Or, in an era of greater gender equality, women may be more likely to compare their lives with those of the men around them, they wrote.[17] "It wasn't clear to us why," Stevenson is quick to point out. "What we were trying to do is document the trend and pose it as something that was important but difficult to understand."

Some see the happiness data as evidence that the feminist movement has let women down. "The idea that you can have it all . . . has not proven to be very family friendly," says Janice Shaw Crouse, a senior fellow at the Beverly LaHaye Institute, a Washington, D.C.-based Christian women's organization that is critical of the feminist movement. "It's not a pretty picture in women's personal lives."

She cites the declining U.S. marriage rate — it hit a record low of 51 percent in 2011 — as a sign of trouble, along with the fact that people are marrying later. The current median age for marriage is about 27 for women and 29 for men.[18] In 1960, by contrast, 72 percent of Americans were married, and the median age of marriage was the early 20s for both men and women.[19]

The reasons for delaying marriage vary; many women put it off until they finish school and get established in

their careers. And many couples live together before marriage, instead of marrying.[20] Marriage, Crouse says, provides the best environment for raising children, forms an important cornerstone of society and makes women happier.

But the happiness data should be viewed in light of contemporary social and economic conditions, says Stephanie Coontz, a professor of history and family studies at Evergreen State College in Olympia, Wash. "In the 1950s and '60s, people were measuring their lives against World War II and the Depression," she says. "People's standards of happiness change."

Higher expectations — and greater anxiety — about their careers, their family's economic well-being, and their ability to provide for the life's big-ticket items, such as a home and their children's college tuition, may account for a decline in women's feelings of happiness, she says. "It's easy for people to say, 'well, maybe we've opened a Pandora's box here.' In fact, I think that's the wrong way to look at it," she says. "We're facing some new challenges — having overcome much worse ones in the past," she says.

Eagle Forum founder Phyllis Schlafly believes the feminist movement devalued marriage and family, to the detriment of women's happiness. "The ones who have planned their life without husband and children are living alone," she says. "And then when they get to be 38 or 40, they realize that life is passing them by. I think there are just so many who are not happy with the choices that they made."

Women are now the sole or primary breadwinner in 40 percent of households with children under 18. In 1960, that was true for just one in 10 households. Nearly two-thirds of these breadwinners are single mothers, whose median family income was $23,000 in 2011, well below the national median income of $57,000 for all families with children. By comparison, among the 37 percent of families in which women out-earned their husbands, the median family income was nearly $80,000.[21]

"There are groups of women who are in significant distress in our society," says Ellen Bravo, the executive director of Family Values at Work, a coalition of groups pressing for mandatory paid sick leave laws. "To say we're better off doesn't mean that we're anywhere near done. If we want to measure the progress of women, we have to measure all women."

Are women limiting themselves?

When it comes to advancing in the workplace, are women victims of a "glass ceiling" or a "sticky floor"?

Plenty of evidence suggests that women encounter systemic barriers on their way up the career ladder — and that they also may impose career limits on themselves, sometimes for the sake of juggling family and professional responsibilities.

Women make up about half of the management ranks at American companies, but relatively few are making it into the executive suite.

In 2012, women held executive officer positions at 14.3 percent of *Fortune* 500 companies.[22] Women still face barriers, internal and external, in reaching the highest levels of leadership and achievement in professional life.

As for female behaviors Facebook COO Sandberg sees as self-limiting, women "systematically underestimate themselves," she said. "Why does this matter? Boy, it matters a lot. Because no one gets to the corner office by sitting on the side — not at the table — and no one gets the promotion if they don't think they deserve their own success or they don't even understand their own success."[23]

But women also face stereotypes. In 2003, Francis Flynn, a professor of organizational behavior at the Stanford University Graduate School of Business, and Cameron Anderson, a professor of leadership and communication at the Haas School of Business at the University of California-Berkeley, conducted a study in which their students were presented the real-life business case of venture capitalist Heidi Roizen, who had leveraged her "outgoing personality . . . and vast professional network" to her advantage.[24]

However, one group read about "Heidi Roizen," the other about "Howard Roizen." The students saw Heidi and Howard as equally competent. But when asked which they liked more, the students chose "Howard."[25]

Research into gender stereotypes bears out such findings. Studies show that women are generally expected to be more nurturing, sympathetic and kind and that when they show dominance or self-promotion they may face social or career-related consequences.[26] Even when women adopt the same career-advancement strategies as men — saying what they want in their careers, asking for opportunities, volunteering to work long hours — they

advance less and their salaries grow more slowly than those of their male counterparts, the studies have found.[27]

Women also are less likely to negotiate for starting salaries or raises, potentially depriving themselves of hundreds of thousands of dollars in lifetime earnings. A study of graduate students indicated that while 57 percent of the male college graduates negotiated for their starting salary, only 7 percent of the women did.[28] Gender socialization explains some of the difference, said Linda Babcock, a professor of economics at Carnegie Mellon University's Heinz College School of Public Policy & Management and the co-author of *Women Don't Ask: Negotiation and the Gender Divide.* While boys are taught to focus on themselves, girls are taught to pay attention to the needs of others first, she said.[29]

Women also may think — correctly, in some cases — that they'll face a backlash for negotiating. Babcock's research revealed a "negotiation penalty" that was 5.5 times higher for women than for men: Both male and female hiring managers were less likely to hire women who negotiated.[30]

"As for the question 'are women limiting themselves?' I think the answer is definitely yes," says Daria Burke, CEO of Black MBA Women, an organization she founded to support aspiring executives. "But external factors play a significant role in our ability to push past the limits that have been set for us."

Women also hesitate to help themselves, according to a study by the London-based Institute of Leadership and Management. "Women managers are impeded . . . by lower ambitions and expectations [of themselves]," the study said. On average, men's higher expectations of themselves and self-confidence help them land management roles three years earlier than women.[31]

Ambivalence toward leadership also keeps women stuck, said Henna Inam, an Atlanta-based executive coach. She identified several typical self-limiting mindsets.

"If we perceive that leadership involves 'exerting power over others,' we are reluctant to lead," she said. "For many women, social acceptance is much more important than for men." Women also may think that accepting a leadership role is too stressful, she said, or that they need to improve themselves before they take on a new challenge, or that they can make a bigger difference in their current role than they could in the upper ranks of the organization.[32]

A study of 60 corporations by management consultant McKinsey & Co. found that a majority of successful women — 59 percent — don't aspire to the top job. When asked why, they gave answers such as "I'm happy doing what I'm doing."[33]

For a lot of women, ambition to climb the career ladder pales in comparison to wanting a balance between work and home life. According to a *New York Times*/CBS News poll, only one-quarter of mothers with children under 18 said they would work full time if money were no object.

"If it were up to me," said Angie Oler, a University of Wisconsin-Madison researcher who switched to part-time work when her first child was born four years ago, "I would never ever go back to full time. . . . I think the world would be a much happier place if we all worked fewer hours, like if everyone worked just four eight-hour days, and I think we'd all still manage to get all of our work done."[34]

For AEI's Sommers such views show that women's relationship to the workplace is "still more tenuous than men's, and not because of oppression. It's because of women's choice, women's freedom."

But women are frequently making those choices inside systems they didn't create, says Williams, of the Hastings College of the Law. Women — and men, for that matter — who want more flexibility in their working lives often are seen as slackers, even when their workplaces offer such arrangements. Moreover, women who leave the workplace to parent full time often face career penalties in the form of lower salaries when they try to return.[35]

The problem, Williams says, is the pervasive, implicit message in many workplaces that "a high-level professional is someone who makes work the central commitment of their lives."[36]

"So long as you have workplaces where the work-devotion ideal remains intact, we're never going to be able to address the 'hours problem,'" Williams says. The "hours problem," she says, is the expectation that to get ahead, workers must devote most of their lives to their jobs.

Among college-educated working mothers ages 25 to 44, she says, only 13.9 percent work more than 50 hours a week, compared to 37 percent of their male cohort (men 25-44, with college educations). It's unrealistic to think that more women will advance to the top of

Women Lag in Some Occupations

Women predominate in mostly traditional female jobs; they represent 98.1 percent of kindergarten teachers and 90.6 percent of nurses (top). And while women represent more than a third of U.S. doctors and surgeons, they account for only 19.7 percent of software developers and 4.1 percent of pilots and flight engineers (bottom). Overall, females now comprise 53.5 percent of the labor force.

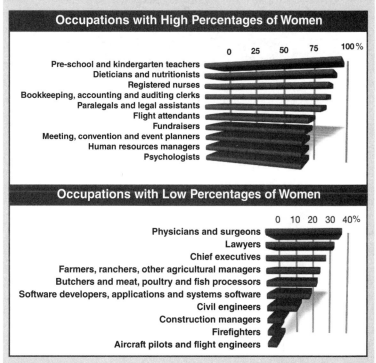

Occupations with High Percentages of Women

Pre-school and kindergarten teachers
Dieticians and nutritionists
Registered nurses
Bookkeeping, accounting and auditing clerks
Paralegals and legal assistants
Flight attendants
Fundraisers
Meeting, convention and event planners
Human resources managers
Psychologists

Occupations with Low Percentages of Women

Physicians and surgeons
Lawyers
Chief executives
Farmers, ranchers, other agricultural managers
Butchers and meat, poultry and fish processors
Software developers, applications and systems software
Civil engineers
Construction managers
Firefighters
Aircraft pilots and flight engineers

Source: "Current Population Survey," U.S. Bureau of Labor Statistics, www.bls.gov/cps/cpsa2012.pdf

AP Photo/*The Republic*/Andrew Laker

Taylor Baker stops to say hello to her 5-month-old daughter, Graesyn Steinkoenig, at the Cummins Childcare Center, part of Cummins Inc., an engine manufacturer, in Columbus, Ind., on Jan. 26, 2012. Baker, who works in the center's office, returned to work seven weeks after having her daughter. Advocates of family-friendly corporate policies say they are good not only for parents and children but also for the economy.

organizations — much less that the needs of ordinary working women will be addressed — without a fundamental shift in how workplaces approach work-life balance.

Should workplaces become more accommodating for women?

The discussion about greater work-life balance often begins with the issue of maternity leave. The United States is the world's only high-income country that doesn't offer a legal right to paid time off after the birth of a child. The Family Medical Leave Act (FMLA), passed in 1993, mandates 12 weeks of job-protected leave to qualified workers, but the leave is unpaid, limited to companies with 50 or more employees and only covers employees who worked at least 1,250 hours in the year before requesting leave. As a result, about 40 percent of workers are not eligible for the benefit.[37]

Congressional Democrats, such as Rep. George Miller of California, have called for extending the FMLA to all workers.[38] While a few states have expanded family and medical leave, federal legislation is not expected to be adopted because of strong opposition from Republicans, who believe such measures would constitute onerous government intrusions into private companies' policies.

Only 11 percent of American workers have access to paid family leave, according to the National Partnership for Women & Families.[39]

"Providing 12 weeks of paid leave is expensive. We should not expect employers to pay for that individually," says Ariane Hegewisch, a study director at the Institute for Women's Policy Research, a Washington think tank that examines the impact of pay equity, immigration and education on women. "It really is something we need to do through social insurance."

A few states, such as California and New Jersey, offer family leave insurance, which — like Social Security or Medicare — is usually funded by a special payroll tax.

Most family-friendly policies in Europe are funded through social insurance. Parental leave policies in other countries vary widely — from Sweden's generous 40 weeks of full-time equivalent paid leave to nearly six years of combined job-protected leave for couples in France and Spain, much of it unpaid. A comparative study of "family friendly" policies in the United States and Europe found that most offered some kind of financial support.[40] Some American companies do offer paid maternity leave, and a few, such as Google and Yahoo, have begun offering paid paternity leave. But they are the exception.

"Employers are not filling the hole left by regulations," says Hegewisch. Laws are needed, she said, "to create a basic floor."

The benefits of "family friendly" policies, according to Hegewisch, include gender equality, lower infant mortality, higher fertility rates, better child health, labor force growth and lower poverty rates.[41] Paid maternity leave could also help the U.S. address its declining birth rate.

Still, says Roger Clegg, general counsel for the Center for Equal Opportunity, a conservative public policy institute, employers have no compelling reason to provide paid leave or other family accommodations. "Individuals should have choices about where they work, and companies should have choices about how to structure their jobs and allow the market to work these things out," Clegg says. "I think it would be a bad thing if we started moving toward the European model. This kind of micromanaging is bad for the economy, bad for economic growth."

In fact, some economists cite high labor costs as a factor in many European countries' ongoing economic woes.[42]

The U.S. Chamber of Commerce led the opposition to the FMLA when it passed in 1993 and opposes paid leave. "Employers have constraints on them," said Marc Freedman, the executive director for labor law policy at the Chamber. Even unpaid leave, he said, is too big a burden for many small companies. While larger companies can accommodate FMLA leave for new parents, he said, it can be difficult for them to track employees' medical leave.[43]

The lack of paid parental leave in the United States may partly explain why women's participation in the labor force has stopped growing, says Francine Blau, a labor economist at Cornell University. It has been at a standstill since the mid-1990s and is falling behind its European counterparts. In 1990, 74 percent of working-age women (16-64) were either employed or looking for a job, the sixth-highest rate among 22 economically advanced countries. By 2010, it had risen to just over 75 percent, while women's labor force participation in other advanced economies had increased on average from 67 percent to nearly 80 percent. Blau and her co-author, Lawrence Kahn, found that the expansion of "family friendly" policies in European countries explained nearly 30 percent of the difference between American women's labor force participation and that of their European counterparts.[44]

"These other countries started with much more aggressive policies of parental leave and part-time entitlements, and expanded those policies over the last 20 years," Blau says. Such generous policies appear to help women "handle both their work and their family responsibilities and increase labor force participation."

But more of the jobs available to European women were part-time, and a larger share of U.S. women are professionals or managers than among their European counterparts.

"We think there probably are some unintended consequences of these [parental leave] policies, if they become extremely generous," Blau says. Women may "spend more time out of the labor force than they otherwise would have and be more likely to work in part-time jobs than they otherwise would have."

"The U.S. may be too low, but other countries may have gone overboard in the other direction."[45]

While work-family policies are good for parents and children, they're also good for the economy as a whole, Blau says. "If we do not fully utilize the skills and talents, our output is not as great as it would be, and we're not as prosperous as we could be," she says.

Paid maternity leave also increases the likelihood that women will return to work once the leave is over, studies show.[46] And a study by one of Blau's graduate students at Cornell, Ankita Patnaik, suggests that encouraging men to take paid paternity leave may have long-term effects on how partners share child care and household duties. Patnaik looked at the long-term effects of Quebec's "use it or lose it" paid parental leave and found that dads who took the leave were more likely to shoulder more of the domestic chores than those who didn't.[47]

BACKGROUND

The Second Wave

When President John F. Kennedy appointed his Presidential Commission on the Status of Women in 1961, political momentum had been growing to address the issue of women's equality. The 26-member commission, headed by former first lady Eleanor Roosevelt, was charged with investigating discrimination against women.

"I don't think he meant to give birth to the modern women's movement," historian Ruth Rosen, a professor emerita at the University of California-Davis, said of Kennedy, "but in effect that's what he did."[48]

For more than 40 years after women won the vote with ratification of the 19th Amendment in 1920, feminism in America had largely faded from public view. The coalition that had fought for suffrage splintered, as one wing, the National Woman's Party, began pursuing an Equal Rights Amendment (ERA), led by suffragist Alice Paul.[49] Another began pushing for legislative changes more narrowly focused on helping to protect working women through the Women's Bureau at the Department of Labor; a third party sought to carve out a more prominent place for women in political parties.[50]

The Women's Bureau, according to historian Georgia Duerst-Lahti, "nurtured a coalition of groups concerned

CHRONOLOGY

1848-1945 *Women press for voting rights and workplace equality.*

1848 First women's rights convention takes place in Seneca Falls, N.Y.

1920 States ratify 19th Amendment, giving women the right to vote. . . . Labor Department's Women's Bureau formed to collect data about working women.

1923 Equal Rights Amendment (ERA) introduced in Congress.

1930 Half of single women and 12 percent of wives are in labor force.

1938 Fair Labor Standards Act establishes rules for a minimum wage, overtime pay and child labor.

1941-1945 Almost 6 million women enter the workforce during World War II.

1960s *Women win landmark victories for equal rights in the workplace.*

1961 President John F. Kennedy establishes Commission on the Status of Women.

1963 Kennedy signs Equal Pay Act. . . . Betty Friedan's *The Feminine Mystique* spurs women's rights movement.

1964 Civil Rights Act outlaws employment discrimination on basis of race, color, religion, sex and national origin.

1966 National Organization for Women founded.

1968 Equal Employment Opportunity Commission bans sex-segregated help-wanted ads.

1970s *Feminist movement spurs political and social change.*

1972 Congress passes Equal Rights Amendment (ERA), sends it to states for ratification. . . . Congress passes Title IX, requiring gender equity in educational programs.

1973 Supreme Court legalizes abortion, energizing women's movement.

1974 Supreme Court rules employers cannot justify lower wages for women.

1978 Pregnancy Discrimination Act bans firing pregnant women or denying them jobs. . . . Labor Department acts to increase the number of women in skilled construction trades.

1982-2000 *ERA fails; unpaid family leave becomes law.*

1982 Equal Rights Amendment falls three states short of 38 needed for ratification.

1986 Supreme Court declares sexual harassment in workplace illegal.

1993 Family and Medical Leave Act entitles eligible employees to take job-protected leave.

2001-Present *Equal-pay fight continues.*

2001 Female Walmart employees file sex-discrimination claim.

2004 Morgan Stanley agrees to pay $54 million in sex-discrimination suit.

2007 Supreme Court throws out woman's pay-discrimination claim because it was not filed within a 180-day deadline from her first paycheck.

2009 President Obama signs the Lilly Ledbetter Fair Pay Act, invalidating the 2007 Supreme Court ruling. The act allows employees to contest pay discrimination 180 days after any discriminatory paycheck.

2011 Supreme Court dismisses *Walmart v. Dukes*, saying it cannot determine whether all 1.5 million plaintiffs were victims of discrimination.

2012 Record number of women elected to Congress — 20 senators and 81 House members.

2013 Census Bureau finds that women are primary breadwinners in 40 percent of U.S. households with children under 18, up from 10 percent in 1960.

with the plight of working women and favoring protectionist legislation, and in the process it kept a spark of activism alive."[51]

By and large, these groups opposed the Equal Rights Amendment because they believed that women needed labor protections, such as maximum work hours and minimum wages, which they feared would be abolished under the ERA. Paul's group, meanwhile, felt that labor standards did not promote equality. "Labor legislation as a form of sex discrimination," she wrote, "is enacting another handicap for women in the economic struggle."[52]

Women's participation in the labor force had been on the rise before World War II, and the war brought about six million women into the workplace between 1940 and 1944 to replace men called up for military service. By the spring of 1944, nearly one-third of all women and girls over age 14 were working, and their ranks in industrial jobs had increased almost 500 percent.

As the war was winding down in 1945, the government waged an aggressive campaign to encourage women to return to their traditional roles as full-time housewives and mothers, or to take jobs in traditional "feminine" (and lower paying) occupations, such as clerical work. But the women were not keen to do so: Polls showed that more than three-quarters of women employed in wartime occupations said they hoped to keep their jobs when the war ended.[53]

Equal-pay legislation, which would ensure equal pay for women doing work that required comparable skills as their male counterparts was proposed in 1945, mainly as a tribute to female wartime workers. But in a postwar economy focused on reintegrating veterans into the workforce, the legislation languished. Large numbers of American women entered or remained in the workforce after World War II. In 1960, nearly 35 percent of American women over age 16 were working, and public opinion — including organized labor — was rallying around the concept of equal pay for equal work.[54]

But until 1963, opposition from business groups blocked the legislation.[55]

In June of 1963, a few months before his Presidential Commission on the Status of Women published its final report, Kennedy signed the legislation amending the 1938 Fair Labor Standards Act. The Equal Pay Act required employers to pay men and women equally for doing the same work. It also allowed for pay differentials based on seniority, merit, quantity or quality of production or a factor other than gender. (Current legislative efforts such as the Paycheck Fairness Act are aimed at closing some of these loopholes.)

A few months later, the presidential commission's final report documented workplace discrimination and recommended equal employment opportunities for women, affordable child care and paid maternity leave. Both developments came in the same year that *The Feminine Mystique* hit book stores, making 1963 an important year in the birth of the modern feminist movement.

Friedan went on to help found NOW in 1966. In 1970 she led the Strike for Women's Equality, a march on the 50th anniversary of women's suffrage that drew an estimated 50,000 women to the streets of New York City and gave the nation its first sweeping visual of the new feminist movement.

Coontz, who explored the impact of *The Feminine Mystique* in her book, *A Strange Stirring: The Feminine Mystique and American Women at the Dawn of the 1960s*, said Friedan's book struck a nerve among women who had left domestic life during World War II but were expected to return to it once the war was over, along with younger women who had watched the expansion of new jobs and educational opportunities in the postwar era only to be told it was abnormal for a woman to want anything other than a traditional role as wife and mother.

"It was a catalyst for stuff that was already coming," she says. "It inspired and had a tremendous emotional impact on women who had at first thought they were neurotic or even crazy for wanting something more out of life," she says.

The movement also attracted an entire generation of young (mostly white) middle-class women who had been raised with the idea that they would go to college but who aspired to defy the stereotype that Friedan depicted in the book. "They create the noise, they politicize these issues, and in effect create the women's movement," Rosen said. "They create the shock troops."[56]

But they were often made to feel unwelcome in the business world. In a recent commentary for *The Washington Post*, former *Post* restaurant critic Phyllis Richman described the discouraging experience of being asked by a Harvard graduate school professor to spell out exactly

Women Still Hold a Fraction of Skilled-Trades Jobs

"There's a big feeling that these are men's jobs."

In the late 1970s, Connie Ashbrook enrolled in a pre-apprenticeship program to become a dump truck driver, her first job toward a career in the skilled trades.

Eventually she became an elevator installer. Her employer was looking for women because the company had a large federal contract and needed to comply with U.S. Department of Labor affirmative action guidelines calling for federal contractors to make a "good faith effort" to hire female workers.

"I always say that I got my job because of affirmative action and all the organizations that fought for equal opportunity, from the civil rights folks . . . to the feminist policymakers and lawyers fighting for women's equal opportunity," says Ashbrook, now executive director of Oregon Tradeswomen, Inc., which provides training and networking opportunities for women. "I kept my job because I was good at it . . . but the door was opened because of those people that believed in justice and equal opportunity."

Women increasingly are an accepted part of construction workplaces, and more women hold key leadership positions in unions and professional organizations than ever before. Despite such gains, however, they still occupy fewer than 3 percent of the nation's skilled trade jobs and apprenticeships.[1]

The construction industry employed 7.1 million people — 5.1 percent of all jobs — in 2011, but women comprised only 2.3 percent of that workforce, which includes electricians, carpenters, bricklayers and other trades.[2] Moreover, the percentage of female skilled apprentices in 2009 was smaller than in 1992, according to the Department of Labor.[3]

Women can earn significantly higher wages in the trades than in other occupations requiring only a high school education. The median weekly income of a male electrician, for example, is $855, which is 159 percent of the median wages of a woman with a high school diploma.[4]

So why aren't more women working in the skilled trades?

"I think there's a big feeling that these are men's jobs," says Francoise Jacobsohn, program director of the Equality Works project at Legal Momentum, a women's advocacy organization. "It's just entrenched discrimination."

The Department of Labor's Office of Federal Contract Compliance Programs (OFCCP) tracks whether federal contractors follow affirmative action guidelines. OFCCP Director Pat Shiu said in March that investigators have found violation rates in the construction industry are significantly higher than in other industries. The "vast majority" of those occurred because companies failed to take the established steps for

how she planned to balance her studies with her family responsibilities if she were to be accepted at Harvard. She replied, 52 years later, in a letter also published in *The Post*: "Before your letter, it hadn't occurred to me that marriage could hinder my acceptance at Harvard or my career," Richman wrote to the professor, William A. Doebele, Jr.[57]

After the 1972 passage of Title IX, the federal civil rights law prohibiting sex discrimination in education, women began heading to college in record numbers.

Women's access to higher education has been the "big advance" for the feminist movement, Smeal, the former NOW president, says. "Down deep, we thought if we could open the doors women would flood in, but we didn't really know. I have to say, once we got the doors open more, it went faster than we probably thought it would have gone."

Women At Work

Still, what women choose to study and the professions they select factor into the persistent wage gap between

ensuring equal opportunity. Her office has beefed up enforcement efforts, she said, and long-awaited Labor Department employment goals for women and minorities will be published this fall.[5]

"I believe that the key to getting more women and minorities in the construction trades is strong enforcement," Shiu said.[6]

"You still run into contractors that say, 'Oh, do I have to take a woman?' says Leah Rambo, director of training for the Sheet Metal Workers Local 28 in New York City. "You tell them, 'Yes you do.' You still have a lot of people who need to be educated."

That goes for the public as well, Rambo says. Girls and women generally don't think of the trades as a career possibility, she says, and they also have to deal with sexual harassment and discrimination.

"A lot of women aren't prepared for that," she said.

Jenna Smith thinks sexual harassment is a major reason women drop out of the skilled trades. "They get worn out," says Smith, who works as the apprentice coordinator at Northwest Line Joint Apprenticeship Training Committee, a multistate organization based in Portland, Ore. "It's a really scary thing to stand up."

Smith remembers her own battle to win her journeywoman license after finishing an apprenticeship as an electricline worker in Eugene, Ore. Smith reported being sexually harassed on the job when she was an apprentice. She was initially denied her journeywoman license, but eventually won an appeal.

Tradeswomen's groups are trying to get more women in the skilled trades, especially in leadership roles, says Carolyn Williams, director of civic and community engagement for the International Brotherhood of Electrical Workers union.

Trainees in Portland, Ore., learn carpentry in a state-certified pre-apprenticeship career class for women sponsored by the group Oregon Tradeswomen.

"Seeing someone who looks like me sends the message that 'there's a place for me here,' " says Williams.

— Michelle Johnson

[1]Timothy Casey, "Still Excluded: There Are Still Virtually No Women in the Federally Created and Supervised Apprenticeship Program for the Skilled Construction Trades," *Legal Momentum*, March 2013, www.legalmomentum.org/sites/default/files/reports/still-excluded.pdf.

[2]"A Databook 2012," U.S. Bureau of Labor Statistics, pp. 29, 38, www.bls.gov/cps/wlf-databook-2012.pdf.

[3]Casey, *op. cit.*, p. 5.

[4]*Legal Momentum* says statistically reliable data on female earnings is unavailable because so few women are employed in the trades.

[5]"Director Shiu Addresses 'Working on Equal Terms' Summit," U.S. Department of Labor Office of Federal Contract Compliance Programs, March 18, 2013, www.dol.gov/ofccp/addresses/Director_address_WETS_March182013.htmp.

[6]*Ibid.*

men and women. Women, especially women of color, are overrepresented in occupations considered "women's work" — child care and elder care, for example.

Much of the gender wage gap can be explained by wage differences in "traditionally male" and "traditionally female" occupations.

"Predominantly male jobs, particularly at the higher educated level, tend to pay much more than the female dominated jobs," says Hegewisch, of the Institute for Women's Policy Research. "I think the solution to this is not just to say, "OK, all women should become engineers now. It's also how we can more equitably fund and pay for the jobs that are done primarily by women. We do need librarians and teachers and psychologists and social workers. So it's not just saying women are wrong to go in for those jobs. Neither is there evidence that as soon as men move in, the wages will go up."

But the differences in chosen careers can't explain the entire gender wage gap, and discriminatory wage practices also persist, despite laws meant to prevent them.

'End of Men' Author Charts Women's Growing Power

"We can't have this fixed idea that men are more dominant."

*I*n her 2012 book The End of Men: And the Rise of Women, *Hanna Rosin maps what she sees as a seismic cultural shift — one accelerated by the recent recession, in* which men lost a disproportionate share of jobs.

Women, she says, haven't just pulled even with men in education and social status — they've surpassed them. It's no longer a man's world.

Rosin, a senior editor for The Atlantic, *says the book is "not a triumphalist feminist book that says, 'We won. We have everything.' Things have changed a lot, but the change has mixed results."*

Here is an edited transcript of CQ Researcher's *Michelle Johnson's interview with Rosin.*

Q: How have feminists responded to your book?

A: There's been a mixed reaction. I have had to think about why the resistance, why the idea that we are doing well feels to many people like a betrayal of feminism. In an era of feminism in the 1970s, you would cheer at that idea. There was a sense that it was great to be triumphant. Now, as we get closer to more and more power, I think there's a sense that it's dangerous to say we're triumphant. I thought people would say, 'What about CEOs? There are so few women CEOs.' But it was more the mood that surprised me. From more working-class women to middle-class women, the sort of striving women who write me, the response is like, 'Duh, this is completely obvious,' or 'Thank you for laying it out.' And those women would not call themselves feminists. One surprise is that men have reacted pretty positively to the book.

Q: At the beginning of writing the book, you thought that a world dominated by women would be more gentle or nurturing, but what you saw happening with women didn't seem "the result of fixed values or traits." You note the rise in arrest rates among women for violent crime, particularly among juveniles.

A: It seems that these traits exist along a continuum, so as women gain more power, they start to show some of the traits of the more powerful. One of the more surprising findings for me was just looking at the violence statistics. We can't have this fixed idea that men are more aggressive, more dominant, more powerful, and women are weaker

In 2009, President Obama signed the Lilly Ledbetter Fair Pay Act, reversing a Supreme Court ruling from two years earlier. Ledbetter, a supervisor at a Goodyear Tire and Rubber Co. plant in Gadsden, Ala., had been paid less than her male counterparts for years but didn't know about the gap until she received an anonymous tip. Her complaint to the Equal Employment Opportunity Commission eventually made its way to the Supreme Court, which said she had failed to file the complaint within 180 days from when the discrimination first occurred. The Ledbetter law extended the statute of limitations for employees to contest pay discrimination to 180 days after any discriminatory paycheck.[58]

But a pay gap persists, even among women who do not choose traditionally female occupations. According to a 2012 study by the American Association of University Women, an inexplicable gap of about 7 percent remained between men and women with identical experience, education and occupational status one year after graduation from college or after obtaining advanced degrees, even after controlling for every known variable.[59]

And the gap has appeared to widen over time, even among high earners. The gap is driven in part by the choices that women often make when trying to balance work and family, experts say. Harvard University economists Claudia Goldin and Lawrence F. Katz examined the "career cost" of having a family among both women and men in business, medicine and law. They found that women pay a higher cost for having a family than men do. For example, while earnings for males and females with an

and more vulnerable. We move along the continuum. We can move a lot further than we think.

Q: You also write that you had this mental image of an imaginary comic book duo, "Cardboard Man" and "Plastic Woman," but they aren't fixed gender traits.

A: I think part of the reason that women have been more flexible in responding to changes in the economy is because they've been the underdogs. They've had to hustle. They've had to work twice as hard and fit into the cracks and struggle and struggle. Those two things are connected. Men have had a kind of entitlement to position, so they haven't had to struggle. But there certainly have been periods after World War II when men . . . behaved in ways that I'm describing women behaving now. They came back from war, bought up farms, went to school, got lots of degrees. They were really hustling in that brief period after the war. So no, I don't think those traits are innate.

Q: Ellen Bravo, executive director of Family Values at Work, talks about "the feminization of work." That is, more jobs are temporary, part-time or on contract — something that has been more common for women — and that it's affecting everyone. Would you use that term?

A: The fundamental structures of the economy have changed. It's not like a bunch of men lost their jobs and they'll get them back. The way the economy works and what it values has changed drastically, from a manufacturing economy to a service and information economy. Jobs

Hanna Rosin, author of "The End of Men: And the Rise of Women."

Courtesy Hanna Rosin

can change at any moment, because technology can make jobs obsolete in a second. But the key element is the ability to adapt, which effectively means go to school and get whatever degree you need for whatever is happening at the moment. And that's something that women are doing much better than men.

— *Michelle Johnson*

MBA were similar immediately after graduation, a substantial wage gap between them existed 10 to 16 years after graduation, when the women's earnings fell to about 55 percent of the men's.[60]

Women with children were much more likely to take time out of the workforce or work part time — 24 percent fewer hours than men or women without children — and MBA moms who dropped out cited family, not career, as the reason, according to Goldin and Katz.[61]

They also found that high-powered career women increasingly are going into specialties that allow greater flexibility, even if it means lower incomes. Many women are choosing specialties that allow them to schedule or control their own hours — such as veterinary medicine, pharmacy and other medical specialties — and slowly are

helping to make those professions more flexible, the Harvard researchers found.[62]

Sharing the Load

As a group, working dads are doing more around the house. A March report from the Pew Research "Social and Demographic Trends" found that fathers spend twice as much time doing household chores as they did in 1965 — from about four hours to 10 hours a week. Mothers in two-parent families put in about 18 hours a week, down from 32 hours in 1965. But while both parents spend more time with their children than parents did in 1965, moms spend more than dads do.[63]

They also tend to carry more of the emotional weight of running a family, says Kerry Fierke, an assistant professor at the University of Minnesota College of Pharmacy.

"We're the ones who send the birthday cards and keep the house set and take on a lot of responsibilities. I'm always working with women on how to shed some of those responsibilities," Fierke says. She dropped off the management track in corporate health care a few years ago and now focuses on healthcare leadership issues, especially for women.

While she and her husband share housework and child care fairly equally, she says, "I do more of the management part of it."

Men may be doing more, but they're also more likely than women to report work-family conflicts and less likely to take advantage of flexible work options offered by their employers, says Williams, of Hastings College of the Law.[64] "Men who take parental leave, much less go part-time, encounter career penalties because they are seen as more feminine," she says.

Yet many younger men, particularly college-educated couples, are taking a more hands-on approach to fathering. Fatherhood has gone from a "provide, protect scenario to a team effort, especially nowadays with couples raising children where both work full time," said 37-year-old Jeremy Foster, an online creative director and designer in Kansas City, Mo.[65]

In single-parent families, however, the "team effort" often involves a logistical juggling act in which children spend time at day care and with a combination of extended family members and friends.

Full-time day care is too expensive for many families, costing more than half the annual income of a family of three living at the poverty level ($18,530). Single parents are not the only ones who struggle, however. In 40 states (plus the District of Columbia), infant day care costs more than 10 percent of the median income for a married couple.[66]

Child care in the United States is also largely unregulated, often resulting in haphazard conditions and low pay for workers. A 2007 survey by the National Institute of Child Health Development rated the majority of day care centers as "fair" or between "poor and good."[67]

Except for a brief period during World War II, when day care centers were set up for women who worked in wartime factories, the United States has never had a national child care system. In 1965, Congress created Head Start, a federal program that provides early childhood education for low-income families. In 1971, Congress passed the Comprehensive Child Care Act, which would have set up a federally subsidized national day care system with standards for quality and money for training and facilities. President Richard M. Nixon, who initially supported the legislation, ultimately vetoed it, declaring that it would promote "communal approaches to child rearing over the family-centered approach."[68]

Head Start expanded during the Clinton administration and serves more than 1 million children in 50 states, but a comprehensive federal child care system has never gained momentum as a national policy issue. Some blame the feminist movement for focusing more on fighting sex discrimination and promoting abortion rights at the expense of working mothers' needs. Friedan herself echoed that criticism in her 1981 book *The Second Stage*, saying that pushing for family-friendly workplace policies was "the new feminist frontier."[69]

Obama has proposed spending $75 billion over 10 years to create a "universal pre-K" system, in which the federal government would provide states with matching funds to set up programs for 4-year-olds, funded with higher cigarette taxes.[70]

CURRENT SITUATION

Leadership Gap

Women such as Facebook's Sandberg and Anne-Marie Slaughter, a former high-ranking State Department official and professor of politics and international affairs at Princeton University, argue that true gender equity won't be possible until a critical mass of women wield power at the highest levels of political and corporate life.

In a widely debated article in *The Atlantic*, "Why Women Still Can't Have It All," Slaughter wrote that the best hope for improving the lot of all women, and for closing what some call "'a new gender gap'" — measured by well-being rather than wages — is to close the leadership gap: to elect a woman president and 50 women senators; to ensure that women are equally represented in the ranks of corporate executives and judicial leaders. Only when women wield power in sufficient numbers will we create a society that genuinely works for all women. That will be a society that works for everyone."[71]

AT ISSUE

Are women better off than they were 50 years ago?

YES Eleanor Smeal
President, Fund for the Feminist Majority; Former President, National Organization for Women

Written for *CQ Researcher*, July 2013

Of course American women are better off today than 50 years ago! As a proud feminist activist for more than 40 years, I don't claim to be an impartial observer. Although inequities remain and the struggle is far from over, women's advancements are revolutionary.

In education, women have soared, both academically and athletically. In the 1960s women comprised a third of students enrolled in college, and some 60 percent never graduated. When I first began speaking for equality, women made up just 3 percent of the lawyers and 8 percent of the medical doctors. Feminists fought restrictive quotas that limited the number of women entering not only professional schools, but college itself. We were taunted with the ditty, "women don't want to be doctors or lawyers, they want to marry them."

Today such taunts are gone. Women are some 57 percent of college graduates and a majority of medical and law students. Women earn some 60 percent of the master's degrees and 52 percent of the doctorates.

In 1963 women were just 20 percent of the paid workforce; today we are nearly half. Women-owned businesses now employ more people than *Fortune* 500 companies combined. Women did not have equal credit opportunities until 1975, and the Pregnancy Discrimination Act did not pass until 1978. Fifty years ago a woman could be fired if she became pregnant. This was a typical fate for pregnant teachers, flight attendants and many more. Today's laws prohibit this practice.

Advances in birth control and abortion, and access to them, have improved women's health, economic well-being and educational opportunities. Women's longevity and maternal health have increased, while infant mortality and morbidity have decreased.

Fifty years ago domestic violence was treated as a personal problem, not talked about in public. Rape was considered a crime of passion, not a crime of violence. That day is over. Feminists at the state and federal levels have passed and are passing laws to combat such violence. Rates of violence, although still high, have been reduced. Sexual assault in the military and on college campuses is at intolerable levels, but an aware public is insisting on change.

Yes, the world is changing for women. Today the movement is worldwide. The need is still great, but the vision, hope and odds for winning women's equality have never been better.

NO Phyllis Schlafly
Founder and President, Eagle Forum

Written for *CQ Researcher*, July 2013

Whether women are better off today depends on what the goals in life are: to be rich, to be important, to achieve the aims of feminism, or to be happy. Women will have different answers. But because the trigger for this question is the 50th anniversary of the feminist movement, perhaps we should answer in that context.

The goal of the women's liberation movement, as it labeled itself when it was launched in 1963 by Betty Friedan's book *The Feminine Mystique*, was to move all fulltime homemakers out of their homes and into the labor force. This was not based on any economic argument; the feminist rationale was that the home was a "comfortable concentration camp" to which wives and mothers were confined by the patriarchy. As Supreme Court Associate Justice Ruth Bader Ginsburg wrote in her book *Sex Bias in the U.S. Code*, "the concept of husband-breadwinner and wife-homemaker must be eliminated from the Code to reflect the equality principle."

The separation of marriage from a recognition of the complementary roles of mother and father, plus the easy divorce laws, brought about the unfortunate separation of babies from marriage. So now 41 percent of births in the United States are illegitimate. Generous federal handouts give women an incentive to look to Big Brother for financial support instead of to husbands and fathers.

A National Bureau of Economic Research working paper by University of Pennsylvania economists reported that women's happiness has declined measurably since 1970. One theory advanced by the authors is that the feminist movement "raised women's expectations" (in other words, sold them a bill of goods), making them feel inadequate when they fail to have it all.

Women's unhappiness is better explained by the fact that the feminist movement taught women to see themselves as victims of the patriarchy and that their true worth will never be recognized, so success in life is forever beyond their reach.

It's sad to read feminists' self-psychoanalysis. Their principal problem was that they took women's studies courses in college where they learned to plan a career in the workplace without any space or time for marriage or babies, at least until the women are over age 40 and their window of opportunity has closed. So they don't have the companionship of a husband in their senior years or grandchildren to provide a reach into the future.

At the current rate of growth, however, it would take more than 70 years for women to pull equal with men in leadership roles.[72]

Burke, of Black MBA Women, cites studies that correlate female leadership with better financial performance by companies as proof that the gender leadership gap needs to close.[73] "Organizations run by women perform better, and not just a little bit," she says. "The same thing goes for companies that have diverse leadership. You look at Wall Street and who ran it into the ground, and it was largely middle-aged white men."

For Sandberg, the leadership issue is a feminist issue. She is one of relatively few high-profile business executives to call herself a feminist, and she came in for some withering criticism, some of it from feminists who see her as too elitist to speak to the average woman's experiences. Others applaud her for speaking up.

"The truth is, feminism could use a powerful ally," wrote feminist author Jessica Valenti in an op-ed for *The Washington Post*.[74]

Though Sandberg identifies as a feminist today, she didn't think of herself that way in college. "But I think we need to reclaim the 'F word' if it means supporting equal opportunities for men and women," she said during an interview with *The Harvard Business Review* in April.[75]

Williams, of Hastings College of the Law, says perhaps "executive feminism" is just what the feminist cause needs in order to advance on behalf of other women. "More women in power might well lead to greater success in other arenas," she said in a recent blog post for *The Harvard Business Review*.[76]

Female leaders aren't immune to trouble, however. For example, the board of Hewlett-Packard forced out Carly Fiorina as CEO over her business decisions. Other powerful businesswomen, such as lifestyle maven Martha Stewart and hotel magnate Leona Helmsley, ran into legal trouble for their business practices. Stewart went to prison for insider trading, and Helmsley served time for tax evasion and fraud.

Legislative Efforts

Many grass-roots feminists today are focusing on policies that they believe would benefit a wide swath of working American families. Bravo's Family Values at Work coalition of groups in 21 states is pushing for state and local measures to provide paid sick leave. Some 44 million Americans lack paid sick leave, and millions of others can't use their sick days to care for others, such as a sick child or parent. Some 60 percent of Latinos, the fastest-growing segment of the American workforce, get no sick leave.[77]

In 2011, Connecticut became the first state to adopt a sick-leave law, and San Francisco, Portland, Chicago and Seattle have adopted similar local measures. A recent New York City ordinance extends sick leave to about 1 million workers, and hundreds of thousands more get job-protected sick leave without pay.

"Many millions of workers are going without the protections they need in terms of sick days and family leave, so the present market hasn't worked, particularly for those at the middle and lower ends of the income ladder," says Vicki Shabo, director of Work and Family Programs for the National Partnership for Women and Families, a Washington, D.C.-based group that advocates for issues including paid family leave, paid sick leave and wage equity.

Shabo's group is working with House and Senate Democrats to push the Healthy Families Act, first introduced in 2004 by the late Sen. Edward M. Kennedy. The measure would allow workers in businesses with at least 15 employees to earn up to seven job-protected, paid sick days a year. The bill was reintroduced in 2013, by Connecticut Rep. Rosa DeLauro in the House and Iowa's Tom Harkin in the Senate. Both bills are stuck in committee and face widespread opposition among Republicans and pro-business advocates, who do not believe in a mandate for paid sick time.

"Republicans want to ensure that working families have the flexibility to get the health care they need, but we don't think the answer is a 'one size fits all' government mandate," said Michael Steel, a spokesman for House Majority Leader John Boehner, R-Ohio.

"It represents the intrusion of the federal government into the benefits policies of millions of companies, large and small," said Republican Rep. Tom Price of Georgia during hearings on the bill in 2009.[78]

Randel K. Johnson, the vice president for labor, immigration and employee benefits at the U.S. Chamber of Commerce, said his group was worried that the legislation could later be expanded. "Some say, 'What's seven days of paid sick leave?' My concern is it would never be just seven days. A year from now it will be 14 days, and then 21," said Johnson.[79]

A 2013 report by the Employment Policies Institute, a conservative think tank, said in places where paid leave laws have gone into effect, such as San Francisco, workers already are losing jobs.[80]

Democrats also would like to update the 1993 Family and Medical Leave Act to provide 12 weeks of paid, job-protected leave for new parents or workers facing family medical emergencies. And they have introduced the Paycheck Fairness Act, which would close loopholes in the 1963 Equal Pay Act. Advocates cite problems with how courts have interpreted the law's provision allowing pay differentials based on factors other than gender as evidence that the law needs to be clarified.[81] But political observers say the measure stands little chance of advancing this year.[82]

In the absence of federal action, some states are taking on the issues of equal pay and workplace flexibility. For example, as part of a larger measure fixing loopholes in Vermont's equal pay law, legislators recently enacted a measure that provides safeguards against retaliation for employees requesting flexible work hours.[83]

OUTLOOK

More Jobs

The aging of America is likely to influence the job market for women. The U.S. Bureau of Labor Statistics projects that most of the 30 fastest-growing occupations through 2020 are in female-dominated fields, such as health care, child care and education.[84]

As the baby boom generation ages, the need for home-health and personal-care aides is expected to grow by 70 percent by 2020, creating an estimated 1.3 million additional jobs.[85]

Hegewisch, at the Institute for Women's Policy Research, also expects many women to work beyond the traditional retirement age of 65, in part because they will need to supplement their retirement incomes. Older women are much more likely than older men to be poor: More than 60 percent of women 65 or older have insufficient income to cover basic expenses.[86]

Jobs in post-secondary education also are projected to grow — by 17 percent — but it is unclear whether those will be full-time positions with benefits or follow the current trend of adjunct and part-time instruction, she says.

The National Urban League's Hardy expects significant growth in the number of female entrepreneurs. Passage of the Affordable Care Act, designed to make health insurance available to all, is expected to help boost the ranks of the self-employed by 11 percent once it is fully implemented.[87] The Urban League found that women own nearly half of all black-owned businesses and employ nearly a quarter of all employees at black-owned companies.[88] Women own nearly 35 percent of all Hispanic-owned businesses.[89]

"They are really being employers and job creators," Hardy says. Entrepreneurship is seen as a key way to address unemployment in communities of color, and women are leading the way, she says.

"As we look at barriers to growth, [we] have to start focusing on technology and health care and education," Hardy says.

In the new economy, the best jobs may be the ones that can't be outsourced easily, writes *End of Men* author Rosin, and women are poised to do well.

"The sure bets for the future," she wrote, "are still jobs that cannot be done by a computer or someone overseas. They are the jobs that require human contact, interpersonal skills and creativity, and these are all areas where women excel."[90]

NOTES

1. "Rewind with Michael Enright," CBC, March 7, 2013, from an interview originally broadcast in 1964 on the CBC program "Take Thirty," www.cbc .ca/rewind/sirius/2013/03/07/betty-friedan/.

2. "Usual Weekly Earnings of Wage and Salary Workers," U.S. Bureau of Labor Statistics, April 2103, www.bls.gov/news.release/pdf/wkyeng.pdf.

3. See "The Gender Wage Gap by Occupation," Institute for Women's Policy Research, April 2013, www.iwpr.org/initiatives/pay-equity-and-discrimi nation.

4. Sheryl Sandberg, *Lean In: Women, Work, and the Will to Lead* (2013), p. 7.

5. Heather Boushey, Ann O'Leary and Sarah Jane Glynn, "Our Working Nation in 2013: An Updated Agenda for Work and Family Policies," Center for

American Progress, February 2013, www.american
progress.org/issues/labor/report/2013/02/05/517
20/our-working-nation-in-2013/.

6. "Bachelor's, master's, and doctor's degrees conferred
by degree-granting institutions, by sex of student
and discipline division: 2009-10," *U.S. Digest of
Education Statistics*, Table 290, National Center for
Education Statistics, *U.S. Department of Education*,
2011, http://nces.ed.gov/programs/digest/d11/
tables/dt11_290.asp.

7. Eileen Parker and Kim Patton, "A Gender Reversal
on Career Aspirations," Pew Social & Demographic
Trends, April 19, 2012, p. 7, www.pewsocialtrends
.org/files/2012/04/Women-in-the-Workplace.pdf.

8. Phyllis Schlafly, "Obama's Pre-K Power Grab," Eagle
Forum, June 26, 2013, www.eagleforum.org/publi
cations/column/obamas-pre-k-power-grab.html.
Also see Heather Boushey and Joan C. Williams,
"The Three Faces of Work-Family Conflict: The
Poor, the Professionals, and the 'Missing Middle,'"
Center for American Progress and the Center for
WorkLife Law, University of California, Hastings
College of the Law, 2010, www.americanprogress.
org/wpcontent/uploads/issues/2010/01/pdf/three
faces.pdf.

9. "Women in America: Indicators of Social and
Economic Well-Being," White House Council on
Women and Girls, March 2011, p. 21. National
Center for Education Statistics, Table 32. "Degrees
Conferred by Institutes of Higher Education, by
level of degree and sex of student: 1949-50 to 1993-
94," National Center for Education Statistics, http://
nces.ed.gov/pubs98/yi/yi32.pdf.

10. "Degrees conferred by degree-granting institutions
by level of degree and sex of student: Selected years,
1869-70 through 2020-21," National Center for
Education Statistics, Table 283, http://nces.ed.gov/
programs/digest/d11/tables/dt11_283.asp?
referrer=list.

11. See "Projections of Education Statistics to 2021,"
National Center for Education Statistics, Table 21,
p. 60. http://nces.ed.gov/pubs2013/2013008.pdf.

12. See Hanna Rosin, *The End of Men and the Rise of
Women* (2012), pp. 145-149.

13. "The Wage Gap Over Time," National Committee
on Pay Equity, www.pay-equity.org/info-time.html.

14. "The Simple Truth About the Gender Pay Gap,
2013 Edition," American Association of University
Women, www.aauw.org/files/2013/02/The-Simple-
Truth-2013.pdf.

15. For more, see Shierholz's presentation at a 2011
Institute for Women's Policy Research roundtable:
"Women and Jobs in the Great Recession and its
Aftermath," www.iwpr.org/roundtable-on-women-
and-economy-files/Shierholz%20IWPR%202011
.pdf.

16. Betsey Stevenson and Justin Wolfers, "The Paradox
of Declining Female Happiness," *American Economic
Journal: Economic Policy*, August 2009, Vol. 1, Issue
2. A working paper version is available through the
National Bureau of Economic Research, www.nber
.org/papers/w14969.

17. *Ibid.*

18. D'Vera Cohn, "Love and Marriage," Pew Research
Social & Demographic Trends, Feb. 13, 2013,
www.pewsocialtrends.org/2013/02/13/love-and-
marriage/.

19. D'Vera Cohn, "Marriage Rate Declines and
Marriage Age Rises," Pew Research Social &
Demographic Trends, Dec. 14, 2011, www.pewso
cialtrends.org/2011/12/14/marriage-rate-declines-
and-marriage-age-rises/.

20. Casey E. Copen, Kimberly Daniels and William D.
Mosher, "First Premarital Cohabitation in the
United States: 2006-2010, National Survey of
Family Growth," National Center for Health
Statistics, April 4, 2013, www.cdc.gov/nchs/data/
nhsr/nhsr064.pdf.

21. Wendy Wang, *et al.*, "Breadwinner Moms," Pew
Social & Demographic Trends, May 28, 2013, www
.pewsocialtrends.org/files/2013/05/Breadwinner_
moms_final.pdf.

22. "2012 Catalyst Census: Fortune 500 Women Executive
Officers and Top Earners," Dec. 11, 2012, www.cata
lyst.org/knowledge/2012-catalyst-census-fortune-
500-women-executive-officers-and-top-earners.

23. Sheryl Sandberg, "Why We Have Too Few
Women Leaders," TEDWomen, December 2010,

www.ted.com/talks/sheryl_sandberg_why_we_have_too_few_women_leaders.html.

24. The case study was conducted by Kathleen McGinn and Nicole Tempest, "Heidi Roizen, Harvard Business School, Case Study #9-800-228" (2009). As cited in Sandberg, p. 39.

25. Sandberg, *Lean In, op. cit.*, p. 39.

26. Madeline E. Heilman and Tyler G. Okimoto, "Why Are Women Penalized for Success at Male Tasks? The Implied Communality Deficit," *Journal of Applied Psychology*, 2007, Vol. 92, No. 1, pp. 81-92. See also L. A. Rudman "Self-promotion as a risk factor for women: The costs and benefits of counterstereotypical impression management," *Journal of Personality and Social Psychology*, 74, 1998, pp. 629-645; and L. A. Rudman, and P. Glick "Prescriptive gender stereotypes and backlash toward agentic women," *Journal of Social Issues*, 57, 2001, pp. 743-762.

27. Nancy M. Carter and Christine Silva, *The Myth of the Ideal Worker: Does Doing All the Right Things Really Get Women Ahead?* (2011), p. 2.

28. Linda Babcock and Sara Laschever, *Women Don't Ask: Negotiations and the Gender Divide* (2003).

29. "Interview with Linda Babcock and Sara Laschever," *The Woman's Connection*, www.youtube.com/watch?v=RcZn7zYGrp8.

30. Hanna Riley Bowles, Linda Babcock and Lei Lai, "Social incentives for gender differences in the propensity to initiate negotiations: Sometimes it does hurt to ask," *Organizational Behavior and Human Decision Processes*, 103, 2007, pp. 84-103.

31. Helen Mayson, "Ambition and Gender at Work," Institute of Leadership and Management, 2013, https://www.i-l-m.com/Insight/Inspire/2013/May/ambition-gender-key-findings.

32. Henna Inam, "Five Mindsets that Keep Women Ambivalent About Leading," www.transformleaders.tv/why-i-dont-want-to-be-1/.

33. Joanna Barsh and Lareina Yee, "Unlocking the Full Potential of Women at Work," McKinsey & Co., 2012.

34. Catherine Rampell, "Coveting Not a Corner Office, But Time At Home," *The New York Times*, July 7,

2013, www.nytimes.com/2013/07/08/business/coveting-not-a-corner-office-but-time-at-home.html.

35. See Jeremy Staff and Jeylan T. Mortimer, "Explaining the Motherhood Wage Penalty During the Early Occupational Career," *Demography*, Vol. 49, No. 1, February 2012, pp. 1-21.

36. For more, see Mary Blair-Loy, "Cultural Constructions of Family Schemas: The Case of Women Finance Executives," *Gender and Society*, Vol. 15, No. 5, October 2001, pp. 687-709.

37. Tara Siegel Bernard, "In Paid Family Leave, U.S. Trails Much of the Globe," *The New York Times*, Feb. 23, 2013, www.nytimes.com/2013/02/23/your-money/us-trails-much-of-the-world-in-providing-paid-family-leave.html.

38. "Rep. Miller on House Floor: "Extend FMLA Benefits to All Americans," Feb. 13, 2013, http://democrats.edworkforce.house.gov/blog/rep-miller-house-floor-extend-fmla-benefits-all-americans.

39. "Paid Family and Medical Leave: An Overview," National Partnership for Women & Families, April 2012, www.nationalpartnership.org/site/DocServer/PFML_Overview_FINAL.pdf?docID=7847.

40. Ariane Hegewisch and Janet C. Gornick, "The Impact of 'Family Friendly' Policies on Women's Employment Outcomes and the Costs and Benefits of Doing Business," World Bank, June 2010.

41. *Ibid.*

42. For background, see Sarah Glazer, "Social Welfare in Europe," *CQ Global Researcher*, Aug. 1, 2010, pp. 185-210.

43. Jennifer Ludden, "FMLA Not Really Working for Many Employees," NPR, Feb. 5, 2013, www.npr.org/2013/02/05/171078451/fmla-not-really-working-for-many-employees.

44. Francine D. Blau and Lawrence Kahn, "Female Labor Supply: Why is the U.S. Falling Behind?" *The American Economic Review*, American Economic Association, May 2013, p. 251.

45. For background, see Sarah Glazer, "Mothers' Movement," *CQ Researcher*, April 4, 2003, pp. 297-320.

46. Hegewisch and Gornick, *op. cit.*

47. Ankita Patnaik, "Merging Separate Spheres: The Role of Policy in Promoting Dual Earner, Dual Career Households," Working Paper, Social Science Research Network, http://papers.ssrn.com/sol3/papers.cfm?abstract_id=2179070.

48. "Conversations With History: Ruth Rosen," University of California, June 12, 2008, www.youtube.com/watch?v=Bw2Zf1XUPWY.

49. For background, see Sarah Glazer, "Women's Rights," *CQ Global Researcher*, April 3, 2012, pp. 153-180.

50. Cynthia E. Harrison, *On Account of Sex: The Politics of Women's Issues, 1945-1968* (1989), p. 120.

51. Georgia Duerst-Lahti, "The Government's Role in Building the Women's Movement," *Political Science Quarterly*, Vol. 104, No. 2, Summer 1989, pp. 249-268, 251.

52. Harrison, *op. cit.*, p. 122.

53. Union polls found that 85 percent of female union members planned to continue working after the war; Women's Bureau studies found that almost 80 percent of women working in the Detroit area and in Erie County, N.Y., hoped to keep their jobs (CIO News, July 30, 1945, clipping, in folder "S.1178," box H1, Wayne Morse papers, University of Oregon), as cited in Harrison, *op. cit.*

54. George H. Gallup, *The Gallup Poll: Public Opinion, 1935-1971* (1972), Vol. 1, p. 322. Also see Claudia Goldin, "The Female Labor Force and American Economic Growth," in Stanley L. Engerman and Robert E. Gallman, eds., *Long-Term Factors in American Economic Growth* (1986), www.nber.org/chapters/c9688.pdf.

55. Harrison, *op. cit.*, p. 51.

56. "Conversations With History: Ruth Rosen," *op. cit.*

57. Phyllis Richman, "Answering Harvard's Question About My Personal Life, 52 Years Later," *The Washington Post*, June 6, 2013, http://articles.washingtonpost.com/2013-06-06/opinions/39784052_1_graduate-school-letter-52-years.

58. The case is *Ledbetter v. Goodyear Tire & Rubber Co. Inc.*, 550 U.S. __ (May 29, 2007). For background, see Thomas J. Billitteri, "Gender Pay Gap," *CQ Researcher*, March 14, 2008, pp. 241-264.

59. Christianne Corbett and Catherine Hill, "Graduating to a Pay Gap: The Earnings of Men and Women One Year After Graduation," American Association of University Women, 2012, p. 21, www.aauw.org/files/2013/02/graduating-to-a-pay-gap-the-earnings-of-women-and-men-one-year-after-college-graduation.pdf.

60. Claudia Goldin and Lawrence F. Katz, "The Career Cost of Family," paper prepared for the Workplace Flexibility 2010 conference at the Georgetown School of Law, p. 11, http://workplaceflexibility.org/images/uploads/program_papers/goldin_formatted_12-12-10.pdf.

61. *Ibid.*, pp. 11-12.

62. For background, see Sarah Glazer, "Telecommuting," *CQ Researcher*, July 19, 2013, pp. 621-644.

63. Kim Parker and Wendy Wang, "Modern Parenthood: Roles of Moms and Dads Converge as They Balance Work and Family," Pew Research Social & Demographic Trends, March 14, 2013, www.pewsocialtrends.org/2013/03/14/modern-parenthood-roles-of-moms-and-dads-converge-as-they-balance-work-and-family/.

64. Ellen Galinsky, Kerstin Aumann and James T. Bond, "Times Are Changing: Gender and Generation at Work and Home," Families and Work Institute, 2009, http://familiesandwork.org/site/research/reports/Times_Are_Changing.pdf, as cited in "Our Working Nation in 2013," *op. cit.*

65. The Associated Press, "New Dads: Diaper Duty's Just the Start," NPR, June 12, 2013, www.npr.org/templates/story/story.php?storyId=191021263.

66. "Parents and the High Cost of Child Care," Child Care Aware of America, 2012, www.naccrra.org/sites/default/files/default_site_pages/2012/cost_report_2012_final_081012_0.pdf.

67. "The NICHD Study of Early Child Care and Youth Development," National Institute of Child Health and Human Development, National Institutes of Health, 2006, p. 11, https://www.nichd.nih.gov/publications/pubs/documents/seccyd_06.pdf.

68. Abby J. Cohen, "A Brief History of Federal Financing for Child Care in the United States," *Financing Child Care*, Vol. 6, No. 2, Summer/Fall 1996,

http://futureofchildren.org/publications/journals/article/index.xml?journalid=56&articleid=326&sectionid=2177.

69. Betty Friedan, *The Second Stage* (1981), p. 90.

70. Lyndsey Layton, "Paying for preschool with a $1 a pack cigarette tax," *The Washington Post*, April 10, 2013, http://articles.washingtonpost.com/2013-04-10/local/38434932_1_cigarette-tax-r-j-reynolds-tobacco.

71. Anne-Marie Slaughter, "Why Women Still Can't Have It All," *The Atlantic*, July 2012, www.theatlantic.com/magazine/archive/2012/07/why-women-still-cant-have-it-all/309020.

72. Melissa Stanger, "Number of Women Leaders Will Equal Men in 2085," *Business Insider*, Dec. 11, 2012, www.businessinsider.com/number-of-women-leaders-will-equal-men-in-2085-2012-11.

73. For example, see "The Bottom Line: Corporate Performance and Women's Representation on Boards," Catalyst, October 2007, http://catalyst.org/knowledge/bottom-line-corporate-performance-and-womens-representation-boards.

74. Jessica Valenti, "Sheryl Sandberg isn't the perfect feminist: So what?" *The Washington Post*, March 1, 2013, http://articles.washingtonpost.com/2013-03-01/opinions/37366536_1_sheryl-sandberg-jessica-valenti-vanity-project.

75. "Now Is Our Time," *Harvard Business Review*, April 2013, http://hbr.org/2013/04/now-is-our-time/ar/1.

76. Joan C. Williams and Rachel W. Dempsey, "The Rise of Executive Feminism," *Harvard Business Review blog*, March 28, 2013, http://blogs.hbr.org/cs/2013/03/the_rise_of_executive_feminism.html.

77. "Latino Workers and their Families Need Paid Sick Days," National Partnership for Women and Families, April 2013, www.nationalpartnership.org/site/DocServer/Latinos_and_Paid_Sick_Days_Fact_Sheet_English.pdf?docID=8544.

78. "Price Statement: H.R. 2339, the Family Income to Respond to Significant Transitions Act, and H.R. 2460, the Healthy Families Act," http://edworkforce.house.gov/news/documentsingle.aspx?DocumentID=173150.

79. Steven Greenhouse. "Bill Would Guarantee Up to 7 Paid Sick Days," *The New York Times*, May 15, 2009, www.nytimes.com/2009/05/16/health/policy/16sick.html?_r=0.

80. Michael Saltsman, "Mandatory Paid Leave: A Remedy Worse Than the Disease," Employment Policies Institute, April 2013, www.epionline.org/oped/mandatory-paid-leave-a-remedy-worse-than-the-disease/.

81. For more background, see www.nwlc.org/sites/default/files/pdfs/factorotherthan_sexfactsheet_5.29.12_final.pdf.

82. See entries for the House and Senate versions of the Paycheck Fairness Act on GovTrack.us: "Tracking the U.S. Congress": www.govtrack.us/congress/bills/113/s84 and www.govtrack.us/congress/bills/113/hr377.

83. "Gov. Shumlin signs into law equal pay legislation to eliminate pay inequity and create family-friendly workplaces," press release, May 14, 2013, http://governor.vermont.gov/newsroom-gov-peter-shumlin-signs-equal-pay-act.

84. "The 30 occupations with the largest projected employment growth, 2010-20," Bureau of Labor Statistics, U.S. Department of Labor, www.bls.gov/news.release/ecopro.t06.htm.

85. *Ibid.*

86. "Doing Without: Economic Security and Older Americans," Wider Opportunities for Women, No. 2: Gender, March 2012, www.wowonline.org/documents/OlderAmericansGenderbriefFINAL.pdf.

87. Linda J. Blumberg, Kevin Lucia and Sabrina Corlette, "The Affordable Care Act: Improving Incentives for Entrepreneurship and Self-Employment," The Urban Institute Health Policy Center, May 2013.

88. Lucy J. Reuben, "Make Room for the New 'She Eos': An Analysis of Businesses Owned by Black Females," The State of Black America 2008, In the Black Women's Voice, National Urban League, 2008, p. 118.

89. Data is based on a 2007 Census Bureau survey of business owners, the most current data available, www.latinamarketplace.com/index.php?node=316.

90. Rosin, *op. cit.*, pp. 139-140.

BIBLIOGRAPHY

Selected Sources

Books

Coontz, Stephanie, *A Strange Stirring: The Feminine Mystique and American Women at the Dawn of the 1960s*, Basic Books, 2011.
An historian interviews nearly 200 women on Betty Friedan's seminal 1963 work, *The Feminine Mystique*.

Friedan, Betty, *The Feminine Mystique*, W. W. Norton, 1963.
A groundbreaking feminist examines the dissatisfaction of U.S. housewives helping to fuel the modern women's movement.

Rosen, Ruth, *The World Split Open: How the Modern Women's Movement Changed America*, Penguin Books, 2000.
An historian documents the multiple threads of feminism from the early 1960s through the 1990s.

Rosin, Hanna, *The End of Men And the Rise of Women*, Riverhead Books, 2012.
A national correspondent for *The Atlantic* argues that women have surpassed men by almost every measure.

Sandberg, Sheryl, *Lean In: Women, Work, and the Will to Lead*, Alfred A. Knopf, 2013.
Facebook's chief operating officer has drawn both praise and scorn for questioning why so few women are leaders.

Articles

Burke, Daria, "What Lean In Means for Women of Color," *The Huffington Post*, April 25, 2013, www.huffingtonpost.com/daria-burke/what-lean-in-means-for-wo_b_3150201.html.
The founder and CEO of Black MBA Women reflects on Sheryl Sandberg's core messages in her book *Lean In*.

Cohn, Jonathan, "The Hell of American Day Care," *The New Republic*, April 15, 2013, www.newrepublic.com/article/112892/hell-american-day-care#.
An investigation finds a poorly regulated, expensive daycare system in the United States.

Gunn, Dwyer, "The Flex Time Ruse: Does Working Flexibly Harm Women?" *Slate*, March 28, 2013, www.slate.com/articles/double_x/doublex/2013/03/flex_time_is_not_the_answer.html.
A journalist writes that "family friendly" policies can have unintended consequences on women's long-term career prospects.

Slaughter, Anne-Marie, "Why Women Still Can't Have It All," *The Atlantic*, July 2012, www.theatlantic.com/magazine/archive/2012/07/why-women-still-cant-have-it-all/309020/.
A former high-ranking State Department official ignites a fierce debate about gender equality and women's choices.

Reports and Studies

"Fifty Years After the Equal Pay Act: Assessing the Past, Taking Stock of the Future," National Equal Pay Task Force, The White House, June 2013, www.whitehouse.gov/sites/default/files/image/image_file/equal_pay-task_force_progress_report_june_10_2013.pdf.
An Obama administration panel analyzes law, policy, economic trends and demographics since President Kennedy signed the Equal Pay Act in 1963.

Barsh, Joanna, and Lareina Lee, "Unlocking the Full Potential of Women At Work," McKinsey & Co., 2012, www.mckinsey.com/client_service/organization/latest_thinking/women_at_work.
An analysis of 60 large corporations reveals that for women to advance, top leadership must demonstrate a commitment to gender diversity in the workplace.

Beninger, Anna, and Nancy M. Carter, "The Great Debate: Flexibility vs. Face Time: Busting the Myths Behind Flexible Work Arrangements," Catalyst, July 8, 2013, www.catalyst.org/knowledge/great-debate-flexibility-vs-face-time-busting-myths-behind-flexible-work-arrangements.
A business think tank finds that flexible work arrangements help recruit and retain top talent, especially women.

Blau, Francine, and Lawrence Kahn, "Female Labor Supply: Why is the U.S. Falling Behind?" National Bureau of Economic Research, Working Paper No. 18702, January 2013, www.nber.org/papers/w18702.

Economists find that the expansion of "family-friendly" policies in other economically advanced countries explains nearly 30 percent of the decrease in U.S. women's labor force participation relative to the other nations.

Shriver, Maria, "The Shriver Report: A Woman's Nation Changes Everything," Center for American Progress, October 2009, www.americanprogress.org/issues/women/report/2009/10/16/6789/the-shriver-report/.
A journalist joins forces with a liberal think tank to examine the economic, social and health impacts of women as breadwinners.

Williams, Joan C., and Heather Boushey, "The Three Faces of Work-Family Conflict: The Poor, the Professionals, and the Missing Middle," Center for American Progress, January 2010, www.american progress.org/wp-content/uploads/issues/2010/01/pdf/threefaces.pdf.
The founding director of the Center for WorkLife at the University of California Hastings College of the Law (Williams) and the chief economist at the Center for American Progress examine the impact of policy on the largest segment of working American families.

For More Information

Catalyst, 120 Wall St., 15th Floor, New York, NY 10005; 212-514-7600; www.catalyst.org. A nonprofit organization that works to expand opportunities for women in business.

Center for Women and Work, Rutgers University School of Management and Labor Relations, 50 Labor Center Way, New Brunswick, NJ 08901-8553; http://smlr.rutgers.edu/smlr/CWW. Focuses on policy issues for women's advancement in the workplace.

Center for WorkLife Law, Hastings College of the Law, University of California, 200 McAllister St., San Francisco, CA 94102; 415-565-4640; www.worklifelaw.org. Focuses on workplace discrimination against women.

Concerned Women for America, 1015 15th St., N.W., Suite 1100, Washington, DC 20005; 202-488-7000; www.cwfa.org. A Christian women's organization focused on policy that supports traditional marriage and opposes abortion.

Eagle Forum, P.O. Box 618, Alton, IL 62002; 618-462-5415; www.eagleforum.org. A conservative organization that helped to defeat ratification of the Equal Rights Amendment and continues to oppose feminist causes.

Economic Policy Institute, 1333 H St., N.W., Washington, DC 20005-4707; 202-775-8810; www.epi.org. A nonprofit, nonpartisan think tank that focuses on economic policy for low- and middle-income workers.

Family Values at Work, 207 E. Buffalo St., Suite 211, Milwaukee, WI 53202; 414-431-0844; www.familyvaluesat work.org. A coalition of state groups that advocate mandatory paid sick leave.

Feminist Majority Foundation, 1600 Wilson Blvd., Suite 801, Arlington, VA 22209; 703-522-2214; www.feminist .org. Works to advance women's equality.

Institute for Women's Policy Research, 1200 18th St., N.W., Suite 301, Washington, DC 20036; 202-785-5100; www.iwpr.org. Conducts research on women, including pay equity, immigration and education.

LeanIn.org, P.O. Box 1452, Palo Alto, CA 94302-1452; leanin.org. A social network aimed at encouraging women to pursue their ambitions; created by Facebook COO Sheryl Sandberg.

Legal Momentum, 395 Hudson St., New York, NY 10014; 212-925-6635; legalmomentum.org. Focuses on workplace rights for women.

MomsRising, www.momsrising.org. An online community of more than 700 bloggers who focus on issues such as parental leave, flexible work and daycare.

National Partnership for Women and Families, 1875 Connecticut Ave., N.W., Suite 650, Washington, DC 20009; 202-986-2600; www.nationalpartnership.org. Advocates for family leave and other family-friendly policies.

6

Youth Unemployment

Alan Greenblatt

President Obama greets 18-year-old Christian Champagne at a White House ceremony to unveil his My Brother's Keeper initiative on Feb. 27, 2014. To be funded over five years by $200 million in foundation grants, the program will address problems facing black youths, including lack of school readiness and high unemployment. More than one in four African-Americans between ages 16 and 24 were unemployed in 2013.

From *CQ Researcher*, March 14, 2014.

Getty Images/Chip Somodevilla

Deanna Mullenax worked for four years at what she describes as "Chicago's first punk rock bakery," moving up from counter person to general manager of all four locations. Then the owners abruptly shut everything down.

For the next six months, Mullenax left 30 resumes per week with potential employers but couldn't get a bite. "It's unbelievable just how cut-throat it's become in the job world," says Mullenax, 24. "You get told 'no' so many times, you're like, I'm-going-to-volunteer-the-rest-of-my-life-and-go-live-with-my-parents." Finally she landed a job at another bakery.

Mullenax's experience last year highlights a serious problem. Dealing with unemployment rates persistently in the double digits since 2008, young people are not just struggling to find work but to start their lives as adults in general, delaying starting families and buying homes — or even renting. Nearly 30 percent of American adults under 35 are living with their parents, according to a recent Gallup survey.[1]

"If you don't have much financial security, you're not setting up your own household, getting married and having your own kids," says Daniel J. Mitchell, a senior fellow at the Cato Institute, a libertarian think tank.

Unemployment among youths 16-24 — which soared above 20 percent in 2010 and was at 14.4 percent in February — is not as dire as in countries such as Spain or Greece, where more than half of young people are out of work, but the situation is worse than it has been in decades.[2]

Experts say persistent youth unemployment can have broad, long-lasting economic, social and political effects, ranging from

Youth Unemployment Raises Tax Burdens

Residents of six mostly Southeastern states pay the highest levies per taxpayer due to unemployment among 18- to 34-year-olds. Residents in Kentucky, Alabama and North Carolina pay the most — more than $80 a year. The costs reflect foregone, or lost, federal and state income taxes and Social Security and Medicare revenue, along with welfare and unemployment insurance expenses.

Per-Taxpayer Cost of Unemployed 18- to 34-year-olds

Source: Rory O'Sullivan, Konrad Mugglestone and Tom Allison, "In This Together: The Hidden Cost of Young Adult Unemployment," Young Invincibles, January 2014, Table B.13, http://tinyurl.com/qjvw8gg

billions of dollars in lost wages and government income-tax revenues, to the delay of first-time home purchases and creation of a generation of risk-averse entrepreneurs and workers.

"What's actually happening with young people is they're not only dealing with the short-term impacts of unemployment, but it's hitting them at a time when it's really important for them to step into adulthood," says Tahir Duckett, national young-worker coordinator for the AFL-CIO, the nation's largest federation of labor unions. "That's actually holding the economy back in a major way," he says. "Not buying their first houses, living at home with their parents — that's a drag on the entire economy."

"The delay in reaching adulthood will have a lasting impact on U.S. society and the economy," said Maureen Conway, executive director of the Economic Opportunities Program at the Washington-based Aspen Institute, an education and policy-studies think tank.

"They are not out there making these typical, middle-class expenditures," she said. "That is a huge problem when you think of where demand is going."[3]

Instead, nearly 5.8 million of the nearly 40 million Americans ages 16 to 24 are "disconnected" — they're not in school and not working, says Russell Krumnow, managing director of Opportunity Nation, a coalition of groups concerned with youth unemployment. "That's 15 percent of that cohort totally on the sidelines" of the economy.

In the wake of the recent recession, a majority of middle-class Americans believes their children will not do better than they have, writes Joel Kotkin, an author and expert on urban trends at Chapman University, in Orange, Calif. Many are "as pessimistic about the future as are optimistic," he writes. With fewer young people able to afford a home, he continues, some experts have theorized that America's economy is shifting to a "rentership society," in which a small minority of wealthy Americans own all of the property and rent it to the lower classes. If such trends continue, he adds, it could lead to "the proletarianization of the American middle class."[4]

After previous recessions, it took a decade or more for young people's wages to catch up to where they otherwise would have been. Already, the so-called millennial generation — those born between 1978 and 2000 — will suffer $20 billion in lost wages over the next decade due to today's high unemployment, according to the Center for American Progress, a liberal think tank in Washington.[5]

"The best data we have shows the negative impact of starting out your career in an economy like this one," but those studies were done during a downturn not "nearly as bad as this one," says Heidi Shierholz, an economist at the Economic Policy Institute, a labor-backed think tank in Washington. "If anything, it's probably going to be worse for this cohort."

Even college graduates are struggling to find jobs commensurate with their education levels — although unemployment is far worse for people without college degrees and minorities.

Young people with low-income backgrounds or who spent time in jail face especially high barriers to employment.

In February, President Obama held a White House press conference to announce a federal task force that will address the problems of black male youths. Known as My Brother's Keeper, the program has garnered pledges of more than $200 million from various foundations over the next five years to address issues that keep young black men from succeeding, such as poor schooling, lack of mentors and encounters with the criminal justice system.[6]

Even kids who appear to have every advantage are struggling to find meaningful, well-paying work. The experience of so many young people being unemployed is making millennials more risk-averse — and therefore less likely to start new businesses that would create future jobs.

"Startup businesses create 3 million jobs a year," says Timothy Kane, an economist and research fellow at the Hoover Institution, a conservative think tank at Stanford University. "If that number starts to decline, that's where you're really seeing just an absence of opportunities for people to get started."

And the job losses may not be temporary, according to economist Tyler Cowen in his 2013 book *Average Is Over*. While the 2007-2009 financial crash was a "very bad" one-time event, he writes, it revealed in stark terms fundamental shifts in the economy — including greater competition from abroad and increasingly advanced technology — signaling that many middle-class jobs will not be coming back.[7]

In her 2013 book *End of the Good Life*, which charts the effects of the financial crisis on her generation, 29-year-old Dow Jones reporter Riva Froymovich says the millennials should expect lower wages and less job

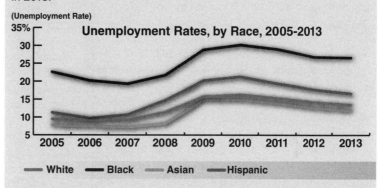

Youth Unemployment Hits Minorities Hardest

Unemployment rates rose for young people (ages 16-24) between 2005 and 2013, with African-Americans and Hispanics hit the hardest during the 2007-09 recession. Joblessness nearly doubled between 2007 and 2010 for Hispanics and soared to more than 30 percent for African-Americans. Although rates have fallen since then, more than one in four African-Americans between 16 and 24 were unemployed in 2013.

(Unemployment Rate)

Unemployment Rates, by Race, 2005-2013

White — Black — Asian — Hispanic

Source: "Labor Force Statistics from the Current Population Survey," U.S. Department of Labor, Bureau of Labor Statistics, www.bls.gov/cps/data.htm

security than their peers in China or Brazil, while coping with a higher cost of living.[8]

Meanwhile, the number of 20- to 24-year-olds working part time because they can't find full-time work has more than doubled in the past decade.[9] Young people now are competing not only with their peers but often against experienced older workers who are eager for any job they can get in a weak market. Thus, during the recession and its aftermath, "you get this really pretty stunning decline in earnings and labor force participation for young people," says Anthony Carnevale, director of the Center on Education and the Workforce at Georgetown University.

Part of high youth unemployment can be traced to government workforce cutbacks demanded by budget-cutting state and federal lawmakers. The Army, for instance, which has traditionally provided entry-level jobs and training to youths from economically challenged towns, is planning to shrink its active-duty force to the smallest size since 1940 as it winds down from the war in Afghanistan. Meanwhile, high youth unemployment is costing federal and state governments $25 billion annually in foregone, or lost, tax revenues and increased government spending on social safety net programs, according to the youth-advocacy group Young Invincibles.

A potential silver lining is that many young people who could not find jobs have been "sheltering" in school, receiving more education and presumably the skills to take on more demanding jobs. Recent Census Bureau data show that the number of adults who completed at least some graduate school increased by nearly 25 percent between 2008 and 2013 — from 29 million to 36 million — more than the 30 million people who completed a bachelor's degree during that period.[10]

"We are the most educated group of 20-somethings in history," Froymovich writes.[11]

However, Kane, the Hoover economist, warns that the country might be experiencing an "education bubble," with too many people starting college but not gaining marketable skills — or even a degree. "Right now, every year, too many kids are dropping out of college with a lot of debt, no work experience and no degree," he says. Still, most politicians emphasize the need for young adults to attain more education and training, with employers demanding higher skill levels — which vary widely by occupation, but generally involve more technology and communication ability than was true a decade or two ago.

"In order to have middle-income, middle-paying jobs — the kinds of jobs that allow people to get ahead — you have to have [a] higher level of training and skill acquisition and education than ever before," Florida Republican Sen. Marco Rubio said last month on the "PBS NewsHour." "We have too many people that don't have those skills. And, in fact, the people who would most benefit from acquiring those skills are the ones least likely to get it because of its cost or because of the way the system is structured."[12]

All that extra education is expensive, however. Overall student debt is at a record high. And, while college graduates continue to have lower unemployment rates than their less-educated peers, a degree is no guarantee of a job. The number of college graduates working for minimum wage, or less, has more than doubled in the past five years.

As policymakers ponder ways of putting more young people to work, here are some of the questions they are debating:

Is high youth unemployment here to stay?

Youth unemployment has been running about double the overall national rate since the recent recession. But then, it nearly always does. "Youth unemployment is almost entirely a product of high unemployment in general," says Hoover's Kane.

Sarah Ayres, a policy analyst at the Center for American Progress, agrees. "Young people have always had a harder time in the workforce than older people," she says. "It's a much tougher prospect now because there just aren't enough jobs to go around."

In other words, the current high unemployment numbers for youths may just be symptomatic of what's been happening in the economy as a whole. And much of the recent drop in the unemployment rate has come not because people are securing jobs, but because many are simply giving up and leaving the workforce, according to census data.

Young people would be able to find jobs — if only there were more jobs to find, suggests Catherine Ruetschlin, a policy analyst with Demos, a liberal think tank in New York City. She notes that about half the jobs created over the past year are in low-wage sectors that are most likely to hire young people, namely, leisure and hospitality, retail and health and education services.

Nothing is "independently attacking young workers," says the Economic Policy Institute's Shierholz. "Young workers have high unemployment relative to older workers right now, but they always do."

Still, deeper changes may be happening in entry-level employment that will continue to affect young people's chances after the current economic cycle has run its course, Georgetown's Carnevale suggests. Many more jobs now require some form of postsecondary education, just to get hired, he says. "The requirements have gone up," he says. "The whole business of getting on the job track has become harder."

There are all kinds of skills that people learn on the job that aren't taught in classrooms, says Kane — including the basics, such as showing up on time and communicating well with co-workers. It's a buyer's market, and many employers would rather not bother hiring people who are green.

"I'll hire someone who's 27, and he's fine," a car rental manager told economics writer Megan McArdle. "But if

I hire someone who's 23 or 24, they need everything spelled out for them, they want me to hover over their shoulder."[13]

There's little expectation that workers will stay with a company throughout their careers, or even for a significant number of years, so employers don't want to spend money training people who might then take their skills elsewhere. "They don't want to make the investment and lose it," says Arne Kalleberg, a sociologist at the University of North Carolina-Chapel Hill who studies employment issues. A major structural change is that "employers are increasingly reluctant to train people. The job ladders we were used to seeing in the first 30 years after World War II are largely gone."

All of this creates ripple effects. Older workers are taking better-paying jobs, meaning more college graduates are working for minimum wage. That's crowding out people with less education. The share of people ages 25 to 32 with only a high school diploma who are living in poverty has grown from 7 percent in 1979 to 22 percent today.[14]

"You have 45-year-olds taking jobs that maybe in the past would have gone to young people, because they're out of work and desperate for income," says Krumnow, of Opportunity Nation. "We're still in the hole multiple millions of jobs from the Great Recession," he says. "As that cascades down, it's going to hit young people the hardest."

Ruetschlin agrees that in a tough job market there is some advantage to being older and more experienced. "The folks [young people] are competing against may have had more of a chance to work in the sector," she says. "It really is just an easier weeding-out process for human resources departments that are flooded by applicants."

> **"There's a huge, underlying structural problem in terms of preparing youths, in particular male youths and male youths of color, for jobs. It has always been bad, but it's worse now."**
>
> — *Betsy Brand,*
> *Executive Director, American Youth Policy Forum*

"There's a huge, underlying structural problem in terms of preparing youths, in particular male youths and male youths of color, for jobs," says Betsy Brand, executive director of the American Youth Policy Forum, a nonprofit group that advocates policies that improve outcomes for youth. "It has always been bad, but it's worse now."

That may be a greater challenge for young people "in communities where there are no jobs, especially inner-city minority communities," Carnevale says. The problems are compounded for those who haven't completed high school, let alone attained a college degree or who have been incarcerated.

Can government do more to put young people to work?

The problem of youth unemployment — along with joblessness in general — is a high priority among policymakers in Washington and around the country.

In February, President Obama directed Vice President Joseph Biden to oversee an overhaul of the plethora of federal job training programs. "The first thing is, let's create more jobs," Obama said in a Jan. 30 speech on the economy in Wisconsin. "Number two, we've got to train Americans with the skills to fill those jobs."[15]

Not everyone is convinced that the government should be in the business of providing job training in the first place. Job training programs — which tend to offer instruction in specific sets of skills, such as dental work or manufacturing — sound great in theory, says Kane, the Hoover economist, but have a poor track record of moving people into permanent employment.

A 2011 Government Accountability Office (GAO) study found that, as of 2009, the federal government ran 47 workforce training programs, administered by nine agencies, at an annual cost of $18 billion.[16] Little is known, however, about their effectiveness, because only five had measured their results in terms of placing people in jobs, the report said.

"In 2012, [Republican] Sen. Tom Coburn's office examined workforce training in Oklahoma and found that Job Corps [a longstanding youth training program] spends $76,000 per participant to place youth in jobs that are often minimum wage and don't

Young and Hopeful

Young job-seekers attend a job fair in Denver sponsored by Urban Peak, a nonprofit group serving homeless youths (top). Hundreds of job-seekers turn out for a job fair at City College of San Francisco, sponsored by the Southeast Community Facility Commission (bottom). As part of his effort to boost youth employment, President Obama, in his State of the Union address in January, called for "more apprenticeships that set a young worker on an upward trajectory for life."

require training," *The Wall Street Journal* noted in February. "Culinary students have been put to work as funeral attendants, tour guides, baggage porters and telemarketers."[17]

Last year, the House approved a bill that would streamline 35 sometimes overlapping job training programs, essentially turning them into state block grants. The Senate Committee on Health, Education, Labor & Pensions passed a different version of the legislation in July that would address the issue differently, but it has yet to be called up for floor action.

There's still a role for government in preparing workers, especially with employers generally not offering on-the-job training, says the University of North Carolina's Kalleberg, author of the 2011 book *Good Jobs, Bad Jobs.*

Like many observers, Kalleberg is encouraged by the growth of public-private partnerships in which employers join with community colleges and other government entities to train young people with real-world skills for jobs available in their communities. "Vocational education has always been looked down upon as a lower-status thing than a four-year degree," he says. "That's the gap we need to fill, and government needs to provide opportunities."

Aside from job training, there's a debate about whether government spending could help ease unemployment by spending more money on, for example, infrastructure improvements and expanding the economy. But federal agencies have experienced a de facto hiring freeze for the past three years, and federal employment is down by nearly 90,000 positions over the past year.[18] Similarly, state and local governments have shed 500,000 jobs since the beginning of the recession in 2007.[19]

Young workers have become "collateral damage of the deficit hawks' single-minded focus on debt," says Duckett of the AFL-CIO. "Most of the job losses that have happened over the past four years are government jobs that are being shed" due to government cutbacks aimed at controlling the national debt.

Under the Pentagon's current budget proposal, the ranks of the active-duty Army would be reduced to as low as 450,000 troops — from a high of 570,000 during the Iraq and Afghanistan wars.[20] That eliminates a potential avenue for many young people, particularly those in rural areas who have looked to the military as an employer of last resort.

Michael Strain, an economist at the American Enterprise Institute, a conservative think tank in Washington, contends that rather than having the government create jobs, it should subsidize employment for the young by giving tax credits to companies that hire young people.

"We want to make it easier for firms to be hiring young people. That's a major challenge," he says, and federal money could help. "We should be thinking about wage subsidies or earned-income tax credit expansions," Strain says. "That will draw more people into jobs, into the labor force, and will make some of these jobs that don't pay much more appealing."

Mitchell, of the Cato Institute, rejects the idea that government should take an active role in boosting employment. The best way for government to create jobs, he says, is simply to get out of the way. Like the Hoover Institution's Kane, he worries that government mandates — such as minimum wage requirements and health benefit mandates under the Affordable Care Act — are making the cost of hiring new workers prohibitive in many cases.

But policymakers in both parties seem wedded to the idea of helping young people prepare for the contemporary — and future — work force. Democrats like the idea of using government programs to help address training needs. Republicans favor education in general, believing that it calls on individuals to take responsibility for self-improvement, rather than relying on outside aid.

"Preparing people with skills for the 21st century is something both parties want to own," says Krumnow, of Opportunity Nation.

Will high youth unemployment have a lasting effect on society?

James Roy, 26, has spent the past six years trying to pay off $14,000 in student debt. He's bounced from job to job and is now working at a coffee shop in a Chicago suburb.

"It seems to me that if you went to college and took on student debt, there used to be greater assurance that you could pay it off with a good job," he said. "But now, for people living in this economy and our age group, it's a rough deal."[21]

Roy may take a long time getting on his feet. A recent study by the Federal Reserve Bank of Boston found that workers who are unemployed for various lengths of time earn substantially lower wages for nearly 20 years. After 10 years, those who were out of work for less than six

More Young Adults Live with Parents

The number of 18- to 24-year-olds living at home rose 10 percent over the past five years. Experts say the increase is due at least in part to limited job opportunities and increased college enrollment.

Percent of 18- to 24-year-olds Living at Home

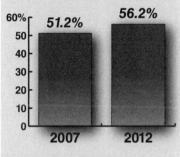

Source: "A Rising Share of Young Adults Live in Their Parents' Home," Pew Research Center, Aug. 1, 2013, p. 4, http://bit.ly/1dYeG7m

months earn 9 percent less than those who have been at work continuously. And workers who were out of work for more than six months still earned wages that were 32 percent less.[22]

"The cohort as a whole is worse off, and those significant scarring effects last a very long time — one to two decades," says Shierholz, of the Economic Policy Institute.

Already, it's taking young workers several more years before they earn the national median wage (they reach it at age 30 now, compared to age 26 back in 1980).[23] The fact that young people spend years earning less money is having a broad impact.

Retailers that cater to teens are seeing a big drop in spending.[24] Adults in their 20s are less likely to live on their own, get married and start families. A Gallup survey released in February found that 14 percent of adults between the ages of 24 and 34 — "those in the post-college years, when most young adults are trying to establish independence" — are living at home with their parents.[25]

One economic problem compounds another. With student debt having tripled over the past decade to $1 trillion, some analysts believe it is hampering home sales to first-time buyers. "It's going to have an extraordinary dampening effect on young peoples' ability to borrow for a home, and that's going to impact the housing market and the economy at large," said David H. Stevens, chief executive of the Mortgage Bankers Association.[26]

Wealth among younger families is still down considerably from pre-recession levels, with housing being a major cause, according to the St. Louis Federal Reserve. "The homeownership rate among younger families has plunged, reflecting [foreclosures and] delayed entry into homeownership among newly formed households," write researchers William R. Emmons and Bryan J. Noeth. "The house-price gains that have helped many older families to rebuild homeowners' equity have been overshadowed among younger families by the ongoing retreat from homeownership."[27]

AP Photo/Detroit News/John M. Galloway

Real estate agent Courtney Dunford, center, shows a home to first-time buyers Matthew Slate and Catherine Feltner in Waterford, Mich., on May 11, 2013. With unemployment high among young Americans, many are unable to buy a home, or even to rent. Nearly 30 percent of American adults under age 35 are living with their parents, according to a recent Gallup Poll.

In addition to not buying homes, young people also are moving less. From the 1980s to the 2000s, the percentage of people 18 to 24 who moved across state lines dropped by 41 percent — a sign of diminished economic opportunity, since jobs are the primary reason people move.[28]

In general, today's young people are apt to be risk-averse, says Neil Howe, founder and president of LifeCourse Associates, a consulting firm that studies generational trends. "We definitely see evidence that entrepreneurship has ebbed among millennials," he says.

Not all aspects of the trend are bad, he says, noting that all manner of youth risk indicators are down, including violent crime, alcohol use and teen pregnancy.

However, some question whether the economic and cultural effects of high youth unemployment will be lasting. "We don't know what this generation of folks is going to look like 10 years from now," the AFL-CIO's Duckett says.

Others see the impact of high youth unemployment as the result of longstanding trends — and not just due to the 2007-09 recession. The development of a "new life stage" for young adults from about 18 to 29 years of age has been happening for decades, says Jeffrey Arnett, a psychologist at Clark University, in Worcester, Mass., who has written several books and articles about what he calls "emerging adulthood."

The age at which people get married or buy their first home has been ticking steadily upward over the past 20 years or more, he says. "People are not adolescents any more, but they're not really settled into a stable adulthood" either, he says. For example, Pew Research Center data indicate that 13 percent of 25- to 32-year-olds — called Generation Xers — were living at home in 1995, while 12 percent of late baby boomers in that age range lived with their folks in 1986.[29]

"I don't want to dismiss the effects of this recession — it was a severe one," Arnett says. "It is more difficult for young people, no doubt. But we just don't know how that's going to influence their economic lives, or any other aspect of their lives, 20, 30 or 40 years from now."

BACKGROUND

Early Youth Labor

Children have always worked, from the earliest days of hunting and gathering and animal tending. Later, medieval guilds employed children, with boys indentured to masters to learn trades, while girls learned domestic skills.[30]

In colonial times, child labor was valued as a way of teaching hard work and frugality.[31] A Virginia statute of 1646 commended England's "laudable custom" of binding out children for work "for the better educating of youth in honest and profitable trades . . . and also to avoid sloth and idleness wherewith such young children are easily corrupted."[32]

But attitudes began to change during the 19th and 20th centuries, as education became compulsory for all children. Based partly on humanitarian concerns — but also motivated by the competition from cheap child labor — workingmen's associations began pushing for free and compulsory education for children.[33] In 1892, the Democratic Party adopted as part of its platform a plank calling for the prohibition of "employment in factories of children under 15 years of age."[34] According to the 1900 census, however, 1.8 million children between the ages of 10 and 15 were still working.[35]

As the 20th century dawned, employers needed workers with more education and greater skills. By 1912, 38 states had adopted child labor laws, limiting hours for children or the age at which they could start working.[36] The Fair Labor Standards Act in 1938 established nationwide restrictions on children working before age 16.

Meanwhile, by the 1930s children were required to stay in school, on average, until age 16 — up from 14 in 1900.[37] By 1940, more than half of 18-year-olds completed high school — an increase from less than 10 percent in 1900.[38]

While teenage work in the past had been largely the province of the lower classes, after World War II wealthier teens began buying cars and wanted money to buy gas, meals and consumer goods. Youngsters working and attending school at the same time — previously unheard of and still a rarity in other countries — became the norm in the United States. By 1980, 44 percent of 16- and 17-year-old boys both worked and went to school, and 41 percent of girls. In 1947, those numbers had been 27 percent for boys and 21 percent for girls.[39]

The teenagers helped fill a growing number of retail and other service-sector jobs that required odd hours. And what may have been bad for adults — part-time work at odd hours — was often a good fit for youths.

As work became common for adolescents, an opportunity gap began to open among racial groups. During the 1940s and '50s, the unemployment rate for black and white kids was roughly the same.[40] By the mid-1960s, however, the jobless rate for African-American youths was 1.5 times that of whites. By the mid-1970s, it was up to three times as high.[41] While the unemployment rate for young white males remained at between 10 and 15 percent from 1955 to 1978, for nonwhite males it ranged between 16 and 31 percent.[42]

Policymakers began viewing youth unemployment primarily through the lens of helping poor and minority communities.

"Employment opportunities play a major role in determining whether [civil] rights are meaningful," President John F. Kennedy wrote in a 1963 message to Congress. "There is little value in a Negro's obtaining the right to be admitted to hotels and restaurants if he has no cash in his pocket and no job."[43]

Job Corps

In 1964, Congress created the Job Corps, which offers free education and training aimed at helping low-income youths earn a high school diploma and find jobs.

Job Corps is still around, but many other training programs have come and gone. In 1977, Congress passed the Youth Employment and Demonstration Projects Act, which funded four major new programs aimed primarily at helping low-income minorities transition from school to work.

These programs served 750,000 youths, but they proved to be short-lived, due to their mixed results.[44] The programs could keep young people working as long as they were heavily subsidized by the government, but had little success transitioning them into permanent, private-sector employment.

President Ronald Reagan, who took office in 1981, was skeptical about federal job programs. In his first budget, he proposed eliminating funding for public service jobs under the Comprehensive Employment and Training Act.[45] That law, known as CETA and first passed in 1973, had been revised eight times during its short existence, but moving young people out of subsidized employment into private-sector jobs proved continually elusive.

In 1982, CETA was replaced by the Job Training Partnership Act (JTPA), which sought to put people to work through private investments. A variety of local business-school partnerships were formed during this period — with schools promising to make high school graduates employable and companies pledging to hire them — but these were largely ad hoc affairs and not always successful. As with other federal job training programs, the JTPA compiled a mixed track record in terms of not just training young people but launching them into careers in which they stayed employed.

In 1983, just 45 percent of black men who were 16 to 21 years old and out of school were working, compared with 73 percent of whites.[46] A National Bureau of Economic Research study of black youth unemployment in 1986 said: "One of the more depressing results of the study is our finding that youths whose families received assistance from major public programs for disadvantaged families did worse in the job market."[47]

The problems with job training programs over the years have varied, but they tend to have several flaws in common. Often, they are not well designed to train workers with the skills they need, or they suffer from some mismatch between the skills that are taught and the needs of local employers. Critics of the programs, in fact, say that they do a poor job of identifying skills gaps that the marketplace is not already addressing.

CETA programs were generally less concerned with job training and more with creating work, such as community

CHRONOLOGY

1970s-1980s *Federal job training programs fail to produce permanently employed workers, prompting policymakers to try new approaches.*

1973 Comprehensive Employment and Training Act (CETA) provides summer jobs for low-income high school students and short-term fulltime jobs at public agencies and nonprofits for the long-term unemployed.

1977 Youth Employment and Demonstration Projects Act provides $1 billion annually for job training programs to serve 750,000 youths, primarily low-income minorities.

1980 Seeking extra money, teenagers begin working in large numbers: 44 percent of boys and 41 percent of girls in school are working, up from 27 percent and 17 percent, respectively, in 1947. Number of employed black male teens has dropped to 30 percent, from more than 40 percent in the 1960s.

1981 President Ronald Reagan proposes eliminating funding for public service jobs under CETA.

1982 Job Training Partnership Act reduces funding for employment and training programs and turns much of the responsibility over to states.

1984 National Urban League finds that the unemployment rate for those 16 to 24 is more than triple that for those 25 or older.

1989 Funding for worker education and job training programs falls from $33 billion to $28 billion during the Reagan presidency.

1990s-2000s *As the baby boom generation is absorbed into the workforce, policymakers shift attention from unemployed youth to college and career readiness.*

1993 President Bill Clinton creates AmeriCorps, which gives stipends and scholarships to youths who do community service work.

1994 School-to-Work Opportunities Act creates apprenticeships for high school graduates who have not completed college.

1998 Workforce Investment Act encourages business participation in workforce development programs.

2006 Congress reauthorizes main career and technical education law, focusing more on vocational students' academic achievement.

2009 American Recovery and Reinvestment Act provides $1.2 billion for employment and training of low-income youths and allows 21- to 24-year-olds to take summer jobs. . . . President Obama unveils $12 billion American Graduation Initiative, meant to boost community college funding and increase graduation rates; little of it is ever funded.

2010s *Interest grows in vocational training as postrecession, high youth unemployment lingers.*

2010 Congress passes a law offering a tax credit and payroll tax exemptions to small businesses that hire unemployed workers. . . . White House forecasts that over the next decade, 80 percent of new jobs will require higher education or workplace training.

2012 White House announces Summer Jobs+, aiming to help 180,000 teens and young adults get jobs using a streamlined database and employers' pledges. . . . A partnership among Chicago, Philadelphia and San Francisco intends to create 110,000 summer jobs and internships for low-income youths.

2013 House passes bill to streamline 35 duplicative federal job training programs, mostly by transforming them into state grants. Senate committee passes a related bill, but it goes nowhere.

2014 Obama asks Vice President Joseph Biden to lead an overhaul of federal job training programs (Jan. 28). . . . Republican Tennessee Gov. Bill Haslam proposes offering two years of free community college or technical training for all new students (Feb. 4). . . . Obama announces $750 million in donations from private companies to improve classroom technology (Feb. 3). . . . Obama announces a $200 million, five-year initiative called My Brother's Keeper to help black youths (Feb. 27).

cleanup programs. They weren't structured to lift people to the next level of skills. JTPA programs often sought to get results quickly and so placed the most capable people in jobs, without offering as much training as promised to those with less ability or education.

"There needed to be a much fuller, creative approach," says Dorothy Stoneman, founder and CEO of the Somerville, Mass.-based YouthBuild USA, which puts young people to work building homes — while offering them academic instruction — in nearly every state.

School-to-Work

Once the baby boom generation (born between 1946 and 1964) had largely been absorbed into the workforce, policymakers shifted their concerns away from high youth unemployment to the broader issue of how best to prepare all youths for careers.[48]

In 1993, President Bill Clinton created AmeriCorps, a program that offered a stipend and scholarships to young people who spent a year doing community service work. The following year, he signed the School-to-Work Opportunities Act, which sought to place young people who hadn't finished college into career apprenticeships.

However, unemployment rates remained high among minority youths who did not attend college. In his autobiography, Clinton says that the national unemployment rate of 6.5 percent in 1994 was "misleading." Unemployment for college graduates was only 3.5 percent, he noted, but more than 5 percent for people with more than two years of college but not a degree, over 7 percent for high school graduates and more than 11 percent for high school dropouts.[49]

In 1998, Congress passed the Workplace Investment Act, which offered not just job placement but a variety of elements aimed at helping young people succeed, including tutoring, occupational skills training, adult mentoring and a minimum of 12 months of follow-up with individuals.

Still, with the economy booming throughout the 1990s, youth unemployment faded as an area of policy concern.

That changed after the recession struck the economy in 2007 and went into overdrive in 2008. The federal stimulus package enacted in 2009 included $1.2 billion for employment and training of low-income youths, with preference that they be hired that summer. By November 2009, states had placed 314,000 young people in summer jobs, at a cost of $717 million.[50]

CURRENT SITUATION

My Brother's Keeper

On Feb. 27, President Obama announced an initiative to address problems facing black male youths. Known as My Brother's Keeper, the program has garnered pledges of $200 million over the next five years from a variety of foundations. Along with business leaders and others, the foundations will seek solutions for issues such as early childhood development, school readiness, educational opportunity and the criminal justice system.

At a White House event, Obama called the challenge of creating success among young black males a "moral issue for our country," noting that they are more likely than other groups to be illiterate or suspended from school — and were almost certain to encounter the criminal justice system, whether as victim or suspect.

"This is not a one-year proposition," Obama said. "It's not a two-year proposition. It's going to take time. We're dealing with complicated issues that run deep in our history, run deep in our society and are entrenched in our minds."[51]

Of more than 2,500 school-based arrests in Chicago during a six-month period in 2011 and 2012, 75 percent of the arrests involved black students. Nationwide, black youths represent 16 percent of the youth population, but they account for 28 percent of juvenile arrests and 37 percent of the detained population.[52]

"This is one of the issues that we as a country are going to have to tackle head-on," says Ruetschlin, the Demos policy analyst. "We're going to have to admit that there's a problem with lack of opportunities for non-white workers."

That presents a problem for society as a whole, since young, non-whites are a growing share of the potential workforce. Whites will no longer make up a majority of the U.S. population by 2042, according to the Census Bureau. Minorities already represent a majority of newborns.[53]

"We have seen no gains in the post-civil rights era," Ruetschlin says. "African-American unemployment is consistently double that for white workers."

Apprenticeships Are Spreading Beyond the Skilled Trades

Popular in Europe, the practice has been "undervalued and underutilized" here.

Jack Dorsey and Jim McKelvey wanted to launch a company that enables businesses to process credit card payments from mobile devices. But they found that their hometown of St. Louis lacked enough people with the right programming skills. So they started Square, which is now a multibillion-dollar enterprise, in San Francisco instead.

Still, the entrepreneurs wanted to do something to improve the economy at home, so they formed an apprentice program to match young people without computer science degrees with experienced programmers at St. Louis companies, including Enterprise Rent-A-Car, Monsanto and Panera, the bakery and restaurant chain.

"To be in the position where you have the job but you don't have the degree, it's once in a lifetime," said Terrence Bowen, who was placed as an apprentice program developer at Clearent, a credit card payment-processing company. "In spite of knowing how much I didn't know, Clearent still took me on because they saw potential."[1]

The idea came to McKelvey because he had once apprenticed as a glass blower (even though he found a career in business ultimately more profitable). Apprenticeships, or paid worker training, traditionally have been associated with skilled trades in manufacturing and construction and are far more prevalent in Europe. But the idea of matching young people with companies where they can gain experience — and often course credit — is hot right now, spreading into many more occupations such as financial services, food preparation and health care.

In his State of the Union address in January, President Obama called for "more apprenticeships that set a young worker on an upward trajectory for life." In subsequent speeches, he said the nation should move away from "train and pray" programs that don't necessarily lead to employment. "What we need to do is look at where are the jobs and take a job-driven approach to training," he said at a General Electric facility in Wisconsin.[2] Governors have been touting the idea as well.

Apprenticeships provide employers with relatively low-cost labor, since apprentices typically make 50 to 60 percent of the wages they'll earn after mastering a skill, according to Sarah Ayres, a policy analyst with the Center for American Progress, a liberal think tank. Apprenticeships can run from one to six years, but the average length of a registered apprentice program is four years.[3]

Apprentices go on to earn good salaries, she says, without having taken on the heavy burden of debt often associated with four-year college degrees. A 2012 study by Mathematica Policy Research, a Princeton social policy research firm, found that people who complete apprentice programs registered with the Department of Labor earn an average of $240,037 more over the course of their careers than those from similar backgrounds who didn't participate in such programs.[4]

"Clearly, apprenticeships are a win-win: They provide workers with sturdy rungs on that ladder of opportunity and employers with the skilled workers they need to grow their businesses," wrote Labor Secretary Thomas E. Perez. "And yet in America, they've traditionally been an

Shierholz, the Economic Policy Institute economist, says disparate effects can be seen even when there is no deliberate discrimination. Minorities tend to live in communities where less opportunity is available, and generations of poverty have made the chance to get ahead through personal and professional networks less likely.

"At a time when jobs are scarce, your job-finding networks can be even more important," Shierholz says.

"Minorities have less access to fruitful job-finding success, which matters at a time when jobs are so weak."

Even in areas where more positive outcomes are available for African-American and Hispanic youths, they often meet with less success than whites. In 11 states, not a single African-American took the Advanced Placement (AP) exam in computer science last year. The same was true for Hispanics in eight states. That means

undervalued and underutilized tool in our nation's workforce development arsenal."[5]

There were only 330,578 registered apprentices in the United States last year — less than 40 percent as many as in Great Britain, which has a population one-fifth the size. By contrast, more than half of young people ages 15 to 19 prepare for future work through apprenticeships in European countries such as Norway, Germany, Switzerland and Austria.[6] (In the United States, most formal apprenticeships don't start until people are in their 20s and typically have no connection to high school vocational programs.)

The United States will never have apprentice programs on the scale of those countries, says Anthony Carnevale, director of the Georgetown University Center on Education and the Workforce. "In the American case, we don't have a European system where workforce development is jointly run by employers, schools, unions and government," Carnevale says. "Without that, we're not going to have [large-scale] apprenticeships."

In fact, the number of apprenticeships in the United States has been trending down since the 1950s, he says, dropping by a third over the past decade.

"The Europeans do it and it's very powerful, with 60 or 70 percent of the kids leaving high school with job skills," Carnevale says. "People see that and say, 'My God, this really works,' and promote it here, but nothing ever happens."

He notes that President Bill Clinton promoted the idea during the 1990s — he called it "school-to-work" — but nothing much came of it because the interests of all the parties involved — educators, employers, labor unions and the government — didn't always line up.

Ayres suggests that rather than seeking to overhaul the education system, as Clinton was trying to do, building demand among businesses is the way to go. Once individual businesses get involved, she says, they love the idea.

"For years, businesses have been saying they can't find workers with the skills to fit their jobs," Ayres says. "We think

Experienced programmers at several companies in St. Louis, including Panera, participate in an apprenticeship program to help young people without computer science degrees.

this is a good way to provide businesses with good workers, while providing workers with long-term, good-paying careers."

— Alan Greenblatt

[1]Lindsay Toler, "Launch Code: How 42 'Unqualified' People Landed Dream Tech Jobs in St. Louis," *Riverfront Times*, Jan. 2, 2014, http://tinyurl.com/ludmnkr.

[2]"Remarks by the President on Opportunity for All and Skills for America's Workers," Jan. 30, 2014, http://tinyurl.com/lxkxowb.

[3]"Registered Apprenticeship," Employment and Training Administration, U.S. Department of Labor, http://tinyurl.com/pffmqz3.

[4]Debbie Reed, *et al.*, "An Effectiveness Assessment and Cost-Benefit Analysis of Registered Apprenticeship," Mathematica Policy Research, July 25, 2012, http://tinyurl.com/lfcefd2.

[5]Thomas E. Perez, "Apprenticeship: Pathway to Opportunity," *The Huffington Post*, Jan. 31, 2014, http://tinyurl.com/nk7eghr.

[6]Peter Downs, "Can't Find Skilled Workers? Start an Apprentice Program," *The Wall Street Journal*, Jan. 17, 2014, http://tinyurl.com/k7s7jbg.

their enrollment in computer AP classes was limited, or nonexistent.[54]

A recent University of Southern California study found that even at the state's best high schools, Asian and white graduates were much more likely to attend four-year colleges than Hispanics. Nearly half of the Hispanics who graduated from top-performing high schools — 46 percent — enrolled at a community college after graduation, compared with 19 percent of Asians and 27 percent of whites.[55]

Dual System

Carnevale, the Georgetown scholar, has found that African-Americans and Hispanics are attending college in greater numbers, but there is a wide disparity among the quality of institutions they attend, compared with those whites attend.[56]

Good Job Without a Degree? It's Complicated

Some occupations don't require college, but they do demand top-notch skills.

Most Americans do not finish college. With so many jobs requiring some form of higher education, does that mean they're doomed to have stunted careers?

Not necessarily.

There's no question that college graduates will earn, on average, more during their careers than those who have only a high school diploma, says Tony Lee, publisher of the job-search website CareerCast.com. And those with college degrees are also far less likely to be unemployed, even in today's economy.

But not attending or finishing college doesn't mean you can't earn a living. "If you have the aptitude and interest, you don't need a degree to have a . . . fruitful, rewarding career," says Lee.

Many vocations, such as carpentry, plumbing or medical secretary, do not require a college degree. And, in addition to these longstanding occupations, some newer fields, such as Web development, also do not require a four-year degree.

"There are still jobs that don't require any postsecondary education, but they do require skills like communications or teamwork and the ability to solve problems," says Betsy Brand, executive director of American Youth Policy Forum, a professional-development organization in Washington.

Still, the education requirements for most jobs have increased, Brand notes. But too often, people confuse the need for postsecondary education with a full, four-year degree. A rising share of today's jobs do require some sort of training or education past high school — but that may be a one-year certificate program at a community college, or an apprenticeship in a skilled trade.

"If you go through an IBEW [International Brotherhood of Electrical Workers] apprentice program, those are good jobs, high-paying jobs that have benefits, that are certainly available without a college degree," says Tahir Duckett, national young-worker coordinator for the AFL-CIO, the nation's largest labor union federation.

Many of the occupations that the Bureau of Labor Statistics projects will grow the fastest over the next decade do not require a college degree. They include electrical helpers, home health care aides and insulation workers.

Last year, William J. Bennett, a former Republican secretary of Education, wrote a book questioning whether college degrees were worthwhile investments for everyone. He pointed out that the proliferation of college graduates has made degrees less valuable (depending on the field) and that many graduates of two-year community colleges earn more than those with four-year degrees. By 2018, Bennett estimates, 14 million jobs will require something more than a high school diploma but less than a college degree.[1]

"I don't think the solution is to send everybody to college," says Michael Strain, a resident scholar at the conservative American Enterprise Institute. "We should take a hard look at the skills employers are looking for." Often those skills can be obtained by getting a two-year degree, he says.

"We're seeing the evolution of a dual-system in higher education today, where increasingly students from low-income families and students of color are going to far less endowed and resourced community colleges and four-year schools," says Dianne Piche, senior counsel at the Leadership Committee on Civil Rights, in Washington.

College promotes social mobility for relatively few low-income students, mainly because so few of them attain degrees, according to Andrew P. Kelly, director of the Center for Higher Education Reform at the conservative American Enterprise Institute think tank. Over the past decade, less than 15 percent of students from the bottom income quartile earned a bachelor's degree, compared with 61 percent of those in the top quartile.[57]

Numerous policymakers are looking for ways to make higher education more affordable and universal. Sen. Rubio likes the idea of private investors paying tuition in exchange for a share of a student's future earnings — say, 4 percent over 10 years.

He also suggests that the college-accreditation model be changed to allow work experience to count toward a degree. Traditional colleges and universities will remain at the heart of the education system, he says, but in an

But not all such jobs pay enough to support families comfortably, however. The opportunity for people to make a good living at a factory job with only a high school education, or less, is just about gone, says Arne Kalleberg, a University of North Carolina-Chapel Hill sociologist who studies employment issues and wrote the 2011 book *Good Jobs, Bad Jobs.*

"There's been growth in high-wage, high-skilled jobs, and huge growth in low-wage occupations," he says. "There's been a hollowing out of the middle."

Moreover, even some employers looking to fill relatively low-paid positions expect applicants to have college diplomas. That's increasingly true when college grads are competing for jobs they might have spurned during times of more robust employment.

"A 'diagnostic medical sonographer' " — one of the jobs expected to grow fastest over the next decade —"is a highly skilled job that doesn't require college training in the sense that you can learn everything you need to do the job in a manner of months," writes *Forbes* contributor Pascal-Emmanuel Gobry. "[But] once there are enough college graduates who can become diagnostic medical sonographers, you can see why employers would rationally toss out of the pile any résumés that don't have a college degree on them."[2]

In other words, even for jobs that don't strictly require a college degree, people who never went to college might end up competing with those who did graduate, or even those who hold advanced degrees. (Of course, the reverse is sometimes the case: College graduates sometimes are waved away from jobs for which employers say they're overqualified.)

"We don't have enough jobs requiring degrees even for those young people with a college degree," says Heidi Shierholz, an economist at the Economic Policy Institute, a liberal think tank in Washington. "You have a ton of young people coming out with a college degree, in a job that doesn't require it."

Many of the jobs being created in today's economy are in the low-paying service sector, such as restaurants, retail and home health care. Dana Dreher, for instance, has a master's degree in social work but can't find a job in her field, so she's working as a waitress at a steakhouse. She earns about $20,000 a year, including tips. "There's so much variability" in what she takes home each day, she said. "Sometimes I have to ask myself, 'Am I going to pay my rent, or my utilities?' "[3]

As of 2012, about 284,000 college graduates were working for the minimum wage or less, more than twice the pre-recession level of 167,000 in 2006, according to the Bureau of Labor Statistics. Among their number were 30,000 people like Dreher who have master's degrees — a threefold increase from 2006.[4]

"These are not necessarily good jobs, but those are the jobs being created in the economy," says Catherine Ruetschlin, who analyzes labor markets at Demos, a liberal think tank.

— Alan Greenblatt

---

[1]Brooke Berger, "Why a College Degree May Not Be Worth It," *U.S. News & World Report*, May 9, 2013, tinyurl.com/pao6mf2.

[2]Pascal-Emmanuel Gobry, "The Jobs of the Future Don't Require a College Degree," *Forbes*, May 7, 2013, http://tinyurl.com/ckmbqzz.

[3]Steven Greenhouse, "Proposal to Raise Tip Wages Resisted," *The New York Times*, Jan. 26, 2014, tinyurl.com/kvgactm.

[4]Danielle Kurtzleben, "Twice as Many College Grads in Minimum Wages Jobs as Five Years Ago," *U.S. News & World Report*, Dec. 5, 2013, tinyurl.com/qy4pbuj.

---

era of economic disruption, greater flexibility is required. "People should be allowed, through internships and work study and online courses and classroom courses and life and work experience, to be able to package all of that together into the equivalent of a degree."[58]

Numerous lawmakers and policy analysts emphasize that while four-year degrees are important, they may not be ideal or even appropriate — or attainable — for everyone. But with increasing numbers of jobs requiring skills and preparation that aren't offered in high school, many are emphasizing the need for some sort of post-secondary education and training.

"There's no state where there's low educational achievement and a high income," said Arkansas state Sen. Keith Ingram.[59]

Republican Gov. Scott Walker of Wisconsin, in his State of the State address in January, highlighted the fact that skilled-trade apprenticeships have gone up 34 percent in Wisconsin over the past year. Republican Tennessee Gov. Bill Haslam, in his Feb. 3 State of the State address, proposed making two years of community college or technical training free for any state resident with a high school diploma or the equivalent, without regard to academic credentials or financial need.

Should the minimum wage be lower for teenagers?

YES
Michael R. Strain
Resident scholar,
American Enterprise Institute

Written for *CQ Researcher*, March 2014

when I was 15, I had a minimum wage job at a local grocery store. I would collect stray shopping carts in the parking lot, clean the restrooms and do other low-skill chores.

I earned about five bucks per hour. Looking back on it, there is no way that I provided $5 per hour of value to the store. They may have been hoping that I would stay on for three or four years, learning the ropes and eventually generating at least as much value per hour as I cost them in wages. But I left when the summer ended and went on to a glorious career as a lifeguard.

When I showed up at the grocery store I had never held a job before. I didn't know how to interact with my coworkers, deal with customers or take instruction from my boss. I wasn't professionally socialized at all. I didn't have any hard skills, either. I couldn't work the cash register, manage inventory, make marketing and product-placement decisions or even cook in the in-store restaurant.

Given their lack of skills, a high minimum wage for young workers provides a disincentive for firms to hire them. (Would you pay a worker more than he is worth?) And without a first job, it's pretty tough to get a second job.

Compounding the problem, computers and robots are becoming more and more capable of replacing humans. I use self-checkout machines at grocery stores all the time now. Do you? That used to be a human cashier, you know. The pressure on businesses to invest in equipment instead of hiring a human being will grow.

Some teenage workers are heads of households. For them, I would want a lower minimum wage paired with federal transfer payments to supplement their labor-market earnings. In the United States, no one who works full time and heads a household should live in poverty, even teenagers.

A lower minimum wage will help these young workers get their start, ensure that firms are willing to hire them even given their relative lack of skills, learn soft and hard skills and remain competitive with machines — and one day get a second, better-paying job.

Keep young workers working, and keep them out of poverty. As we go forward, a lower minimum wage is an important part of achieving that goal.

NO
Jack Temple
Policy Analyst,
National Employment Law Project

Written for *CQ Researcher*, March 2014

with the teen unemployment rate stuck above 20 percent — three times higher than the national average — there is no question young jobseekers face severely limited opportunities for gaining much-needed work experience. But for teens already grappling with an unforgiving job market, it would make things worse if those young workers lucky enough to secure a job have to absorb a pay cut, which is precisely what a sub-minimum wage for teen workers would entail.

Under federal law, employers are already permitted to pay teens a much lower minimum wage of $4.25 per hour for their first 90 days of work. Expanding the window of time that employers may pay this sub-minimum wage — or eliminating the cut-off period altogether — would drive down wages for teen workers without making any progress toward job creation.

The reality is that high teen unemployment has been driven by macroeconomic trends shaping the labor market that have nothing to do with the minimum wage. Teens now face increasing competition from adult workers older than 55, many of whom cannot afford to retire and are turning to low-wage jobs to make ends meet. At the same time, government funding that supports teen summer jobs has been cut significantly in recent years. Cutting the minimum wage for teens would do nothing to reverse these broad trends.

Census data show that half of all college students work at least 20 hours per week, with one in five working full time year-round as they struggle with high costs and debt. These students deserve a higher minimum wage that will allow them to cover more costs, finish school more quickly and take out fewer loans. They also deserve the same wage for doing the same work as their adult co-workers.

Raising the minimum wage has proved an effective approach for boosting incomes, including for teen workers, without reducing employment. A 2011 study examined every state and federal minimum wage increase over the past two decades and found that even during difficult economic periods increases in the minimum wage boosted pay without reducing employment.

The federal minimum wage has remained stuck at just $7.25 per hour for nearly five years, making it nearly impossible for many to afford the basics. America's lowest-paid workers — all of them — are long overdue for a raise.

Meanwhile, cities such as Cleveland and San Francisco are providing small savings accounts to students as early as kindergarten, believing even $50 put away toward college is enough to spark expectations about actually attending. A recent National Bureau of Economic Research study found that a $1,000 increase in tax refunds received by families in the spring of students' high school senior year increased college enrollment the next fall by 2 to 3 percentage points.[60]

But for all the homage politicians pay to higher education, they haven't always backed it up with cash. Over the past 25 years, measured in real dollars, state support for public colleges and universities has dropped from $8,500 per student to $5,900, according to the State Higher Education Executive Officers association. State spending on higher education has dropped by 10.6 percent over the past five years — including cuts of nearly 50 percent in Arizona, Florida and New Hampshire.[61]

Although some naysayers question the value of college, given the ever-increasing costs of a degree, employers are still willing to pay a premium for people with college degrees, says Georgetown's Carnevale.

"In the old days, work ethic was enough to get you in a job, and then you learned on the job," he says. "Now, the on-ramp is tougher and tougher, because of [skill] requirements." The age at which the average young American earns the national average has risen from 26 to 30 years since the 1990s, he points out.

A recent Pew Research Center study found that college graduates ages 25 to 32 working fulltime are earning about $17,500 more than employed young adults with only a high school diploma. College-educated millennials are also much less likely to be unemployed than their less-educated peers (3.8 percent compared with 12.2 percent).[62]

But are all college degrees created equal? In a January speech promoting job training programs, Obama said, "I promise you, folks can make a lot more, potentially, with skilled manufacturing or the trades than they might with an art history degree."

The president soon apologized to the nation's humanities majors. And the Association of American Colleges and Universities recently put out a report indicating that humanities and social science majors, although they may struggle at first, can end up making as much or more

> "We're facing a really dire sort of future in 10 years. That's what we're going to continue to see, folks paying for more and more school, incurring more and more debt to fight it out for fewer and fewer jobs."
>
> — Tahir Duckett,
> National Young-Worker Coordinator, AFL-CIO

later in life than people with more "practical" degrees in sciences or engineering. Going on to get graduate degrees is the key.[63]

An increasing number of colleges and universities are working with state governments and regional employers to craft programs that will train graduates for jobs in their areas. But leaders in the higher education field say their role is not simply to act as job-training facilities.

It's not that university presidents want to churn out more art history majors, medievalists or Shakespeare scholars. Rather, they insist that a broader education helps prepare students not just for the first job that might be available after graduation but for a lifetime of problem-solving, communication and continuing education.

"We are understandably quite focused on jobs, but we sometimes forget that a person's last job may not be related to her first job," says Molly Corbett Broad, president of the American Council on Education, a higher education advocacy association. "If we want to continue to sustain prosperity in this increasingly competitive global economy, we're going to have to continue up the value chain of skills and knowledge," she says.

OUTLOOK

'Second Machine Age'

Every generation responds differently to enormous societal challenges, says Howe, the Lifecourse Associates president. Unlike earlier generations, he says, today's young people have no desire to grow up fast and become more independent.

"The world is horrible out there," he says. "Thinking about that kind of world, if we have a period of extreme economic crisis and unrest long enough, like in the '30s and '40s, we might see young people extremely desirous of not rocking the world."

Young people today have reason to be a bit gun shy. They've faced bad job markets for more than five years — a big percentage, or in some cases all, of their working lives.

"At the rate of average employment growth we had last year, adding an average of 185,000 jobs a month, we would see the economy recovering to pre-recession levels in 2019 or 2020," says Ruetschlin, the Demos policy analyst. "That means a full decade of labor-market disadvantages for young people."

Such a timeframe is long enough for yet another recession to hit, further imperiling young people's chances of success. Even when they do get jobs, today's young adults will be doing worse than they would have for years to come, says Shierholz, the Economic Policy Institute economist. "The larger economy will have recovered from the Great Recession, but the cohort that entered the labor market during it will not," she says.

Like other economists, she expects the American labor force to continue shrinking. "Extrapolating from current trends, I would expect that there will be fewer people working, and that the problems we have would be larger," says Strain, the American Enterprise Institute economist.

In their new book *The Second Machine Age*, MIT researchers Erik Brynjolfsson and Andy McAfee say many more jobs done by humans can be done by robots and software.[64] A recent Oxford University paper says two-thirds of the tasks performed in the 10 jobs expected to grow the fastest over the next decade will soon be automated, including personal care aides and janitors and cleaners.[65]

It's dangerous trying to predict the economic future, says Arnett, the Clark University psychologist, but other trends affecting young people — such as delays in getting married and having children — are likely to continue.

"Having observed this for 20 years, what's striking to me is the consistency of the patterns," Arnett says. "Every year, more and more people are getting more and more education, in response to the realities of the labor market."

He takes heart from history. A century ago, he notes, young people were not universally expected to get a high school education. Now, that's taken for granted. The same sort of thing needs to happen with higher education, he says. "In the early 20th century, there was a recognition that people need more education," he says. "That's what we need to recognize in the early 21st century."

Of course, the question of how to pay for college remains central. "We're facing a really dire sort of future in 10 years," says Duckett, from the AFL-CIO. "That's what we're going to continue to see, folks paying for more and more school, incurring more and more debt to fight it out for fewer and fewer jobs."

An alternative scenario, Duckett suggests, could play out if the federal government invests more in infrastructure and in spending that aids young people generally. But Washington isn't going to do much to address such issues, suggests Kalleberg, the University of North Carolina sociologist — in part because of the political paralysis that is likely to continue at least through the Obama years.

"Americans do not have enough tolerance of big government for things to come out of Washington," he says.

Despite increasing concerns about income inequality, there will be little appetite for anything that smacks of income redistribution, says Carnevale, the Georgetown scholar. Instead, leaders in both parties will continue to talk about creating opportunity. "Jobs and upward mobility are not a hard sell on either side," he says. "It fits with the American narrative."

But despite all the attention being paid to higher education and workplace apprenticeships, says Ayres of the Center for American Progress, what's really needed to address employment needs is simple: jobs.

"You can educate people all you want and have a great, educated workforce, but if there aren't enough jobs to go around, if businesses feel that they don't have enough customers, we're not going to create jobs, and we're not going to have full employment," she says.

NOTES

1. Jeffrey M. Jones, "In U.S., 14% of Those 24 to 34 Are Living at Home," Gallup, Feb. 13, 2014, tinyurl.com/pmzvwbh.

2. Harry J. Holzer, "Not Your Father's Shop Class," *Washington Monthly*, November-December 2013, http://tinyurl.com/lbh4c5m. For background, see Reed Karaim, "Youth Unemployment," *CQ Global*

Researcher, March 6, 2012, pp. 105-128, http://bit .ly/1fcX1Pd.

3. Caroline Porter, "Millennials Face Uphill Climb," *The Wall Street Journal*, Sept. 30, 2013, http://tinyurl .com/n8tuy3u.

4. Joel Kotkin, "The Millennial Generation's New American Dreams," *The Pittsburgh Post-Gazette*, Nov. 30, 2013, tinyurl.com/kw23lzs.

5. Sarah Ayres, "Middle-Out for Millennials," Center for American Progress, October 2013, http://tinyurl .com/kdbngnz.

6. Dana Ford, "Obama unveils 'My Brother's Keeper,' opens up about his dad, drugs and race," CNN, Feb. 27, 2014, http://tinyurl.com/ncdkn89.

7. Tyler Cowen, *Average Is Over* (2013), p. 3.

8. Riva Froymovich, *End of the Good Life* (2013), p. 5.

9. *Ibid.*, p. 80.

10. Jessica Davis, "Beyond a Bachelor's Degree: Big Gains for Graduate School Attainment," U.S. Census Bureau, Feb. 4, 2014, http://blogs.census .gov/2014/02/04/beyond-a-bachelors-degree-big-gains-for-graduate-school-attainment/.

11. Froymovich, *op. cit.*, p. 10.

12. "Closing the Gap," NewsHour, Feb. 12, 2014, www .pbs.org/newshour/bb/closing-gap-sen-marco-rubio-education-fewer-broken-families-can-change-income-inequality/.

13. Megan McArdle, "Why Writers Are the Worst Procrastinators," *The Atlantic*, Feb. 12, 2014, tiny-url.com/klaxlx4.

14. Katherine Peralta, "College Graduates Taking Low-Wage Jobs Displace Less Educated," Bloomberg, March 6, 2014, tinyurl.com/nyln54f.

15. "Remarks by the President on Opportunity for All and Skills for America's Workers," Jan. 30, 2014, www.whitehouse.gov/the-press-office/2014/01/30/ remarks-president-opportunity-all-and-skills-americas-workers.

16. "Multiple Employment and Training Programs," Government Accountability Office, January 2011, www.gao.gov/assets/320/314551.pdf.

17. "Biden's 47 Job Training Flavors," *The Wall Street Journal*, Feb. 18, 2014, http://on.wsj.com/1nppW2W.

18. "Current Employment Statistics Highlights," Bureau of Labor Statistics, Feb. 7, 2014, www.bls.gov/web/ empsit/ceshighlights.pdf.

19. Niraj Choksi, "Most Government Jobs Are Local (And So Are the Cuts)," *The Washington Post*, Aug. 26, 2013, www.washingtonpost.com/blogs/govbeat/ wp/2013/08/26/most-government-jobs-are-local-and-so-are-the-cuts/.

20. Helene Cooper and Thom Shanker, "Pentagon Officials Say They're Willing to Assume the Risks of a Reduced Army," *The New York Times*, Feb. 24, 2014, www .nytimes.com/2014/02/25/us/politics/pentagon-officials-say-theyre-willing-to-assume-risks-of-a-reduced-army.html.

21. Porter, *op. cit.*

22. Daniel Cooper, "The Effect of Unemployment Duration on Future Earnings and Other Outcomes," Federal Reserve Bank of Boston, Jan. 13, 2014, www .bostonfed.org/economic/wp/wp2013/wp1308.pdf.

23. Porter, *op. cit.*

24. Elizabeth A. Harris, "Retailers Ask: Where Did Teenagers Go?" *The New York Times*, Jan. 31, 2014, www.nytimes.com/2014/02/01/business/retailers-ask-where-did-teenagers-go.html.

25. Jones, *op. cit.*

26. Dina ElBoghdady, "Student Debt May Hurt Housing Recovery by Hampering First-Time Buyers," *The Washington Post*, Feb. 7, 2014, http://wapo.st/1cSTUF. For background, see Marcia Clemmitt, "Student Debt," *CQ Researcher*, Oct. 21, 2011, pp. 877-900.

27. William R. Emmons and Bryan J. Noeth, "Housing Crash Continues to Overshadow Young Families' Balance Sheets," Federal Reserve Bank of St. Louis, February 2014, http://bit.ly/1ekDj1Z.

28. Timothy Noah, "Stay Put, Young Man," *The Washington Monthly*, November-December 2013, http://tinyurl.com/polf9xu.

29. Jordan Weissmann, "Indisputable Evidence That Millennials Have It Worse Than Any Generation in 50 Years," *TheAtlantic.com*, Feb. 11, 2014, http:// bit.ly/1iYYu9F.

30. Walter I. Trattner, *Crusade for the Children* (1970), p. 21.

31. Ellen Greenberger and Laurence Steinberg, *When Teenagers Work* (1986), p. 11.

32. Trattner, *op. cit.*, p. 25.

33. Greenberger and Steinberg, *op. cit.*, p. 12.

34. Trattner, *op. cit.*, p. 33.

35. *Ibid.*, p. 41.

36. Philip Dray, *There Is Power in a Union: The Epic Story of Labor in America* (2010), p. 254.

37. Greenberger and Steinberg, *op. cit.*, p. 13.

38. *Ibid.*, p. 14.

39. *Ibid.*, p. 15.

40. Albert J. Pautler Jr., *High School to Employment Transition* (1994), p. 4.

41. Martin A. Levin and Barbara Ferman, *The Political Hand: Policy Implementation and Youth Employment Programs* (1985), p. 1.

42. Rob Fiddy, ed., *Youth, Unemployment and Training* (1985), p. 139.

43. Quoted in Sar A. Levitan and Garth L. Mangum, *Federal Training and Work Programs in the Sixties* (1969), p. 6.

44. Fiddy, *op. cit.*, p. 144.

45. Lou Cannon, *President Reagan: Role of a Lifetime* (1991), p. 241.

46. Richard B. Freeman and Harry J. Holzer, eds., *The Black Youth Employment Crisis* (1986), p. 3.

47. *Ibid.*, p. 15.

48. Robert I. Lerman, "Improving Career Outcomes for Youth," Urban Institute, July 2000, p. iv.

49. Bill Clinton, *My Life* (2004), p. 590.

50. Jeanne Bellotti, *et al.*, "Reinvesting in America's Youth: Lessons From the 2009 Recovery Act Summer Youth Employment Initiative," U.S. Department of Labor, Feb. 26, 2010, http://1.usa.gov/1npt26U.

51. Michael D. Shear, "Obama Starts Initiative for Young Black Men, Noting His Own Experience," *The New York Times*, Feb. 27, 2014, http://nyti.ms/1cbYQLk.

52. Ivory A. Toldson, PhD., "School Security Boosts Student Insecurity?" *The Root*, Nov. 30, 2012, www.theroot.com/articles/politics/2012/11/security_at_black_schools_metal_detectors_might_do_harm.html. For nationwide arrest data, see www.whitehouse.gov/blog/2014/02/27/my-brother-s-keeper-new-white-house-initiative-empower-boys-and-young-men-color.

53. Tony Cox, "U.S. Will Have Minority Whites Sooner, Says Demographer," NPR, June 27, 2011, http://tinyurl.com/avt52fy.

54. Emily DeRuy, "No African-Americans, Hispanics or Girls Took the AP Computer Science Exam in Some States," *Fusion.net*, Jan. 10, 2014, http://tinyurl.com/kzyqaa7.

55. Adopho Guzman-Lopez, "Even From State's Best High Schools, Latinos Mostly Go to Community College," KPCC, Jan. 6, 2014, http://tinyurl.com/kbn82ry.

56. Anthony P. Carnevale and Jeff Strohl, "White Flight Goes to College," Poverty & Race Research Action Council, September-October 2013, www.prrac.org/pdf/SeptOct2013Carnevale_Strohl.pdf.

57. Andrew P. Kelly, "Does College Really Improve Social Mobility," *Brookings Social Mobility Memos*, Feb. 11, 2014, www.brookings.edu/blogs/social-mobility-memos/posts/2014/02/11-college-improve-social-mobility.

58. Stephanie Czekalinski, "Rubio: Here's How to Make College Affordable," *National Journal*, Feb. 10, 2012, www.nationaljournal.com/next-america/education/rubio-here-s-how-to-make-college-affordable-20140210.

59. "The Crippling Effects of the Dysfunction in D.C.," Capitol Ideas, January-February 2014, www.csg.org/pubs/capitolideas/2014_jan_feb/issuesfacingstates_south.aspx.

60. Dayanand S. Manoli and Nicholas Turner, "Cash-on-Hand & College Enrollment: Evidence from Population Tax Data and Policy Nonlinearities," *NBER Working Paper No. 19836*, January 2014, http://nber.org/papers/w19836.

61. Suzanne Weiss, "States Are Searching for Ways to Control the Ever-Increasing Costs of a College Education," *State Legislatures*, February 2014, www.ncsl.org/research/education/higher-ed-aches.aspx.

62. "The Rising Cost of Not Going to College," Pew Research Center, Feb. 11, 2013, www.pewsocial trends.org/2014/02/11/the-rising-cost-of-not-going-to-college/. For background, see Robert Kiener, "Future of Public Universities," *CQ Researcher*, Jan. 18, 2013, pp. 53-80.

63. Beckie Supiano, "How Liberal Arts Majors Fare Over the Long Haul," *The Chronicle of Higher Education*, Jan. 22, 2014, http://chronicle.com/article/How-Liberal-Arts-Majors-Fare/144133. For background, see Marcia Clemmitt, "Humanities Education," *CQ Researcher*, Dec. 6, 2013, pp. 1029-1052.

64. Erik Brynjolfsson and Andy McAfee, *The Second Machine Age: Work, Progress, and Prosperity in a Time of Brilliant Technologies* (2014).

65. Derek Thompson, "The Fastest Growing Jobs of This Decade," *The Atlantic Cities*, Jan. 28, 2014, www .theatlanticcities.com/jobs-and-economy/2014/01/ fastest-growing-jobs-decade/8229/

BIBLIOGRAPHY

Selected Sources

Books

Cowen, Tyler, *Average Is Over: Powering America Beyond the Age of Stagnation*, Dutton, 2013.
A George Mason University economist predicts middle-class jobs will continue to disappear.

Froymovich, Riva, *End of the Good Life: How the Financial Crisis Threatens a Lost Generation — and What We Can Do About It*, Harper Perennial, 2013.
A *Wall Street Journal* reporter finds diminishing career opportunities, even as young people are burdened by student debt and tax policies that favor aging baby boomers.

Articles

"Biden's 47 Job Training Flavors," *The Wall Street Journal*, Feb. 18, 2014, tinyurl.com/mzse69r.
Federal job training programs often waste money and fail to prepare people for jobs, the newspaper editorializes.

Dewan, Shaila, "In Jobless Youth, U.S. Is Said to Pay High Price," *The New York Times*, Jan. 6, 2014, tinyurl.com/lqf8tur.
High unemployment among youths is costing the government $25 billion in foregone income tax revenues, in addition to increased costs such as unemployment benefits.

Harris, Elizabeth A., "Retailers Ask: Where Did Teenagers Go?" *The New York Times*, Jan. 31, 2014, tinyurl.com/k326qul.
With unemployment for older teens above 20 percent, sales have plunged for retailers that appeal to younger shoppers.

Kurtzleben, Danielle, "Twice as Many College Grads in Minimum Wage Jobs as Five Years Ago," *U.S. News & World Report*, Dec. 5, 2013, tinyurl.com/qy4pbuj.
Nearly 285,000 college graduates were working at or below the minimum wage in 2012.

Meyerson, Harold, "The Forty-Year Slump," *American Prospect*, Nov. 13, 2013, tinyurl.com/mm8lbzu.
The economy has grown by 18 percent since 2000, but median household income has dropped as low-wage occupations have grown.

Noah, Timothy, "Stay Put, Young Man," *The Washington Monthly*, November-December 2013, www.washingtonmonthly.com/magazine/november_ december_2013/features/stay_put_young_ man047332.php.
In contrast with historic patterns, Americans of all ages and stripes are becoming less likely to move. The percentage of young adults annually migrating across state lines is down more than 40 percent since the 1980s.

Ross, Andrew S., "Ranks of 'Gig Economy' Swell With Mobile Workforce," *San Francisco Chronicle*, Oct. 26, 2013, tinyurl.com/k3clwnd.
For more than 20 million Americans who work on freelance, contractual or contingent projects, "work is no longer a place."

Weissmann, Jordan, "Indisputable Evidence That Millennials Have It Worse Than Any Generation in 50 Years," *TheAtlantic.com*, Feb. 11, 2014, tinyurl.com/ ksnlvfz.
No matter their level of education, Americans 25 to 32 years old in 2013 had worse unemployment than prior generations at that stage of life.

Studies and Reports

"The Rising Cost of Not Going to College," Pew Research Center, Feb. 11, 2014, tinyurl.com/kznjdwf.
Researchers say the disparity in economic outcomes between college and high school graduates and dropouts has never been greater in modern times.

"Youth and Work: Restoring Teen and Young Adult Connections to Opportunity," Annie E. Casey Foundation, December 2012, tinyurl.com/c8d2nv4.
Youth employment has been at a low ebb, with only half of Americans aged 16 to 24 working in 2011.

Abel, Jaison R., Richard Deitz and Yaqin Su, "Are Recent College Graduates Finding Good Jobs?" Federal Reserve Bank of New York, tinyurl.com/menvluv.
College graduates ages 22 to 27 are more likely to be underemployed than 15 years ago.

Carnevale, Anthony P., Andrew R. Hanson and Artem Gulish, "Failure to Launch: Structural Shift and the New Lost Generation," Georgetown University Center on Education and the Workforce, September 2013, tinyurl .com/lhkndbj.
Today's young people are suffering a "lost decade" in job opportunities and wages.

Cooper, Daniel, "The Effect of Unemployment Duration on Future Earnings and Other Outcomes," Federal Reserve Bank of Boston, Jan. 13, 2014, tinyurl .com/kflrtby.
An economist finds that people unemployed for more than six months earn less than their peers for nearly 20 years.

Olinsky, Ben, and Sarah Ayres, "Training for Success: A Policy to Expand Apprenticeships in the United States," Center for American Progress, Dec. 2, 2013, tinyurl.com/khyr52k.
Researchers say apprenticeships can help meet demand for skilled labor while offering workers a chance at high wages.

For More Information

AFL-CIO, 815 16th St., N.W., Washington, DC 20006; 202-637-5000; www.aflcio.org. The nation's largest federation of unions; trains young workers through apprentice programs and maintains young workers' groups and a Young Workers Advisory Council.

American Youth Policy Forum, 1836 Jefferson Place, N.W., Washington, DC 20036; 202-775-9731; www.aypf.org. Professional-development organization that provides avenues for lawmakers and youths to share viewpoints about policies to improve outcomes for young people.

Center for Labor Market Studies, Northeastern University, 360 Huntington Ave., Boston, MA 02115; 617-373-2000; www.northeastern.edu/clms/. Sponsors and conducts research on labor market trends, including training programs and the employment situation of low-income youths.

Center on Education and the Workforce, Georgetown University, Suite 5000, Box 571444, 3300 Whitehaven St., N.W., Washington, DC 20007; 202-687-4971; cew.georgetown.edu. Studies links among education, career qualifications and workforce demands.

John J. Heldrich Center for Workforce Development, Rutgers University, 30 Livingston Ave., New Brunswick, NJ 08901; 732-932-4100; www.heldrich.rutgers.edu/. Studies and consults with workforce programs that aim to improve training and education.

Opportunity Nation, 200 Clarendon St., 9th Floor, Boston, MA 02116; 850-400-0036; www.opportunitynation.org. Bipartisan organization composed of more than 250 nonprofit groups, businesses and educational and faith-based institutions working to expand economic opportunity.

U.S. Department of Labor, 200 Constitution Ave., N.W., Washington, DC 20210; 866-4-USA-DOL. Federal department responsible for a number of job training programs and enforcement of fair labor laws and standards.

Young Invincibles, 1411 K St., N.W., 4th Floor, Washington, DC 20005; 202-534-3560; younginvincibles.org. Advocacy group that addresses health-coverage and youth-unemployment issues.

YouthBuild USA, 58 Day St., Somerville, MA 02144; 617-623-9900; youthbuild.org. Guides more than 250 programs that educate and train young people, putting them to work building affordable housing in nearly every state.

7

Abortion Debates

William Wanlund

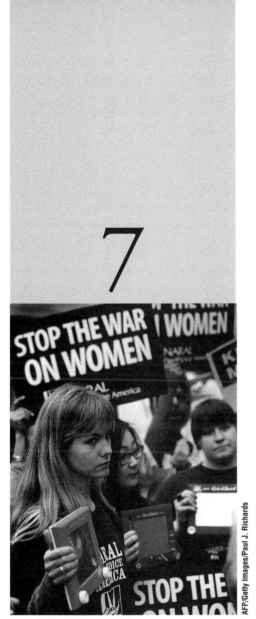

Members of NARAL Pro-Choice America protest at a hotel in Washington hosting a fundraiser for Republican presidential hopeful Mitt Romney on March 22, 2012. The protesters were objecting to Romney's proposal to stop federal support for the abortion rights/family planning group Planned Parenthood of America. The federal government's sweeping, new health-care reform law – dubbed Obamacare – requires that health insurance plans cover contraception. Later this month the U.S. Supreme Court will hear a challenge to the law by companies with religious objections to birth control.

From *CQ Researcher*,
March 21, 2014.

The Falls Church Healthcare Center is facing a financial crisis, according to director Rosemary Codding.

A state law enacted in 2011, she says, requires the small Northern Virginia abortion clinic to abide by the same building and safety standards that apply to new hospital construction. She says regulations stemming from the law will require $1.5 million in renovations to the facility, such as enlarging a janitor's utility closet, expanding laundry facilities and upgrading heating, ventilation and air conditioning equipment.

Codding is suing the state over the regulations, arguing they are unreasonable and "include things that have absolutely no impact on health, patient safety or the well-being of our small staff." On Oct. 9 a judge rejected the state's effort to have Codding's case thrown out; a circuit court in Arlington, Va., is scheduled to hear the case April 29.

Abortion-rights activists say the Virginia law is among 205 similar measures enacted in 29 states since 2011 designed to restrict the number of abortions performed in the United States. The new laws — which, among other things, require abortion providers to have admitting privileges and/or transfer agreements with local hospitals or impose structural requirements on clinics — are partly responsible for the more than 70 abortion facilities in 30 states that have closed or stopped offering abortions since 2010, say opponents of the laws.[1]

But lawmakers who support such laws say they are designed to protect patients. "This is not about banning abortion in Virginia,"

Republican state Sen. Jill Holtzman Vogel said when the law was passed. "It is simply caring for women who are about to have an invasive surgical procedure and creating an environment for them . . . to have [the procedure] in a place that's safe."[2]

After decades of trying to get the Supreme Court to weaken its 1973 *Roe v. Wade* decision legalizing abortion, opponents of abortion rights have turned their focus on the states, supporting new regulations for abortion clinics, anti-abortion candidates for the legislatures and shorter periods during a pregnancy when legal abortions can be performed. The ultimate goal, the groups say, is to test the limits of the Supreme Court's landmark decision and possibly even get the ruling overturned. Abortion-rights groups are suing dozens of states over the laws, contending they impose unreasonable demands on abortion providers, making it more difficult for women to get safe, legal and affordable abortion care.

Further fueling the debate, the federal government this year is implementing its sweeping health-care reform law, which requires that health insurance plans cover contraception. Companies with religious objections to birth control are suing the government over the requirement, a case that will be argued before the Supreme Court later this month and which some say could have far-reaching implications on the availability of birth control.

Polls show most Americans still want abortion to be legal, but regional differences in attitudes are growing. A Pew Research Center survey conducted last July found that 54 percent of Americans say abortion should be legal in all or most circumstances, while 40 percent said it should be illegal all or most of the time. Opposition to legal abortion was highest — 52 percent — in the South Central states and lowest — 20 percent — in New England, according to the survey. The disparity between the two regions has risen 19 percentage points since 1996.[3]

The number of abortions performed each year has been declining since 2000 and fell 13 percent between 2008 and 2011 (the latest year for which statistics were available), according to a March report from the Guttmacher Institute, a policy research organization that supports abortion rights.[4]

Those numbers do not yet reflect the impact of the new state laws, say experts. A 2012 Centers for Disease Control and Prevention (CDC) report attributed a 9 percent drop in pregnancy rates between 1990 and 2008 to improved contraception and economic instability.[5] But Carol Tobias, president of the anti-abortion organization National Right to Life (NRL), says the abortion rate is falling because "pro-life legislative efforts at the state and federal level" have "raised awareness about the humanity of the unborn child."[6]

As for the new rules like the ones Codding is challenging, a sensational case in Pennsylvania last year heightened the debate over the need for new regulations. Philadelphia abortion doctor Kermit Gosnell was sentenced to life in prison without parole in May 2013 after being convicted in the gruesome deaths of a patient and three babies born alive during late-term abortions at a filthy clinic.[7]

"For many years, abortion providers have been treated as a special class," Tobias says. "They have hidden behind the idea that . . . abortion should somehow be treated differently from other surgical procedures. As a result, we end up with situations . . . where abortionists are allowed to operate in substandard conditions that put women at risk."

The new state regulations are "common-sense requirements" that mandate such things as improved sanitary conditions, working emergency equipment and larger hallways and rooms so emergency personnel can quickly access patients in distress, says Michael New, a political scientist and adjunct scholar with the Charlotte Lozier Institute, a Washington policy research organization that opposes abortion.

But abortion-rights activists — who call the new measures TRAP laws, for targeted regulation of abortion providers — say they are designed to make it too expensive or logistically impossible for abortion clinics to stay open. "The TRAP laws we are challenging make it harder for good providers to continue providing abortion services, which means that women have less access to legal abortion," says Julie Rikelman, litigation director at the Center for Reproductive Rights, a New York-based legal advocacy organization that supports women's access to abortion. "TRAP laws are designed to seem benign, but they're not."

Jennifer Dalven, director of the Reproductive Freedom Project at the American Civil Liberties Union (ACLU), says, "more and more, we are seeing politicians pass laws that either directly ban abortion or are backdoor bans that purport to protect women's health but in fact are laws designed to shut down women's health centers and outlaw abortion."

In Texas, at least a third of the state's abortion providers, mostly in rural areas, have stopped providing abortion services since the state passed one of the country's toughest abortion clinic laws last year. Among other things, it requires doctors performing abortions to be accredited at a hospital within 30 miles of the abortion clinic. By March of this year, only 24 abortion facilities were still operating in Texas, a state with a population of more than 26 million people.[8]

The American Medical Association and the American College of Obstetricians and Gynecologists, which oppose the Texas law, wrote in a legal brief that: "There is simply no medical basis to impose a local admitting-privileges requirement on abortion providers." The law "does not serve the health of women in Texas, but instead jeopardizes women's health by restricting access to abortion providers and denying women well-researched, safe, evidence-based and proven protocols for the provision of medical abortion."[9]

Abortion-rights supporters have challenged the Texas law in court, and the Fifth U.S. Circuit Court of Appeals heard the case on Jan. 6. Both sides expect the case to eventually reach the Supreme Court.[10]

A Bloomberg News investigation found that abortion clinics have been closing in record numbers across the country since the new state laws went into effect but that only about a third of closings have been due to the new laws. The rest closed due to demographic changes, declining demand, industry consolidation, doctor retirements and crackdowns on unfit providers, the news service said.[11]

The warring sides in the abortion debate are gearing up for an active 2014 election season, as state legislature and congressional races get underway. Erika West, political director of NARAL Pro-Choice America, a Washington, D.C.-based advocacy organization that supports abortion rights, told a press conference that, with national politics largely at a standstill due to a highly polarized government, the organization would focus on races for state offices and support candidates who advocate abortion rights.[12]

But NRL's Tobias thinks abortion-rights proponents will face "an uphill battle" in trying to affect state-level elections, given the recent successes of anti-abortion

groups in getting states to adopt new abortion laws. "People in the states are electing pro-life legislators because they support pro-life laws."[13]

As supporters and opponents of abortion rights carry their messages into the 2014 election campaigns, here are some key questions being asked:

Will the strategy of restricting abortions at the state level lead to *Roe v. Wade* being overturned?

In the 2010 mid-term elections, voters swept Republicans by the hundreds into state legislatures. Republicans won 675 new seats and wrested control of 11 legislatures from Democrats, according to the National Conference of State Legislatures (NCSL). After the elections, 25 state legislatures were in GOP hands, and 11 governorships had flipped from Democratic to Republican control. [14]

It was a moment that James C. Bopp Jr., a conservative Indiana lawyer and general counsel for National Right to Life, had been waiting for since 2007, when he and law firm colleague Richard E. Coleson wrote an 11-page strategy memo for anti-abortion activists. The ultimate target was getting *Roe v. Wade* overturned.

"Astute pro-life leaders . . . have been working hard to get pro-life officials elected," wrote Bopp and Coleson, so that "over the long term, there might emerge a majority on the Supreme Court willing to overrule *Roe*. [That] has been a powerful motivator for pro-life political activism."[15]

Encouraged by the prospect of a more sympathetic Supreme Court and emboldened by the wave of social conservatives elected to state office, abortion opponents began focusing on state legislatures, pushing for the new abortion clinic laws. Since 2011, states enacted 205 laws that the Guttmacher Institute says restrict access to abortion, compared to 189 over the previous decade. In 2013 alone, 70 abortion-restricting measures were enacted in 22 states, according to the institute.[16]

Donna Crane, policy director for NARAL Pro-Choice America, says the tough laws were a hidden agenda among the social conservatives elected in 2010. "In the 2010 elections, a crop of really conservative, anti-choice [candidates] ran for office, and they ran cleverly [by] talking about jobs and the economy because in 2010 that was really on top of everyone's mind," she says. "But after they got into office, they immediately . . . began attacking the issue of reproductive freedom."

States Limit When Women Can Get Abortions

Since the Supreme Court in 1992 allowed states to restrict abortions after fetal viability, 42 states have enacted laws limiting when a pregnant woman can get an abortion. A law pending in Mississippi would be the most restrictive, banning abortions at 18 weeks of pregnancy. Thirteen other states banned abortions as early as 20 weeks, but since medical professionals generally say fetal viability, or survival, cannot occur before 23 weeks, several of those laws already have been challenged in court and the cases are expected to be appealed to the Supreme Court.

State Abortion Bans, by Length of Pregnancy

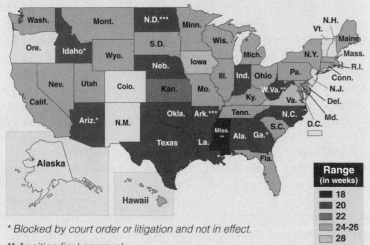

Range (in weeks): 18, 20, 22, 24-26, 28

* Blocked by court order or litigation and not in effect.

** Awaiting final approval.

*** North Dakota and Arkansas passed 6-week and 12-week restrictions, respectively, which were blocked by federal judges.

Source: "State Policies on Later Abortions," Guttmacher Institute, March 1, 2014, http://tinyurl.com/k83kfmk; see also Niraj Chokshi, "West Virginia's legislature passes a 20-week abortion ban," The Washington Post, March 10, 2014, http://tinyurl.com/lpzacw6; Jeff Amy, "Mississippi Senate passes amended 20-week abortion ban," The Associated Press, March 11, 2014, http://tinyurl.com/kmbpmg8; Erik Eckholm, "Judge Blocks North Dakota Abortion Restrictions," The New York Times, July 22, 2013, http://tinyurl.com/msavshk.

unprecedented level of abortion advocacy at the federal level and a hostility to defending life."

Anti-abortion groups found that the state legislatures were an appropriate venue for carrying out the debate. "States truly are the laboratories of democracy," she says. "We are seeing real policy innovation at the state level."

John Green, director of the Ray C. Bliss Institute of Applied Politics at the University of Akron, says using state legislation to reduce the availability of abortion "can be effective in reducing the number of abortions, but it won't make such procedures illegal." Ultimately, he says, "it depends on how the courts rule."

In fact, some of the new laws have been designed to confront *Roe v. Wade* head-on, say anti-abortion activists, specifically by challenging the court on how many weeks into a woman's pregnancy she can legally obtain an abortion. In 1992, the Supreme Court allowed states to restrict abortions after fetal viability, which medical professionals generally occurs between 23 and 28 weeks. A new Arkansas law bans abortions after 12 weeks of pregnancy, however, and a North Dakota law bans the procedure after a fetal heartbeat is detected, usually at about the six-week point. And nine states have banned abortions after 20 weeks.

Courts have blocked both the Arkansas and North Dakota laws, and in January the Supreme Court refused to review a lower court decision barring an Arizona 20-week ban from taking effect, thus striking down the law.[17]

Still, some legislators believe the time is right for a direct challenge to *Roe*. "When is enough enough?" asked Republican state Sen. Jason Rapert, who sponsored the Arkansas law. "It's time to take a stand."[18]

The "dominant theme" in the last three years for abortion-rights supporters, she says, has been "dealing with these guys who are just hell-bent on taking away a woman's right to choose."

But Charmaine Yoest, president and CEO of Americans United for Life, which opposes abortion, says the switch to "a state-based approach has made sense from a political perspective," because there had been "an

Republican Texas Governor Rick Perry has said that one of his goals as governor was to "make abortion, at any stage, a thing of the past."[19]

Does emergency contraception cause abortion?

Emergency contraception — pills taken after intercourse to prevent pregnancy — have been available in the United States since 1999, when the Food and Drug Administration (FDA) approved the sale of levonorgestrel, a high dose of progestogen hormones, the basis for many birth control pills. Marketed as Plan B One-Step and its generic versions, My Way and Next Choice One Dose, the medication is available without prescription on pharmacy shelves.

Often called the "morning-after pill," the drug, if taken within five days — ideally, within 72 hours — after unprotected sex, works primarily by delaying ovulation, or the release of an egg from the uterus.

The availability of the drug was potentially an important development for women who did not want to have a child but who did not want an abortion either. About 5.8 million American women used the morning after pill from 2006 to 2010, according to a CDC report.[20]

Abortion-rights supporters say scientific studies have proved that the pill only prevents a pregnancy from occurring and does not end an existing pregnancy.

Many medical experts, including the American College of Obstetricians and Gynecologists (ACOG), say pregnancy does not occur until an egg is fertilized in the uterus and then implanted in the lining of the woman's uterus, which does not happen until several days after intercourse.[21] "Review of evidence suggests that emergency contraception cannot prevent implantation of a fertilized egg," so it does not cause an abortion, according to an ACOG committee report.

But many abortion opponents believe that life begins at fertilization, not at implantation, so they say

States Tighten Laws for Providers

At least 29 states in the past four years have enacted laws to regulate abortion clinics that supporters say are designed to protect patients and opponents say aim to make it more difficult for women to get safe, legal and affordable abortions. Among other things, the laws require that abortion clinic doctors have admitting privileges and transfer agreements with local hospitals or require clinics to meet the same structural standards as ambulatory surgical centers.

States with Recent Laws on Abortion Clinics

Source: "Targeted Regulation of Abortion Providers," Guttmacher Institute, March 1, 2014, http://tinyurl.com/mnhuenr

the definition of pregnancy does not address the question of when life begins. And the morning-after pill, they say, can cause an abortion if an egg was released into the uterus before the pills were taken.

"It is scientifically undisputed that a new human organism begins at fertilization," the Catholic Medical Association and other organizations of health care professionals opposing abortion have stated. "[If] a drug or device can work after fertilization, by blocking the implantation of a developing human embryo, [it] might not end a 'pregnancy' . . . but it does end the life of a unique human being."

Interpretation of a government-approved description of the pill's effects also plays a role in the dispute. FDA's product information label for Plan B One-Step says the medication "will not work if you are already pregnant and will not affect an existing pregnancy." However, the label also says the product may work "by preventing attachment [of a fertilized egg] to the uterus" — and that possibility rankles abortion opponents.

Nonprescription emergency contraception (EC) medication has been available in the United States since 1999, marketed as Plan B One-Step and its generic versions, My Way and Next Choice One Dose. The availability of EC's was seen as an important development for women who did not want a child but did not want to have an abortion. But abortion opponents say the so-called morning-after pill can go beyond contraception in some cases and cause an abortion. According to a federal report, 5.8 million women used the pill from 2006 to 2010.

The American Association of Pro-Life Obstetricians and Gynecologists has said, "Terminating a human embryo is abortion, whether before or after its implantation into the uterus."[22]

Many scientists say the FDA's labeling doesn't reflect the latest scientific knowledge about Plan B. ACOG and other health care professional organizations have written that the label's statement about preventing attachment of a fertilized egg "has not been updated since the product was originally approved in 1999 and . . . does not reflect the most current research [showing] that Plan B . . . functions by inhibiting or postponing ovulation. . . . It does not prevent fertilization or implantation" so it does not cause an abortion."[23]

A Princeton University study published in February left some room for doubt. It found that emergency contraceptives do not cause abortions under the implantation definition of pregnancy accepted by ACOG and the FDA. However, according to the study, "To make an informed choice, women must know that [although the drugs] prevent pregnancy primarily by delaying or inhibiting ovulation and inhibiting fertilization . . . it is not scientifically possible to definitively rule out that [the drugs] may inhibit implantation of a fertilized egg in the [uterus]." However, the study also found "no available evidence" of that happening.[24]

Biochemist Diana Blithe, program director for the Contraceptive Development Research Centers Program at the National Institute of Child Health and Human Development, said the possibility of Plan B One-Step's effect on implantation no longer belongs on the label. "As a scientist, I would definitely take [the implementation reference] off of emergency contraception," she said.[25]

The FDA has announced no plans to change the label's wording, although Acting Assistant Commissioner for Media Affairs Erica Jefferson says that if a woman is already pregnant when she takes the pill, "that is — when the fertilized egg has attached to the uterine wall — the drug will not cause the pregnancy to end."

The agency is "aware of emerging data" suggesting that Plan B "does not inhibit or prevent implantation of the fertilized egg" and can change a drug's labeling, but it must be "at the request of a company to reflect new information from clinical trials or other scientific sources," Jefferson says.

Should employers with religious objections be able to exclude coverage for abortions and birth control expenses in company health insurance plans?

Under the new, comprehensive health care reform law — the Affordable Care Act (ACA) — for-profit companies must include coverage for physician-prescribed and FDA-approved contraceptive services for women enrolled in company insurance plans. The coverage must be free — that is, an employee does not have to provide a co-payment or a deductible — so the employer ends up paying for insuring the services.

The law "is designed to ensure that health care decisions are made between a woman and her doctor," White House press secretary Jay Carney said Nov. 26, 2013. "The president believes that no one, including the government or for-profit corporations, should be able to dictate those decisions to women."[26]

But two businesses, whose owners object to contraception on religious grounds, have sued the federal government over the birth control mandate, claiming it interferes with their constitutional right to practice their religion. Although the two cases, which will be heard together by the U.S. Supreme Court on March 25, are based on similar arguments, lower courts arrived at different conclusions in their rulings on the cases.

One case was filed by the owners of the arts-and-crafts chain Hobby Lobby, who say they apply biblical principles to their company's management. The owners say they don't object to providing coverage for certain forms of contraception, such as diaphragms, condoms or sterilization surgery, which prevent an egg from being fertilized. However, they do object to emergency contraception drugs such as Plan B One-Step which, they say, can prevent fertilized embryos from implanting in the uterus and therefore — under their definition — constitutes an abortion.

Hobby Lobby's owners said they are faced with either refusing to offer their 13,000 employees the comprehensive coverage required by ACA, which would subject them to fines of $1.3 million a day, or dropping employee insurance altogether, which would cost them $26 million in fines.[27]

Hobby Lobby lawyer Kyle Duncan said, "No one should be forced to give up their constitutionally protected civil rights just to go into business. . . . [T]he government's efforts to strip this family business of its religious rights represent a gross violation of the Religious Freedom Restoration Act [RFRA, a 1993 federal law intended to remove obstacles to an individual's religious practice] and the First Amendment."[28]

The 10th U.S. Circuit Court of Appeals in Denver agreed with Hobby Lobby, concluding that a corporation has a constitutional right of religious expression and thus is not required to cover abortion services or contraception.[29] Appealing the decision to the Supreme Court, the Justice Department argued that RFRA is not "a sword . . . to deny employees of for-profit commercial enterprises the benefits and protections of generally applicable laws."[30]

The American Civil Liberties Union, which supports the government position, wrote in a "friend of the court" brief, "Although the business owners are certainly entitled to their religious beliefs, the companies are not permitted to invoke those beliefs to discriminate against their female employees. Just as the companies' owners would not be able to use religion to hire only men, or refuse to pay their female employees equally, they should not be allowed to use religion to violate a contraception rule that is designed to promote gender equality."[31]

The other case involves Conestoga Wood Specialties Corp., a cabinet maker in East Earl, Pa., owned by a

The new Affordable Care Act requires employers to provide free contraception services for employees in company insurance plans. Owners of the Hobby Lobby chain and another firm object to contraception and have sued the government to overturn the mandate, contending it interferes with their constitutional right to practice their religion. The U.S. Supreme Court will hear arguments in the case on March 25.

AP Photo/Ed Andrieski

Mennonite family opposed to contraception and abortion. The company employs 950 workers; the owners say their faith requires them to apply their religious principles to their business practices.[32] In ruling that the company was not exempt from the ACA mandate, the Third U.S. Circuit Court of Appeals wrote, "We simply cannot understand how a for-profit, secular corporation — apart from its owners — can exercise religion."[33]

But Randall Wenger, one of Conestoga's attorneys, said in announcing the company's decision to appeal the case to the Supreme Court, "How can the government tell families operating businesses that they can no longer apply their convictions in the workplace? Living consistently with one's beliefs is a basic tenet of a free society."[34]

Some churches and other religiously affiliated organizations also oppose the contraception mandate. In response to their complaints, the White House in 2012 exempted "churches, other houses of worship and similar organizations" from paying for their employees' contraception coverage on the basis of the employer's religious objections; in those cases, the insurance companies would cover the costs.[35]

Despite the exemption, some employers maintain that the ACA's contraception requirement requires them to violate their religious convictions that forbid the

Regional Divide on Abortion Grows

The regional disparity in attitudes about abortion nearly doubled between 1995 and 2013. The difference between those in New England who broadly support legal abortion compared to those in the South Central region rose from 18 percentage points to 35 during that period.* As support for abortion in all or most cases grew in New England, it declined in the South Central states.

Percentage Who Favor Legal Abortion in All or Most Cases, by Region

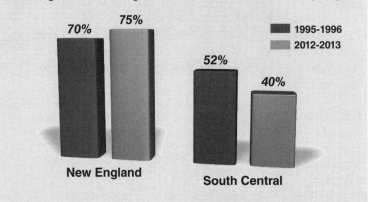

* *New England includes Connecticut, Massachusetts, Maine, New Hampshire, Rhode Island and Vermont. South Central region includes Alabama, Arkansas, Kentucky, Louisiana, Mississippi, Oklahoma, Tennessee and Texas.*

Source: "Widening Regional Divide over Abortion Laws," Pew Research Center, July 29, 2013, http://tinyurl.com/pwg3fcl

practice of birth control. The Little Sisters of the Poor, an order of Catholic nuns which operates nursing and assisted living facilities for the elderly, sued the government over a requirement to sign a form requiring their insurance company to provide the contraception coverage. Signing the form, the sisters said, would violate their religious convictions by making contraception available to their female employees.[36]

On Jan. 21, 2014, the Supreme Court ruled that the Little Sisters should not be required to sign the form before their case is resolved in the courts. Instead, a written notice to the Department of Health and Human Services would suffice, stating that as a religious order they have "religious objections to providing coverage for contraceptive services." The court made clear its ruling was not "an expression of [its] view" of the case's merits. The case is pending before the 10th U.S. Circuit Court of Appeals in Denver.[37]

In a case raising similar issues, the Chicago-based Seventh Circuit on Feb. 21 denied the University of Notre Dame's request for a temporary injunction exempting it from ACA's contraception requirement, which the university said forced it to go against its religious beliefs. The court wrote, "while a religious institution has a broad immunity from being required to engage in acts that violate the tenets of its faith, it has no right to prevent other institutions, whether the government or a health insurance company, from engaging in acts that merely offend the institution."[38]

The Justice Department has argued that, "To opt out of providing contraceptive coverage, Little Sisters need only certify that they are nonprofit organizations that hold themselves out as religious and that, because of religious objections, they are opposed to providing coverage for some or all contraceptive services . . . [there is] no substantial burden on their exercise of religion."[39]

But George Mason University professor Helen Alvaré, a strong abortion opponent who teaches family law and religion and the law, has written, "Legally, the [contraception] Mandate has put the Catholic Church in the exemption-seeking business — the business of seeking *not* to comply with laws billed as advancing human rights for women. This is a position more than disagreeable to anyone pushed to take it."[40]

BACKGROUND

Banning Abortion

During the 18th and early 19th centuries, abortions were illegal only after "quickening," or when a woman could feel movement of the fetus, generally considered to occur around the fourth month of pregnancy. Drugs and other medications that induce abortions were widely available; practitioners were also beginning to offer surgical abortions.

In 1857, the American Medical Association (AMA) began campaigning to make abortion at any stage of pregnancy illegal, partly on moral grounds, partly out of concern for patients' health and partly to limit competition from homeopaths and midwives, according to historian James C. Mohr. By 1880, every state had banned abortion except when needed to protect the life of the mother.

But illegal abortion remained an option, although it carried serious risks, such as poisoning from untested and unregulated medications and surgical procedures carried out under unsanitary conditions. In 1930, abortion was the official cause of death for nearly 2,700 women, or 18 percent of childbirth-related deaths recorded that year.[41] The actual number of abortion-related deaths is unknown.

"Many deaths from illegal abortion would go unlabeled as such because of careless or casual autopsies, lack of experience and ability of autopsy surgeons, and simply the shame and fear associated with abortion's illegality," according to a study by NARAL Pro-Choice America.[42]

Childbearing in general was dangerous, as well. In her book *When Abortion Was a Crime*, historian Leslie Reagan wrote, "The mortality associated with abortion must be assessed within the context of overall maternal mortality. In the 1920s, observers believed that at least 20,000 women died each year due to [childbirth-related] causes."[43]

By the 1960s perhaps as many as 1.2 million illegal abortions were being performed each year.[44]

In 1962, a high-profile case brought the issue out from the shadows. Sherri Chessen — known as Miss Sherri, host of the Phoenix, Ariz., edition of the popular "Romper Room" children's TV show — was pregnant with her fifth child and suffering from severe morning sickness.

> **"I was hardly thinking 50 years ahead to what impact my decision would have on the world of the future. . . .
> It was simply the perfect storm for this long-delayed debate to be brought to the forefront."**
>
> **— Sherri Chessen,**
> *who had a controversial abortion in 1962 after taking the drug thalidomide and learning her child would be born severely deformed.*

Hoping to quell the debilitating nausea, she took a tranquilizer that had been prescribed for her husband while he was on a business trip to England. The drug, thalidomide, was not available in the United States. A few weeks later, she saw a newspaper account of babies being born in England with grotesque deformities after their mothers had taken an unnamed tranquilizer during pregnancy. Eventually she learned that the drug was thalidomide. Her doctor told her the odds were significantly against her delivering "a normal baby."

At the time, abortion was illegal in Arizona except to save a woman's life. Even though Chessen's life was not in danger, the doctor recommended terminating the pregnancy, calling it a "therapeutic" abortion. She agreed; he made the arrangements.

Her situation soon became national, then international, news. Fearing prosecution, the hospital canceled the procedure. So Chessen sought an abortion overseas and received permission to have the procedure done in Sweden. The obstetrician who performed it told her the baby was too badly deformed to have survived.[45]

Lee Epstein, a professor of law and political science at the University of Southern California, wrote that Chessen's "situation evoked sympathetic reactions . . . and, in essence, led to the creation of an American abortion reform movement."[46]

Chessen told *CQ Researcher* she "was not a spearhead, but a catalyst." She says she was just "a mother . . . with four small children to care for, and was facing the possibility of knowingly giving birth to what was described to me as 'a head and a torso.' I was hardly thinking 50 years ahead to what impact [my] decision [would] have on the world of the future. . . . It was simply the perfect storm for this long-delayed debate to be brought to the forefront."

A Gallup poll conducted in September of 1962 showed that 52 percent of Americans thought Chessen "had done the right thing," while 32 percent called it "the wrong thing." Sixteen percent were unsure or had no opinion.[47]

Decriminalizing Abortion

With the Chessen case, America's decades-old conversation about abortion, which had focused mostly on moral perspectives, expanded to incorporate other medical, legal and political concerns. In 1967 the newly established National Organization for Women (NOW)

CHRONOLOGY

1973-1989 *Supreme Court establishes constitutional right to abortion, igniting ongoing political battles. Court later upholds some restrictions, strikes down others.*

1973 Supreme Court's landmark *Roe v. Wade* decision establishes constitutional right to abortion. . . . In *Doe v. Bolton*, the court strikes down a Georgia law requiring a woman to get approval from three physicians before having an abortion.

1976 Congress passes Hyde Amendment banning the use of Medicaid and other federal funds for abortions.

1979 Supreme Court rules unconstitutional a Missouri law requiring abortions be performed in hospitals after the first trimester.

1983 Supreme Court declares unconstitutional an Ohio law requiring a 24-hour waiting period before an abortion, parental consent for abortions on girls under 15 and that abortions after the first trimester be performed in a hospital.

1989 Supreme Court strikes down a Washington state law declaring that "life begins at conception."

1990s *Court broadens states' right to regulate abortions; abortion opponents try to get the court to chip away at Roe.*

1992 In *Planned Parenthood v. Casey*, the Supreme Court reaffirms *Roe*'s holding that states may not ban abortions but upholds mandatory 24-hour waiting periods and parental-consent laws.

1996 Congress passes law banning late-term abortions (also called "partial birth" abortions); President Clinton vetoes the bill.

2000-2007 *U.S. abortion rate declines steadily.*

2003 President George W. Bush signs partial birth abortion legislation.

2007 Supreme Court upholds the constitutionality of the partial birth abortion ban.

2010-Present *Social conservatives push for more state regulations on abortion; abortion coverage becomes issue in debate over comprehensive health care law.*

2010 Congress passes Affordable Care Act (ACA) in March, requiring Americans to have health insurance . . . . In November voters elect hundreds of social conservatives to state legislatures and governors' mansions.

2011 Federal government says insurance companies must cover women's contraceptives under the ACA. . . . Number of abortions reaches lowest level since *Roe v. Wade* — a 25 percent drop from the 1990 all-time high.

2012 Supreme Court in June upholds the ACA but says states can decide the level of abortion coverage each woman must receive. . . . Owners of Hobby Lobby craft stores and Conestoga Wood Specialties Corp. sue the government on religious grounds over the ACA's contraception mandate. . . . White House exempts churches and religious organizations from paying for employees' contraception coverage.

2013 States enact 70 laws regulating abortion, compared to 189 over the entire previous decade. . . . Tenth U.S. Circuit Court of Appeals rules that Hobby Lobby does not have to provide contraception coverage for employees, but Third Circuit rules that Conestoga Wood Specialties does. Both decisions are appealed to the Supreme Court, which agrees to hear them together. . . . House of Representatives in June passes the Pain-Capable Unborn Child Protection Act, which would ban abortions after the 20th week of pregnancy; a companion bill in the Senate is given little chance of passage.

2014 Supreme Court in January gives religious organizations temporary relief from complying with the ACA contraception mandate while the issue is being resolved in the courts and refuses to review a lower court decision striking down an Arizona ban on abortions at 20 weeks of pregnancy. . . . Supreme Court will hear arguments in Hobby Lobby and Conestoga cases on March 25.

adopted a Bill of Rights that included "the right of women to control their own reproductive lives" by decriminalizing abortion.

Religious organizations also were taking sides. Conservative denominations such as Roman Catholics and the Lutheran Church's Missouri Synod took strong stands against legalizing abortion out of respect for human life. More liberal denominations, including Methodists and the United Church of Christ, supported abortion rights.[48]

In 1970 the AMA, which had led the 19th-century effort to criminalize abortion, reconsidered its position and declared that decisions about abortion should be left to the "sound clinical judgment" of the physician and the consent of the "informed patient." The evolution of the AMA's position presents "a portrait of a profession — like the society it served — on the cusp of change," wrote legal affairs journalist Linda Greenhouse and law professor Reva B. Siegel.[49]

States soon began to loosen their abortion restrictions. Beginning in 1970, Alaska, Hawaii, New York and Washington repealed their antiabortion statutes and allowed abortions on request before fetal viability, generally, during the first trimester. Of the four, however, only New York did not impose a 30-day residency requirement on the patient, making it a destination for out-of-state women who could afford the trip.[50]

A study by an economic research organization found a "robust association" between distance to New York and abortion rates in the pre-*Roe v. Wade* years, with abortion rates falling "11.9 percent for every hundred miles a woman lived from New York."[51]

In 1973, the landmark Supreme Court *Roe* decision establishing a woman's constitutional right to abortion was based on a woman's right to privacy under the 14th Amendment, which limits the activities of government officials as they affect citizens.[52]

In 1976, in response to the concerns of abortion opponents, Congress passed legislation that became known as the Hyde Amendment, which prohibits the use of funds appropriated for the Department of Health and Human Services to pay for an abortion except in the case of rape, incest or when the woman's life is endangered. The amendment primarily affects Medicaid, the health care program for low-income individuals, which is funded jointly by states and the federal government.

In 1992 a more conservative court, led by Chief Justice William Rehnquist, in *Planned Parenthood of Southeastern Pa. v. Casey*, reaffirmed *Roe*'s "essential principle" of the right to abortion without undue state interference but also found that states could impose certain reasonable requirements, including a 24-hour waiting period and parental consent for minors. The decision effectively broadened the rights of states to regulate abortion.[53]

Also in 1992, Democrat Bill Clinton was elected president. He said abortion decisions "should be left to a woman, her conscience, her doctor and her God" and that "abortion should not only be safe and legal, it should be rare."[54] With a supporter of abortion rights in the White House, and a Supreme Court apparently unwilling to reverse *Roe*, abortion opponents "moved away from the all-or-nothing attitude" of trying to overturn *Roe* outright, a tactic they had concluded "would simply generate more court decisions re-endorsing *Roe*," says David Garrow, a history and law professor at the University of Pittsburgh. Instead, he says, they adopted a strategy of "chipping away at the margins."

Without directly challenging *Roe*'s precepts, states began passing legislation making access to abortion more difficult — for example by forbidding the use of public funds for abortion; restricting private insurance coverage for abortions; mandating waiting periods between gynecological counseling and performance of an abortion; and requiring parental consent before a minor could get an abortion.

It's the kind of incremental, long-term approach that anti-abortion strategist Bopp of National Right to Life favors. "The Supreme Court's current makeup assures that a declared federal constitutional right to abortion remains secure for the present," he and Coleson wrote in their 2007 memo. "Eschewing incremental efforts to limit abortion where legally and politically possible makes the error of not saving some because not all can be saved. It also makes the strategic error of believing that the pro-life issue can be kept alive without such incremental efforts."[55]

Challenging *Roe*

A bill passed by the House of Representatives last June 18 — the Pain-Capable Unborn Child Protection Act — would ban abortions after the 20th week of pregnancy and directly challenge *Roe*'s gestation strictures.

Compromise Remains Elusive in Abortion Debate

Politicians "benefit from keeping the divisiveness alive."

In March 1993, David Gunn, a physician in Pensacola, Fla., who performed abortions, was shot to death by Michael F. Griffin as he shouted "Don't kill any more babies," the first of five killings or attempted killings of U.S. abortion providers over the next two years. He was convicted of murder and sentenced to life in prison.

"The 1990s was a tumultuous decade," says Mary Jacksteit, a specialist in conflict resolution. "The abortion issue was very divisive and disruptive at the local level."

Jacksteit and Sister Adrienne Kaufmann, a Benedictine nun, thought there might be a way to reduce the conflict through dialogue between activists on both sides of the debate. In the months following Gunn's murder they founded the Network for Life and Choice under the sponsorship of Search for Common Ground, a conflict prevention organization in Boston.

For them, common ground didn't mean legislating agreement and defining what was and was not permissible; their goal was to make the debate more civil. "We wanted to know, 'How can we wage this battle [over abortion rights] without being violent, by finding areas where we agree?'" Jacksteit says. "We were very focused on changing the relationships between advocates and opponents."

"We found people, both pro-life and pro-choice, who wanted to have a serious discussion without destroying relationships or being ugly or violent," Jacksteit says. With funds mostly from grants from philanthropic foundations, Jacksteit and Kaufmann by 1999 had brought their program of workshops and public forums to 20 cities. By then, however, the abortion conflict was out of the headlines, Jacksteit says, and "the foundation world became bored with the issue. In 1998, when [abortion doctor Barnett Slepian] was killed in Buffalo, it wasn't page one news."

With foundation grants disappearing, the two women sought funding from advocacy organizations on both sides of the abortion issue. "We had good conversations, but no traction because at that level of advocacy, you raise money by demonizing the other side," not by "quiet, reasonable discussion," Jacksteit says. The network closed up shop in 1999.

Today, Jacksteit says she sees no prospect of movement toward common ground "as long as politics in Washington and in the states are so polarized.[1] Until that overall dynamic changes, I don't see anything happening very soon."

Even an effort in 2009 to get legislation passed that aimed "to reduce the need for abortion while preserving the right to have one" could not get support from both sides. Rachel Laser, then-director of the culture program at Third Way, a liberal Washington think tank, worked on legislation with U.S. Reps. Tim Ryan of Ohio, who called himself a "pro-life Democrat," and Rosa DeLauro, D-Conn., who supported

Sen. Lindsey Graham, R-S.C., who introduced a companion bill in the Senate on Nov. 7, said, "We are choosing today to speak up for all babies at 20 weeks, and trying to create legal protections under the theory that if you can feel pain, the government should protect you from being destroyed by an abortion."[56]

The measure's supporters cited research concluding that fetuses can feel pain at that stage, but that theory is controversial. Dr. Paul Ranalli, a University of Toronto neurologist, has said, "At 20 weeks, the fetal brain has the full complement of brain cells present in adulthood, ready and waiting to receive pain signals from the body, and their electrical activity can be recorded by standard electroencephalography."[57]

Dr. Nicholas Fisk, a senior maternal-fetal medicine specialist at Royal Brisbane and Women's Hospital in Australia, once considered early fetal pain a possibility.[58] But the former president of the International Fetal Medicine and Surgery Society later revised his opinion, saying recent neurological research convinced him pain "is not possible at all" before 24 weeks.[59]

The fetal pain bill, with broad support among Republicans, is considered unlikely to clear the Democratic-controlled Senate and faces a likely presidential veto. In a

abortion rights. They crafted a bill to provide funds for increased access to contraception, expanded public information about adoption, increased health care coverage for pregnant women and broadened access to comprehensive sex education. The legislation had the backing of abortion rights groups such as NARAL Pro-Choice America and Planned Parenthood, as well as some evangelical Christian leaders who opposed abortion.

But major anti-abortion groups did not endorse it because, they believed, "Planned Parenthood and NARAL wouldn't back a so-called 'common ground' bill unless it included abortion services," said Charmaine Yoest, president and CEO of Americans United for Life, which calls itself "the nation's premier pro-life legal team."[2] The bill died in committee.

Laser says it failed because it tried "to depoliticize an issue that a lot of politicians thrive on." Politicians "are not interested in calming the debate," she says, because "they benefit from keeping the divisiveness alive," since extremists on both sides are most likely to vote and to make campaign contributions.

Like Jacksteit, Laser is pessimistic about the near-term chances for reaching common ground, which she defines as shared values both sides can agree on "while staying true to their core values." Laser calls the current political climate "challenging," and says, "We have not seen the end of finding

Florida Department of Corrections

Michael F. Griffin, above, shot and killed David Gunn, a physician who performed abortions in Pensacola, Fla., in 1993. Gunn was the first of five abortion providers killed or attempted to be killed over the next two years. Griffin was convicted and sentenced to life in prison.

shared values on abortion, but right now it doesn't seem as though some major effort is going to emerge."

A 2011 Gallup poll found "plenty of common ground" between the two sides. For instance, 86 percent of adults favoring abortion rights and 87 percent opposing them agreed in requiring informed consent for women seeking abortions, and 79 percent and 94 percent, respectively, agreed with making abortion illegal in the third trimester.

Ted Jelen, a political science professor at the University of Nevada, Las Vegas, says polls show that "most people think abortion should be legal but restricted."

However, Jelen says, the fact that "both sides are able to frame their positions in terms of rights — the fetal right to life versus the maternal right to choose—"makes it difficult for the two sides to come together. 'Rights' is a very powerful symbol in American politics."

— *William Wanlund*

[1] For background, see Tom Price, "Polarization in America," *CQ Researcher*, Feb. 28, 2014, pp. 193-216.

[2] Press release, "AUL: So-Called 'Common Ground' Ryan-DeLauro Bill Would Actually Force All 50 States to Pay for Abortion," Americans United for Life, Aug. 7, 2009, http://tinyurl.com/kt7yr26.

statement, the Obama administration has said the measure "would unacceptably restrict women's health and reproductive rights and is an assault on a woman's right to choose."[60]

In January 2013, Obama signed legislation permitting military servicewomen to use their government insurance to pay for an abortion in case of rape or incest. Previously, military insurance had covered only abortions performed to save the woman's life; servicewomen who wanted to terminate a non-life-threatening rape- or incest-caused pregnancy had to pay for the procedure themselves.

Defense Department figures show 467 reports of rape of service members during the fiscal year beginning Oct.

1, 2011. However, the department also estimates that fewer than 15 percent of military sexual-assault victims report the attack to a military authority, due to stigma "and other barriers that deter reporting."[61]

The Senate legislation was sponsored by Sen. Jeanne Shaheen, D-N.H., who also has co-sponsored a pending bill to make the same benefits available to Peace Corps volunteers.[62] According to agency statistics, 212 rapes or attempted rapes were reported by volunteers during the decade 2001-2010.[63]

The bill "is a matter of basic fairness," said Cecile Richards, president of the pro-choice Planned Parenthood

Federation of America. "It will ensure that a woman serving in the Peace Corps will have the same access to abortion if she is the victim of rape or incest, or when her life is endangered, as women in the armed services and many other women covered by federal health programs."[64]

However, Americans United for Life president Yoest said in a statement that, rather than resorting to abortion, more attention should be paid to protecting the volunteers. "Rather than addressing the egregious security concerns that we should all have for these young women who are being sent in dangerous situations, the Obama administration and their allies are using the horrific events in [their] lives to expand federal involvement in abortion."[65]

The Peace Corps legislation was approved last July 25 by the Senate Appropriations Committee for inclusion in the overall State Department and foreign relations appropriations bill, which has not been scheduled for a vote by the full Senate.

Meanwhile, in 1999, the Food and Drug Administration approved emergency contraceptives for prescription-only sale in the United States.

In 2006 the agency partially removed the pill's prescription requirement, making it available without a prescription to women over 18, and by prescription to those 17 and younger. In June 2013, under pressure from federal courts and finding no medical evidence that the drug was harmful, the agency dropped the age restriction altogether.[66]

CURRENT SITUATION

Abortion and the ACA

As expansion of public and private insurance under the Affordable Care Act (ACA) got underway Jan. 1, controversy has intensified over how the new law treats abortion services.[67]

One aspect of the controversy revolves around the health insurance exchanges — the government-supervised "marketplace" of insurance plans from which potential ACA enrollees can choose federally subsidized health

Philadelphia abortion doctor Kermit Gosnell was sentenced to life in prison without parole after being convicted in the deaths of a patient and three babies born alive during abortions at a filthy clinic. The sensational 2013 case heightened the controversy over tough, new state regulations on abortion clinics. Abortion opponents say they are needed to protect women's health. Abortion-rights advocates contend the laws are unreasonable and designed to put abortion clinics out of business.

AP Photo/Philadelphia Police Department

insurance. The plans are offered by private companies, but the marketplaces are run by either the states or the federal government.[68]

Abortion opponents contend that, because the ACA subsidizes some insurance premiums for policies that include abortion coverage, it is subsidizing abortions with taxpayer money in violation of the Hyde Amendment. The 1976 law prohibits the use of funds appropriated for the Department of Health and Human Services to pay for an abortion except in the case of rape, incest or when the woman's life is endangered. The amendment primarily affects Medicaid.

In March 2010 Obama issued an executive order intended to ensure that the ACA was consistent with the amendment. If abortion is covered in an exchange insurance plan, the order said, the policyholder must pay a separate premium out of her own pocket for that service.[69] Moreover, under the ACA, states may exclude abortion coverage from plans offered in their health insurance exchanges. As of Feb. 1, nearly two dozen states had prohibited their state exchanges from covering most abortions.[70]

However, Americans United for Life announced in a statement that the ACA circumvents Hyde because "insurance plans in the new state exchanges are permitted to cover abortion unless states prohibit it." Thus, the group said, "many Americans will be railroaded into paying directly for abortions with their insurance premiums — sometimes without their knowledge and consent."[71]

According to an analysis by the Charlotte Lozier Institute, the research organization opposed to abortion rights, the ACA will result in an annual net increase of up to 111,500 insured abortions that are either fully publicly funded through Medicaid or heavily subsidized through the state health insurance exchanges, depending on how many women forego insurance and pay out-of-pocket."[72]

Upcoming Elections

As Republican politicians prepare for next fall's midterm elections, the party hopes its candidates will strike the right tone in their public comments about abortion.

Abortion Debate Takes to the Road

"Choose Life" license plates available in 29 states.

Randy Harris, a Florida county commissioner, was stuck in traffic in 1996 when he found himself thinking about an environmental message on the license plate of the vehicle ahead of him. If a plate can carry a "Protect the Panthers" message, he wondered, why not one that says "Choose Life" to promote adoption as an alternative to abortion?

Getting the Florida legislature to approve the idea, however, wasn't easy. At first, lawmakers wouldn't even move a bill out of committee, and in 1998 Democratic Gov. Lawton Chiles rejected the plates as politically divisive. But the following year Republican Gov. Jeb Bush signed legislation allowing sales of the plates, although a court challenge delayed their distribution until 2000.

"Adoption is as worthy a cause as [Bush] can think of," his spokesman said at the time.[1]

Since Florida became the first to adopt Choose Life plates, 28 other states have done so. As of December 2013, some 910,000 Choose Life plates had been bought or renewed nationally, raising nearly $20 million for organizations that promote adoption instead of abortion, according to Choose Life America, a group formed in 2011 to promote the sale of plates to fund adoptions as an alternative to abortion.[2]

But efforts to win state approval of the plates have been difficult at times. Last July, Rhode Island's Democratic governor, Lincoln Chafee, vetoed Choose Life legislation that would have sent $20 of the $40 cost of each plate to a Christian CareNet crisis pregnancy center that opposes abortion rights.

The function of a license plate is "to register and identify a motor vehicle," Chafee wrote in his veto message to lawmakers. "It is my belief that state participation in the transmission of funds to this organization would violate the separation of church and state, one of the fundamental principles upon which our state was founded."[3]

Likewise, in December 2012, a federal judge ruled that North Carolina's offering of a Choose Life license plate "in the absence of a pro-choice alternative" amounts to "viewpoint discrimination" and violates the First Amendment.[4]

North Carolina appealed the decision to the Fourth U.S. Circuit Court of Appeals, which rejected the appeal in February. The state attorney general's office was reviewing the decision, a spokeswoman said.[5]

While more than half of the states offer Choose Life plates, only four have offered plates with a pro-choice message. That's "not surprising," says Elizabeth Nash, state issues manager at

Virginia offers both "Choose Life" license plates, which help fund adoption agencies, and "Trust Women-Respect Choice" plates, which fund gynecological exams and related services.

the Guttmacher Institute, a research organization that supports abortion rights.

"Pro-choice and pro-life license plate efforts come from different motivations," Nash says. Choose Life plates help fund adoption agencies and similar organizations, while pro-choice plates are "more of a messaging piece" promoting family planning, she says.

Virginia offers both Choose Life plates and plates with the slogan, "Trust Women/Respect Choice." Funds from sales of the latter are used for gynecological exams and sexually transmitted disease testing and follow-up care — but not for abortion-related services — at Planned Parenthood centers in Virginia.[6]

Tarina Keene, executive director of NARAL Pro-Choice Virginia, says, "We really don't feel like a license plate is the place to be promoting a political agenda." However, she says, her organization saw the Choose Life plate as a challenge that needed to be answered, so NARAL and other organizations that support abortion access lobbied for the pro-choice plate. It was approved by the state legislature in 2010.

— *William Wanlund*

[1]David Nitkin, "Gov. Bush Signs Controversial License Law," *Orlando Sentinel*, June 9, 1999, http://tinyurl.com/m4lbz97.

[2]"Newsletter," Choose Life America, Inc., Dec. 12, 2013, http://tinyurl.com/n8rr5yy.

[3]"Rhode Island Governor Vetoes 'Choose Life' License Plates," *Governing.com*, July 17, 2013, http://tinyurl.com/pduo8z6.

[4]Opinion, U.S. District Court for the Eastern District of North Carolina, Western Division, *ACLU of North Carolina v. State of North Carolina*, Dec. 7, 2012, http://tinyurl.com/qyelt7q.

[5]Dan McCue, "Anti-Abortion License Plates in N.C. Tossed," Courthouse News Service, Feb. 14, 2014, http://tinyurl.com/n99ty6f.

[6]"Support Trust Women/Respect Choice License Plates," fact sheet, Planned Parenthood, http://tinyurl.com/pdxdwre.

Abortion Rate at 38-Year Low

The abortion rate in 2011 — about 16 per 1,000 women between the ages of 15 and 44 — was the lowest since 1973, the year the Supreme Court legalized abortion. The rate peaked in 1981 at 29 abortions per 1,000 women, and has generally fallen since then. Between 2008 and 2011, the abortion rate fell by 13 percent.

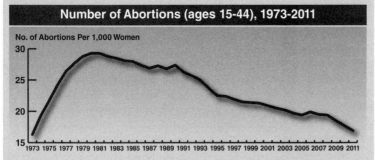

Number of Abortions (ages 15-44), 1973-2011

No. of Abortions Per 1,000 Women

Sources: Rachel Jones and Kathryn Kooistra, "Abortion Incidence and Service Availability in the United States, 2008," Perspectives on Sexual and Reproductive Health, Guttmacher Institute, March 2011, http//tinyurl.com/mnxrghj; 2008-2011 data is from Rachel Jones and Jenna Jerman, "Abortion Incidence and Service Availability in the United States, 2011," Perspectives on Sexual and Reproductive Health, Guttmacher Institute, March 2014, http//tinyurl.com/plk68q2.

In their 2012 Senate campaigns Rep. Todd Akin in Missouri and Richard Mourdock in Indiana made controversial assertions about rape and abortion that contributed to their defeat by their Democratic opponents.[73] In Virginia's 2013 gubernatorial election, Democrats portrayed Republican candidate Ken Cuccinelli as hostile to women for his opposition to abortion and stands on other issues. Cuccinelli lost the women's vote by 9 percentage points, which contributed to his defeat by Democrat Terry McAuliffe in an election decided by a vote difference of 2.5 percent.[74]

Republican Virginia state Sen. Stephen Martin said on Feb. 24, 2014, "once a child does exist in your womb, I'm not going to assume a right to kill it just because the child's host (some refer to them as mothers) doesn't want it," prompting Democratic colleague Barbara Favola to say Martin's comment showed a "total lack of respect for women."[75]

"Republicans have struggled in the past on a whole range of reproductive issues. They haven't talked about those issues with a whole lot of understanding of the situation that women sometimes find themselves in," says Kate Gage, a partner in Burning Glass Consulting of Alexandria, Va., which advises Republican candidates on women voters. "We saw what happened in 2012 with candidates like Mourdock and Akin. It's like they've never even spoken to women who've been in these situations. When talking about these issues, you have to understand that women who are facing an unwanted pregnancy are women in real crisis."

Gage says she tells candidates, "It's important to communicate with more than a woman's reproductive system. Let's talk to women's brains and their pocketbooks and about issues that they confront on a day-to-day basis."

By alleging that the ACA and its abortion provisions are examples of fiscal irresponsibility, Republicans think they can tap into conservative anger over excessive government spending. For many lawmakers, abortion "ties into the issue they want to be talking about this election, which is Obamacare," said Tom McClusky, using the nickname Republicans have given the ACA. McClusky is vice president for government affairs for the March for Life, which opposes abortion.[76]

Ted Jelen, a political science professor at the University of Nevada, Las Vegas, who researches the politics of abortion, doesn't think abortion will be "terribly important" in the 2014 general elections but could have a major impact on who gets on the fall ballot. The abortion issue "might have an impact on some Republican primary races" this spring, he says, when activists on the issue "are more likely to turn out."

Clyde Wilcox, a professor of government at Georgetown University in Washington, says if abortion becomes an election issue it will favor Republicans, because abortion is the only "culture war" issue that "Republicans seem to be making inroads with."

Public opinion is trending "massively in a liberal direction" on issues such as same-sex marriage and legalization of marijuana, he says, "but on abortion, the trend is, if anything, slightly more conservative. The public is generally in favor of . . . what they see as moderate restrictions on abortion. At the same time, the public is generally

Do abortion limits disproportionately harm low-income women?

YES
Heather D. Boonstra
Senior Public Policy
Associate, Guttmacher Institute

Written for *CQ Researcher*, March 2014

NO
Helen Alvaré
Professor of Family Law and Law and Religion,
George Mason University School of Law

Written for *CQ Researcher*, March 2014

Restrictions on abortion fall hardest on low-income women, who already are disadvantaged in a variety of ways, including lacking access to the information and services necessary to prevent unplanned pregnancy in the first place. Indeed, low-income women bear a disproportionate burden from unintended pregnancies. In 2008, the rate of unintended pregnancy among poor women was more than five times that of women with an income of at least 200 percent of the federal poverty level (137 vs. 26 per 1,000 women, ages 15-44). As a result, low-income women are disproportionately likely to be faced with the decision about whether to seek an abortion.

Some abortion restrictions — such as the Hyde Amendment, which sharply limits abortion coverage for women who rely on Medicaid for insurance — specifically target low-income women. The impact of these restrictions is significant. Unable to use their coverage, poor women living at or near the poverty line often have to postpone an abortion because of the time it takes to scrape together the funds to pay for the procedure. Moreover, one in four women enrolled in Medicaid who would have had an abortion if coverage were available is forced to carry a pregnancy to term.

Other anti-abortion measures — such as pre-viability abortion bans, unwarranted doctor and clinic regulations and limits on the provision of medication abortion — have forced clinics in many states to close and otherwise cut off access to abortion in rural communities. In states or regions with these restrictions, getting to an abortion provider is not easy, especially for those with few resources. Raising money not only for the procedure but also for transportation, a hotel and child care — more than six in 10 women obtaining an abortion already are mothers — are challenges that, although surmountable, may cause a serious delay that only increases risk.

Simply put, restrictions on abortion make it more costly — financially and in terms of women's health and safety. It is cruel and ultimately self-defeating for governments to interfere with women's decision-making. Rather than coercing poor women to carry an unwanted pregnancy to term, we should focus on supporting all of a woman's pregnancy decisions: empowering poor and low-income women to prevent unintended pregnancy through access to high-quality contraceptives; supporting women so they can raise their children with dignity; and ensuring they can access safe and timely abortion care.

people seeking easier abortion access for poor women dwell on the apparently popular ends they pursue: avoiding creating children who are unwelcome and avoiding child poverty and the associated taxpayer expenditures. They also champion "empowering" poor women to make decisions without the interference of the state, or of men who may not have their best interests in mind. These ends seem to exude concern for the poor and for women's equality.

The problems with this position, however, are profound: They concern both the "means" proposed and the collateral effects.

First, abortion advocates refuse to squarely face the means they endorse to reach their ends. Abortion destroys human life. This is not mere "opinion," but a fact acknowledged by everyone from the Guttmacher Institute to the Planned Parenthood Federation to abortion providers far and wide. Solicitude on behalf of the poor is one thing; working to ensure access to aborting poor children is another. If anything, legal abortion is more disturbing today than 40 years ago, before ultrasound machines began depicting the human victim.

Second, an "abortion-access-for-the-poor" campaign is waist-high in collateral damage. No matter how strenuously the National Institutes of Health avoids the question, or abortion advocates flatly deny it, abortion scars many women. European studies give us some idea of the how and who, but in the United States we know about it more from the thousands of women flooding post-abortion distress programs.

There is also the matter of how abortion changes the "marketplace" for sex and marriage by its ultimate divorcing of sex from children. Well-off Americans have managed to avoid the nonmarital parenting and abortion rates that legal abortion facilitates, but the poor have not.

Finally, the pursuit of abortion access for the poor — who are already a disproportionately aborted population — smells of class disdain. The vocal "concern" for more abortion among the poor doesn't reflect what poor women seek for themselves: marriage and marital childbearing, stable work and transcendent meaning in their lives.

When it comes to abortion among the poor, both the poor and the public should trust the people and institutions who renounce the violence of abortion, while also running a massive network of social service programs for women, children and families. Don't trust the interest groups that have spent most of their enormous economic and social capital working to secure easier access to the abortion of poor children.

> "Republicans have struggled in the past on a whole range of reproductive issues. They haven't talked about those issues with a whole lot of understanding of the situation that women sometimes find themselves in."
>
> — Kate Gage,
> Political Consultant, Alexandria, Va.

favorable to abortion being legal and available to them and their families."

In 2008, Wilcox co-authored a study that found that abortion was one of the rare issues over which a voter might change political allegiances depending on a party's presentation of its views of the subject. "Partisanship moves when parties send clear signals on issues about which many in the public care deeply," the authors wrote.[77] But Wilcox thinks voters' attitudes have solidified since that report was published. "Really, we don't know anything about abortion today we didn't know before," he says. "People who were going to switch parties on this have already switched. I don't think there's going to be a lot more party-switching on this issue."

In a 2012 Gallup poll, 17 percent of registered voters surveyed said a candidate's position on abortion would be "decisive" in how they voted. Forty-five percent considered abortion "one of many important issues," while 34 percent didn't see it as a major issue. Overall, 48 percent considered themselves "pro-life" and 45 percent described themselves as "pro-choice," giving the electorate "a slight pro-life tilt," according to Gallup.[78]

OUTLOOK

Pushback?

On a blustery Saturday morning in December, Chuck Weichbrecht stood on the sidewalk outside the Falls Church Healthcare Center, displaying a placard with the image of a bloody, dismembered fetus to people entering the building and to motorists passing by.

Weichbrecht's graphic poster is a controversial medium for his message: That the public should be

conscious of the facts of abortion. "If people find these pictures horrifying, isn't the act [of abortion] itself even more horrifying?" he asks.

Weichbrecht, who says he is a devout Christian, believes the images "make people more conscious of the consequences" of abortion. "These are the last images they see before they go inside to kill their babies."

Center director Codding, who calls herself "a woman of faith," sometimes confronts the demonstrators. "I tell them that I'm praying for them so they can understand the true meaning of being a Christian and open their hearts to understanding and supporting our women," she says.

The drama playing out at this suburban clinic illustrates the passion that is likely to continue to accompany the abortion debate in the United States. And much of that dialogue is taking place in communities, state legislatures and the courts, rather than in Congress.

According to Elizabeth Nash, state issues manager at the Guttmacher Institute, in the first two months of this year, legislators in 14 states introduced 51 provisions in support of abortion rights, the heaviest volume of abortion-rights legislation since the early 1990s. The measures would either repeal new abortion restrictions or ease access to abortion.

"We're probably seeing the beginning of an effort to push back against all of these abortion restrictions," Nash says. And "most of these bills are being introduced in states where abortion rights have not been treated favorably over the past few years, such as Arizona, Virginia, Ohio and Nebraska. What this says to me is that the sponsors of these bills really want to stand up and say enough is enough."

For instance, she notes, the Virginia Senate voted this year to repeal a restrictive abortion law. Although the measure was defeated in the House of Delegates, Nash says, "It marks a change in how abortion may be dealt with at the state level. There's momentum, an effort to stop this wave of restrictions."

"I think we are at a potential turning point," said Suzanne Goldberg, director of the Center for Gender and Sexuality Law at Columbia University. "Either access to abortion will be dramatically restricted in [2014] or perhaps the pushback will begin."[79]

Dan McConchie, vice president of government affairs at Americans United for Life, isn't concerned about the surge in abortion rights legislation. "We had a strategy that lined up with where the American people are," he said. "What's being offered by the other side is not something that the American people appear to embrace."[80]

Abortion opponent Tobias, meanwhile, said she is "very encouraged" by developments on the state level. "We've been gaining ground in recent years with laws that are a stronger challenge to *Roe*," she said, referring to the new laws that limit the period during which a woman can get an abortion. "I think it is more difficult to get an abortion in the country today."[81]

Jelen, at the University of Nevada, Las Vegas, doesn't think the Supreme Court will overturn *Roe v. Wade*, at least not during Chief Justice John Roberts' term. "Roberts is very concerned about the court's legitimacy and the value of precedent," Jelen says. "I think you can expect to see *Roe* chipped away at over a period of time, but not being necessarily overturned outright."

NOTES

1. Esmé E. Deprez, "The Vanishing Abortion Clinic," *BloombergBusinessweek*, Nov. 27, 2013, http://tinyurl.com/pbef3xo.

2. Rosalind S. Helderman, "Virginia assembly says abortion clinics should be regulated as hospitals," *The Washington Post*, Feb. 25, 2011, http://tinyurl.com/o567hzf.

3. "Widening Regional Divide over Abortion Laws," Pew Research Center for the People and the Press, July 29, 2013, http://tinyurl.com/pwg3fcl.

4. Rachel K. Jones and Jemma Jerman, "Abortion Incidence and Service Availability in the United States, 2011," *Perspectives on Sexual and Reproductive Health*, The Guttmacher Institute, March 2014, http://tinyurl.com/plk68q2. Also see Karen Pazol, *et al.*, "Abortion Surveillance — United States, 2010," *Morbidity and Mortality Weekly Report*, Centers for Disease Control and Prevention, Nov. 29, 2013, http://tinyurl.com/nlrcs7m.

5. Stephanie J. Ventura, *et al.*, "Estimated Pregnancy Rates and Rates of Pregnancy Outcomes for the United States, 1990-2008," *National Vital Statistics Report*, Vol. 60, No. 7, June 20, 2012, http://tinyurl.com/7xous32.

6. Tatiana Bergum, "Report: Abortions Drop 32 Percent From All-Time High as Roe Turns 41," LifeNews.com, Jan. 21, 2014, http://tinyurl.com/krgrjzt.

7. Jon Hurdle, "Doctor Starts His Life Term in Grisly Abortion Clinic Case," *The New York Times*, May 15, 2013, http://tinyurl.com/o4vwm56.

8. Manny Fernandez, "Abortion Law Pushes Texas Clinics to Close Doors," *The New York Times*, March 6, 2014, http://tinyurl.com/pbx8zdh.

9. Christy Hoppe, "Appeals court taking up Texas law that's shuttered abortion clinics," *Dallas News*, Jan. 5, 2014, http://tinyurl.com/l2xw74q.

10. Becca Aaronson, "5th Circuit Court of Appeals Weighs Abortion Rules," *The Texas Tribune*, Jan. 7, 2014, http://tinyurl.com/kd8s2f6.

11. Esmé E. Deprez, "Abortion Clinics Close at Record Pace After States Tighten Rules," Bloomberg News, Sept. 3, 2013, http://tinyurl.com/mxcp7yl.

12. Blake Neff, "NARAL shifts strategy to fight 'backward momentum' on abortion," *The Hill*, Jan. 14, 2014, http://tinyurl.com/lssopka.

13. *Ibid.*

14. Karen Hansen, "A GOP wave washed over state legislatures on Election Day," *Red Tide*, National Council of State Legislatures blog, December 2010, http://tinyurl.com/mopvyab. Also see Corey Dade, "GOP's 'Sweet' Wins in Governors' Races May Pay Off," NPR, Nov. 8, 2011, http://tinyurl.com/lwja4pd.

15. James Bopp, Jr. and Richard E. Coleson, "Memorandum, To Whom It May Concern, Re: Pro-Life Strategy Issues," Bopp, Coleson and Bostrom, Aug. 7, 2007, http://tinyurl.com/krpgept.

16. Elizabeth Nash, *et al.*, " Laws Affecting Reproductive Health and Rights: 2013 State Policy Review," The Guttmacher Institute, http://tinyurl.com/mlkngn.

17. *Ibid.*

18. Erik Eckholm, "Arkansas Adopts a Ban on Abortions After 12 Weeks," *The New York Times*, March 7, 2013, http://tinyurl.com/cyzbxk9.

19. Manny Fernandez, "Abortion Law Pushes Texas Clinics to Close Doors," *The New York Times*, March 6, 2014, http://tinyurl.com/mc6ws9f.

20. Amicus Curiae Brief of the Catholic Medical Association, *Kathleen Sebelius, et al. v. Hobby Lobby Stores, Inc., et al.*, American Bar Association Preview of United States Supreme Court Cases, http://tinyurl.com/q9hl36a.

21. Rachel Benson Gould, "The Implications of Defining When a Woman Is Pregnant," *The Guttmacher Report on Public Policy*, May 2005, Volume 8, Number 2, http://tinyurl.com/pxxm8w5.

22. News release, "FDA Decision on Plan B is Bad Medicine for Women," American Association of Pro-Life Obstetricians and Gynecologists, undated, http://tinyurl.com/nv7hgbj.

23. "Sebelius v. Hobby Lobby and Conestoga Wood Specialties Corp. v. Sebelius — Consolidated," Docket No's. 13-354 and 13-356 American Bar Association Preview, http://tinyurl.com/mazujqv.

24. James Trussell, *et al.*, "Emergency Contraception: A Last Chance to Prevent Unintended Pregnancy," Princeton University, February 2014, http://tinyurl.com/mgawwsg.

25. Pam Belluck, "Abortion Qualms on Morning-After Pill May Be Unfounded," *The New York Times*, June 5, 2012, http://tinyurl.com/l93eugn.

26. "Statement by the White House Press Secretary Regarding Sebelius v. Hobby Lobby Stores, Inc.," White House, Nov. 26, 2013, http://tinyurl.com/n6jxcez.

27. Appellants' brief, *Hobby Lobby Stores v. Sebelius, et al.*, Nov. 20, 2012, http://tinyurl.com/nd592au.

28. News release, "Hobby Lobby Supreme Court Brief Counters Government 'Divide and Conquer' Attempt to Violate Business Owners' Religious Rights," The Becket Fund for Religious Liberty, Feb. 10, 2014, http://tinyurl.com/mz33plx.

29. Opinion, Tenth U.S. Circuit Court of Appeals, *Hobby Lobby Stores et al., vs. Kathleen Sebelius, et al.*, June 17, 2013, http://tinyurl.com/kvjt2up.

30. Lawrence Hurley, "Obama asks high court to review contraception mandate ruling," Reuters, Sept. 19, 2013, http://tinyurl.com/khbvqf4.

31. American Civil Liberties Union, *et al.*, Amicus Curiae brief, *Sebelius v. Hobby Lobby, Inc.* and *Conestoga Wood Specialties Corp., et al., v. Sebelius*, http://tinyurl.com/poop7q9.

32. Michelle Bauman, "Mennonite-owned wood manufacturer sues over contraception mandate," Catholic News Agency, Dec. 11, 2012, http://tinyurl.com/kfl8oqa/.

33. Opinion, *Conestoga Wood Specialties Corp., et al. v. Secretary of Health and Human Services, et al.*, United States Court of Appeals for the Third Circuit, July 26, 2013, http://tinyurl.com/lbgffdp.

34. Press release, "Conestoga Wood Products Lawyers Appeal to Supreme Court," Woodworking Network, Sept. 19, 2013, http://tinyurl.com/mup2ruk.

35. Office of the White House Press Secretary, "Fact Sheet: Women's Preventive Services and Religious Institutions," Feb. 10, 2012, http://tinyurl.com/6r8p3gn.

36. Lyle Denniston, "Analysis: The Little Sisters case and EBSA Form 700," *Scotusblog.com*, Jan. 4, 2014, http://tinyurl.com/pzp34va.

37. Lyle Denniston, "Partial Win for Little Sisters," *Scotusblog.com*, Jan. 24, 2014, http://tinyurl.com/lrct2op.

38. Elizabeth LaForgia, "Federal appeals court rules against Notre Dame in contraception case," *Jurist*, Feb. 23, 2014, http://tinyurl.com/mos96cn.

39. Steve Kenny and Robert Pear, "Justice Blocks Contraception Mandate on Insurance in Suit by Nuns," *The New York Times*, Dec. 31, 2013, http://tinyurl.com/nywxqse.

40. Helen Alvaré, "No Compelling Interest: The 'Birth Control' Mandate and Religious Freedom," *Villanova Law Review*, Vol. 58, No. 3, 2013, pp. 379-436, http://tinyurl.com/msd9gw4.

41. Rachel Gould Benson, "Lessons from Before Roe: Will Past be Prologue?" *The Guttmacher Institute, Report on Public Policy*, March 2003, Volume 6, Number 1, http://tinyurl.com/o63ht.

42. "The Safety of Legal Abortion and the Hazards of Illegal Abortion," NARAL Pro-Choice America, Jan. 1, 2014, http://tinyurl.com/2352qjc.

43. Leslie J. Reagan, *When abortion was a crime: Women, Medicine and Law in the United States, 1867-1973* (1997), p. 77.

44. "Medical and Social Health Benefits Since Abortion Was Made Legal in the U.S.," Planned Parenthood Federation, November 2009, http://tinyurl.com/yavm4w7.

45. Unless otherwise noted, the account of Sherri Chessen's abortion experience is drawn from Linda Greenhouse, "A Never-Ending Story," *The New York Times*, Sept. 5, 2012, http://tinyurl.com/lvladq2.

46. Lee Epstein, "The Impact of the ACLU Reproductive Freedom Project," paper presented at the Midwest Political Science Association meeting, April 15-18, 1981, http://tinyurl.com/p4ele3b.

47. Brian E. Fisher, *Abortion: The Ultimate Exploitation of Women* (2013), p. 60.

48. Ernest Ohlhoff, "Abortion: Where Do the Churches Stand?" *Pregnant Pause.com*, Sept. 12, 2000, http://tinyurl.com/pvzs82.

49. Linda Greenhouse and Riva Siegel, *Before Roe v. Wade: Voices that Shaped the Abortion Debate Before The Supreme Court's Ruling* (2010), p. 25.

50. Rachel Benson Gould, "Lessons from Before Roe: Will Past Be Prologue?" *The Guttmacher Report on Public Policy*, March 2003, Volume 6, Number 1, http://tinyurl.com/pnbz933.

51. Theodore Joyce, Ruoding Tan and Yuxiu Zhang, "Back to the Future? Abortion Before & After Roe," National Bureau of Economic Research, *Working Paper No. 18338*, August 2012, http://tinyurl.com/qds86et.

52. Text of decision, *Roe v. Wade*, U.S. Supreme Court, Jan. 22, 1973, Cornell University Law School Legal Information Institute, http://tinyurl.com/meufhlt.

53. Text of decision, *Planned Parenthood of Southeastern Pennsylvania v. Casey*, U.S. Supreme Court, June 29, 1992, Cornell University Law School Legal Information Institute, http://tinyurl.com/nwdqm7y.

54. William J. Clinton, speech accepting the Democratic nomination for president, Aug. 30, 1996, http://tinyurl.com/pu5ve6d.

55. Bopp memo, *op. cit.*

56. Seth McLaughlin, "Graham introduces 'historic' 20-week abortion ban; says no primary politics at play," *The Washington Times*, Nov. 7, 2013, http://tinyurl.com/pqe5v2l.

57. "Babies Feel Pain," Wisconsin Right to Life, http://tinyurl.com/ojjpa5m.

58. Anne Murphy Paul, "The First Ache," *The New York Times*, Feb. 10, 2008, http://tinyurl.com/qfs24qn.

59. Pam Belluck, "Complex Science at Issue in Politics of Fetal Pain," *The New York Times*, Sept. 17, 2013, http://tinyurl.com/m9tdqj2.

60. Statement of Administration Policy, "H.R. 1797: Pain-Capable Unborn Child Protection Act," Executive Office of the President, Office of Management and Budget, June 17, 2013, http://tinyurl.com/ofj87jx.

61. "Department of Defense Annual Report on Sexual Assault in the Military, Fiscal Year 2012," Vol. I, http://tinyurl.com/pzwgguj.

62. Lisa Rein, "Women's health groups want Peace Corps volunteers to have insurance coverage for abortions," *The Washington Post*, April 25, 2013, http://tinyurl.com/czqyt9g.

63. "Final Report: Review of the Peace Corps' Implementation of Guidelines Related to Volunteer Victims of Rape and Sexual Assault," Office of the Inspector General, Peace Corps, September 2012, http://tinyurl.com/nz9lcw9.

64. Press release, "Planned Parenthood Applauds the Introduction of the Peace Corps Equity Act," Planned Parenthood, April 25, 2013, http://tinyurl.com/qfa4cdc.

65. Rein, *op. cit.*

66. The story of LNG's evolution from a strictly controlled prescription medication to a non-prescription over-the-counter product is laced with charges of political interference in FDA's regulatory process touching the presidential administrations of George W. Bush and Barack Obama. A website operated by Princeton University's Office of Population Research and the Association of Reproductive Health Professionals offers a timeline: http://tinyurl.com/3o2g9y7. See also Marc Kaufman, "FDA Official Quits over Delay on Plan B," http://tinyurl.com/a3nmx; Gardiner Harris, "Plan to Widen Availability of Morning-After Pill Is Rejected," *The New York Times*, Dec. 7, 2011, http://tinyurl.com/chaqgqk; and Maggie Fox, "Judge refuses to delay ruling on Plan B," NBC News, May 12, 2013, http://tinyurl.com/p9uqp45.

67. Text of the Affordable Care Act can be found at http://tinyurl.com/pqukxj4.

68. Fact sheet, "What is the Health Insurance Marketplace?" Healthcare.gov, http://tinyurl.com/moyadrv.

69. "Executive Order 13535 — Patient Protection and Affordable Care Act's Consistency with Longstanding Restrictions on the Use of Federal Funds for Abortion," Office of the White House Press Secretary, March 24, 2010, http://tinyurl.com/y9tb6jg.

70. Most states allow exceptions in cases of rape or incest, or where the health or safety of the fetus or mother are at risk; two states, however — Louisiana and Tennessee — prohibit any abortion coverage under policies sold in those states. "Restricting Insurance Coverage of Abortion," The Guttmacher Institute, March 1, 2014, http://tinyurl.com/qfozmlu.

71. Press release, "AUL Says the Anti-Life Policies Intertwined Throughout Obamacare Require its Repeal," Americans United for Life, Sept. 17, 2013, http://tinyurl.com/k4goac2.

72. Charles A. Donovan, "Multi-State Health Plans: A Potential Avenue to Tens of Thousands of Publicly Subsidized Abortions," Charlotte Lozier Institute, September 2013, http://tinyurl.com/pfhv9bg.

73. Transcript, remarks of Missouri Senate candidate Todd Akin on Abortion, Aug. 19, 2012, http://tinyurl.com/cfk9u8b. Also see press release, "NARAL Pro-Choice America Calls on Gov. Romney to Withdraw His Endorsement of Senate Candidate Richard Mourdock," NARAL Pro-Choice America, Oct. 24, 2012, http://tinyurl.com/pvl9hsp.

74. Dana Blanton, "Exit polls: McAuliffe wins in Virginia with strong support among women," Fox News, Nov. 6, 2013, http://tinyurl.com/mrh7a6b.

75. Petula Dvorak, "Pregnant women as hosts? Sure, state Sen. Stephen Martin, why not?" *The Washington Post*, Feb. 27, 2014, http://tinyurl.com/kvnm7ps.

76. Jeremy W. Peters, "Parties Seize on Abortion Issues in Midterm Race," *The New York Times*, Jan. 20, 2014, http://tinyurl.com/o2x98rm.

77. Mitchell Killian and Clyde Wilcox, "Do Abortion Attitudes Lead to Party Switching?" *Political Research Quarterly* 61.4 (2008): 561-572, JSTOR, Nov. 16, 2010, http://tinyurl.com/qf7nfpd.

78. Lydia Saad, "Abortion Is Threshold Issue for One in Six U.S. Voters," Gallup, Oct. 4, 2012, http://tinyurl.com/q2qx74r.

79. Erik Eckholm, "Access to Abortion Falling as States Pass Restrictions," *The New York Times*, Jan. 3, 2014, http://tinyurl.com/lyrewgd.

80. Esmé E. Deprez, "Abortion-Rights Backers on Offense After 3-Year Drubbing," Bloomberg, Feb. 24, 2014, http://tinyurl.com/poah87y.

81. Erik Eckholm, "Access to Abortion Falling as States Pass Restrictions," *The New York Times*, Jan. 3, 2014, http://tinyurl.com/qbrdu6r.

BIBLIOGRAPHY

Selected Sources

Books

D'Antonio, William V., Michele Dillon and Mary L. Gautier, *American Catholics in Transition*, Rowman and Littlefield, 2013.
Three sociologists report on American Catholics' beliefs, attitudes and behavior by tracking surveys conducted at six-year intervals, beginning in 1987.

Forsythe, Clarke, *Abuse of Discretion: The Inside Story of Roe v. Wade*, Encounter, 2013.
The general counsel of Americans United for Life examines the deliberations that led to the landmark 1973 Supreme Court decision that legalized abortion, which he calls "a unique combination of impulses, errors and miscalculations."

Greenhouse, Linda, and Reva Siegal, *Before Roe v. Wade: Voices that Shaped the Abortion Debate Before the Supreme Court's Ruling*, Kaplan Publishing, 2010.
A journalist (Greenhouse) and a law professor examine both sides of the abortion debate in the run-up to *Roe v. Wade*, using excerpts from primary sources, including articles, speeches, pamphlets, legal briefs and other documents.

Levine, Philip, *Sex and Consequences: Abortion, Public Policy, and the Economics of Fertility*, Princeton University Press, 2004.
An economics professor looks at how increased access to abortion affects individuals' sexual behavior.

Reagan, Leslie J., *When Abortion Was a Crime: Women, Medicine, and Law in the United States,*

1867-1973, University of California Press, 1997 (also available online: http://tinyurl.com/p5v2dd3).
A law and history professor at the University of Illinois examines the history and enforcement of abortion laws in the United States before the Supreme Court's *Roe v. Wade* decision legalized the procedure.

Articles

Alvaré, Helen M., and Meg T. McDonnell, "Why pro-lifers keep fighting abortion," *The Washington Post*, March 1, 2013, http://tinyurl.com/cmgs9wg.
The president and the communications director of the Chiaroscuro Institute, an educational organization that opposes abortion, explain why they believe the anti-abortion struggle is worth waging.

Beckwith, Francis J., "Thomson's 'Defense of Abortion' at Forty," *The Catholic Thing*, Aug. 6, 2011, http://tinyurl.com/nkftbz8.
A professor of philosophy and church-state studies rebuts a famous 1971 defense of abortion's morality (see Thompson, below).

Fowler, Anne, *et al.*, "Talking With the Enemy," *The Boston Globe*, Jan. 28, 2001, http://tinyurl.com/pzel752.
Six activists — three from each side of the abortion debate — describe the successes and frustrations of their five years of secret meetings as they searched for ways to communicate constructively and respectfully about abortion.

Leonhardt, David, "In Public Opinion on Abortion, Few Absolutes," *The New York Times*, July 17, 2013, http://tinyurl.com/ld8nydy.
An economics journalist advises taking a critical look at public opinion surveys on the abortion issue.

Levs, Josh, "Gosnell horror fuels fight for abortion laws," CNN, May 14, 2013, http://tinyurl.com/o3spc7p.

Revelations of murder and other illegal acts at a Philadelphia women's health care center led to a widespread push for tighter state restrictions on abortion clinics.

Tarico, Valerie, "Abortion As a Blessing, Grace, or Gift — A Renewed Conversation about Reproductive Rights," *Ethical Technology*, Dec. 12, 2013, http://tinyurl.com/l3k6twd.
A psychologist argues that abortion is a moral and ethical act.

Thomson, Judith Jarvis, "A Defense of Abortion," *Philosophy and Public Affairs*, Vol. 1, No. 1., Autumn 1971, pp. 47-66, http://tinyurl.com/ppc43.
Granting for argument's sake that a fetus has a right to life, a philosopher offers a classic defense of the morality of abortion.

Reports and Studies

"Fact Sheet: Induced Abortion in the United States," Guttmacher Institute, February 2014, http://tinyurl.com/5wley.
A research organization that supports abortion rights summarizes information pertaining to abortion safety, laws and other topics.

Joyce, Theodore J., Tan Ruoding and Yuxiu Zhang, "Back to the Future? Abortion Before and After Roe," Working Paper 18338, National Bureau of Economic Research, August 2012, http://tinyurl.com/pa9vn2o.
Economists conclude that overturning *Roe v. Wade* would have resulted in 73,000-182,000 unintended births in 2007.

Klick, Jonathan, and Thomas Stratmann, "Abortion Access and Risky Sex Among Teens: Parental Involvement Laws and Sexually Transmitted Diseases," *Journal of Law, Economics and Organization*, Vol. 24, No. 1, 2008, p. 2.
A law professor and a political economist find evidence that abortion laws requiring parental consent lead to less-risky sexual behavior among teenagers.

For More Information

American Civil Liberties Union Reproductive Freedom Project, 125 Broad St., New York, NY 10004; 212-549-2500; https://www.aclu.org/reproductive-freedom. Active in litigation, advocacy and public education to protect women's access to abortion.

Americans United for Life, 655 15th St., N.W., Washington, DC 20005; 202-289-1478; http://aul.org/. Advocacy organization that litigates and provides information in opposition to abortion.

Centers for Disease Control Abortion Surveillance System, 1600 Clifton Rd., Atlanta, GA 30333; 800-232-4636; www.cdc.gov/reproductivehealth/data_stats/Abortion.htm. Federal agency that tracks the number and characteristics of women seeking legal abortions.

Charlotte Lozier Institute, 1707 L St., N.W., Washington, DC 20036; 202-223-8073; www.lozierinstitute.org/. Provides information and offers leadership training in opposition to abortion.

Guttmacher Institute, 125 Maiden Lane, New York, NY 10038; 212-248-1111; https://www.guttmacher.org/. Provides information, research and analysis on abortion issues; supports access to abortion.

NARAL Pro-Choice America, 1156 15th St., N.W., Washington, DC 20005; 202-973-3000; www.naral.org/. Provides information and lobbies in favor of access to abortion.

National Right to Life, 512 10th St., N.W., Washington, DC 20004; 202-626-8800; www.nrlc.org/. Provides information and lobbies in opposition to abortion.

Planned Parenthood Federation of America, 434 West 33rd St., New York, NY 10001; 212-541-7800; www.plannedparenthood.org/. Provides reproductive health care services and information; supports access to abortion.

8

Big Data and Privacy

Tom Price

Actor Kunal Nayyar wears Google glasses to the 65th Annual Primetime Emmy Awards in Los Angeles on Sept. 22, 2013. Part of the big data revolution, the glasses contain a computer that can take pictures, respond to voice commands, search the Internet and perform other functions. Along with the nonstop collection of data come concerns about loss of privacy.

From *CQ Researcher*, October 25, 2013.

When Peter Higgs and François Englert won the Nobel Prize for physics this month, they were honored for a theory they published nearly a half-century ago but was not confirmed until March.

Higgs, of Scotland's University of Edinburgh, and Englert, of Belgium's Université Libre de Bruxelles (Free University of Brussels), had independently theorized that matter obtains mass from an unknown energy field that permeates the universe. Higgs suggested it is composed of an undiscovered subatomic particle, which became known as the Higgs boson. To confirm the theory, scientists needed to find that particle.

They finally succeeded largely with the help of so-called big data — the collection and analysis of enormous amounts of information by supercomputers, often in real time. Physicists analyzed trillions of subatomic explosions produced at the European Organization for Nuclear Research's Large Hadron Collider, a 17-mile circular underground tunnel that crosses the border between Switzerland and France. There, protons are fired at each other at nearly the speed of light, shattering them into other subatomic particles, including the Higgs.[1]

To analyze the results of those collisions, scientists needed computing capability that was "of larger scale and faster than ever before," says Joe Incandela, a University of California, Santa Barbara, physics professor who led one of the two collider teams searching for the Higgs. The collider can generate up to 600 million

Big Data Reveals Sources of Racist Tweets

Geographers at Humboldt State University in Arcata, Calif., used big data to create an interactive "Geography of Hate" map revealing where racist Twitter traffic originated. Hot spots predominated in the Midwest, South and Northeast, often in rural areas.

Where Most Racist Tweets Originated, June 2012-April 2013

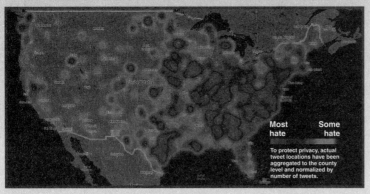

Source: Monica Stephens, "Geography of Hate," Humboldt State University, http://users.humboldt.edu/mstephens/hate/hate_map.html#

collisions per second, and the teams' servers can handle 10 gigabytes* of data a second.[2]

The search for the Higgs boson is just one of a vast array of discoveries, innovations and uses made possible by the compilation and manipulation of big data. The explosively emerging field could radically advance science, medicine, social science, crime-fighting and corporate business practices. But big data is controversial because of its potential to erode individual privacy, especially in the wake of recent revelations that the National Security Agency (NSA) is collecting massive amounts of personal information about Americans and others around the world. Critics want privacy controls on big data's use, while proponents say its benefits outweigh its risks.

Big data has led to cutting-edge medical discoveries and scientific breakthroughs that would have been impossible in the past: links between genetic traits and medical conditions; correlations among illnesses, their causes and potential cures; and the mapping of the human genome.

Big data also is a boon to businesses, which use it to conduct consumer marketing, figure out when machines will break down and reduce energy consumption, among other purposes. Governments mine big data to improve public services, fight crime and track down terrorists. And pollsters and political scientists use it to analyze billions of social media posts for insights into public opinion.

Even humanities scholars are embracing big data. Historians tap big data to gain new perspectives on historical figures. Other scholars use it to study literature. In the past, researchers investigating literary trends might read 10 books and conclude that "these books from this era show us how literature is different" from another era, says Brett Bobley, director of the National Endowment for the Humanities Office of Digital Humanities. "Today, a researcher could study thousands of books and look at how language changes over time, how the use of gender changes, how spelling changes."

Uses of big data involve businesses, governments, political organizations and other groups vacuuming up massive amounts of personal information from cell phones, GPS devices, bank accounts, credit-card transactions, retail purchases and other digital activities. The data often are gleaned from search engines, social networks, email services and other online sources. The mountains of information compiled in this manner — and the way they are analyzed and put to use — generate much of the criticism of big data, particularly after former NSA computer specialist Edward Snowden revealed in June that the agency has been collecting Americans' telephone and email records, and *The New York Times* revealed that the Drug Enforcement Administration had ordered AT&T to hand over vast amounts of records about its customers' telephone and computer usage.[3]

---

*A gigabyte is 1 billion bytes. A byte is eight bits. A bit is one action of a computer switch. A byte commonly is equivalent to a single alphanumeric character.

Most Americans View Data Collection Negatively

More than half of Americans polled in May and June said the massive collection and use of personal information by government and business have a "mostly negative" impact on privacy, liberty and personal and financial security.* The polling was done just before former National Security Agency computer specialist Edward Snowden in June revealed widespread NSA domestic spying. Fewer than 40 percent of the respondents see the use of big data as "mostly positive." Fewer than half trust how the government uses their personal data, and nearly 90 percent support the so-called "right to be forgotten."

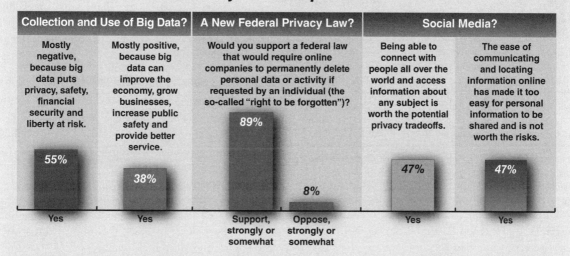

What is your viewpoint on . . .

Collection and Use of Big Data?		A New Federal Privacy Law?		Social Media?	
Mostly negative, because big data puts privacy, safety, financial security and liberty at risk.	Mostly positive, because big data can improve the economy, grow businesses, increase public safety and provide better service.	Would you support a federal law that would require online companies to permanently delete personal data or activity if requested by an individual (the so-called "right to be forgotten")?		Being able to connect with people all over the world and access information about any subject is worth the potential privacy tradeoffs.	The ease of communicating and locating information online has made it too easy for personal information to be shared and is not worth the risks.
55%	38%	89%	8%	47%	47%
Yes	Yes	Support, strongly or somewhat	Oppose, strongly or somewhat	Yes	Yes

Note: Totals do not add to 100 because don't know/refused to answer responses are not included.

* Pollsters contacted 1,000 people by telephone between May 29-June 2, 2013.

Source: "Allstate/National Journal/Heartland Monitor Poll XVII," June 2013, www.theheartlandvoice.com/wp-content/uploads/2013/06/HeartlandTopline-Results.pdf

"I don't really want to live in a total surveillance state where big brother knows everything I do and has all that information at its fingertips," says John Simpson, privacy project director for Consumer Watchdog, a consumer advocacy organization in Santa Monica, Calif. Sen. Jay Rockefeller, D-W.Va., has introduced a measure to allow Internet users to prohibit websites from collecting any of their personal information except when needed to provide a requested service to that person. Even then, the identity of the user would have to be kept secret or the information would have to be deleted after the service was performed. The bill awaits action in the Senate Committee on Commerce, Science and Transportation.[4]

Big data differs from old-fashioned data partly in the massive volume of the information being collected. But other distinctions exist as well. Big data computers often crunch vast amounts of information in real time. And they can reach beyond structured databases — such as a company's customer list — to make sense of unstructured data, including Twitter feeds, Facebook posts, Google searches, surveillance-camera images and customer browsing sessions on Amazon.com.

As a result, Internet platforms, such as Facebook or Google, act as big data "sensors," gathering information about people just as a thermometer gathers temperature information. In addition, Internet-connected optical,

Getty Images/John Moore

Police at New York City's counterterrorism center monitor more than 4,000 security cameras and license plate readers in the Financial District and surrounding parts of Lower Manhattan. Vast amounts of data are collected and stored by police departments and other government agencies. For example, law enforcement agencies store photos taken by cameras mounted on patrol cars and on stationary objects. Governments store photos made for driver's licenses and other identification documents. Many images are stored indefinitely and can now be searched with facial-recognition technology across multiple databases.

electronic and mechanical sensors are being installed in ever-increasing numbers and locations.

Viktor Mayer-Schonberger and Kenneth Cukier offer striking illustrations of the size of the data being collected — and the speed with which the volume of that information is growing — in their 2013 book *Big Data: A Revolution that Will Transform How We Live, Work, and Think*. If all the world's data were distributed among everyone on Earth, they write, each person would have 320 times more information than existed in third-century Egypt's Alexandria Library. If today's information were stored on stacks of compact disks, the stacks would stretch from Earth to the moon five times.

In 2000, only one-fourth of the world's information was stored digitally. Today 98 percent is, and the amount of digital data is doubling every two to three years, according to Mayer-Schonberger, a professor at Oxford University's Internet Institute, and Cukier, data editor of *The Economist*.[5] According to IBM, 90 percent of the world's data has been created in the last two years, and that information is growing by 2.5 quintillion bytes each day.[6] (A quintillion is 1 followed by 18 zeroes.)

For example, rapidly improving telescopes linked to powerful computers and the Internet are doubling the world's compilation of astronomical data each year and making it available to astronomers around the globe. Until it suffered a major malfunction in May, the Kepler Space Telescope, for instance, measured the light of 170,000 stars every 30 minutes in search of changes indicating the presence of planets, according to Alberto Conti, a scientist for the Space Telescope Science Institute at Johns Hopkins University.[7]

As advances in technology relentlessly expand big data's capabilities, here are some questions that scientists, business executives, privacy advocates and government officials are debating:

Do big data's benefits outweigh the risks?

Mario Costeja was shocked when a Google search on his name returned an 11-year-old Spanish newspaper notice about a financial transgression. Costeja, a Spaniard, had become delinquent on social security contributions, creating a debt that landed him in legal trouble in 1998 but that he had long since paid.

In a case still pending, Costeja asked a court to order the newspaper to remove the notice from its online archives and Google to block the notice from search results. The court ruled in the newspaper's favor, but the Google ruling remains undecided.[8]

Costeja's plight reveals a key drawback to big data: Once something enters an online database, it can be impossible to erase. Before digital databases and powerful search engines, the newspaper notice that Costeja encountered in 2009 would have existed only as a yellowed clipping in the newspaper's "morgue," or perhaps been buried in microfilm or old newspapers stored in a few libraries.

But with today's search engines capable of instantly exploring every database connected to the Internet, old transgressions can be found by anyone with a computer connection. And polls indicate that people are concerned about losing control of information once it gets collected and stored.

Of 1,000 Americans surveyed this year, 55 percent perceive a "mostly negative" impact from the collection and use of personal information. Two-thirds complain they have little or no control over information collected about them. Three-fifths believe they can't correct erroneous data. Conducted for the Allstate insurance company and *National Journal*, and just before the NSA domestic spying became public, the poll found that only 48 percent of Americans trust how governments, cell-phone companies and Internet providers use that information.[9]

Simpson of Consumer Watchdog says big data can harm individuals, especially if the information is erroneous or used to draw incorrect conclusions. Organizations can collect information from a variety of sources, then use it to "put together a profile about you that potentially could be used against you," he says. Analysis might conclude, for example, that "you're probably a health risk because you go to all these sites about losing weight, and we can see you're buying too much booze.

"Similarly, you can slice and dice the data you get from the Web and other sources and produce something that might be used to determine whether you should get a job, whether you should get a loan, or what rate you have to pay if you get the loan."

With sophisticated enough analysis, organizations might "red-line people," just as neighborhoods, suggests Jules Polonetsky, executive director and co-chair of the Future of Privacy Forum, a Washington-based think tank. Such "Web-lining," as some are calling it, can cause people to pay more for health insurance if they have traits associated with certain illnesses, he explains, or a person's credit rating could be affected by his Facebook friends' financial histories.

Those are "probabilistic predictions that punish us not for what we have done, but what we are predicted to do," said Mayer-Schonberger, the Oxford professor.[10]

But Jeff Jarvis, a City University of New York journalism professor who writes frequently about big data, says critics focus too much on the negatives while ignoring the positives. For example, while many deplore facial recognition technology as an invasion of privacy that can empower stalkers and other predators, Jarvis explains, "facial recognition technology also can be used to find lost children or people on Alzheimer's alert or criminals or terrorists."

And despite the negative attitudes toward big data uncovered by the Allstate/*National Journal* survey, some poll respondents saw value in the technology. Nearly half said the privacy tradeoffs are a fair price for being able to connect with people around the world and access information about almost any subject within seconds. More than two-thirds said the collection and analysis of information about them would likely lead them to receive more information about interesting products and services and better warnings about health risks. Nearly two in five said big data could enable government and business officials to make better decisions about expanding businesses, improving the economy, providing better services and increasing public safety.[11]

Scientists in Boston, for example, are using probabilistic predictions to try to prevent suicide. Funded by the federal government's Defense Advanced Research Projects Agency, the scientists are monitoring social media and text postings by volunteers who are active-duty military personnel or veterans. The scientists' computers watch for keywords associated with suicide in an effort to create an automated system that will alert caregivers, relatives or friends when suicide-linked expressions are observed.[12]

The Financial Industry Regulatory Authority — a self-regulating body for the securities industry — has turned to big data to catch up with the rapid technological changes occurring in financial markets. In August 2012, the agency employed software that scans trading activity for patterns that indicate suspicious practices. Results led the agency to launch 280 investigations by July 2013.[13]

Is big data speeding the erosion of privacy?

Security technologist Bruce Schneier, who has declared that "the Internet is a surveillance state," is doubtful about protecting privacy in the era of big data.

"If the director of the CIA can't maintain his privacy on the Internet," Schneier said, "we've got no hope."[14]

Schneier, a fellow at Harvard Law School's Berkman Center for Internet and Society, was referring to David Petraeus, who stepped down as director of the spy agency last November as his extramarital affair with former military intelligence officer Paula Broadwell was becoming public. The couple — presumably experts in covert actions — had taken steps to conceal their relationship. To avoid blazing email trails, they left messages to each other in the draft folder of a shared Gmail account. And when Broadwell sent threatening emails to a woman she thought was a rival for Petraeus' attention, she used a fake identity and accessed the Internet from hotel networks rather than her home. But big data tripped them up.[15]

Analyzing email metadata — addresses and information about the computers and networks used by the senders (but not message content) — the FBI traced Broadwell's threatening messages to several hotels. From hotel records, they found one guest who had stayed at those hotels on the dates the emails were sent: Broadwell.[16]

Combining Internet data with offline data occurs constantly across the globe, as companies build dossiers on their customers to offer personalized products and services and to target advertising or sell the information to others.

"This is ubiquitous surveillance," Schneier said. "All of us [are] being watched, all the time, and that data [are] being stored forever. . . . It's efficient beyond the wildest dreams of George Orwell," whose novel *1984* introduced the world to the all-seeing "Big Brother."[17]

Internet users voluntarily post photos of themselves and their friends on social media. Surveillance cameras take photos and videos of people in public and private places. Police departments store photos taken by cameras mounted on patrol cars and on stationary objects. Governments store photos made for driver's licenses and other identification documents. Some police cruisers are equipped with devices that enable remote searches of photo databases. Many of those images are stored indefinitely and can now be searched with facial-recognition technology across multiple databases.

Phone companies store call records, and mobile phone companies store records of where phones were used. Analysis of those records can reveal where a phone was at any time, down to a specific floor in a specific building.[18]

Big-data companies say they protect the identities of individuals behind the data. But scientists say even "anonymized" phone records — those with users' names removed — can reveal identities.

Many phone numbers are listed in public directories. Researchers at the Massachusetts Institute of Technology (MIT) and Belgium's Université Catholique de Louvain discovered that they could identify anonymized cell phone users 95 percent of the time if they knew just four instances of when and where a phone was used.[19] Companies' privacy policies also can be meaningless if

they accidentally release information or if their business partners don't honor the policies.

For example, due to a computer bug, Facebook allowed unauthorized people to access the phone numbers and email addresses of 6 million users and nonusers between mid-2012 and mid-2013. The social network admitted that it had been secretly compiling data about users from sources beyond Facebook and had been gathering information about nonusers as well.[20]

In 2010, the network had admitted that many third-party applications available through Facebook were collecting data on users and that the apps' makers were passing the information on to advertisers and tracking companies, contrary to Facebook's stated policy. Some also were collecting and distributing information about the app-users' friends.[21]

Such revelations have left many Americans worried about their privacy. In the Allstate/*National Journal* poll, 90 percent of Americans said they have less privacy than previous generations, and 93 percent expect succeeding generations to have even less.[22] An 11-nation survey by Ovum, a London-based business and technology consulting firm, found that two-thirds of respondents would like to prevent others from tracking their online activities.[23]

"Everything we do now might be leaving a digital trail, so privacy is clearly on the way out," says David Pritchard, a physics professor at MIT who studies teaching effectiveness by mining data gathered during massive open online courses (MOOCs), which MIT and other universities offer for free over the Internet.[24]

By recording and analyzing students' keystrokes, Pritchard can see what page of an online textbook they viewed, for how long and what they did before and after that. He can also see who participated in the course's online forum. Comparing such study habits with performance on tests will enable him to "figure out what tools students use to get problems right or wrong," he says. But he is quick to note that he obtains students' permission to monitor their keystrokes for the study.

While many people value their personal privacy, he says, "We're going to have to work a lot harder to maintain some aspects of it."

Others say concerns about big data speeding the loss of privacy are overblown.

Patrick Hopkins, a philosopher who focuses on technology, advocates a pragmatic approach. "We need to get realistic about privacy in the information age. This notion of privacy being an inalienable right is recent," says Hopkins, who chairs the Millsaps College Philosophy Department in Jackson, Miss., and is an affiliate scholar with the Institute for Ethics and Emerging Technologies, an international organization based in Hartford, Conn., that studies technology's impact on society. "It's not in the Constitution. It's not in the French Declaration of Rights," he says, referring to the "Declaration of the Rights of Man and of the Citizen," adopted by the French National Assembly in 1789.[25] "I'm only worried about privacy if there's something that's going to harm me."

"These days, I know if I drive down a street I will be monitored," says Hopkins. "That does not bother me. There's no harm to me, and I might benefit" if surveillance catches a criminal.

Similarly, he's not bothered by the government mining big data in search of terrorists. "Asking if you're willing to give up your privacy for security is a false dilemma," Hopkins says. "It's not like you have 100 percent of one and zero percent of the other. I would be willing to give up a bit of privacy for security."

Citing surveys showing that young people are less worried about privacy than their elders, Mike Zaneis, senior vice president for public policy at the Interactive Advertising Bureau, a New York-based trade association for the online advertising industry, says, "It's not because they don't care about privacy. It's that they understand the value of the exchange, and they are willing to give up more information as long as they are receiving some benefit."

Andreas Weigend — former chief scientist at Amazon.com who now directs Stanford University's Social Data Lab — says many people's notion of privacy is "romantic" and "belongs in the Romantic Age. We need to

Health Care Providers, Employers Most Trusted to Protect Data

Consumers said they trusted doctors, hospitals and employers the most to handle individuals' personal data responsibly, according to a poll taken in late May and early June. Political parties, the media and social media websites were trusted the least. The poll was conducted just before Edward Snowden's revelations that the National Security Agency has been spying on private citizens.

How much do you trust these groups or people to use information about you responsibly?

	A great deal/some	Not much/ not at all
Health care providers	80%	20%
Employers	79	19
Law enforcement	71	28
Insurance companies	63	35
Government	48	51
Cell phone/Internet providers	48	50
Political parties	37	61
Media	29	69
Social media sites	25	70

Note: Totals do not add to 100 because don't know/refused to answer responses are not included.

Source: "Allstate/National Journal/Heartland Monitor Poll XVII," June 2013, www.theheartlandvoice.com/wp-content/uploads/2013/06/HeartlandTopline-Results.pdf

understand a 21st-century notion of privacy, and it can't be what some people wish was the case."

Should the federal government strengthen its regulation of big data?

Privacy advocates and big data businesses both view Europe as instructive in debates about government regulation — but in different ways. Many privacy advocates want the United States to adopt Europe's stronger regulatory approach, and business advocates want Europe to become more like the less-regulated U.S.

The United States has laws that protect certain kinds of data, such as financial and medical records, while all European countries have broad right-to-privacy laws. For example, many European countries require

Jeff Jarvis, a City University of New York journalism professor, says critics focus too much on the negatives of big data while ignoring the positives. While many deplore facial recognition as an invasion of privacy that can empower stalkers, the technology also can be used to find lost children, as well as criminals or terrorists, he says.

organizations to obtain permission before collecting information about an individual and allow those individuals to review and correct the data.[26] Last year, the United Kingdom forbade online organizations from tracking individuals' Web activities without consent. And the European Union (EU) is considering regulations that would apply to all 28 member states.[27]

Zaneis, of the Interactive Advertising Bureau, says U.S. residents' privacy is guarded adequately by the laws regulating data gathered for specific purposes, including protecting children's online privacy.

The Federal Trade Commission is charged with protecting Americans' privacy, Zaneis says, and the marketing industry has an effective self-regulatory regime. For instance, he says, more than 95 percent of online advertising companies participate in a program that enables consumers to prevent their information from being sent to third parties for marketing purposes.

That's not good enough for many privacy advocates, however. Individuals should not have to opt out of data-collection programs, they argue. Instead, they contend, companies should have to ask individuals to opt in. Critics also maintain that self-regulation is inadequate.

"This isn't something the free market can fix," argued Schneier, of Harvard's Berkman Center for Internet and Society. "There are simply too many ways to be tracked" by electronic devices and services. "And it's fanciful to

expect people to simply refuse to use [online services] just because they don't like the spying."[28]

Supporting Schneier's contention, Forrester Research reported that just 18 percent of Internet users set their browsers to ask organizations not to track their online activities — a request the organizations can, however, legally ignore.[29] Zaneis says most people don't change their default settings — whether to opt in or opt out.

Privacy advocates want to do much more than block information to third parties. In the United States, Consumer Watchdog supports Sen. Rockefeller's proposal to enable individuals to ban Internet sites from collecting information about them online except when the collection is necessary to provide a requested service to the individual.[30]

Americans "should be empowered to make their own decisions about whether their information can be tracked and used online," Rockefeller said when he introduced the legislation in March.[31] Consumer Watchdog's Simpson would extend that right to all data, not just online data. "You as a consumer should have the right to control what data companies collect from you and how to use it, and if you don't want them to collect it you ought to be able to say 'no,' " he argues. "Right now, we have this insidious ecosystem that's based on spying on people without them really knowing who's looking and what they're doing and that they're putting together giant dossiers on you."

Americans also want the right to remove online data that they don't like. Fully 89 percent of respondents in the Allstate/*National Journal* survey supported this so-called "right to be forgotten."[32]

Computer scientist Jaron Lanier — an early developer of virtual reality technology who currently works at Microsoft Research — suggests that people should be paid for their data. The value of that personal information probably runs to $1,000 or more a year, he estimates. Companies already compensate consumers for the information they give up when using club cards at grocery stores and other retailers, by giving them "member" discounts, he notes.

But it's not just the value of online advertising that counts, Lanier says. "What if someone's medical records are used to make medicine?"

Zaneis argues that Internet users already are compensated via the services they receive free on the Web.

"Ninety-nine percent of the content and services that we consume online are offered for free to the consumer," he says. "They're paid for by the consumer giving something. Sometimes it's data. Sometimes it's their eyeballs on advertising." If many people blocked access to their data, he says, it could kill the Internet as we know it.

Stanford's Weigend calls that "the underlying concept [of the Internet]: Give to get."

Jim Harper, director of information policy studies at the Cato Institute, a libertarian think tank in Washington, says government should stay out of the debate. "I put the burden on people to maintain their own privacy," he says. "It's the responsibility of Web users to refuse interaction with sites they don't want to share information with, to decline to share cookies," which are small files that a website places in a computer's browser to identify the browser on future visits. "Don't post online things you don't want posted online.

"When you walk outside your house, people can see you and gather what they learn and use it any way they want. I think the online world has to work the same."

Jarvis, the journalism professor, argues that Internet users have an obligation to share their information with the websites they use. "You have an impact on the sustainability of the properties whose content you're getting," he says. By blocking your information, "you are choosing to make yourself less valuable to that property. You've made this moral choice not to support these sites." News media, which are struggling to survive as it is, would be especially damaged if readers withheld information needed to make ads more valuable, he adds.

Jarvis does not argue against all privacy laws, such as those protecting medical records, for instance. And he favors extending first-class mail's privacy guarantee to all private communication. But "we should not be legislating according to technology, because [technology] can be used for good as well as bad," he continues. "We shouldn't regulate the gathering of information" online because that would be restricting what people can learn and know. "We should regulate behavior we find wrong."

Jarvis also calls for respecting "publicness" as well as privacy. "The right to be forgotten has clear implications for the right to speak," he says. "If I take a picture of us together in public, and you, say, force me to take that picture down [from the Internet], you're affecting my speech."

Deciding how to regulate big data is "quite complex," Hopkins, of Millsaps College, says. "We need to recognize what the costs would be."

BACKGROUND

Data Overload

In mid-1945, as World War II slogged toward its end, Vannevar Bush, director of the U.S. Office of Scientific Research and Development and later a key advocate for creation of the National Science Foundation, conjured up the future of big data and the so-called Information Age.

In a lengthy essay in *The Atlantic* entitled "As We May Think," Bush wrote:

"The summation of human experience is being expanded at a prodigious rate, and the means we use for threading through the consequent maze . . . is the same as was used in the days of square-rigged ships. . . . The investigator is staggered by the findings and conclusions of thousands of other workers — conclusions which he cannot find time to grasp, much less to remember."[33]

Technology probably will solve the problem, Bush suggested, hinting at future inventions such as desktop computers, search engines and even Google's new Glass headgear, eyeglasses that contain a computer that can take pictures, respond to voice commands, search the Internet and perform other functions as wearers move from place to place. Bush envisioned a miniature automatic camera that a researcher would wear on his forehead to make microfilm photographs as he worked. He also predicted that one day a microfilmed *Encyclopaedia Britannica* could be kept in a matchbox and a million books in part of a desk.

Perhaps most striking, he suggested the personal computer and the search engine in a desk-sized contraption he dubbed the "memex." "On the top are slanting translucent screens, on which material can be projected for convenient reading," he wrote. "There is a keyboard, and sets of buttons and levers." Inside are all those compressed documents, which the memex user will call to a screen the way the brain remembers — through "association of thoughts" rather than old-fashioned indexing, as search engines do today.

Bush knew a great deal about data, having invented the differential analyzer — a mechanical computer for working

C H R O N O L O G Y

1960s–1995 *Development of Internet opens new ways to create and gather data.*

1967 Defense Department's Advanced Research Projects Agency (ARPA) funds research that leads to creation of the Internet.

1969 UCLA and Stanford Research Institute establish the first ARPANET link.

1980 Computer scientist I. A. Tjomsland declares that data expand to fill the available storage space. . . . Phrase "big data" is first used in print.

1989 Internet opens to general public.

1991 Commercial activities are allowed on Internet for first time. . . . Point-and-click navigation invented. . . . World Wide Web name coined.

1992 Bill Clinton-Al Gore presidential/vice presidential campaign makes Internet an effective political tool.

1994 First White House website launched.

1995 Library of Congress puts legislative information online.

1997–Present *Big data becomes major force through use of search engines, social media and powerful computers.*

1998 Google search engine goes online. . . . American information scientist Michael Lesk predicts increase in storage capacity will mean no data will have to be discarded.

2000 A quarter of the world's stored data has been digitized.

2002 LinkedIn business-networking site launched.

2003 More data created this year than in all previous human history.

2004 "TheFacebook" is launched for Harvard undergraduates. . . . Flickr photo-sharing platform goes online. . . . Walmart is storing 460 terabytes (460 trillion bytes) of data about its customers. Other large retailers also are storing large amounts of data.

2005 YouTube video-sharing site created.

2006 Twitter goes online. . . . Facebook opens to anyone age 13 or over.

2007 AT&T begins giving police access to U.S. phone records dating back to 1987 for use in criminal investigations.

2008 Sen. Barack Obama uses big data to win presidential election.

2010 Super-secret National Security Agency (NSA) processes 1.7 billion intercepted communications daily. . . . Google discloses that cars taking street-level photos for Google maps also captured information from unprotected Wi-Fi networks. . . . Conservative activists turn Tea Party into political force using social media.

2012 Google fined $22.5 million for bypassing browser privacy controls. . . . U.S. government launches $200 million Big Data Research and Development Initiative to advance technologies needed to analyze and share huge quantities of data. . . . Financial Industry Regulatory Authority taps big data to uncover suspicious securities practices. . . . NSA begins building $2 billion facility for processing big data. . . . Federal Trade Commission (FTC) begins inquiry into data brokers' activities. . . . Social media activism helps prolong Republican presidential nominating process. . . . Obama intensifies use of big data to win re-election.

2013 After strong negative customer reaction, Facebook temporarily backs away from plan to utilize users' pictures and postings in ads. . . . Google fights lawsuit over reading Gmail content. . . . Survey reveals 55 percent of Americans see "mostly negative" impact from collection of big data about people. . . . FTC official says people should be able to restrict use of their data in commercial databases. . . . Acxiom data broker lets people correct and delete information in its database. . . . Tapping Medicare's big data, U.S. government reports what 3,000 U.S. hospitals charge for 100 different treatments. . . . Ninety percent of world's data have been created in the last two years, and data are growing by 2.5 quintillion bytes daily. . . . Ninety-eight percent of world's data are stored digitally.

complex equations — in 1931. But he was far from the first to bewail data overload and to seek ways of addressing it. The Old Testament book of Ecclesiastes laments: "Of making many books there is no end; and much study is a weariness of the flesh."[34] The first-century AD philosopher Lucius Annaeus Seneca grumbled that "the abundance of books is distraction."[35] By the 15th century, Europeans felt crushed under information overload after German printer Johannes Gutenberg invented mechanical printing with moveable type — the printing press.

"Suddenly, there were far more books than any single person could master, and no end in sight," Harvard University historian Ann Blair observed of Europe after Gutenberg's invention around 1453.

Printers "fill the world with pamphlets and books that are foolish, ignorant, malignant, libelous, mad, impious and subversive," the Renaissance humanist Erasmus wrote in the early 16th century, "and such is the flood that even things that might have done some good lose all their goodness. . . . Is there anywhere on earth exempt from these swarms of new books?"[36]

The products rolling off the presses did not overwhelm scholars for long, however. New technologies were developed to address the challenges the presses had created: public libraries, large bibliographies, bigger encyclopedias, compendiums of quotations, outlines, indexes — predecessors of *Reader's Digest*, *Bartlett's Familiar Quotations* and Internet aggregators, Blair noted.

That always happens, the late science historian Derek Price said, because of the "law of exponential increase," which he propounded while teaching at Yale University in 1961. Scientific knowledge grows exponentially because "each advance generates a new series of advances," he said.[37]

Before the Internet and powerful computers made today's big data possible, some scholars saw it coming. In 1980, computer scientist I. A. Tjomsland proclaimed a corollary to Parkinson's First Law (Work expands so as to fill the time available for its completion.) "Data expands to fill the space available," he said, because "users have no way of identifying obsolete data," and "the penalties for storing obsolete data are less apparent than are the penalties for discarding potentially useful data."[38]

In 1997, while working on an electronic library project called CORE (Chemical Online Retrieval Experiment),

information scientist Michael Lesk predicted that advances in storage capacity would create unlimited space for data.

"In only a few years, we will be able [to] save everything — no information will have to be thrown out, and the typical piece of information will never be looked at by a human being," said Lesk, who now is a professor of library and information science at Rutgers University.[39]

Birth of Big Data

Technological advances often come about through government initiatives. For instance, the 1890 U.S. Census used machine-read punch cards for the first time to tabulate the results, enabling the complete census to be reported in one year instead of eight. That, according to *Big Data* co-authors Cukier and Mayer-Schonberger, was the beginning of automated data processing.[40]

In Vannevar Bush's time, government demand drove the development of computing machines in efforts to crack enemy codes during World War II. After the war, U.S. spy agencies sought ever-more-powerful technology to collect, store and process the fruits of their espionage.

By 2010, the NSA was processing 1.7 billion intercepted communications every day. In 2012, it began construction of a $2 billion facility in Utah designed to deal with the huge amounts of data it collects.[41]

U.S. national security concerns also drove the creation and initial development of the Internet. The Defense Advanced Research Projects Agency funded the efforts in order to facilitate information exchange among military research facilities. The first Internet link occurred when a University of California, Los Angeles, computer logged onto a Stanford Research Institute computer 360 miles away on Oct. 29, 1969.

Although the concept of an "information explosion" had been around since 1941, the phrase "big data" was used first by the late University of Michigan sociologist Charles Tilly in a 1980 paper for the university's Center for Research on Social Organization, according to the *Oxford English Dictionary*. "None of the big [social history] questions has actually yielded to the bludgeoning of the big-data people," Tilly wrote of historians using computers and statistics.[42]

The Internet didn't open to the general public until the late 1980s, when MCI Mail and CompuServe offered

Crunching Data Sheds New Light on History

"Big data allows us to ask questions that were not possible before."

Big data can be used for more than plumbing databases for consumer preferences about dish soap or spying on citizens' phone calls. Sometimes supported by grants from the National Endowment for the Humanities, scholars in history and literature, for example, are digging into new databases of old documents to reexamine common assumptions about authors and important historical figures.

Researchers at Stanford University, for instance, have discovered that England was much less important to French philosopher Voltaire and the French Enlightenment than was commonly thought.

Tapping into Oxford University's digitized collection of 64,000 letters written by 8,000 historical figures from the early 17th to mid-19th centuries, the Stanford team analyzed the letters' metadata — the names, addresses and dates, but not their content — and discovered little communication between Voltaire and the English.

Using big data "allows us to ask questions that were simply not possible to be asked in a systematic manner before, and to analyze our data in ways that would have been impossible or incredibly difficult to do," explains Dan

Edelstein, a Stanford associate professor of French and history. The analysis of the Oxford papers "allowed me to see Voltaire's correspondence network in a new light and to formulate hypotheses that I probably would not have hit upon."

Similarly, Caroline Winterer, a Stanford history professor and director of the Stanford Humanities Center, and her colleagues probed the papers of Benjamin Franklin, collected by Yale University scholars beginning in 1954 and digitized with support from the Packard Humanities Institute, in Los Altos, Calif. Their findings challenged the perception of Franklin as a cosmopolitan figure, at least before 1763, when he returned to America after a six-year stay in England. Almost all of the letters Franklin received while in England were from England or America.[1]

Living in London made Franklin "a typical Anglo-Atlantic figure" rather than "an international man of mystery," Edelstein explains, because "the American colonies and England really had shared a culture at this time."

email services. The public's first full-service Internet access came through a provider called "The World" in 1989.

The early '90s saw the beginnings of commercial activity on the Internet and the coining of the term World Wide Web. The additions of point-and-click browsing and graphics increased the Internet's popularity.[43]

Data and Politics

During the 1992 presidential campaign, former Arkansas Gov. Bill Clinton and his running mate, Sen. Al Gore of Tennessee, turned the Web into a campaign tool, then launched the first White House website in 1994. In 1995, the Library of Congress started an online legislative information website —Thomas.gov — named after former President Thomas Jefferson, who sold his personal book collection to the library after the British burned Congress' original holdings during the War of 1812.

In 2003, Vermont Gov. Howard Dean scaled new heights in Internet campaigning by organizing supporters,

publicizing campaign events and raising funds online. The efforts made him the most successful fundraiser in the history of the Democratic Party and enabled him to take an early lead in the campaign for the 2004 Democratic presidential nomination.

Dean's quest for the nomination failed. But four years later, Illinois Sen. Barack Obama took a quantum leap over Dean, winning the White House after raising a record $500 million online and making the Internet and big data an integral part of his campaign. Obama compiled more than 13 million email addresses, attracted a million-member audience for text messages, and created a 90-worker digital staff to contribute to communication, fundraising and grassroots organizing. He campaigned on Facebook, Twitter and YouTube, and even bought ads in video games.[44]

Mark McKinnon, an adviser to George W. Bush's 2000 and 2004 campaigns, described the Obama run as a "seminal, transformative race" that "leveraged the Internet in ways never imagined."[45]

Analyzing big data, however, does not replace traditional scholarship, Edelstein says. "To find out if you're on the right track, you need to contextualize your results and to interpret them, and that means being very familiar with your data and with the scholarship of your period. When you see England doesn't seem to be that important in Voltaire's map [of correspondence], that only means something if you already are familiar with certain scholarship about Voltaire that establishes England as an important place for him.

"What does it mean that you don't see a lot of letters there?" he asks. "It could mean he didn't care about England. It could mean he had other sources of information about England. Could it be we just lost the letters to England? You have to spend time in rare-books collections figuring out these questions." They concluded that "there's not really a good reason why more of the English letters would have been lost than his [other] letters."

Brett Bobley, who runs the national endowment's Office of Digital Humanities, says big data techniques greatly expand what humanities scholars can accomplish.

"Humanities scholars study books, music, art — and those very objects that they study are increasingly in digital format," he explains. "If you study the Civil War and you read old newspapers, now you can digitally access thousands and thousands of newspaper pages from the Civil

Computer analysis of letters received by Benjamin Franklin during a six-year stay in England challenged perceptions of the famed founding father as a cosmopolitan figure.

War era, and you can use digital tools to analyze the data in those newspapers far more than you could possibly read in your lifetime."

— Tom Price

[1]Claire Rydell and Caroline Winterer, "Benjamin Franklin's Correspondence Network, 1757-1763," Mapping the Republic of Letters Project, Stanford University, October 2012.

Two years later, conservative activists employed online social media to turn the Tea Party into a political force that helped Republicans take control of the U.S. House. In 2012, social media activism helped dark-horse candidates stay alive to prolong the 2012 Republican presidential nominating contest. But Obama — adding a robust social media presence to his big-data mix of information-collection, data-processing and Internet communication — won a second term.

Social media — now a major source of big data — emerged in the early 2000s, with the LinkedIn business networking site launching in 2003 and Facebook (first called TheFacebook) beginning to serve Harvard undergraduates in 2004. The Flickr photo-sharing platform went online in 2004 and the YouTube video-sharing site in 2005. Twitter launched in 2006, and Facebook opened to anyone 13 or older that same year.[46]

A decade earlier, Stanford University graduate students Larry Page and Sergey Brin began to build a search engine. They went online in 1997 with the name Google, a play on the number googol, which is 1 followed by 100 zeroes. Page and Brin chose the brand to represent the massive challenge of trying to search the entire Internet.[47] Google became the most profitable Internet company on the *Fortune* 500 list by continually innovating and adding new products and services, such as the Google+ social media platform, Google Maps and the street-level and satellite photos that accompany the maps.[48]

It also stumbled into some significant controversies, such as when it was discovered that Google cars taking street-level photos in 2010 also were collecting information from unprotected Wi-Fi networks, including email addresses and passwords. The Federal Trade Commission (FTC) fined the company $7 million for improper data collection that Google said was unintentional.[49] Last year, the FTC fined Google another $22.5 million for bypassing privacy controls on Apple's Safari browser.[50]

In the days before electronic computers, keypunch operators entered data on machine-readable cards. The U.S. government used punch cards in 1890 to tabulate census results, enabling the complete results to be reported in one year instead of eight, which some scholars mark as the beginning of automated data processing.

While online businesses such as Google and Facebook are famous — or infamous — for their use of big data today, brick-and-mortar retailers have been mining customer data since before some online companies were born. By 2004, for example, Walmart had loaded 460 terabytes of customer data onto its computers — more than twice as much information as was then available on the Internet and enough to begin predicting consumer behavior "instead of waiting for it to happen," according to Linda Dillman, the company's chief information officer.[51]

Target, too, has collected vast amounts of information about its customers for years and uses it to focus its marketing. For example, having determined what products pregnant women frequently buy at which stage of pregnancy, the retailer can predict which of its customers are pregnant and send promotions to them precisely when they'd likely be interested in certain products.

The process can have unintended consequences, however, such as when an angry father demanded to know why Target was sending coupons for baby clothes to his teenage daughter, only to learn later that she was expecting.[52]

CURRENT SITUATION

Hunting Criminals

After a summer-long public focus on the National Security Agency's surveillance practices, September brought additional revelations about government spying — this time by domestic law enforcement agencies employing big data strategies, primarily to hunt for criminals.

The New York Times reported that since 2007 AT&T had given federal and local police access to U.S. phone records — including phone numbers, locations of callers and date, time and duration of the calls — dating back to 1987.[53] Under the federally funded program, called the Hemisphere Project, four AT&T employees are embedded in joint federal-local law enforcement offices in Atlanta, Houston and Los Angeles, the newspaper said. They tap into AT&T's database whenever they receive "administrative subpoenas" from the Drug Enforcement Administration. The data are used to investigate a variety of crimes, however, not just drug cases.

The AT&T database contains records of every call that passes through the company's switches, including those made by customers of other phone companies. The AT&T's database may be larger than the NSA's — which stores records of phone numbers, date, time and duration of almost all U.S. calls but deletes them after five years — and it grows by about 4 billion calls a day. Justice Department spokesman Brian Fallon said the project "simply streamlines the process of serving the subpoena to the phone company so law enforcement can quickly keep up with drug dealers when they switch phone numbers to try to avoid detection."

Officials said the phone records help them find suspects who use hard-to-trace throwaway cell phones. Daniel Richman, a former federal prosecutor who teaches law at

Columbia University, described the project as "a desperate effort by the government to catch up" with advancing cell-phone technology.

September also brought disclosures that the NSA surveillance looked at more Americans' records than had previously been reported. Documents released in a lawsuit revealed that, from May 2006 to January 2009, the NSA improperly revealed phone numbers, date, time and call duration information about Americans who were not under investigation. The NSA gave the results of database queries to more than 200 analysts from other federal agencies without adequately shielding the identities of the Americans whose records were revealed.

The agency also tracked phone numbers without establishing "reasonable and articulable suspicion" that the numbers were tied to terrorists, as was required by a federal court order that allowed the NSA data collection.[54]

'Reclaim Your Name'

Just as the Justice Department is trying to catch up with criminals using cell-phone technology, regulatory agencies are trying to keep up with the technology employed by industries they oversee. The Federal Trade Commission, for instance, is investigating how data brokers operate. Such companies collect information about people, then sell it to others.

The commission asked nine companies about the kind of information they gather, the sources of the information, what they do with it and whether they allow individuals to view and correct the information or to opt out of having their information collected and sold.[55]

In August, FTC Commissioner Julie Brill called on the data broker industry to adopt a "Reclaim Your Name" program, which would enable people to see their information stored in companies' databases, learn how the information is gathered and used, prevent companies from selling it for marketing purposes and correct errors.

The proposal would not allow individuals to demand that the companies erase the information. Nevertheless, Brill said, it would address "the fundamental challenge to consumer privacy in the online marketplace: our loss of control over our most private and sensitive information."[56]

One data broker is opening the curtain on some of its practices — perhaps to its detriment. Scott Howe, chief executive of Arkansas-based Acxiom Corp., announced in late August that people can visit a new website, aboutthedata.com, to see and even change some of the information Acxiom has collected about them. Site visitors can discover the sources of the data, correct errors, delete some information and even tell the company to stop collecting and storing data about them, though to do so they first must provide Acxiom with personal information, including their address, birth date and last four digits of their Social Security number.

Acxiom collects a wide range of information about some 700 million individuals worldwide, including contact and demographic information, types of products purchased, type and value of residence and motor vehicles and recreational interests.[57] It gathers the information from public records, directories, Internet activity, questionnaires and from other data-collection companies. Acxiom sells the information to companies, nonprofits and political organizations that use it in marketing, fundraising, customer service, constituent services and outreach efforts.

Howe acknowledged Acxiom is taking a risk by letting people review their information. They could falsify information about themselves, for instance. And, if a significant number asked to be deleted from the database, "it would be devastating for our business," he said. "But I feel it's the right thing to do."

Aboutthedata.com also could lead to new business opportunities, Howe added. In the future, the site might invite visitors to volunteer more information about themselves. And Acxiom could make its database more valuable by allowing visitors to specify what kinds of advertising they'd like to see.[58]

Others in the marketing industry disagree. Adopting Brill's proposals "would lead to more fraud and limit the efficacy of [marketing] companies," according to Linda Woolley, CEO and president of the Direct Marketing Association, a trade organization for the direct marketing industry.[59]

Big data companies also are clashing with Web browser producers who make it easier for Internet surfers to keep their information secret and prevent tracking of their online activities. Microsoft now ships Internet Explorer with its do-not-track feature turned on. Mozilla plans to ship new versions of its Firefox browser with a default setting to block third-party cookies, but it's still working out the details. Internet Explorer, Firefox and other browsers allow users to set other restrictions on cookies. Randall

From Yottabytes to Googolplexes: Big Data Explained

For some, it's "writing zeroes until you get tired."

The term big data showed up this year in an old-school database — the *Oxford English Dictionary*, which defined it as "data of a very large size, typically to the extent that its manipulation and management present significant logistical challenges; [also] the branch of computing involving such data."[1]

Big data's information databases are so massive they require powerful supercomputers to analyze them, which increasingly is occurring in real time. And big data is growing exponentially: The amount of all data worldwide is expanding by 2.5 quintillion bytes per day.

In addition to analyzing large, traditional databases, big-data practitioners collect, store and analyze data from unstructured databases that couldn't be used in the past — such as email messages, Internet searches, social media postings, photographs and videos. The process often produces insights that couldn't be acquired in any other way.

Analyses of big data can uncover correlations — relationships between things that may or may not establish cause and effect. Some analysts say the lack of clear cause and effect is a weakness, but others say mere correlations often are sufficient to inform decisions.

"Correlations are fine for many, many things," says Jeff Hawkins, cofounder of Grok, a company that makes software for real-time data analysis. "You don't really need to know the why . . . as long as you can act on it." For instance, he continues, "You don't really need to understand exactly why people consume more energy at 2 in the afternoon" in order to decide whether to buy or sell it at that time of the day. "If I'm just trying to make a better pricing strategy," the correlation is enough.

Databases are measured in "bytes," which describe the amount of computer action required to process them. A byte is eight bits. A bit is one action of a computer switch. A byte commonly is equivalent to a single alphanumeric character.

Discussing big data requires huge numbers with unfamiliar names, such as:

- **Quadrillion:** 1 followed by 15 zeroes.
- **Quintillion:** 1 followed by 18 zeroes.
- **Sextillion:** 1 followed by 21 zeroes.
- **Septillion:** 1 followed by 24 zeroes.
- **Terabyte:** 1 trillion bytes.
- **Yottabyte:** 1 septillion bytes.
- **Googol:** 1 followed by 100 zeroes (the inspiration for the Google search engine's name).

Rothenberg, president and CEO of the Interactive Advertising Bureau (IAB), called Microsoft's do-not-track decision "a step backwards in consumer choice." Because it is set by default, he said, it doesn't represent a consumer's decision.[60]

The digital advertising industry's code of conduct currently does not require companies to honor do-not-track signals, but the Digital Advertising Alliance established a committee in October to formulate a policy on do-not-track settings by early next year. The alliance is a consortium of six advertising industry trade groups.[61]

The IAB also charged that Mozilla's plan to block third-party cookies would disrupt targeted advertising.

"There are billions and billions of dollars and tens of thousands of jobs at stake in this supply chain," Rothenberg said.[62] Blocking the cookies would be especially damaging to small online publishers that depend on the cookies to sell ads to niche audiences, he added. "These small businesses can't afford to hire large advertising sales teams [and] can't afford the time to make individual buys across thousands of websites."[63]

Brendan Eich, Mozilla's chief technology officer, defended the planned cookie-blocking. "We believe in putting users in control of their online experience, and we want a healthy, thriving Web ecosystem, [and] we do not see a contradiction," he said.[64]

- **Googolplex:** 1 followed by a googol zeroes — that is, 1 followed by 100 zeroes 100 times.

Googol and googolplex exist primarily for mathematical amusement. The 9-year-old nephew of Columbia University mathematician Edward Kasner, Milton Sirotta, coined the terms. The boy defined googolplex as a 1 followed by "writing zeroes until you get tired," Kasner related in the 1940 book *Mathematics and the Imagination*, which he wrote with fellow mathematician James Newman.[2]

Other big data jargon includes:

- **Metadata:** Information about information. With email, for instance, metadata include the addresses, time sent, networks used and types of computers used, but not the message content.

Many who collect metadata — including companies and government investigative agencies — say they don't invade privacy because they don't collect the content or identify specific individuals. But critics say metadata can reveal a great deal about an individual. Analyzing records of phone calls between top business executives could suggest a pending merger, calls to medical offices could hint at a serious illness and records of reporters' communications might reveal the identity of confidential sources, according to mathematician Susan Landau, a former Sun Microsystems engineer and author of *Surveillance or Security? The Risks Posed by New Wiretapping Technologies*.[3]

- **Cookie:** A small file, inserted into a computer's browser by a website, which identifies the browser. Different kinds of cookies perform different functions. They can relieve users of the need to provide the same identification information each time they visit a website. Cookies also can track the browser's activities across the Internet. A visited website can allow another, unvisited website to place a cookie — which is called a third-party cookie – into a computer without the Web surfer's knowledge.

- **Do not track:** A request a browser can send to a visited website asking that the site not set a tracking cookie. The site can ignore the request.

- **The cloud:** Computing and computer storage capabilities that exist beyond the user's computer, often accessed through the Internet.

- **Opt in and opt out:** Telling a website that you do or don't want to do something. Online companies tend to prefer the opt-out system, because the Web surfer specifically has to request that a site not set a cookie or track a browser. Privacy advocates tend to prefer the opt-in system.

- **Analytics:** The process of finding insights in data.

— *Tom Price*

[1] *Oxford English Dictionary* (2013), www.oed.com/view/Entry/18833#eid301162177.

[2] Edward Kasner and James Newman, *Mathematics and the Imagination* (2001), p. 23; Eric Weisstein, "Edward Kasner (1878-1955)," *Eric Weisstein's World of Science*, Wolfram Research, http://scienceworld.wolfram.com/biography/Kasner.html.

[3] Jane Mayer, "What's the Matter with Metadata?" *The New Yorker*, June 6, 2013, www.newyorker.com/online/blogs/newsdesk/2013/06/verizon-nsa-metadata-surveillance-problem.html.

Privacy advocates applauded. "This is a really good move for online consumers," said Jeff Chester, executive director of the Center for Digital Democracy, a consumer-privacy advocacy group in Washington.[65]

While spying and advertising by big data companies stir up controversies, many big-data accomplishments go unnoticed by the public. Because of super-speedy computers, enormous databases and powerful sensors, scientists, technicians, business managers and entrepreneurs daily push out the frontiers of science, business and daily life. Some are even pushing past databases — employing computers, sensors and software to collect and analyze data simultaneously.

Maximizing big data's benefits requires real-time analysis of information streamed from sensors, says Jeff Hawkins, cofounder of Grok, a company that has developed software to do just that. The data explosion is happening in part because of an increase in data sources, he says, noting that "pretty much everything in the world is becoming a sensor." Sensors are collecting data from buildings, motor vehicles, streets and all kinds of machinery, Hawkins says, and much of it needs to be analyzed immediately to be worthwhile.

"Data coming off a windmill might get (analyzed) every minute," Hawkins explains. "Server data might be every 10 seconds. Trying to predict pricing in some marketplace

Are new laws needed to prevent organizations from collecting online personal data?

YES   John M. Simpson
Director, Privacy Project,
Consumer Watchdog

Written for *CQ Researcher*, October 2013

Privacy laws simply have not kept pace with the digital age and must be updated to protect us as we surf the Web or use our mobile devices. People must be able to control what, or even whether, organizations collect data about them online.

Suppose you went to the library and someone followed you around, noting each book you browsed. When you went to a store, they recorded every item you examined and what you purchased. In the brick-and-mortar world, this would be stalking, and an obvious invasion of privacy.

On the Internet such snooping is business as usual, but that is no justification. Nearly everything we do online is tracked, often without our knowledge or consent, and by companies with whom we have no relationship. Digital dossiers may help target advertising, but they can also be used to make assumptions about people in connection with employment, housing, insurance and financial services — and for government surveillance.

Americans increasingly understand the problem. The Pew Research Center released a poll in September that found 86 percent of Internet users have taken steps online to remove or mask their digital footprints. Some 68 percent of respondents said current laws are not good enough to protect our online privacy.

So, what can be done? In February 2012 President Obama issued a report, *Consumer Privacy in a Networked World*, that called for a Consumer Privacy Bill of Rights that includes the right of consumers "to exercise control over what personal data companies collect from them and how they use it." He called for legislation to enact those rights. It is long past time to introduce and pass it.

All four major browsers can now send a "do not track" message to sites their users visit. However, companies are not required to comply, and most do not.

Sen. Jay Rockefeller, D-W.Va., has introduced a "do not track" bill that would require compliance. But with Congress mired in partisan gridlock, state-level "do not track" legislation – perhaps enacted through the ballot initiative process in a progressive state such as California — is another option.

Stopping Internet companies from tracking users online will not end online advertising or break the Internet, but it will force advertisers to honor our personal boundaries. A "do not track" mechanism would give consumers better control and help restore everyone's confidence in the Internet. That's a win-win for consumers and businesses alike.

NO   Jim Harper
Director, Information Policy Studies,
The Cato Institute

Written for *CQ Researcher*, October 2013

There is no question that Internet users should be able to stop organizations from collecting data about them. The question is how.

Most people think that new sets of legal rights or rules are the way to put Internet users in the driver's seat. Ideas range from mandatory privacy notices, to government regulation of data collection, to a radical new legal regime in which people own all data about them. But these ideas founder when it comes to administration, and their proponents misunderstand what privacy is and how people protect it.

We can learn about online privacy from offline privacy. In the real world, people protect privacy by controlling information about themselves. We have ornate customs and habits around how we dress; when and where we speak; what we say, write or type; the design of houses and public buildings; and much more. All of these things mesh our privacy desires with the availability of information about us. Laws, such as contract and property laws, back up the decisions we make to protect privacy.

Protecting privacy is harder in the online world. Many people do not understand how information moves online. And we don't know what consequences information sharing will have in the future. What's more, privacy interests are changing. (Make no mistake: People — even the young — still care about privacy.)

The way to protect privacy online is by using established legal principles. When Internet service providers, websites or email services promise privacy, the law should recognize that as a contract. The law should recognize that a person's data — contact information in a phone or driving data in a car — belong to that person.

Crucially, the government should respect the contracts and property concepts that are emerging in the online environment. This is not an entirely new idea. In a 1929 Fourth Amendment case, U.S. Supreme Court Justice Pierce Butler weighed in against wiretapping, saying, "The contracts between telephone companies and users contemplate the private use of the facilities employed in the service. The communications belong to the parties between whom they pass."

When Internet users learn what matters to them and how to protect it, the laws and the government should protect and respect their decisions. This is the best way to let Internet users stop organizations from collecting data about them.

or demand for energy use in a building might be hourly or every 12 to 16 minutes."

Grok never runs into privacy issues because "we don't save data," Hawkins says. "We look at data, we act upon it and we throw away the data."

OUTLOOK

'Internet of Things'

People familiar with big data agree that the amount of information processed and the speed and sophistication with which it can be analyzed will increase exponentially. Huge amounts of data will be generated by what many are calling the "Internet of Things" — the online linking of sensors installed on more and more inanimate objects.

"There are going to be billions of sensors," Grok's Hawkins says, "maybe hundreds of billions. We are going to see the world become more efficient, more reliable. In the future, your refrigerator should be able to say: I should precool myself by about 3 degrees so, when the price of electricity goes up in the afternoon, I don't have to run."

Google Chairman Eric Schmidt predicts that everyone on Earth will be online by the end of the decade, but he concedes that won't be all good. In a book written with Jared Cohen, director of Google Ideas, the company's think tank, Schmidt acknowledges that threats to privacy and reputation will become stronger.[66]

Noting the old advice to not write down anything you don't want to read on a newspaper's front page, Schmidt and Cohen broaden it to "the websites you visit, who you include in your online network, what you 'like,' and what others who are connected to you say and share." They foresee privacy classes joining sex-education classes in schools and parents sitting children down for "the privacy-and-security talk even before the sex talk."[67]

The Cato Institute's Harper expects the collection of personal data to increase indefinitely, but "there still remain huge amounts of information that people keep to themselves, and that's not going to change. From every thought that crossed your mind at breakfast to your reasons for watching the television programs you did tonight — all that personal information that's part of what gives your life meaning — nobody knows that unless you tell them."

Hopkins from Millsaps College says, "it will become easier and cheaper to find information out about people in ways that our laws and ancestors never conceived of," noting the threat to privacy that would occur if nefarious individuals [such as peeping Toms or thieves "casing a joint"] could own drones.[68]

"Courts and public policymakers are going to have to decide if we're going to try to limit technology to things you could have done in 1950 or 1750, or are we going to have to give up the notion that we could have the same kinds of privacy expectations that we had a century ago," Hopkins says. People probably will accept less privacy, he says, "because of the incredible ease of use and personal benefits" that come from sharing the data. "I suspect we'll just get used to it."

Zaneis, of the Interactive Advertising Bureau, also doesn't expect tighter data controls, because government can't keep up with the speed of technological advances. "There's going to be evolution and change at such a rapid pace that legislators and regulators can't keep pace," he says, contending that industry self-regulation will fill the gap.

Consumer Watchdog's Simpson concedes that privacy advocates won't get everything they want. "But I think we're going to see some serious protections put in place," he says, because the NSA revelations have generated "tremendous pushback" against privacy invasion.

But Polonetsky, of the Future of Privacy Forum, says, "Technology probably is going to solve this before policymakers do," citing how browser manufacturers are developing privacy protections for their users.

Similarly, Mark Little, the principal consumer analyst for the Ovum consulting firm, warns big data companies that they could run into "hurricane-force disruptions" of their data collection. "Marketers should not be surprised if more and more consumers look to alternative privacy ecosystems to control, secure and even benefit from their own data," he said.[69]

NOTES

1. For background, see Tom Price, "Globalizing Science," *CQ Global Researcher*, Feb. 1, 2011, pp. 53-78.

2. "Computing," European Organization for Nuclear Research, Http://home.web.cern.ch/about/computing.

3. For background, see Chuck McCutcheon, "Government Surveillance," *CQ Researcher*, Aug. 30, 2013, pp. 717-740.

4. "Bill Summary & Status, 113th Congress (2013-2014), S.418, All Congressional Actions," Library of Congress, http://thomas.loc.gov/cgi-bin/bdquery/D?d113:1:./temp/~bd9qWL:@@@X|/home/LegislativeData.php.

5. Viktor Mayer-Schonberger and Kenneth Cukier, *Big Data: A Revolution that Will Transform How We Live, Work, and Think* (2013); James Risen and Eric Lichtblau, "How the U.S. Uses Technology to Mine More Data More Quickly," *The New York Times*, June 9, 2013, p. 1, www.nytimes.com/2013/06/09/us/revelations-give-look-at-spy-agencys-wider-reach.html?_r=0.

6. Risen and Lichtblau, *ibid.*

7. Ross Andersen, "How Big Data Is Changing Astronomy (Again)," *The Atlantic*, April 19, 2012, www.theatlantic.com/technology/archive/2012/04/how-big-data-is-changing-astronomy-again/255917.

8. Juliette Garside, "Google does not have to delete sensitive information, says European court," *The Guardian*, June 25, 2013, www.guardian.co.uk/technology/2013/jun/25/google-not-delete-sensitive-information-court; Katherine Jacobsen, "Should Google be accountable for what its search engine unearths?" *The Christian Science Monitor*, June 25, 2013, www.csmonitor.com/Innovation/2013/0625/Should-Google-be-accountable-for-what-its-search-engine-unearths.

9. "New Poll Shows Americans Anxious About Privacy," Allstate/*National Journal/The Atlantic/Heartland Monitor* Poll, June 13, 2013, www.magnetmail.net/actions/email_web_version.cfm?recipient_id=615749555&message_id=2731423&user_id=NJG_NJMED&group_id=526964&jobid=14264751.

10. Farah Stockman, "Big Data's big deal," *The Boston Globe*, June 18, 2013, p.11, www.bostonglobe.com/opinion/2013/06/18/after-snowden-defense-big-data/7zH3HKrXm4o3L1HIM7cfSK/story.html.

11. "New Poll Shows Americans Anxious About Privacy," *op. cit.*

12. Vignesh Ramachandran, "Social Media Project Monitors Keywords to Prevent Suicide," *Mashable*, Aug. 20, 2013, http://mashable.com/2013/08/20/durkheim-project-social-media-suicide.

13. Dina ElBoghdady, "Wall Street regulators turn to better technology to monitor markets," *The Washington Post*, July 12, 2013, www.washingtonpost.com/business/economy/wall-street-regulators-turn-to-better-technology-to-monitor-markets/2013/07/12/ab188abc-eb25-11e2-aa9f-c03a72e2d342_story.html.

14. Bruce Schneier, "The Internet Is a Surveillance State," CNN, March 16, 2013, www.schneier.com/essay-418.html.

15. Max Fisher, "Here's the e-mail trick Petraeus and Broadwell used to communicate," *The Washington Post*, Nov. 12, 2012, www.washingtonpost.com/blogs/worldviews/wp/2012/11/12/heres-the-e-mail-trick-petraeus-and-broadwell-used-to-communicate.

16. Schneier, *op. cit.*

17. *Ibid.*

18. Risen and Lichtblau, *op. cit.*

19. Niraj Chokshi and Matt Berman, "The NSA Doesn't Need Much Phone Data to Know You're You," *National Journal*, June 6, 2013, www.nationaljournal.com/nationalsecurity/the-nsa-doesn-t-need-much-phone-data-to-know-you-re-you-20130605.

20. Gerry Shih, "Facebook admits year-long data breach exposed 6 million users," Reuters, June 21, 2013, www.reuters.com/article/2013/06/21/net-us-facebook-security-idUSBRE95K18Y20130621; Violet Blue, "Firm: Facebook's shadow profiles are 'frightening' dossiers on everyone," ZDNet, June 24, 2013, www.zdnet.com/firm-facebooks-shadow-Fprofiles-are-frightening-dossiers-on-everyone-7000017199.

21. Emily Steel and Geoffrey A. Fowler, "Facebook in Privacy Breach," *The Wall Street Journal*, Oct. 17, 2010, http://online.wsj.com/article/SB10001424052702304772804575558484075236968.html.

22. "New Poll Shows Americans Anxious About Privacy," *op. cit.*

23. Mark Little, " 'Little data': Big Data's new battleground," *Ovum*, Jan. 29, 2013, http://ovum.com/2013/01/29/little-data-big-datas-new-battleground.

24. For background, see Robert Kiener, "Future of the Public Universities," *CQ Researcher*, Jan. 18, 2013, pp. 53-80.

25. For background, see "Declaration of the Rights of Man and of the Citizens," "Lectures in Modern European Intellectual History," *The History Guide*, www.historyguide.org/intellect/declaration.html.

26. Bob Sullivan, " 'La difference' is stark in EU, U.S. privacy laws," MSNBC, Oct. 19, 2006, www.nbcnews.com/id/15221111/ns/technology_and_science-privacy_lost/t/la-difference-stark-eu-us-privacy-laws/#.UlxnkhDhDpc.

27. Thor Olavsrud, "EU data protection regulation and cookie law — Are you ready?" *ComputerworldUK*, May 24, 2012, www.computerworlduk.com/in-depth/security/3359574/eu-data-protection-regulation-and-cookie-law—are-you-ready.

28. Schneier, *op. cit.*

29. Natasha Singer, "A Data Broker Offers a Peek Behind the Curtain," *The New York Times*, Aug. 31, 2013, www.nytimes.com/2013/09/01/business/a-data-broker-offers-a-peek-behind-the-curtain.html?adxnnl=1&ref=natashasinger&adxnnlx=1378241984-ftuN93sEdSPgKXyXIEdZZw.

30. "Section-by-Section Summary of the Do-Not-Track Online Act of 2013," U.S. Senate Committee on Commerce, Science and Transportation, www.commerce.senate.gov/public/?a=Files.Serve&File_id=95e2bf27-aa9b-4023-a99c-766ad6e4cf12.

31. "Rockefeller Introduces Do-Not-Track Bill to Protect Consumers Online," Office of Sen. Jay Rockefeller, March 1, 2013, www.rockefeller.senate.gov/public/index.cfm/press-releases?ID=deb2f396-104e-46a0-b206-8c3d47e2eed3.

32. "New Poll Shows Americans Anxious About Privacy," *op. cit.*

33. Except when noted otherwise, information for this historical section was drawn from Uri Friedman, "Big Data: A Short History," *Foreign Policy*, November 2012, www.foreignpolicy.com/articles/2012/10/08/big_data; Gil Press, "A Very Short History of Big Data," *Forbes*, May 9, 2013, www.forbes.com/sites/gilpress/2013/05/09/a-very-short-history-of-big-data; Ann Blair, "Information overload, the early years," *The Boston Globe*, Nov. 28, 2010, www.boston.com/bostonglobe/ideas/articles/2010/11/28/information_overload_the_early_years/?page=1.

34. Ecclesiastes 12:12, Holy Bible: King James Version, University of Michigan Library Digital Collections, http://quod.lib.umich.edu/cgi/k/kjv/kjv-idx?type=DIV1&byte=2546945.

35. Blair, *op. cit.*

36. *Ibid.*

37. Press, *op. cit.*

38. *Ibid.*

39. Michael Lesk, "How Much Information Is There In the World?" 1997, www.lesk.com/mlesk/ksg97/ksg.html.

40. Mayer-Schonberger and Cukier, *op. cit.*, p. 22.

41. Jessica Van Sack, "Nothing to fear now, but soon . . ." *The Boston Herald*, June 11, 2013, p. 2.

42. *Oxford English Dictionary* (2013), www.oed.com/view/Entry/18833#eid301162177. Gil Press, "Big Data News: A Revolution Indeed," *Forbes*, June 18, 2013, www.forbes.com/sites/gilpress/2013/06/18/big-data-news-a-revolution-indeed.

43. For background, see Marcia Clemmitt, "Internet Regulation," *CQ Researcher*, April 13, 2012, pp. 325-348.

44. Tom Price, "Social Media and Politics," *CQ Researcher*, Oct. 12, 2012, p. 922.

45. For background, see Tom Price, "Social Media and Politics," *CQ Researcher*, Oct. 12, 2012, pp. 865-888.

46. For background, see Marcia Clemmitt, "Social Media Explosion," *CQ Researcher*, Jan. 25, 2013, pp. 81-104.

47. "Our history in depth," Google, www.google.com/about/company/history. For background, see David Hatch, "Google's Dominance," *CQ Researcher*, Nov. 11, 2011, pp. 953-976.

48. "Fortune 500, 2013," CNN Money, http://money.cnn.com/magazines/fortune/fortune500/2013/full_list/index.html?iid=F500_sp_full.

49. Brian Fung, "Google Street View's covert collection of consumers' Wi-Fi data in 2010," *National Journal*, June 21, 2013, www.nationaljournal.com/tech/

you-know-who-else-inadvertently-gathered-your-electronic-data-20130621.

50. Phil Rosenthal, "Deeper into data mine we go, privacy plundered," *Chicago Tribune*, Aug. 12, 2012, p. 1, http://articles.chicagotribune.com/2012-08-12/business/ct-biz-0812-phil-privacy—20120812_1_apple-s-safari-google-privacy.

51. Constance L. Hays, "What Wal-Mart Knows About Customers' Habits," *The New York Times*, Nov. 14, 2004, www.nytimes.com/2004/11/14/business/yourmoney/14wal.html?_r=1&pagewanted=all&position=.

52. Mayer-Schonberger and Cukier, *op. cit.*, p. 57.

53. Scott Shane and Colin Moynihan, "Drug Agents Use Vast Phone Trove, Eclipsing N.S.A.'s," *The New York Times*, Sept. 1, 2013, www.nytimes.com/2013/09/02/us/drug-agents-use-vast-phone-trove-eclipsing-nsas.html?_r=1&.

54. Ellen Nakashima, Julie Tate and Carol Leonnig, "NSA broke privacy rules for 3 years, documents say," *The Washington Post*, Sept. 11, 2013, p. 1.

55. "FTC to Study Data Broker Industry's Collection and Use of Consumer Data," Federal Trade Commission, Dec. 18, 2012, www.ftc.gov/opa/2012/12/databrokers.shtm.

56. Julie Brill, "Demanding transparency from data brokers," *The Washington Post*, Aug. 15, 2013, www.washingtonpost.com/opinions/demanding-transparency-from-data-brokers/2013/08/15/00609680-0382-11e3-9259-e2aafe5a5f84_print.html.

57. Adam Tanner, "Finally You'll Get To See The Secret Consumer Dossier They Have On You," *Forbes*, June 25, 2013, www.forbes.com/sites/adamtanner/2013/06/25/finally-youll-get-to-see-the-secret-consumer-dossier-they-have-on-you/.

58. Singer, *op. cit.*

59. Linda Woolley, letter to FTC Commissioner Julie Brill, Aug. 19, 2013, http://blog.thedma.org/2013/08/19/dma-responds-to-op-ed-attacking-commercial-data-use.

60. "'Do Not Track' Set to 'On' By Default in Internet Explorer 10 — IAB Response," Interactive Advertising Bureau, May 31, 2012, www.iab.net/InternetExplorer.

61. Al Urbanski, "New Do Not Track Group Makes Progress in San Francisco," *Direct Marketing News*, Oct. 11, 2013, www.dmnews.com/new-do-not-track-group-makes-progress-in-san-francisco/article/315995.

62. Craig Timberg, "Firefox moves forward with tracking blocker," *The Washington Post*, June 20, 2013, p. 14.

63. "IAB Accuses Mozilla of Undermining American Small Business & Consumers' Control of Their Privacy with Proposed Changes to Firefox," Interactive Advertising Bureau, March 12, 2013, www.iab.net/about_the_iab/recent_press_releases/press_release_archive/press_release/pr-031213?gko=2dce8.

64. Brendan Eich, "C is for Cookie," Mozilla, May 16, 2013, https://brendaneich.com/2013/05/c-is-for-cookie.

65. Timberg, *op. cit.*

66. Eric Schmidt and Jared Cohen, *The New Digital Age: Reshaping the Future of People, Nations and Business* (2013).

67. Doug Gross, "Google chairman: 6 predictions for our digital future," CNN, April 23, 2013, www.cnn.com/2013/04/23/tech/web/eric-schmidt-google-book.

68. For background, see Daniel McGlynn, "Domestic Drones," *CQ Researcher*, Oct. 18, 2013, pp. 885-908.

69. Little, *op. cit.*

BIBLIOGRAPHY

Selected Sources

Books

Jarvis, Jeff, *Public Parts*, Simon & Schuster, 2011.
A journalism professor who writes frequently about big data and the Internet makes the case for sharing, which he calls "publicness," and putting aside certain notions of privacy.

Lanier, Jaron, *Who Owns the Future?* Simon & Shuster, 2013.
A Microsoft Research computer scientist argues that people should be paid for the information they share online and off.

Mayer-Schonberger, Viktor, and Kenneth Cukier, *Big Data: A Revolution That Will Transform How We Live, Work, and Think*, Houghton Mifflin Harcourt, 2013.
An Oxford professor (Mayer-Schonberger) and *The Economist*'s data editor examine big data's impact on the world, highlighting both its opportunities and threats.

Morozov, Evgeny, *To Save Everything, Click Here: The Folly of Technological Solutionism*, Public Affairs, 2013.
A self-described "digital heretic" challenges the utopian visions of "digital evangelists" and warns that many fruits of cutting-edge technology come with high costs.

Smolan, Rick, and Jennifer Erwitt, eds., *The Human Face of Big Data*, Against All Odds Productions, 2012.
Combining photographs, illustrations and essays, this remarkable coffee-table book shows big data at work in the real world, from obtaining new insights into health care costs to compiling detailed statistics from every Major League Baseball pitch.

Articles

Blair, Ann, "Information overload, the early years," *The Boston Globe*, Nov. 28, 2010, www.boston.com/bostonglobe/ideas/articles/2010/11/28/information_overload_the_early_years/?page=1.
A Harvard historian explains how since biblical times humankind has felt oppressed by too much data, then learned to cope.

Egan, Erin, "Proposed Updates to our Governing Documents," Facebook, Aug. 29, 2013, www.facebook.com/notes/facebook-site-governance/proposed-updates-to-our-governing-documents/10153167395945301.
Facebook officials announce plans for a revised privacy policy that says users automatically permit their posts and photos to be used in ads. Thousands of users express outrage.

Scola, Nancy, "Obama, the 'big data' president," *The Washington Post*, June 14, 2013, www.washingtonpost.com/opinions/obama-the-big-data-president/2013/06/14/1d71fe2e-d391-11e2-b05f-3ea3f0e7bb5a_story.html.

A journalist who covers technology and politics documents President Barack Obama's embrace of big data in both his campaign and his administration.

Stahl, Lesley, "A Face in the Crowd: Say goodbye to anonymity," CBS News, May 19, 2013, www.cbsnews.com/2102-18560_162-57599773.html.
In a report on facial-recognition surveillance, the veteran CBS correspondent walks into a store, is recognized by a surveillance camera and, moments later, her cell phone receives a text with a special deal offered by the store, based on her shopping history and Facebook "likes."

Reports and Studies

"Big Data, Big Impact: New Possibilities for International Development," World Economic Forum, 2012, www3.weforum.org/docs/WEF_TC_MFS_BigDataBigImpact_Briefing_2012.pdf.
An organization best known for annually convening international leaders in Davos, Switzerland, explores how analyzing big data could predict crises, identify needs and help devise ways to aid the poor.

"Kenneth Cukier and Michael Flowers on 'Big Data,'" Foreign Affairs Media Conference, Council on Foreign Relations, May 9, 2013, www.cfr.org/health-science-and-technology/foreign-affairs-media-conference-call-kenneth-cukier-michael-flowers-big-data/p30695.
The Economist's data editor (Cukier) and New York City's chief analytics officer discuss how the city uses big data to improve services, as well as some downsides to the massive collection and analysis of information.

"Self-Regulatory Principles for Online Behavioral Advertising," American Association of Advertising Agencies, American Advertising Federation, Association of National Advertisers, Direct Marketing Association, Interactive Advertising Bureau, July 2009, www.aboutads.info/resource/download/seven-principles-07-01-09.pdf.
Five advertising industry trade associations join together to issue "consumer-friendly standards" for collecting information online and using it to target advertising to individuals. The organizations said they would report uncorrected violations to government agencies and the public.

Rainie, Lee, Sara Kiesler, Ruogu Kang and Mary Madden, "Anonymity, Privacy, and Security Online," Pew Research Center, Sept. 5, 2013, www.pewinternet.org/Reports/2013/Anonymity-online.aspx.

A survey by the nonpartisan think tank finds that most Americans want the ability to be anonymous online, but many don't think it's possible.

For More Information

Berkman Center for Internet and Society at Harvard University, 23 Everett St., 2nd Floor, Cambridge, MA 02138; 617-495-7547; www.cyber.law.harvard.edu. Research center that studies aspects of the Internet, including commerce, governance, education, law, privacy, intellectual property and antitrust issues.

Consumer Watchdog, 2701 Ocean Park Blvd., Suite 112, Santa Monica, CA 90405; 310-392-0522; www.consumerwatchdog.org. National consumer advocacy organization that promotes privacy of personal data.

Future of Privacy Forum, 919 18th St., N.W., Suite 901, Washington, DC 20006; 202-642-9142; www.futureofprivacy.org. Think tank that convenes discussions, publishes papers and advocates policies to protect privacy of data on and offline.

Institute for Ethics and Emerging Technologies, Williams 119, Trinity College, 300 Summit St., Hartford, CT 06106; 860-297-2376; 860-297-2376; www.ieet.org. Think tank that studies and debates ethical implications of new technologies.

Interactive Advertising Bureau, 116 East 27th St., 7th Floor, New York, NY 10016; 212-380-4700; www.iab.net. Trade association for companies that sell online advertising; promulgates an industry code of conduct.

Pew Internet & American Life Project, 1615 L St., N.W., Suite 700, Washington, DC 20036; 202-419-4500; www.PewInternet.org. Research center that conducts frequent public opinion surveys as it studies how the Internet affects Americans.

9

Domestic Drones

Daniel McGlynn

NASA uses Global Hawk drones to monitor tropical storms and other weather events. Small drones typically fly at 400 feet or less, while big ones like the Global Hawk can reach 60,000 feet. Potential commercial uses for drones are quickly expanding beyond public safety and law enforcement to include mapping, pipeline monitoring and real estate photography. Agriculture is expected to be one of the biggest drone users in the future, monitoring crops and tracking livestock.

From *CQ Researcher*, October. 18, 2013.

When catastrophic floods hit Boulder, Colo., in mid-September, Chris Miser used an unmanned aerial vehicle (UAV), or drone, to help the Boulder Emergency Operations Center survey the damage.

Miser, a former Air Force captain who owns an unmanned-aircraft business, had just finished showing disaster response crews footage of washed out roads and flooded homes when he received a call from the Federal Emergency Management Agency. FEMA officials told Miser the agency controlled the airspace over the disaster area and that he would be arrested if he didn't stop his drone flights.

"It makes sense to shut down the airspace during a disaster," Miser said. "What was irritating was how they did it. All the helicopters were up in the mountains and canyons doing search and rescue. I was in the flatlands, where there was nobody else up in the air. They didn't ask if I was a hobbyist or a professional. They didn't ask if I was taking live video or still shots. They just said no drone flights, or I'd be arrested."[1]

Miser's attempt to fly his Falcon unmanned aircraft underscores many of the issues surrounding the introduction of drones in U.S. skies. Unmanned aircraft already are operating in American airspace on a limited basis, mainly on scientific research and public-safety missions. The Federal Aviation Administration (FAA), which regulates the nation's airspace, estimates that once it completes new rules governing when and where commercial drones can fly — and who can operate them — 7,500 such aircraft will be flying in the United States within the first five years.[2]

The control and guidance system technology that makes unmanned flight possible has become smaller, cheaper and more

Domestic Drones Vary in Size, Capability

Small unmanned aircraft systems (UAS) often are used for search and rescue missions, wildlife tracking and surveillance. They typically weigh less than 55 pounds, fly at 400 feet or less and within the operator's view and can remain airborne for only a few hours, although some can fly longer and beyond the operator's sight. Some larger drones can reach 60,000 feet or more and remain aloft for days. They may be used for NASA research projects, border surveillance or military training.

Uses for Unmanned Aircraft

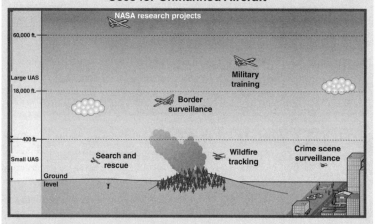

Source: "Unmanned Aircraft Systems: Measuring Progress and Addressing Potential Privacy Concerns Would Facilitate Integration into the National Airspace System," Government Accountability Office, September 2012, www.gao.gov/assets/650/648348.pdf

But the boom in domestic drones has triggered wide-ranging debates among legislators and civil liberties advocates about safety, privacy and how best to regulate an emerging technology that can be economically productive but also invasive and dangerous to other aircraft or people on the ground.

Drones, which usually are remote-controlled, range in size and complexity, from tiny bird-sized aircraft built by hobbyists to multimillion-dollar commercial jets that fly at 60,000 feet with military-grade sensing and data-collection capabilities. Their military predecessors are the stealthy — and lethal — drones that have been used since 2004 for controversial strikes against suspected terrorists in such countries as Pakistan, Afghanistan and Yemen.[4] Today's drones are getting smaller and more sophisticated: Some domestic and military ones under development are tiny, insect-like low-flying robots.[5]

Currently, research universities, state and local law enforcement agencies and federal agencies such as the U.S. Geological Survey, U.S. Forest Service and Department of Homeland Security can operate drones on a limited basis in U.S. airspace. Hobbyists can fly drones for noncommercial purposes up to 400 feet in altitude, but the craft must remain within sight of the operator. Private companies, however, have been eagerly pushing for permission to operate drones on a widespread commercial basis. Congress has given the FAA until 2015 to devise rules to safely integrate drones into U.S. aviation.

"Unmanned aircraft is going to be a game changer," says Alan Palmer, director of the Center for UAS [unmanned aircraft systems] Research, Education and Training at the University of North Dakota's John D. Odegard School of Aerospace Sciences, the first college program to offer a four-year degree in unmanned aerial systems operations. "When unmanned aircraft are allowed

powerful in recent years. In the United States, small companies, such as Miser's, have sprouted up to develop drones for specific uses. Miser's hand-launched Falcon, which has an eight-foot wingspan and weighs 9.5 pounds, is designed for public safety applications such as disaster response and search and rescue missions. A pair of Falcons costs $55,000.

Potential commercial uses for drones are quickly expanding beyond public safety and law enforcement to include mapping, oil and gas pipeline monitoring and real estate photography. The Association for Unmanned Vehicle Systems International, an advocacy group in Arlington, Va., predicts that agriculture will be one of the biggest domestic markets for drone technology.[3] The aircraft are suited, for example, to monitoring crops, tracking livestock and helping manage development-threatened wildlife, experts say.

[in domestic airspace], great things are going to happen. It will be very similar to the explosion of cell phones and how that has changed the way we communicate."

However, civil liberties groups worry that the ability of drones to conduct surveillance activities could allow the government, law enforcement officials and private individuals to circumvent Fourth Amendment protections against unreasonable search and seizure — protections traditionally viewed as undergirding privacy rights.[6]

"The prospect of cheap, small, portable flying video-surveillance machines threatens to eradicate existing practical limits on aerial monitoring and allow for pervasive surveillance, police fishing expeditions and abusive use of these tools in a way that could eventually eliminate the privacy Americans have traditionally enjoyed in their movements and activities," lawyers for the American Civil Liberties Union (ACLU) told a Senate panel in March.[7]

Drones flying in domestic airspace also raise concerns about public safety. While the technology might be appropriate for battlefield settings, critics argue that flying drones over populated areas is potentially dangerous because they may interfere with conventional aircraft. In addition, cases of drone software malfunctions have been documented during computer-controlled flight.[8] Critics cite reports and studies that compare the safety records of drones to piloted airplanes. Those include a report for Congress showing that the accident rate for drones used by the Department of Homeland Security, which operates a fleet of 10 unmanned craft mainly for border security operations, was "historically multiple times higher" than the rate for manned aircraft.[9]

Critics also say operators of remote-controlled craft are unable to follow a fundamental FAA safety guideline for all pilots: to "see and avoid" — that is, to be able to spot other aircraft in the air and take evasive steps to avoid collision.

Proponents of unmanned aircraft, however, say sensing systems and ground-based radar enable unmanned aerial systems to "detect and avoid" hazards, making them as safe as a piloted craft. They also say unmanned aircraft have been in regular use by the military for more than a decade, during which the technology has matured.

"The real challenge is not technological," said Ian Glenn, CEO of ING Robotic Aviation, a Canadian drone manufacturer. "The real challenge is regulatory acceptance. . . . We are able to be as good as manned

aviation. So the issue is how to get federal aviation authorities around the world to get their minds around it."[10]

Under the FAA Modernization and Reform Act of 2012, Congress charged the agency with setting up six sites across the country to test how drones will interact with traditional aircraft. Aerospace industry leaders say they welcome the law because its passage and implementation signal the opening of U.S. airspace to unmanned craft.

But critics say the FAA is ill-equipped to deal with the privacy issues surrounding domestic drone use. "The FAA has zero expertise or experience regulating privacy issues," says Ben Gielow, general counsel and government relations manager for the Association of Unmanned Vehicle Systems International. "If you want to rent an airplane, you can fly it wherever you want as long as you meet the FAA safety guidelines. We don't want to see the FAA say who can fly based on whether the mission" violates privacy, he says.

In the absence of explicit federal drone regulations, 42 states have introduced legislation pertaining mainly to privacy or to prohibitions against unmanned aircraft being weaponized by law enforcement agencies. In 2010, the Department of Homeland Security considered equipping its drones with "nonlethal" weapons, such as tear gas or pellets guns, but the department said it has since abandoned the idea.[11]

As domestic drones come into wider use, here are some of the issues under debate:

Can drones fly safely in domestic airspace?

Some 70,000 aircraft ply U.S. skies every day.[12] By 2032, consumer air travel is expected to double, meaning even more airplanes.[13] The FAA predicts that as many as 30,000 drones may be operating in U.S. airspace by 2030.[14] Safety experts question how many flights the air traffic control system can handle before accident rates increase — especially during the early years of integration, when unmanned aircraft technology would still be maturing.

Already, several military drones have run into trouble in domestic airspace. In 2006, an unarmed Predator drone, operated by the U.S. Customs and Border Protection agency from a base in Sierra Vista, Ariz., crashed while patrolling the U.S. border with Mexico. The cause was attributed to operator error.[15] And three years

Most Americans Support Unarmed Domestic Drones for Policing Borders

Most U.S. adults support using domestic drones — but not armed ones — for border security, according to a 2013 Monmouth University poll. A slight majority believes law enforcement officials should be able to use armed drones in hostage situations, however. Nearly 70 percent say they would be somewhat or very concerned about their own privacy if law enforcement agencies began using drones equipped with cameras and recording equipment, and a strong majority said authorities should be required to obtain a court order before using drones.

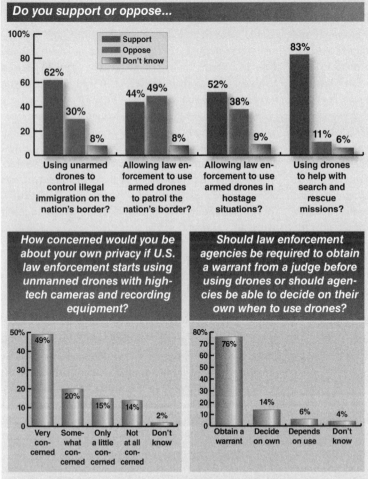

Source: "National: U.S. Supports Unarmed Domestic Drones," Monmouth University Poll, Aug. 15, 2013, www.monmouth.edu/assets/0/32212254770/ 32212254991/32212254992/32212254994/32212254995/30064771087/409a ecfb-3897-4360-8a05-03838ba69e46.pdf

ago, the U.S. military almost shot down one of its own helicopter-like drones after the craft's communication link failed and it began rapidly approaching a no-fly zone around Washington, D.C. The drone's operators were able to re-establish control before the aircraft had to be destroyed.[16]

Unmanned aircraft systems "pose technological, regulatory, workload and coordination challenges that affect their ability to operate safely and routinely in the national airspace system," the Government Accountability Office, the investigative arm of Congress, wrote in 2008.[17] And in 2010, the Congressional Research Service, which provides unbiased policy research for Congress, wrote that unmanned aerial vehicles "suffer accident rates multiple times higher than manned aircraft."[18]

But some analysts downplay the risks. "It's inevitable that drones will crash," wrote Pierre Hines, a former Army intelligence officer and member of the Truman National Security Project, a national defense think tank in Washington. "I've experienced it during military operations overseas, and it will happen when drones operate domestically. But piloted planes also crash, and it hasn't led to them being categorically banned, and there is little evidence to suggest that drones are inherently more dangerous. . . . The FAA should move forward in integrating drones with as much risk mitigation as possible, while keeping in mind that eliminating all risk is impractical."[19]

Moreover, say drone proponents, unmanned aircraft have become more sophisticated in the past decade, in large part because of their expanded military uses. Accident rates for Predator drones — capable of flying at

50,000 feet and shooting laser-guided Hellfire missiles when so equipped — are comparable to those of F-16 fighter jets when they were in the same stage of development, according to *The Washington Post*, which cited Air Force data.[20]

"Right now, we're in the nineteen-teens relative to manned aviation," said Peter Singer, a widely cited expert on drone warfare, comparing the current state of unmanned aircraft to the first years of piloted flight. "The common mistake historically is that the first generation is the way it will always be," added Singer, a fellow at the Brookings Institution, a centrist think tank in Washington. "We're going to figure this out, but almost every new technology isn't originally set up the optimal way," he said, referring broadly to the current state of drone technology.[21]

One stark difference between military drone use and potential domestic drone applications is the popularity of small drones used by hobby fliers. Recreational drone users typically want to tinker with the technology or use the vehicles for creative purposes such as filmmaking or photography. But they may not have the aviation background of military drone pilots, or even the skills of operators of more advanced civilian drones. For decades U.S. airspace under 400 feet in altitude belonged to model-aircraft enthusiasts. They developed standards based on good practice and common sense, such as picking safe locations for flying, not using new or untested equipment around people or crowds and keeping their aircraft within sight at all times.

In 1981, the FAA issued model-aircraft operating standards, which were guidelines rather than official regulations. Anticipating the current domestic drone boom, the FAA in 2007 required larger model aircraft to have a special permit for flight in domestic airspace higher than 400 feet. The FAA also prohibited remote-controlled aircraft from performing commercial activities such as for-profit aerial photography.[22]

The model aircraft community has an exemplary safety record, says Timothy Reuter, founder of the Washington, D.C., Drone User Group, which promotes the use of lightweight drones, and co-founder of Drone U, a drone education project hosted by the New America Foundation, a centrist think tank in Washington, D.C. Reuter thinks the airspace below 400 feet should be opened to commercial drones weighing less than 10 pounds with no restrictions on commercial activities.

Pilot Ned White used his drone, Silver Fox, to help monitor Washington state's Mount St. Helens volcano in October 2004. Unmanned surveillance craft have proved their value in scientific applications, but civil liberties groups worry that the ability of drones to conduct surveillance activities could enable the government, law enforcement officials and private individuals to circumvent privacy rights under the Constitution's Fourth Amendment.

AP Photo/Don Ryan

"It seems strange to me that it would be safe for recreational users to have access to the airspace, while professionals, who would presumably spend more time at the controls and be more careful about what they are doing, are banned," he says.

Nonetheless, two recent high-profile accidents by small-drone users have raised concerns. In August a drone filming a bull-running event in Virginia crashed into four spectators, causing only minor injuries.[23] In September, a 19-year-old New York man remotely piloting a small helicopter was killed when the rotors sliced off part of his skull.[24]

Reuter acknowledges the hazards of flying unmanned aircraft but says the potential benefits for innovation and applications by small-business owners, such as photographers, outweigh the dangers. "It's not that we can eliminate all risk from all activities, but we need balance," he says. "We haven't eliminated all risk from driving a car, but we've found the right balance between economic activity and minimizing risks."

Will domestic drones infringe on personal privacy?

In late October 2012, Seattle police officials held an informal public meeting to talk about two drones their department had purchased with a Department of Homeland Security grant: a pair of 3.5-pound Draganflyer X6 helicopters for $80,000. The intent, the police said, was to replace the department's more expensive manned helicopter operations.[25] But when they tried to explain the need for the drones, members of the audience began shouting back.

"We are not going to tolerate this in our city," a protester yelled. "This is unacceptable."[26]

Four months later a committee of the Seattle City Council held another meeting, this time to get public feedback on a city ordinance that would bar the police from using drones for surveillance or flights over public assemblies.[27] Despite the ordinance's intent, the public rebelled against the very idea that police would employ unmanned aircraft under any circumstance. The next day, Seattle Mayor Mike McGinn said the city would return the drones to the manufacturer and end the program.[28]

Despite what happened in Seattle, few Americans oppose using drones for public safety missions, such as firefighting or search and rescue operations, according to an August opinion poll by the New Jersey-based Monmouth University Polling Institute.[29] But privacy advocates fiercely object to law enforcement personnel using drones for surveillance and data gathering.

Unmanned aircraft systems (UAS) can perform "highly advanced and near-constant surveillance through live-feed video cameras, thermal imaging, communications intercept capabilities and back-end software tools, such as license plate recognition, Global Positioning System (GPS) tracking and facial recognition," wrote Jennifer Lynch, a staff attorney with the Electronic Frontier Foundation, a digital-privacy advocacy organization in San Francisco that opposes police drone activity without a warrant. "They can amass large amounts of data on private citizens, which can then be linked to data collected by the government and private companies in other contexts."[30]

Echoing sentiments by other drone advocates, Reuter of the Drone User Group says existing laws are sufficient to deal with emerging drone technology. "Rather than having laws on any one technology, we should be focusing on the rules about data capture," he says, referring to methods for monitoring and capturing information. "A greater threat to privacy is the fact that everyone has a camera in their pocket right now," Reuter says.

Gielow, of the Association of Unmanned Vehicle Systems International, says "Everyone is treating this like a whole new technology, and it's not." Sensors detecting location, motion, heat already exist in cell phones and traffic cameras and other devices, he says, "so it's deploying these sensors in a new way." Some digital privacy advocates have suggested that all unmanned aircraft have a license plate of sorts, such as the so-called "N" number — or tail number — required on conventional aircraft. The number links to key information about the aircraft, such as its place of origin and owner.

"If we're going to put cameras on drones and let just about anyone with a few hundred bucks fly them around our neighborhoods, recording video of anyone in our backyards and doing who-knows-what with them, shouldn't there at least be a way to identify who the drone belongs to?" asked Joseph Lorenzo Hall, senior staff technologist at the Center for Democracy & Technology, a digital privacy organization in Washington.[31]

At the federal and state levels, the idea of restricting drone use through new legislation has bipartisan support.[32] Two drone-related privacy bills were introduced in Congress this year.

The Drone Aircraft Privacy and Transparency Act of 2013 would require the FAA to obtain and post online a "data collection statement" from each drone operator before issuing a license. The statement would provide detailed information about where drone operators are based and what kinds of data they would be collecting.

The Preserving American Privacy Act of 2013 would prohibit drones from photographing people without their consent when they are on private property.[33]

During the 2012 state legislative sessions, only a few states were concerned with drones, but this year some 42 states introduced 90 different pieces of drone legislation, says Allie Bohm, an advocacy and policy strategist at the

> "Unmanned aircraft can be used for education or to take beautiful photos, but right now because we have only seen this technology in the context of war, people feel threatened. We are trying to change that public perception."
>
> — *Timothy Reuter,*
> *Founder, Washington, D.C., Drone User Group*

ACLU. So far nine states have passed laws that limit the use of drones by private citizens or law enforcement officials.[34]

Bohm says many state lawmakers think the federal government is not moving quickly enough to address privacy concerns about drones, particularly to restrict their use by police. Most of the state privacy-related bills, Bohm says, would require police to obtain a warrant based on probable cause before they could use a drone to investigate a crime on private property.

"There are truly amazing uses for drones that we have no objection to," Bohm says, "but the trick is to put in place protections so that drones are not just flying around collecting data. There needs to be a reasonable suspicion of criminal activity on public property and probable cause for a search on private land.

"We also need to talk about how the data collected can be used — that is, how we can use this technology without turning into a surveillance society."

Some privacy advocates say that allowing individual states to develop privacy guidelines for drone use is the best approach. "Many think Congress should establish the necessary nationwide regulations to govern both law enforcement and civilian drone use. That thinking, however, is wrong," wrote Margot Kaminski, executive director of the Information Society Project at Yale Law School. Instead of a federal approach, Kaminski advises "a state-based approach to privacy regulation that governs drone use by civilians, drawing on states' experience regulating other forms of civilian-on-civilian surveillance. This approach will allow necessary experimentation in how to best balance privacy concerns against First Amendment rights in the imminent era of drone-use democratization."[35]

Can drones be effectively regulated?

The FAA's congressionally mandated task of developing comprehensive domestic drone regulations by 2015 is challenging for several reasons.

Drones Gather Intelligence on Hurricanes

The National Aeronautics and Space Administration deploys Global Hawk drones — large unmanned aircraft systems (UAS) that can fly over hurricanes at 60,000 feet and stay airborne for more than 24 hours. Studying how hurricanes form and progress improves scientists' ability to forecast these giant weather systems.

Collecting Hurricane Data

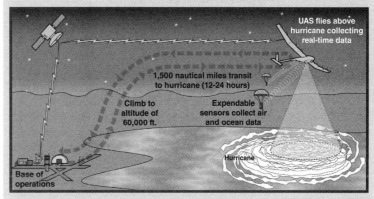

Source: "Unmanned Aircraft Systems: Measuring Progress and Addressing Potential Privacy Concerns Would Facilitate Integration into the National Airspace System," Government Accountability Office, September 2012, www.gao.gov/assets/650/648348.pdf

As a safety regulator, the FAA has to figure out how drones can fly in U.S. skies without endangering conventional aircraft or people on the ground. Beyond that, lawmakers must decide who can fly — professional pilots, hobbyists, licensed operators — as well as where and when they can fly.

A complexity of domestic drone regulation is that drones range in size from small, relatively inexpensive hand-launched vehicles weighing only a few pounds and controlled by hobby pilots to more sophisticated aircraft weighing several thousand pounds that require runways, control rooms and professionally trained pilots. While the FAA is well-suited to handle the latter, based on its history of regulating conventional aircraft, some drone advocates question the agency's ability to regulate all forms of unmanned aircraft.

"In a certain way, I don't think the FAA is equipped to handle this," says Reuter of the Drone User Group. "They are used to dealing with a small group of people who are highly trained and keep up on the safety

Impact of Unmanned Aviation Forecast at $82 Billion by 2025

Direct U.S. spending on drones will climb from about $1.2 billion in 2015 to more than $5 billion in 2025, according to the Association for Unmanned Vehicle Systems International. It expects nationwide economic impact from the boom to hit $10 billion a year in 2015 and total $82 billion from 2015-2025. Because of agricultural uses, such as crop monitoring, California, Washington state, Texas, Florida and Arizona will feel the biggest effects of the industry's growth. The association expects the industry to generate more than 100,000 jobs by 2025.

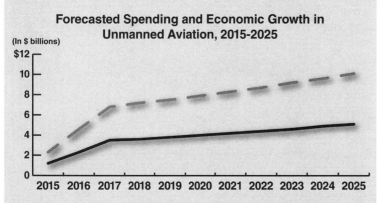

Forecasted Spending and Economic Growth in Unmanned Aviation, 2015-2025

Source: "The Economic Impact of Unmanned Aircraft Systems Integration in the United States," Association for Unmanned Vehicle Systems International, March 2013, http://higherlogicdownload.s3.amazonaws.com/AUVSI/958c920a-7f9b-4ad2-9807-f9a4e95d1ef1/UploadedImages/New_Economic%20Report%202013%20Full.pdf

literature." Do-it-yourself drone pilots and people interested in using drones to run small businesses will not necessarily have a background in aviation safety or protocol, he says. Rather than create an elaborate licensing system, Reuter points to existing drone community guidelines as a good model to create rules for hobby drone fliers.

The Academy of Model Aeronautics (AMA), an Indiana-based group that promotes flying small, unmanned hobby aircraft, has developed safety guidelines for its 150,000 members. The guidelines require operators to maintain visual contact with their aircraft, avoid flying over crowds or power lines and take other steps to minimize injury or property damage in the event of a malfunction or accident.[36]

In a similar fashion, the International Association of Chiefs of Police (IACP), a Virginia-based group of 20,000 law enforcement professionals, created drone guidelines in 2012 for police departments. The guidelines state that police should obtain warrants when people being pursued have a reasonable expectation of privacy; retain drone-collected data only if it relates to a crime; notify the public about drone activity; ban the weaponizing of drones; and be held accountable for misuse of drones.

But guidelines do not carry the same weight as enforceable regulations. Already, reports have surfaced of drone operators skirting the existing FAA ban on commercial drone activity. Some farmers and ranchers have begun using drones to monitor their land and livestock, regardless of their permit status. "The FAA doesn't have inspectors running around the heartland looking for people with UAVs [unmanned aerial vehicles]," said Rory Paul, chief executive of Volt Aerial Robotics, a St. Louis company that operates small drones used for agriculture and remote sensing.[37]

Some states are concerned about weaponized drones in domestic airspace. So far 17 states have proposed prohibiting law enforcement departments or other government agencies from operating weaponized drones, prompted in part by reports that the Customs and Border Protection agency was considering using Department of Homeland Security (DHS) drones along the Mexican border. DHS has since said it will not arm its 10 drones.[38]

James Williams, an FAA official charged with integrating drones into domestic airspace, said in February that the agency already has rules on the books "that would prohibit weapons from being installed on a civil aircraft. We don't have any plans on changing them for unmanned aircraft."[39]

There currently are no reported cases of federal, state, or local law enforcement agencies using weaponized drones within the United States.

BACKGROUND

Early Drones

Inventors have been tinkering with drones since before the Wright brothers flew the first successful manned airplane near Kitty Hawk, N.C., in 1903.[40] For instance, Samuel Langley, then director of the Smithsonian Institution, built and flew for short distances a steam-powered unmanned aircraft he called an aerodrome.[41]

Until recently, though, the drive to develop unmanned aircraft came from the worlds' militaries, which wanted to use them to deliver bombs or scout positions. Early unmanned aircraft clumsily delivered ordinance and had an extremely high rate of failure.[42] But in the 1990s, drones began using advanced materials and sophisticated software, changing how wars are fought. By the early 2000s, drone technology had become an important part of the U.S. military arsenal. In 2004, the Central Intelligence Agency used a Predator drone in Pakistan to conduct the first targeted killing of suspected terrorists.[43]

One of the first civilian drones — the Aerosonde, designed for high altitude weather research — made headlines in 1998. Engineers at the Insitu Group, a company in Washington state, developed the aircraft for only $15,000. Weighing a mere 29 pounds, it had a 10-foot wingspan, a one-cylinder engine and basic software for the plane's guidance system and autopilot.[44]

Seeking to call attention to their young company, the Aerosonde's engineers used the plane to make the first unmanned flight across the Atlantic Ocean. They launched four of the aircraft from the roof of a speeding rental car in Newfoundland, on Canada's east coast, and one reached Ireland, marking an unmanned aircraft milestone.[45] (The other three craft never made it to the landing spot.)

Also in the 1990s the FAA began allowing unarmed military drones to fly in domestic airspace to monitor wildfires, but only in areas with low levels of air traffic.[46]

In 2005, the U.S. Customs and Border Protection Agency (CBP) used Department of Homeland Security funds to purchase six Predator drones for surveillance and tracking of illegal crossings on the U.S.-Mexican border.[47] Stationed in Arizona, Florida, Texas and North Dakota (for northern border security), the drones can stay aloft for 20 hours.[48] But despite the crafts' advanced sensor

Local drone enthusiasts gather for the Maryland Fly In in Laytonsville, Md., on July 27, 2013. Hobbyists can fly drones for noncommercial purposes up to 400 feet in altitude, but the craft must remain in sight of the operator. Private companies, however, have been pushing to operate drones on a widespread commercial basis. Congress has given the Federal Aviation Administration until 2015 to safely integrate drones into U.S. aviation.

Getty Images/*The Washington Post*/Bill O'Leary

and surveillance technology, "The use of UAVs has resulted in fewer alien apprehensions per flight hour than the use of manned aircraft," the Congressional Research Service said in 2010.[49]

In July 2013, the Electronic Frontier Foundation obtained documents from the CBP showing that the CBP had been flying drone missions for other government agencies. The agencies included the FBI, Immigration and Customs Enforcement, U.S. Marshals Service, U.S. Coast Guard, Minnesota Bureau of Criminal Investigation, North Dakota Bureau of Criminal Investigation and Texas Department of Public Safety.

"These missions ranged from specific drug-related investigations, searches for missing persons, border crossings and fishing violations to general 'surveillance imagery' and 'aerial reconnaissance' of a given location," Lynch, the foundation's attorney, wrote after the documents were released.[50]

The CBP flew its Predator drones 30 times for other government agencies in 2010; by 2012 that number had jumped to 250, according to the agency's documents.

Not all of those missions were law enforcement-related, according to the Government Accountability Office. The CBP Predator drones also have provided the National Oceanic and Atmospheric Administration with videos of damaged infrastructure, such as dams and bridges, to identify flood risks, the GAO said.[51]

CHRONOLOGY

1917-1940s *Development of military and civilian aviation puts pressure on airspace, reveals need for coordinated safety rules. Drone research is conducted primarily for military applications.*

1917 U.S. military investigates drones for battlefield use.

1926 Air Commerce Act makes secretary of Commerce responsible for developing air traffic control rules.

1938 Civil Aeronautics Act gives federal government more control of airspace regulation.

1946 In *United States v. Causby*, Supreme Court defines airspace above private land as public space.

1950s-1980s *Regulation of U.S. airspace keeps pace with growing air traffic.*

1958 Federal Aviation Act creates Federal Aviation Agency, with responsibility for civil aviation safety.

1966 Congress creates Department of Transportation. . . . Federal Aviation Agency becomes Federal Aviation Administration (FAA).

1982 FAA guidelines say remote-control aircraft must stay within sight of the operator and fly below 400 feet.

1986 In *California v. Ciraolo*, Supreme Court says police aerial observations of private property without a warrant did not violate the Fourth Amendment protection against unreasonable searches and seizures.

1990-2007 *Regular use of drone technology in warfare begins. Civilian use of drones emerges.*

1990 FAA allows unmanned aircraft to fight a wildfire, one of the first uses of domestic drones.

1995 Global Positioning System (GPS), which drones use for navigation, becomes fully operational.

1998 The Aerosonde, one of the first unmanned aircraft developed solely for civilian weather research and remote sensing, crosses the Atlantic, a first for unmanned aircraft.

2001-2010 Domestic drone use becomes more common for law enforcement and scientific research.

2004 First documented drone strike by the U.S. military occurs in Pakistan.

2005 Department of Homeland Security purchases six Predator drones for Customs and Border Protection surveillance, triggering questions about safety, effectiveness and privacy.

2007 FAA bans commercial use of remote-controlled aircraft below 400 feet, limiting development of lightweight drones.

2011-Present *Aerospace companies and do-it-yourself aviation enthusiasts continue to develop nonmilitary drone technology. . . . FAA begins permitting system to regulate unmanned aircraft used in domestic airspace for such tasks as firefighting and border patrol. In United States v. Jones, Supreme Court sets legal precedent for prolonged surveillance.*

2011 Predator drone aircraft dispatched by Department of Homeland Security helps North Dakota sheriff track and arrest cattle thieves, marking a first in U.S. law enforcement.

2012 FAA Modernization and Reform Act requires FAA to develop regulations for unmanned aircraft to fly in U.S. airspace by 2015. FAA creates Unmanned Aircraft Systems Integration Office and announces plan to create six test sites but misses the first two deadlines for implementation, blaming privacy concerns for the delays. . . . Supreme Court holds in *United States v. Jones* that prolonged use of GPS tracking without a warrant violates the Fourth Amendment.

2013 Drone-related legislation introduced in 42 states. . . . FBI admits using domestic drones eight times since 2006 for surveillance in kidnapping cases, search and rescue operations, drug interdictions and fugitive investigations, and twice in national security cases. . . . Seattle Police Department cancels its drone program. . . . Association for Unmanned Vehicle Systems International estimates drones will generate $82 billion impact in U.S. from 2015-2025

Flights Help Biologists Study Wildlife Habitat

Drones fly to the rescue of pygmy rabbits.

Before development forced them into isolated pockets of dense sagebrush, pygmy rabbits once ranged widely through the American West. The rabbits — the smallest in North America — are listed in Washington state as a federally protected endangered species, and they also are at risk in other states.

The rabbits' vulnerability has prompted plans by wildlife biologists to breed the animals in captivity and release them in the wild. Boise State University biological sciences professor Jennifer Forbey is using drone aircraft to help carry out that mission.

"Pygmy rabbits are a sensitive species, so finding a better way to assess habitats was one of our goals," Forbey says. "Most people start on the ground . . . and get really small snapshots of what's going on, but in a few hours with a UAS [unmanned aircraft system] we can cover a wide area."

Using drones from the University of Florida's Unmanned Aircraft Systems Research Program to scout out a vast Bureau of Land Management (BLM) tract in Idaho, Forbey has targeted optimum sites for release of the rabbits.

She got the idea to use drones several years ago, when a team from the U.S. Geological Survey (USGS), which uses the aircraft for mapping and other research projects, came to Boise to test a small, hand-launched aircraft, the Raven.[1] "They came out and showed us what kinds of images they could get of the landscape," Forbey says.

The USGS uses drones elsewhere in similar conservation contexts, such as studying whooping cranes. In places like Africa, conservationists are using drones to track wildlife poachers.

Soon after the visit from the USGS, Forbey secured a National Science Foundation grant to use the drones in her research. She also found that University of Florida scientists were linking pictures of landscape being studied with the land's GPS coordinates. That enabled Forbey to pinpoint spots that have appealing pygmy rabbit habitat characteristics.

The Florida team also was flying drones that had special infrared imaging equipment. "It's like getting the fingerprint of a plant, which tells us about the nutritional quality of the area, so we are getting a good idea of the foodscapes," Forbey says.

An unmanned aircraft is retrieved off Key Largo, Fla.,during a National Oceanic and Atmospheric Administrationtest of drones' ability to monitor environmental conditionsand wildlife in marine sanctuaries.

The downside of using drones for scientific research is the lag time involved, Forbey says. Her research team must file paperwork with the BLM and inform the public through press releases of plans to fly unmanned aircraft. The flight team from the University of Florida also has to make sure it has the proper paperwork for a certificate of authorization from the Federal Aviation Administration (FAA). "There's definitely a hindrance," Forbey says. "It takes about a year of planning."

But for now, the wait seems worth it, given the results, Forbey says. The team is able to quickly pinpoint locations that will provide good forage and cover for the rabbits, she says.

"Without this technology, it wouldn't be possible to do this kind of research," Forbey says, referring to studying wildlife habitat on a large scale. "We are trying to answer questions that people have been wanting to answer for a long time."

— Daniel McGlynn

[1]U.S. Geological Survey, National Unmanned Aircraft Systems Project Office, http://rmgsc.cr.usgs.gov/UAS.

Air Rights

Prior to the FAA's oversight, U.S. airspace was governed solely by common law — nonstatutory law based on customary practice or legal precedent.[52]

When aviation became an important means of transportation and commerce in the 1920s, Congress began to pass laws expressly designed to regulate use of the skies and promote commercial flights. The 1926 Air Commerce Act required the secretary of Commerce to encourage air commerce through safety rules, a system of licensing pilots and establishment of a navigation system for aircraft.[53] The Civil Aeronautics Act of 1938 created the Civil Aeronautics Administration within the Commerce Department to strengthen and expand rules about aircraft, pilots and air traffic control and to govern operations of commercial airports. The legislation also created an independent safety board, which investigated accidents involving aircraft and recommended ways to prevent future accidents.[54]

In 1946, the Supreme Court, in *Causby v. the United States*, established a legal precedent for property rights above private land. The plaintiff, Thomas Lee Causby, a chicken farmer near Greensboro, N.C., sued the U.S. government for damages to his business, claiming military planes operating from a nearby airport were causing his chickens to die prematurely. Causby invoked the so-called takings clause of the Fifth Amendment, which bars the government from taking private property for public use without compensation.

The Supreme Court ruled that Causby was entitled to damages because the proximity of the aircraft to his farm caused "a direct and immediate interference with the enjoyment and use of the land."[55] In a separate part of their ruling, the court struck down the common law understanding of airspace and private property, stating that if it stood, "every transcontinental flight would subject the operator to countless trespass suits. Common sense revolts at the idea."[56]

The court, however, stopped short of delineating where private property ends and public airspace begins. The justices merely stated, "If the landowner is to have full enjoyment of the land, he must have exclusive control of the immediate reaches of the enveloping atmosphere."[57]

In 1958, following a mid-air collision over the Grand Canyon two years earlier that killed 128 people, Congress created the Federal Aviation Agency. Its mission was to develop a more robust system of air traffic control and better aircraft navigation systems. In 1967, the agency was transferred to the new Department of Transportation and renamed the Federal Aviation Administration. By the mid-1970s, the FAA had developed a complex array of radar and computer systems to aid air traffic controllers. Air traffic increased drastically beginning in 1978, when the airline industry was deregulated and ticket prices dropped because of increased competition among airlines. To keep pace with an increasing number of flights, the FAA implemented a semi-automated air traffic control system, which began relying on computers and radars to track aircraft.[58]

In 1982, the FAA created the National Airspace Plan, a 20-year effort to update air traffic control and air navigation systems across the country. But nine years later, the FAA needed a new plan to incorporate technological advancements in radar, communication and weather forecasting equipment.[59]

In 2003, Congress passed the Century of Aviation Reauthorization Act, which outlined the Next Generation Air Transportation System (NextGen). In 2004, the secretary of Transportation established the interagency Joint Planning and Development Office (JPDO) within the FAA. Both the NextGen and JPDO were created to develop a plan for updating the integration and regulation of emerging aerospace technologies and applications, such as unmanned aerial systems.[60]

Privacy Precedents

The Supreme Court has ruled on several cases that relate to privacy and surveillance issues inherent in widespread use of unmanned aerial systems.

> **"Unmanned aircraft is going to be a game changer. It will be very similar to the explosion of cell phones and how that has changed the way we communicate."**
>
> — *Alan Palmer,*
> *Director, Center for Unmanned*
> *Aircraft Systems Research, Education and*
> *Training, John D. Odegard School of Aerospace*
> *Sciences, University of North Dakota*

In 1986 the court ruled in *Dow Chemical Co. v. United States* that "the taking of aerial photographs of an industrial plant complex from navigable airspace is not a search prohibited by the Fourth Amendment."[61] Dow, which makes consumer, agricultural and industrial chemicals, had sued the Environmental Protection Agency (EPA) for taking aerial photos of one of its facilities in Midland, Mich., claiming the photographs constituted a warrantless government search and thus violated the Fourth Amendment. The EPA had taken photos of an outdoor area at a 2,000-acre Dow chemical plant site after being denied a follow-up visit to a routine inspection.

The same year, the court made a similar ruling. In *California v. Ciraolo*, defendant Dante Carlo Ciraolo complained that Santa Clara, Calif., police lacked a warrant when they took aerial photos of his illegal marijuana-growing operations, located in his fenced backyard, and then prosecuted him. The Supreme Court found that Ciraolo's expectation of privacy was unreasonable and that the photographs did not violate the Constitution because they were taken from public airspace.

In *Kyllo v. United States*, decided in 2001, police had charged Danny Kyllo with illegally growing marijuana in his house. But before they had obtained a warrant to search the house, they had used thermal imaging technology to scan its exterior and found a high level of heat emissions coming from inside — a clue that lights used in marijuana-growing operations were in the home.

The Supreme Court ruled that the thermal imaging of Kyllo's house constituted an illegal search because — unlike photographs obtained from a public space — the use of thermal imaging equipment to obtain information about the inside of a home violated a reasonable expectation of privacy.

"While the technology used in the present case was relatively crude, the rule we adopt must take account of more sophisticated systems that are already in use or in development," the court wrote.[62]

In 2012, the Supreme Court decided another technology-related case with privacy implications. In *United States v. Jones*, law enforcement agents installed a GPS tracking device on the vehicle of Antoine Jones and tracked him for a month. The court overturned Jones' conviction on a drug conspiracy charge, ruling that the government's surveillance was unconstitutional.[63]

Experts say that although none of the privacy cases involved evidence gathered by drones, the rulings suggest

Eye in the Sky

An unarmed U.S. Customs and Border Patrol (CBP) Predator drone takes off on a surveillance flight near the Mexican border on March 7, 2013, from Fort Huachuca in Sierra Vista, Ariz. (top). The craft typically fly an average of 12 hours per day at about 19,000 feet. A CBP pilot flies a Predator over southern Arizona from a base at Fort Huachuca (bottom). Drones search for drug smugglers and immigrants crossing illegally from Mexico into the United States.

that in the eyes of the judicial system navigable airspace is public space, and images collected through common means, such as a camera, are considered reasonable grounds for permitting further searches by police. But the rulings also suggest that in the Supreme Court's view, extended surveillance or obtaining of data through technology not widely used by the public is, for now, unreasonable and thus not permitted by the government under the Fourth Amendment.

"The Constitution will prove a much stronger measure of protection against government UAS [unmanned aircraft systems] privacy abuses than is widely appreciated," wrote John Villasenor, a nonresident senior fellow in governance studies at the Brookings Institution's Center for Technology Innovation and a professor of electrical engineering at the University of California, Los Angeles.[64]

CURRENT SITUATION

FAA Testing

In July the Federal Aviation Administration (FAA) certified the first drones for commercial use — one manufactured by Chicago-based Boeing and the other by California-based AeroVironment. Both aircraft weigh less than 50 pounds, have a 4.5-foot wingspan and are designed to monitor oil and gas equipment in rural areas.[65]

Meanwhile, the FAA continues to work toward its 2015 deadline for integrating unmanned aircraft into the national airspace system by researching best practices and procedures for drones to safely operate alongside traditional aircraft. When the agency announced it was creating six test sites to study how drones operate — required under the 2012 FAA Modernization and Reform Act — 24 states submitted proposals to host the new proving grounds. Aerospace officials see the proposals as an indication that the American public may be ready for domestic drones.

"The test sites are a very good idea," says Gielow of the Association of Unmanned Vehicle Systems International. "The states involved understand that UAS is the future of aerospace. These test sites . . . will provide the FAA with the data they don't have about safety and effective integration. We view these test sites as a good first step."

> **"The trick is to put in place protections so that drones are not just flying around collecting data. There needs to be a reasonable suspicion of criminal activity on public property and probable cause for a search on private land."**
>
> — *Allie Bohm,*
> *Advocacy and Policy*
> *Strategist, American Civil Liberties Union*

However, in part due to overall privacy concerns about drones, the FAA is behind schedule in selecting the six sites. Initially, the agency had planned to identify them by August 2012 but now says it won't announce them until the end of this year. "We are working to move forward with the proposals for the six test sites as we evaluate options with our interagency partners to appropriately address privacy concerns regarding the expanded use of UAS," FAA Administrator Michael Huerta wrote to Congress in 2012, explaining the delays.[66]

Meanwhile, the number of applications is growing rapidly for Certificate of Waiver or Authorization (COA) permits to fly drones on specialized public safety and research missions. In 2009, the FAA approved 146 COAs; by early 2013 that had risen to 327.[67]

The list includes permits granted to sheriff departments across the country, universities and federal agencies. In addition, drone manufacturers can apply for a different kind of permit, a Special Airworthiness Certificate (SAC), to fly aircraft in domestic airspace. In 2012, 36 SACs were issued to drone manufacturers, including companies such as General Atomics Aeronautical Systems, which makes Predator and Reaper drones for the military.[68]

The rules for operating unmanned aircraft under a COA are strict. Domestic drones must be kept in the operator's line of sight at all times, either from the ground or from a manned aircraft. Drones normally are permitted to operate only during daylight hours, and operators must communicate with local air traffic control authorities.[69]

Economic Impact

Advocates of integrating drones into the national airspace system often cite the potential economic benefits of unmanned aircraft.

"This is an emerging technology, and it's going to have a number of economic impacts," U.S. Rep. Mike Turner, R-Ohio, said in August at a drone trade show in Washington, D.C. Referring to Ohio's history as an automobile manufacturing state, Turner said, "Traditional manufacturing bases will become suppliers for the UAS chain."[70]

A 2013 report by the Association for Unmanned Vehicle Systems International estimated that domestic drone integration will create more than 70,000 jobs — 34,000 of them in manufacturing — during the first three years unmanned aircraft operate in U.S. airspace. The report predicted that in the first three years drone manufacturing, maintenance, and associated activities will have an economic impact of $13.6 billion, followed by growth worth $82.1 billion between 2015 and 2025. By 2025, more than 100,000 jobs will be attributable to the industry, the report estimated. Moreover, it said, growth in the manufacturing and support-technician sectors will generate $482 billion in tax revenue in the first decade of integration.[71]

However, Philip Finnegan, director of corporate analysis for the Fairfax, Va., Teal Group, which provides market analysis for the defense and aerospace industries, advises caution in projecting economic growth for the domestic unmanned aircraft market. "It is important to remember that people on both sides of the debate have an interest in exaggerating the number of UAVs out there," he says. "A new technology will take time to prove itself. In the military market, performance is key; in the civilian market cost is really important. It's a very different market."

"There will be gradual adoption of systems where they make economic sense," he continued. UAVs "will be huge" in agriculture, he says, "but not every farmer will buy one. Then there will be a market for systems in mapping and imaging, but it will be growing throughout the decade."

Public Perception

As news stories continue to cover emerging applications for domestic drones, from the outlandish — such as unmanned take-out food delivery systems — to more practical tasks such as monitoring oil and gas pipelines for leaks, the public seems to be warming up to the idea that drones can have nonmilitary uses.

In a June 2012 poll by the Monmouth University Polling Institute, 80 percent of respondents supported using unmanned aircraft to help with search and rescue missions. About two-thirds supported using drones to track down criminals (67 percent) and to control illegal immigration on the border (64 percent).[72]

"Americans clearly support using drone technology in special circumstances, but they are a bit leery of more routine use by local law enforcement agencies," said Patrick Murray, director of the polling institute.[73]

A survey this past June by Duke University's Institute for Homeland Security Solutions showed almost the same results. It found that 57 percent of Americans think integrating drones into domestic airspace, regardless of the application, is a good idea. More than two-thirds

(67 percent) said they would favor using unmanned systems for homeland security operations, and 88 percent said they supported using unmanned aircraft in search and rescue missions.[74]

However, 67 percent said they were concerned about constant surveillance or privacy issues — a finding similar to that of the Monmouth poll.

OUTLOOK

Early Start?

Although both sides in the domestic drone debate are looking anxiously at the 2015 airspace-integration date, even drone supporters concede that the skies will not suddenly fill with unmanned aircraft.

"We will probably crawl, walk and then run," says unmanned vehicle systems advocate Gielow.

In the meantime, some domestic drone services may begin operating before the FAA permits full integration in 2015. In July, the FAA announced that it would allow two types of unmanned aircraft to conduct limited commercial activities. Both drones weigh less than 55 pounds, are four-and-a-half feet long and have wingspans of about 10 feet.

One type, the ScanEagle X200, manufactured by Insitu (now a subsidiary of Boeing), will conduct ice floe surveys and whale monitoring off the coast of Alaska for the oil company CononcoPhillips.[75]

The second type of drone, PUMA, is manufactured by AeroVironmental and will be used to monitor oil spills and wildlife in the Beaufort Sea area.[76]

While the nation's airspace continues to open for various domestic drone applications, the biggest challenge for privacy and safety advocates will be to ensure that the proposed regulations keep pace with drone technology and its emerging applications. Both advocates and skeptics of drones agree that laws or rules should focus more on what kind of data can be captured and how that data can be used rather than trying to tailor laws to a specific technology.

As the public sees more positive uses for drones, perceptions may continue to evolve, says drone advocate Reuter. "Part of the reason we want to teach people to [build and fly drones] is that it normalizes the activity, and people will realize that it's not just for invading privacy," he says.

Should drone surveillance by police always require a warrant?

YES — Amie Stepanovich
Associate Litigation Counsel, Electronic Privacy Information Center (EPIC)

From Testimony before Subcommittee on Oversight, Investigations, and Management, House Committee on Homeland Security, July 19, 2012

An unmanned aircraft, or drone, is an aerial vehicle designed to fly without a human pilot on board. Drones can either be remotely controlled or autonomous. Drones can be weaponized and deployed for military purposes. Drones can also be equipped with sophisticated surveillance technology that makes it possible to identify individuals on the ground. Gigapixel cameras used to outfit drones are among the highest definition cameras available and can provide "real-time video streams at a rate of 10 frames a second." On some drones, sensors can track 65 different targets across a distance of 65 square miles. Drones may also carry infrared cameras, heat sensors, GPS, sensors that detect movement and automated license plate readers. Drones are currently being developed that will carry facial-recognition technology . . . .

In [2005, EPIC] observed, "the use of [drones] gives the federal government a new capability to monitor citizens clandestinely, while the effectiveness of the . . . surveillance planes in border patrol operations has not been proved." Today, drones greatly increase the capacity for domestic surveillance.

Much of this surveillance technology could, in theory, be deployed in manned vehicles. However, drones present a unique threat to privacy. Drones are designed to undertake constant, persistent surveillance to a degree that former methods of surveillance were unable to achieve. Drones are cheaper to buy, maintain and operate than helicopters or other forms of aerial surveillance. Drone manufacturers have recently announced new designs that would allow drones to operate for more than 48 consecutive hours, and other technology could extend the flight time of future drones out into weeks and months. Also, "by virtue of their design, size, and how high they can fly, [drones] can operate undetected in urban and rural environments." . . .

An amendment to the National Defense Authorization Act of 2013, introduced by Congressman Jeff Landry, R-La., and passed by the House, would prohibit information collected by drones operated by the Department of Defense from being used in court as evidence if a warrant was not obtained. In June [2012], . . . Rep. Austin Scott, R-Ga., introduced legislation to expand this protection, requiring all law enforcement to first obtain a warrant before conducting any criminal surveillance. . . . These measures are not sufficient to protect the myriad of privacy interests implicated by increased drone use. . . . [However,] a first step would be the consideration and passage of Rep. Scott's bill. . . .

NO — Gregory S. McNeal
Associate Professor, Pepperdine University School of Law

From Testimony before Subcommittee on Crime, Terrorism, Homeland Security and Investigations, House Committee on the Judiciary, May 17, 2013

The looming prospect of expanded use of unmanned aerial vehicles, colloquially known as drones, has raised understandable concerns regarding privacy. Those concerns have led some to call for legislation mandating that nearly all uses of drones be prohibited unless the government has first obtained a warrant. Such an approach would exceed the requirements of the Fourth Amendment and lead to perverse results that in some instances would prohibit the use of information when gathered by a drone, but would allow the same information to be admitted if gathered by nearly any other means.

Such a technology-centric approach to privacy misses the mark — if privacy is the public policy concern, then legislation should address the gathering and use of information in a technology-neutral fashion. . . .

Congress should reject calls for a blanket requirement that all drone use be accompanied by a warrant: Proposals that prohibit the use of drones for the collection of evidence or information unless authorized by a warrant are overbroad and ill-advised. Such legislation treats the information from a drone differently than information gathered from a manned aircraft, differently than that gathered by a police officer in a patrol car, or even from an officer on foot patrol. Under current Fourth Amendment jurisprudence, police are not required to shield their eyes from wrongdoing until they have a warrant, [so] why impose such a requirement on the collection of information by drones?

For example, imagine a police officer was on patrol in her patrol car. While driving she witnesses the car in front of her strike a pedestrian and speed off. Until witnessing the crime she did not have probable cause, or even reasonable suspicion, to believe the vehicle in front of her would be involved in a crime.

Let's further assume that her dash camera recorded the entire incident. That video may be used as evidence against the driver in a subsequent criminal proceeding, but under broadly worded proposals mandating a warrant for drone usage, the same piece of evidence if gathered by a drone would be inadmissible in court. Why? . . .

What public policy goal is advanced by the suppression of evidence of a crime when documented by a drone when the same evidence, if recorded by a dashcam, observed from an airplane, or viewed from a neighboring home, would be admissible in court?

"Unmanned aircraft can be for education or to take beautiful photos, but right now because we have only seen this technology in the context of war, people feel threatened. We are trying to change that public perception."

Law enforcement activities using drones likely will remain controversial, however. Besides sharing the Predator drones with other government agencies, the Customs and Border Protection agency says it wants to increase its fleet from its current 10 drones to 24 by 2016 to fly surveillance missions along the Southern border 24 hours a day, seven days a week. The plan has increased privacy advocates' concerns about the United States becoming a surveillance society.[77]

Apart from integrating drones into the nation's airspace, the FAA also is updating requirements for aviation infrastructure and flight guidance equipment, such as replacing ground-based navigation systems with a GPS-based system.[78] The new capabilities will allow autonomous drones, which rely heavily on software and GPS, to be more easily integrated into the current National Airspace System.

"We are limited only by our imaginations," says Palmer, at the University of North Dakota's Center for Unmanned Aerial Systems. "To us this is the same as the emergence of the jet engine. It will change the way we travel and do business."

NOTES

1. John Galvin, "Officials halt drone operator trying to aid Colorado responders," *Popular Mechanics*, Sept. 17, 2013, www.popularmechanics.com/outdoors/survival/stories/officials-shut-down-drone-operator-trying-to-aid-colorado-rescuers-15936242.

2. "FAA aerospace forecast fiscal years 2013-2033," Federal Aviation Administration, 2013, p. 66, www.faa.gov/about/office_org/headquarters_offices/apl/aviation_forecasts/aerospace_forecasts/2013-2033/media/2013_Forecast.pdf.

3. "Economic Impact of unmanned aircraft systems integration in the United States," Association for Unmanned Vehicles International, March 2013, http://higherlogicdownload.s3.amazonaws.com/AUVSI/958c920a-7f9b-4ad2-9807-f9a4e95d1ef1/UploadedImages/New_Economic%20Report%202013%20Full.pdf.

4. For background, see Thomas J. Billitteri, "Drone Warfare," *CQ Researcher*, Aug. 6, 2010, pp. 653-676. See also, Mark Mazzetti, "A secret deal on drones, sealed in blood," *The New York Times*, April 6, 2013, www.nytimes.com/2013/04/07/world/asia/origins-of-cias-not-so-secret-drone-war-in-pakistan.html?pagewanted=all&_r=0.

5. Judy Dutton, "Drones' future: Supersonic swarms of robot bugs," *Danger Room*, *Wired.com*, June 22, 2012, www.wired.com/dangerroom/2012/06/ff_futuredrones/.

6. For background, see Chuck McCutcheon, "Government Surveillance," *CQ Researcher*, Aug. 30, 2013, pp. 717-740.

7. "Written Statement of the American Civil Liberties Union," American Civil Liberties Union, March 20, 2013, www.aclu.org/files/assets/aclu_statement_domestic_drones_senate_judiciary032013_final.pdf.

8. Kyle VanHemert, "Navy lost control of drone over DC due to 'software issue,' " *Gizmodo*, Aug. 26, 2010, http://gizmodo.com/5622500/navy-lost-control-of-drone-over-dc-due-to-software-issue.

9. Chad C. Haddal and Jeremiah Gertler, "Homeland security: Unmanned Aerial Vehicles and Border Surveillance," Congressional Research Service, July 8, 2010, www.fas.org/sgp/crs/homesec/RS21698.pdf.

10. Patrick Marshall, "The tech that will make drones safe for civilian skies," GCN, July 12, 2013, http://gcn.com/Articles/2013/07/12/Drone-UAV-sense-and-avoid-technologies-civilian-airspace.aspx?Page=1.

11. Somini Sengupta, "U.S. border agency allows others to use its drones," *The New York Times*, July 3, 2013, www.nytimes.com/2013/07/04/business/us-border-agency-is-a-frequent-lender-of-its-drones.html?pagewanted=all&_r=0.

12. "Sequestration: The effects on aviation and everyday travel," National Air Traffic Controllers Association, December 2012, www.natca.org/ULWSiteResources/natcaweb/Resources/file/Legislative%20Center/SeqFINAL.pdf.

13. Rob Lovitt, "FAA predicts airline passenger travel to double by 2032," NBC News, March 8, 2012,

www.nbcnews.com/travel/faa-predicts-airline-passenger-travel-double-2032-372819.

14. "FAA aerospace forecast fiscal years 2010-2030," Federal Aviation Administration, p. 48, www.faa.gov/data_research/aviation/aerospace_forecasts/2010-2030/media/2010%20Forecast%20Doc.pdf.

15. Ed Lavandera, "Drones silently patrol U.S. borders," CNN, March 12, 2010, www.cnn.com/2010/US/03/12/border.drones/index.html. For background on U.S. border security, see Reed Karaim, "Border Security," *CQ Researcher*, Sept. 27, 2013, pp. 813-836.

16. Richard Conniff, "Drones are ready for takeoff," *Smithsonian*, June 2011, www.smithsonianmag.com/science-nature/Drones-are-Ready-for-Takeoff.html?c=y&page=2.

17. "Unmanned Aircraft Systems: Federal Actions Needed to Ensure Safety and Expand Their Potential Uses within the National Airspace System," Government Accountability Office, May 2008, www.gao.gov/new.items/d08511.pdf.

18. Haddal and Gertler, *op. cit.*

19. Pierre Hines, Truman National Security Project, http://trumanproject.org/expert-directory/#expert-28768476.

20. Craig Whitcock, "Drone crashes mount at civilian airports," *The Washington Post*, Nov. 30, 2012, www.washingtonpost.com/world/national-security/drone-crashes-mount-at-civilian-airports-overseas/2012/11/30/e75a13e4-3a39-11e2-83f9-fb7ac9b29fad_story.html.

21. Dan Parsons, "Air Force F-35s, drones may square off in budget battle," *National Defense*, February 2012, www.nationaldefensemagazine.org/archive/2012/February/Pages/AirForceF-35s,DronesMaySquareOffinBudgetBattle.aspx.

22. For background, see Federal Aviation Administration, "Unmanned Aircraft Operations in the National Airspace System," Feb. 6, 2007, www.faa.gov/about/initiatives/uas/reg/media/frnotice_uas.pdf.

23. Martin Weil, "Drone crashes into Virginia bull run crowd," *The Washington Post*, Aug. 26, 2013, http://articles.washingtonpost.com/2013-08-26/local/41446472_1_drone-tomato-fight-public-event.

24. Pervaiz Shallwani, Sarah Armaghan and Danny Gold, "Remote controlled helicopter kills man in Brooklyn," *Metropolis* blog, *The Wall Street Journal*, Sept. 5, 2013, http://blogs.wsj.com/metropolis/2013/09/05/remote-control-helicopter-kills-man-in-brooklyn/.

25. Jonathan Kaminsky, "Seattle police plan for helicopter drones hits severe turbulence," Reuters, Nov. 27, 2013, www.reuters.com/article/2012/11/27/us-usa-drones-seattle-idUSBRE8AQ10R20121127.

26. Christine Clarridge, "Protesters steal the show at Seattle police gathering to explain intended use of drones," *The Seattle Times*, Oct. 25, 2012, http://seattletimes.com/html/localnews/2019526462_drones26m.html.

27. Christine Clarridge, "Heated hearing airs distrust over SPD drones," *The Seattle Times*, Feb. 6, 2013, http://seattletimes.com/html/localnews/2020303926_policedronesxml.html.

28. Christine Clarridge, "Seattle grounds police drone program," *The Seattle Times*, Feb. 7, 2013, http://seattletimes.com/html/localnews/2020312864_spd-dronesxml.html.

29. "National: U.S. supports unarmed domestic drones," Monmouth University Poll, Aug. 15, 2013, www.monmouth.edu/assets/0/32212254770/32212254991/32212254992/32212254994/32212254995/30064771087/409aecfb-3897-4360-8a05-03838ba69e46.pdf.

30. Letter from Jennifer Lynch, Electronic Frontier Foundation staff attorney, to the Aerospace States Association, May 31, 2013, www.eff.org/sites/default/files/eff_asa_model_drone_legislation_letter.pdf.

31. Joesph Lorenzo Hall, " 'License plates' for drones?" Center for Democracy and Technology, March 8, 2013, www.cdt.org/blogs/joseph-lorenzo-hall/0803license-plates-drones.

32. "Lawmakers eye regulating domestic surveillance drones," Foxnews.com, May 19, 2013, www.foxnews.com/politics/2013/05/19/congress-eyes-regulating-drones/.

33. Alissa M. Dolan and Richard M. Thompson III, "Integration of drones into domestic airspace: Selected legal issues," Congressional Research Service, April 4 2013, www.fas.org/sgp/crs/natsec/R42940.pdf.

34. Dana Liebelson, "Map: Is your state a no-drone zone," *Mother Jones*, Sept. 30, 2013, www.motherjones.com/politics/2013/09/map-are-drones-illegal-your-state.

35. Margot E. Kaminski, "Drone federalism: Civilian drones and the things they carry," California Law Review Circuit, April 26, 2013, http://ssrn.com/abstract=2257080.

36. For background, see Academy of Model Aeronautics, National Model Aircraft Safety Code, effective Jan. 1, 2014, www.modelaircraft.org/files/105.pdf.

37. Matt Haldane, "U.S. slowly opening up commercial drone industry," Reuters, Aug. 8, 2013, www.reuters.com/article/2013/08/08/us-usa-drones-commercial-idUSBRE97715U20130808?irpc=932.

38. Jennifer Lynch, "Customs and Border Protection considered weaponizing drones," Electronic Frontier Foundation, July 2, 2013, www.eff.org/deeplinks/2013/07/customs-border-protection-considered-weaponizing-drones. See also, Jillian Rayfield, "Over forty states are considering laws to regulate domestic drone use," *Salon*, www.salon.com/2013/06/14/over_forty_states_are_considering_laws_to_regulate_domestic_drone_use/.

39. Jeff Schogol, "FAA: No armed drones in U.S. airspace," *AirForceTimes Flightlines* blog, Feb. 13, 2013, http://blogs.militarytimes.com/flightlines/2013/02/13/faa-no-armed-drones-in-u-s-airspace/.

40. Nick Turse, "A drone-eat-drone world," *The Nation*, May 31, 2012, www.thenation.com/article/168159/drone-eat-drone-world#.

41. William S. Dietrich II, "The Wright way to fly," *Pittsburg Quarterly*, summer 2010, www.pittsburghquarterly.com/index.php/Historic-Profiles/the-wright-way-to-fly1.html.

42. For background, see Billitteri, *op. cit.*

43. Mazzetti, *op. cit.*

44. Conniff, *op. cit.*

45. *Ibid.*

46. Riya Bhattacharjee, "Are you being watched? The future of domestic drones," MSN News, March 6, 2013, http://news.msn.com/us/are-you-being-watched-the-future-of-domestic-drones?stay=1. Also see Dan Parsons, "Booming unmanned aircraft industry straining to break free of regulations," *National Defense*, May 2013, www.nationaldefensemagazine.org/archive/2013/May/Pages/BoomingUnmannedAircraftIndustryStraingtoBreakFreeofRegulations.aspx.

47. Sengupta, *op. cit.*

48. *Ibid.*

49. Haddal and Gertler, *op. cit.* The authors cite: "A review of remote surveillance technology along U.S. land borders," Office of the Inspector General, OIG-16-15, Department of Homeland Security, December 2005.

50. Jennifer Lynch, "Customs and Border Protection logged eight-fold increase in drone surveillance for other agencies," Electronic Frontier Foundation, July 3, 2013, www.eff.org/deeplinks/2013/07/customs-border-protection-significantly-increases-drone-surveillance-other.

51. Testimony of Gerald L. Dillingham, director of Physical Infrastructure Issues, Government Accountability Office, before the Subcommittee on Oversight, Committee on Science, Space, and Technology, House of Representatives, "Unmanned aircraft systems, continued coordination, operational data, and performance standards needed to guide research and development," Feb. 15, 2013, www.gao.gov/products/GAO-13-346T.

52. Alissa M. Dolan and Richard M. Thompson II, "Integration of drones into domestic airspace: Selected legal issues," Congressional Research Service, April 4 2013, www.fas.org/sgp/crs/natsec/R42940.pdf.

53. Flight Procedures Branch, *Instruments Procedure Handbook*, Federal Aviation Administration, Department of Transportation, 2007, www.faa.gov/regulations_policies/handbooks_manuals/aviation/instrument_procedures_handbook/media/CH-01.pdf.

54. *Ibid.*

55. "United States v. Causby," The Oyez Project at IIT Chicago-Kent College of Law, accessed Sept. 13, 2013, www.oyez.org/cases/1940-1949/1945/1945_630.

56. *Ibid.*

57. *Ibid.*

58. U.S. Department of Transportation, *op. cit.*

59. "A brief history of the FAA," Federal Aviation Administration, www.faa.gov/about/history/brief_history/.

60. *Ibid.*

61. Villasenor, *op. cit.*

62. *Ibid.*

63. *Ibid.*

64. *Ibid.*

65. Haldane, *op. cit.*

66. "A letter to members of Congress from Michael P. Huerta, Federal Aviation Administration to members of Congress," Nov. 1, 2012, http://higherlogic-download.s3.amazonaws.com/AUVSI/958c920a-7f9b-4ad2-9807-f9a4e95d1ef1/UploadedFiles/FAA%20Response%20to%20Congressional%20Unmanned%20Systems%20Caucus%20on%20Test%20Site%20Delay%20-%20112812.pdf.

67. Federal Aviation Administration, Fact sheet — "Unmanned Aircraft Systems," Feb. 19, 2013, www.faa.gov/news/fact_sheets/news_story.cfm?newsId=14153. For further background, see Electronic Frontier Foundation, "FAA releases new drone list — Is your town on the map?" Feb. 7, 2013, www.eff.org/deeplinks/2013/02/faa-releases-new-list-drone-authorizations-your-local-law-enforcement-agency-map.

68. "FAA list of Special Airworthiness Certificates — Experimental Category," Electronic Frontier Foundation, www.eff.org/document/faa-list-special-airworthiness-certificates-experimental-categorysacs.

69. *Ibid.*

70. Andrea Peterson, "States are competing to be the Silicon Valley of drones," *The Washington Post*, Aug. 19, 2013, www.washingtonpost.com/blogs/the-switch/wp/2013/08/19/states-are-competing-to-be-the-silicon-valley-of-drones/.

71. "The economic impact of unmanned aircraft systems integration in the United States," Association for Unmanned Vehicle Systems International (AUVSI), March 2013, www.auvsi.org/econreport.

72. U.S. supports some domestic drone use," Monmouth University Poll, June 2012, www.monmouth.edu/assets/0/32212254770/32212254991/32212254992/32212254994/32212254995/30064771087/42e90e6a27c0968b911ec51eca6000.pdf.

73. *Ibid.*

74. "Unmanned aircraft and the human element: Public perceptions and first responder concerns," Institute for Homeland Security Solutions, Duke University, June 2013, http://sites.duke.edu/ihss/files/2013/06/UAS-Research-Brief.pdf.

75. Ed Crooks, "Conoco in landmark Alaska drone flight," CNBC, Sept. 25, 2013, www.cnbc.com/id/101060663.

76. "One giant leap for unmanned-kind," Federal Aviation Administration, July, 26, 2013, www.faa.gov/news/updates/?newsId=73118.

77. Lynch, "Customs and Border Protection logged eight-fold increase in drone surveillance for other agencies," *op. cit.*

78. "NextGen Implementation Plan 2013," Federal Aviation Administration, www.faa.gov/nextgen/implementation/.

BIBLIOGRAPHY

Selected Sources

Books

Benjamin, Medea, *Drone Warfare: Killing by Remote Control*, OR Books, 2012.
The cofounder of Code Pink, an American political and peace-activist organization, and organizer of Drones Watch, a watchdog group, examines the human costs and potential outcomes of drone warfare.

Boghosian, Heidi, *Spying on Democracy: Government Surveillance, Corporate Power and Public Resistance*, City Lights Publishers, 2013.
The executive director of the National Lawyers Guild documents how corporations and government intelligence agencies mine data from sources as diverse as surveillance cameras, unmanned drones, iris scans and medical records.

Piddock, Charles, *Drones: Are They Watching You?* The Media Source, 2013.

A technology writer provides a history of drone use and describes their role in recent U.S. military operations as well as their domestic integration and potential future applications.

Singer, Peter W., *Wired for War: The Robotics Revolution and Conflict in the 21st Century,* **Penguin, 2009.**
A Brookings Institution senior fellow looks at the implications of using advanced technology, and drones specifically, in warfare.

Articles

Anderson, Chris, "How I Accidentally Kickstarted the Domestic Drone Boom," *Wired,* **June 22, 2012, www.wired.com/dangerroom/2012/06/ff_drones/all/.**
The former editor of *Wired* started an open-source lightweight drone business, called 3D Robotics, that shows how inexpensive, off-the-shelf technology can be used to build compact and powerful drones for under $1,000.

Bennett, Brian, "Police Employ Predator Drone Spy Planes on Home Front," *Los Angeles Times,* **Dec.10, 2011, http://articles.latimes.com/2011/dec/10/nation/la-na-drone-arrest-2011121.**
A North Dakota sheriff's use of a Department of Homeland Security Predator drone to help him arrest cattle rustlers has prompted questions about the use of spy drones by law enforcement authorities.

Conniff, Richard, "Drones are Ready for Takeoff," *Smithsonian,* **June 2011, www.smithsonianmag.com/science-nature/Drones-are-Ready-for-Takeoff.html.**
The writer describes the first unmanned trans-Atlantic flight and the two engineers behind early innovations in civilian unmanned aircraft.

Greene, Susan, "Colorado's Mesa County a National Leader in Domestic Drone Use," *The Colorado Independent,* **June 6, 2013, www.coloradoindependent.com/127870/colorados-mesa-county-a-national-leader-in-domestic-drone-use.**
While some law enforcement agencies have encountered resistance to their use of drones, the Mesa County Sheriff's Office in western Colorado is pressing ahead with its drone program, which helps with search and rescue and to reconstruct crime scenes using aerial photography.

Sengupta, Somini, "U.S. Border Agency Allows Others to Use its Drones," *The New York Times,* **July 3, 2013, www.nytimes.com/2013/07/04/business/us-border-agency-is-a-frequent-lender-of-its-drones.html?pagewanted=all.**
The Department of Homeland Security has lent Predator drones to other government agencies and has considered eventually equipping drones used for border patrol with nonlethal weapons, according to public documents.

Reports and Studies

"The Economic Impact of Unmanned Aircraft Systems Integration in the United States," Association for Unmanned Vehicle Systems International, March 2013, www.auvsi.org/econreport.
A drone advocacy organization estimates huge economic benefits from greater use of domestic drones and says agricultural use offers the greatest potential.

Dolan, Alissa M., and Richard M. Thompson II, "Integration of Drones into Domestic Airspace: Selected Legal Issues," Congressional Research Service, April 4, 2013, www.fas.org/sgp/crs/natsec/R42940.pdf.
Domestic drone integration presents several legal issues, ranging from private-property rights to privacy considerations and potential federal preemption of state aviation laws.

Singer, Peter W., "The Predator Comes Home: A Primer on Domestic Drones, their Huge Business Opportunities, and their Deep Political, Moral, and Legal Challenges," Brookings Institution, March 8, 2013, www.brookings.edu/research/papers/2013/03/08-drones-singer.
The Brookings senior fellow, who directs the think tank's Center for 21st Century Security and Intelligence, says "a huge set of ripple effects . . . will emerge from the opening up of the airspace to domestic drones."

Villasenor, John, "Observations From Above: Unmanned Aircraft Systems and Privacy," *Harvard Journal of Law & Public Policy,* **April 2014, www.harvard-jlpp.com/wp-content/uploads/2013/04/36_2_457_Villasenor.pdf.**
The author outlines how a handful of Supreme Court decisions might inform future drone-related privacy laws.

For More Information

American Civil Liberties Union, 125 Broad St., 18th Floor, New York, NY 10004; 212-549-2500; www.aclu .org. Advocates for personal liberties, including privacy rights.

Association for Unmanned Vehicle Systems International, 2700 S. Quincy St., Suite 400, Arlington, VA 22206; 703-845-9671; www.auvsi.org. Promotes unmanned aircraft systems and related technology.

Center for Democracy & Technology, 1634 I St., N.W., #1100, Washington, DC 20006; 202-637-9800; www.cdt. org. Focuses on Internet freedom and related technology issues.

Drone User Group Network, www.dugn.org. Promotes civilian uses of drones for beneficial purposes.

Electronic Frontier Foundation, 815 Eddy St., San Francisco, CA 94109; 415-436-9333; www.eff.org. Advocates for privacy and other digital rights.

Electronic Privacy Information Center, 1718 Connecticut Ave., N.W., Suite 200, Washington, DC 20009; 202-438-1248; www.epic.org. Focuses on emerging civil liberties issues.

U.S. Department of Transportation, Federal Aviation Administration, 800 Independence Ave., S.W., Washington, DC 20591; 1-866-835-5322; www.faa.gov. Regulates unmanned aircraft systems.

10 Voting Controversies

Kenneth Jost

Voters in Miami wait to cast ballots in the presidential election on Nov. 6, 2012. A bipartisan commission that President Obama created, partly in response to overlong delays at some polling places, recommended on Jan. 22, 2014, that states upgrade voting machines to keep pace with technological change. The commission also wants more states to adopt online voter registration and allow voting before Election Day — either in person or by absentee ballots.

From *CQ Researcher*, February 21, 2014.

Getty Images/*El Nuevo Herald*/David Santiago

Ith the 2012 presidential campaign underway, Republican legislators in the battleground state of Pennsylvania pushed through a new law requiring voters to show a photo ID before casting their ballots. GOP lawmakers minimized the likely impact of the law, approved on a party-line vote, saying that only 90,000 Pennsylvanians lacked the kind of government-issued photo identification required by the law.

In a damning decision two years later, however, a state court judge found that the law — on hold pending a legal challenge — could disenfranchise up to 5 percent of the state's electorate, or as many as 400,000 otherwise qualified voters. In a 103-page ruling issued on Jan. 17, Judge Bernard McGinley faulted state agencies for doing little to tell voters about the new requirement or the procedures for obtaining a qualifying identification.

McGinley also said the state had failed to show the need for the photo-ID procedure, which GOP legislators said would help prevent voter fraud at polling places. The state "wholly failed to show any evidence of in-person voter fraud," McGinley wrote.[1]

The Pennsylvania law is one of more than 20 state measures establishing or tightening voter-ID requirements passed since 2005. The issue has split the two major political parties. In sponsoring these measures, Republicans say they are needed to prevent fraud and protect the integrity of elections. Democrats say the laws are not needed and are being pushed in order to reduce voting among groups that skew Democratic in elections, especially Latinos and African Americans.[2]

Nearly Three Dozen States Have Voter-ID Laws

Thirty-five states have passed voter-ID laws, although some laws are not currently in effect, either because they are too new or because they are being challenged in court. State laws vary widely as to the kinds of identification accepted, with 13 states — since 2005 — requiring photo IDs and others accepting such items as a Social Security card, a birth certificate or a utility bill. State laws also vary as to voters who show up without identification. In some states, for instance, a voter can cast a ballot, but it won't be counted until the voter returns with a qualifying ID.

States That Have Enacted Voter-ID Laws

Source: "Voter Identification Requirements," National Conference of State Legislatures, Feb. 12, 2014, www.ncsl.org/research/elections-and-campaigns/voter-id.aspx#al

aimed at meeting the court's objection that the use of a "coverage formula" dating from the 1960s to determine the jurisdictions subject to preclearance was unconstitutional. Voter-ID laws, however, would be exempt from the new preclearance provision.[3]

Traditional civil rights and civil liberties groups are strongly supporting the proposed rewrite, as are many Democrats on Capitol Hill. Despite Sensenbrenner's role, some of his leading Republican colleagues oppose the bill, as do some conservative election law experts and advocates.

Elections in the United States have been under intense scrutiny ever since the presidency was awarded to George W. Bush in 2000 on the basis of a highly disputed vote count in the pivotal state of Florida. Two years later, Congress passed and Bush signed into law the Help America Vote Act, aimed at helping states upgrade voting machines and improve vote-counting procedures.[4]

A decade later a bipartisan commission that President Obama created in part as a response to reports of overlong delays at some polling places in the 2012 presidential election says states need to upgrade voting machines again to keep pace with technological change. The Presidential Commission on Election Administration, which released its recommendations on Jan. 22, also wants more states to adopt online voter registration and allow voters to cast ballots before Election Day — either in person or by absentee ballots.

As a new benchmark, the commission recommends that no voter should have to wait in line more than 30 minutes to cast a ballot. The 15-member group was cochaired by experienced election lawyers from both major parties: Democrat Robert Bauer and Republican Benjamin Ginsberg, who served as chief lawyers for the Obama and Romney presidential campaigns, respectively, in 2012.[5]

The two parties are also divided for the most part on a new issue created by the Supreme Court's June 2013 decision to nullify a key provision of the federal Voting Rights Act used to police racially discriminatory election practices in some parts of the country. The decision in *Shelby County v. Holder* effectively nullified a requirement that eight states and localities in four others had to obtain "preclearance" from the Justice Department or a federal court in Washington before instituting any change in election law, procedure or practice.

A bipartisan bill cosponsored by Senate Judiciary Committee Chairman Patrick J. Leahy, D-Vt., and former House Judiciary Committee Chairman James Sensenbrenner, R-Wis., would reimpose the preclearance requirement on states or localities with a recent history of racial discrimination in voting procedures. The bill is

By deliberately sidestepping the politically contentious issues of voter-ID laws and the Voting Rights Act rewrite, the commission is winning applause for striking a bipartisan chord. "The commission's report is an indication that in a huge core [of election issues] there isn't a split," says David Becker, director of the elections initiative at the Pew Charitable Trusts.

"There's only a split on these highly volatile issues," says Becker, formerly an attorney with the Justice Department's voting rights section. There is "wide agreement," he adds, on "a large core of reform that could have a huge impact on our democracy."

The partisan divide continues, however, in Pennsylvania and other states over voter-ID laws. Pennsylvania's Republican governor, Tom Corbett, who signed the measure into law on March 14, 2012, says the state will appeal McGinley's ruling even as Democrats are urging him not to.

McGinley's ruling cheered opponents of the new crop of voter-ID laws after challenges in several other states had fallen short. The decision may have limited impact, however, because McGinley based it on provisions of Pennsylvania law and the state's constitution guaranteeing equal voting rights.

The judge rejected claims by the plaintiffs, individual voters, the League of Women Voters and the Pennsylvania conference of the NAACP, that the law violated equal-protection clauses in the Pennsylvania and U.S. constitutions. McGinley also found no impermissible partisan motivation in enactment of the law despite the remark by the Republican leader in the Pennsylvania House of Representatives three months after the measure was adopted that it would help Republican Mitt Romney carry the state in November 2012. With the law blocked from taking effect, Obama carried the state with about 52 percent of the vote.

Voting issues are in play in courts and legislatures in several states as well as on Capitol Hill in Washington. Voter ID laws are being challenged in at least four other

Most States Have Expanded Voting Laws

Twenty-seven states and the District of Columbia allow voters to cast ballots before Election Day and to get an absentee ballot without giving a reason, called "no-excuse" balloting. Six states, mostly in the South, allow only early voting, and Minnesota has adopted only no-excuse absentee voting.

States with Early Voting and No-Excuse Absentee Voting

Allows early voting
Allows no-excuse absentee voting
Allows both

Source: "Absentee and Early Voting," National Conference of State Legislatures, www.ncsl.org/research/elections-and-campaigns/absentee-and-early-voting.aspx#no_excuse

states — Kansas, North Carolina, Texas and Wisconsin — while legislatures in some states are gearing up to consider tightening voter identification procedures.

"It's definitely an ongoing battle," says Tova Wang, a senior fellow and election reform expert at the liberal advocacy group Demos headquartered in New York City.

Myrna Pérez, deputy director of election programs at the Brennan Center for Justice, a liberal think tank at New York University School of Law, thinks the wave of new voter ID laws may have crested. "Our hope is that given how much outrage there has been over attempts at voter suppression, some folks will think twice before engaging in such efforts," she says.

Conservative election law experts bristle at the accusation that new ID laws are aimed at voter suppression. "That's ridiculous," says Hans von Spakovsky, a senior fellow at the conservative Heritage Foundation in Washington and a former member of the Federal Election Commission (FEC). "We've had election after election" in states with voter ID laws, von Spakovsky says, "and turnout did not go down after those laws went into effect."

Pérez, one of Obama's two pending nominees to the U.S. Election Assistance Commission (EAC), the agency created in 2002 to help states upgrade voting machines, also says some state legislatures are likely to move toward easing voting requirements. A new Brennan Center report finds more bills to expand voting rights introduced in state legislatures for 2014 than measures to narrow access to voting.[6]

Von Spakovsky, who has criticized Pérez as "a radical, left-wing activist with absolutely no experience in election administration," says civil rights litigation hampers election officials' efforts to improve voting procedures. "They are constantly being sued in what I consider to be unwarranted lawsuits, particularly by civil rights organizations," he says.[7]

Meanwhile, the partisan divide in Washington over election issues is so deep that it threatens the very existence of the EAC. The four-member commission has been short of a quorum — which requires three members — since 2010 and has had no members at all since 2011. Pérez and a second Obama nominee, Thomas Hicks, appear headed toward likely Senate confirmation after protracted delays, but Republicans are refusing to offer

Experienced election lawyers from both major parties, Republican Benjamin Ginsberg, right, and Democrat Robert Bauer, are co-chairs of the Presidential Commission on Election and Administration. As a new benchmark, the commission recommends that no voter should have to wait in line more than 30 minutes to cast a ballot.

candidates for seats reserved for GOP members because they believe the agency should be abolished.

As voting and election issues percolate in Washington and around the country, here are some of the questions being debated:

Should Congress revive the Voting Rights Act's preclearance requirement for some states and localities?

With the Voting Rights Act's preclearance requirement in effect, Texas was denied permission in 2012 to put into effect its strict photo-ID voting law enacted the year before. Both the Justice Department and a three-judge federal court said the state had failed to prove that the law would not have a "retrogressive" effect on voting by Latinos and African-Americans.

When the Supreme Court effectively nullified the preclearance requirement in June 2013, however, Texas officials immediately announced they would put the law into effect. The Justice Department responded just two months later with a suit, still pending, seeking to block the law under the Voting Rights Act's general prohibition — found in Section 2 — against racial discrimination.

Civil rights advocates seeking to reinstate the preclearance requirement say the Supreme Court's decision has weakened efforts to prevent racial discrimination in voting. The ruling eliminated "a very effective mechanism of preventing states from enacting restrictions that take away voting rights from minorities," says Wang, the election law expert at Demos.

The Brennan Center's Pérez agrees. "Section 2 is an important and helpful tool, but it does not have the scope or the functions of Section 5," she says, referring to the preclearance provision.

Conservative groups that applauded the Supreme Court's decision see no need to revive a preclearance process. "There is no need for preclearance because there are powerful remedies in the rest of the Voting Rights Act that provide remedies for discrimination," says the Heritage Foundation's von Spakovsky.

Roger Clegg, president and general counsel of the Center for Equal Opportunity, which opposes racial preferences, agrees. "The only difference between Section 2 and Section 5 is that under Section 5 the defendant has to prove his innocence before he's allowed to make a voting change," Clegg says. "Now, if someone doesn't like a voting change, they have to come into court and prove a civil rights violation, which is the way every other civil rights statute works."

The Supreme Court decision did not outlaw preclearance; it only invalidated the coverage formula set out in the act's Section 4, which was based on minority voting turnout during the 1960s. To meet the court's objections, sponsors of the proposed rewrite crafted a new formula based on recent Voting Rights Act violations.

Under the proposed formula, a state would be subject to preclearance if it had five voting rights violations within the most recent 15-year period, at least one of which was committed by the state itself. A local jurisdiction would be covered if it had three voting rights violations within the most recent 15-year period or one such violation along with "persistent and extremely low minority voter turnout." Initially, only four states would be covered under that formula: Georgia, Louisiana, Mississippi and Texas.

The bill also would continue to allow a court to impose a preclearance requirement on a jurisdiction under the so-called bail-in procedure, but under a relaxed burden of proof. The existing bail-in procedure requires proof of intentional racial discrimination; the bill would allow preclearance to be imposed based on so-called disparate impact on minorities without proof of intentional discrimination.

Supporters of the bill say some form of preclearance is still needed. "We know that there are still efforts to restrict voting rights in our country," says Pérez.

Conservative groups disagree. "There's no case to be made that we need Section 5 at all," says Clegg.

The bill also includes a new provision requiring jurisdictions to disclose, among other items, any changes in voting procedures within 180 days of a federal election. And it retains the attorney general's existing authority to assign federal observers to elections. But in a concession to political reality sponsors decided to protect photo-ID laws from any need to obtain preclearance.

Civil rights groups supporting the bill regret the exemption for photo-ID laws. "Many of them are clearly discriminatory and do violate the Voting Rights Act and the Constitution for that matter," says Wang. From the opposite side, Clegg worries that even with a supposed exemption, the Justice Department could go after photo-ID laws by including them along with other election law changes in a Section 2 suit or a bail-in procedure.

Richard Hasen, an election law expert at the University of California-Irvine Law School and publisher of the influential *Election Law Blog*, disagrees with the Supreme Court's decision and calls the proposed rewrite "sensible." He also regrets that Congress did not revise the coverage formula after the Supreme Court raised constitutional doubts about the law in an earlier ruling in 2009.

The formula in the new bill might be upheld, Hasen says, but some other parts might not be — specifically, extending the bail-in procedure to unintentional discrimination. And, in any event, Hasen doubts that Congress will approve the bill in the current session.

Should courts strike down voter photo-ID laws?

With Republicans controlling the legislature and governor's office for the first time in years, Indiana became the second state in 2005 (after Georgia) to enact a law requiring virtually all citizens to present a government-approved photo ID to vote. A legal challenge to the law, brought by Democrats and civil liberties advocates, reached the U.S. Supreme Court three years later.

The court's 6-3 decision in April 2008 upheld the law after finding the state's interest in detecting voter fraud to outweigh any burdens on voters. The ruling left the door open, however, to further challenges to the Indiana law.[8]

In the six years since the Supreme Court's decision, the number of states with similarly strict photo-ID voting requirements has grown to 11, according to the National Conference of State Legislatures. Legal challenges have proliferated, but the issues remain much the same. Supporters and opponents disagree sharply on the need for the laws in the first place and the resulting burdens on would-be voters as well as lawmakers' motives in adopting the measures.

Supporters of the laws depict the measures as self-evidently useful in preventing voter fraud at the polling place. To prove the point, the conservative guerrilla filmmaker James O'Keefe had an assistant use a hidden camera to record him posing as Attorney General Eric Holder at Holder's voting place in Washington, D.C., in April 2012. O'Keeefe offered to go get identification, but the election official said there was no need.

Online Registration Gains in Popularity

Nineteen states have legislation allowing online voter registration, and six states offer limited online voter registration. For example, registered voters in New Mexico and Ohio can update an existing registration record online, but new applications still must be made on paper.

States That Allow Online or Limited Online Registration
(as of February 2014)

Allows full online registration

Allows limited online registration

Source: "Online Voter Registration," National Conference of State Legislatures, www.ncsl.org/research/elections-and-campaigns/electronic-or-online-voter-registration.aspx

O'Keefe stopped before asking for a ballot, but John Fund, a *National Review* columnist and co-author with the Heritage Foundation's von Spakovsky of a book on election fraud, wrote that the episode shows that it is "comically easy to commit voter fraud in person."[9] Von Spakovsky says voter-ID laws also can prevent other kinds of fraud, including voting by noncitizens, voting under false registration or casting ballots in more than one state.

Opponents of the law repeatedly emphasize the lack of evidence of any measurable amount of voter impersonation fraud. In the Pennsylvania case, lawyers from the office of Democratic Attorney General Kathleen Kane defended the law, but stipulated that there were "no specific incidents of voter ID fraud" leading up to its passage.

"The only fraud uncovered in this case is the ID law itself," Witold Walczak, legal director of the ACLU of Pennsylvania and one of the lawyers for the plaintiffs, said after the decision.[10]

Curtis Gans, a longtime U.S. elections expert, faults advocates on both sides. "Those who say there's no fraud are just wrong," says Gans. "Those who say there's huge fraud in elections are also wrong."

Opponents also say the voter-ID laws impose significant burdens on citizens who lack the most common form of government-issued photo identification — a driver's license — and have to obtain an ID specifically for voting. "There's going to be some segment of the population for whom it will be difficult to get the kind of identification they need," says Wang, the election law expert at Demos.

In its decision refusing to preclear the Texas voter-ID law, the three-judge federal court in Washington noted that Texans in some rural counties would have to travel 100 miles or more to obtain a voter ID. Moreover, the court said, the burden "will fall most heavily on the poor."[11]

Supporters of the law counter with evidence that they say show voter-ID laws have not hurt turnout in states where they have been enacted and that few would-be voters have actually been turned away at the polls. "All the claims that they will suppress votes are just not true," says von Spakovsky. He calls the opponents' arguments "hysterical."

A statistical expert who testified for Texas in the voter-ID case agrees that voter-ID laws are unlikely to significantly affect turnout. "As a practical matter you're very unlikely to see voter-ID have substantive or demonstrable impact on aggregate turnout rates," says Daron Shaw, an associate professor of government at the University of Texas-Austin.

Matt Baretto, an associate professor of political science at the University of Washington in Seattle who has testified for plaintiffs in challenging voter-ID laws, says turnout depends on a host of factors other than identification requirements. But he says the laws definitely have an impact. "There are empirically millions of eligible voters who don't have photo IDs," he says.

Baretto says supporters of voter-ID laws are making "a circular argument" when they point to the low number of would-be voters turned away. "The effect happens before you show up at the polling place," he says. "If you don't have the ID, you don't go to the polling place."

Hasen, the election law expert at UC-Irvine, discounts the claimed rationales for voter-ID laws. "These laws are motivated by an interest in moderately depressing the vote and as a means of firing up the base by accusations of fraud," Hasen says. But Hasen, who favors a national voter-identification program, stops short of calling for the current laws to be struck down. "I can't make a blanket normative statement about what courts ought to do," he says.

Should states make registration and voting easier?

Arizona was already a leader among states in using technology to improve government services in 2002 when it became the first state to allow online voter registration. A decade later, about 70 percent of voter registration in the state was done online instead of with paper forms, at a considerably lower cost and with fewer errors.

Experts are enthusiastic about the new procedure, which has now spread to around 20 states and could gain further ground now that the presidential commission has endorsed it. "Online registration is a no-brainer," says election law expert Hasen. The National Conference of State Legislatures calls online registration "the bipartisan trend in elections."[12]

Even so, some conservatives are raising red flags. The Heritage Foundation's von Spakovsky has no objections to online registration to change a voter's address or other information but opposes the practice for a voter's initial registration. "That is a recipe for voter fraud," von Spakovsky says. "You can't check identity online. You can't verify they are who they really are."

Von Spakovsky is also unenthusiastic about early voting and flatly opposes expanding so-called "no-excuse absentee voting" — two of the other steps recommended by the presidential commission. "I don't have a problem with more early voting if states want to devote the resources needed to do that, von Spakovsky says. "But you're making campaigns more expensive because campaigns have to mount get-out-the-vote efforts over a longer time."

A demonstrator in Columbia, S.C., on Feb. 26, 2013, urges the U.S. Supreme Court not to nullify Section 5 of the Voting Rights Act, which requires South Carolina and other states with histories of discriminatory voting practices to get federal preclearance before approving new voting laws. In June 2013, however, the high court effectively nullified the requirement. A bipartisan bill would reimpose preclearance. Civil rights and civil liberties groups strongly support the proposed rewrite; some leading Republicans oppose it, as do some conservative election law experts and advocates.

As for absentee balloting, von Spakovsky again sees the likelihood of increased fraud. "Fraud most often occurs with absentee ballot voting," he says. "They're the easiest ones to steal." In the book he co-authored, von Spakovsky labels absentee ballots the "tool of choice" of vote thieves.[13]

Some of von Spakovsky's concerns are seconded by Gans, the longtime U.S. voting expert. Eased rules for absentee voting are "an enhancement to fraud," Gans says. "You can buy votes and have proof that you bought something. It lends itself to the pressured vote. You can resist the pressure of peers in the voting booth. It's harder to do that in the living room."

Gans sees no risk of increased fraud in early, in-person voting, but he also questions the supposed benefit of increased turnout. "There's no evidence it enhances turnout," Gans says. The experience in states with early voting so far has been mixed, he says. As for eased absentee voting, Gans says the evidence indicates that the practice actually hurts turnout.

Becker, the Pew Trusts election expert, firmly rejects von Spakovsky's fears of fraud from online registration. "There isn't a shred of evidence to support that argument," Becker says.

"Online registration offers something paper registration does not," Becker continues. The process requires personal data from the voter that can be computer-checked against motor vehicle records or other government information. "That's something you can't do with a paper form," Becker says.

Pew has not studied early voting in detail, but Becker sees some benefits. "The research seems to support the view that early voting can reduce some of the burdens on Election Day," he says. And he says there is no evidence of increased risk of in-person voter fraud given the use of the same check-in procedure as on Election Day itself.

In presenting the commission's report, co-chairs Bauer and Ginsberg said elections ought to be viewed as a problem of professional administration and voters in effect as the government's customers. "There are a number of things that go to helping the voter experience and the way that they vote, an issue that both Republicans and Democrats agree on," Ginsberg said on the "PBS NewsHour," with Bauer seated beside him.[14]

Liberal advocacy groups generally applauded the commission's recommendations. Michael Waldman, president of the Brennan Center, said in a prepared statement that the commission's report "marks a significant advance in the way we think about voting."

Some liberal groups, however, also had reservations. Wang, the reform expert with Demos, is enthusiastic about online registration, but adds, "It's not going to do very much for the segments of the population who are left out." Katherine Culliton-Gonzalez, director of voter protection at the New York-based Advancement Project, which is litigating voter-ID law challenges in Pennsylvania and Wisconsin, calls the commission's report "excellent" but complains it does not address issues of racial discrimination in voting. She favors a national "best practices" law that would prohibit any voting or election procedures shown to have a discriminatory impact on racial or ethnic minorities.

The commission also underscored what it calls the "impending crisis in voting technology." Voting machines bought 10 years ago are about to reach the end of their useful lives, the report says.

Despite praise for the commission's report, whether its recommendations are adopted depends on the actions of hundreds of state and local election officials. Costs also will be an issue for some of the recommendations, but Becker is optimistic that election administrators will make sure money is not a problem for some changes.

"I'm already hearing discussions [from officials] trying to find ways to have the best of both worlds," Becker says. "You can save money and improve performance. It doesn't have to cost money."

BACKGROUND

"Forces of Democracy"

Voting rights were very limited when the United States was founded and were determined by individual state governments, which for the most part allowed suffrage only to propertied white men. As states began to loosen wealth and property requirements in the 19th century, the French commentator Alexis de Tocqueville predicted that "forces of democracy" would result inexorably in an expanding suffrage. The further gains in voting rights — for freed slaves, immigrants, women, and young people — were won, however, only after long and hard-fought battles in the courts, Congress, state legislatures and streets.[15]

States began to dismantle colonial era property qualifications for voting soon after the Revolution. As the nation's population grew, states eased or eliminated the laws rapidly in the 19th century, often in response to demands by the new immigrants. Despite the liberalized voting rules, however, 12 states continued to bar "paupers" from voting until the late 1800s.

C H R O N O L O G Y

1960s-1970s *Voting Rights Act changes election rules in South, elsewhere.*

1965-1966 Voting Rights Act passed by Congress, signed by President Lyndon B. Johnson (Aug. 6, 1965); upheld by Supreme Court (March 7, 1966); preclearance provision (section 5) requires four Deep South states to get permission to make any voting, election law changes.

1970 Congress reauthorizes Voting Rights Act, with preclearance provision.

1971 Twenty-Sixth Amendment guarantees 18-year-olds right to vote.

1975 Congress reauthorizes Voting Rights Act; adds provision to protect "language minorities;" extends preclearance provision.

1980s-1990s *Voting Rights Act reauthorized; "motor voter" bill adopted.*

1980 Supreme Court limits nationwide Voting Rights Act provision (section 2) to intentional discrimination (April 22).

1982 Voting Rights Act reauthorized for 25 years, amended to prohibit "disparate impact" discrimination (no proof of intent required).

1992 President George H.W. Bush vetoes National Voter Registration Act — the so-called motor voter law — to require states to allow voter registration at driver's license offices, welfare agencies (July 2).

1993 With Democrat Bill Clinton in White House, Congress again passes National Voter Registration Act; signed by Clinton (May 20); mandatory provision takes effect 1995.

2000s-Present *Voting procedures become partisan battleground.*

2000 Supreme Court ends disputed recount of presidential ballots in Florida; ruling in *Bush v. Gore* ensures Electoral College victory for George W. Bush (Dec. 12).

2002 Arizona is first state to allow voter registration online. . . . Help America Vote Act provides federal

money, authorizes federal standards for upgrading election technology (signed Oct. 29).

2005 Georgia, Indiana pass new voter-ID laws requiring government-approved photo identification to cast ballots.

2006 Congress reauthorizes Voting Rights Act in near-unanimous votes; preclearance provision extended 25 years (signed July 27). . . . Missouri Supreme Court throws out state voter-ID law (Oct. 16).

2008 Supreme Court upholds Indiana voter photo ID law (April 28). . . . Senate race in Minnesota between Republican incumbent Norm Coleman and Democratic challenger Al Franken goes to recount; after legal challenge, Franken declared winner in July 2009.

2009 Supreme Court skirts challenge to Voting Rights Act; warns Congress to consider revising preclearance coverage formula (June 22); Congress fails to act.

2011 Eight states adopt or strengthen voter ID laws; five others vetoed by Democratic governors. . . . U.S. Election Assistance Commission is left with no commissioners after remaining two members' terms expire.

2012 Federal court delays South Carolina voter ID law until after 2012 elections (Oct. 10). . . . Minnesota voters reject voter ID law (Nov. 6).

2013 Supreme Court throws out Voting Rights Act's coverage formula for preclearance (June 25); Senate, House Judiciary Committees hold hearing on restoring provision (July 17, 18). . . . Texas restores voter ID law; Justice Department sues to block (Aug. 22). . . . Justice Department sues to block North Carolina voter ID law, due to take effect in 2016 (Sept. 30). . . . Tennessee Supreme Court upholds voter ID law (Oct. 17).

2014 Voting Rights Act rewrite introduced; bill would impose preclearance on four states (Jan. 16). . . . State court judge throws out Pennsylvania voter ID law (Jan. 17). . . . Presidential Commission on Election Administration calls for online registration, expanded early voting, election technology upgrades (Jan. 22). . . . Wisconsin Supreme Court to hear arguments on voter-ID law (Feb. 25); ruling in federal court case awaited.

Outmoded Voting Machines Pose "Impending Crisis"

Presidential commission says current technology no longer meets election needs.

Barely 10 years ago, state and local election administrators used billions of federal dollars to upgrade the machines used to tabulate election results. But in today's world of high-tech products, a decade is a lifetime — or maybe two. So the state-of-the-art voting machinery bought before the smartphone and computer tablet era is now sadly out of date.

The situation amounts to an "impending crisis in voting technology," according to the Presidential Commission on Election Administration. Machines purchased 10 years ago "are now reaching the end of their natural life cycle," the commission said in its report issued Jan. 22, "and no comparable federal funds are in the pipeline to replace them." Besides fiscal constraints, election administrators face other obstacles in upgrading vote-counting technology, including out-of-date standards and a relatively small number of manufacturers.[1]

"Everything doesn't last as long as it used to," says Doug Lewis, executive director of the National Association of Election Officers. "Yet we've been locked into this thinking that election equipment should last eight to 10 to 12 years."

As Lewis recalls, the clunky lever machines that date from the late 19th century and remained in use through the 1950s and '60s are now museum pieces — although a few were pulled out of storage in the New York City mayoral primary in September. All but gone as well are the punch-card voting systems of the sort that malfunctioned so critically in Florida's presidential election in 2000.

The Help America Vote Act, enacted in 2002 in response to the *Bush v. Gore* fiasco, provided federal funds for state and local election agencies to replace the lever and punch-card devices with optical-scan or touch-screen machines. The act also created the Election Assistance Commission (EAC) and authorized it to establish voluntary certification standards for states to use in purchasing voting machines.

In its report, the presidential commission quoted state and local election officials as saying that available machines no longer meet their current needs and that voting machine manufacturers sympathize with the officials' problems. But manufacturers and election agencies alike are hampered by

---

African-American slaves were not allowed to vote, and so-called freedmen were allowed to vote in only five Northern states: Massachusetts, New Hampshire, New York, Rhode Island and Vermont. New York's property qualification, however, limited the impact of its provision. The 13th Amendment, ratified in 1865, freed the slaves but did not require states to grant them the right to vote. Nor did the 15th Amendment, narrowly ratified in 1870, which only prohibited states from using "race, color, or previous condition of servitude" to restrict whatever voting rights they granted in general.

Supreme Court decisions in the 1870s blunted enforcement of the 15th Amendment; a decade later, partisan divisions doomed a Republican-backed bill in Congress to authorize federal monitoring of state elections. Left alone, Southern and border states responded with an array

of measures and stratagems to keep African-Americans from voting, including literacy tests and poll taxes. So-called grandfather clauses allowed whites to bypass such requirements if they could show that their grandfathers had voted. In the same era, Northern and Western states threw up barriers to voting to immigrants.

Women's suffrage, deliberately omitted from both the 14th and 15th Amendments, made little headway until Western territories and states began allowing women to vote in the 1890s and early 1900s. By the 1910s, both parties supported women's suffrage, but Congress approved the eventual 19th Amendment only after an initial defeat and a special session convened by President Woodrow Wilson in 1919. Ratification was completed on Aug. 18, 1920, on the strength of a single-vote margin in the Tennessee House of Representatives.

EAC standards that have not been updated since 2005, in part because of the partisan impasse over the commission's role that has left the four-member commission without a quorum since 2010. Republicans in Congress want to abolish the EAC and are refusing to designate candidates for the two seats reserved for GOP nominees.

Election technology reformers envision a new world of tablet-like voting machines that 21st century voters will see as thoroughly familiar. "The device on which you record your choice would look like something you use every day," explains David Becker, director of the Pew Charitable Trusts' elections initiative.

The machines could use off-the-shelf software that could be updated without replacing the machines themselves. In addition, the machines could be used for multiple purposes instead of being stored in warehouses in two-year cycles.

For now, however, the EAC standards — voluntary but adopted by many states — are designed for the self-contained voting systems brought into service a decade ago. And the presidential commission said concerns about security among the computer science community have slowed manufacturers' interest in innovation.

Inevitably, cost is also a factor. "These things are not free," says Becker. Lewis says a new voting system can cost from $2 million for a small locality to $240 million for a major metropolitan jurisdiction.

Lewis laments that the United States tends to stay "behind the curve" on voting technology. "In the rest of

A woman votes on Nov. 6, 2012, in Manassas, VA. Voting machines were upgraded nationwide a decade ago, but the Presidential Commission on Election Administration says that they are now out of date and that there are no federal funds designated to replace them.

America, we go for the latest and greatest technology," he says. "In terms of voting we're stuck in the past."

— *Kenneth Jost*

[1]"The American Voting Experience: Report and Recommendations of the Presidential Commission on Election Administration," Jan. 22, 2014, pp. 11-13, 62-67, www.supportthevoter.gov/files/2014/01/Amer-Voting-Exper-final-draft-01-09-14-508.pdf. For coverage, see Martha T. Moore, "Digital voting machines are aging out of use," *USA Today*, Feb. 3, 2014, p. A4.

Women faced no special barriers to voting after ratification of the 19th Amendment, but blacks continued to be denied voting rights in practice in many Southern and border states. The Supreme Court in 1944 gave blacks an important victory by prohibiting all-white Democratic primaries or conventions in the one-party South. Literacy tests and poll taxes remained in place, however, even as the civil rights movement made progress on other fronts, including racial desegregation in schools and public accommodations.

Physical intimidation and violence also were used in the South to keep blacks from voting, notably on "Bloody Sunday" (March 7, 1965) when police in Selma, Ala., used nightsticks and tear gas to disperse a voting rights march as it set out toward the state capital in Montgomery. National outrage over the incident provided the catalyst

for President Lyndon B. Johnson to propose and Congress to pass the strongest federal voting rights law in history. The Voting Rights Act of 1965 prohibited discrimination in voting nationwide and imposed the preclearance requirement on four Deep South states with histories of racial discrimination in voting: Alabama, Georgia, Louisiana and Mississippi. Upheld by the Supreme Court less than a year later, the act helped increase black registration by 1970 to more than 50 percent in all Deep South states.[16]

Congress reauthorized the Voting Rights Act in 1970 and included a provision extending the right to vote to 18-year-olds in all federal, state and local elections — a response to Vietnam War-era student activism. A constitutional challenge resulted in a split Supreme Court decision later that year limiting the provision to federal elections. The prospect of different voting rolls for federal

Leadership Vacuum Stymies Election Agency

Partisan infighting leaves Election Assistance Commission lacking a quorum.

Arizona, Georgia and Kansas faced an unusual problem when they asked the federal Election Assistance Commission (EAC) for permission to revise a federally prescribed voter registration form to include a state law requirement for proof of citizenship. The problem: the EAC had no Senate-confirmed commissioners to act on the request, the result of a partisan impasse that has left the commission without a quorum for nearly four years and with no members at all for two.

When Congress created the four-member panel in 2002, it specified that the House and Senate majority and minority leaders should each nominate a commissioner to be appointed by the president. Republicans have refused to designate candidates since 2010 as commissioners' terms have expired and have been able to thwart Senate confirmation of Democratic nominees.

The Senate is trying to ease the impasse somewhat by getting ready to move the nominations of two Democratic voting-rights advocates toward a floor vote. But even if Thomas Hicks and Myrna Pérez are confirmed, the EAC will still be shy of the three members required for a quorum as long as Republicans refuse to submit candidates for the two seats reserved for GOP nominees.

House Republicans have waged a long campaign to abolish the agency, created in the Help America Vote Act, passed in 2002 after the *Bush v. Gore* presidential election fiasco. GOP lawmakers, led by Rep. Gregg Harper of Mississippi, contend that the EAC has accomplished its original goal of helping states fund new voting technology. Harper calls the agency, with about 30 employees and an $11 million operating budget in 2013, a "bloated bureaucracy."[1]

Democrats say the commission is still needed. When the House Committee on Administration voted to kill the agency on June 5, the panel's top Democrat, Pennsylvania's Robert Brady, said the commission has "an important, valuable role" and was "worth reauthorizing."

Hicks, senior elections counsel for the House Administration Committee and a former staffer with the public interest group Common Cause, was nominated by President Obama in March 2010 on the recommendation of House Democratic Leader Nancy Pelosi. Pérez, senior counsel at the Brennan Center for Justice at New York University School of Law, was nominated in June 2011 on the recommendation of Senate Democratic Leader Harry Reid.

After his reelection, Obama renominated Hicks and Pérez on June 11, 2013, and they appeared before the Senate Rules Committee for a second confirmation hearing on Dec. 11. As acting chairman, Sen. Angus King, an independent from Maine who caucuses with Democrats, said both were "well qualified." The committee's top Republican,

versus state elections prompted state election administrators to join in urging adoption of what became the 26th Amendment, setting the minimum voting age at 18 nationwide.[17]

Congress reauthorized the act again in 1975 and expanded the preclearance provision to jurisdictions with low voting rates by "language minorities." The provision generally required bilingual voting materials in jurisdictions with significant language minorities and extended preclearance requirements to Texas and parts of six other states: Alaska and South Dakota (Native Americans) and Arizona, California, Florida and New York (Hispanics). As the decade ended, however, the Supreme Court intervened with a contentious decision that threatened to blunt the usefulness of the act in expanding minorities' rights in voting and elections.

Election Mechanics

Congress and two Republican presidents — Ronald Reagan and George W. Bush — approved long extensions and significant expansions of the Voting Rights Act in 1982 and 2006, respectively. Throughout that period, the Justice Department increasingly used the act's preclearance provision to affect election procedures in covered jurisdictions. Meanwhile, Congress twice turned to improving election mechanics: first with the Democratic-backed 1993 law to facilitate voter registration and then in 2002 with a bipartisan bill enacted after the *Bush v. Gore* controversy

Sen. Pat Roberts of Kansas, also acknowledged the nominees' qualifications, but reiterated the GOP goal of abolishing the agency. "The EAC has fulfilled its purpose and should be eliminated," Roberts said.[2]

The EAC rankled Republicans when a draft staff report prepared in 2006 cast doubt on allegations from GOP lawmakers about voting place fraud, which GOP lawmakers cite as the reason for stricter voter photo-ID laws. The draft report stated that there was "widespread but not unanimous agreement that there is little polling place fraud." The commission revised the final report, however, to state, in its executive summary, that "there is a great deal of debate on the pervasiveness of fraud."[3]

Election law watchers say the lack of leadership at the top has combined with turnovers in the major staff positions of executive director and general counsel to bring the EAC to a virtual standstill. Among other issues, the lack of a quorum is preventing the adoption of new certification standards for voting machines; the new standards are needed, according to the just-released report by the Presidential Commission on Election Administration, to allow replacement of technologically obsolete equipment.[4]

Arizona, Georgia and Kansas encountered the agency's leadership vacuum when they asked for permission to revise the federally prescribed voter registration form for federal elections to include instructions to provide proof of U.S. citizenship to vote in state elections. The commission's 46-page memorandum rejecting the request, issued on Jan. 17, was signed by Alice Miller as chief operating officer and acting executive director.[5]

The leadership vacuum will continue for at least a little while. The Senate Rules Committee was due to vote on the Hicks and Pérez nominations on Feb. 12, but had to put off the action because of the lack of a quorum until after the Senate's Presidents Day recess. With a Democratic majority, the committee is certain to approve the nominations, but Republicans could use a number of parliamentary maneuvers to delay or possibly prevent a floor vote.

— Kenneth Jost

---

[1]See Deborah Barfield Berry, "House panel OKs ending Election Assistance Commission," *USA Today*, June 5, 2013, www.usatoday.com/story/news/politics/2013/06/04/house-panel-approves-eliminating-election-commission/2389737/; other background drawn from story. See also U.S. Election Assistance Commission, "2013 Activities Report," www.eac.gov/assets/1/Documents/2013%20Activities_Report%20_FINAL%20website%20version,%201-31-14.pdf.

[2]The 59-minute hearing can be viewed at http://tinyurl.com/l9b8pfj.

[3]See Ian Urbina, "U.S. Panel Is Said to Alter Finding on Voter Fraud," *The New York Times*, April 11, 2007, p. A6.

[4]See "The American Voting Experience: Report and Recommendations of the Presidential Commission on Election Administration," Jan. 9, 2014, pp. 62-66, www.youtube.com/watch?v=xCUMXpU6N3k.

[5]"Memorandum of Decision Concerning State Requests to Include Additional Proof-of-Citizenship Instructions on the National Mail Voter Registration Form," U.S. Election Assistance Commission, Jan. 17, 2014, EAC-2013-0004, www.eac.gov/assets/1/Documents/20140117%20EAC%20Final%20Decision%20on%20Proof%20of%20Citizenship%20Requests%20-%20FINAL.pdf.

---

to establish and help states meet minimum standards for administration of elections.

Civil rights supporters were disappointed in 1980 when the Supreme Court ruled that the Voting Rights Act's nationwide provision, Section 2, prohibited only intentional racial discrimination.[18] After maneuvering between the Democratic-controlled House and Republican-controlled Senate, Congress expanded the definition of discrimination by prohibiting any voting practice that had the effect of denying a racial, ethnic or language minority an equal opportunity to participate in the political process.

The 1982 reauthorization also extended the preclearance provision, Section 5, for another 25 years. Congress in 1992

extended the bilingual election assistance provisions — due to expire that year — until 2007 as well.

The Supreme Court blessed Section 2's expanded definition of racial discrimination in a 1986 decision that applied the provision to so-called "vote dilution" — defined as any election practice that reduced the ability of a cohesive racial or ethnic minority to elect candidates of their choice.[19] The Justice Department responded by applying this expanded definition to a growing number of election practices, both in suits initiated under Section 2 and in preclearance review under Section 5.

As one important consequence, the Justice Department began pressing states in the South to draw legislative and congressional districts with majority African-American or

Voters fill out ballots at a polling station in San Francisco on Nov. 6, 2012. Douglas Lewis, executive director of the National Association of Election Officials, sees a trend toward liberalizing voter access through online registration and early voting. Online registration "is coming one way or another," he says. Giving voters more opportunities to cast ballots early is "also of value."

Latino populations to facilitate election of minority legislators. The Supreme Court in the 1990s cut back on this use of the Voting Rights Act, however, by limiting the extent to which race could be considered in drawing district lines. But the expanded definition of racial discrimination also allowed the Justice Department to require preclearance of seemingly minor ground-level voting changes — such as moving a polling place away from a location convenient to minority voters.

In the meantime, Democrats in Congress had succeeded in enacting the so-called motor voter bill, formally the National Voter Registration Act. The law stemmed from efforts of two liberal college professor activists, Frances Fox Piven and Richard Cloward, who thought it possible to increase voter turnout by allowing registration at motor vehicle departments or other government agencies.

President George H. W. Bush vetoed the Democratic-backed legislation on July 2, 1992. With Democrat Bill Clinton in the White House, however, the Democratic-controlled Congress quickly passed the measure again and Clinton signed it into law on May 20, 1993. About half the states already allowed registration through motor vehicle departments, but Republicans arguing against the bill warned the measure would be expensive and invite fraud.

Congress's second major initiative on the mechanics of elections followed the embarrassing spectacle of Florida's disputed recount in the *Bush v. Gore* election in 2000.[20] Bush's 537-vote victory in the election-deciding state of Florida was certified and then left standing by the U.S. Supreme Court after a month of recounts and litigation that highlighted poorly designed ballots and inconsistent standards for tallying disputed votes. Responding to the controversy, a privately sponsored commission co-chaired by former presidents Jimmy Carter and Gerald R. Ford issued a report in July 2001 calling for, among other changes, creation of a new federal agency to oversee federal responsibilities for nationwide elections.[21]

Republicans and Democrats argued about provisions of the Help America Vote Act for more than a year until finally achieving strong bipartisan majorities for the version that Bush signed into law on Oct. 29, 2002.

As enacted, the law consigned punch card and lever voting machines to the waste heap and authorized $3.9 billion in federal money to help states and localities replace machinery, train poll workers and computerize registration lists. New identification requirements led major Latino groups and the American Civil Liberties Union (ACLU) to oppose the final bill, but the act required election officials to establish procedures for would-be voters challenged at the polls to cast provisional ballots and to have their votes counted after presenting sufficient evidence later.

Congress returned to the Voting Rights Act in 2005 as the act's preclearance provision was set to expire the next year. Fearing potential review by the Supreme Court, the House and Senate judiciary committees assembled up-to-date evidence on, among other factors, black vs. white turnout and registration in covered and uncovered jurisdictions. The evidence was ambiguous: African American turnout and registration had seemingly increased to comparable levels as whites; and the Justice Department was denying fewer requests to preclear election changes — only 92 objections in the previous 10 years.

Even so, the political difficulties entailed in rewriting the coverage formula led Congress in the end to leave it unchanged and extend the preclearance provision for another 25 years. Lawmakers in both chambers approved the bill by overwhelming margins — 390-33 in the House,

98-0 in the Senate — and President Bush signed it into law in a photo-op ceremony on July 27, 2006.[22]

"Voting Wars"

The bipartisan support for extending the Voting Rights Act was not enough to deflect the constitutional challenge to the law or prevent the Supreme Court's eventual decision to neuter the preclearance provision by throwing out the act's coverage formula. In the meantime, voting controversies intensified as Republicans pushed and Democrats resisted new state voter-ID laws, eventually challenging them in court. In addition, some high-profile close elections were settled only after contentious and litigious recounts akin to *Bush v. Gore.* For his book chronicling the decade, election law expert Hasen chose an apt title: *The Voting Wars.*[23]

Laws requesting voters to present identification were on the books in 14 states as of 2001 but were lightly enforced, according to the National Conference of State Legislatures.[24] Would-be voters without identification were allowed to cast ballots after signing an affidavit or having an election official or other voter vouch for their identity. The strict laws pioneered by Georgia and Indiana in 2005 demanded a photo ID and required anyone without one to cast a provisional ballot that would be counted only if the citizen returned to the elections office with proper identification within a matter of days.

Indiana's law survived a legal challenge intact, but Georgia eased its enforcement provisions a bit to win preclearance from the Justice Department and eventually a favorable ruling in federal court. Meanwhile, however, the Missouri Supreme Court struck down a photo-ID law just as it was about to take effect for the November 2006 election.

Legislative activity spiked again in 2011 as eight states adopted new or strengthened identification requirements. In five other states, however, Democratic governors vetoed photo-ID bills. And in November 2012 Minnesota voters rejected a proposed constitutional amendment that would have required a photo ID to cast a ballot; the measure failed by about 100,000 votes out of nearly 3 million cast.

In the meantime, Minnesota had provided the country a rerun of sorts of the *Bush v. Gore* battle with its November 2008 contest between incumbent Republican Sen. Norm Coleman and his Democratic challenger, former television comedian Al Franken. As Hasen relates the story, Coleman held a 725-vote lead after an initial Election Night tabulation. The margin fell to 215 votes after a statewide canvass completed on Nov. 18 — so narrow as to trigger a mandatory recount under state law. After counting more than 900 wrongly rejected absentee ballots, the state's canvassing board certified Franken the winner by 225 votes, but Coleman contested the election in state court.

The Minnesota Supreme Court ruled for Franken, allowing him to be sworn in on July 2009. Hasen comments that the Minnesota rivals appeared to change positions as the vote count shifted. Coleman initially called for "a healing process" after the close vote before launching his court challenge once Franken was certified the winner. For his part, Franken switched from a "count every vote" position while he was behind to a "strict compliance" stance once he had gained the lead.[25]

By Franken's swearing in, the Supreme Court had added to election-related issues by sending a strong signal to Congress that the Voting Rights Act might be constitutionally defective. The court's June 22, 2009, decision in *Northwest Austin Municipal Utility District No. 1 v. Holder* stemmed from a challenge brought by a local utility district in suburban Austin, Texas, that chafed under the Justice Department's preclearance review of the relocation of a polling place. The utility district argued that Congress was wrong to subject Texas and other Southern states to preclearance requirements long after they had dropped the blatantly discriminatory practices in effect before 1965.

Conservative justices appeared sympathetic to the position in oral arguments, but the court skirted the issue in an 8-1 decision written by Chief Justice John G. Roberts Jr. The ruling merely gave local jurisdictions a greater opportunity to "bail out" of the preclearance provision. Roberts added, however, that the preclearance requirement raised "serious constitutional questions." [26]

Congress's failure to rewrite the coverage formula set the stage for a new challenge, this one by Shelby County, Ala., a predominantly white county in the Birmingham metropolitan area. As in the earlier case, a three-judge federal district court upheld the constitutionality of the preclearance requirement, but the

Supreme Court's 5-4 decision on June 26, 2013 — again written by Roberts — faulted Congress for an "irrational" decision to subject states and local jurisdictions to preclearance based on 40-year-old statistics.

With no coverage formula, the preclearance provision was reduced to a dead letter. Vermont's Sen. Leahy among others vowed to revive the provision, and committee hearings were held within the month in both the House and Senate. By the end of the year, however, lawmakers working on the issue were still talking behind the scenes about how to fashion a bill that might command bipartisan support in the Republican-controlled House and Democratic-controlled Senate.

CURRENT SITUATION

Court Cases

Civil rights groups are voicing optimism about legal challenges to state voter-ID laws, but supporters of the measures believe they will survive court tests.

With legal challenges pending in five states, opponents of photo-ID laws won the most recent round in Pennsylvania and are hopeful as suits in Wisconsin reach critical stages. Judges have yet to rule on pending suits in Texas and North Carolina brought separately by civil rights groups and the U.S. Justice Department or in a recently filed private suit in Kansas.

In Wisconsin, a federal judge is expected to rule soon on a challenge to the state's photo-ID law after presiding over a two-week trial in November. In the meantime, the Wisconsin Supreme Court decided to hear consolidated cases brought by the League of Women Voters and the state NAACP on Feb. 25 after a state appellate court upheld the law in one of the suits.

In Pennsylvania, lawyers for Gov. Corbett filed a motion before Judge McGinley on Jan. 27 urging him to reconsider his decision ruling the state's law unconstitutional. The lawyers argued that problems in making voter-ID cards available did not require the law to be struck down. But they also said that if McGinley does not change his mind, the law should be put on hold to avoid confusion in this year's primary and general elections.

The Justice Department and civil rights groups are separately challenging photo-ID requirements in both

North Carolina and Texas. The Texas law will be in effect in the March 4 statewide party primaries because the Supreme Court's decision on the Voting Rights Act lifted the need for federal preclearance. The NAACP and Mexican American Legislative Caucus sued the state in federal court in Corpus Christi challenging the photo-ID requirement in September, the month after the Justice Department had filed its similar suit in the same court.

The department also filed suit in September challenging North Carolina's new voting law, shortly after the state's Republican governor, Pat McCrory, signed it into law. The government's suit challenges not only the photo-ID requirement, but also other provisions that reduce early voting by one week, limit same-day registration and tighten procedures for counting provisional ballots. The League of Women Voters and the North Carolina branch of the A. Philip Randolph Institute had filed a comparable suit in state court just days after McCrory signed the bill.

In Kansas, Topeka attorney Jim Lawing is representing two voters who are challenging the photo-ID requirement in state court after being prevented from casting ballots in 2012. Secretary of State Kris Kobach, a Republican known for promoting measures to require proof of citizenship for voting, moved to have the case tried in federal court instead. Lawing is opposing the move; the issue is pending.

In all of the cases, state officials are defending the laws, with the Wisconsin suits closest to resolution pending a possible appeal to the U.S. Supreme Court. In Wisconsin, as in Indiana in 2005, the photo-ID law was adopted in 2011 shortly after Republicans gained control of both legislative chambers and the governor's office. The law requires specified forms of government-issued photo IDs; a voter without qualifying identification may cast a provisional ballot, but must provide the right kind of identification by the end of the week for the vote to be counted.

The NAACP and League of Women Voters filed separate suits challenging the law and won rulings to strike it down. In the league's case, however, an intermediate appellate court upheld the law in March 2013. With the NAACP case pending at a different appellate court, the state's Supreme Court decided to hear both cases on Feb. 25. In the meantime, U.S. District Court Judge Lynn

Should Congress pass the proposed Voting Rights Act rewrite?

YES

Sen. Chris Coons, D-Del.
Member, Senate Judiciary Committee

Written for *CQ Researcher*, February 2014

We've come a long way since the Voting Rights Act was adopted in 1965, but we're not yet where we need to be. Discrimination still exists, and we'll never stop it by pretending it doesn't.

The Supreme Court's *Shelby County v. Holder* decision last June left a dangerous gap in our voter protections by gutting the preclearance system that allowed the Department of Justice to stop proposed discriminatory voting changes before they take effect. Since then, numerous jurisdictions have implemented voting changes that the preclearance system would have blocked. More are on the way, and together these changes serve as a sad reminder that Voting Rights Act protections are still critically necessary.

The Voting Rights Amendments Act of 2014 will restore the vitality of the law in jurisdictions where aggressive voting rights enforcement is still needed. The Supreme Court threw out the old formula for deciding which jurisdictions were subject to preclearance because it was based on 50-year-old data. This bill would base preclearance on a formula that looks clearly and soberly at the modern challenges facing voters.

Detractors criticized the old preclearance formula for applying only to the old South — even jurisdictions that no longer discriminate — while not covering states and counties in which race- or language-based discrimination has emerged over the past 50 years. This bill responds to those charges, as well. Jurisdictions with a history of discrimination but that no longer propose and enforce discriminatory practices will now no longer be subject to preclearance. Jurisdictions that enact new, discriminatory voting laws will be eligible for preclearance, whether or not they have been subject to preclearance in the past.

This bill also makes voting rights and elections more transparent, ensuring the public has access to basic information about polling places, election law changes and redistricting, so voters can feel confident elections are fair.

Under the leadership of Judiciary Chairman Patrick Leahy, Sen. Dick Durbin and Reps. James Sensenbrenner, John Conyers and John Lewis, we've crafted a bipartisan bill designed to be both effective and able to pass this Congress. It's practical, can become law and would survive future legal scrutiny.

It is a modern voting rights bill to confront modern voting rights challenges. It's time for Congress to pass this legislation and restore our democracy's fundamental promise of free and fair access to the ballot box.

NO

Rep. Lynn Westmoreland, R-Ga.
Member, Committee on Financial Services, Tea Party Caucus

Written for *CQ Researcher*, February 2014

Everyone agrees that the significant burdens imposed by preclearance under the Voting Rights Act were desperately needed when they were passed in 1965. But that was nearly 50 years ago. Since its passage, we have seen dramatic changes across the country, especially in the South, that point to the fact that the law needed updating. Georgia has four African-American members of Congress and some of the highest minority voter turnout in the country. In fact, in November 2012, a higher percentage of registered African-American women turned out to vote than registered white women or men.

Because of the major changes since the dark days of the 1960s, the Supreme Court's ruling in *Shelby County v. Holder* last year that the preclearance formula used under Section 5 of the Voting Rights Act was unconstitutional should not have come as a surprise. This law used outdated information to set the formula for preclearance and punished certain areas of the country for the sins of their fathers and grandfathers. To put it in perspective, a person who became eligible to vote the year the law was adopted became eligible for Medicare last year.

I pushed hard to update the coverage formula — the portion the court struck down — when the law was reauthorized in 2006. Unfortunately, my pleas fell on deaf ears. I applaud my colleague from Wisconsin Rep. Jim Sensenbrenner for attempting to update the law, but unfortunately cannot agree with his method.

First and foremost, the proposed update doesn't change the scope of preclearance, which is a huge burden to jurisdictions and was a major consideration in the Supreme Court's decision on the old formula. Second, it continues to punish entire states for the actions of counties — even if the state government has no control over its counties, as is the case in Georgia. Third, it backdates coverage to include any election changes made since the formula was overturned last year, punishing states at a time when they didn't realize they would be punished. Fourth, it defines which races will be the "majority" and "minority" for all time, even if that is not true in a particular state or jurisdiction, making the law less able to account for changing conditions. Finally, it disproportionately punishes states that were under the unconstitutional formula because all existing objections raised under the old preclearance system still count toward coverage — something that is not true for other states.

Adelman has under advisement a comparable suit, filed by the League of United Latin American Citizens, among other groups, after a two-week trial in November and filing of briefs in December.[27]

The Advancement Project is providing lawyers in the Pennsylvania case and the federal case in Wisconsin. Culliton-Gonzalez calls the ruling in Pennsylvania "a great victory" and feels optimistic about Wisconsin. "I feel like the tide has turned," she says.

The Heritage Foundation's von Spakovsky, however, feels the challengers will come up short. "We're going to have years and years of experience with states, which will show that claims against [photo-ID laws] are hot air," he says.

Shift in Legislation?

State lawmakers are throwing more bills into the hopper this legislative season to ease access to voting than measures to make it harder to participate in elections, according to a compilation by the Brennan Center for Justice.

The center, which strongly backs moves to increase access to voting, counts 190 bills introduced in 31 states in that direction so far in 2014, nearly four times greater than the 49 bills to restrict access to voting introduced or carried over from the previous year.

The trend is less pronounced, however, when counting only bills that the center considers "active" — based on hearings or other action. The center counts 12 "expansive" bills active in seven states on such topics as modernizing voter registration and increasing early voting opportunities. The center counts five "restrictive" bills active in four states, primarily bills to establish or tighten photo-ID requirements.[28]

"The beginning of 2014 shows real momentum toward improving our elections, both in the states and nationally," the center says in introducing the report. At the federal level, the report notes the introduction of the bipartisan Leahy-Sensenbrenner measure in the House and the Senate to revive the Voting Rights Act provision requiring some states and localities to obtain preclearance before any voting or election law change.

Using the Brennan Center's terminology, however, the proposed rewrite of the Voting Rights Act was not "active" as of early February. Despite the photo-op introduction of the bill in January, neither the House nor Senate Judiciary panel has scheduled hearings on the bill.

The Heritage Foundation's von Spakovsky discounts the center's reading of the political climate on the issues. "They're declaring victory before they've achieved victory," he says after quickly reviewing the center's report. "I actually don't think that they're winning momentum."

The apparent trend toward liberalizing voting laws comes after a year when the opposing election-law camps swapped victories, according to the National Conference of State Legislatures. In its report for 2013, the group noted the enactment of strict photo-ID laws in Arkansas and North Carolina offset by adoption of online registration in Illinois and West Virginia. Virginia enacted laws adopting both practices.

Same-day registration was adopted in Colorado, the conference reports, but eliminated as part of North Carolina's omnibus election law overhaul. Colorado also moved toward all-mail elections, while Florida restored early-voting opportunities to what had been available before a restrictive 2010 enactment.

The head of the organization for local election administrators also sees a trend toward liberalizing voter access through online registration and early voting, as recommended by the Bauer-Ginsberg election law reform commission. Online registration "is coming one way or another," says Doug Lewis, executive director of the National Association of Election Officials. Giving voters more opportunities to cast ballots early is "also of value," he says.

In addition to online registration and early voting, the Brennan Center favorably notes bills introduced in 11 states to allow students under age 18 to preregister so they are registered as soon as they reach voting age. The center also applauds introduction of bills in seven states to make it easier for felons to regain voting rights.

The center's list of restrictive bills include proposals to require proof of citizenship for voting, to limit voter registration mobilization drives and to make it easier to remove voters from registration rolls.

Lewis applauds the presidential commission for "a credible job of looking at a limited number of issues" in its report. Like the commission, Lewis says long wait times are a problem for some voters—though he says 97 percent of voters cast ballots within 14 minutes. He says the commission's recommendation that no voter should wait more than 30 minutes to cast a ballot is "not a bad goal," but says election administrators think a one-hour limit is more achievable.

Like the commission, Lewis sees a "looming crisis" in voting technology. "The biggest danger to American elections today is state and local governments trying to force equipment to be used longer than it was designed for," Lewis says. But he fears that fiscally strapped state and local governments may continue to defer needed replacement of outdated equipment.

OUTLOOK

Continuing Debates

When Texans go to the polls in party primaries on March 4 to choose candidates for congressional and state offices, it will be the biggest test to date of a strict voter photo-ID law. And Republicans and Democrats in Texas are differing on the likely impact of the law just as the two major parties disagree nationwide on the need for such measures.

Texas, second in population to California, is the nation's biggest state to require voters to present a government-approved photo identification before casting a ballot. Democrats in Texas are warning the law will confuse voters and dampen turnout, while Republicans are discounting the fears.

As evidence, GOP leaders, including Greg Abbott, state attorney general and leading contender for the party's gubernatorial nomination, point to the turnout in the November 2013 statewide balloting on constitutional amendments. With the ID law in effect, turnout averaged about 1.1 million votes on nine measures, around 50 percent higher than the average turnout of 672,000 in a comparable election two years earlier with 11 amendments to be voted on.

Still, the Democratic majority on the Dallas County Commissioners Court was concerned enough about voter turnout to approve $145,000 in October for an informational mailing to explain the new law. The court was debating a second appropriation of $165,000 in February as the primaries approached. The court's lone Republican opposed the expenditures.

Whatever the turnout may be in the March 4 races, the arguments over the impact of voter-ID laws in Texas and elsewhere appear likely to continue, unresolved. Shaw, the University of Texas political scientist, notes that turnout can be affected by any number of factors — from the level of interest in the contests themselves to Election Day weather and transportation conditions. "It's hard to disentangle" the effect of any single factor, Shaw says.

The parties are also likely to continue to fight over proposals to enact or to tighten ID requirements, according to election law expert Hasen. "There are fundamental disputes over whether to make voting easier," he says. "Democrats want to make voting easier. They see voting as about the allocation of power among equals. Republicans see voting more as a test to determine the best candidate — in which case imposing hurdles weeds out voters who are least informed."

The opposing camps also differ on the likely course of court rulings on voter-ID laws. Supporters, such as the Heritage Foundation's von Spakovsky, predict most laws will be upheld, while the Advancement Project's Culliton-Gonzalez and other opponents expect more victories like the one in Pennsylvania.

The Pennsylvania ruling, however, gives the state government a chance to revive the law if sufficient resources are provided to help voters obtain qualifying identification. For his part, Baretto, the University of Washington professor who testified for the plaintiffs in the Pennsylvania case, expects courts to examine ID laws with "more scrutiny," even in cases where the laws are not struck down.

In Washington, supporters of the proposed rewrite of the federal Voting Rights Act are working behind the scenes to try to muster Republican support that the bill will need to advance in the GOP-controlled House. Without referring specifically to the bill, Vice President Joe Biden used a Martin Luther King Day appearance to call for reviving the Voting Rights Act in the wake of the Supreme Court's decision last year. For his part, Attorney General Holder went before a criminal justice reform symposium at Georgetown Law School in Washington to call for restoring voting rights for felons.[29]

As for the rest of the nation's election machinery and procedures, more attention is on the agenda, but the prospects for concrete action are cloudy. Online registration may advance, given its claimed advantages of greater accuracy at less expense. But the parties' opposing views on whether to make voting easier raise doubts about the presidential commission's recommendations for more early and no-excuse absentee voting. And fiscal realities threaten the commission's urgent recommendation to upgrade vote-counting technology.

The nation got a wake-up call on the problems of administering elections in 2000, according to Becker, head of the Pew elections initiative. Despite the mixed forecast for changes, he sees the past decade-plus of debates as necessary and useful.

"America should be a model for the world in democracy," Becker says, "and that means harnessing technology to build an election system that is as accurate, convenient, cost-effective and efficient as possible."

NOTES

1. See *Applewhite v. Commonwealth*, 330 M.D. 2012 (Jan. 17, 2014), www.pacourts.us/assets/files/setting-647/file-3490.pdf?cb=a5ec29. For coverage, see Karen Langley, "Judge Declares Voter ID Law is Invalid," *Pittsburgh Post-Gazette*, Jan. 18, 2014, p. A-1; Amy Worden, "Pa. voter ID law struck down," *The Philadelphia Inquirer*, Jan. 18, 2014, p. A1; Rick Lyman, "Pennsylvania Voter ID Law Struck Down as Judge Cites Burdens on Citizens," *The New York Times*, Jan. 18, 2014, p. A12. Some background drawn from Charles Thompson, "State nears requiring that voters show IDs," *Patriot News* (Harrisburg, Pa.), March 13, 2012, p. A1.

2. For a detailed list and chronology, see "Voter Identification Requirements," National Conference of State Legislatures (regularly updated), www.ncsl.org/research/elections-and-campaigns/voter-id.aspx. For previous coverage, see these *CQ Researcher* reports by Peter Katel: "Voter Rights," May 18, 2012, pp. 449-476; "Voting Controversies," Sept. 15, 2006, pp. 745-768.

3. The case is *Shelby County v. Holder*, 570 U.S. —— (June 25, 2013), www.supremecourt.gov/opinions/12pdf/12-96_6k47.pdf. For coverage, see Kenneth Jost, *Supreme Court Yearbook 2012-2013*.

4. See Kathy Koch, "Election Reform," *CQ Researcher*, Nov. 2, 2001, pp. 897-920.

5. "The American Voting Experience: Report and Recommendations of the Presidential Commission on Election Administration," Presidential Commission on Election Administration, Jan. 22, 2014, www.supportthevoter.gov. For coverage, see Scott Wilson,

"Election commission recommends changes," *The Washington Post*, Jan. 23, 2014, p. A4.

6. "Voting Laws Roundup 2014," Brennan Center for Justice, Feb. 6, 2014, www.brennancenter.org/analysis/voting-laws-roundup-2014#ftn4.

7. Von Spakovsky's earlier quote from Lachlan Markay, "Critics Blast Obama Nominee for Election Assistance Commissioner," *The Washington Free Beacon*, June 11, 2013, http://freebeacon.com/critics-blast-obama-nominee-for-election-assistance-commissioner/.

8. The decision is *Crawford v. Marion County Board of Elections*, 533 U.S. 188 (2008). For an account, see Kenneth Jost, *Supreme Court Yearbook 2007-2008*.

9. John Fund, "Why We Need Voter-ID Laws Now," *National Review Online*, April 9, 2012, www.nationalreview.com/articles/295431/why-we-need-voter-id-laws-now-john-fund. Fund stresses that O'Keefe did not violate the law because he did not explicitly identify himself as Holder or request a ballot. The book co-authored by Fund and von Spakovsky is *Who's Counting? How Fraudsters and Bureaucrats Put Your Vote at Risk* (2012).

10. Quoted in "Democracy Prevails in Pennsylvania Voter ID Trial," Advancement Project, Jan. 17, 2014, www.advancementproject.org/news/entry/democracy-prevails-in-pennsylvania-voter-id-trial.

11. *Texas v. Holder*, 12-cv-128, U.S. Dist. Ct.-Dist. Col., (Aug. 30, 2012), pp. 46-47, www.scribd.com/doc/104429876/Texas-v-Holder.

12. See "Online Voter Registration," National Conference of State Legislatures, November 2013, www.ncsl.org/research/elections-and-campaigns/electronic-or-online-voter-registration.aspx. The report includes a link to the 55-minute Nov. 12 webinar, "Online Voter Registration: The Bipartisan Trend in Elections."

13. Fund and von Spakovsky, *op. cit.*, chap. 6.

14. "Reforming the voting process to improve access," "PBS NewsHour," Jan. 23, 2014, http://video.pbs.org/video/2365162592/.

15. Historical background drawn in part from Alexander Keyssar, *The Right to Vote: The Contested History of Democracy in the United States* (rev. ed, 2010). See also Katel, "Voter Rights," *op. cit.*

16. The Supreme Court decision is *South Carolina v. Katzenbach*, 383 U.S. 301 (1966).

17. The Supreme Court decision is *Oregon v. Mitchell*, 400 U.S. 112 (1970).

18. The decision is *Mobile v. Bolden*, 446 U.S. 55 (1980). The ruling threw out a lower court order that found the city of Mobile, Ala., had violated the Voting Rights Act by changing from a district to an at-large system for electing members of the city's governing body.

19. The decision is *Thornburg v. Gingles*, 478 U.S. 30 (1986). The decision sustained a lower court decision that threw out several multimember legislative districts in North Carolina.

20. For background, see Koch, *op. cit.*

21. "To Assure Pride and Confidence in the Electoral Process," National Commission on Federal Election Reform, August 2001, http://web1.millercenter.org/commissions/comm_2001.pdf. The commission was co-sponsored by the University of Virginia's Miller Center on Public Affairs and the Century Foundation; the report was presented to President Bush at the White House on July 31, 2001.

22. For a detailed dissection of the reauthorization, see Nathaniel J. Persily, "The Promise and Pitfalls of the New Voting Rights Act," *Yale Law Journal*, Vol. 117, No. 2 (November 2007), pp. 174-253, http://yalelawjournal.org/images/pdfs/606.pdf.

23. Richard L. Hasen, *The Voting Wars: From Florida 2000 to the Next Election Meltdown* (2012).

24. "Voter ID: Where Are We Now?" The Canvass, National Conference of State Legislatures, April 2012, www.ncsl.org/documents/legismgt/elect/Canvass_Apr_2012_No_29.pdf.

25. Hasen, "Margin of Litigation," *op. cit.*, pp. 131-133.

26. For an account, see Kenneth Jost, *Supreme Court Yearbook 2008-2009*.

27. See Patrick Marley, "High court to take up cases on voter ID," *Milwaukee Journal Sentinel*, Nov. 21, 2013, p. B1; Bruce Vielmetti, "Legal filings hone voter ID arguments," *Milwaukee Journal Sentinel*, Dec. 25, 2013, p. B1.

28. "Voting Laws Roundup 2014," *op. cit.* States with active "expansive" bills are California, Colorado, Kentucky, Massachusetts, Nebraska, New York and Washington; states with active "restrictive" bills are Nebraska, New Hampshire, Washington and Wisconsin. Also see "2013 Election Legislation Enacted by State Legislatures," National Conference of State Legislatures, Jan. 14, 2014, www.ncsl.org/research/elections-and-campaigns/wrap-up-2013-election-legislation-enactments.aspx.

29. See Dave Boyer, "Biden hits voter ID laws at event to honor King," *The Washington Times*, Jan. 21, 2014, A3; Matt Apuzzo, "Holder Urges States to Lift Ban on Felons' Voting," *The New York Times*, Feb. 12, 2014, p. A17.

BIBLIOGRAPHY

Selected Sources

Books

Fund, John H., and Hans von Spakovsky, *Who's Counting? How Fraudsters and Bureaucrats Put Your Vote at Risk*, Encounter Books, 2012.
Fund, a columnist with *National Review Online*, and von Spakovsky, a senior fellow with the conservative Heritage Foundation and former Federal Election Commission member, contend that voting fraud is spreading in the United States. They call for voter-ID laws, among other steps, to safeguard the integrity of elections, and they criticize liberal-backed proposals such as same-day voter registration as invitations to fraud. Includes notes. Fund also is author of *Stealing Elections: How Voting Fraud Threatens Our Democracy* (2d ed.), Encounter Books, 2008.

Hasen, Richard L., *The Voting Wars: From Florida 2000 to the Next Election Meltdown*, Yale University Press, 2012.
A nationally prominent election law expert at the University of California-Irvine School of Law details the controversies over administration of elections beginning with the presidential vote recount in Florida in 2000 and continuing through the 2010 election cycle. Includes notes. Hasen also publishes the comprehensive *Election Law Blog* (http://electionlawblog.org/).

Keyssar, Alexander, *The Right to Vote: The Contested History of Democracy in the United States* (rev. ed.), Basic Books, 2010 (originally published 2000).

A professor of history and public policy at Harvard University's Kennedy School of Government traces the history of voting issues from the limited suffrage in the country's early history through the hard-fought battles over expanding voting rights from the mid-19th century to the present day. Includes appendix material, detailed notes.

May, Gary, *Bending Toward Justice: The Voting Rights Act and the Transformation of American Democracy*, **Basic Books, 2013.**

A professor of history at the University of Delaware details the events leading to the enactment of the Voting Rights Act of 1965. Includes notes.

Wang, Tova Andrea, *The Politics of Voter Suppression: Defending and Expanding Americans' Right to Vote*, **Cornell University Press, 2012.**

An election-law expert at the liberal advocacy group Demos criticizes voter-ID laws among other proposals as attempts at "voter suppression."

Articles

Lee, Suevon, "Everything You've Ever Wanted to Know About Voter ID Laws," *Pro Publica*, Nov. 5, 2012, www .propublica.org/article/everything-youve-ever-wanted-to-know-about-voter-id-laws.

A question-and-answer format provides a thorough explanation of the origin of and controversy over voter-ID laws.

Toobin, Jeffrey, "Annals of Law: Holder v. Roberts," *The New Yorker*, Feb. 17, 2014, www.newyorker.com/reporting/2014/02/17/140217fa_fact_toobin.

A legal analyst depicts Attorney General Eric Holder as deeply committed to using suits against Texas and North Carolina to restore the power of the Voting Rights Act to prevent discriminatory voting practices.

Hearings

"From Selma to Shelby County: Working Together to Restore the Protections of the Voting Rights Act," *U.S.*

Senate Judiciary Committee, July 17, 2013, www.judiciary.senate.gov/hearings/hearing.cfm?id=6ae289b2466e2489f90d6b42c9d8d78f.

The hearing included testimony by two of the House co-sponsors of the proposed rewrite of the Voting Rights Act and three private witnesses.

"The Voting Rights Act After the Supreme Court's Decision in Shelby County," U.S. House Judiciary Subcommittee on the Constitution and Civil Justice, July 18, 2013, http://judiciary.house.gov/index.cfm/hearings?ID=3798FE70B5F1-C18F-30C6-70FAF7EBCA5C.Committee.

The hearing included testimony by four private individuals.

Reports and Studies

"The American Voting Experience: Report and Recommendations of the Presidential Commission on Election Administration," January 2014, www.support thevoter.gov/files/2014/01/Amer-Voting-Exper-final-draft-01-09-14-508.pdf.

The bipartisan, 10-member commission called for online registration, expanded early or absentee voting and improved voting technology; commissioners were unanimous in the 112-page report, but did not address photo-ID proposals.

"Building Confidence in U.S. Elections: Report of Commission on Federal Election Reform," September 2005, www1.american.edu/ia/cfer/report/full_report .pdf.

The private commission called for photo IDs for all voters, verifiable paper trails for election results and impartial administration of elections.

On the Web

Election Law @ Moritz, http://moritzlaw.osu.edu/electionlaw/.

The Ohio State University's Moritz College of Law maintains a website with "information and insights on the laws governing federal, state, and local elections."

For More Information

Advancement Project, 1220 L St., N.W., Suite 850, Washington, DC 20005; 202-728-9557; www.advancement project.org. The multiracial civil rights organization works with community organizations on election reform and other issues.

American Civil Liberties Union, 125 Broad St., New York, NY 10004; 212-549-2500; www.aclu.org/voting-rights. The ACLU's Voting Rights Project participates in litigation against photo-ID laws and other election issues; also provides news, analysis and research reports.

Brennan Center for Justice at New York University School of Law, 161 Avenue of the Americas, New York, NY 10013; 646-292-8310; www.brennancenter.org. The nonpartisan law and policy institute publishes research, analysis and litigation documents on major election law issues.

Election Assistance Commission, 1335 East West Highway, Suite 4300, Silver Spring, MD 20910; 301-563-3919; www .eac.gov. The federal agency is an independent bipartisan commission established in 2002 to assist states and localities in improving election administration and implementing provisions of the Help America Vote Act.

Fair Elections Legal Network, 1825 K St., N.W., Suite 450, Washington, DC 20006; 202-331-0114; http://fairelec tionsnetwork.com. The network of lawyers works to remove barriers to voting and improve election administration across the United States.

Heritage Foundation, 214 Massachusetts Ave., N.E., Washington, DC 20002; 202-546-4999; www.heritage.org/ issues/legal. The conservative think tank advocates stricter ID requirements for voting.

Mexican American Legal Defense and Educational Fund (MALDEF), 634 S. Spring St., Los Angeles, CA 90014; 213-629-2512; www.maldef.org. The longtime civil rights organization works on voting rights issues affecting Latinos.

NAACP, 4805 Mt. Hope Drive, Baltimore, MD 21215; 877-622-2798; www.naacp.org. The longtime civil rights organization participates in voting rights advocacy at the federal, state and local levels.

NAACP Legal Defense and Educational Fund, 99 Hudson St., 16th floor, New York, NY 10013; 212-219-1900; www.naacpldf.org. The organization — separate from the NAACP — litigates on voting rights issues in federal and state courts.

National Association of Election Officials, 21946 Royal Montreal Drive, Suite 100, Katy, TX 77450; 281-396-4309; http://electioncenter.org. The professional association represents government employees who serve in voter registration and elections administration.

National Association of Secretaries of State, 444 North Capitol St., N.W., Suite 401, Washington, DC 20001; 202-624-3525; www.nass.org. The association represents secretaries of state from the 50 states, the District of Columbia, Puerto Rico and American Samoa, most of whose offices have responsibility for administering elections in their jurisdictions.

National Conference of State Legislatures, 7700 East First Pl., Denver, CO 80230; 303-364-7700; www.ncsl.org. The nonpartisan organization furnishes the most complete and up-to-date information on states' voter-ID laws and other election-related measures.

Project on Fair Representation, c/o Project Liberty, 109 N. Henry St., Alexandria, VA 22314; 703-505-1922; www .projectonfairrepresentation.org/. The project sponsored the litigation that resulted in the Supreme Court's decision to invalidate the Voting Rights Act's preclearance coverage formula.

True the Vote, P.O. Box 27368, Houston, TX 77227; http:// truethevote.org. The Web-based organization supports photo-ID laws and organizes a nationwide network of election-watchers.

U.S. Department of Justice, 950 Pennsylvania Ave., N.W., Washington, DC 20530; 202-514-2000; www.justice.gov. The Justice Department's Voting Section is responsible for enforcing federal laws regarding voting rights.

11

Housing the Homeless

Peter Katel

A Times Square church offers sanctuary from the cold to a homeless man in New York City. Street people represent only the public face of homelessness. Since the early 1980s, large numbers of single-parent families, veterans and mentally ill people have become homeless.

Getty Images/Spencer Platt

Kimberly Mahan had just spent her remaining $3 on a large package of Ramen noodles. It was 2012, and Mahan was stuck in Farmington, N.M., pushing a stroller stuffed with six clothes-filled backpacks for herself and her two young children.

Mahan realized she had no idea how to reach Albuquerque, the state's biggest city, where she hoped to restart her life. She also had no idea of what she was going to do once she got there. "I looked up to the sky and said, 'OK, God, what am I supposed to do?' " she remembers.

A few days later, Mahan made it to Albuquerque, thanks to strangers who gave her rides and money after spotting the family on roadsides. Police officers picked up Mahan and her children and took them to Joy Junction, an evangelical Christian family shelter that provides food, clothing and Bible-based counseling.

Mahan's 180-mile journey began when her husband left, she says, depriving the family of its breadwinner. Mahan, 40, had worked for years in stores and fast-food restaurants but quit after her second child was born. Now, after nearly two years at Joy Junction, she wants to land a job and rent an apartment.

"I hope to have me and my kids back on our feet pretty soon," she says, citing the shelter's policy of allowing residents time to rebuild their lives.

"Typically, you're not going to see [homeless families] on the street," says Carmela J. DeCandia, director of the National Center on Family Homelessness, a think tank in Waltham, Mass.

Homeless single people, on the other hand, can be found in the streets and parks of cities big and small, often to the despair and

From *CQ Researcher*,
October 10, 2014.

Majority of Homeless Lives in 5 States

California accounted for more than 20 percent of the nation's homeless population in 2013, and 13 percent lived in New York. Collectively, those two states, along with Florida (8 percent), Texas (5 percent) and Massachusetts (3 percent), had 51 percent of the total.

State Shares of National Homeless Population, 2013

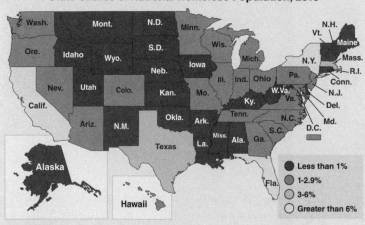

Legend:
- Less than 1%
- 1-2.9%
- 3-6%
- Greater than 6%

Source: Meghan Henry, Alvaro Cortes and Sean Morris, "The 2013 Annual Homeless Assessment Report (AHAR) to Congress: Part 1 Point-in-Time Estimates of Homelessness," U.S. Department of Housing and Urban Development, November 2013, p. 8, http://tinyurl.com/qd89wa8.

questions: What exactly is homelessness? Should the definition be limited to street people or include those temporarily living with friends or relatives? The answers lead to an even bigger question: How can homelessness be ended?

Counting the homeless population remains an inexact science. The U.S. Department of Housing and Urban Development (HUD) conducts an annual one-night "point-in-time" count of the homeless. According to HUD's figures, about 610,000 Americans were homeless on a single night in 2013 — a 9.2 percent drop from 2007. HUD also found that between 2012 and 2013 the homeless population fell 3.7 percent.[2]

According to another HUD assessment, nearly 1.5 million Americans used a homeless shelter at some point in 2012 — down since 2007, despite a jump between 2009 and 2010. And 36 percent of those were homeless families — the same percentage that showed up in the "point in time" census.[3]

outrage of residents, business owners and politicians. In the tourism mecca of Honolulu, Mayor Kirk Caldwell calls street people a threat.

"It's time to declare a war on homelessness, which is evolving into a crisis," Caldwell, a Democrat, wrote in *The Honolulu Star-Advertiser* in June. "We cannot let homelessness ruin our economy and take over our city."[1]

But street people represent only the public face of a socioeconomic tragedy that has been intensifying since the early 1980s, when several developments came together. Those include a punishing recession; rises in the divorce rate and number of single-parent families; and changes in mental health care that resulted in more mentally ill people becoming homeless.

Ambitious goals set in the 2000s by the George W. Bush administration to end chronic homelessness within 10 years remain unfulfilled, in part because of the steep recession of 2007-09.

With homelessness entrenched in the national landscape, the debate has focused on the most basic of

But HUD's point-in-time count "underestimates the scope of the problem because it misses many people who have found their own refuges outside of formal shelters," says Marybeth Shinn, a social psychologist and the chair of the Human & Organizational Development Department at Vanderbilt University's Peabody College of Education and Human Development in Nashville, Tenn., because it misses many people who have found their own refuges outside of formal shelters.

Shinn helped conduct a study that concluded a point-in-time count in New York City in 2005 missed up to 41 percent of homeless people who were not living in shelters.[4]

HUD itself acknowledges that its numbers fall short of producing a full picture. While HUD-funded housing programs — from shelters to permanent housing — aid more than 1 million people a year, "the total number of persons who experience homelessness may be twice as high," HUD said.[5]

Apart from the difficulties of physically counting the homeless, the HUD numbers reflect a definition of homelessness that some consider too narrow. HUD includes people who are:

- Living in dwellings unfit for human habitation, in emergency shelters or in temporary housing; or
- Leaving such a place;
- Facing loss of their housing within 14 days;
- Living in families with children or unaccompanied youths who haven't had a lease in the past 60 days and have moved two or more times during that period;
- Fleeing domestic violence.[6]

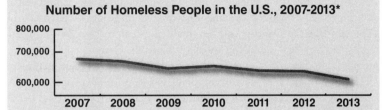

Homelessness Fell Despite Economic Woes

The number of homeless Americans fell from nearly 672,000 in 2007 to 610,000 in 2013, a decline of 9 percent, despite the 18-month recession that began in December 2007.

Number of Homeless People in the U.S., 2007-2013*

* Calculated as "point-in-time counts," which are one-night estimates of both sheltered and unsheltered homeless populations measured during the last week of January each year.

Source: Meghan Henry, Alvaro Cortes and Sean Morris, "The 2013 Annual Homeless Assessment Report (AHAR) to Congress: Part 1 Point-in-Time Estimates of Homelessness," U.S. Department of Housing and Urban Development, November 2013, p. 6, http://tinyurl.com/qd89wa8.

"HUD does not include . . . people who are doubled up," says Nan Roman, president and CEO of the National Alliance to End Homelessness, a Washington-based advocacy and research organization, using the term for people who lose their homes and move in with family or friends. "It includes people in imminent risk of homelessness, but we just haven't figured out a way to count people who would have to leave where they are within 14 days."

Yet, for many people, doubling up is the last step before homelessness. HUD's 2012 annual shelter-based count noted that 66 percent of homeless adults with children had lived with family or friends before entering shelters.[7]

Although not counted by HUD, some of those doubled-up people are tallied by the U.S. Department of Education, which reported that 1.3 million children were homeless during the 2012-13 school year, the most recent figure available. Seventy-five percent of those were doubled-up, 6 percent were in motels and 16 percent in shelters.[8]

"It's a subterranean problem," says Lauren Voyer, a senior vice president at HAPHousing, a Springfield, Mass.-based nonprofit that helps people rent or buy affordable housing. "A lot of families working in low-wage situations who can't get the money together to get

an apartment are living in motels. If you are in that situation, you are living without a home."

But others worry that expanding HUD's definition to include doubled-up people could overwhelm the capacity of programs for the homeless. "Doubled-up is its own problem," says Dennis Culhane, a professor of social policy and psychology at the University of Pennsylvania in Philadelphia. "Calling it homeless doesn't solve it. We have a lot of people in this country living in unaffordable, crowded housing," he continues. And relabeling it would only increase "the competition for the tiny resources we have."

Scarce resources, in fact, are the core problem, experts agree. "We still don't have enough affordable housing," says Eric Tars, senior attorney at the National Law Center on Homelessness & Poverty, an advocacy and research organization in Washington. However, as his organization and others advocate, if the federal income tax deduction for mortgage interest were reduced, as has been proposed by some economists, "we could take the savings and reinvest them in affordable-housing programs."

The Obama administration is trying several things aimed at reducing homelessness. On a broad scale, its "Opening Doors" strategy — a sequel to the Bush administration's plan to end homelessness in 10 years — calls for eliminating family homelessness by 2020 by providing affordable or subsidized housing in various forms. It also calls for veterans and homeless individuals who have spent years on the streets to be housed by the end of next year, mainly by placing them in facilities with mental-health and other services.[9]

For the "chronically" homeless, HUD's Housing First doctrine makes providing permanent housing as quickly as possible the top priority, with no qualifying requirements, such as first achieving sobriety. Housing First programs also provide mental health and other services.

Lori Thomas, a professor of social work at the University of North Carolina, Charlotte, says data from Housing First programs for chronically homeless adults show that getting them from shelters into real homes should be the first step. "They need housing to stabilize them to get them working on substance abuse and other issues," she says. "They could never get to that before, because their basic needs were not being met."

Thomas has been assessing the results of a "permanent supportive housing" operation in Charlotte aimed at helping chronically homeless men. That model, with on-site services, embodies the Housing First approach for permanently disabled people. By contrast, other programs — called transitional housing — offer short-term housing aid for up to two years to individuals and families.[10]

Back in Albuquerque, Mahan has now found a part-time job and is hoping for a range of help as she seeks a home for herself and her kids. She stresses she'll need rental assistance from somewhere, as well as psychological aid. "Before I leave here," she says, "I need a support system."

As lawmakers, homeless advocates and academics try to end homelessness, here are some of the questions they are debating:

Does unemployment cause most homelessness?

Experts agree that poverty is the main cause of homelessness. But poverty has many dimensions. Economic factors, including a combination of poor education and joblessness or underemployment, can lead to poverty and homelessness. And social problems such as substance abuse or mental illness can make it difficult to keep a job or afford housing.

An interim HUD report last year on an ongoing study of 2,307 homeless families showed that only 17 percent of the adults were working at the outset of the study, and many of those were working 30 hours a week or less. Likewise, a 1999 study by the Urban Institute, a nonpartisan think tank in Washington, found that only 29 percent of homeless families had paid work in the past month.[11]

Shinn of Vanderbilt University says economic factors — particularly income inequality and rising housing costs — drive many into homelessness. "There are lots of people who are very poor and paying way too much of their income toward rent or are doubled up with other people because they can't afford independent housing," she says.

Data on what causes family homelessness are inconclusive, says Shinn, a principal researcher in the ongoing HUD study. But homelessness became a bigger national issue some 30 years ago, when economic conditions changed, she notes. Many economists say Reagan-era tax cuts contributed to widening disparities in income as the economy continued its march from an industrial model with plenty of well-paid union jobs to an economy dominated by non-union service-oriented jobs. "The change is income inequality and the rising cost of housing," Shinn says. "Anything you can do to raise incomes at the bottom and lower housing costs at the bottom will reduce homelessness."

Peter Gagliardi, president and CEO of HAPHousing, the Springfield nonprofit, notes the loss of traditional jobs that used to define once-thriving factory towns in New England and elsewhere. In Springfield, for instance, several "big employers in the heart of the city that allowed people to walk to work" are now gone, he says. Those employers included board-game-maker Milton Bradley and the Springfield Armory, a then-government-owned firearms manufacturer. Nowadays, he says, "when jobs exist they don't pay enough to cover housing, food and health care. There is a huge, almost unseen, group of families who are in the worst-case housing situation."

Yet, social factors are important, too. DeCandia of the National Center on Family Homelessness says economic trends only partly explain homelessness. "There is a complex interplay between factors like lack of housing and poverty and trauma, domestic violence," she says.

Having a disability or a disabled family member can keep a homeless adult from working, contributing to the low employment rate among adults in homeless families.

One study found that 39 percent of homeless adults in families were themselves disabled and/or caring for a relative with a disability that limited the caretaker's ability to work, compared with only 4.5 percent of adults ages 18-44 in the population as a whole.[12]

DeCandia says some families "don't report major mental health issues or major trauma," but they can be "really struggling on the poverty cliff." One thing, she says, "can send them over the edge: loss of a job, or they're hit with a health crisis in the family and can't work regularly." Her organization studied 294 female-headed homeless families in four metropolitan areas of upstate New York and found that 93 percent of the mothers had a history of trauma, most the result of physical assault.[13]

Jessica Williams, who is staying at Albuquerque's Joy Junction with her husband, their newborn son and two older sons, says low wages, combined with a landlord's dishonesty, played a part in their homelessness. "He was going to rent us a house," she says, "and he took our $500 deposit and called us later and said he'd found somebody else."

Williams acknowledged that she had been addicted to cough syrup with codeine, which hurt her employability. Still, both she and her husband found jobs in stores, which allowed them to stay in motels for several weeks. At one, she says, she met someone else who had lost money to an unscrupulous landlord.

"If it's not addiction," she says, "if it's not the economy, it's people."

Is Housing First the best way to keep people from reverting to homelessness?

The name of the doctrine sounds common-sensical and humane. "Housing First" programs are based on the belief that problems a homeless individual or family faces cannot be solved until they are no longer living in the street or a crowded shelter. Hence, people should not be subject to sobriety or drug tests or other requirements as a condition of obtaining housing.[14]

The strategy originated in New York City in 1992 with a program called Pathways to Housing, which provided subsidized permanent housing combined with psychiatric care or drug treatment for chronically homeless individuals. The model later was extended to other categories of homeless persons.[15]

Getty Images/Spencer Platt

Formerly homeless Air Force veteran Barbara Barnes once slept in one of these bunks at the women's quarters at the New England Center for Homeless Veterans in Boston. Nationwide, nearly 140,000 vets stayed in shelters at one time or another in 2012, down from nearly 150,000 in 2009. The administration is planning to expand its programs for veterans housing to serve 200,000 vets annually. "We're not going to stop until every veteran who has defended America has a home in America," President Obama said in August.

Housing First helps people find long-term housing — other than shelters — as soon as possible and sees that as essential to preventing them from remaining homeless or returning to homelessness. Under that broad concept, a more tactically focused approach, called Rapid Re-Housing, provides short-term financial assistance to allow homeless people or families to acquire temporary housing within 30 days of becoming homeless and to enter a homeless assistance program. The idea is to deal with the immediate burden that finding a rental can place on financially stretched people. Subsidies can be a flat amount or income-based, with households paying a fixed percentage of their earnings for rent. Subsidies typically run for four to six months.[16]

HUD and other agencies — among them the Justice Department, which helps homeless victims of domestic violence and related crimes — use both the Housing First and Rapid Re-Housing approaches. HUD alone serves about 1 million people, including chronically homeless adults and families at imminent risk of homelessness.[17]

Thomas, of the University of North Carolina, says shelters can be counterproductive because of the lack of privacy and the mandatory schedules that participants must abide by. "I've had people tell me they'd rather be

Over One-Fifth of Homeless Are Children

Nearly 23 percent of all homeless people in the United States in 2013 were under 18, and teenagers and children made up nearly a third of those living in shelters. Eighty percent of those living on the street were 25 or older.

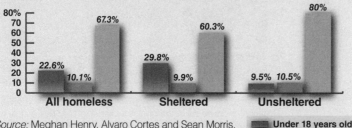

Share of U.S. Homeless Population by Age Group, 2013

Source: Meghan Henry, Alvaro Cortes and Sean Morris, "The 2013 Annual Homeless Assessment Report (AHAR) to Congress: Part 1 Point-in-Time Estimates of Homelessness," HUD, November 2013, p. 6, http://tinyurl.com/qd89wa8

in the street," she says. In shelters, "people surrender a lot of their dignity" because of strict rules.

The fundamental idea behind Housing First and Rapid Re-Housing, Thomas says, is that homeless people "need housing to stabilize them, to get them working on substance abuse or other issues. We are going to try to get [you] into housing that you can stay in for the rest of your life, not contingent on following anything but minimal rules — no harm to yourself or others."

But families struggling with poverty, employability and lack of education don't qualify for lifetime supportive housing, so rapidly rehousing them may not keep them from another bout of homelessness, some experts argue.

Ralph da Costa Nunez, president and CEO of the Institute for Children, Poverty & Homelessness in New York City, says Housing First does not work as a one-size-fits-all strategy. "Housing First is terrific for those ready to be housed first," he says. "Eighteen to 22 percent of families in shelters are working poor, with a long work history, and you'll never see them again." Another group of families needs help polishing their job skills and can move into permanent housing relatively quickly, Nunez continues.

But he sees an inherent problem with the relatively short-term nature of assistance available under Rapid Re-Housing models. "The hard-core group churns through the system forever, and it's growing larger and

larger," says Nunez, who advocates turning shelters into temporary housing with educational, job-training and other services on-site. "We do them an injustice by simply putting them in housing and seeing them come back. This is not simply a homeless issue; we have to face that."

Culhane of the University of Pennsylvania responds that homelessness is exactly what the word says. "The homeless system is not equipped to solve the problems of poverty," he says, even though homeless people, and poor people in general, may have acute needs, ranging from mental and physical health care to education and financial-management advice.

Homelessness agencies can connect people with services, he adds. But he argues against trying to duplicate those services by, for example, setting up dental clinics in homeless shelters. "The homeless system's job should be to solve the homeless problem," Culhane says. "The person is without shelter and should then be returned to some kind of housing."

DeCandia of the National Center on Family Homelessness takes the opposite stance. "Homelessness is not just about lack of housing," she says. "It is embedded in a pattern of residential instability. It is a crisis of housing, but it is not separate from other issues."

Debate should not center on where services are provided, DeCandia says. "There are things that a shelter system and a homeless system can do in the way they create an environment that supports people when they move on, whether that is in a week or three months."

Should homeless families receive bigger or longer-lasting housing subsidies?

The inability of people at the bottom of the socioeconomic ladder to afford housing is at the heart of homelessness, whatever the other contributing factors may be.

Federal Section 8 programs — created in 1974 to provide subsidies for low-income renters — and similar, smaller-scale subsidy programs have only enough funds to help about 23 percent of the population that is eligible for assistance, according to two Washington think tanks: the liberal Center on Budget and Policy Priorities and the centrist Bipartisan Policy Center.[18]

In Massachusetts, for instance, 5,400 families are at the end of their two-year state-funded HomeBASE rental assistance. "If I could figure out a way to pay market rate, I would," a homeless Boston mother of two, Altia Taylor, told a state legislative committee last year. "If I could own my own home, I would. I would have done it a long time ago."[19]

Waiting lists for state-administered Section 8 funds are years long. To solve that problem, Republican and Democratic members of a housing strategy panel assembled by the Bipartisan Policy Center recommended last year that "our most vulnerable households, those with extremely low incomes . . . [be] assured access to housing assistance if they need it."[20]

Many congressional Republicans disagree. "Yes, there are some people that probably need and do need housing assistance," Rep. Randy Neugebauer, R-Texas, said last year at a hearing of the House Financial Services Committee. "But this [Section 8] program is on a course that's not sustainable." He cited a 10 percent increase between 2003 and 2013 — from 3 million to 3.3 million — in the number of families participating in the two main Section 8 programs.[21]

Advocating tax cuts and rollbacks of federal regulations on business as ways to stimulate economic growth — and criticizing Democrats for opposing such measures — Neugebauer said, "More and more people are falling off the economic ladder. . . . And so just making the net bigger and bigger is not the long-term solution for many of those families." The long-term solution for those families, he said, "is to keep them on the economic ladder, so that they don't need a safety net."[22]

Democrats on the committee insisted that immediate prevention of homelessness should take priority over longer-term anti-poverty measures. "Full funding of these programs will help keep impoverished Americans, most especially the future of our country, our children, from being pushed onto the streets or forced to live out of cars," said Rep. Carolyn Maloney, D-N.Y.[23]

Maloney denied that Democrats oppose easing regulations on business, but said that leaning too far in that direction, by loosening supervision of the financial industry, could lead to a repeat of the stock market crash of 2008 and thus increase poverty. In any case, she said,

homeless people are not in a position to pull themselves up the ladder. "If you don't have and you can't afford housing," she said, "you can't afford going to school."

Others homeless advocates question whether Section 8 subsidies by themselves can do anything more than ensure housing. "I'd like to say that we just need more housing subsidies," says Gagliardi of HAPHousing. "But, ultimately, the solution has to be to address poverty head-on."

That effort, he says, must involve creating or teaching skills for jobs that pay more than minimum wage. "A McDonald's job, a Wal-Mart job — if it's a second job, it's sustaining, but if it's the only one, it doesn't work," he says. Citing the Massachusetts minimum hourly wage of $8, he adds, "You just have to do the math."

Those concerns aside, some homelessness and housing experts argue that experimenting with various forms and levels of rent subsidies, including temporary subsidies to families under Rapid Re-Housing programs, could expand the beneficiary pool.

However, Shinn of Vanderbilt University asks: "Is a short-term subsidy enough?"

"Wouldn't it be nice if that were true; then there would be much more to go around."

Shinn urges researchers to look into whether smaller subsidies, which provide less assistance than Section 8, would keep beneficiaries housed while allowing more people to enter the program. The idea, she acknowledges, is "heresy" among advocates for the homeless. But, she says, "I think it's worth experimenting with different structures."

BACKGROUND

"I Ain't Got No Home"

In Elizabethan England, they were known as the strolling poor: vagabonds who took to the highways in search of food, shelter and jobs. In colonial America, village watchmen were responsible for shooing away the wandering poor before they could enter town and become a burden to town charities.[24]

Things were little better in an industrializing America, which saw the emergence of large slums populated by growing numbers of homeless migrants and workers. Single men labeled as "tramps" and "hobos" — the latter looking for work, the former uninterested in working — traveled throughout the country in the late 19th century.

After the stock market crashed in 1929, thousands of banks failed, causing the Great Depression, massive unemployment and a spike in homelessness. By 1933, 1.2 million people were without homes, according to a nationwide census by the private National Center on Care of the Transient and Homeless.[25]

Nature added to the misery: The Dust Bowl — a combination of drought, heat and howling wind that struck the Great Plains — destroyed farms and led some 400,000 people from Oklahoma, Texas, Arkansas and Missouri to flee to California's fertile Central Valley in the mid-1930s.[26] Californians reacted much as their colonial forebears: They tried to keep out the migrants, whom authorities lumped together as "Okies" and "Dust Bowl refugees."

Even without formal anti-Okie policies, police in California earned a reputation for brutal treatment of homeless migrants. In the words of folk singer Woody Guthrie, who together with novelist John Steinbeck, was one of the best-known chroniclers of the migration: "I ain't got no home, I'm just a-roamin' 'round/Just a wandrin' worker, I go from town to town/And the police make it hard wherever I may go/And I ain't got no home in this world anymore."[27]

In 1939, three California district attorneys began enforcing a 1933 state law, the Indigent Act, which made it illegal to help destitute persons enter the state. The U.S. Supreme Court in 1941 overturned that law, making clear that states could not bar people from entry.[28]

Elsewhere in America, the Roosevelt administration's "New Deal" recovery measures financed federal construction projects that would provide shelter and jobs for millions of unemployed "transients" roaming the countryside.[29] Perhaps the best-known was the Civilian Conservation Corps (CCC), open to boys and men ages 16 to 24, as well as up to 25,000 World War I veterans. Participants received housing in newly built camps, food and a small wage for working on flood protection, dams, road-building and other infrastructure projects. By the time the program ended in 1942, about 3 million had served in the CCC.[30]

In a second anti-homelessness measure, Congress appropriated $500 million for grants to states to provide shelter, jobs and other "necessities of life to persons in need . . . whether resident, transient, or homeless." The latter phrase, writes Neil Larry Shumsky, a history professor at Virginia Tech in Blacksburg, marked the first time the federal government explicitly recognized homelessness as a social ill, and it authorized states to help people who were not residents of those states.[31]

The law setting up the fund also created the Federal Transient Program, designed to help states establish relief projects. The program created camps similar to those established by the CCC, but it was a short-lived effort, lasting only until 1935.

Emptying Asylums

In the 1950s, a time of relative prosperity, homelessness again was seen as a problem largely confined to alcoholic single men. President John F. Kennedy undertook some anti-poverty programs in the early 1960s, and his successor, Lyndon B. Johnson, expanded those efforts into his signature War on Poverty program.

Under the program, defined by large-scale nationwide anti-poverty efforts, private and public agencies attempted to end homelessness by broadening the range of services available to the predominantly male homeless population. But projects to reduce the number of people living in poverty took precedence.

Those efforts coincided with another government initiative: decreasing reliance on state psychiatric hospitals (known as "insane asylums" and "mental institutions") for treating mentally ill people. Often dubbed "snake pits," the hospitals had reputations for squalor and abuse or neglect of patients, making legislators increasingly reluctant to fund them. Meanwhile, doctors' associations were promising that new-generation tranquilizers would make hospitalization unnecessary for most patients.

However, "deinstitutionalization," as the process became known, had the unintended consequence of significantly increasing the homeless population.[32] The effort was championed by Kennedy, who had a developmentally disabled sister. The Mental Retardation Facilities and Community Mental Health Centers Construction Act of 1963 sought to replace "custodial mental institutions" with "therapeutic centers," Kennedy said when signing the legislation.[33]

Experts viewed the initial results of the statute and subsequent similar measures as successful. From 1956 to 1980, the hospital population of mentally ill patients dropped from 559,000 to 154,000.[34] But the strategy depended on the availability of space in community-based treatment centers. And by the 1970s, evidence was mounting that nonhospital mental health treatment facilities were in short supply. Two big states, New York and California, saw motels, boarding houses, jails and streets fill up with people discharged from psychiatric hospitals.[35]

In late 1980, shortly before losing his re-election bid, President Jimmy Carter signed the Mental Health Systems Act, designed to expand the number of community mental health centers. But upon taking office in 1981, President Ronald Reagan got Congress to repeal the law. Funds destined for federal mental health centers were combined with other mental health care grants into "block grants" to states, with few conditions for the states to meet. The Reagan administration also launched a review of disability-payment cases, leading to the removal of about 500,000 people from the rolls, many of them mentally ill. However, Congress passed the Disability Benefits Reform Act of 1984, which made such removals more difficult.[36]

Reagan was skeptical of community mental health centers and of services for homeless people, whose situations, he suspected, often reflected personal choice rather than underlying economic or psychological problems.[37]

But the number of homeless people continued to climb due to the effects of deinstitutionalization and the cutback in community mental health services. By 1988, the National Institute of Mental Health reported that between 125,000 and 300,000 people with chronic mental illness were homeless.[38]

Myriad economic problems and profound socioeconomic shifts during the early 1980s added to the homelessness problem. The recession of 1981-82 —the most severe since the 1930s — saw the unemployment rate soar to 10.8 percent in late 1982. Meanwhile, high interest rates and, later in the decade, the failure of more than 700 of the nation's savings and loans institutions made homeownership even tougher for the working poor.[39]

Reagan and Congress responded to the recession and the subsequent economic boom by cutting taxes in a series of measures culminating in the Tax Reform Act of 1986. The same period saw the beginning of the widely documented growth in income inequality, though experts argue over whether the new tax structure created the trend, or — as some say — failed to soften the effects of changes occurring in the economy.

Homeless people sleep on the sidewalk in the Skid Row area of Los Angeles. The city's new anti-homelessness initiative, Operation Healthy Streets, marks a break with Los Angeles' past and the enforcement-heavy anti-homelessness approaches taken by other cities. The initiative provides immediate services for homeless people, such as mental health appointments and enrollment in Medicaid.

At the same time, the number of single-mother families was increasing at a time when the number of manufacturing jobs was decreasing. Plus, a rising divorce rate and widespread adoption of no-fault divorce laws left many divorcees destitute if they lacked marketable job skills.[40]

The "New Homeless"

As the 1990s began, cities began filling up with homeless people to an extent not seen since the Depression. A 1991 study led by Martha Burt, a longtime researcher on homelessness at the Urban Institute, found that between 1981 and 1989 the overall homelessness rate, based on the availability of shelter space, in the nation's 182 largest cities (with populations of 100,000 or more) tripled — from 5 per 10,000 residents to 15 per 10,000. By 1989, 45 cities had rates higher than 20 per 10,000, and seven (including Washington, D.C., and New York) had rates of more than 40.[41]

The rise in homelessness spawned political and legal movements to provide services, prevent homelessness and protect the homeless from what advocates considered repressive police measures. As early as 1972, the U.S. Supreme Court had ruled that vagrancy laws, long used as an enforcement tool against the homeless, encouraged "arbitrary and erratic arrests and convictions."[42]

CHRONOLOGY

1933-1941 *Great Depression causes mass homelessness, triggering government programs to combat it.*

1933 With some 1.2 million people homeless, Congress creates, at the request of President Franklin D. Roosevelt, the Civilian Conservation Corps, putting jobless men to work on federally funded projects. . . . Congress provides $500 million for state programs to aid the needy.

1935 Families made homeless by the Depression and the Dust Bowl begin trekking to California.

1939 Three California prosecutors begin enforcing a law prohibiting indigent people from entering the state.

1941 U.S. Supreme Court strikes down California law barring indigents.

1963-1984 *Deinstitutionalization of the mentally ill and cuts to safety-net programs for the poor lead to surge in homelessness.*

1963 President John F. Kennedy signs Mental Retardation Facilities and Community Mental Health Centers Construction Act, designed to treat the mentally ill in community clinics instead of "insane asylums."

1970s As deinstitutionalization takes effect, New York and California see formerly hospitalized people flood cheap lodgings, jails and streets.

1979 New York State Supreme Court rules the state must provide shelter for the homeless.

1980 President Jimmy Carter signs Mental Health Systems Act to expand community mental health centers to treat deinstitutionalized patients.

1981 At the urging of President Ronald Reagan, Congress repeals the community mental health centers law, consolidating all mental health program funding into block grants for states to administer.

1984 Reagan says some people are homeless "by choice."

1987-1996 *Homelessness becomes part of national landscape, prompting various aid measures.*

1987 Growth in homelessness prompts Congress to pass McKinney-Vento Homeless Assistance Act, designed to help the homeless find housing by creating job-training programs.

1988 Up to 300,000 mentally ill people are homeless, the National Institute of Mental Health reports.

1991 Urban Institute says that homelessness tripled between 1981-89.

1992 A New York program pioneers Housing First strategy, combining permanent housing with mental health treatment.

1996 Ninth U.S. Circuit Court of Appeals upholds Seattle ordinances against sitting or lying on downtown sidewalks at certain hours.

2002-Present *Wars in Iraq and Afghanistan focus new attention on homeless veterans, as federal strategy shifts to ending homelessness.*

2002 George W. Bush administration establishes strategy of ending chronic homelessness in 10 years.

2010 Obama administration continues the end-homelessness strategy, vowing to end chronic and veteran homelessness by the end of 2015, and family homelessness by 2020.

2012 Department of Housing and Urban Development reports the number of people using homeless shelters is down 6.3 percent since 2007. . . . Department of Education counts 1.1 million homeless public school students in 2011-12 school year.

2013 One-night "point-in-time" count shows 7 percent drop in number of homeless veterans and a 3.7 percent overall decline in homelessness.

2014 Hawaii's Oahu enacts ordinances designed to keep homeless people out of tourist areas. . . . Police in Albuquerque, N.M., kill homeless schizophrenic man who was camping illegally. . . . Homeless Iraq veteran is arrested for trying to break into the White House.

In 1979, when New York City was experiencing the first effects of what would become a national trend of growing homelessness, lawyer Robert Hayes won a crucial class-action lawsuit on behalf of six homeless men. The suit — which attacked a city policy of forcing homeless people to find shelter — cited a Depression-era amendment to the state constitution that said "aid, care and support of the needy are public concerns and shall be provided by the state and . . . its subdivisions."[43] The initial court victory led the city to acknowledge its obligation to provide shelter to all homeless men (and, later, women). By 1988, New York shelters could take in up to 10,000 people.[44]

In 1987, advocacy campaigns coupled with the growth in homelessness led to passage of the McKinney-Vento Homeless Assistance Act, which created so-called Continuum of Care programs designed to help the homeless acquire housing.[45]

But the law was based on a definition of homelessness that some experts criticized as too limited. It defined a homeless person as someone without a "fixed, regular and adequate nighttime residence," or someone of low income whose nighttime residence was a shelter. That definition excluded "doubled-up" persons living with relatives or friends. The definition did include people at imminent risk of losing their homes within seven days, but advocates argued that many at-risk people did not meet that seven-day requirement. In effect, that definition severely limited programs designed to help people who were at risk of becoming homeless.[46]

New Strategies

The first major new anti-homelessness initiative since the 1987 McKinney-Vento Act was adopted in 2002. Borrowing the idea from a 2000 proposal by the National Alliance to End Homelessness, the George W. Bush administration declared a goal of ending one form of homelessness — chronic homelessness — within 10 years. It assigned this ambitious task to a revived U.S. Interagency Council on Homelessness, which had been inactive for six years.[47]

The council's director, Philip F. Mangano, enthusiastically adopted the Housing First doctrine, to the applause of some mayors whose cities were struggling with homelessness. "When you ask the consumer what they want," he said at the end of the Bush administration, "they don't

simply say a bed, blanket and a bowl of soup. They say they want a place to live."[48]

For chronically homeless individuals, permanent supportive housing — low-rent dwellings with access to substance-abuse counseling and mental health treatment — was seen as the best approach. HUD adopted a policy, still in effect, of favoring Homeless Assistance Grant applicantions from organizations or agencies that provide permanent supportive housing for disabled individuals or families with a disabled adult. That policy effectively addressed the chronically homeless, the nonpartisan Congressional Research Service found, because individuals with a disability are often the ones who are homeless for long, recurring periods.[49]

But Bush's overall housing policy also included efforts to increase homeownership for low- and moderate-income people. Those efforts, supported by Democrats and the lending industry, eventually helped to trigger a housing bubble and the financial crisis of 2007-09, when home prices and the mortgage market collapsed and 2.8 million homes were foreclosed in 2009 alone.[50]

The number of people in homeless shelters rose less drastically, by 2.2 percent between 2009 and 2010, largely because those who lost their homes initially went to rental housing or to stay with friends or family.[51] "We didn't see a lot of foreclosed families ending up in shelters," says Gagliardi of HAPHousing.

However, later research showed that about 20 percent of foreclosures hit rental properties, and 40 percent of families facing eviction from foreclosed apartment buildings were renters, the National Center on Homelessness & Poverty said in 2012. "The problem may only continue to worsen as renters represent a rising segment of the U.S. population," the center concluded.[52]

For children, consequences of foreclosures include frequent moves that tend to lower academic performance, as well as family stress that can bring on "negative behaviors," a former poverty specialist at the federal Health and Human Services Department concluded in a report for the Brookings Institution think tank.[53]

Congress responded in 2009 with the Helping Families Save Their Homes Act, which expanded the definition of homelessness to include people staying in motels or hotels at the expense of a government agency or a charity.[54] Under the new definition, unsuitable places to sleep included cars, parks, abandoned buildings, bus and train stations and campgrounds.

Albuquerque Struggles to Help the Homeless

Needs far exceed the capacity of current services.

On a hot September morning in Albuquerque's hardscrabble South Valley, a group of 30 homeless men and women sit in a large dining hall at a family shelter and talk about how Jesus is helping them rebuild their lives.

"I'm still healing," says a woman in her 40s. "God has shown me how wonderful and merciful he is; my addiction and behaviors made me lose a lot." The shelter's chaplain, Gene Shiplet, leads the program from his desk on the stage, reading Bible passages about leaving bad associates behind. He encourages his flock to participate, complimenting them on their testimonies.

Welcome to the "Life Recovery" program at Joy Junction, New Mexico's largest shelter for homeless families. Staff of the donor-funded project, which opened in 1986, say they won't turn away non-Christians or the non-religious. But for those who stay, the religious message is unavoidable.

"Things get so bad in peoples' lives that they turn to abuse of alcohol or drugs to escape the pain and dull their senses," says founder and CEO Jeremy Reynalds. "You have to give someone a replacement, a reason for living, someone or something they can turn to to make life worth living. For us as evangelicals, that means having a relationship with Jesus Christ."

A few miles north, in downtown Albuquerque, the head of the state's biggest service center for the homeless is also a man of God. But the Rev. Russell "Rusty" Smith, an Episcopal priest and the executive director of St. Martin's Hospitality Center, takes a secular approach to the center's work.

"Religion doesn't belong in basic human care," Smith says at a coffee shop staffed by a St. Martin's client who is learning job skills. "This is a human response to a human need. I am so opposed to introducing preaching to people in need."

Regardless of whether help comes with Bible readings, no one disputes the need for homeless services in New Mexico's biggest city. Its history has been intertwined with homelessness since the 1930s, when the city was a key stop on Route 66, the fabled highway used in the 1930s by migrants heading to California to escape the Dust Bowl.[1]

"66 is the mother road, the road of flight," John Steinbeck wrote in *The Grapes of Wrath*, as he traced the highway from Arkansas to California, where it wound through "Tucumcari and Santa Rosa and into the New Mexican mountains to Albuquerque, where the road comes down from Santa Fe."

But the Dust Bowl refugees were only passing through. This year in Albuquerque, a schizophrenic homeless man, James Boyd, was shot dead by police, and two homeless Navajo men, Allison Gorman and Kee Thompson, were bludgeoned to death, allegedly by teenagers, as they slept.[2]

Extraordinarily, one of the accused teenagers had been homeless himself. "It's so hard that he could do that to

---

And the seven-day limit on loss-of-housing risk was doubled to 14 days. People fleeing domestic violence, sexual assault or other such dangers, and who were unable to find new housing immediately, also were added to the definition.[55]

The increase in homelessness in 2008-09 prompted the Obama administration to adopt and expand its predecessor's objective of ending homelessness. In a 2010 strategy document, "Opening Doors," the administration set a five-year timetable for ending homelessness among the chronically homeless, as well as veterans. The administration also announced a plan to

end homelessness in 10 years for families, youth and children.[56]

"In many respects, this current period of economic hardship mirrors the early 1980s, when widespread homelessness reappeared for the first time since the Great Depression," the strategy document said.[57]

The administration also has focused on reducing homelessness among veterans, through services such as HUD's Veterans Affairs Supportive Housing program (VASH).

"Since 2008, we've housed more than 73,000 veterans through the HUD-VASH program, which provides housing vouchers to help homeless veterans pay for permanent,

someone where . . . I mean, like I said, we came from there," Victor Prieto, the father of a 15-year-old who is charged with killing the Navajo men, told Albuquerque's KOB-TV.[3]

According to the city's count, Albuquerque typically had 1,170 homeless people on any one night last year — in a city with about 556,000 people — down 28 percent from 2011. But under the U.S. Department of Education's more expansive definition of homelessness, Albuquerque's public schools enrolled more than 6,000 homeless students during the 2011-12 academic year, according to the school system's Homelessness Project.[4]

Support services in Albuquerque are "highly fragmented [and] underfunded," making it difficult for people to navigate multiple services, according to the New Mexico Coalition to End Homelessness, which includes St. Martin's.

Substance-abuse counseling is one of those services. Reynalds says nearly everyone who shows up at Joy Junction comes with a tormented personal history that usually involves alcohol or drugs. "The BBC came to do a segment retracing *The Grapes of Wrath*, and they wanted to find people who were at Joy Junction purely for lack of money," he says. "We were able to scrape up three people."

For the homeless, Smith argues, substance abuse can be a vital form of survival. "If I was living on the streets, I'd be blitzed every day," he says. "Eating pizza from a dumpster, you can only do that if you're drinking."

St. Martin's offers substance-abuse counseling and other mental health services, along with a day lounge, showers, a laundry and storage space. However, says Monet Silva-Caldwell, the center's development director, "that is not what St. Martin's is all about. We want to get them into housing."

To that end, St. Martin's screens willing clients for a variety of small-scale housing programs that are available. They include "permanent supportive housing" — 142 apartments with mental health services on-site — and subsidized housing for as long as two years in 10 two-bedroom apartments. A new program funded by United Way offers three months of rental assistance and job-search help to people in imminent danger of homelessness.

But the staff at both St. Martin's and Joy Junction say the needs far exceed the capacity of current services. St. Martin's has registered 6,200 people for its day services since August 2013. Joy Junction houses about 300 men, women and children a night.

While Reynalds acknowledges the evangelical nature of Joy Junction's therapeutic services, he draws some lines. "There is a proclivity in some religious missions to say, 'Have your gospel, and then we'll feed you,' " he says. "I have always been strongly opposed to that. We want to take care of your physical needs and then feed you spiritually."

— *Peter Katel*

---

[1]John Steinbeck, *Grapes of Wrath* (1939), http://tinyurl.com/nyas79c.

[2]Ryan Boetel, "Teenage attacker to homeless victims, 'Eat mud,' " *Albuquerque Journal*, July 23, 2014, http://tinyurl.com/ly6mg5j; Rick Nathanson, "James Boyd's dark journey," *Albuquerque Journal*, March 30, 2014, http://tinyurl.com/knkw5rr.

[3]Quoted in Lindsey Bever, "One teen charged with killing two homeless men was once homeless himself, his father said," *The Washington Post*, July 22, 2014, http://tinyurl.com/mge76l4/.

[4]"A Community Response to Homelessness in Albuquerque 2013-2017," New Mexico Coalition to End Homelessness, updated September 2014, p. 5, http://tinyurl.com/mv5h6fq.

---

stable housing," first lady Michelle Obama wrote in an op-ed in July.[58] Nearly 140,000 veterans stayed in shelters at one time or another in 2012, down from nearly 150,000 in 2009.[59]

But that number is still large. And, at a time when 1.4 million Afghanistan and Iraq vets are no longer on active duty, studies of past veteran cohorts show that psychological effects of wartime service often show up as late as 10 years after leaving the military.[60]

Culhane of the University of Pennsylvania, who is a consultant to the Department of Veterans Affairs, says the agency is planning to expand VASH and other

programs to serve 200,000 people a year. Results so far show that "homelessness has gone down dramatically among veterans," he says.

"We're not going to stop until every American who has defended America has a home in America," President Obama said in a speech to the American Legion in August.[61] The administration's goal is to end homelessness among veterans next year.

But some congressional Republicans and homelessness experts doubt that target can be met and question how much progress is being made. "There has been an incredible outlay of resources, and other than VA statistics, we

Motels Become Transitional Housing

"Families crowd into rooms, living week to week."

When the Democratic Party held its national convention in Charlotte, N.C., in 2012, homeless shelters saw a sudden influx of families.

"We had a big displacement of homeless families," says social work professor Lori Thomas of the University of North Carolina, Charlotte, because they were shut out of where they'd been living — motels. As anyone involved in the world of the homeless knows, motels play an important role for those who have lost their housing.

"Over the years, I've seen motels end up becoming their housing," says Carmela J. DeCandia, director of the National Center on Family Homelessness in Waltham, Mass., "because they can pay night to night or week to week and because there is no security deposit or credit check."

"People in motels are shelter people," says Ralph da Costa Nunez, president and CEO of the Institute for Children, Poverty & Homelessness in New York City.

But Nan Roman, president and CEO of the National Alliance to End Homelessness in Washington, says families with no resources who can't find room at a shelter are likely to sleep at a friend's or relative's house, or in a car. "People in motels have got money, though they've probably got a cash flow problem," she says. "They need help but probably have income."

The motel-living trend got national exposure three years ago, when "60 Minutes" ran a hard-hitting piece on families in Central Florida whose incomes were too low for them to live anywhere except in motels. "In Seminole County, near Orlando, so many kids have lost their homes

that school buses now stop at dozens of cheap motels where families crowd into rooms, living week to week," CBS reporter Scott Pelley said.[1]

In Albuquerque, N.M., as in Orlando, some incomes leave people very close to the edge. Jeremy Reynalds, a pastor and the director of Joy Junction, an Albuquerque family shelter that sends a food truck to serve families living in local motels, says some of those who eat the free meals have only enough to pay for lodging. Jessica Williams, a Joy Junction resident with her husband and their newborn, says they stayed at a Motel 6 "until we ran out of money and came here."

The Albuquerque mayor's office cracked down on substandard motels in 2008, reducing, at least for a while, the stock of available motel housing, Reynalds remembers.[2] "I sympathized with what they were doing," he says, because some of the motels had safety hazards. But he adds, "It's like payday loans; they take advantage of the poor, but if they weren't there, what would take their place?"

No one knows how many homeless people are living in motels nationwide. The closest thing to a census of that population is the U.S. Department of Education's count of 64,930 public school students living in hotels and motels during the 2011-12 school year. That figure does not include the students' parents and preschool-age siblings, or any motel-dwellers not attending school.[3]

Massachusetts appears to have the best data of the states, because a state law guarantees homeless families a "right to shelter," and Massachusetts turned to motels when shelters

really don't have specifics on the programs' effectiveness, outcomes and sustainability," Rep. Jeff Miller, R-Fla., chairman of the House Veterans' Affairs Committee, told *The New York Times*.[62]

In the fiscal year ending this past September, the VA has budgeted $5.4 billion for clinical health services for homeless vets, and $1.4 billion on other programs for the homeless. For the new fiscal year, the administration wants a 17.8 percent increase for the VA's homelessness efforts, including $1.64 billion for housing and homelessness-prevention programs. Overall, since 2010, the

administration has spent $4 billion on homeless-vet housing programs, including apartment rentals.[63]

Homelessness among veterans has been an embarrassing issue since the Vietnam War ended. VA research based on 2009 data concluded that veterans were overrepresented among the homeless, and that the possibility of a veteran becoming homeless rose after the draft ended in 1973. Male veterans were 1.25 times more likely to be homeless than non-veterans, and women veterans were 2.1 times more likely than non-veteran women.[64]

filled up. Last year, the state was housing more than 2,000 families, including 2,008 school-age children, in motels and hotels, at a cost of $48.1 million, according to the New England Center for Investigative Reporting.[4]

The nine-member family of Sergio and Rosa Serrano was living in a Days Inn in Shrewsbury. For the children, "it's not good, but what are you going to do?" Sergio Serrano, an unemployed and partially disabled construction worker, told the center. "They want to be outside, but they can't. They have no place to play."[5]

New York City also requires that the homeless have shelter. The city, which has the state's greatest number of homeless residents, at one point took over buildings whose owners were in default on tax obligations. One shelter near John F. Kennedy International Airport is a former Best Western motel.[6]

At the other end of the country, San Jose, Calif. — another city with a large homeless population and high housing costs — is planning to pay motel bills for "transitionally homeless" people. The motel subsidies could last up to one year for those with good employment prospects who have qualified for rental-assistance vouchers but can't find a place to live.[7]

The paucity of affordable housing in places like New York, Massachusetts and San Jose, which as home to the lucrative high-tech industry has famously high housing costs, makes it difficult for families working at the low end of the job market.

"We have a lot of families working in low-wage situations who can't get the money together to get into an apartment, and who are living in motels," says Lauren Voyer, a senior vice president at HAPHousing, a Springfield, Mass.-based nonprofit that helps people rent or buy affordable housing. "If you're in that situation, you're living without a home."

— Peter Katel

Theresa Muller, a homeless woman in Kissimmee, Fla., prepares to move out of the cluttered motel room she shared with her boyfriend, father and three children. They were planning in August to move to a home in a neighboring county.

[1]Scott Pelley, "Homeless Children: The Hard Times Generation," "60 Minutes," June 20, 2011, http://tinyurl.com/pwwvmwc.

[2]Dan Mckay, "Mayor Brings in New Team," *Albuquerque Journal*, July 8, 2008, http://tinyurl.com/ntp79r2.

[3]"Education for Homeless Children and Youth Program," U.S. Department of Education, updated August 2013, http://tinyurl.com/osbmbwq. For background, see Marcia Clemmitt, "Homeless Students: Should Aid Programs Be Expanded?" *CQ Researcher*, April 5, 2013, pp. 305-328.

[4]Rupa Shenoy, "Homeless in motels: How some families are hanging on," New England Center for Investigative Reporting (in the *Worcester Telegram & Gazette*), Feb. 23, 2014, http://tinyurl.com/qdfnafk.

[5]Quoted in *ibid.*

[6]Ian Frazier, "Hidden City," *The New Yorker*, Oct. 28, 2013, http://tinyurl.com/npr83gk.

[7]Alice Yin, "Homeless Programs Take Different Paths to Address Crisis," *San Jose Inside*, Aug. 27, 2014, http://tinyurl.com/ndulwu5.

The most extensive research so far on veteran homelessness is several decades old and focused on Vietnam vets, the Congressional Research Service reported. That 1984-88 study did not find a direct connection between post-traumatic stress disorder (PTSD) and homelessness. However, some of the issues contributing to PTSD — including substance abuse and unemployment — were risk factors for homelessness.

Data on the mental health of Afghanistan and Iraq veterans do point to a high potential for homelessness in their ranks. Two studies found that between 14 percent

and 17 percent of those veterans showed signs of PTSD and depression.[65]

CURRENT SITUATION

Arresting the Problem

Several new ordinances in Hawaii aim to crack down on the growing number of homeless people, seen as a threat to tourism — the economic lifeblood of Oahu Island, home to Honolulu, Pearl Harbor and the famous Waikiki beaches.

One law makes it a crime to sit or lie on sidewalks in the Waikiki area, punishable by a $1,000 fine and up to 30 days in jail. Another law makes it a petty misdemeanor to urinate or defecate on Waikiki's streets or in other public places on the island.

These realities clash with the island paradise image promoted by tourism business leaders. "There's an expectation for Waikiki, for Hawaii. It's a dream," said Helene "Sam" Shenkus, marketing director of the Royal Hawaiian Center, a popular shopping mall. "And because they're families, and it's their money, they don't have to come here."[66]

Honolulu Mayor Kirk Caldwell pushed through the ordinances after announcing measures to open more public restrooms and add more shelter space for homeless people. Still, Oahu has 4,400 beds for an estimated homeless population of 4,700.

The County of Honolulu, which includes the entire island, is planning to expand homeless shelter space, and when proposing the measures Caldwell described them in humane, rather than punitive, terms. But the American Civil Liberties Union of Hawaii said the "sit-lie" ordinance criminalizes "basic human functions [and] in the absence of options for shelter violates the Eight Amendment prohibition against cruel and unusual punishment."[67]

While Honolulu's status as a tourism mecca made its homelessness crackdown newsworthy, less glamorous cities have been adopting similar measures for years, especially after the Ninth U.S. Circuit Court of Appeals in 1996 rejected a challenge to Seattle's ordinance banning aggressive panhandling and sitting or lying on downtown sidewalks at certain times.[68]

According to the National Law Center on Homelessness & Poverty, 53 percent of U.S. cities now ban sitting or lying in certain public places; 65 percent prohibit loitering in specific places; 43 percent prohibit sleeping in vehicles; 57 percent bar camping in certain public places and 34 percent ban all camping within city limits.

Although such anti-homelessness laws may restore some degree of order in cities, they can have other consequences. A mentally ill homeless man shot and killed by police in Albuquerque last March was illegally camping in the Sandia Mountain foothills at the eastern edge of town. The shooting of James Boyd, 38, added to discontent over the police department's reliance on force and raised questions about the effectiveness of services for homeless people with mental illness.[69]

The Rev. Russell "Rusty" Smith, an Episcopal priest who is executive director of the St. Martin's Hospitality Center in Albuquerque, which offers a variety of aid to the homeless, but not overnight shelter, said Boyd had frequented the center but had refused services. Smith said he couldn't disclose details of Boyd's history. But schizophrenics who take medication often quit when they feel better, Smith added. In any event, "the reason that he was up in the hills is that he felt safe there," Smith said.

Ordinances designed to keep the homeless out of downtowns and parks often are enacted in response to citizens who say they feel threatened by the proximity of large numbers of homeless people. In San Francisco, enforcement of the city's anti-homelessness ordinances is lax, and public urination and defecation and screaming at passersby is common, according to the *San Francisco Chronicle*. "If you're very tolerant of inappropriate behavior, you're pretty likely to keep getting more of it," Bill McConnell, a former behavioral health division staffer for the city, told the newspaper in June.[70]

But Tars of the National Law Center on Homelessness & Poverty says, "Criminalizing [homelessness] is at least three times as costly as providing shelter or housing." However, officials would have to allocate a budget line to housing or shelter, he points out, while the costs of criminalization can be hidden in police, court and emergency room budgets.

In any case, not all municipal enforcement efforts to curb homelessness are successful in the courts. In June, the Ninth U.S. Circuit Court of Appeals threw out a Los Angeles ban on living in vehicles.[71]

Alternate Approach

Los Angeles, as it happens, has embarked on an anti-homelessness strategy that marks a break with its own past and with enforcement-heavy options chosen by other cities.

"I don't consider homelessness breaking the law," Los Angeles Police Capt. Mike Oreb told the *Los Angeles Times*. "We're not the homeless police."[72]

In September, a month after Los Angeles city and county launched a drive to remove health hazards and provide immediate help to the 3,500 homeless people who live on Skid Row, officials said the effort had succeeded in providing emergency housing for 42 people; removing 3.5 tons of waste and hazardous material,

Is Housing First the best approach to ending homelessness?

YES
Nan Roman
*President and CEO, National
Alliance to End Homelessness*

Written for *CQ Researcher*, October 2014

Research indicates that Housing First is the most effective and least costly way to end homelessness for a majority of people. The strategy, which helps people experiencing homelessness to quickly obtain housing, supported with rental assistance and services, eliminates lengthy and costly stays in homeless programs. Data indicate that Housing First prevents relapses into homelessness better than any other approach.

Housing First is based on two premises: that homelessness is traumatic and damaging and should be as brief as possible, and that all people benefit from the stability of a home. The importance of a home is backed by evidence. The Centers for Disease Control and Prevention found that housing is essential to good health. Children do better in school when they have a permanent place to live, and services and treatment are more effective when people are in a home.

For families, homelessness is typically an economic issue. They are poor, and housing is expensive. In the past we addressed their homelessness by providing a temporary place to stay and social services that did little to help them with their immediate problem — the lack of a home. Today, Housing First for families reverses this process by helping families move back into housing after a short stay in a shelter and then providing them with services. It works. Housing First shortens the time families are homeless by up to 50 percent and does a better job of preventing returns to shelter than any other approach we have tried.

Housing First also works for those with more persistent problems. A minority of homeless people, mostly single adults, are disabled. It is neither realistic nor humane to expect them to address their challenges while living in shelters or on the streets. Housing First gets them into permanent supportive housing — housing with services attached — and studies indicate that it is significantly less expensive than leaving them on the street ($29,000 a year per person less in one Seattle cost study).

There is, of course, no one-size-fits-all solution to any problem, and Housing First is no exception. Youths and young parents experiencing homelessness, as well as people who need a sober recovery environment and some victims of domestic violence, may benefit from specialized transitional housing.

But on the whole, people who become homeless want, and need, to be housed again. And that is exactly what Housing First does.

NO
Ralph da Costa Nunez
*President and CEO, Institute for
Children, Poverty & Homelessness*

Written for *CQ Researcher*, October 2014

As an across-the-board solution to the problem of homelessness, no. Individuals and families become homeless for a variety of reasons, and to assume that one approach is going to work for everyone is misguided.

Housing First is a well-intentioned approach: get people out of shelter and into housing as quickly as possible. However, the implementation of a Housing First approach has varied widely between communities and among various populations, and it has had some unintended consequences.

For chronically homeless individuals, Housing First has usually meant placement into housing with long-term assistance, such as permanent supportive housing with ongoing services. Once placed, individuals have a reasonable expectation that they will be able to remain housed.

However, for families, this is simply not the case. For them, Housing First has generally taken the form of rapid rehousing: usually a voucher or subsidy that offers short-term rental support, as well as help finding housing. Services are usually limited in scope and duration, if they exist at all, and rarely address the underlying causes of their homelessness. For some families, this is the right amount of support. But for many others who struggle with limited educations and job skills, domestic violence or mental health challenges, rapid rehousing offers at best only brief stability.

New York City has spent almost 10 years and unknown millions of dollars rapidly rehousing families. There is daily proof that this approach does not work. Two-thirds of all families who enter a shelter have been there before. It is hard to argue that these families were ever truly helped or cost-effectively rehoused the first time around.

Although proponents of rapid rehousing often claim impressive success rates, these outcomes are usually conveniently measured at the six- or 12-month mark, while rental supports are still in place. The real proof of success will be if these families remain housed over the long term. Until those results are measured, governments will continue spending millions of dollars on an unproven idea. Only time and data will tell.

Sadly, the unintended consequences of Housing First for America's 1.8 million homeless children are yet to come. Housing instability has proven not only to have negative effects on their education and health, but also increases the likelihood that they may themselves become homeless as adults. When Housing First puts the long-term needs of families last, the more important question to ask is, Can we afford to pay that price?

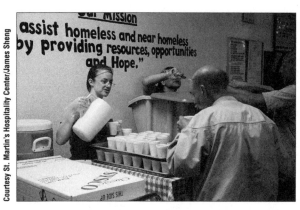

St. Martin's Hospitality Center in Albuquerque, N.M., the state's biggest service center for the homeless, does not provide housing but offers other assistance, such as hot meals and substance-abuse counseling.

including syringes, needles and knives; and granting approval for six people to obtain permanent housing.[73]

The Skid Row sweep also identified 80 people who needed immediate medical care and 27 who required mental health attention.[74]

The Operation Healthy Streets project will involve further sweeps of the area, both to remove trash and provide immediate services such as mental health appointments and enrollment in Medicaid, the state-run, federally subsidized health insurance program for low-income Americans.[75]

Some experienced police officers had been calling for a new approach, one that doesn't rely on police to be mental health workers. "The police have been asked for years to be the answer to the issues stemming from mental illness in the communities we serve," Deon Joseph, a Los Angeles Police Department senior lead officer with 16 years' service on Skid Row, wrote in the *Los Angeles Downtown News*.

"It is not the LAPD that has failed the mentally ill or the public," he wrote. "It is our society that has failed them. A society that has closed down hospitals. A system that is slow to create more housing-plus-care locations."[76]

OUTLOOK

"A Human Right"

Homelessness experts have accumulated vast experience in human suffering. But some of them are hopeful, citing the new federal emphasis on ending homelessness as a

recognition that homelessness should not be seen as an unsolvable problem.

"We have been doing a lot of work on housing as a human right, and after many years of feeling that we were banging our heads against the wall, the federal government has become more responsive [to our argument]," says Tars of the National Law Center on Homelessness & Poverty. He cites the U.S. Interagency Council on Homelessness' adoption of the doctrine.[77]

Eventually, Tars says, acknowledgment of housing as a fundamental right will combine with the pressure created by the shortage of affordable housing to force the government to fill the gap. "We don't have to go all the way to subsidized housing or public housing for every American," he says. "It can be done in a market-based system, with a safety net that ensures that no one is without that essential human need."

Tars and others advocate getting the business sector involved by providing incentives for builders to construct affordable rental housing — similar to the mortgage interest income tax deduction that encourages taxpayers to buy a house.

"The private sector is very good at building housing," Sheila Crowley, president and CEO of the National Low Income Housing Coalition, said in a telephone conference call for journalists in March. But under current conditions, she added, "if you could make money housing people [with very low incomes], somebody would have figured out how to do that by now. You can't make money at it. It has to have a public subsidy in order to be able to achieve that goal."

If the amount homeowners can deduct in mortgage interest payments were reduced even slightly, she said, the resulting increased revenues could be used to "solve the housing problems of the very poorest."[78]

Other developments are perhaps more promising. Smith of St. Martin's Hospitality Center said the Affordable Care Act (ACA) — known as "Obamacare" — has made an enormous and immediate difference to the homeless men and women he sees by expanding eligibility for access to Medicaid, reducing reliance on a local nonprofit, Albuquerque Health-Care for the Homeless. "It has been life-changing," he says. "A year and a half ago, most of our clients received medical care through Health-Care for the Homeless and the emergency room, and when they were dealing with a chronic illness they didn't go. Now, at least 30 percent of our clients have signed up with the ACA."

Gagliardi of HAPHousing in Springfield, Mass., points to a small resurgence of jobs that pay more than minimum wage. "This area used to be known for precision manufacturing, then it all went away," he says. "Now it's coming back, and they can't find enough qualified people. Community colleges and vocational schools are out to produce them. If, in fact, there really is a return to work for people at a decent wage, that will make a huge difference."

Culhane of the University of Pennsylvania praises the development of rapid rehousing and permanent supportive housing projects. "From the treatment perspective, these are very good cures," he says. "We need to scale that up, and we are seeing that happen incrementally every year."

Da Costa Nunez of the Institute for Children, Poverty & Homelessness in New York is similarly optimistic about the centers operated by Homes for the Homeless, a nonprofit that he also heads, which combine transitional housing with after-school and jobs programs. The nonprofit already operates four "family inns" along those lines for New York City.

The institute also is building a major center in the Bronx, whose job training efforts will include an on-site culinary training institute as well as educational and child-care programs open to the surrounding community. "We are not building shelters," he says. "We are building something that is part of the community. It's time to take the word 'shelter' out and think of it as a residential community resource center."

Yet the poverty underlying homelessness remains severe. "We need to

Statement of Ownership Management, Circulation

Act of Aug. 12, 1970: Section 3685, Title 39, United States Code

Title of Publication: CQ Researcher. Date of filing: October 1, 2014. Frequency of issue: Weekly (Except for 3/28, 5/23, 7/4, 8/15, 8/22, 11/28, 12/19, 12/26/14). No. of issues published annually: 44. Annual subscription price for high schools: $1,077. Annual subscription price for college/university: $1,162. Location of known office of publication: SAGE Publications, Inc., 2455 Teller Road, Thousand Oaks, CA 91320. Names and addresses of publisher, editor and managing editor: Publisher, SAGE Publications, Inc., 2455 Teller Road, Thousand Oaks, CA 91320; Managing Editor, Thomas J. Billitteri, CQ Press, an imprint of SAGE Publications, Inc., 2300 N Street, N.W., Suite 800, Washington, D.C. 20037. Owner: SAGE Publications, Inc., McCune Inter-Vivos Trust, David F. McCune, 2455 Teller Road, Thousand Oaks, CA 91320. Known bondholders, mortgagees and other security holders owning or holding 1 percent or more of total amount of bonds, mortgages or other securities: None.

Extent and Nature of Circulation	Average Number of Copies of Each Issue During Preceding 12 months	Actual Number of Copies of Single Issue Published Nearest to Filing Date
A. Total number of copies printed (Net press run)	476	469
B. Paid and/or requested circulation		
(1) Paid/requested outside-county mail subscriptions stated on Form 3541	374	369
(2) Paid in-county subscriptions stated on Form 3541	0	0
(3) Sales through dealers and carriers, street vendors, counter sales, and other non-USPS paid distribution	0	0
(4) Other classes mailed through the USPS	0	0
C. Total paid and/or requested circulation	374	369
D. Free distribution by mail (Samples, complimentary, and other free copies)		
(1) Outside-county as stated on Form 3541	0	0
(2) In-county as stated on Form 3541	0	0
(3) Other classes mailed through the USPS	0	0
E. Free distribution outside the mail (Carriers or other means)	0	0
F. Total free distribution	0	0
G. Total distribution	374	369
H. Copies not distributed	102	100
I. Total	476	469
J. Percent paid and/or requested circulation	100%	100%

revisit the adequacy of welfare payments to families, especially those with preschool-age kids," Culhane says. "Poverty among young families remains a problem. But these are things that can be solved."

Others stress the need to expand the stock of affordable housing. "If we don't do something about that, people are going to keep losing housing and being homeless," says Roman of the National Alliance to End Homelessness. "But I do think we could end homelessness in the way we know it now, and make it a very brief, rare one-time-only event."

NOTES

1. Quoted in Adam Nagourney, "Honolulu Shores Up Tourism With Crackdown on Homeless," *The New York Times*, June 22, 2014, http://tinyurl.com/pcmuvcm.

2. "The 2013 Annual Homelessness Assessment Report (AHAR) to Congress: Part 1, Point-in-Time Estimates of Homelessness," U.S. Department of Housing and Urban Development, p. 7, http://tinyurl.com/qd89wa8.

3. "2012 Annual Homeless Assessment Report (AHAR) to Congress, Volume II," U.S. Department of Housing and Urban Development, September 2013, pp. 1-7, 3-7, http://tinyurl.com/l6j268s.

4. Kim Hopper, *et al.*, "Estimating Numbers of Unsheltered Homeless People Through Plant-Capture and Postcount Survey Methods," *American Journal of Public Health*, August 2008, http://tinyurl.com/oan68g3.

5. "Homelessness Assistance," U.S. Department of Housing and Urban Development, undated, http://tinyurl.com/d5kejj3.

6. "Changes in the HUD Definition of 'Homeless,'" National Alliance to End Homelessness, Jan. 18, 2012, http://tinyurl.com/pswbcak. For background, see Marcia Clemmitt, "Homeless Students," *CQ Researcher*, April 5, 2013, pp. 305-328.

7. *Ibid.* "Changes in the HUD Definition," p. 41; "The 2012 Annual Homeless Assessment Report to Congress," Vol. II, *op. cit.*, pp. 3-14.

8. "Education for Homeless Children and Youth Program: Consolidated State Performance Report Data," National Center for Homeless Education, September 2014, http://tinyurl.com/ktbhbhh; "Laws & Guidance/Elementary & Secondary Education — Part C — Homeless Education," U.S. Department of Education, updated Sept. 15, 2004, http://tinyurl.com/36jhv5x.

9. "Opening Doors: Federal Strategic Plan to Prevent and End Homelessness," U.S. Interagency Council on Homelessness, 2010, p. 4, http://tinyurl.com/n6z52dn.

10. "Homeless Emergency Assistance and Rapid Transition to Housing: Continuum of Care Program, A Rule by the Housing and Urban Development Department on 7/31/2012," *Federal Register*, July 31, 2012, http://tinyurl.com/pro9rwa.

11. "Interim Report: Family Options Study," U.S. Department of Housing and Urban Development, March 2013, p. xiv, http://tinyurl.com/mtohsek; Martha R. Burt, *et al.*, "Homelessness: Programs and the People They Serve," Urban Institute, August 1999, p. 29, http://tinyurl.com/lx7o62u.

12. *Ibid.*, "Interim Report," p. 56.

13. Maureen A. Hayes, Megan Zonneville and Ellen Bassuk, "The SHIFT Study: Final Report," National Center on Family Homelessness, 2010, pp. 18-19, http://tinyurl.com/m3t9uhc.

14. "Rapid Re-Housing: A History and Core Components," National Alliance to End Homelessness, April 22, 2014, http://tinyurl.com/n8u5w7p.

15. Libby Perl, *et al.*, "Homelessness: Targeted Federal Programs and Recent Legislation," Congressional Research Service, Feb. 3, 2014, p. 23, http://tinyurl.com/l5x3tma; "Housing First," National Alliance to End Homelessness, undated, http://tinyurl.com/qcu7qvw; "McKinney-Vento Homeless Assistance Success Stories," National Alliance to End Homelessness, February 2006, http://tinyurl.com/n3ubo5q.

16. "Rapid Re-Housing: A History and Core Components," National Alliance to End Homelessness, April 22, 2014, http://tinyurl.com/n8u5w7p; "Rapid Re-Housing: Creating Programs that Work," National Alliance to End Homelessness, July 2009, pp. 41-43, http://tinyurl.com/k887hp5.

17. "Homelessness Assistance," U.S. Housing and Urban Development Department, *op. cit.*; Perl, *et al.*, *op. cit.*, summary, p. 13.

18. "Chart Book: Federal Housing Spending Is Poorly Matched to Need," Center on Budget and Policy Priorities, Dec. 18, 2013, http://tinyurl.com/nxgpdyc; "Housing America's Future: New Directions for National Policy," Housing Commission, Bipartisan Policy Center, February 2013, pp. 10-11, http://tinyurl.com/mm9tum6.

19. Quoted in Steve LeBlanc, "In Mass., A Tough Quest to End Family Homelessness," The Associated Press, Jan. 1, 2014, http://tinyurl.com/k435udf.

20. "Housing America's Future," *op. cit.*, p. 11; "Policy Basics: Section 8 Project-Based Rental Assistance," Center on Budget and Policy Priorities, Jan. 25, 2013, http://tinyurl.com/qe4x8eo; "Policy Basics: The Housing Choice Voucher Program," Center on Budget and Policy Priorities, May 14, 2014, http://tinyurl.com/mrjcxkm.

21. "Rep. Jeb Hensarling Holds a Hearing on Sustainable Housing Finance System," House Committee on Financial Services, CQ Transcriptions, July 18, 2013.

22. *Ibid.*

23. *Ibid.*

24. Peter Charles Hoffer, *Law and People in Colonial America* (1998), p. 8.

25. Martha R. Burt, *Over the Edge: The Growth of Homelessness in the 1980s* (1993), p. 3.

26. James N. Gregory, " 'The Dust Bowl Migration' Poverty Stories, Race Stories," http://faculty.washington.edu/gregoryj/dust%20bowl%20migration.htm.

27. Woody Guthrie, "I Ain't Got No Home," 1938, http://tinyurl.com/plt3dp6; John Steinbeck, *The Grapes of Wrath* (1939).

28. James N. Gregory, *American Exodus: The Dust Bowl Migration and Okie Culture in California* (1989), pp. 98-99; *Edwards v. California*, 314 U.S. 160 (1941), http://tinyurl.com/mbbzyha.

29. Ella Howard, *Homeless: Poverty and Place in Urban America* (2013), Kindle edition, no page numbers.

30. Neil Larry Shumsky, *Homelessness: A Documentary and Reference Guide* (2012), pp. 147-151; "CCC Brief History," CCC Legacy, undated, http://tinyurl.com/cbgc6oz.

31. Quoted in *ibid.*, p. 150.

32. Chris Koyanagi, "Learning From History: Deinstitutionalization of People with Mental Illness As Precursor to Long-Term Care Reform," Henry J. Kaiser Family Foundation, August 2007, http://tinyurl.com/lxmwgp6; Richard D. Lyons, "How Release of Mental Patients Began," *The New York Times*, Oct. 30, 1984, http://tinyurl.com/b894wpq.

33. "Remarks on signing mental retardation facilities and community health centers construction bill, Oct. 31, 1963," John F. Kennedy Presidential Library and Museum, http://tinyurl.com/lget9yx; Martin Weil, "Rosemary Kennedy, 86; President's Disabled Sister," *The Washington Post*, Jan. 8, 2005, http://tinyurl.com/yb47jgo.

34. Koyangi, *op. cit.*, p. 4.

35. E. Fuller Torrey, "Ronald Reagan's shameful legacy: Violence, the homeless, mental illness," Salon, Sept. 29, 2013, http://tinyurl.com/lr4s422.

36. *Ibid.*; for background see Barbara Mantel, "Mental Health Policy," *CQ Researcher*, May 10, 2013, pp. 425-448.

37. Quoted in Howard, *op. cit.*

38. Torrey, *op. cit.*

39. For background, see "The S&L Crisis: A Chrono-Bibliography," Federal Deposit Insurance Corporation, http://tinyurl.com/masdhwx.

40. Howard, *op. cit.*; Marc Labonte, "The 2007-2009 Recession: Similarities to and Differences from the Past," Congressional Research Service, Oct. 6, 2010, http://tinyurl.com/msqquca; David Kocieniewski, "Since 1980s, the Kindest of Tax Cuts for the Rich," *The New York Times*, Jan. 18, 2012, http://tinyurl.com/ou3tg6e; William A. Galston, "Stop Blaming the Tax Code for America's Inequality Problem," *The New Republic*, via Brookings Institution, April 19, 2012, http://tinyurl.com/qgzmp78; "History of the US Tax System," U.S. Department of the Treasury, undated, http://tinyurl.com/79oer4b.

41. Martha R. Burt, "Causes of the Growth of Homelessness During the 1980s," 1991, from "Understanding Homelessness: New Policy and

Research Perspectives," Fannie Mae Foundation, 1991, 1997, pp. 182-183, http://tinyurl.com/lrzckm2.

42. *Papachristou v. City of Jacksonville*, 405 U.S. 156 (1972), http://tinyurl.com/mh95nlp; ibid., Burt, "Causes of the Growth."

43. Quoted in Ian Frazier, "Hidden City," *The New Yorker*, Oct. 28, 2013, http://tinyurl.com/npr83gk; for background, see Peter Katel, "Housing the Homeless," *CQ Researcher*, Dec. 18, 2009, pp. 1053-1076.

44. *Ibid.*, Katel.

45. Shumsky, *op. cit.*, pp. 234-235; "Continuum of Care (CoC) Program," HUD Exchange, U.S. Housing and Urban Development Department, undated, http://tinyurl.com/o2myeut.

46. Rosemary Chapin, *Social Policy for Effective Practice: A Strengths Approach* (2010), p. 177; Maria Foscarinis, "Homelessness in America: A Human Rights Crisis," *Journal of Law in Society*, Wayne State University, 2012, p. 517, http://tinyurl.com/of6rrl2.

47. Libby Perl, *et al.*, "Homelessness: Targeted Federal Programs and Recent Legislation," Congressional Research Service, Feb. 3, 2014, pp. 22-24, http://tinyurl.com/l5x3tma.

48. Quoted in Derek Kravitz, "Homelessness Official Wins Praise With Focus on Permanent Housing," *The Washington Post*, Dec. 30, 2008, http://tinyurl.com/lbd766q.

49. *Ibid.*, pp. 23-24.

50. Jo Becker, Sheryl Gay Stolberg and Stephen Labaton, "Bush drive for home ownership fueled housing bubble," *The New York Times*, Dec. 21, 2008, http://tinyurl.com/7emvj3z.

51. "Foreclosure to Homelessness 2009: the forgotten victims of the subprime crisis," National Coalition for the Homeless, 2009, http://tinyurl.com/mknpp3.

52. "Eviction (Without) Notice: Renters and the Foreclosure Crisis," National Law Center on Homelessness & Poverty, December 2012, p. 6, http://tinyurl.com/l7ebrxa. Les Christie, "Record 3 million households hit with foreclosure in 2009," CNN Money, Jan. 14, 2010, http://tinyurl.com/ybqrkje.

53. Julia B. Isaacs, "The Ongoing Impact of Foreclosures on Children," Brookings Institution, April 2012,

pp. 5-6, http://tinyurl.com/pw8feh3; Julia Isaacs, [professional biography], Urban Institute, http://tinyurl.com/jvqauv7.

54. *Ibid.*, pp. 4-5; Christie, *op. cit.*

55. Perl, *et al.*, pp. 5-6.

56. *Ibid.*, pp. 24-25; "Opening Doors," *op. cit.*, p. 4.

57. *Ibid.*, "Opening Doors."

58. Michelle Obama, "Let's end veteran homelessness once and for all," McClatchy Newspapers, July 30, 2014, www.mcclatchydc.com/2014/07/30/234885_lets-end-veteran-homelessness.html?rh=1.

59. "The 2012 Annual Homeless Assessment Report to Congress, Vol. II," *op. cit.*, pp. 4-7.

60. Libby Perl, "Veterans and Homelessness," Congressional Research Service, Nov. 29, 2013, p. 39, http://tinyurl.com/n6sncq4.

61. Quoted in Erica E. Phillips and Ben Kesling, "Number of Homeless Veterans in the U.S. Falls Over Past Four Years," *The Wall Street Journal*, Aug. 26, 2014, http://tinyurl.com/mhw5dv2.

62. Quoted in Dave Philipps, "Many Veterans Adapt to a Strange World, One With Walls," *The New York Times*, Sept. 20, 2014, http://tinyurl.com/lfokh8h.

63. *Ibid.*; Phillips and Kesling, *op. cit.*; "Proposed Fiscal year 2015 Budget Fact Sheet: Homelessness Assistance, U.S. Interagency Council on Homelessness, undated, http://tinyurl.com/lnmb8lg.

64. Perl, "Veterans and Homelessness," *op. cit.*, pp. 12-14.

65. *Ibid.*, pp. 16-17.

66. Quoted in Cathy Bussewitz, "Honolulu Approves Plan to Move Homeless," The Associated Press (via *Minneapolis Star-Tribune*), Sept. 11, 2014, http://tinyurl.com/mnen5hz; Mileka Lincoln, "Mayor Caldwell signs homeless bills into law," KGMB, KHNL, Sep. 17, 2014, http://tinyurl.com/n22pxv7.

67. Quoted in Lincoln, *ibid.*, "Mayor Caldwell"; Kirk Caldwell, "Together we can resolve problem of homelessness in Honolulu," *Honolulu Star-Advertiser*, June 1, 2014, http://tinyurl.com/ok2g4rt; Bussewitz, *ibid.*

68. "A Dream Denied: The Criminalization of Homelessness in U.S. Cities, Case Summaries,"

National Coalition for the Homeless, National Law Center on Homelessness & Poverty, January 2006, http://tinyurl.com/ol32u9y; Heather Knight, "San Francisco looks to Seattle: Did sidewalk sitting ban help?" *San Francisco Chronicle*, in *Seattle Post-Intelligencer*, March 29, 2010, http://tinyurl.com/ohyjxef.

69. Russell Contreras, "Albuquerque Police Release New Video of James Boyd Shooting," The Associated Press (via *The Huffington Post*), June 12, 2014, http://tinyurl.com/qdozuvc; Rick Nathanson, "James Boyd's dark journey," *Albuquerque Journal*, March 30, 2014, http://tinyurl.com/knkw5rr.

70. Quoted in Heather Knight, "A decade of homelessness: Thousands in S.F, remain in crisis," *San Francisco Chronicle*, June 28, 2014, http://tinyurl.com/ncb94my.

71. Quoted in Maura Dolan and Gale Holland, "Appeals court panel ends L.A. ban on homeless living in vehicles," *Los Angeles Times*, June 19, 2014, http://tinyurl.com/oxfye5v.

72. Quoted in Gale Holland, "L.A. leaders are crafting new plan to help homeless on skid row," *Los Angeles Times*, July 15, 2014, http://tinyurl.com/kmsh8rg.

73. Gale Holland, "Skid row sweep finds many homeless with medical, psychiatric needs," *Los Angeles Times*, Sept. 11, 2014, http://tinyurl.com/o7c5d4p.

74. *Ibid.*

75. Holland, "L.A. leaders," *op. cit.*

76. Deon Joseph, "Skid Row Cop: Downtown Is in a Mental Health State of Emergency," *Los Angeles Downtown News*, June 30, 2014, http://tinyurl.com/nbh5ckq.

77. "U.S. Department of Housing and Urban Development Statement on the U.S. Participation in the United Nations' Universal Periodic Review," U.S. Department of Housing and Urban Development, 2010, http://tinyurl.com/qhec7kq.

78. "The National Low Income Housing Coalition Holds a Teleconference on a Report Regarding the Affordable Rental Housing Shortage," *SEC Wire*, March 24, 2014 (via Nexis).

BIBLIOGRAPHY
Selected Sources
Books

Howard, Ella, *Homeless: Poverty and Place in Urban America*, **University of Pennsylvania Press, 2013.**
A history professor at Armstrong State University in Savannah, Ga., chronicles homelessness and government responses to it from the late 19th century on, focusing on New York's Bowery.

Reynalds, Jeremy, *A Sheltered Life: Take It to the Streets*, **West Bow Press, 2013.**
The English-born founder of a homeless shelter in Albuquerque recounts his own brief homelessness and describes the lives of some of the people he and his colleagues have helped.

Shumsky, Neil Larry, *Homelessness: A Documentary and Reference Guide*, **Greenwood, 2012.**
A history professor at Virginia Tech in Blacksburg depicts the course of homelessness throughout the country's history.

Articles

Frazier, Ian, "Hidden City," *The New Yorker*, **Oct. 28, 2013, http://tinyurl.com/npr83gk.**
A detailed first-person account by a magazine writer describes the lives of New York City's homeless.

Joseph, Deon, "Skid Row Cop: Downtown Is in a Mental Health State of Emergency," *Los Angeles Downtown News*, **June 30, 2014, http://tinyurl.com/nbh5ckq.**
A Los Angeles police officer writes about the horrific conditions in which thousands of the city's mentally ill homeless people live, calling it an indictment of American society.

Knight, Heather, "A decade of homelessness: Thousands in S.F. remain in crisis," *San Francisco Chronicle*, **June 27, 2014, http://tinyurl.com/l8s7bye.**
Despite a 10-year-old pledge by the city's then-mayor to end homelessness, San Francisco continues to struggle with the problem.

Nathanson, Rick, "James Boyd's dark journey," *Albuquerque Journal*, **March 30, 2014, http://tinyurl.com/knkw5rr.**

A mentally ill homeless man shot to death by Albuquerque police had shuttled between jails and a psychiatric hospital for years.

Olsen, Hanna Brooks, "Homelessness and the Impossibility of a Good Night's Sleep," *The Atlantic*, Aug. 14, 2014, http://tinyurl.com/oykcjn7.
A Seattle writer explores an unknown facet of homelessness: the debilitating effects of never getting a restful night's sleep, whether the person is in a shelter or on the street.

Phillips, Erica E., and Ben Kesling, "Number of Homeless Veterans in the U.S. Falls Over Past Four Years," *The Wall Street Journal*, Aug. 26, 2014, http://tinyurl.com/mhw5dv2.
The number of homeless veterans has dropped sharply, but ending it by next year (as the Obama administration wants) seems unlikely.

Shenoy, Rupa, "Homeless in motels: How some families are hanging on," New England Center for Investigative Reporting, in the *Worcester Telegram & Gazette*, Feb. 23, 2014, http://tinyurl.com/qdfnafk.
Journalists investigate the difficulties of family life in a motel room and the Massachusetts state government's attempts to meet its obligation to shelter homeless families.

Reports and Studies

"Meeting the Child Care Needs of Homeless Families — How Do States Stack Up?" Institute for Children, Poverty & Homelessness, July 2014, http://tinyurl.com/lz8zsr2.

A New York-based think tank reports that child care, needed by homeless mothers who must work to acquire housing, receives little attention in most states' homelessness programs.

"No Safe Place: The Criminalization of Homelessness in U.S. Cities," National Law Center on Homelessness & Poverty, July 2014, http://tinyurl.com/plgfed2.
Cities are passing laws that effectively penalize homelessness, reports a Washington-based advocacy organization that opposes the trend both as inhumane and a waste of money.

Abt Associates, "Family Options Study, Interim Report," U.S. Housing and Urban Development Department, March 2013, http://tinyurl.com/19cxnpx.
The first installment of a study of more than 2,300 homeless families reports on their characteristics and the services that are available to them. A second installment is intended to provide data on which services are most effective as permanent solutions to homelessness.

Henry, Meghan, Dr. Alvaro Cortes, and Sean Morris, "The 2013 Annual Homeless Assessment Report to Congress, Part I: Point-in-Time Estimates of Homelessness," http://tinyurl.com/qd89wa8, and "The 2012 Annual Homeless Assessment Report to Congress, Vol. II: Estimates of Homelessness in the United States," Office of Community Planning and Development, U.S. Department of Housing and Urban Development, September 2013, http://tinyurl.com/l6j268s.
These annual reports detail point-in-time counts and data on shelter use.

For More Information

Institute for Children, Poverty & Homelessness, 44 Cooper Square, New York, NY 10003; 212-358-8086; www.icphusa .org. Think tank that researches links between homelessness and poverty and its effects on families.

National Alliance to End Homelessness, 1518 K St., N.W., 2nd Floor, Washington, DC 20005; 202-638-1526; www .endhomelessness.org. Advocacy group and research center that helped popularize the idea of ending homelessness, rather than simply sheltering the homeless.

National Center on Family Homelessness, c/o American Institutes for Research, 201 Jones Rd., Waltham, MA 02451; 781-373-7080; familyhomelessness.org. Think tank that explores causes and effects of homelessness on parents (single mothers, for the most part) and children, and effectiveness of treatment methods.

National Law Center on Homelessness & Poverty, 2000 M St., N.W., Washington, DC 20036; 202-638-2535; www .nlchp.org. Opposes laws that penalize homeless people; advocates that housing be defined as a human right.

U.S. Department of Veterans Affairs, 810 Vermont Ave., N.W., Washington, DC 20420; 877-424-3838; www.va.gov/ homeless. Runs a separate site with information on programs aimed at homeless vets.

U.S. Interagency Council on Homelessness, 1275 1st St., N.E., Washington, DC 20002; 202-708-4663; www.uscih .gov. The coordinating arm of federal anti-homelessness efforts that publishes updates of strategy on fighting homelessness.

12

Paying
College Athletes

Reed Karaim

Northwestern's Warren Long celebrates after blocking a punt in a game against Maine in Evanston, Ill., on Sept. 21, 2013. In a potentially historic decision, a regional director of the National Labor Relations Board concluded that Northwestern players spend so much time on football that they should be considered university employees. Results of an April 25 vote by the players on whether to unionize may not be known for months.

Getty Images/Chicago Tribune/John J. Kim

From *CQ Researcher*,
July 11, 2014.

O n the morning of April 25, the 76 scholarship players on the Northwestern University football team may have fundamentally changed college athletics: They voted on whether to unionize.

The unprecedented vote followed a regional National Labor Relations Board (NLRB) ruling that, because of the demands of their sport, the players were employees of the university.[1]

The ruling applies only to private schools, and the results of the vote may not be known for months. Because Northwestern, in Evanston, Ill., has appealed the ruling to the national NLRB, the ballot boxes were impounded to await that judgment as well as possible court appeals.[2]

If the initial decision is upheld and if players voted for a union, they will be able to bargain collectively over compensation and workplace rules. But regardless of the vote, the NLRB ruling marks a significant shift in the perception of college athletics. The regional NLRB director concluded that the time Northwestern players spend on football — 40 to 50 hours a week during the season, even more during training camp — and other special demands placed on them mean they are not primarily students who play sports, but laborers working for the university.[3]

The ruling has reignited a long-simmering debate over whether college athletes, especially in the money-making sports of Division I football and basketball — the top tier of collegiate competition — deserve greater compensation for their efforts than scholarships. Some analysts say these athletes deserve to be paid, especially in light of how much money — billions of dollars from TV contracts alone — is being made off their labor. Others say paying players would destroy college athletics: profitable programs could recruit the best athletes,

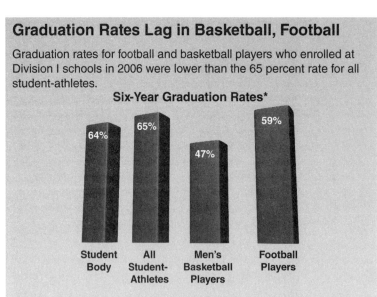

Graduation Rates Lag in Basketball, Football

Graduation rates for football and basketball players who enrolled at Division I schools in 2006 were lower than the 65 percent rate for all student-athletes.

Six-Year Graduation Rates*

- Student Body: 64%
- All Student-Athletes: 65%
- Men's Basketball Players: 47%
- Football Players: 59%

* Federal six-year graduation rate for students enrolling in 2006 at Division I schools; football players are those in the Football Bowl Subdivision schools, which are the top athletic tier of Division I, including both public and private schools.

Source: NCAA Research Staff, "Trends in Graduation-Success Rates and Federal Graduation Rates at NCAA Division I Institutions," NCAA, October 2013, pp. 20, 23, http://tinyurl.com/ngs93le.

cost of going to school — current athletic scholarships don't cover all expenses — along with better health care and more support for their academic work.

But other advocates go further, saying athletes warrant payment that better reflects their importance to school athletic programs. The NCAA refused requests for an interview for this *CQ Researcher* report.

The stakes are high for both athletes and institutions of higher learning. College sports in America is a multibillion-dollar industry. The most recent TV contract for rights to show the NCAA March Madness Basketball Tournament was for $10.8 billion over 14 years. [5] And broadcasters pay the top college football conferences — groups of schools that regularly play against each other — more than $200 million each annually, with each team in some conferences receiving $20 million or more. [6] Playing in a post-season bowl game brings in even more millions. The Southeastern Conference (SEC) alone received nearly $52 million last season in bowl game payouts — revenue the schools split, largely from TV contracts. [7]

The money has rippled down through college athletics, with escalating coaches' salaries and construction of bigger and better sports facilities. Top coaches earn salaries in the millions of dollars, often many times the salary of their university's president. Nick Saban, coach of the University of Alabama's football team, the Crimson Tide, recently received a raise to $6.9 million a year.[8] In 2013, the university's president, Judy Bonner, earned $535,000.[9] Shortly after Saban's contract was announced, the University of Kentucky gave men's basketball coach John Calipari a new seven-year contract worth $7.5 million a year.[10] Salaries for athletic directors and assistant coaches also have soared.

In addition, top schools have embarked on building sprees to construct new practice and playing facilities, part of a nonstop competition to lure the best athletes and thus more fans. Brand-new McLane Stadium at

creating ever-greater competitive differences, and schools would be forced to trim or end unprofitable sports.

The National Collegiate Athletic Association (NCAA) — the powerful nonprofit organization that makes and enforces rules for college sports — is opposed to paying athletes. "Most university presidents, most college presidents that I've talked to, are not particularly interested in continuing sports as they exist now if [college athletes] are going to be converted to employees that are hired," Mark Emmert, NCAA president, said earlier this year. [4]

But Ramogi Huma, a former college football player and president of the College Athletes Players Association (CAPA), the group seeking to unionize players, says the NLRB ruling exposes the "myth" of amateurism for big-time college athletics. "They are already paid," he says. "They're paid to play. The schools require them to provide a service for receiving their scholarships. So the question is what is fair compensation and treatment for their services."

CAPA is not asking that college players be paid a professional salary, Huma says, but that they receive the full

Baylor University, in Waco, Texas, scheduled to open in August, exemplifies the high-end upgrades. It will have a new locker room, a state-of-the-art scoreboard, 39 premium suites with catered food service and 79 "loge boxes" that provide a semi-private viewing experience for a premium price.[11] "I'm not kidding you. It's going to change the whole image of Baylor," said coach Art Briles.[12]

Supporters of high-profile sports programs say athletic prominence helps with university fundraising and student recruitment, but critics say the money athletics raises goes overwhelmingly to athletics, not academics, and can even hurt other efforts by forcing senior administrators to spend extra time wooing sports supporters.

In contrast, the lifestyle of college athletes remains highly restricted by NCAA rules and guidelines established by individual athletic programs. Full scholarships pay tuition and room and board but can fall short of the complete cost of attending school, by several thousand dollars annually at some institutions. During the NCAA tournament last April, Shabazz Napier, star of the national champion Huskies basketball team at the University of Connecticut, discussed the impact of scholarship limits, which, coupled with his lack of money, he said, sometimes left him short of food.

"There are hungry nights that I go to bed and I'm starving," Napier said.[13] At the time, NCAA rules restricted the meals and snacks that could be provided for scholarship athletes.

Many athletic scholarships are granted only for one year, renewed at the discretion of coaches. A player who doesn't perform can find himself cut loose. Medical care most often does not extend beyond college, and a player who is seriously injured can face considerable long-term expenses.

In addition, while under scholarship, athletes are subject to an array of NCAA rules that restrict their ability to earn outside income, accept gifts or profit by selling autographs

Athletes Could Be Worth Big Money

If top college basketball and football players were paid like professionals, they would make hundreds of thousands of dollars per year, according to an advocacy group that favors paying athletes. For instance, under the systems used to share revenue between players and teams in the National Basketball Association and National Football League, a University of Louisville men's 2011-12 basketball team member who received a $17,000 scholarship would have been paid $1.6 million, and a University of Texas football player who received a $21,000 scholarship would have made nearly $570,000.

Market Value for Top Student Athletes, Basketball, 2011-12		
School	**Market Value per Player**	**Value of Athletic Scholarship**	**Difference**
Louisville	$1,632,103	$17,370	$1,614,733
Syracuse	$995,722	$52,244	$943,478
Duke	$987,144	$55,245	$931,899
UNC	$923,510	$17,629	$905,881
Kentucky	$830,718	$19,928	$810,790

Market Value for Top Student Athletes, Football, 2011-12		
School	**Market Value per Player**	**Value of Athletic Scholarship**	**Difference**
Texas	$567,922	$21,090	$546,832
Michigan	$466,145	$23,150	$442,995
Alabama	$448,554	$20,481	$428,073
Auburn	$442,167	$19,790	$402,377
Georgia	$410,236	$19,258	$390,978

Source: Ramogi Huma and Ellen J. Staurowsky, "The $6 Billion Heist: Robbing College Athletes Under the Guise of Amateurism," National College Players Association and Drexel University Sport Management, 2012, p. 13, http://tinyurl.com/nu2khpt.

or memorabilia connected to their role as a player. They must maintain a minimum grade-point average, which differs depending on the institution, and make progress toward graduating based on a schedule established by the NCAA.[14] Violating the rules can cost athletes their chance to compete and put scholarships at risk.

Until recently, players also haven't shared in the financial rewards collected by universities and the NCAA from merchandising that traded on the players' popularity. Universities and the NCAA make millions of dollars selling video game rights, jerseys, T-shirts and more. But players had not received a share of this money until this June, when the NCAA and EA Sports, the video game maker, agreed to pay $20 million and $40 million, respectively, to former college athletes whose likenesses have been used in video games.[15]

Those payments resulted from out-of-court settlements in two class-action lawsuits among several brought to give college athletes a share of the money being made from college sports. In the most highly publicized case, still unresolved, former University of California-Los Angeles (UCLA) basketball player Ed O'Bannon is asking a U.S. District Court to strike down NCAA restrictions that prevent athletes from profiting off their name and likeness.[16]

For college athletes who succeed on the professional level, the rewards of the training and experience they gained in college can be considerable. But even in the best programs, only a small minority of football and basketball players end up playing professionally.[17]

Congress and a few states have considered legislation to liberalize scholarship rules and improve the treatment of college athletes, but the bills do not propose that students be paid like professional athletes.

Recently, the NCAA has made some changes it says are intended to bolster the success of "student-athletes on the playing field, in the classroom and in life after college."[18] Shortly following Napier's comment about going to bed hungry, the NCAA announced that all Division I student-athletes would be allowed unlimited meal benefits. NCAA President Emmert also has called for providing a $2,000 annual stipend to scholarship athletes to help them cover incidental expenses, although so far he has been unable to get the university presidents who control the NCAA to agree.

The NCAA and its supporters say such relatively modest changes could improve the situation for scholarship players while maintaining their amateur status. But critics say the changes fall short of providing equitable treatment, given the demands placed on players and the money now being made in college sports.

As the debate about the future of college sports continues, here are some of the key questions being considered:

Should college athletes be paid?

Most opponents of directly paying college athletes don't claim the current system is perfect. Many say they support more liberal scholarship benefits, including a stipend that provides players with enough money to cover the full cost of college. But they believe allowing athletes to collect a paycheck for playing would destroy the idea of the "student-athlete" and create several additional problems.

"It is my strong belief that universities should not be in the business of running professional teams and semi-pro teams," says Amy Perko, executive director of the Knight Commission on Intercollegiate Athletics, which was created in 1989 by the charitable Knight Foundation to keep college sports true to the educational mission of universities. Paying players would mean schools were essentially operating professional teams under the banner of an institution of higher learning, she says.

Instead, Perko says, the commission believes the college athletic system needs reform in the opposite direction: putting the "student" in student-athlete first by re-emphasizing academics. To that end, she adds, the commission supports giving students more time for classes and a greater chance of completing school with a meaningful degree.

However, those who support paying college athletes say college sports already are operated as professional businesses — but the only participants expected to be amateurs are the players. Richard Southall, director of the College Sports Research Institute at the University of South Carolina in Columbia, says the NCAA has tried to have it both ways by promoting a term the association originated: "the collegiate model" of athletics. "In the collegiate model, professionalism, and generating as much revenue as possible, is good, even morally justified," he says, "but it's immoral for the college athlete to get paid."

Southall says the demands placed on players at the top levels of college sports, particularly football and basketball, mean "they've been employees for a long time." He says they should be able to seek the best deal they can get for their labor. In non-revenue-producing sports, athletes might play for a scholarship or for free, but in sports that bring in millions of dollars, athletes would have a chance to negotiate for more. "In some sports, they'd get compensated, and in some they wouldn't, and that's okay," Southall says. "I don't know exactly what [compensation] would look like, but what I know is that college athletes should have the right to bargain for it."

But some analysts believe the current system provides adequate recompense for college athletes. "Colleges are already compensating their student athletes with tuition, room, board, coaching, nutritional support and physical trainers that can exceed $100,000 per year in value.

Student athletes are already paid, and the current system is pretty close to as fair as we are going to get," wrote Jeffrey Dorfman, a University of Georgia economist.[19]

However, an analysis by *FiveThirtyEight*, a statistics and polling website, found that the top college quarterbacks are worth more than $3 million annually to their schools.[20] Another study commissioned by the National College Players Association (NCPA), which advocates for better treatment of student-athletes, found that the value of scholarships falls far short of how much football and basketball players at the top schools would command on the open market.

Football players in the Football Bowl Subdivision of Division I (the top 125 schools) would receive an average of $178,500 annually for the years 2011-15, above and beyond their scholarships, while basketball players at those schools would receive $375,000 per year, according to the NCPA study, which was co-authored by Huma, founder and president of NCPA and also president of unionization advocate CAPA, and Ellen Staurowsky, a sports management professor at Drexel University in Philadelphia.[21]

"We should be past the time when we fall for the NCAA party line that suggests that a 'free education' is adequate compensation for college athletes who generate billions of dollars in revenue for corporate marketing and media partners," Staurowsky wrote.[22]

Some experts, however, say rewarding football and basketball players based on market value would be unfair to other athletes. Ann Mayo, director of the Center for Sport Management at Seton Hall University in South Orange, N.J., says athletes in other sports, such as swimming or track and field, are no less dedicated than those in the money-making sports. Yet because many athletes in the non-revenue-generating sports know they will not go pro, they concentrate on taking advantage of the educational opportunity provided by their scholarship.

"You're not going to pay everybody. There's not enough money for that," she says. "But there are a lot of student-athletes in other sports who love their sport, but also love the classes they are taking and are doing really well. These are the people who probably aren't going to get paid for all their hard work. On the surface, it looks like the people who are doing what they are supposed to be doing, who are the true student-athletes, are probably not going to get paid."

Top Division I coaches such as Nick Saban of the University of Alabama football team earn millions of dollars annually, reflecting the vast sums colleges with top teams receive from TV broadcasting rights. Saban received a raise recently to $6.9 million a year. Alabama President Judy Bonner's salary was $535,000 in 2013. Soon after, the University of Kentucky gave men's basketball coach John Calipari a new seven-year contract worth $7.5 million a year.

Kristi Dosh, ESPN's sports business reporter, says paying college athletes could destroy competitive balance, because the most successful schools would be able to offer much bigger paychecks. Pro sports uses a player draft process that favors the worst teams in order to maintain balance, she notes, but the less successful college teams would simply be left out in the cold.

Dosh also says paying players could run afoul of Title IX, the federal legislation that bars discrimination by gender in education. Paying just football or men's basketball players, she says, is likely to end in expensive litigation if female athletes aren't treated the same. "My understanding from talking to Title IX experts is . . . if you're going to give any kind of cash stipend, then you really have to do it across the board," Dosh says.[23]

But others say Title IX's requirement of equal educational opportunity, does not apply if some college athletes become university employees. "The argument that we can't pay our employees so we can provide opportunities through Title IX is an invalid labor law analysis," says the University of South Carolina's Southall.

Can colleges and universities afford to pay student-athletes?

Given the billions of dollars paid to the NCAA and colleges and universities for broadcast rights to basketball,

Spending on Football Surges

Spending on Division I football players has nearly doubled from 2005 to 2012, to more than $115,000 per player. Academic spending for all full-time students at those schools increased just 30 percent.

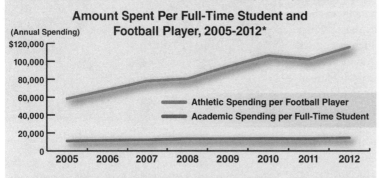

Amount Spent Per Full-Time Student and Football Player, 2005-2012*

(Annual Spending)

Athletic Spending per Football Player
Academic Spending per Full-Time Student

* At schools in the Division I Football Bowl Subdivision (FBS)

Source: Data reported by NCAA member schools; Athletic & Academic Spending Database for NCAA Division I, Custom Reporting Results, 2005-2012, Knight Commission on Intercollegiate Athletics, http://tinyurl.com/mbw489s.

football and, more modestly, other college sports, it may be hard to imagine schools can't afford to pay athletes. But athletic directors and other experts say big TV contracts disguise the financial reality of college sports.

Out of 335 Division I college sports programs, says Andrew Zimbalist, an economics professor at Smith College in Northampton, Mass., "You have 23 that have an operating surplus, but probably only half a dozen that are making money if you include capital costs," for buildings and other infrastructure. "You're really talking about a handful of schools that have a surplus."

The median Division I athletic program loses $11 million a year on an operating basis, Zimbalist says, in part because of how the financial rewards from college sports are distributed. "It functions very much like a winner-take-all system," he explains. "You get the superstar programs like Texas, USC [University of Southern California], Alabama that run away with the lion's share of the money. And then you get the other programs that are trying to compete with them but can't keep up, so their expenses run up, but their revenues don't go up commensurately."

Spending millions more to pay players would only exacerbate a difficult financial situation for schools that are already subsidizing athletics, he says. "If you expand

[athletic costs] by millions of dollars, that means you're draining the academic budgets even more than you currently are, and I don't think that's desirable," Zimbalist says.

But Huma, the NCPA and CAPA president, says, "The idea that there's not enough revenue out there is ridiculous." The major conferences recently signed television deals worth an additional $1.2 billion over their previous deals, he says. He also notes that schools already share athletic revenue in a variety of ways. If the NCAA is seriously worried about the schools that aren't making money, he says, the association could institute a revenue-sharing program that would distribute the money more equitably.

Daniel Mahony, a dean and professor at the College of Education, Health and Human Services at Kent State University in Ohio, counters that many schools are already having a tough time reining in the cost of athletics, particularly coaches' salaries. He notes the NCAA lost a class-action lawsuit in 1998 after it tried to limit the salaries of assistant coaches.[24] "They have enough trouble with coaches, and if you now started paying college athletes commensurate with what their value is, that's going to cause even more problems," he says.

However, some analysts say universities have the money but have chosen to spend it on coaches' salaries and upgraded facilities. Coaches' salaries in the top sports conferences have risen 500 percent since 1985, and universities and colleges spent $5 billion on new buildings and other improvements in the last five years, Stanford economist Roger Noll noted in testimony in June in the antitrust suit filed by former UCLA basketball star Ed O'Bannon.

Paying players would be a wiser investment, Noll said. "It's much more efficient to pay people for what they're producing than it is to create a competition for the right to exploit them," he said.[25]

But other experts argue that even in successful Division I sports programs, the money made by football and basketball has to be stretched farther than most people realize.

Division I schools often support more than 20 different sports teams for men and women. "If you have 21 programs, there are two that make money. That's football and men's basketball. The other 19 don't make money. The amount they're going to bring in . . . isn't even going to pay for the coaches' salaries," says Jim Livengood, a retired athletic director at the University of Arizona in Tucson and other schools. "Yet those programs are just as valuable an experience to the student-athlete, just as valuable a lifetime skill as football and basketball."

For schools with financially self-sufficient athletic programs, the money from football and basketball allows them to compete in the other sports, Livengood says. He says changing that could have a disastrous effect on a university's athletics. "Who knows that within our own athletic programs we wouldn't have a revolt," he says.

But Huma says the situation in Division II, the second tier of college athletic competition, proves universities can maintain the other sports on their own. "In Division II, you're talking about almost 300 schools, none of which generate revenue overall from sports, yet they have teams across the board," he says. "If you needed big-time football and basketball to subsidize the other sports, then Division II would not exist."

Howard Nixon, a recently retired professor of sociology at Towson University in Maryland and the author of *The Athletic Trap: How College Sports Corrupted the Academy*, believes spinning off the big-money sports as separate, for-profit entities could resolve the question of their impact on a school's budget while allowing greater compensation for the athletes. "You'd create these semi-autonomous enterprises, kind of like the university hospital. They have to pay for themselves," he says. "It's a short step from being a minor league team, but you still maintain a connection to the universities."

Other sports teams would compete more like those in Division III, the smallest schools, which do not award athletic scholarships and make fewer demands on their players. This would maintain those sports as amateur enterprises, while the athletes who are making money for the school by playing football or basketball could be paid or otherwise fairly compensated. "It would remove the hypocrisy," Nixon says. "People have said it's unaffordable. I have said it's about being fair to the athletes. . . . You be fair to the athletes and then figure out how to make it work. You've certainly figured out a way to pay the coaches."

The Connecticut Huskies celebrate after defeating the Kentucky Wildcats 60-54 in the NCAA Men's Final Four Championship in Arlington, Texas, on April 7. The big game caps the NCAA's three-week March Madness basketball tournament, which last year helped boost NCAA revenue to more than $912 million.

Are academic standards for college athletes strict enough?

In early June, Rashad McCants, a player on the University of North Carolina's 2004-05 national championship basketball team, told ESPN's "Outside the Lines" that he was able to maintain his academic eligibility only because tutors wrote some of his term papers and he signed up for bogus classes that never met.[26]

Coach Roy Williams and others at the university have denied that McCants' claims are representative of the experience of UNC players.[27] But the story is the latest in a long line of tales of academic fraud or cheating to keep star athletes playing. The scandals have fed a debate about academic standards for athletes. A college education is the principal benefit that most scholarship athletes receive in return for their efforts on the field, but critics say many athletic programs do little to make sure their players receive a meaningful education.

Rather than paying college athletes as employees, some experts say universities and the NCAA should stiffen admission and academic standards to make sure athletes are competing in the classrooms and not just on the playing field.

Gerald Gurney, a professor at the University of Oklahoma who specializes in academic reform and ethics in athletics, has emerged as a leading critic of current standards. The NCAA has changed its academic standards many times, but a key moment occurred in 2003, when the NCAA stopped requiring a minimum test score on the ACT and SAT college admission tests. Admission is now based on a sliding scale — the lower the test score, the higher the high school grades required.

The change was, in part, a result of concern about the lower rate of admissions for minority students, but Gurney says the results show only a minimal improvement in minority admissions. However, high-school grade inflation, special prep schools that cater to athletes with easy grades and the free pass given some gifted athletes in high school mean the standards allow unprepared students to qualify for college admission.

In addition, studies have found that a disproportionate share of athletes are "special admissions," which means universities waived standard admissions requirements to allow the student to enroll.[28]

Gurney says the process needs reform. "The answer always begins with admission standards. They are too low. They are admitting athletes who are underprepared for college," he says. "If I had an answer, I'd say we shouldn't admit kids who cannot read. But I'm also a realist. If a kid runs a 4.3 [seconds in the 40-yard dash] he's likely to be admitted." In that case he adds, the athlete shouldn't be eligible to compete his first year. "We ought to spend that time remediating him or her so they have a chance to succeed academically," he says.

But Billy Hawkins, a kinesiology professor at the University of Georgia in Athens and the author of *The New Plantation: Black Athletes, College Sports, and Predominantly White NCAA Institutions*, says it's unfair to expect athletes from troubled, poorly funded public schools to meet tougher college admission standards —"unless they're able to change what's going on in the public schools: the high schools, the middle schools, the elementary schools," he says. "If they can't impact that, they are just trying to narrow the gate and not addressing what's really going on."

Gurney says he is not talking about denying admission, but rather requiring unprepared scholarship athletes to focus on academics until they have acquired the skills to handle college classwork. "This would not punish the athlete. It holds them out because they're not ready to get that education," he says. "This is not rocket science. It's basic. We must have students who are ready for college before we can educate them."

Many observers also criticize the academic guidance provided to college athletes, particularly in football and basketball. Gurney and others say athletes often are steered into the least demanding classes and majors, a phenomenon known as "major clustering."

Earlier this year, Mary Willingham, an academic counselor at the University of North Carolina, gained national attention when she said many of that school's athletes were taking advantage of special classes with almost non-existent requirements in order to remain eligible despite serious academic deficiencies. "They're leaving here, our profit-sport athletes, without an education," Willingham said. "They're significantly behind the level of reading and writing that's required."[29]

Livengood, the former athletic director at the University of Arizona and other schools, says universities and the NCAA should take steps to see that the academic schedules of athletes are set up so they can obtain a meaningful degree. "I contended the whole time I was AD [athletic director] that we look at really preparing kids for things they want to study, things they could really see as a career, a vocation, not just things that make their practice schedule easier," he says.

But other observers say the best solution might be to reduce, or even eliminate, academic requirements while athletes are concentrating on sports. "I don't think you can expect a student-athlete to maintain anywhere from a 50- to 70-hour work week and also maintain an academic schedule," says the University of Georgia's Hawkins, who believes the number of credits athletes are required to take should be reduced during the sports season.

Some analysts would go even further. Rather than having students try to play sports and study at the same time, says the University of South Carolina's Southall, "Why not let them go to school later, when they have time and can be a full-time student?"

The NCAA responds to criticism of the academic performance of athletes by citing graduation rates for all student-athletes, which the NCAA says are rising and higher than in the general student body. As proof it is making progress, the association also points to changes it has made in its requirements for athletes to stay on track academically. "More student-athletes than ever before are earning their college degrees, and we are gratified to see our reform efforts impact the lives of those we serve," NCAA President Emmert said in a press release.[30]

However, critics point out, the NCAA has developed its own method of measuring graduation rates, which differs from the federal standard. The NCAA says its measure, "the graduation success rate," is a more accurate way of determining how many college athletes graduate. But not counting players who transfer out of a program or leave for certain other reasons paints a false picture, critics say. "They're trying to drive the numbers up," says Southall. When you look at the players in football and basketball, in particular, the real statistics "clearly show that college athletes don't graduate at the same rate as the student population as a whole," he says. "They just don't."

BACKGROUND

Early Competition

The first athletic competition between U.S. universities took place in 1852, when Harvard and Yale students met in a rowing match on Lake Winnipesaukee in New Hampshire. Commerce played a role in college sports from the very beginning. The race was sponsored and paid for by a railroad that hoped to promote excursions to the area.[31]

Scholars of sports history say the idea that college athletics was once the province of amateurs playing simply for the love of the game isn't borne out by the historical record. "An amateur, noncommercial model has never existed in American intercollegiate sport. . . . There never was an age of innocence," says Ronald A. Smith, a professor emeritus of sports history at Pennsylvania State University and the author of *Pay for Play: A History of Big-Time College Athletic Reform.*

In fact, in the 1855 race against Yale, Harvard used a rower who had already graduated, requiring the two schools to work out eligibility rules for future meets.[32] As college football and other sports began to grow in popularity early in the 20th century, the rewards provided to athletes also became more direct. "There's been payment of athletes throughout the history of college athletics," says Kent State's Mahony, an expert in sports history and management. "The NCAA didn't come around until 1905 and didn't start penalizing anybody until the 1950s; college sports was largely unregulated until then."

A 1929 Carnegie Foundation study of 112 schools found that 81 ignored NCAA recommendations and provided compensation to student-athletes "ranging from

open payrolls to disguised booster funds to no-show jobs at movie studios," according to Pulitzer Prize-winning historian Taylor Branch.[33] In 1939, freshman football players at the University of Pittsburgh went on strike because the upperclassmen on the team were getting paid more than they were.[34]

In 1948 the NCAA tried to establish a "Sanity Code" limiting athletic aid to scholarships based on need. The plan failed when several schools refused to follow it, and the NCAA membership voted not to penalize them.[35] It would take a new series of scandals in the 1950s for the NCAA to gain real authority.

Scandals and Television

In 1951 college sports were rocked by a succession of scandals. Early in the year, players from four different New York schools, including City College, which had won the previous year's NCAA basketball tournament, were booked for conspiring with gamblers to fix some games by "point-shaving," in which players conspire to keep the score closer than the point spread established by bookies.[36] In August, a cheating scandal at West Point, the U.S. Military Academy, resulted in the expulsion of many members of the football team.[37]

But after a point-shaving scandal hit the University of Kentucky, the reigning national basketball champion and a pre-eminent basketball program, the NCAA was able to assert added control over college sports. Walter Byers, NCAA executive director, moved quickly to impose penalties, without waiting to call a full convention of NCAA schools.

Then, despite questions about the NCAA's legal authority to punish schools, he persuaded the University of Kentucky to accept an unprecedented penalty: A one-year suspension for the basketball team.[38] Writing in *The Atlantic*, historian Branch said the move established a precedent and "created an aura of centralized command for an NCAA office that barely existed."[39]

At the same time, colleges had failed to grasp the financial potential of television, then in its infancy. Rather than negotiate individual contracts, NCAA member schools voted to ban televising football games except those licensed though the NCAA. In 1952, NBC agreed to pay $1.14 million for a one-year package of weekend games. The NCAA got 12 percent of the proceeds, but, importantly, the contract established the NCAA's control over television

C H R O N O L O G Y

1852-1905 *Intercollegiate athletics become popular; questions arise about amateurism and fair play.*

1852 Harvard and Yale face off in a crew race held on Lake Winnipesaukee, N.H., the first intercollegiate sporting contest in America. The event is sponsored by a railroad company.

1879 Eastern colleges form a conference for baseball to establish rules following the use of professional players by Brown and graduate students by Harvard.

1905 The Intercollegiate Athletic Association of the United States, forerunner of the National Collegiate Athletic Association (NCAA), is formed when 68 institutions meet to reduce the violence of college football.

1910-1948 *NCAA emerges as the main governing body of college sports, but struggles to impose rules.*

1910 The Intercollegiate Athletic Association becomes the NCAA.

1929 The Carnegie Foundation surveys 112 schools and finds 81 providing inducements to student-athletes that include direct pay, money from boosters or no-show jobs.

1939 Freshman football players at the University of Pittsburgh go on strike because they are getting paid less than other members of the team.

1948 The NCAA's new "Sanity Code" restricts aid to athletes to scholarships based on financial need, but the effort fails through lack of support and is eventually repealed.

1951-1972 *Television changes the financial picture; Title IX boosts women's sports.*

1951 Scandals involving point-shaving in basketball (to fix games for gamblers) and falsifying players' grades in football rock college sports.

1952-53 NBC signs a deal with the NCAA for a restricted football contract, limiting games and sharing revenue among schools. . . . The NCAA gains credibility when it suspends the University of Kentucky's basketball team for the entire season for player involvement in point-shaving.

1972 Title IX, which bars gender discrimination in education, becomes law, significantly expanding opportunities for women in college sports.

1984-1986 *TV deals bring big money; concern grows about academic performance.*

1984 U.S. Supreme Court strikes down the NCAA's TV football contracts as restraint of trade. Universities and conferences cut their own multimillion-dollar deals. . . . NCAA study finds that academic standards of freshman scholarship athletes, on average, are far below those of nonathletes.

1986 NCAA adopts Proposition 48, establishing eligibility standards for incoming athletes.

2003-Present *NCAA defends the idea of the student-athlete; players turn to lawsuits.*

2003 NCAA changes its eligibility requirements for athletes to eliminate minimum college entrance exam test scores.

2009 Ed O'Bannon, a former UCLA basketball player, sues the NCAA for prohibiting college athletes from sharing in revenue generated from their names and likenesses. . . . Associated Press survey finds that football players in top college programs are more than 10 times more likely to be granted special admission compared with other students.

2014 Regional National Labor Relations Board official rules that Northwestern University football players are school employees and can unionize (March). . . . Lawyers for former and current players announce two new lawsuits against NCAA, arguing it illegally restricts compensation for college athletes (May). . . . EA Sports, a video game company, and the NCAA agree to pay former college athletes for use of their likenesses in video games. . . . O'Bannon lawsuit goes to trial (June).

The Other Student-Athletes

Most who play college sports are not big-time basketball or football stars.

Viewers who tuned into a big college sports event during the last year had a good chance of seeing a National Collegiate Athletic Association (NCAA) advertisement that celebrated athletes whose future was not on the playing field.

"There are more than 450,000 student-athletes, and the majority of them will go pro in something other than sports," the ad proclaimed.

At a moment when the NCAA is fighting in the courts to defend the idea of the unpaid amateur student-athlete, the advertising campaign can be seen as an effort to steer attention away from the demands placed on athletes in big-time college sports and the billions of dollars that are made off their performances on the field. But the ads also reflect the larger reality of college sports.

Star athletes such as Johnny "Johnny Football" Manziel, Texas A&M's quarterback last year, may be the face of college sports to most fans. But their experiences and those of other athletes in football and men's basketball in Division I, the top tier of athletic competition, are not representative.

The largest number of college athletes — more than 170,000 — compete in Division III, which is made up of smaller schools that do not provide athletic scholarships and require shorter practices and playing seasons with less travel. That means players can concentrate more on academics. Division II, the middle tier of athletic competition, includes nearly 110,000 more athletes, very few of whom have pro prospects.[1]

Even in Division I, scholarship football and basketball players amount to fewer than a quarter of the roughly 170,000 athletes competing within the division. The NCAA conducts 38 different national Division I championships for everything from rifle shooting to water polo.

In Division I men's basketball and football, graduation rates for players trail those of the general student body, according to statistics compiled by the NCAA, but in other sports, athletes graduate at a higher rate than other students. Women college athletes do particularly well, with graduation rates in Division I — around 80 percent for many sports. The graduation rate for women athletes in the division exceeds the rate for women students overall by about 7 percentage points.[2]

That doesn't mean that balancing the demands of athletics and academics is easy, says Daniel Mahony, a dean at Kent State University in Ohio and an expert in sports management. "I wouldn't discount that these other athletes are having some

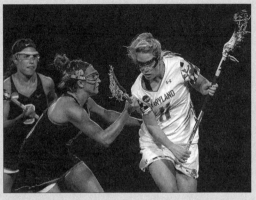

Maryland's Brooke Griffin (11) moves against Kasey Mock of Syracuse during the NCAA Division I Women's Lacrosse Championship in Towson, Md., on May 25. Maryland won, 15-12. Opponents of paying college athletes say that even the most successful Division I football and basketball programs are stretched more than many people realize, often supporting more than 20 different sports teams for men and women.

problems, too," he says. "I have taught enough athletes to tell you that a lot of them are gone more than the football players [for games or meets], so they can struggle, too."

But in general, say many who have worked with college athletes, players in the lesser-known sports manage their priorities in order to get an education while also competing. "Certainly, for the great majority of athletes . . . their total experience has been a positive one, and, in many cases, one in which the system works," says Amy Perko, executive director of the Knight Commission on Intercollegiate Athletics, which works to keep college sports true to the educational mission of universities.

"We still think there need to be improvements," she adds. "But one of the issues that has created problems over the years has been to try and apply a solution for one sport to all the sports. We need to move beyond that, and more clearly define the issues in particular sports."

— Reed Karaim

---

[1] Statistics on participation rates in the different divisions and different sports can be found at www.ncaa.org.

[2] "Trends in Graduation Success Rates and Federal Graduation Rates at NCAA Division I Schools," NCAA, October 2013, http://tinyurl.com/ngs93le.

Alabama Leads in Athletic Program Profit

The athletic departments at the University of Alabama, University of Iowa and University of Texas-Austin are the most profitable among NCAA Division I schools. Only about 14 percent of those schools generated more than $1 million in profit in 2012, calculated by subtracting operating expenses for all sports from total sports revenue.

Most Profitable University Athletic Departments, NCAA Division I, 2012

School	Revenue	Expenses	Profit
Alabama	$143,393,059	$109,071,197	$34,321,862
Iowa	106,703,779	76,839,138	29,864,641
Texas-Austin	165,691,486	138,205,604	27,485,882
Notre Dame	108,509,683	88,846,780	19,662,903
Oklahoma	123,805,661	106,340,398	17,465,263
Florida	129,505,644	11,4024,962	15,480,682
California-Berkeley	91,815,125	76,362,086	15,453,039
Kansas	93,114,168	79,720,038	13,394,130
Michigan	122,742,252	111,363,181	11,379,071
Kansas State	69,250,204	58,118,494	11,131,710

Source: "The Equity in Athletics Data Analysis Cutting Tool," U.S. Department of Education, Office of Postsecondary Education, http://ope.ed.gov/athletics

rights. By the 1960s, Byers had negotiated college football's television contract up to $3.1 million, more than the National Football League got at the time.[40]

In the 1980s, the most successful college football programs revolted against the NCAA monopoly and sued. In 1984 the Supreme Court ruled that the NCAA's football broadcast contract constituted an illegal restraint of trade.[41] But by then, money from the March Madness basketball tournament, which the NCAA continued to control, was providing a healthy new stream of revenue to the organization.[42]

The growing popularity of college basketball and football also greatly increased the money coming into universities, especially those that had built a national reputation. The pressure increased on universities and coaches to recruit and enroll the best athletes in those sports. Through the 1980s and '90s stories of under-the-table payments to athletes by boosters or even assistance by coaches that violated NCAA rules appeared repeatedly in the news.

Author Smith of Penn State views those scandals as part of an ongoing history that refutes the idea that amateurism was ever at the heart of college sports. "I don't think it's changed that much," he says, "but what has happened is there is a lot more money for recruiting now,

coaches have multimillions to fly here there and everywhere. Coaches' salaries are also so high that it puts a huge amount of pressure on them to win because they're going to fire them if they don't."

The NCAA, however, has continued to hold to its idea of amateurism, expanding efforts to keep the "student-athlete," a term it coined, from directly sharing in the growing amount of money in university athletics. The term was crafted, at least in part, to help colleges fight workers'-compensation claims from injured athletes.[43]

"500-Page Rulebook"

In the 1950s, after a player for the Fort Lewis A&M Aggies in Colorado died from a football-induced head injury, his widow sued for workers' compensation. The case was a test of the idea of the student-athlete. If players' responsibilities were akin to those of students working in other university jobs, they would be eligible for benefits. But if players were viewed as students engaged in an extracurricular activity, then they would not be eligible. The Colorado Supreme Court eventually agreed with the college, ruling the widow was not eligible for compensation because football was not a business enterprise.[44]

As the amount of money produced by college football and basketball programs has increased, the notion that they are amateur, noncommercial enterprises has generated heated criticism. But the NCAA has continued to police college athletes and athletic departments to preserve the idea of the unpaid student-athlete.

Over the years, NCAA rules about which benefits athletes can and cannot receive have proliferated. "The power-happy NCAA has a nearly 500-page rulebook, which results in micromanagement of coaches and athletes, excessive limitations on student-athletes' lives and budgets," wrote David Davenport, a research fellow at the Hoover Institution, a conservative think tank based at Stanford University in California.[45]

Infractions include offenses that could provide one team with a competitive advantage over another or could be a corrupting influence, such as college boosters giving gifts or cash to players. But the NCAA rulebook also deals with

NCAA Makes Rules, Runs Championships

Annual revenue tops $900 million, most of it from "March Madness."

The National Collegiate Athletic Association has long been a lightning rod for criticism. Among other things, members of the media and the academic community have ridiculed the nonprofit association for rules regulating players' lives that can seem arbitrary and petty.

But making and enforcing rules for college athletics is only part of NCAA activities. The association, which is governed by a board of college presidents and chancellors, has more than 1,100 member colleges and universities of all sizes that agree to compete under its umbrella.

The organization has a broad charter. From its 142,000-square-foot headquarters in Indianapolis, which it rents from the city for $1 a year, the NCAA's 500 employees oversee a variety of sports enterprises, including marketing efforts and merchandising contracts. The NCAA also "conducts 89 national championships in 23 sports across Divisions I, II and III," according to its website.[1]

But by far the signature event for the association, and the source of 84 percent of its annual revenue, is the Division I men's basketball tournament, which the NCAA operates and from which it collects hundreds of millions of dollars for broadcast rights. The three-week "March Madness" tournament has helped the NCAA increase its revenue from about $500 million in 2005 to more than $912 million last year. In the last 15 years, salaries and benefits for NCAA employees have more than doubled, from $20 million to $49 million. The NCAA has 86 employees that make more than $100,000 annually, including President Mark Emmert, who gets about $1.6 million a year, according to *The Indianapolis Star*.[2]

Those numbers have led to charges the association and its employees are getting rich while college athletes toil for scholarships that fail to cover the true cost of school. *New York Times* columnist Joe Nocera is one of many observers who have campaigned against what he has called the "glaring, and

NCAA President Mark Emmert reportedly earns about $1.6 million a year. To counter charges that the NCAA and its employees are getting rich at the expense of student-athletes, the NCAA says 90 percent of its revenue goes to its member institutions.

Getty Images/Jamie Squire

increasingly untenable discrepancy between what football and basketball players get and what everyone else in their food chain reaps."[3]

The NCAA counters that 90 percent of the money it takes in goes to its member institutions through a variety of programs. A large share is returned to schools and conferences that participate in the March Madness tournament, but a variety of programs do support the athletes more directly. Last year, this included $73.5 million for a Student Assistance Fund, which makes money available to Division I athletes for costs associated with family emergencies, academic supplies, uncovered medical expenses, clothing and other expenses. The association provided another $25 million to enhance academic support programs for athletes at Division I schools. One of the largest revenue-sharing programs returned $188 million to schools in Division I for their scholarship funds.[4] The NCAA also spends another $63 million to support grants and services for college athletes at the Division II and III levels.

As for salaries, NCAA Chief Financial Officer Kathleen McNeely told *The Indianapolis Star* they are comparable to others in the field of sports management.

"We have a lot of lawyers at the NCAA," McNeely said.[5] With one ongoing and two pending antitrust lawsuits, as well as a National Labor Relations Board case it has appealed, that is one NCAA expense that can be expected to rise.

— Reed Karaim

[1] "Championships," NCAA, http://tinyurl.com/n9ysf42.

[2] Mark Alesia, "NCAA approaching $1 billion per year amid challenges by players" *The Indianapolis Star*, March 27, 2014, http://tinyurl.com/q6qeqk6.

[3] Joe Nocera, "Let's Start Paying College Athletes," *The New York Times Magazine*, Dec. 30, 2011, http://tinyurl.com/82jorry.

[4] "Investing where it matters," NCAA, http://tinyurl.com/n5tooy8.

[5] Alesia, *op. cit.*

much smaller matters. For example, coaches face restrictions on when and how often they can text recruits. In one incident, the University of Oklahoma suspended its recruitment of a player when it determined that assistant coach Bruce Kittle had inadvertently pocket-dialed the player on his cell phone in violation of NCAA rules.[46]

Until the NCAA recently revised its rules, the association seemed obsessively concerned with what food could be given to players. At one point, schools could provide bagels to players, but not spreads or toppings such as cream cheese.[47] In another case, the University of Tennessee declared that during a trip women's basketball players had each accidently received $3 more in per diem than they were allowed for lunch. To set matters right, the school had each student donate $3 to charity.[48]

The seemingly petty nature of many rules has led to widespread criticism and ridicule. "The NCAA is very paternalistic," says the University of Georgia's Hawkins, referring to how the organization restricts the lives of players while limiting their ability to profit from their own labor. "That's why I call it a plantation system."

NCAA President Emmert has acknowledged that the NCAA rulebook is complex, but he has said the organization is working to simplify it. Meanwhile, the NCAA has bolstered its enforcement staff, he said, and is aggressively focusing on serious violations. "We set up a penalty structure that reinforced the serious concerns . . . so there was much greater emphasis on those and not so much worry about little things," Emmert told *USA Today.*[49]

But some critics believe the NCAA remains primarily concerned with the public image of college athletics. "They spend three times as much money on PR [public relations] as they do on enforcement," says Kent State's Mahony. "They are primarily an organization designed to promote college athletics. There are some who would argue that they want to catch just enough people to get the appearance of enforcement without really changing things."

CURRENT SITUATION

Athletes in Court

On June 9, roughly five years after it was filed, an antitrust lawsuit by former UCLA basketball star Ed O'Bannon against the NCAA finally came to trial.

In U.S. District Court in Oakland, Calif., Judge Claudia Wilken will decide whether O'Bannon and other current and former college athletes have the right to share in the money made from the use of their likenesses on television broadcasts and in video games. A ruling is expected in early August.[50]

The case is one of three antitrust lawsuits now pending against the NCAA. In March, former West Virginia football player Shawne Alston sued the NCAA and five major football conferences, claiming they are breaking antitrust laws by capping athletic scholarships below the full cost of attending school.[51]

Later in March, sports labor lawyer Jeffrey Kessler filed another antitrust lawsuit on behalf of a group of current college football and basketball players. Kessler's suit goes further than the other suits, claiming the NCAA unlawfully limits compensation to players to the value of a scholarship. Kessler told ESPN the objective "is to strike down permanently the restrictions that prevent athletes in Division I basketball and the top tier of college football from being fairly compensated for the billions of dollars in revenue that they help generate."[52]

Kessler has a track record of success in high-profile sports cases, including the legal battle that helped to bring free agency to NFL players.[53] But his lawsuit and Alston's could be years away from trial. The O'Bannon case has the most immediate potential for changing how the NCAA and college athletic departments operate.

Despite his college success, O'Bannon struggled in professional basketball, playing just two years in the NBA and several years for a succession of foreign teams before retiring at age 32. He was working for a car dealership in Las Vegas when he saw himself portrayed in a college basketball video game. He was bothered that no one had asked his permission and that he wasn't receiving any money for use of his likeness.[54]

According to the trial brief, O'Bannon's lawyers hope to prove that the NCAA, its member institutions and business partners "have conspired to deprive college athletes in Division I men's basketball and football of any portion of the revenues earned through the licensing of those athletes' names, images, and likenesses in television broadcasts, rebroadcasts, game clips and videogames."[55]

The lawyers are seeking an injunction against NCAA rules that prohibit universities from paying players for use of their name and likeness. "Free-market forces" would then determine whether schools decide to compensate athletes for these rights, the filing states.

The NCAA's lawyers are expected to counter that its rules are necessary to protect the amateur nature of college sports, maintain competitive balance among schools and provide more scholarships to more student-athletes.[56]

Still, right before arguments in the O'Bannon case began, the NCAA settled another video game-rights case by agreeing to pay $20 million to current and former players for the use of their likenesses. The suit had originally been brought by former Arizona State and Nebraska quarterback Sam Keller.[57]

That agreement followed one by EA Sports, originally named as a codefendant in the O'Bannon case, in which EA agreed to pay $40 million, minus legal fees, to former college athletes who played as far back as 2003. The size of the payments will depend on the number of players who file claims, but many players could receive up to $951 for each year they appeared in a video game.[58]

Even some opponents of paying college athletes believe the players are entitled to share the money made from their image or name. "There are really only two groups of people who can't make money off of their own celebrity," says Kent State's Mahony. "That's prisoners and student-athletes, and when you're grouped with prisoners, you have to question if that's a fair rule, especially if you haven't done anything wrong."

Legislative Measures

The partisan gridlock that has paralyzed Capitol Hill on a range of issues makes it unlikely lawmakers will pass legislation to change how the NCAA and college athletics operate anytime soon. But two bills have been introduced that would address some of the concerns expressed by the National College Players Association and many athletes.

The National Collegiate Athletics Accountability Act, sponsored by Reps. Charlie Dent, R-Pa., and Joyce Beatty, D-Ohio, would require NCAA member institutions to guarantee four-year athletic scholarships to recipients. Schools now have that option, but some offer only year-to-year scholarships for some athletes.[59]

Dent said students' fear of losing their scholarships could make them hide injuries, such as concussions. The bill also would require NCAA members to perform baseline concussion tests on athletes who play high-contact

A lawsuit brought by former UCLA and Dallas Mavericks player Ed O'Bannon is one of three antitrust actions pending against the NCAA. O'Bannon's suit went to trial on June 9, about five years after he filed it. He is arguing that current and former college athletes have the right to share in the money made from the use of their likenesses on TV broadcasts and in video games.

Getty Images/Allsport/Stephen Dunn

sports. In addition, the NCAA would have to provide colleges and students with the chance for an administrative hearing and appeal before the association could issue penalties for alleged rules violations.[60] If the NCAA or member schools did not follow the legislation's requirements, they could lose some federal funding.

"This bill will ensure that students — the individuals the NCAA is charged to protect — will, once again, come first in college athletics," Reps. Dent and Beatty said in a written statement.[61] The legislation has been referred to the House Committee on Education and the Workforce but has yet to be considered.

Another House bill, the Collegiate Student-Athlete Protection Act, would require college athletic programs that receive at least $10 million from media rights to provide their athletes with guaranteed benefits, including financial aid to continue in school if they lose their

Should student-athletes be paid?

YES

Emmett Gill
Assistant Professor, University of Texas at San Antonio; National Coordinator, Student-Athletes Human Rights Project

Written for *CQ Researcher*, July 2014

college athletes do not necessarily need to receive a paycheck directly from their universities, but they should retain the ability to use their name, likeness and brand to generate uncapped income during and after their college career. The $2,000 stipend the NCAA proposed in 2012 is the same amount it proposed in 1999. All college athletes should be able to receive money to appear in a chip-and-dip commercial, have their own bubble gum card or operate their own sports camp.

The importance of amateurism is not a worthy argument because, as Martin Luther King Jr. said, there are just and unjust laws. Justice refers to fairness. Is it fair that coach Nick Saban of the University of Alabama recently signed a $55.2 million contract, but Tyrone Protho, the Crimson Tide wide receiver celebrated for making "The Catch" in 2005, fractured both bones in his lower leg in his next game? Saban is wealthy and Protho is in debt and out of football.

The argument that the value of a scholarship is sufficient compensation is invalid — look at the wretched diplomas from the University of North Carolina. Forty-five percent of UNC male athletes are clustered into three social science majors, the football players are on campus 11 months of the year and at least 7 percent are unable to read well.

If you compete at Oklahoma State University, it's a potential pathway to prison. Over the past four months, four Oklahoma State athletes were arrested for alleged crimes from outraging public decency to armed robbery.

However, allowing college athletes to participate in the free market neutralizes Title IX concerns about sex discrimination because the policy mandates only equal opportunities. Proponents of pay for play rightfully argue that everyone else makes money off college athletes and that the extracurricular activity is really a form of employment.

Even more compelling is that a free market in college athletics will provide athletes with the internship of a lifetime — the opportunity, the coursework and the platform to build a brand that can feed them, their families and their communities for generations.

If athletes can participate in the booming free market in college athletics, then maybe they will pursue business degrees, honor the morality clauses in their endorsement contracts and avoid arrests, and if all goes well, leave school with a trust fund instead of a load of debt.

student-athletes should not be paid. There is a misperception that all athletic programs are profitable, and institutions are

NO

Horace Mitchell
President, California State University, Bakersfield; member, NCAA Division I Board of Directors

Written for *CQ Researcher*, July 2014

making money hand-over-fist. The truth is that only a fraction of programs are profitable, while most operate at a cost to the institution.

The question arises primarily in reference to student-athletes in the sports of football and basketball at NCAA Division I institutions with high-profile, high-income athletic programs. The argument is that because such institutions receive millions of dollars from the performance (labor) of student-athletes, they should be paid.

However, student-athletes are not employees or professional athletes who are paid salaries and incentives for a career in sports. They are students who gain access to a college education through their participation in sports, for which they earn scholarships to pay tuition, fees, room and board and other allowable expenses. A high percentage of student-athletes graduate without the burden of student loans that most students accumulate and must repay.

Student-athletes are amateurs who choose to participate in intercollegiate athletics as part of their educational experience, thus maintaining a distinction between student-athletes who participate in the collegiate model and professional athletes who might be students as well. Participation in collegiate sports is not a student-athlete's job. His or her ability to compete is contingent upon continued enrollment and academic eligibility. Because these athletes are not employees, it follows that they should not be unionized.

It is clear that, in addition to their academic course loads, student-athletes' physical conditioning, practice, travel and competition schedules make it difficult for many of them to take on part-time employment to supplement their institutional aid as do other students. So, perhaps the question is, "Is it reasonable that student-athletes should have additional resources that are typical for students who work part-time during the academic year?" The answer to that question is, "Yes."

It is both reasonable and fair, because scholarships do not cover all living expenses, and many student-athletes do not have the opportunity to earn income to cover those expenses or to afford simple social outings with friends, an important component of college life, student well-being and personal development. Athletic scholarships should be increased to cover the full cost of attendance for both male and female student-athletes, but student-athletes should not be paid.

scholarship for reasons other than academic failure or behavioral misconduct. The bill would also provide greater medical benefits and health care guarantees for student-athletes.[62]

"It shouldn't be a situation where you have a kid who has a dream, and then all of the sudden because the school gets a new coach or they have players that might be a little bit better than them, they're just tossed to the side," Rep. Tony Cárdenas, D-Calif., said.[63] The legislation has also been referred to the Education and Workforce Committee.

At a May hearing by the same House committee on the consequences of unionizing college athletes, both Democrats and Republicans criticized the NCAA for failing to address athletes' concerns. But members of the two parties expressed different views on unionization, with Republicans clearly opposed, illustrating the difficulty Congress is likely to face finding a consensus approach to college athletic reform.[64]

State Proposals

Cárdenas's bill was modeled in part on a 2012 California law. The Student Athlete Bill of Rights requires schools to pay the health insurance premiums of low-income athletes and cover medical expenses for players for up to two years after they graduate.

It also has provisions to boost graduation rates for scholarship athletes. If a school's graduation rate for athletes, for each team, is less than 60 percent, the school must extend scholarships for a year after a player has exhausted his or her athletic eligibility. Like Cárdenas's proposed national legislation, the California law applies to schools bringing in $10 million or more annually in media rights — just a handful of the state's biggest public and private universities.[65]

According to the National Conference of State Legislatures, several states have considered other bills regulating college athletes in recent years, but none has become law.[66]

NCAA Faces Revolt

While battling to preserve its vision of college athletics in the courts and facing unhappy lawmakers on Capitol Hill, the NCAA also is confronting discontent in its own membership. Mounting frustration among the five most successful athletic conferences (Big Ten, Southeastern [SEC], Atlantic Coast [ACC], Pac 12 and Big 12) broke

Ramogi Huma, a former college football player, is president of the College Athletes Players Association, which is seeking to unionize players. He contends that the recent ruling by a regional National Labor Relations Board director exposes the "myth" of amateurism for big-time college athletics. CAPA is not asking for professional salaries for college athletes, just that they receive the full cost of going to school, and better health care and academic support.

into the open this spring when SEC Commissioner Mike Slive said if the conferences aren't granted more autonomy within Division I, they will move to create their own "Division IV," with its own scholarship rules.

The five conferences propose increasing aid to scholarship athletes up to the full cost of attending school. They also would provide more comprehensive medical coverage and offer incentives for athletes to return to school and get their degrees. The schools in the five conferences say the proposed changes are necessary to head off the lawsuits pending against the NCAA and its members and to treat athletes more fairly. But the moves have been resisted by other Division I schools that fear they could not afford them.[67]

ESPN's Dosh says the conferences are not actually likely to bolt. "It would take a lot of time and expensive effort to form their own division, to come up with rules and hire people to run things," she says, adding that she thinks the intent is really to let other schools know the extent of their frustration. Dosh says she thinks an agreement will be reached that grants the five conferences more autonomy while remaining in Division I.

OUTLOOK

How Much Change?

The final NLRB decision on the right of Northwestern football players to unionize and the U.S. District Court's ruling on the O'Bannon antitrust suit will play big roles in determining the future of college athletics. But regardless of the rulings in those cases and others, some longtime observers of college sports believe a basic change is taking place.

Former Rutgers football player Eric LeGrand leaves the field after participating in the coin toss before a game between Rutgers and Army at Yankee Stadium on Nov. 12, 2011, in New York City. LeGrand was paralyzed during a kickoff return in October 2010. Proposed legislation in the House would require college athletic programs that receive at least $10 million from media rights to provide greater medical and health care guarantees to student-athletes.

Getty Images/Patrick McDermott

"I'm more optimistic than I've been before in my 31 years in athletics, because what I see now is a movement of athletes who are tired of empty promises and snail-paced bureaucracy and simply demanding what is right," says the University of Oklahoma's Gurney. College athletes won't be satisfied until they receive fairer treatment, he adds, including scholarships that cover the full cost of attending school, and "a chance at a real education."

But Kent State's Mahony is pessimistic about the NCAA's willingness to embrace real reform. "If you look at its history, the tradition of the NCAA is to try to make as little change as possible because the system is working for the NCAA administrators and the coaches," he says. "They'll try to do the least amount they possibly can to make this go away."

The University of South Carolina's Southall thinks college sports are likely to move toward a "hybrid model" in which the revenue-producing sports at some schools become more professional, with players getting salaries or greater compensation of some form, while other sports even at the same school operate on a more amateur basis. "The fundamental difference will be college athletes having more voice," he says.

However, the Knight Commission's Perko does not see big changes ahead for most college athletics. "The vast majority of programs really fall outside the huge influx of money and commercial interest that we've seen," she says, "so the vast majority will still be guided by the principles of running athletic programs that are aligned with the educational mission of the university." The question, she says, is what changes will come to the athletic programs that are the beneficiaries of "huge media contracts — whether those programs will evolve to become even more commercial or professionalized than they already are."

But even at schools that remain committed to big-time sports, Huma of the National College Players Association says changes will largely be invisible to fans. Players will have unionized, he says, but work stoppages will be rare, and fans will still recognize college sports.

"Ten years from now it's going to look very similar in terms of the product. You're still going to have games going on, still going to have the excitement," he says. "But you're also going to have a sense of peace because you're going to know that if a player is injured on the field or the court, they're not going to be stuck with their medical bills, they're not going to lose their scholarship, they're actually going to have a chance to complete their degree."

But Livengood, the former athletic director, predicts the escalating costs of staying competitive will cause some colleges and universities to rethink their commitment to athletics. "Down the road," he says, "I think we'll see a great number of schools saying it's too expensive to compete."

A reordering of priorities, Livengood adds, won't necessarily be bad for higher education. "As important as athletics is, and I do believe it can do so many things, it's not the reason and never should be that a college exists," he says, "and I think we might have lost our way a bit on that."

NOTES

1. Dan Wolken, "Northwestern football players cast votes on union," *USA Today*, April 25, 2014, http://tinyurl.com/lramper.

2. *Ibid.*

3. The full text of the ruling by Peter Sung Ohr, NRLB regional director, which includes a more complete look at the circumstances that led him to reach his conclusion, can be found under case number "13-RC-121359" on the NRLB website, http://tinyurl.com/kv3uzzq.

4. "Emmert: NCAA doesn't want athletes to be employees," The Dan Patrick Show, April 21, 2014, http://tinyurl.com/k3btw6d.

5. "Time Warner Joins CBS in $10.8 Billion March Madness TV Deal," Fox Business, April 22, 2010, http://tinyurl.com/mcbomg7.

6. Kristi Dosh, "A comparison: Conference TV deals," ESPN, March 19, 2013, http://tinyurl.com/l5ea6o2.

7. Chris Smith, "The SEC Is Already Bowl Season's Biggest Winner Thanks To $52 Million Payout," *Forbes*, Dec. 10, 2013, http://tinyurl.com/latmz68.

8. Steve Berkowitz, "Nick Saban to make $6.9 million as part of new contract," *USA Today*, June 3, 2014, http://tinyurl.com/qxtdp8d.

9. Ken Roberts, "University of Alabama's president earns about $2 million less than Auburn University's president," *Tuscaloosa News*, May 14, 2013, http://tinyurl.com/mzgm2cm.

10. Daniel Uthman, "John Calipari, Kentucky agree to $52 million contract extension," *USA Today*, June 5, 2014, http://tinyurl.com/mr64qdg.

11. "McLane Stadium," Baylor University, http://tinyurl.com/lop3y44.

12. Pete Roussel, "Photos: New stadiums and expanded venues in college football," *247sports.com*, May 21, 2014, http://tinyurl.com/mol6v82.

13. Sara Ganim, "UConn guard on unions: I go to bed 'starving,' " CNN, April 8, 2014, http://tinyurl.com/pppjc8a.

14. "Remaining Eligible: Academics," NCAA, http://tinyurl.com/ln9kfyp.

15. The Associated Press, "NCAA settles with former athletes," ESPN, June 9, 2014, http://tinyurl.com/kzgx6z4.

16. Stewart Mandel, "Judge allows Ed O'Bannon v. NCAA to proceed to trial," *Sports Illustrated*, Feb. 20, 2014, http://tinyurl.com/lvr4map.

17. "Probability of Competing Beyond High School," NCAA, http://tinyurl.com/k4cd4fo.

18. "Reform efforts," NCAA.org, http://tinyurl.com/k2sat6j.

19. Jeffrey Dorfman, "Pay College Athletes? They're Already Paid Up To $125,000 Per Year," *Forbes*, Aug. 29, 2013, http://tinyurl.com/q97f9nb.

20. Seth Gitter and Peter Hunsberger, "How Much College Quarterbacks Are Worth," *FiveThirtyEight*, May 20, 2014, http://tinyurl.com/p9tsjlv.

21. Ramogi Huma and Ellen Staurowsky, "The $6 Billion Heist: Robbing Student Athletes Under the Guise of Amateurism," National College Players Association and Drexel University Sports Management, 2012, http://tinyurl.com/n7akd63.

22. Ellen Staurowsky, " 'Should College Athletes Get Paid?' is the Wrong Question," *The Atlantic*, Sept. 19, 2011, http://tinyurl.com/mznvq4m.

23. For background see Chanan Tigay, "Women and Sports," *CQ Researcher*, March 25, 2011, pp. 265-288.

24. Kirk Johnson, "Assistant Coaches Win N.C.A.A. Suit; $66 Million Award," *The New York Times*, May 5, 1998, http://tinyurl.com/ktvmkxo.

25. Ben Strauss, "In Testimony Against N.C.A.A., Economics Professor Suggests Players Should Be Paid," *The New York Times*, June 12, 2014, http://tinyurl.com/mrn5frr.

26. Matt Bonesteel, "Former North Carolina basketball player Rashad McCants recounts academic fraud at the school," *The Washington Post*, June 6, 2014, http://tinyurl.com/q3g4spc.

27. "Williams: McCants doesn't ring true," ESPN, June 8, 2014, http://tinyurl.com/jw2eft3.

28. Jeff Barker, " 'Special admissions' bring colleges top athletes, educational challenges," *The Baltimore Sun*, Dec. 22, 2012, http://tinyurl.com/pobnzdx; and The Associated Press, "Report: Admissions exemptions benefit athletes," ESPN, Dec. 30, 2009, http://tinyurl.com/y8vxouc.

29. "Counselor: Some UNC student-athletes read at 3rd, 4th grade level," CNN, updated Jan. 28, 2014, http://tinyurl.com/pw2d7t6.

30. Michelle Brutlag Hosick, "Division I Student-Athletes Make The Grade," NCAA, Oct. 24, 2013, http://tinyurl.com/l5bgljl.

31. "Harvard-Yale Boat Race Turns 150," *Harvard Magazine*, May-June 2002, http://tinyurl.com/q49lor.

32. Ronald A. Smith, *Pay for Play: A History of Big-Time College Athletic Reform* (2012), p. 213.

33. Taylor Branch, "The Shame of College Sports," *The Atlantic*, October 2011, http://tinyurl.com/lv7kpcu.

34. *Ibid.*; Nick Veronica, "College sports and money: Decades-old issues remain unresolved," *Pittsburgh Post-Gazette*, June 16, 2013, http://tinyurl.com/kfehaeo.

35. Smith, *op. cit.*, p. 221.

36. Joe Goldstein, "Explosion: 1951 scandals threaten college hoops," ESPN Classic, Nov. 19, 2003, http://tinyurl.com/7rdaojg.

37. Smith, *op. cit.*, p. 221.

38. Branch, *op. cit.*

39. *Ibid.*

40. *Ibid.*

41. Ben Strauss, "30-Year-Old Decision Could Serve as Template for N.C.A.A. Antitrust Case," *The New York Times*, June 13, 2014, http://tinyurl.com/qgl6s98.

42. Branch, *op. cit.*

43. *Ibid.*

44. *Ibid.*

45. David Davenport, "The Real March Madness: Unions, Money and Power in College Athletics," *Forbes*, March 28, 2014, http://tinyurl.com/p68gwcf.

46. Ryan Aber, "OU releases list of self-reported NCAA violations," *The Oklahoman*, Feb. 18, 2014, http://tinyurl.com/lc3p4nq.

47. Holly Anderson, "Vital bagel rule update: NCAA food-monitorings of the future," *Sports Illustrated*, Jan. 22, 2013, http://tinyurl.com/b6n6ox5.

48. Evan Woodbery, "UT releases self-reported minor NCAA rules violations," *govolsxtra.com*, July 9, 2013, http://tinyurl.com/lufe6az.

49. Brent Schrotenboer, "Emmert sees progress amid 'noise' over NCAA reforms," *USA Today*, April 3, 2013, http://tinyurl.com/memof89.

50. Jon Solomon, "O'Bannon plaintiffs try to make their case in NCAA post-trial brief," CBS Sports, July 2, 2014, http://tinyurl.com/llx8vbm.

51. The Associated Press, "Shawne Alston suing NCAA, others," ESPN, March 6, 2014, http://tinyurl.com/kmwg9st.

52. Tom Farrey, "Jeffrey Kessler files against NCAA," ESPN, March 18, 2014, http://tinyurl.com/p4py95n.

53. *Ibid.*

54. Steve Eder and Ben Strauss, "Understanding Ed O'Bannon's Suit Against the N.C.A.A.," *The New York Times*, June 9, 2014, http://tinyurl.com/py6ejtk.

55. Antitrust Plaintiffs' Trial Brief at 1, *Edward C. O'Bannon Jr. v. National Collegiate Athletic Association (NCAA)*; Electronic Arts, Inc.; and Collegiate Licensing Company, Case No. 4:09-cv-3329 CW, June 3, 2014.

56. Eder and Strauss, "Understanding Ed O'Bannon's Suit Against the N.C.A.A.," *op. cit.*

57. Ben Strauss and Steve Eder, "N.C.A.A. Settles One Video Game Suit for $20 Million as a Second Begins," *The New York Times*, June 9, 2014, http://tinyurl.com/nwlxpxd.

58. The Associated Press, "Former NCAA athletes to get $40 million in videogames lawsuit settlement," *Los Angeles Times*, June 1, 2014, http://tinyurl.com/qal5r9g.

59. Brad Wolverton, "Bill in Congress Aims to Give NCAA Athletes Greater Protections," *The Chronicle of Higher Education*, Aug. 1, 2013, http://tinyurl.com/o4kqrnm.

60. Xander Zellner, "Lawmakers introduce bill for NCAA changes," *USA Today*, Aug. 1, 2013, http://tinyurl.com/nc29sfp.

61. Wolverton, *op. cit.*

62. Mike Singer, "Act proposed to protect NCAA athletes at high-revenue schools," CBS Sports, Nov. 20, 2013, http://tinyurl.com/m4ojnh5.

63. *Ibid.*

64. Steve Berkowitz, "House panel grills college leaders on unionization," *USA Today*, May 8, 2014, http://tinyurl.com/pjvfwyn.

65. Dennis Dodd, "California passes Student-Athlete Bill of Rights," CBS Sports, Oct. 9, 2012, http://tinyurl.com/qah2svw.

66. The National Conference of State Legislatures reviewed the states' actions on bills regulating college athletes at the request of *CQ Researcher*.

67. "SEC ponders 'Division IV,' " ESPN, May 30, 2014, http://tinyurl.com/k2ub6uf.

BIBLIOGRAPHY

Selected Sources

Books

Dosh, Kristi, *Saturday Millionaires: How Winning Football Builds Winning Colleges*, Wiley, 2013.
An ESPN sports-business reporter says successful football programs can benefit universities without degrading academics and calls the idea that college players could be paid like employees a myth.

Hawkins, Billy, *The New Plantation: Black Athletes, College Sports, and Predominantly White NCAA Institutions*, Palgrave Macmillan, 2010.
A kinesiology professor at the University of Georgia examines how racial attitudes influence the treatment and expectations surrounding black athletes at predominantly white universities.

Nixon, Howard, *The Athletic Trap: How College Sports Corrupted the Academy*, Johns Hopkins University Press, 2014.
A former Towson University sociology professor argues that the amount of money poured into college athletics has bred corruption in sports programs and diverted resources from academics.

Smith, Ronald, *Pay for Play: A History of Big-Time College Athletic Reform*, University of Illinois Press, 2010.
A professor emeritus of sports history at Penn State University traces the history of college athletics reforms from their earliest days to recent efforts to regulate what has become a multibillion-dollar industry.

Articles

Berkowitz, Steve, "House panel grills college leaders on unionization," *USA Today*, May 8, 2014, http://tinyurl.com/pjvfwyn.
Members of Congress criticize the NCAA's treatment of athletes during a hearing examining the consequences of allowing college athletes to unionize.

Branch, Taylor, "The Shame of College Sports," *The Atlantic*, October 2011, http://tinyurl.com/cuye4nh.
A civil rights historian outlines the long history of scandals and cheating in college sports and argues universities should pay athletes.

Delsohn, Steve, "UNC's McCants: 'Just show up, play,' " ESPN, June 6, 2014, http://tinyurl.com/kq5cpl5.
A former University of North Carolina basketball star tells ESPN that tutors wrote his term papers and he took bogus classes to maintain academic eligibility.

Gitter, Seth, and Peter Hunsburger, "How Much College Quarterbacks Are Worth," *FiveThirtyEight*, May 20, 2014, http://tinyurl.com/p9tsjlv.
Each of the nation's top college quarterbacks is worth more than $3 million, based on an analysis of how much they helped their teams win.

Gurney, Gerald, and Richard Southall, "NCAA Reform Gone Wrong," *Inside Higher Ed*, Feb. 14, 2013, http://tinyurl.com/luughyv.
A former University of Oklahoma athletics director and a professor of sport administration at the University of North Carolina say NCAA reforms have made it easier for academically unprepared athletes to be admitted to universities and colleges.

Strauss, Ben, and Steve Eder, "College Players Granted Right to Form Union," *The New York Times*, March 26, 2014, http://tinyurl.com/q79ou7l.
The National Labor Relations Board ruled that Northwestern University football players are university employees and have the right to unionize and bargain collectively.

Strauss, Ben, and Steve Eder, "Understanding Ed O'Bannon's Suit Against the N.C.A.A.," *The New York Times*, June 9, 2014, http://tinyurl.com/py6ejtk.
A lawsuit brought by a former University of California, Los Angeles, basketball star against the NCAA argues that players should be able to negotiate "fair market value" for use of their likenesses in broadcasts and videogames.

Reports and Studies

"Restoring The Balance: Dollars, Values, and the Future of College Sports," Knight Commission on Intercollegiate Athletics, June 2010, http://tinyurl.com/nexwqro.
A study by a watchdog group concludes institutions in major athletic conferences spend four to 11 times more per athlete than regular students and calls for rebalancing spending to prioritize academics.

"Trends in Graduation-Success Rates and Federal Graduation Rates at NCAA Division I Institutions," NCAA Research Staff, *NCAA*, October 2013, http://tinyurl.com/ngs93le.
A presentation by the NCAA compares student-athlete graduation rates at Division I schools by sport, race and gender between 1995 and 2006.

Huma, Ramogi, and Ellen J. Staurowsky, "The $6 Billion Heist: Robbing College Athletes Under the Guise of Amateurism," National College Players Association and Drexel University Sport Management, 2012, http://tinyurl.com/nu2khpt.
A study commissioned by a group working on behalf of student-athletes concludes the NCAA is denying football and basketball players billions of dollars they would receive in an open market.

For More Information

College Sports Research Institute, 2012 Carolina Coliseum, University of South Carolina, Columbia, SC 29208; 803-777-0658; http://csri-sc.org. Studies business and social aspects of college athletics.

Knight Commission on Intercollegiate Athletics, 910-551-6809; www.knightcomission.org. Works to emphasize academic values and ensure that college athletic programs operate within the educational mission of their colleges and universities; formed by the John S. and James L. Knight Foundation in 1989 in response to a series of scandals in college sports.

National Collegiate Athletic Association (NCAA), 700 W. Washington St., P.O. Box 6222, Indianapolis, IN 46206; 317-917-6222; www.ncaa.org. Regulates college athletics, setting standards for student athletes and college programs; conducts national championships in 23 sports across Divisions I, II and III.

National College Players Association (NCPA), P.O. Box 6917, Norco, CA 92860; 951-898-0985; www.ncpanow .org. Promotes interests of former and current college athletes, including adequate compensation for their efforts.

National Labor Relations Board (NLRB), 1099 14th St., N.W., Washington, DC 20570; 202-273-1000; www.nlrb. gov. Federal agency charged with safeguarding employees' rights to organize and with preventing and remedying unfair labor practices

13

Regulating Lobbying

Chuck McCutcheon

Howard Dean, a former presidential candidate and chairman of the Democratic National Committee, is now a "senior strategic adviser" for a Washington law firm that lobbies for health care and drug companies. Increasing numbers of lobbyists are calling themselves advisers to skirt a 2007 law passed in response to the Jack Abramoff lobbying scandal. There are now more such unregistered "shadow lobbyists" in Washington than registered lobbyists. Congress has shown little interest in recent years in closing loopholes in lobbying laws.

From *CQ Researcher*, June 6, 2014.

Nearly a decade ago, presidential candidate Howard Dean thrilled Democrats with his vow to stand up to the special interests in Washington. Lately, however, some Democrats have been accusing him of lobbying on behalf of those same interests.

Although not a registered lobbyist, Dean is a "senior strategic adviser" at McKenna, Long & Aldridge, a Washington law firm that lobbies on behalf of health care and pharmaceutical companies. Last July, in a *Wall Street Journal* column, he criticized a cost-control panel set up as part of President Obama's health-care overhaul. Left-leaning publications rebuked him: "Dean has found a home in the K Street establishment he once held in such disdain," wrote *The New Republic*, referring to the downtown area where many lobbying firms are located.[1]

Dean told *Time*: "I dare say some of the clients think [the column] is great, but I don't write stuff because the clients like it. I write stuff because I believe it."[2]

But one of Dean's drug company clients told the publishing company BioCentury that Dean had been "very helpful" in his firm's efforts to loosen federal regulations on drug development. Another said Dean "has been a great addition to our team."[3]

Dean's situation offers a window into the ongoing transformation of the lobbying industry in Washington. Increasingly, its practitioners are trying to influence the opinions of the public, the regulators and politicians without registering as lobbyists or having to formally disclose their contacts and income. The result, say government watchdogs, is a shadow world of lobbying that taxpayers know little about and that creates a potentially ripe environment for abuse.

Finance, Health Sectors Spent Most on Lobbying

The finance, health and business sectors spent the most on lobbying in 2013, more than 10 times as much as organized labor, whose expenditures on lobbying have shrunk over time as the number of unionized jobs has dwindled.

Lobbying Expenditures by Sector, 2013

Sector	Amount
Finance/Insurance/Real Estate	$488,112,892
Health	$483,078,712
Misc. Business*	$481,983,886
Communications/Electronics	$393,044,474
Energy/Natural Resources	$357,730,595
Transportation	$223,271,514
Other**	$218,932,399
Agribusiness	$151,730,315
Single-Issue Causes	$146,419,518
Defense	$134,507,531
Construction	$48,850,975
Labor	$46,457,560

*Includes manufacturing, textiles, steel, chemical, consumer retail, restaurants, gambling, tourism, food and beverages

** Includes retirees, educators, government employees, nonprofit organizations, religious groups and members of the armed forces

Source: "Ranked Sectors, 2013" Center for Responsive Politics, undated, http://tinyurl.com/okwphbh

the growth will be" in the future, predicted Carter Eskew, founding partner of the lobbying and public relations firm Glover Park Group.[4]

Instead, Rehr says, lobbying now requires a broader set of skills, the kind that public relations firms possess. "Lobbyists and public relations professionals no longer work in silos," said an invitation to a recent Public Relations Society of America event. "Instead, we are expected to offer integrated services and bottom-line results in a seamless manner."[5]

And lobbying does produce big bottom-line results. In 2012 and 2013, for instance, Whirlpool Corp. invested $1.8 million in lobbying for legislation to create energy tax credits for making high-efficiency appliances — credits worth an estimated $120 million.[6] And a 2009 study found that for every dollar spent on lobbying for a 2004 bill that provided tax breaks for large multinational corporations, companies received more than $220 as the result of beneficial language added to the bill.[7]

To achieve similar results, well-connected "advisers" such as Dean and former Senate Majority Leaders Tom Daschle, a Democrat, and Bob Dole, a Republican, are generously rewarded. Daschle reportedly makes more than $2.1 million a year.[8] Such advisers are among the so-called "shadow lobbyists" or "unlobbyists" — a group that by 2013 had grown larger than the number of registered lobbyists, according to one estimate. Watchdog groups say the growth stems largely from loopholes in lobbying laws and lax enforcement.[9]

Congress has shown little interest in closing those loopholes, and many predict it will take a major scandal before lawmakers make a serious effort to close them. The current system is the result of previous attempts to clean up the industry following earlier scandals.

The Lobbying Disclosure Act defines a lobbyist as someone who earns at least $2,500 from lobbying over a three-month period, whose services include contacting

"Today, to be really effective, a lobbyist not only has to be thinking about the inside game — going to Capitol Hill — but the outside game," says David Rehr, a former lobbyist who now studies the industry as an adjunct professor at George Washington University's Graduate School of Political Management. The outside game, he says, includes "forming coalitions, getting third parties to augment your research or your economic arguments" and coordinating media coverage through opinion articles, such as Dean's *Wall Street Journal* column.

Even the word "lobbying" is considered passé. The American League of Lobbyists — the main trade organization for the influence industry — changed its name last fall to the Association of Government Relations Professionals. And, the traditional practice of "relationship lobbying," based on head-to-head meetings to try to persuade elected officials, "is dead, or at least not where

more than one person on behalf of a client and who spends at least 20 percent of his or her time for each client on lobbying activity.

Both the number of registered lobbyists and the amount of money reported as spent on lobbying have declined in recent years. Data from the Center for Responsive Politics, a Washington watchdog group, shows the number of registered lobbyists dropped 17 percent from 2007 to 2013, to around 12,300. Meanwhile, the amount reported as being spent on lobbying dropped from a high of $3.55 billion in 2010 to $3.23 billion last year.[10] And in the first three months of this year, the amount reported as spent on lobbying was lower than in any quarter in four years.[11]

However, those figures do not include shadow lobbyists' work, which is not required to be reported. If their statistics are included, one political scientist estimates, the amount spent on lobbying tops $6 billion a year — and is on the rise.[12]

Registered lobbyists face multiple challenges. Extreme political polarization means fewer bills are being considered, so the opportunities to lobby Congress have dwindled, while the special-interest earmarks in appropriations bills that once created big business for K Street are largely gone. And more than any other recent chief executive, President Obama has taken steps to curtail lobbyists' access and influence within the executive branch, such as barring them from serving on federal advisory boards.

Meanwhile, lobbyists are fighting a persistent image problem. In a December 2013 Gallup poll, lobbying scored lowest among 22 professions on honesty and ethical standards. Just 6 percent of those surveyed said lobbyists had high or very high standards — fewer than members of Congress (8 percent) and car salespersons (9 percent).[13]

"The lobbying profession . . . symbolizes a deep conflict of American values," wrote former *Washington Post* managing editor Robert G. Kaiser in his 2009 book *So Much Damn Money: The Triumph of Lobbying and the*

Corrosion of American Government. "Lobbying is corrupt and deplorable . . . until one's own ox is gored or threatened; at which point, let the lobbying begin!"[14]

Lobbyists' image took a severe hit in the mid-2000s, with a scandal surrounding the activities of Jack Abramoff. Once one of Washington's top lobbyists, Abramoff served 43 months in prison after being convicted of conspiring to bribe Republican elected officials, among other charges.[15] Rep. Bob Ney, R-Ohio, went to prison in connection with the scandal, and a number of congressional and George W. Bush administration officials were convicted of various related crimes.

But lobbyists say their profession is scorned because the public doesn't understand it. After the Gallup poll appeared, former Republican Mississippi Gov. Haley Barbour and Ed Rogers of BGR Group, a Washington government-affairs firm, wrote a response explaining three overlooked aspects of lobbying.

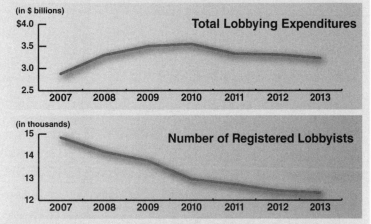

Fewer Lobbyists, But Spending Still High

Spending on lobbying peaked in 2010 at $3.6 billion, while the number of registered lobbyists fell by 17 percent between 2007 and 2013. But according to the Sunlight Foundation watchdog group, the spending figures do not reflect fees paid to "shadow lobbyists" — advisers hired to influence policy but not required to disclose their fees or clients. When they are included, the total spent on lobbying may have been as high as $6.7 billion in 2012, the group estimated.

Source: "Lobbying Database," Center for Responsive Politics, http://tinyurl.com/cbyu 433; also see Tim LaPira, "How much lobbying is there in Washington?" Sunlight Foundation (blog), Nov. 25, 2013, http://tinyurl.com/mzkgm3f

Lobbying Group Defends Name Change

Lobbyists today "have so many more responsibilities."

Members of the main Washington trade group for lobbyists say the group's new name — which doesn't include the word "lobbyist" — isn't an attempt to disguise what they do but simply an effort to show how much the industry is changing.

Last fall the 1,100-member American League of Lobbyists voted to rename itself the Association of Government Relations Professionals (AGRP). Eighty-three percent of those voting supported the change.

Group members said the action reflects how lobbyists today do much more than the traditional efforts to influence how lawmakers write, and vote on, legislation. They now have to actively use social media, form alliances with grassroots organizations and public affairs firms and develop other innovative ways to represent their clients.

"If you're a lobbyist now, you have so many more responsibilities," says Monte Ward, the organization's president.

Ward said the idea of renaming the association had been discussed since 2000. It was the subject of several focus groups in which he and other lobbyists discussed how much the profession has evolved.[1] "It just made sense to change the name to reflect the reality of D.C.," says Robert Hay Jr., an AGRP board member.

Paul Miller, a former president of the group, opposed the name change at first: "I thought if you were a lobbyist and you were afraid to call yourself a lobbyist, you shouldn't be one," he says. But he voted for the new name, he explains, because "I realized the profession has changed."

Going forward, Ward said he wants the association to focus on increasing educational opportunities for lobbyists. That includes getting more people in the industry to take part in AGRP's lobbying certification program, which it set up in 2006 in response to the Jack Abramoff scandal. Abramoff, a former lobbyist for American Indian tribes, was convicted of mail fraud, conspiracy to bribe public officials and tax evasion and served 43 months in prison.[2]

The certification program is open to association members, who pay $1,636, as well as nonmembers, who are charged slightly more. It requires enrollees to complete five one-day core courses and six electives within two years of signing up. One of the courses covers ethics training, which association members say lends credibility to those who graduate.

The group tells lobbyists on its website that obtaining a certificate "will set you apart as the cream of the crop. That's because this is the only certificate program that offers mastery of government relations strategies and best practices, the legislative process plus practical know-how for getting results while meeting the highest standards of ethics and professionalism."[3]

Organization members often defend the lobbying profession in the news media. In particular, they frequently counter criticisms from Abramoff, who has drawn considerable publicity with his accusations that lobbyists still engage in the kind of payola practices that sent him to prison. In a speech

The first, they wrote, is identifying who to talk to: "The growth of bureaucracy is making it harder for a company or even an industry, much less an individual, to find out what is actually going on in government, and harder still to move the needle on any given measure." The second is providing lawmakers with solid information. "[T]he majority of policymakers want to thoroughly understand the policy and politics of whatever issue is on the table." The third is telling the truth: "If you want to be invited back to talk about an issue with members of Congress, government officials and other policymakers, you need to be credible."[16]

Contrary to what some voters believe, lobbyists do not always get their way. A broad coalition of powerful interest groups, ranging from Catholic and evangelical organizations to the U.S. Chamber of Commerce, has been lobbying the House heavily for months to follow the Senate in adopting a comprehensive immigration reform bill. But House Republican leaders have resisted the idea, and it is considered unlikely that a bill will pass before the November midterm elections.

Some lobbyists, finding less work at the federal level, are turning to the states, where disclosure laws vary widely. Nearly half of the states do not require registered lobbyists to file activity reports quarterly as they must at the federal level, and eight states require activity reports

last year at Georgetown University, he said: "I figured that I wasn't really doing anything wrong, because every lobbying firm on Capitol Hill was giving the same improper benefits. I was just doing it on a much larger scale."[4]

Miller, who was the group's president when the Abramoff scandal broke in 2005, says the ex-lobbyist has no sincere interest in bettering the lobbying industry — and that if he did he would donate some of his income from speaking fees and book royalties to the certification program. "For a guy who screwed the entire profession, he should consider an apology to all of us following the rules," Miller says. "At the end of the day, Jack Abramoff is a crook and only out for himself."

In response, Abramoff accused association members of "Orwellian doublespeak" if they think he should donate to the lobbying certification program when they already are guilty of prospering in ethically suspect ways. Miller's suggestion "that the true path to reform is through donations to his organization would be funny if he were not serious," Abramoff wrote in an email. "His problem does not lie only with Jack Abramoff, but rather with a nation which will no longer condone special-interest money buying legislative results."[5]

Despite the low regard with which polls show the American public holds lobbyists, Ward says he's confident the group can help persuade people that the profession is essential and ethical. He contends he's already seeing some evidence of it.

"It's an educational process," he says. "When I talk about what we do to people and say, 'Here's what a lobbyist does' — once you go through that process, they often go, 'They do provide a valuable service.' "

— ***Chuck McCutcheon***

Former lobbyist Jack Abramoff served 43 months in prison for conspiracy to bribe public officials and other crimes. Abramoff says lobbyists still engage in illegal and unethical practices, a charge the industry vigorously denies.

AFP/Getty Images/Jewel Samad

[1]Holly Yeager, "Lobbyists' Lobbying Group Wants a New Name — One That Doesn't Mention Lobbying," *The Washington Post*, Oct. 15, 2013, http://tinyurl.com/prvpvyo.

[2]For background, see Susan Schmidt, *et al.*, "Investigating Abramoff: Special Report," *The Washington Post*, undated, http://tinyurl.com/8chq6.

[3]"Lobbying Certificate Program," Association of Government Relations Professionals, http://tinyurl.com/oh5hrqu.

[4]Sam Abrams, "Abramoff Talks Lobbying," *The Hoya* (Georgetown University), Oct. 11, 2013, http://tinyurl.com/o5vvc38.

[5]Chuck McCutcheon, "Abramoff Still Biggest Thorn in Lobbying Industry's Side," CQ Press First Street Research Group blog, March 15, 2012.

only once a year, according to a 2011 survey by the Sunlight Foundation watchdog group.[17]

Meanwhile, lobbying is becoming more international, as trans-border issues such as data privacy and financial regulation assume greater prominence. "There's more U.S. lobbying in the national and regional governments across the world; we never used to have that before," says Nicholas Allard, an ex-lobbyist who is now dean of Brooklyn Law School.

Allard is among those hoping that lobbyists' reputations improve as more of them consider a future in politics. Democrat Terry McAuliffe was elected Virginia's governor in 2013, and Republican David Jolly won a special House election in Florida's 13th District in March — both after overcoming heavy criticism of their lobbying backgrounds.[18]

As lobbyists, lawmakers, watchdog groups and others debate changes in the lobbying industry, here are some of the questions under discussion:

Do current laws sufficiently regulate lobbying?

Since 1946, Congress has approved four separate measures to regulate lobbyists' contacts with congressional members. Each required lobbyists to register with both the House and Senate and to disclose receipts and expenditures.

The most recent was the Honest Leadership and Open Government Act (HLOGA) of 2007, adopted in response to the Abramoff bribery scandal. The law substantially revised the Lobbying Disclosure Act, adopted 12 years earlier. It refined the thresholds and definitions of lobbying activities and doubled — to four — the number of yearly reports required for registered lobbyists and lobbying firms. It also required additional disclosures, created new semi-annual campaign contributions reports and required lobbying coalitions and associations to file disclosures.[19]

Senate Majority Leader Harry Reid, D-Nev., hailed the law in 2009 for providing "an unprecedented level of disclosure — both in quantity and quality — of the activities of lobbyists as they seek to influence federal policymaking." Reid said the law addresses "one of the glaring weaknesses revealed by the Abramoff scandal — the lack of effective enforcement that helped lead to an attitude among some that the rules could be ignored with impunity."[20]

However, watchdog groups, lobbyists and those who study the industry say the law is rife with deficiencies. "HLOGA doesn't do much," says Paul Miller, a former president of the Association of Government Relations Professionals, the main Washington trade group for lobbyists. "You're never going to be able to legislate morality. There are just too many creative people who can find loopholes and jump through them."

For instance, Miller and others say, lobbyists are required to disclose only money spent on lobbying in excess of $12,500 per quarter. "Groups that spend $12,499 or less in a quarter need not disclose," said the Center for Responsive Politics, "and we know little about the ways they are trying to influence public policy."[21]

And grassroots lobbying activities, such as when an interest group organizes "fly outs" of its members to Washington, D.C., do not have to be reported. For instance, the Christian Coalition reported spending up to $6.4 million a year on lobbying in 1998, but after the faith-based group stopped reporting its grassroots spending, its official tally was just $10,000 for 2013 and nothing for 2011 or 2012, said the Center for Responsive Politics.[22]

Lobbying experts say the offices that register lobbyists — the House clerk and secretary of the Senate — perform largely clerical duties, making sure that what lobbyists submit shows up in the database. "They only look into cases where disclosures have already arrived in their office and

they suspect error," said Timothy LaPira, a James Madison University political scientist who studies lobbying.[23]

Moreover, the U.S. Attorney's Office for the District of Columbia, which is responsible for enforcing lobbying violations, has only four attorneys handling the issue, and their workloads include health care and housing fraud, false claims and other cases. "We have no ability to know if somebody doesn't register unless some insider or a competitor comes and says, 'We have reason to believe that this individual or this group is lobbying,' " said Keith Morgan, the office's deputy chief.[24]

When Obama took office in 2009, he barred registered lobbyists from joining his administration. But experts say many lobbyists decertified themselves to avoid those and other restrictions, even though they continued to do similar work, many for the same employers.[25]

In a 2013 report for the Sunlight Foundation, LaPira estimated that for every registered lobbyist at least one "shadow lobbyist" is being paid to influence policy without disclosing fees or clients. Assuming that a shadow lobbyist collects the same amount in fees as a registered lobbyist, LaPira concluded that total spending in the industry did not decline in 2012, but doubled — from $3.1 billion to $6.7 billion.[26]

HLOGA "had sort of a perverse outcome and unintended consequences," LaPira says. "Instead of adding transparency, it's actually decreased transparency."

The use of shadow lobbyists has become known as "the Daschle Loophole," after South Dakota Democratic Sen. Daschle, who was defeated for re-election in 2004, three years before the law was enacted.[27] He is now a senior policy adviser at DLA Piper, a Washington law and lobbying firm. But Daschle said that while he makes speeches, gives advice and does other work for clients related to public policy, he personally doesn't "lobby" by directly approaching ex-colleagues.

"I've never felt comfortable asking my former colleagues for access or for support for things that I want to do," he told *The Hill* newspaper.[28]

Daschle is not the only former legislator to eschew the "lobbyist" tag. During the 2012 Republican presidential primary campaign, Mitt Romney accused former Republican House Speaker Newt Gingrich of Georgia of lobbying Congress on behalf of several clients, including mortgage giant Freddie Mac. Gingrich responded that he did not lobby but provided advice "as a historian."[29]

To some industry observers and lobbyists, however, such explanations are unsatisfactory. "People say to me, 'I don't lobby. I engage in strategic planning and education,' " said Ken Gross, a lawyer who specializes in lobbying laws and ethics. "I say to them, 'That's exactly what lobbying is — if it's for the purpose of influencing legislation or policy, not strategic planning on who's going to win the Super Bowl.' "[30]

Do lobbyists move in and out of government too easily?

Watchdog groups have long complained about the "revolving door" between the government and K Street, saying too many lawmakers and staffers readily move into lucrative lobbying jobs. Critics say it gives the lobbyists privileged access to former colleagues.

People who shift from government to lobbying "are literally cashing in on their Rolodex," said Craig Holman, a lobbyist for the consumer-interest group Public Citizen. "It distorts the legislative process in favor of those who can pay for that Rolodex."[31]

The opposite scenario also occurs. Increasingly, so-called "reverse revolvers" leave corporations and lobbying firms to work in government — sometimes after receiving six-figure bonuses from their former employers — according to Public Citizen and other watchdog groups.

In January 2013, Ambrose "Bruce" Hock joined the Republican staff of the Senate Armed Services Committee after working as an executive and lobbyist at Northrop Grumman Corp. The defense giant gave him up to $450,000 in bonus and incentive pay before he left. Another former lobbyist for the company, Thomas Mackenzie, received even more — $498,334 — when he left to go to work for Republicans on the House Armed Services Committee in 2011.[32]

"The revolving door is maybe the most corrupting element of Washington," said Danielle Bryan, who heads the Project on Government Oversight, a watchdog group.[33]

Defenders of the revolving door, such as Indiana Republican Sen. Dan Coats, say it can provide lobbyists and government with a more informed perspective. Coats went from serving in the Senate to lobbying and then became U.S. ambassador to Germany. He returned to K Street, but later moved back to Indiana and ran successfully for the Senate again in 2010. "Throughout my life, whenever a new door has opened, I chose to accept the challenge," Coats said.[34]

Other lobbyists say colleagues with prior backgrounds on Capitol Hill have helped to offset the declines in longevity among congressional staffers by providing critical knowledge and background needed to shape legislation. "Despite the increase in the scale and complexity of governance, the number of staffers in congressional offices has remained nearly the same over the past 20 years," said Allard, the former lobbyist. "Experience is spread thin."[35]

Former Oregon GOP Sen. Gordon Smith, who took a job as a senior adviser at the law and lobbying firm Covington & Burling after losing his seat in 2008, said he not only deals with Congress but also contacts officials in the judicial and executive branches of government.[36]

In a study for the Sunlight Foundation, analysts Lee Drutman and Alexander Furnas found that most of the growth in lobbyists' fees between 1998 and 2012 came from revolving-door lobbyists. The number of active lobbyists who reported having prior government experience quadrupled during that period, they found.[37]

The Center for Responsive Politics counts more than 400 former House and Senate members who have moved into lobbying or related government-affairs work. Hundreds of their ex-employees also hold such jobs, including 61 one-time staffers for the late Democratic Sen. Edward M. Kennedy of Massachusetts, 50 for former Republican Sen. Kay Bailey Hutchison of Texas and 40 for former Democratic Sen. Max Baucus of Montana.[38]

The number of ex-Baucus staffers working as lobbyists became an issue in 2013, when the Senate Finance Committee — which Baucus chaired at the time — passed a bill to extend tax cuts that otherwise would have expired under the so-called "fiscal cliff." The measure included several tax-related provisions sought by companies for whom Baucus' ex-aides were lobbying.[39]

The Honest Leadership and Open Government Act (HLOGA) bans all lobbying contact for a period of time between government officials and the agency or body where they once worked. The length of time varies, depending on where the official worked and the position held.

The law distinguishes between members of Congress and their staffers and also makes a distinction between "senior" and "very senior" executive branch officials.

Congressional Aides Return as Lobbyists

More former Republican than Democratic legislative aides registered as lobbyists in 2012 and 2013. In 2007, after Democrats took control of both the House and Senate, 53 percent of the 758 aides-turned-lobbyists were Republicans. The number of aides becoming lobbyists typically increases in odd-numbered post-election years, when proposed new legislation creates more lobbying opportunities.

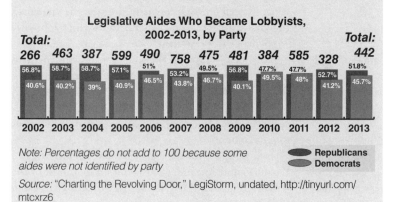

Legislative Aides Who Became Lobbyists, 2002-2013, by Party

	Total: 266	463	387	599	490	758	475	481	384	585	328	Total: 442
Republicans	56.8%	58.7%	58.7%	57.1%	51%	53.2%	49.5%	56.8%	47.7%	47.7%	52.7%	51.8%
Democrats	40.6%	40.2%	39%	40.9%	46.5%	43.8%	46.7%	40.1%	49.5%	48%	41.2%	45.7%
	2002	2003	2004	2005	2006	2007	2008	2009	2010	2011	2012	2013

Note: Percentages do not add to 100 because some aides were not identified by party

● Republicans
● Democrats

Source: "Charting the Revolving Door," LegiStorm, undated, http://tinyurl.com/mtcxrz6

Senators and "very senior" former executive officials, such as Cabinet members, are prohibited from lobbying for two years, while House members, senior congressional staffers and "senior" executive branch employees face a one-year ban. During this so-called "cooling-off period," affected individuals may not engage in any communications aimed at influencing decision-making at their former agency or government body.

Lobbyist Miller says the cooling-off period does an acceptable job of preventing new lobbyists from being able to influence legislation on which they worked as a member or aide. "I don't have an issue with the revolving door," he says. "You've got the two-year cooling-off period for a member or a year for a staffer." If that period were extended any further, he adds, "you're taking away their ability to earn a living."

However, many former lawmakers and top federal officials have joined lobbying firms during the cooling-off periods, usually as senior advisers or in similar positions until they are legally permitted to lobby. Five months after he left office in 2011, former New Hampshire GOP Sen. Judd Gregg, who chaired the Senate Budget Committee, was named an international adviser to the Wall Street investment firm Goldman

Sachs. He later became CEO of the Securities Industry and Financial Markets Association, a trade association for the financial industry.[40]

Watchdogs say it's not always clear what lawmakers are doing during the cooling-off period. "There is no registration or public disclosure required for simply working at a firm that lobbies, and as such, the public may have little to no idea of what former politicians are doing behind the scenes," said the Center for Responsive Politics.[41]

Former Senate Minority Whip Jon Kyl, R-Ariz., in discussing how the lobbying ban would affect him when he joined Covington & Burling in 2013, acknowledged that he couldn't lobby current senators. But, he said, "I'm not prohibited from giving them my best advice."[42]

Most "revolvers" come from Congress, according to researchers LaPira and Herschel Thomas III, a University of Texas-Austin doctoral candidate. Among 1,600 randomly selected lobbyists, nearly two-thirds came from Congress, the researchers found, compared to 23 percent from federal agencies and 9 percent from the White House.[43]

The New York Times reported in February that many former House aides had taken advantage of loopholes in HLOGA to lobby within one year of leaving Capitol Hill. For instance, it found some aides had resisted pay raises to keep their annual salaries below the $130,500 cutoff that would trigger being subject to lobbying restrictions.[44]

Does lobbyists' money have too much influence on policymaking?

Lobbyists and interest groups are commonly caricatured as doling out campaign checks to politicians in exchange for access. But the role that such donations play in directly influencing law or policy remains a subject of debate.

Leon Panetta, who served as a House member from California before becoming CIA director and secretary of Defense, is among those lamenting lawmakers' increasing financial dependence on lobbyists. Members of Congress "rarely legislate; they basically follow the money," said Panetta, who now chairs a California State University public policy institute. "They're spending more and more time dialing for dollars. . . . The only place they have to turn is to the lobbyists."[45]

Panetta's comments came before the Supreme Court's landmark 2010 decision in *Citizens United v. Federal Election Commission*, which struck down limits on corporate political donations and opened the doors for even more spending.

Center for Responsive Politics Executive Director Sheila Krumholz emphasized that money is not given "as a quid pro quo to purchase a vote. But well-placed contributions, money spent on lobbying, well-placed former aides now working to lobby are all assets that can be used by private interests to influence policy."[46]

A recent study that attracted substantial publicity indicated that a lobbying group's campaign contributions can pave the way for access. Two political science graduate students enlisted the help of a liberal organization, CREDO Action, based in San Francisco, which was seeking congressional cosponsors for a bill banning certain chemicals. The group sent two different emails to congressional offices. One had the subject line "Meeting with campaign donors about cosponsoring bill" and said that CREDO members "who are active political donors" were interested in meeting with the member. The second email removed the donor references and replaced them with "local constituents." The researchers found that 12.5 percent of offices responded positively to the first email, while only 2.4 percent did so to the second.[47]

Some political scientists faulted the study's methods. "Like all research in this area, this study is vexed by the problem of demonstrating a causal relationship between money and legislator behavior that is independent of a common underlying ideology," said Jennifer Victor, an assistant professor of public and international affairs at George Mason University in Fairfax, Va.[48]

The HLOGA sought to restrict lobbyists' financial influence in various ways, including barring a lobbyist for a corporate client from planning or paying for a lawmaker's trip. The provision was adopted in response to the free out-of-town and overseas trips that Abramoff and his associates used to ingratiate their clients with members of Congress.

However, the law permits such trips if foreign governments foot the bill, so a lobbyist can pay for a trip on behalf of one of those governments. In addition, nonprofit organizations, some of which have close ties to lobbying shops, also can finance trips. As a result, lawmakers and their aides took more free trips in 2013 than in any year since the restrictions took effect — an estimated 1,887 excursions costing almost $6 million.[49]

But some research disputes the direct correlation between money and the outcome of an issue. University of North Carolina political scientist Frank R. Baumgartner looked at 98 randomly selected cases of lobbying in Washington from 1999 to 2003, examining Federal Election Commission campaign finance reports and other information. He found "virtually no impact of money on outcomes." He said it was because lobbying "is generally about changing the status quo," and that "the huge business and corporate bias that permeates Washington is already built into the policies of the status quo."[50]

Rehr, the former lobbyist, reached a similar conclusion in a survey he conducted in 2013 of more than 700 congressional staffers and 2,200 lobbyists. He asked the most important ways to get access to a member of Congress or their staff. Only 2 percent of staffers and 4 percent of lobbyists said the most important determinant of access was whether a lobbyist's political action committee had donated to the member's campaign. They ranked it last among six measures. The highest-ranking measure cited by both lobbyists and staffers was "providing credible, reliable information."[51]

Money is "a tool," Rehr says. "As a lobbyist, I would rather have it than not. But it doesn't play the dominant role people assume it does."

Lobbyists note that even the most powerful among their ranks don't always get what they want. Before the deep automatic spending cuts known as "sequestration" were scheduled to take effect in 2012, defense contractors including some of the largest political contributors, such as Lockheed Martin Corp. and Raytheon Co., waged fierce lobbying campaigns against the cuts. But sequestration took effect anyway.

"People . . . have accused us of crying wolf," said Dan Stohr, a spokesman for the Aerospace Industries Association, the trade group representing aerospace companies.[52]

Meanwhile, some lobbyists say the perception that they offer money in exchange for access and favors is

Getty Images/Chip Somodevilla

Religious leaders and lay people hold a prayer vigil for immigration reform outside the Capitol Hill office of House Speaker John Boehner, R-Ohio, on Oct. 8, 2013. A broad coalition of Catholic and evangelical groups has been lobbying the House for months to pass a comprehensive immigration reform bill, but House Republican leaders have resisted the idea.

misguided. Instead, they say, the spiraling cost of running for office forces lawmakers to come to wealthy lobbying groups, hat in hand, asking for money. Between 1986 and 2010, the inflation-adjusted cost of winning a seat in the House doubled, while the cost of winning a Senate seat climbed by more than a third, according to a study by the nonpartisan Campaign Finance Institute.[53] In addition to individual candidates, well-funded issue-oriented interest groups are pouring ever-increasing amounts of cash into televised political messages and attack ads, without even mentioning a particular candidate. Yet, the unmentioned candidate then feels pressured to respond to the ads.

As a result, the airwaves during recent campaign seasons, especially in highly competitive districts, have been inundated by political ads. In 2010, the total number of TV political ads for House, Senate and gubernatorial candidates was two-and-a-half times greater than the number of ads for the same category of races in 2002, according to one study. In terms of spending, TV ads in House races cost 54 percent more in 2010 than they did two years earlier, while the cost of Senate race ads rose 71 percent over 2008.[54]

As a result, complain lobbyists, they must host or attend fundraiser after fundraiser. "I do not believe it would be possible to receive more fundraiser invitations," lobbyist Pat Raffaniello said recently.[55]

BACKGROUND

"Lobby Agents"

Lobbying, embedded in the First Amendment's protection of citizens' right "to petition the government for a redress of grievances," has been part of American democracy since its earliest days. In 1792, a lobbyist for Continental Army veterans in Virginia invited other veterans groups to form a coalition to push for better compensation.

The term "lobbying" came into vogue in the 19th century. In 1829, the phrase "lobby-agents" was used to describe favor-seekers who hovered in the lobby of the New York Capitol in Albany. Within a few years, it had been shortened to "lobbyist" and was widely used around the U.S. Capitol.[56]

In a 1987 speech, Sen. Robert C. Byrd, D-W.Va., recalled how many of the first Washington reporters were in fact lobbyists for merchants and shippers, sent to the capital to provide information on pending tariffs. He noted that they worked in a free-wheeling atmosphere: "Clubs, brothels and 'gambling dens' became natural habitats of the lobbyists, since these institutions were occasionally visited by members of Congress, who, far from home, came seeking good food, drink and agreeable company."[57]

In such an environment, scandals flourished. In 1857, *The New York Times* published an exposé charging that lobbyists had rewritten a Pacific railroad bill to take control of federal lands. Four U.S. representatives had to resign after an investigation by the House. In the Credit Mobilier affair 15 years later, several members of Congress were accused of taking stock in return for helping the Union Pacific Railroad obtain large land grants. And in 1906, a *Cosmopolitan* magazine series accused prominent senators of representing special interests rather than the public interest. The resulting political pressure helped enact the 17th Amendment, requiring senators to be elected by the public rather than by state legislatures.[58]

By the end of the 19th century, the reputation of lobbyists was so bad that President William McKinley rebuffed a suggestion from his political mentor, Mark Hanna, that McKinley appoint a friend to his Cabinet with the blunt remark: "Mark, I would do anything in the world for you, but I cannot put a man in my Cabinet who is known as a lobbyist."[59]

In 1876 the House began requiring all lobbyists to register.[60] States also took action: In its 1877 constitution

C H R O N O L O G Y

1800s *States restrict lobbyists as their influence grows.*

1829 The phrase "lobby-agents" is used to describe favor-seekers in New York Capitol lobby.

1872 Credit Mobilier scandal reveals that senators and representatives received railroad stocks for supporting railroad legislation.

1876 House requires lobbyists to register.

1877 Georgia constitution outlaws lobbying of state legislators.

1890 Massachusetts requires lobbyists active on state issues to register.

1940s-1960s *Lobbying regulation evolves in modern political age.*

1946 Federal Regulation of Lobbying Act requires lobbyists to register.

1950 President Harry S. Truman complains about lobbyists' influence. . . . House committee recommends strengthening 1946 law.

1954 Supreme Court upholds 1946 law.

1962 Congress redefines bribery to include offering or taking anything of value to influence a vote.

1970s *Reform-minded lobbying groups blossom in the wake of political and social protest movements.*

1970 Ralph Nader founds watchdog U.S. Public Interest Research Group. . . . Politically oriented lobby groups formed following Watergate scandal.

1978 Ethics in Government Act requires former executive branch officials to wait a year before lobbying former colleagues.

1990s *Congress attempts further regulation of lobbyists.*

1995 Lobbying Disclosure Act broadens definition of lobbying to include contacts with congressional staff and

executive branch officials. . . . Republicans launch K Street Project to influence lobby groups.

1998 Senate committee investigates a program offering lobbyists and other campaign donors coffee with President Bill Clinton, officials.

2000s *Lobbying business booms; President Obama cracks down.*

2003 Newspaper in Alexandria, La., reports Coushatta Tribe's payments of $16 million in one year to lobbyist Jack Abramoff and a public relations firm; investigations follow.

2004 Powerful Pharmaceutical Research and Manufacturers of America (Big Pharma), taps as its new president former Rep. W. J. "Billy" Tauzin, R-La., main sponsor of a 2003 Medicare bill supported by the drug industry.

2006 Abramoff sentenced to six years in prison for mail fraud, conspiracy to bribe public officials and tax evasion; he later becomes an advocate for tough restrictions on lobbying.

2007 Abramoff scandal sparks passage of Honest Leadership in Open Government Act, aimed at further regulating lobbying.

2009 Newly elected President Obama orders appointed members of his administration to refuse gifts from registered lobbyists and permanently refrain from lobbying the administration after leaving government.

2010 Total lobbying spending reaches a record $3.6 billion. . . . House and Senate end special-interest "earmarks" in appropriations bills, which had been a boon for lobbyists.

2013 The 1,100-member American League of Lobbyists votes to rename itself the Association of Government Relations Professionals.

2014 A federal appeals court in January rules that a lower court must hear arguments that Obama's 2009 ban on lobbyists serving on government advisory panels violates lobbyists' First Amendment rights.

Regulation Sought for "Political Intelligence"

But critics see constitutional and other problems.

Information is power, as the saying goes, and in Washington a new form of information — "political intelligence" — is flexing its muscles — and causing controversy.

Some consider it a variation of lobbying and think it should be regulated, though it has nothing to do with influencing laws being written. Instead, political intelligence seeks to help stock market investors by providing up-to-the-minute information about government actions.

Political intelligence came under new scrutiny last year when a Washington brokerage firm, Height Securities, revealed a Medicare funding decision to its clients before the Obama administration formally announced it. The move prompted a surge in the price of health care stocks in the minutes before the market closed.[1]

Political intelligence emerged as an industry in the pre-Internet 1980s, when investment banker Ivan Boesky hired lobbyists to attend committee hearings about a proposed oil merger in 1984, using the information they provided to eventually earn $65 million.

"Investors started to realize that there was money to be made by knowing what was going on in Washington and knowing it as quickly as possible," said Michael Mayhew,

founder of the political-intelligence firm Integrity Research Associates.[2]

Some lawmakers say political intelligence practitioners should be subject to the same regulations as registered lobbyists. "When a political intelligence professional is paid to gather inside information from congressional or agency sources that can be used to make investment decisions, that professional should have to register and disclose his or her activities to the public," Sen. Chuck Grassley, R-Iowa, and Rep. Louise Slaughter, D-N.Y., said in a joint statement last year.[3]

Grassley won Senate approval in 2012 of an amendment requiring registration of political intelligence practitioners. But his amendment, attached to a stock-trading bill, was stripped from the final version of the bill.[4]

Not everyone endorses regulating the practice. A *Bloomberg View* editorial called it a "dumb idea," stressing the difficulty of defining political intelligence. "The Internet has enabled an explosion of insider newsletters and websites that strive to give subscribers government information faster and better than the competition. . . . Would this information count as political intelligence? More broadly, political speech enjoys strong constitutional protection; it's

---

Georgia outlawed any lobbying of state legislators (these prohibitions survived until 1992, though they were not enforced), while Massachusetts in 1890 began requiring lobbyists to register and disclose their expenses.[61]

By 1946, lobbyists were required to disclose basic information about their activities under the Federal Regulation of Lobbying Act, passed as part of a legislative reorganization bill. The Supreme Court in *United States v. Harris* upheld the constitutionality of the law in 1954 but narrowly interpreted its key aspects, including a finding that the law covered only direct contact with legislators and not their aides. [2]

Corporations interested in influencing policy continued to operate behind the scenes. Before its official formation in 1972, the industry group Business Roundtable consisted of executives meeting secretly at a Manhattan social club.

"They were aware that if some journalist from *The Washington Post* got wind of a meeting in a social club of representatives of industrial interests, all hell would break loose," says Benjamin Waterhouse, a University of North Carolina historian and author of the 2013 book *Lobbying America: The Politics of Business from Nixon to NAFTA.* "They said, 'We need to keep this fairly under wraps.' "[63]

The group, no longer secret, now counts as members more than 200 chief executive officers of America's largest companies. But two groups with a similar agenda — the National Association of Manufacturers (NAM) and the U.S. Chamber of Commerce — are better known.

NAM, established in 1895 to expand foreign trade opportunities, became a counterweight in the 1930s to President Franklin D. Roosevelt's New Deal social and economic programs. Its membership has remained constant

hard to see how political intelligence wouldn't merit similar deference," the editorial said.[5]

The Government Accountability Office (GAO), in a report last year, also cited the difficulties of pinpointing how political intelligence is used. "The extent to which investment decisions are based on a single piece of political intelligence would be extremely difficult to measure. . . . Investors typically use multiple sources of information to influence their investment and business decisions," the GAO said.[6]

Slaughter said any proposed legislation to regulate political intelligence would exclude journalists, prompting Reuters media critic Jack Shafer to ask: "But how practical is that? The primary difference between Bloomberg, Reuters, *The Wall Street Journal* and all the other collectors of conventional business-and-government news and the myriad political-intelligence outfits and research firms collecting fine-grain business-and-government information is 1) the price they charge for information and 2) how many clients (or readers) they have."[7]

Grassley, the Senate Judiciary Committee's top Republican, launched an investigation of the Height Securities Medicare information tip and the actions of another political intelligence firm, Capitol Street, which held a conference call with investors in which congressional staffers discussed the likely ruling on the Medicare funding.[8]

Grassley's office said in a statement in April that the investigation stalled because the Obama administration refused to share emails from the Department of Health and Human Services, the Office of Management and Budget and the White House.

Grassley "remains interested in the role of political intelligence firms in obtaining and sharing government information with Wall Street prior to public release and in making these interactions with the government more transparent," the statement said.

— *Chuck McCutcheon*

[1]Tom Hamburger and Dina Elboghdady, "Sen. Grassley: Political Intelligence Firms Need More Transparency, Disclosure," *The Washington Post*, May 9, 2013, http://tinyurl.com/n4rkxnh.

[2]Tim Murphy, "The Fastest-Growing Washington Industry You've Never Heard Of," *Mother Jones*, November/December 2013, http://tinyurl.com/pblr9ot.

[3]"Senator Grassley, Congresswoman Slaughter React to GAO Report on Political Intelligence," Office of Sen. Chuck Grassley, April 4, 2013, http://tinyurl.com/ndvm68b.

[4]"Taking Stock of 'Political Intelligence,' " Office of Sen. Chuck Grassley, April 29, 2013, http://tinyurl.com/lkjw7wf.

[5]"Regulating Political Intelligence is Dumb Idea," *Bloomberg View*, May 28, 2013, http://tinyurl.com/l4c58t3.

[6]"Political Intelligence: Financial Market Value of Government Information Hinges on Materiality and Timing," Government Accountability Office, April 2013, http://tinyurl.com/n7fh4pn.

[7]Jack Shafer, "The Dumb War on Political Intelligence," Reuters, May 8, 2013, http://tinyurl.com/ohabye5.

[8]Hamburger and Elboghdady, *op. cit.*

at around 14,000 companies and subsidiaries. The Chamber, founded in 1912, now has nearly 3,000 state and local chapters.[64] It claims to represent the interests of more than 3 million businesses, but its critics have argued its actual membership is about one-tenth that size.[65]

Nevertheless, the Chamber has become a dominant powerhouse in American politics. During the 2010 election cycle, it spent nearly $33 million on election-related advertisements and other communications, making it the biggest spender other than the national party committees. Most Chamber money promotes Republican candidates or opposes Democrats. However, like other nonprofit business associations, the Chamber does not have to disclose its donors.[66]

Before the 1970s, organized labor was a dominant lobbying force. Its sizeable grassroots campaigns could effectively lobby the president and others directly. The American Federation of Labor was founded in 1886 and merged in 1955 with the rival Congress of Industrial Organizations to form the AFL-CIO, the largest union umbrella group. Although its membership totaled nearly 16 million at the time of the merger, the loss of unionized jobs over the subsequent decades caused the AFL-CIO's membership to dwindle to around 10.5 million.[67]

Watergate Reforms

The Watergate scandal of the 1970s created a clamor for more openness in government, as lawmakers sought to address the public's general concerns about corruption.

A variety of post-Watergate reforms opened most congressional committee meetings to the public, while also increasing the power of subcommittees. As the power

Too Much Power?

Protesters in Washington march to the Department of Justice during a rally against big banks and home foreclosures on May 20, 2013 (top). Bank executives testify about mortgage rules proposed by the new Consumer Financial Protection Bureau before the House Financial Institutions and Consumer Credit Subcommittee on Jan. 14, 2014. Many Americans feel that corporate lobbyists have more influence over – and access to – lawmakers and government officials than average citizens, especially since lobbyists and corporate executives are often called to testify on Capitol Hill on pending legislation. Such concerns intensified following the collapse of the real estate bubble in 2007, leading to hundreds of thousands of homeowner foreclosures.

that once was concentrated in each party's leadership became more diffuse, opportunities to directly lobby more members increased. Many new lobbyist groups were created, and others became even more powerful.

Issue-advocacy groups, which lobby on matters dealing with the government's ability to affect individual freedoms, also began to emerge. Such groups began on the political left, such as the U.S. Public Interest Research Group (U.S. PIRG), founded by consumer advocate Ralph Nader in 1970, and Public Citizen, which Nader established in 1971 to address a broad array of interests, from consumer protection to pension rights. Public Citizen, which became one of the most prominent Washington advocacy groups, conducts both grassroots lobbying and direct lobbying, though it does not endorse candidates or make campaign contributions.

There are also advocacy groups on the political right, with the National Rifle Association regarded as the most powerful. Former Union Army officers founded the NRA after the Civil War with the goal of promoting better marksmanship among citizens.[68] Over time, it took on the cause of defending the rights of all gun owners, developing a lobbying operation that spent more than $3.4 million in 2013.[69]

The NRA spends heavily on issue-advocacy advertisements and publishes a legislative scorecard that rates politicians on their positions on gun rights issues. The group has fought a variety of legislative attempts to restrict firearms, including after the 1999 shootings at Columbine High School in Littleton, Colo., and after the 2012 massacre at Sandy Hook Elementary School in Newtown, Conn. It also has sought to repeal existing gun laws. Many of its members tend to be "single-issue" voters who will look only at a candidate's position on guns in deciding how to vote.[70]

Conservatives depict the American Civil Liberties Union (ACLU) as a liberal interest group, but the organization — founded in 1920 — has defended political speech by groups as diverse as communists and the Ku Klux Klan. Since the Sept. 11, 2001, terrorist attacks, one of the ACLU's main focuses has been to protect individual privacy rights as the government enhances national security. It has lobbied against the USA Patriot Act anti-terrorism law and in favor of proposals to rein in the National Security Agency's domestic eavesdropping activities.[71]

The powerful AARP, formerly the American Association of Retired Persons, spent more than $9.6 million on lobbying in 2013, largely on health-care related issues and on protecting Social Security.[72]

Throughout the 1970s and '80s, most lobbyists did not bother to register, and between 1946 and 1980 the Justice Department prosecuted only six lobbying groups under the Federal Regulation of Lobbying Act. After

Republicans gained control of both houses of Congress in 1994, they enacted the Lobbying Disclosure Act, which made several significant changes, including expanding the definition of lobbying to include contacts between lobbyists and non-elected officials, such as congressional staffers. The law also sought to increase prosecutions for violations by lowering the threshold for minor violations from felonies to misdemeanors.[73]

Scandals Erupt

Republican leaders, meanwhile, relied on certain lobbyists to help them maintain their majority. Early in 1995, a group of GOP lawmakers, lobbyists and strategists launched the K Street Project, in which the advocacy group Americans for Tax Reform created and monitored a database of lobbyists' party affiliations and contributions. At the same time, Republican leaders urged their members to work only with lobbyists from the GOP, while pressuring lobby firms, corporations and trade associations to hire their former Republican staffers and colleagues as lobbyists.

Then-House Majority Leader Tom DeLay, R-Texas, solicited energy industry executives and lobbyists to attend a fund-raising retreat in 2002 shortly before a House-Senate conference committee was to begin work on a national energy bill. The House Ethics Committee admonished DeLay for violating House rules by creating an appearance of impropriety with the timing of the event.[74]

DeLay also had close ties to disgraced lobbyist Abramoff, whose dealings with Indian tribes became the subject of a Senate investigation that concluded he and his business partner, Michael Scanlon, billed six tribes $66 million, much of it through fraudulent overcharges. A former aide to DeLay, Tony Rudy, pleaded guilty to bribing lawmakers while working for Abramoff.[75] Rep. Bob Ney, R-Ohio, also was convicted of corruption charges and served a 30-month jail term. The saga was made into the 2010 movie "Casino Jack" starring Kevin Spacey.

Democrats used the scandal in their successful 2006 effort to reclaim majorities in the House and Senate by promising to "drain the swamp" of what then-Minority Leader Nancy Pelosi, D-Calif., said was widespread GOP corruption.[76] When Pelosi ascended to the speakership of the House in 2007, she helped steer into law the Honest Leadership and Open Government Act (HLOGA), which passed 96-2 in the Senate and 411-8 in the House.[77]

Both the scandal and Abramoff's subsequent calls for further overhauling lobbying regulations put the industry on the defensive. Upon his release from prison in 2010, Abramoff wrote a book and advocated a lifelong ban on legislators and their aides becoming lobbyists, as well as barring lobbyists from making contributions or giving gifts of any amount to any lawmaker. Many lobbyists dismissed those ideas as too draconian.[78]

During his presidential campaign in 2007-08, Obama often condemned the industry, asserting that "special interests" and lobbyists "think they own this government, but we're here today to take it back."[79] He later boasted that lobbyists "won't find a job in my White House." However, news media outlets reported during his first month in office that at least a dozen former lobbyists had been granted waivers in order to work there.[80]

Upon taking office, Obama ordered that appointed members of his administration must refuse gifts from registered lobbyists, imposed a two-year ban on appointees working on issues involving a former employer, and prohibited them from lobbying the administration after leaving government service. He later announced a controversial policy to restrict the number of registered lobbyists serving on federal advisory boards and commissions.[81]

Obama also began releasing White House visitor logs as part of an effort to show he and his aides weren't holding court with lobbyists. Some meetings, however, subsequently were held in a complex just off the White House grounds and thus weren't recorded on those logs. Lobbyists said the move was a deliberate attempt to conceal their visits, but administration officials denied that.[82]

Neither Obama's executive orders nor the HLOGA addressed the longstanding issue of "earmarks," federal money for local projects in lawmakers' home states and districts. Lobbyist Gerald Cassidy pioneered the use of earmarking as a specialty, becoming one of the most powerful figures in Washington. As members of both parties began using them in the 1990s as bargaining chips to pass bills, their use soared from a few dozen each year into the thousands.[83] The most infamous earmark was the proposed $300 million "bridge to nowhere," a project connecting Ketchikan, Alaska, to the island of Gravina. It was never built.[84]

Earmarks were at the center of several political corruption scandals, including one that sent former Rep. Randy "Duke" Cunningham, R-Calif., to jail after he was convicted of accepting bribes in exchange for inserting earmarked provisions sought by lobbyists into spending bills. Cunningham steered government contracts to companies who had plied him with a luxury house, a Rolls-Royce and other gifts.

Earmarks eventually became a prime target of budget-cutting lawmakers and outside groups, and after Republicans regained control of the House in 2010 they pressured their leadership to end the practice. The Senate followed suit, and in 2011 Obama promised to veto any appropriations bill sent to him that contained earmarks.[85]

The loss of earmarks led to a steep drop in business — and in income — for some lobbyists. "The fees I charged for clients seeking earmarks were quadruple what I am able to charge them now," says veteran lobbyist Michael Fulton.

An American Bar Association task force made up of lobbyists and public interest groups released a comprehensive reform proposal in 2011 calling for lowering the threshold by which someone must register as a lobbyist. The group suggested reducing the requirement that lobbyists spend at least 20 percent of their time for a client on lobbying activity to an unspecified "reasonable" percentage. It also called for a two-year prohibition on lobbyists doing any fundraising for members that they lobby. However, Congress did not act on it.[86]

In 2012, Rep. Frank Wolf, R-Va., became concerned about the use of lobbyists by foreign governments, especially those whose interests differed from those of the United States. He introduced a bill to bar ex-presidents and members of Congress from lobbying on behalf of those governments for 10 years after leaving office. The measure drew just one cosponsor, and no action was taken on it.[87]

CURRENT SITUATION

Inaction by Congress

A variety of bills aimed at tightening federal lobbying restrictions have been introduced in the current session of Congress, but in the absence of scandals, lawmakers have shown little interest.

In March, Rep. Mike Quigley, D-Ill., introduced the Transparency in Government Act, which contained some of the Bar Association task force's recommendations. In addition to removing the 20-percent loophole and lowering the yearly lobbyist income ceiling from

$20,000 to $12,000, Quigley's legislation calls for establishing a Justice Department task force to prosecute lobbying violations.

But the measure, which Quigley also had introduced during the previous Congress, had attracted no cosponsors as of June 1.[88] Other lawmakers also had been unable, as of June 1, to attract support for lobbying-related legislation, such as:

- A bill introduced in February by Rep. David Cicilline, D-R.I., to bar former members of Congress from becoming lobbyists had no cosponsors as of June 1.[89]
- A bill introduced in 2013 by Rep. Bill Posey, R-Fla., to extend to five years the cooling-off period on lobbying by ex-members had only three cosponsors as of May.[90]
- A measure introduced in 2013 by Rep. Alan Grayson, D-Fla., requiring corporations to choose between using lobbyists or spending money on political campaigns had no cosponsors as of May.[91]

The Association of Government Relations Professionals also has found House and Senate members unwilling to hold committee hearings on regulating lobbying. Its members support many of the reforms that Quigley has proposed. Howard Marlowe, the group's immediate past president, says members told him they feared it would touch off "partisan acrimony," with both sides accusing each other of being dependent on lobbyists' donations.

"Here's the problem: We're waiting for the next scandal," Marlowe says of the lack of action. "And it's going to come."

Court Decisions

A federal appeals court in January ruled that a lower court must hear arguments that President Obama's 2009 ban on lobbyists serving on government advisory panels violates lobbyists' First Amendment rights. Six lobbyists for trade associations had challenged Obama's order, in which he said lobbyists could exert undue influence if they are on those panels.

The lobbyists sought appointments to the Industry Trade Advisory Committees, which provide the executive branch with input from the business community on trade matters. A U.S. District Court judge had dismissed the case (*Autor v. Pritzker*) in 2012, but the U.S. Court of Appeals for the D.C. Circuit said that decision was "premature."

Is President Obama unfair to lobbyists?

YES Howard Marlowe
*Former President, Association of
Government Relations Professionals*

Written for *CQ Researcher*, May 2014

From the moment he began his race for the presidency, President Obama made demonization of lobbyists one of his signature dishes, so to speak. And during much of his first term, he clearly left the impression that "high-priced lobbyists" are behind every reprehensible legislative cause.

There are at least two sides to every issue, so there are at least two sets of lobbyists battling it out, yet he has attacked only those working for his opposition. He barred lobbyists from holding jobs in his administration and refused to take political contributions from lobbyists. To protest these maneuvers as a grave injustice is akin to lobbing a tennis ball into Obama's court. Pigs squeal when you stick them, don't they? It's in Obama's interest for lobbyists to object.

When the president's rhetoric was fresh, many of us looked to his days as a community activist, law professor, state legislator or U.S. senator for clues to what might have sparked this apparent hatred for lobbyists. We found none. It quickly became apparent that his attacks were the work of a man whose advisers watched public opinion polls carefully. They knew that Obama could attack lobbyists and members of Congress with the assurance that the public held both groups in low esteem. They also knew that he could still raise as much money and have as many meetings as he wanted, as long as they were with unregistered lobbyists — the "unlobbyists."

Aside from this rather expedient hypocrisy, President Obama's anti-lobbyist rhetoric puts the devil's horns on a profession that is an integral part of our representative system of government. We help give voice to the full spectrum of interests from local governments to small businesses and large corporations, to charities, farmers and gun owners. Lobbyists do not succeed unless they combine at least a modest level of expertise with essential ingredients such as honesty and trustworthiness. Members of Congress and their staffs rely on our knowledge of the issues and the legislative process. Like many of the university students I work with now, I got involved with public policy advocacy because I wanted to make a difference.

Before long, this president will "retire" to a millionaire's life of corporate boards and speaking engagements, where rhetoric takes a back seat to fat checks. Perhaps Obama will even become the first ex-president to become a lobbyist. That would surely be the definition of poetic justice.

NO Robert Bauer
*Former White House Counsel (Obama
Administration)*

Excerpted from remarks at the American University Conference on Lobbying Reform in the U.S. and E.U., March 17, 2014

While in the U.S. Senate, when running for president and then while in office, President Obama has often spoken out about the risk to the development and advancement of public policy presented by well-financed lobbying campaigns. And he has been unsparing at times in his description of the problem, such that many have heard from lobbyists that he is offending them and giving a bad name to the processes by which people bring legitimate issues before the government for resolution.

Much of the attention is focused on a particularly controversial measure — the executive order the president signed on Jan. 21, 2009, his first day in office. With that order, he approved unprecedented restrictions on the hiring for senior positions of individuals who had been registered . . . as "lobbyists" any time within the previous two years and also on the lobbying or contacts permitted to Obama administration officials after they return to the private sector.

The first objection is that the president's policy fails to distinguish between good and bad lobbyists and paints everybody whose business it is to shape government policy, through pressure and persuasion, in the same dark colors. It has never been clear how any reform policy that is concerned with the "revolving door" could meet this objection successfully.

As for the broader objection, that the executive order cast aspersions on the craft of lobbying, this, too, does not seem to allow for any practical answer. Either we have revolving-door restrictions or we don't, but if we have them, we will necessarily, by virtue of the restrictions written into our rules and regulations, suggest that — in some ways and in some circumstances — lobbying activity or the role of lobbyists raise issues that are properly addressed by reforms.

To the very real question about shutting out of government service people with much to contribute, the answer lies in administrative flexibility through the waiver process. And perhaps there is other fine-tuning that, with experience and further reflection, could prove useful. For example, the two-year period could be shortened to one year, or other aspects of the policy could be revised to limit its more expansive applications.

For all the controversy over these policies, and indeed because of that controversy, they constructively moved reform, and the debate about reform policy, in a fresh direction when a fresh direction away from old and unproductive quarrels has been needed.

The appeals court instructed the lower court to focus on the justification for distinguishing between corporate employees — who are permitted to serve on advisory panels — and registered lobbyists for those same corporations.[92]

In another high-profile ruling with implications for lobbyists, the U.S. Supreme Court in April struck down so-called aggregate limits on political contributions. The decision, in *McCutcheon v. Federal Election Commission*, allows lobbyists and other contributors — who previously could give no more than $123,000 directly to political candidates and party committees during an election cycle — to spend up to $3.5 million.

The ruling is expected to put lobbyists under even more pressure to contribute vast sums to candidates and causes. Many of them had cited the prior aggregate restriction as a reason for turning down fundraising appeals from lawmakers. One unidentified GOP lobbyist told *The Hill* before the Supreme Court's ruling: "I like the limit because it gives me an excuse not to give more."[93]

Executive Branch

President Obama has not proposed any new crackdowns on lobbying since he won re-election in 2012, but has continued to criticize the profession.

Getty Images/*The Washington Post*/Eva Russo

A demonstrator marches near Washington's K Street — center of the city's lobbying industry — on Oct. 1, 2012, to protest the influence of lobbyists on Congress. Lobbying scored lowest among 22 professions on honesty and ethical standards in a poll in 2013, the same year the American League of Lobbyists changed its name to the Association of Government Relations Professionals.

"Ordinary folks can't write massive campaign checks or hire high-priced lobbyists and lawyers to secure policies that tilt the playing field in their favor at everyone else's expense," he said in a December speech.[94]

However, Obama recently has turned to lobbyists to fill some administration posts. In February he nominated Robert Holleyman, a former leader of the Business Software Alliance, as deputy U.S. trade representative.[95] Earlier he named lobbyist Joseph Hezir as the Department of Energy's chief financial officer.[96]

Federal prosecutors, meanwhile, have filed charges against two lobbying firms. In March, the U.S. Attorney's Office for the District of Columbia filed a complaint against Alexandria, Va., lobbyist Alan Mauk and his firm for allegedly failing to submit dozens of disclosure reports. Nine months earlier, the office had filed a civil suit against a New York consulting firm, Biassi Business Services, charging it with 124 disclosure violations.[97]

State Actions

A handful of states are debating tougher lobbying laws, often in response to scandals and controversies.

Lawmakers in Alabama are barred from lobbying the chamber they worked in for two years after leaving office. The state Senate president pro tem, Republican Del Marsh, introduced a bill extending the ban to both chambers after three House members resigned, with one joining a lobbying firm and two working for political advocacy groups.[98] Senate Democrats successfully added language imposing new limits on lobbying for family members, but a House committee removed that language.[99]

In Illinois, where several lobbying-related scandals have erupted in the past, GOP state Sen. Darin LaHood this year reintroduced a measure he has sponsored since 2011 that would place a one-year ban on legislators becoming lobbyists as well as bar legislators from negotiating lobbying contracts while still in office. LaHood — the son of former U.S. House member and Secretary of Transportation Ray LaHood — said the Democratic majority in the Senate has blocked the measure from coming to a vote, knowing it would pass.[100]

Other states have focused on gifts and donations that lobbyists can give to lawmakers. In Virginia, Democratic Gov. McAuliffe in January imposed a $100 limit on gifts to most executive branch employees following a gift-giving scandal involving his predecessor, Republican

Robert McDonnell. McDonnell and his wife were indicted on charges that they lent the prestige of the governor's office to businessman Jonnie R. Williams Sr. and a company he used to run, Star Scientific, in exchange for gifts and loans. They have pleaded not guilty. State lawmakers subsequently passed a bill limiting the value of gifts to lawmakers and public officials from lobbyists to $250.[101]

In Kentucky, lawmakers this year strengthened an existing ethics law banning lobbyists from contributing to legislators or legislative candidates as well as prohibiting lobbyists' employers and political action committees (PACs) from donating to candidates during the three-month legislative session.[102]

The Philadelphia Inquirer reported in March that four state lawmakers were caught on tape accepting cash from a lobbyist wearing a wire, an incident that spurred hearings to address strengthening Pennsylvania's gift laws. Legislators now are allowed to accept gifts of any amount as long as they disclose gifts of more than $250 and hospitality-related events, such as dinners, that exceed $650.[103]

Meanwhile, the American Legislative Exchange Council (ALEC), a business-oriented group that brings together state lawmakers with corporate executives to try to pass conservative-oriented "model" bills, has been under scrutiny. In April, U.S. Rep. Raúl Grijalva, D-Ariz., asked the Interior Department to investigate the group for what he alleged was unregistered lobbying to change state laws regarding public-land uses.

The group says it does not lobby, and a spokesman dismissed Grijalva's request as "high political theater."[104] But critics say ALEC's leadership is made up of former lobbyists and that its approach of writing model legislation "makes old-fashioned lobbying obsolete."[105]

OUTLOOK

Interest-Group Gridlock

Lobbying is here to stay — and experts say it will become more sophisticated as technology evolves. They also predict groups will devote ever-increasing amounts of time and money to advancing their causes.

"One of the things we need to figure out as a society is what happens when you have so many interests devoting so many resources to politics," says the Sunlight Foundation's Drutman. "There's a kind of interest-group

gridlock where you have so much on both sides of an issue. . . . It crowds out other issues."

As an example, Drutman cited the recurring controversy over whether Congress should pass a resolution labeling as genocide the massacre of hundreds of thousands of Armenians during and following World War I. Armenian-Americans have lobbied persistently in support of such a measure, but Turkey's government has vigorously campaigned against the idea, hiring a lobbying firm led by former House Majority Leader Richard Gephardt, D-Mo.[106]

Experts say future attempts to rein in lobbyists' influence and encourage disclosure of their activities should not replicate old ones. Drutman has proposed that the Library of Congress create a website as the central online forum and clearinghouse for all public policy advocacy.

"Such a website would both level the playing field (it is much cheaper to post a web page than to hire an army of lobbyists to descend on Washington) and increase transparency and accountability (if all positions and arguments are public, everyone knows who is lobbying for what and why). This will result in more democratic and more thoroughly vetted public policy," he said in a research paper.[107]

The Sunlight Foundation also has proposed creating an online disclosure system of lobbying activities.[108] "Congress should examine and craft new lobbying disclosure laws that are strong enough to move at the pace of the influence they are intended to expose," said John Wonderlich, Sunlight's policy director.[109]

Other experts have offered additional suggestions for the future. Yale University law professor Heather Gerken has called for establishing "policy research consultants" for members of Congress and their staffs who can serve as an alternative to lobbyists providing advice on writing and passing bills.

"If we imagine a market-based solution for funding the legislative subsidy — allowing individual members to hire whomever they want — we would avoid the really hard constitutional question involved" in trying to regulate lobbying, she said.[110]

Allard, the former lobbyist who is now Brooklyn Law School's dean, suggests a way to make the information and expertise that lobbyists provide more accessible to small interest groups that cannot afford to hire lobbyists. He advocates having young lawyers work on behalf of such groups in exchange for reducing those individuals' law school debts. "We could adopt programs like Teach for America — you could have Lobby for America," he says.

Allard also says the current campaign-finance system and politicians' demands for donations "may make them more dependent on lobbyists — not for money, but to get the work of legislators done." As a result, he says, "The links between professional lobbying and elections should be better understood. The topic is rich and worthy of considerable further study."

NOTES

1. Jonathan Cohn, "Howard Dean, the Obamacare Payment Board and K Street," *The New Republic*, July 29, 2013, http://tinyurl.com/mqlggap.

2. Kate Pickert, "Howard Dean Defends His Work for Lobbying Firm After Backlash," *Time*, July 30, 2013, http://tinyurl.com/mwce95a.

3. Cohn, *op. cit.*

4. Thomas B. Edsall, "The Unlobbyists," *The New York Times*, Dec. 31, 2013, http://tinyurl.com/obhfm45.

5. "Building Bridges: The Changing Relationship Between Public Relations and Lobbying," Public Relations Society of America, http://tinyurl.com/l35rtwt.

6. Christopher Rowland, "Tax Lobbyists Help Businesses Reap Windfalls," *The Boston Globe*, March 17, 2013, http://tinyurl.com/brwf7ha.

7. Raquel Meyer Alexander, *et al.*, "Measuring Rates of Return for Lobbying Expenditures: An Empirical Case Study of Tax Breaks for Multinational Corporations," *Journal of Law and Politics*, April 8, 2009, http://tinyurl.com/cwzs9z.

8. Lee Fang, "When a Congressman Becomes a Lobbyist, He Gets a 1,452 Percent Raise (On Average)," *The Nation*, March 14, 2012, http://tinyurl.com/7hlh6kq.

9. Tim LaPira, "How Much Lobbying Is There in Washington? It's Double What You Think," Sunlight Foundation (blog), Nov. 25, 2013, http://tinyurl.com/mzkgm3f.

10. "Lobbying Database," Center for Responsive Politics, http://tinyurl.com/cbyu433.

11. Russ Choma, "How Low Can It Go? Another Drop in Lobbying Spending," Center for Responsive Politics, May 1, 2014, http://tinyurl.com/ksh683w.

12. LaPira, *op. cit.*

13. "Honesty/Ethics in Professions," Gallup, undated, http://tinyurl.com/lcer8a.

14. Robert G. Kaiser, *So Much Damn Money: The Triumph of Lobbying and the Corrosion of American Government* (2009), p. 95.

15. For background on the Abramoff scandal, see Peter Katel, "Lobbying Boom," *CQ Researcher*, July 22, 2005, pp. 613-636.

16. Haley Barbour and Ed Rogers, "The Lobbyists' Lament," *Politico*, Dec. 17, 2013, http://tinyurl.com/opnlgun.

17. Melanie Buck, "How Often Is State Lobbying Influence Reported?" Sunlight Foundation (blog), July 20, 2011, http://tinyurl.com/k9qj9la.

18. Byron Tau, "Who Says Lobbyists Can't Win Elections?" *Politico*, March 12, 2014, http://tinyurl.com/kh26jyh.

19. Jacob R. Straus, "Lobbying Registration and Disclosure: Before and After the Enactment of the Honest Leadership and Open Government Act of 2007," Congressional Research Service, April 22, 2011, http://tinyurl.com/jvqhx5g.

20. Harry Reid, "Foreword to the Fourth Edition," *American Bar Association Lobbying Manual*, 2009, http://tinyurl.com/kdaozvu.

21. "The 10 Things They Won't Tell You About Money in Politics," Center for Responsive Politics, undated, http://tinyurl.com/n2admue.

22. *Ibid.*

23. Lee Fang, "Where Have All the Lobbyists Gone?" *The Nation*, Feb. 19, 2014, http://tinyurl.com/kyk2ytp.

24. *Ibid.*

25. Dan Auble, "Waning Influence? Tracking the 'Unlobbyist,' " Center for Responsive Politics, March 18, 2014, http://tinyurl.com/mvhrnoc.

26. LaPira, *op. cit.*

27. Fang, "Where Have All the Lobbyists Gone?" *op. cit.*

28. Elise Viebeck, "Daschle: A Cabinet Secretary in Exile," *The Hill*, April 8, 2014, http://tinyurl.com/kc3pg6a.

29. Glenn Kessler, "Newt Gingrich and Freddie Mac: Is He Being Misleading?" *The Washington Post* (blog), Nov. 17, 2011, http://tinyurl.com/7f4t27x.

30. Eliza Newlin Carney and Kate Ackley, "Ex-Gingrich Adviser Now Trying to Close Lobbying Loopholes," *CQ Roll Call*, Jan. 25, 2012, http://tinyurl.com/7hytfon.

31. Alex Leary, "Florida Lawmakers-Turned-Lobbyists Fuel Revolving Door of Politics," *Tampa Bay* (Fla.) *Times*, May 31, 2013, http://tinyurl.com/oza359d.

32. Lee Fang, "The Reverse Revolving Door: How Corporate Insiders Are Rewarded Upon Leaving Firms for Congress," *The Nation*, May 4, 2013, http://tinyurl.com/bn7yqrw.

33. "How Money Rules Washington," "Moyers & Company," May 17, 2013, http://tinyurl.com/ockrfxq.

34. Mary Beth Schneider, "Bio: Senate Race is Coats' Latest Challenge," *The Indianapolis Star*, Sept. 7, 2010, http://tinyurl.com/lf2n4gy.

35. Nicholas Allard, "Lobbying Is An Honorable Profession: The Right to Petition and The Competition to Be Right," *Stanford Law & Policy Review*, 2008, http://tinyurl.com/lc3wv96.

36. Fredreka Schouten, "Door Still Revolving Between Capitol, Lobbyists," *USA Today*, April 22, 2009, http://tinyurl.com/lk3gye7.

37. Lee Drutman and Alexander Furnas, "How Revolving-Door Lobbyists Are Taking Over K Street," Sunlight Foundation (blog), Jan. 22, 2014, http://tinyurl.com/pu5mpj4.

38. Open Secrets, www.opensecrets.org/revolving.

39. Timothy Carney, "Max Baucus Rewards Ex-Staffers With Tax Breaks for their Clients," *Washington Examiner*, Jan. 4, 2013, http://tinyurl.com/keb27gc.

40. Marcus Baram, "Judd Gregg Hired by Goldman Sachs as International Advisor," *The Huffington Post*, May 27, 2011, http://tinyurl.com/3kulzfb.

41. "The 10 Things They Won't Tell You About Money in Politics," *op. cit.*

42. Catalina Camia, "Ex-Sen. Jon Kyl Joins D.C. Firm's Lobbying Group," *USA Today*, March 6, 2013, http://tinyurl.com/krq8k67.

43. Tim LaPira and Herschel Thomas III, "A Test of Nancy Pelosi's Revolving-Door Hypothesis," *The Washington Post*, Feb. 7, 2014, http://tinyurl.com/l4o8erg.

44. Eric Lipton and Ben Protess, "Law Doesn't End Revolving Door on Capitol Hill," *The New York Times*, Feb. 1, 2014, http://tinyurl.com/kvh5cfe.

45. Kaiser, *op. cit.*, p. 19.

46. "How Money Rules Washington," *op. cit.*

47. Matea Gold, "Ready For a Surprise? Money Does Equal Access in Washington," *The Washington Post* (blog), March 11, 2014, http://tinyurl.com/kr9s2eo.

48. Jennifer Victor, "On Money Buying Access . . ." *Mischiefs of Faction*, March 11, 2014, http://tinyurl.com/ozsavmd.

49. Shane Goldmacher, "Congress Took More Free Trips in 2013 Than In Any Year Since the Abramoff Reforms," *National Journal*, Feb. 3, 2014, http://tinyurl.com/nr4m32r.

50. Frank R. Baumgartner, "Controverting Expectations: New Empirical Evidence on Congressional Lobbying and Public Policy," University of North Carolina at Chapel Hill, March 8, 2013, http://tinyurl.com/plzsj6d.

51. David Rehr, "The 2014 Congressional Communications Report," undated, http://tinyurl.com/qy4wo74.

52. Sara Sorcher, "How the Defense Lobby Became Irrelevant," *National Journal*, Jan. 1, 2014, http://tinyurl.com/knvrqsp.

53. "The Cost of Winning an Election, 1986-2010," Campaign Finance Institute, undated, http://tinyurl.com/jwl6lb4.

54. Robert W. McChesney and John Nichols, "The Bull Market: Political Advertising," *Monthly Review*, April 2012, http://tinyurl.com/o2kgotd.

55. Kevin Bogardus, "Lobbyists Fear Shakedown If Supreme Court Lifts Campaign Contributions

Cap," *The Hill*, Feb. 26, 2013, http://tinyurl.com/kbrtjke.

56. *Guide to Congress* (7th edition), CQ Press (2013), pp. 833-835.

57. Remarks of U.S. Sen. Robert C. Byrd, "Lobbyists," Sept. 28, 1987, http://tinyurl.com/mka3eol.

58. Donald Ritchie, "Congressional Lobbying Scandals: A Top Ten List," Oxford University Press blog, March 14, 2006, http://tinyurl.com/6xdkuf.

59. *Guide to Congress, op. cit.*

60. Remarks of Sen. Robert C. Byrd, *op. cit.*

61. Richard L. Hasen, "Lobbying, Rent Seeking, and the Constitution," *Stanford Law Review*, Jan. 3, 2011, http://tinyurl.com/pfzowr5.

62. *Guide to Congress, op. cit.*, p. 866.

63. Interview with Benjamin Waterhouse, March 26, 2014, http://tinyurl.com/lnyvxrb.

64. *Guide to Congress, op. cit.*, p. 845.

65. Josh Harkinson, "Chamber Rejects Use of Term '3 Million Members,' " *Mother Jones*, Oct. 23, 2009, http://tinyurl.com/yl5aj2u.

66. "U.S. Chamber of Commerce," Center for Responsive Politics, undated, http://tinyurl.com/o29an4a.

67. *Guide to Congress, op. cit.*, pp. 846-847. BAC Local Union 7, "AFL-CIO History," www.baclocal7.org/history.aspx?zone=History&pID=1631.

68. *Ibid.*, pp. 851-857.

69. "National Rifle Association," Center for Responsive Politics, undated, http://tinyurl.com/cttkdb8.

70. Brian Palmer, "Why Is the NRA So Powerful?" *Slate*, Dec. 18, 2012, http://tinyurl.com/cv9h2rv.

71. "ACLU History," American Civil Liberties Union, undated, http://tinyurl.com/ktlgllz. For background, see Chuck McCutcheon, "Government Surveillance," *CQ Researcher*, Aug. 30, 2013, pp. 717-740; and Kenneth Jost, "Remembering 9/11," *CQ Researcher*, Sept. 2, 2011, pp. 701-732.

72. "AARP," Center for Responsive Politics, undated, http://tinyurl.com/ls5cfdk.

73. *Guide to Congress, op. cit.*, p. 867.

74. *Ibid.*, p. 836.

75. *Ibid.*, p. 872.

76. David Espo, "Pelosi Says She Would Drain GOP 'Swamp,'" The Associated Press, Oct. 6, 2006, http://tinyurl.com/jw4cs.

77. "U.S. Senate Roll Call Votes 110th Congress — 1st Session," Secretary of the U.S. Senate, Jan. 18, 2007, http://tinyurl.com/pqt3fpn. Also see "Final Vote Results for Roll Call 763," Clerk of the U.S. House, July 31, 2007, http://tinyurl.com/qhu79st.

78. Chuck McCutcheon, "Abramoff Still Biggest Thorn in Lobbying Industry's Side," CQ Press First Street Research Group blog, March 15, 2012.

79. "Transcript: Sen. Barack Obama's Announcement for President," The Associated Press, Feb. 10, 2007, http://tinyurl.com/nhz7ygx.

80. Kenneth P. Vogel and Mike Allen, "Obama Finds Room for Lobbyists," *Politico*, Jan. 28, 2009, http://tinyurl.com/csf4y8.

81. Jacob R. Straus, "Lobbying the Executive Branch: Current Practices and Options for Change," Congressional Research Service, Oct. 31, 2011, http://tinyurl.com/ozz84rf.

82. Chris Frates, "White House Meets Lobbyists Off Campus," *Politico*, Feb. 24, 2011, http://tinyurl.com/4u9jrgr.

83. Kaiser, *op. cit.*

84. "The Gravina Access Project: A Bridge to Nowhere," Taxpayers for Common Sense, Feb. 9, 2005, http://tinyurl.com/oya5bcj.

85. Guide to Congress, *op. cit.*, p. 874.

86. Dave Levinthal, "Without Scandal, Lobby Reform Stalls," *Politico*, Sept. 14, 2011, http://tinyurl.com/q7x84fm.

87. "H.R.4343," — Foreign Lobbying Reform Act," U.S. House of Representatives 112th Congress, http://tinyurl.com/qxvdslr.

88. See "HR 2425 —Transparency in Government Act of 2014," U.S. House of Representative 113th Congress, http://tinyurl.com/pgp72at.

89. See "H.R.4014 —To amend title 18, United States Code, to prohibit former Members of Congress from engaging in lobbying contacts," U.S. House

of Representative 113th Congress, http://tinyurl
.com/pczc5ax.

90. See "H.R.440 — Stop the Revolving Door in
Washington Act," U.S. House of Representatives
113th Congress, http://tinyurl.com/k2hlw8e.

91. See "H.R.1118 — Pick Your Poison Act of 2013,"
U.S. House of Representatives 113th Congress,
http://tinyurl.com/orjarlz.

92. *Autor v. Pritzker* (12-5379), U.S. Court of Appeals
for the District of Columbia, Jan. 17, 2014, http://
tinyurl.com/m7kk9vv.

93. Bogardus, *op. cit.*

94. "Remarks by the President on Economic Mobility,"
White House Office of the Press Secretary, Dec. 4,
2013, http://tinyurl.com/mk4qe7n.

95. Lee Fang, "Obama Nominates SOPA Lobbyist for
TPP Trade Post," *The Nation*, Feb. 27, 2014,
http://tinyurl.com/os45spw.

96. "President Obama Announces More Key
Administration Posts," White House Office of the
Press Secretary, Oct. 30, 2013, http://tinyurl.com/
o4sn76m.

97. Holly Yeager, "Lobbyist Faces $5 Million Fine for
Allegedly Failing to File Disclosure Reports," *The
Washington Post*, March 18, 2014, http://tinyurl
.com/l3ntp7m.

98. Phillip Rawls, "Alabama Senate Votes to Toughen
State Ethics Law," The Associated Press, Feb. 4,
2014, http://tinyurl.com/ndsu5ey.

99. Max Reiss, "Factcheck: Ad Targets GOP
Leadership," WSFA-TV.com, April 14, 2014,
http://tinyurl.com/mqpphla.

100. Darin LaHood, "LaHood: Time to Stop the
Legislator-to-Lobbyist Revolving Door From
Spinning in Illinois," *RebootIllinois.com*, April 3,
2014, http://tinyurl.com/knc5bqy.

101. Nicholas Kusnetz, "Virginia's Move Toward Ethics
Reform Leaves Many Unimpressed," State Integrity
Investigation, March 11, 2014, http://tinyurl
.com/pxh3war.

102. George C. Troutman, "2014 Changes Will
Strengthen Kentucky Ethics Law," *The Eagle Post*
(Ky.), April 9, 2014, http://tinyurl.com/ltuzouq.

103. Amy Worden, "Toughen Ethics Laws, Advocates
Tell Pa. Legislators," *The Philadelphia Inquirer*,
April 28, 2014, http://tinyurl.com/m7jy2kb.

104. Niraj Chokshi, "One Democratic Congressman
Escalates the Fight Over ALEC," *The Washington
Post* (blog), April 16, 2014, http://tinyurl.com/
o2ycs3m.

105. "ALEC Exposed," The Center for Media and
Democracy, undated, http://tinyurl.com/o6elecn.

106. Dan Eggen, "Armenia-Turkey Dispute Over
Genocide Label Sets Off Lobbying Frenzy," *The
Washington Post*, March 4, 2010, http://tinyurl
.com/ybw9f6j.

107. Lee Drutman, "A Better Way to Fix Lobbying,"
Issues in Governance Studies, Brookings Institution,
June 2011, http://tinyurl.com/lmpchmr.

108. "Real Time Online Lobbying Transparency Act,"
Sunlight Foundation, undated, http://tinyurl
.com/4rnvm8t.

109. "Testimony of John Wonderlich, Policy Director,
Sunlight Foundation," House Energy and
Commerce Committee, Subcommittee on
Oversight and Investigations, May 3, 2011, http://
tinyurl.com/pyaw8qc.

110. Heather Gerken, "Keynote Address: Lobbying as
the New Campaign Finance," *Georgia State
University Law Review*, Summer 2011, http://tiny-
url.com/nvolsap.

BIBLIOGRAPHY
Selected Sources
Books

**Abramoff, Jack, *Capitol Punishment: The Hard Truth
About Washington Corruption From America's Most
Notorious Lobbyist*, WND Books, 2011.**
A convicted ex-lobbyist contends — in an argument that
practicing lobbyists vehemently reject — that corruption
pervades the industry.

**Holyoke, Thomas T., *Interest Groups and Lobbying:
Pursuing Political Interests in America*, Westview
Press, 2014.**

A California State University-Fresno political scientist explains the roles of interest groups and lobbyists in shaping public policy.

Kaiser, Robert G., *So Much Damn Money: The Triumph of Lobbying and the Corrosion of American Government*, Knopf, 2009.
A veteran *Washington Post* reporter and editor traces the career of powerful lobbyist Gerald Cassidy to illustrate how campaign donations have influenced lobbying and politics.

Vance, Stephanie, *The Influence Game: 50 Insider Tactics from the Washington D.C. Lobbying World That Will Get You to Yes*, Wiley, 2012.
A longtime lobbyist discusses the techniques that lobbyists use to achieve short- and long-term goals.

Waterhouse, Benjamin C., *Lobbying America: The Politics of Business From Nixon to NAFTA*, Princeton University Press, 2013.
A University of North Carolina historian details how industry lobby groups emerged in the 1970s and '80s to advance a pro-business agenda.

Articles

Barbour, Haley, and Ed Rogers, "The Lobbyists' Lament," *Politico*, Dec. 17, 2013, http://tinyurl.com/opnlgun.
Two long-time lobbyists explain how their business operates in an attempt to bolster public confidence in the profession.

Becker, Bernie, "From Newspaper Reporter to Advocate," *The Hill*, Oct. 1, 2013, http://tinyurl.com/pzopuku.
Jeffrey Birnbaum went from covering the lobbying industry as a reporter to becoming a lobbyist himself.

Edsall, Thomas B., "The Unlobbyists," *The New York Times*, Dec. 31, 2013, http://tinyurl.com/obhfm45.
A veteran political journalist examines the rise of "strategic advisers" and other unregistered lobbyists.

Fang, Lee, "Where Have All the Lobbyists Gone?" *The Nation*, Feb. 14, 2014, http://tinyurl.com/kyk2ytp.
A journalist who covers money in politics looks at how the lobbying profession has changed in recent years.

Schmidt, Michael S., Eric Lipton and Alexandra Stevenson, "After Big Bet, Hedge Fund Pulls the Levers of Power," *The New York Times*, March 9, 2014, http://tinyurl.com/lh8vnj5.
Hedge fund manager William A. Ackman lobbied vigorously to bring about the collapse of the nutritional-supplement company Herbalife to protect an investment.

Smith, Jennifer, and Elizabeth Williamson, "Lobbying Firm Patton Boggs Fights for Itself," *The Wall Street Journal*, March 9, 2014, http://tinyurl.com/qggtv66.
One of Washington's most powerful lobbying firms has lost ground to competitors.

Reports and Studies

Alexander, Raquel Meyer, *et al.*, "Measuring Rates of Return for Lobbying Expenditures: An Empirical Case Study of Tax Breaks for Multinational Corporations," *Journal of Law and Politics*, April 8, 2009, http://tinyurl.com/cwzs9z.
A Washington and Lee University associate professor of accounting, along with law and business professors from the University of Kansas, finds a significant rate of return among corporations that spent money for lobbying on a 2004 tax bill.

Baumgartner, Frank R., "Controverting Expectations: New Empirical Evidence on Congressional Lobbying and Public Policy," paper presented at the Baldy Center for Law and Social Policy, SUNY Albany Law School, March 8, 2013, http://tinyurl.com/plzsj6d.
A University of North Carolina political scientist looks at 98 randomly selected cases of lobbying and finds "virtually no impact of money on outcomes."

Drutman, Lee, and Alexander Furnas, "How Revolving-Door Lobbyists Are Taking Over K Street," *Sunlight Foundation* blog, Jan. 22, 2014, http://tinyurl.com/pu5mpj4.
Researchers for a watchdog group document how many former elected officials and their staffers are turning to lobbying.

Gerken, Heather, "Keynote Address: Lobbying as the New Campaign Finance," *Georgia State University Law Review*, summer 2011, http://tinyurl.com/nvolsap.

A Yale University law professor discusses how future lobbying reforms might avoid constitutional challenges.

Rehr, David, "The 2014 Congressional Communications Report," http://tinyurl.com/qy4wo74.

A former lobbyist who studies the industry surveys lobbyists and congressional staff members about what types of lobbying are most effective.

For More Information

Association of Government Relations Professionals, 300 North Washington St., #205, Alexandria, VA 22314; 703-960-3011; grprofessionals.org. A trade organization for lobbyists (formerly the American League of Lobbyists).

Center for Congressional and Presidential Studies, American University, Ward 109, 4400 Massachusetts Ave., N.W., Washington, DC 20016-8130; 202-885-3491; www.american.edu/spa/ccps/PAAI.cfm. Sponsors lectures by lobbyists and other experts through the center's Public Affairs and Advocacy Institute.

Center for Public Integrity, 910 17th St., N.W., Suite 700, Washington, DC 20006; 202-466-1300; publicintegrity.org. A nonprofit dedicated to investigative journalism.

Center for Responsive Politics, 1101 14th St., N.W., Suite 1030, Washington, DC 20005; 202-857-0044; www.opensecrets.org. A nonpartisan research group that tracks money in politics and its effect on elections and public policy.

Sunlight Foundation, 1818 N St., N.W., Suite 300, Washington, DC 20036; 202-742-1520; www.sunlightfoundation.org. A nonpartisan research group that tracks lobbying as part of its mission to promote greater transparency in politics.

14

School Discipline

Anne Farris Rosen

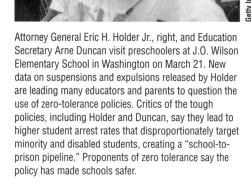

Attorney General Eric H. Holder Jr., right, and Education Secretary Arne Duncan visit preschoolers at J.O. Wilson Elementary School in Washington on March 21. New data on suspensions and expulsions released by Holder are leading many educators and parents to question the use of zero-tolerance policies. Critics of the tough policies, including Holder and Duncan, say they lead to higher student arrest rates that disproportionately target minority and disabled students, creating a "school-to-prison pipeline." Proponents of zero tolerance say the policy has made schools safer.

From *CQ Researcher*,
May 9, 2014.

W hen 15-year-old Dontadrian Bruce of Olive Branch, Miss., was suspended for 21 days in February for holding up two fingers and thumb in a class photo, there was an outcry from schoolmates and the community on social media sites calling for his reinstatement. Bruce, a 10th-grade football player, said he didn't know he was flashing a gang sign, but Desoto County school administrators said the gesture violated the county's school discipline code.

"We're looking at possible revisions for the upcoming school year," said Associate Superintendent Van Alexander. "But safety still has to be the number one priority. It just has to be."[1]

The discipline meted out to Bruce is not uncommon. Although in the past such behavior might have landed students in detention or in the principal's office, today students in the United States are suspended for minor infractions such as disrupting class, not wearing a school uniform, chewing gum or using a cell phone.

Nearly two decades after school administrators began instituting get-tough discipline to stem growing violence and drugs in schools, new data on high rates of suspensions and expulsions are leading many school officials to question the use of so-called zero-tolerance policies and to institute reforms. Critics say overzealous use of such policies, plus a growing police presence in schools, has disproportionately targeted minority and disabled students, in some cases creating a "school-to-prison pipeline." Proponents of zero tolerance, however, say the policies have made schools safer.

In addition, recent school shootings have led some parents and gun-rights groups to call for more armed personnel in schools, but

Blacks Disciplined at Disproportionate Rates

Black students represent 16 percent of total student enrollment (pre-K-12), but 32-42 percent of students suspended or expelled. In comparison, white students also represent between 31-40 percent of students suspended or expelled, but they are 51 percent of the student population.

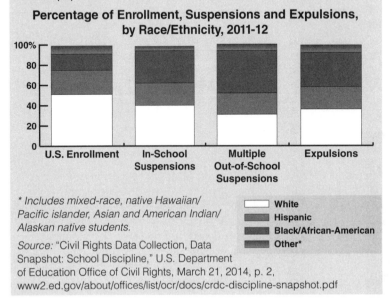

Percentage of Enrollment, Suspensions and Expulsions, by Race/Ethnicity, 2011-12

* Includes mixed-race, native Hawaiian/ Pacific islander, Asian and American Indian/ Alaskan native students.

☐ White
▨ Hispanic
▦ Black/African-American
▨ Other*

Source: "Civil Rights Data Collection, Data Snapshot: School Discipline," U.S. Department of Education Office of Civil Rights, March 21, 2014, p. 2, www2.ed.gov/about/offices/list/ocr/docs/crdc-discipline-snapshot.pdf

some studies show that having police in schools leads to higher student arrest rates. And civil liberties advocates question whether school discipline policies that cover off-campus misbehavior, such as cyberbullying, infringe on students' privacy and civil rights.

Figures released in March show that some 3.5 million students were suspended from U.S. elementary and secondary public schools, mostly for minor offenses, during the 2011-12 school year, the latest data available.[2] Another 130,000 students were expelled, and 260,000 students were referred to law enforcement. And nearly 5,000 preschoolers were suspended once — and 2,500 more than once.[3] Nationwide, 95 percent of out-of-school suspensions are for nonviolent behavior, said U.S. Education Secretary Arne Duncan.[4]

Moreover, according to the newly released figures, suspension rates are disproportionately higher among minority and disabled students. African-Americans are suspended and expelled at three times the rate of whites, and students with disabilities are more than twice as likely to be suspended as students without disabilities.[5]

A recent study shows that although racial disparity in suspensions has existed since the 1970s, the gap between black and white students has widened since schools began expanding the use of zero tolerance.[6]

Those racial disparities occur even at the prekindergarten level, U.S. Attorney General Eric H. Holder Jr. said in releasing the new data on preschool suspensions and expulsions — the first time such data have been collected.[7] "Every data point represents a life impacted and a future potentially diverted or derailed," Holder said.[8] "This administration is moving aggressively to disrupt the school-to-prison pipeline in order to ensure that all of our young people have equal educational opportunities."

The pre-K data is part of an Obama administration effort to reinstitute and expand the government's annual data collection on national school discipline, which was discontinued during the George W. Bush administration. The new information on the sharp rise in suspensions and expulsions has helped spur educators, elected officials and parents to rethink school discipline policies.

"Most people weren't aware of how frequently students were being suspended," says Daniel Losen, director of the Center for Civil Rights Remedies at the University of California at Los Angeles's Civil Rights Project. "The sheer volume raised flags for parents and education policymakers."

"We're at a very exciting stage right now," says Michael Thompson, director of the Council of State Governments' Justice Center, a nonpartisan organization that serves local, state and federal policymakers. "It's clear that we're seeing a substantial growth of momentum across the country as it relates to rethinking school discipline policies."

Others are wary that reforms could sacrifice safety. "The first priority should be on creating a safe and orderly environment for the vast majority of students who want to learn and obey the rules," said Michael Petrilli, executive vice president of the conservative Thomas B. Fordham Institute, a research organization in Washington that promotes educational excellence.[9] "But we should never sacrifice a safe and orderly climate for feel-good efforts for the handful of disruptive students."

The Obama administration is pushing for reforms of zero tolerance discipline, both focusing on data collection and raising awareness about the disproportionate rates of suspensions and expulsions among minority and disabled students. "An African-American kindergartner was given a five-day suspension for setting off a fire alarm, while a white ninth-grader in the very same district was suspended for one day for the same offense," Deborah Delisle, an assistant secretary of Education, told a Senate Judiciary Committee hearing on "Ending the School-to-Prison Pipeline."[10]

The Justice Department also is investigating allegations of high suspension rates, racial disparity in discipline and unlawful use of law enforcement in schools. In Wake County, N.C., for instance, 18 civil rights and education- reform organizations have filed a complaint with the Justice Department against the school system, sheriff's department and seven police departments. The groups allege that African-American students' constitutional civil rights have been violated by the over-use of law enforcement in Wake County schools for minor discipline problems. The school system is reviewing the complaint, but former Wake County School Board Chairman Ron Margiotta defended the board's actions. "We cannot educate students if we can't control what goes on in the schools and in the classrooms," he said.[11]

Several academic and nonprofit organizations say the new research on the pervasiveness and effects of zero tolerance supports their contention that changes are needed. For instance, a study examining at least six years of records of 1 million public secondary school students

in Texas found that nearly 60 percent had been suspended or expelled at least once. It also found that African-American students had a 31 percent higher likelihood of suspension or expulsion than their white or Hispanic counterparts.[12]

In 2012, nationwide numbers showed higher rates of suspension among Latino, disabled, gay and transgender students, as well as African-Americans, often for similar violations.[13]

Some scholars, however, such as Frederick Hess of the conservative American Enterprise Institute (AEI), have said the government is focusing too narrowly on civil rights rather than considering other explanations for disciplinary disparities. The disparities might be the result of "prejudice either overt or intentional," he said, but it also could be that "low income or minority kids are misbehaving at higher rates for whatever reason. My experience is that it's probably some mix of the two."[14]

Hans Bader, a senior attorney specializing in First Amendment and civil rights law at the Competitive Enterprise Institute, a nonprofit organization in Washington that promotes limited government and free enterprise, said the numbers of suspensions largely "reflect actual infraction rates." Trying to bring suspension rates for

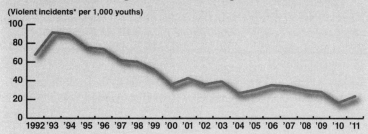

School Violence Declines Over 20 Years

Serious violent crimes and assaults against students ages 12 to 18 fell by about 75 percent since reaching a peak in 1993. School violence reached a 20-year low in 2010 before edging up in 2011.

Violent Crime* Against Students, Ages 12-18, 1992-2011

(Violent incidents* per 1,000 youths)

* Includes serious violent crimes, including rape, sexual assault, robbery and aggravated assault, as well as simple assault.

Source: Simone Robers, Jana Kemp, and Jennifer Truman, "Indicators of School Crime and Safety: 2012," National Center for Education Statistics, U.S. Department of Education, and Bureau of Justice Statistics, June 2013, Table 2.1, http://tinyurl.com/pcvy3xq

minorities closer in line with those of other groups would mean adopting a "de facto racial quota in discipline" that at least one federal court has ruled violates the Constitution's Equal Protection Clause, Bader contended.[15]

But Russell Skiba, a school psychology professor at Indiana University in Bloomington, said the disparity rate is not the result of minority students misbehaving more than their white peers. In one of his own studies, Skiba found that even when controlling for poverty and student behavior, black students were suspended or expelled at rates 1.5 times those of whites.[16]

Some schools are incorporating alternative discipline models for nonviolent offenses, such as antibullying programs, teacher training for positive feedback, manhood-development classes, early intervention and conflict resolution. Another approach, called restorative justice, holds misbehaving students accountable to the victims and the school community.[17] An analysis by Losen shows that many schools use alternative programs and are suspending fewer students than before.[18] Schools in Cleveland and Virginia that introduced some of these alternatives saw an improved sense of safety among students and a decline in suspensions, according to a 2014 study by 26 research collaborators.[19]

"More than ever before, we're seeing a willingness to develop strategies that keep children in the classroom while creating safe, welcoming learning environments that help all students succeed," says Thompson.

Alternatives can be expensive, however. "Superintendents recognize that out-of-school suspension is outdated and not in line with 21st-century education," said Daniel Domenech, executive director of The School Superintendents Association, in Alexandria, Va. But "funds to improve school climate and train school personnel in alternative school discipline can be scarce in today's economic climate."[20]

As schools and the public continue to grapple with student-discipline problems, here are some of the questions that arise:

Has zero tolerance made schools safer?

When schools began adopting zero-tolerance policies in the early-1990s, it was largely to address the rising incidence of violence and drugs in schools. Also, Congress in 1994 mandated that schools expel a student for one year for possessing a weapon at school.[21] Some local administrators, using their authority under the law to modify expulsions on a case-by-case basis, extended strict discipline to a wide variety of misbehavior. A spate of school shootings beginning in the late 1990s also led to demands that schools crack down on troublemakers and post police and armed security guards on campus.

Some school boards also adopted mandatory zero-tolerance punishments for infractions to protect principals and administrators from lawsuits alleging that discipline was being applied unequally based on students' race, disabilities or other factors. Such policies eliminated principals' discretion, it was argued, so they could not be accused of disparate treatment.

Although the juvenile crime rate has dropped since peaking in 1994, and there is less violence in schools today than 20 years ago, the get-tough policies along with the added security staffing has meant more students are being ushered into court and suspended from school.[22] "This sort of tsunami of zero tolerance, get-tough-on-kids approach, and this willingness to kick out the bad kids so the good kids can learn, has seen a dramatic increase," says Losen of the Center for Civil Rights Remedies. "The mentality of zero tolerance has seeped into every little offense."

A growing body of research examining the impact on students and schools of swift and strict penalties has concluded that while such policies are crucial for serious offenses involving weapons, drugs or violence, the use of arbitrary suspension and expulsion for minor violations may not be the best approach to school discipline.

"Two decades of research has confirmed that out-of-school suspensions do not improve student behavior and, in fact, often exacerbate it," says Laura Faer, education rights director for Public Counsel, a law firm in Los Angeles that provides pro bono legal services to schools. "Students who are suspended lose valuable instructional time and are more likely to fall behind in school, drop out and enter the juvenile delinquency system, at great cost to students and taxpayers."

One study showed that students expelled or suspended once were twice as likely to be held back a year and almost three times as likely to end up in the juvenile justice system compared with students of similar characteristics.[23]

Supporters of zero-tolerance policies cite other studies showing that strict, universal discipline helps maintain order and a safe learning environment. Four in 10 educators surveyed by *Education Week* in 2013 said suspensions and expulsions are effective in maintaining a safe environment. Teachers are generally more likely than administrators to see punitive discipline as an effective way to address student behavior.[24]

"Zero-tolerance policies have resulted in countless numbers of badly conceived decisions, such as students suspended for having baseball bats in their car trunks when they play on the baseball team. The [policies] have done a lot of harm," says Andrew Coulson, director of the libertarian Cato Institute's Center for Educational Freedom in Washington. "But if you get rid of very strict discipline, you will not get what you hoped for, which is more sane schools. You will get more chaotic schools and less learning because the alternatives are not done systematically."

For instance, he says, studies show that when out-of-school suspensions are reduced without instituting other changes, such as strong discipline that consistently rewards or punishes behavior, overall student achievement suffers because disruptive students remain in the classroom. "It is unjust to punish innocent students educationally for the actions of a few disruptive students," Coulson says. Keeping unruly students in class "makes it harder for the typical school to be able to teach."

Both sides of the zero-tolerance debate agree there is a place for alternative discipline for minor violations. "I think schools have been pretty safe places and still are," says Losen, "but safer schools are not a result of suspensions. Good relationships are much more important. If [you] invest in the right kind of things — training and behavior modification — you instill more order."

David Osher, an expert on schools and youth development and vice president of the American Institutes for Research, an organization in Washington that conducts behavioral and social science research, said studies show students and teachers perform better when schools improve discipline. Most effective, he says, are programs that focus on self-discipline and healthy behavior, connecting to students rather than removing them from the school community and providing services in a coordinated fashion rather than adding them piecemeal.[25]

Such a multitiered approach to discipline can be expensive, especially since more than two-thirds of states spent less per student in 2013 than before the 2007-2009 recession.[26] "Threadbare school budgets have resulted in the loss of, or inability to hire, much-needed guidance counselors, school social workers and school psychologists," said Randi Weingarten, president of the American Federation of Teachers (AFT), a union representing 1.5 million members, which favors alternatives to suspensions and expulsions.[27] On average, she said, schools have one counselor for every 471 students, a ratio twice as high as recommended.

"After-school, peer-mediation and restorative-justice programs that empower students to resolve conflicts: cut, cut, cut," she says. "Many of the things that help keep students in school and give them a sense of belonging are being taken away."

However, disciplining students by excluding them from class may cost taxpayers more than keeping students in school, says Losen. "Tax dollars are going to be spent on these kids one way or another," he says, "either in schools or later in courts at a much higher cost." In one study, Connecticut estimated it annually costs $14,000 to educate a student compared to $270,000 for juvenile custody.[28]

While studies have found links between student suspensions and criminal behavior, there is no solid proof that suspensions cause a student to get involved in crime later in life, researchers say, since many students arrive at school with problems much larger than educators can address. But Zeph Capo, a former school teacher and vice president of the Houston Federation of Teachers, said that in his experience suspensions do not always improve student behavior or help students succeed.[29]

Others put a positive spin on the consequences of zero-tolerance policies. Cole Alexander, guitarist for the punk rock band Black Lips, said he didn't like being expelled when zero-tolerance policies came to his Georgia high school months after the 1999 shooting at Columbine High School in Littleton, Colo., when two heavily armed students killed a teacher and 12 students. But zero tolerance, he says, gave him motivation to get a job and focus on his now-successful music career.[30]

Should principals be able to discipline students for off-campus behavior?

In a 1980 precedent-setting case, a high school student in Rogers, Ark., left school, got drunk with friends and returned to school to find he was suspended. The student, Pete McCluskey, sued the school board, and his case,

Eighteen-year-old Isabella "Belle" Hankey, left, here with her mother, has filed a multimillion-dollar lawsuit against the school district, town officials and three school administrators, alleging that her repeated complaints about bullying she experienced at Concord-Carlisle High School in Concord, Mass., were ignored. All states except Montana have passed laws requiring school programs to protect students from bullying.

Board of Education of Rogers, Arkansas v. McCluskey, eventually ended up at the U.S. Supreme Court, which ruled in the school's favor.[31]

Since then courts have generally favored schools when it comes to disciplining kids for off-campus behavior, particularly if the behavior disrupts the school climate. But in the age of modern technology, legal issues surrounding discipline for off-campus behavior today are more complicated. Electronic communication can facilitate a climate of bullying as students post hurtful information on the Internet or harass others with text messages both on and off campus. And the legal decisions and laws regarding cyberbullying vary greatly from case to case and state to state.[32]

Traditional schoolyard slurs have taken a new electronic form via tweeting, texting, sexting and cyberbullying. A federal study released in 2012 found that 9 percent of secondary school students said they had been cyberbullied in and out of school.[33] The targets were more likely female middle schoolers — particularly sixth-graders — and white. Another study found that more than one-fifth of secondary students said they had

been cyberbullied, and the same percentage said they had cyberbullied someone.[34]

While studies vary on the frequency of cyberbullying, few experts question the quandary it poses for administrators who must also respect students' First Amendment rights to free speech. Schools have responded in a variety of ways, with most — 91 percent — limiting access to social-networking sites from school computers and banning cell phone use and text messaging during school hours.[35]

But school administrators are grappling with how to respond when off-campus student speech, such as what students say to one another online, causes disruption at school.

"A student does not and should not receive less protection under the Constitution just because their speech is off campus," says Lee Rowland, an attorney for the American Civil Liberties Union in New York. "The Supreme Court has stated time and again that kids do not lose their First Amendment rights simply because they're students. Twenty-four/seven government monitoring of private student speech is both unwise and unconstitutional. We wouldn't accept school officials rifling through a student's personal diary, and we shouldn't accept it simply because the diary is digital."

Finding the right balance between free speech and keeping a school safe can be difficult, said Sarah Levitan Kaatz, a California attorney who specializes in education law. "I don't know a single administrator who wants to violate a student's free-speech right," she said. "But I do know a lot of administrators who wake up every morning wanting to make sure [they provide] a safe school environment for everybody there."[36]

Some groups advocating more regulation of off-campus electronic behavior have said a principal should be able to discipline a student if the student's speech prevents other students — especially legally protected groups such as minorities or disabled students — from receiving an education.

"When student speech is outside of school, officials only have the authority to formally respond if the impact of that speech has, or foreseeably will, substantially disrupt or interfere with the rights of other students at school," says Nancy Willard, director of Embrace Civility in the Digital Age, a nonprofit organization in Eugene, Ore., that helps parents and students address digital bullying. "People should have free speech rights up to the point that they're interfering with other students' rights. That's where the line should be drawn."

Lower court rulings involving off-campus electronic speech have been mixed. One court ruled in favor of a student who sued the school after being expelled for writing rap music at home and publishing it online. Another court ruled in favor of the school district after an eighth-grader sent electronic messages to friends from home depicting violent statements about his English teacher.

"Interestingly, courts have seemingly provided greater speech protections to students for cyber speech than school teachers and employees," said Gretchen M. Shipley, an education technology lawyer in San Diego, Calif. She cited two cases in which courts ruled that schools had overstepped their authority by suspending students whose off-campus cyberbullying did not cause substantial disruption at school.[37]

Usually, the off-campus behavior must have a strong connection to the school setting before principals can discipline. Education lawyers today generally advise schools to take disciplinary action for off-campus activity if one of four criteria is met:

- There is a clear-cut and violent threat;
- The school has solid proof that speech disrupts the school environment;
- A student brings printed versions of the electronic communication to campus;
- Cyber harassment has a significant impact on staff.

All states except Montana have anti-bullying laws, and 48 states prohibit cyberbullying as part of their education codes.[38] A 2013 California law allows suspension or expulsion for electronic bullying, even if it originates outside of school.

More Security Officers in Schools

Nearly 70 percent of students ages 12 to 18 said security guards or police officers were present at their schools in 2011 — up 15 percentage points from 1999.

Percentage of Students With Security Officers at School

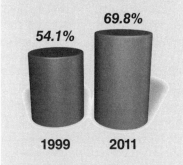

Source: Simone Robers, Jana Kemp, and Jennifer Truman, "Indicators of School Crime and Safety: 2012," National Center for Education Statistics, U.S. Department of Education, and Bureau of Justice Statistics, June 2013, Figure 21.1, http://tinyurl.com/pcvy3xq

Should schools increase the number of armed security officers on campus?

The number of law enforcement personnel on school grounds has increased drastically in the last 15 years, in part because after the Columbine massacre Congress provided federal grants for schools to hire security guards.[39] And whenever there is a high-profile school shooting — such as the 2012 massacre at Sandy Hook Elementary School in Newtown, Conn., when 20 small children and six adults were shot to death — some in the public demand that more school personnel carry guns.[40]

Security staff in schools typically are school resource officers (SROs), uniformed and armed security officers who are sworn municipal law enforcement officers or members of a school district's own security force. SROs carry out the duties of regular officers and can make arrests and respond to incidents. They also have additional duties as mentors and may conduct classes on crime and drug prevention.

Only 1 percent of schools reported having police in 1975. By 2009-2010, 40 percent of schools had law enforcement officers stationed in the building. In a 2011 survey of students, 70 percent reported police officers in their schools. Proponents of increasing the number of armed security personnel said schools are safer now than ever before, and to reduce their presence would deny students and teachers a sense of safety and order. Opponents say more armed guards do not necessarily improve safety and can undermine the school environment by creating a "police state" atmosphere. School staff should not be armed, they say, preferring that only trained police officers carry weapons.

Much of the push for more school security staff has come from the federal government, which has spent more than $811 million to hire school security officers since Columbine. A month after Sandy Hook, President

Obama pledged to put an additional 1,000 trained police officers in schools.

"Each school is different and should have the flexibility to address its most pressing needs," White House guidelines stated. "Some schools will want trained and armed police; others may prefer increased counseling services. Either way, each district should be able to choose what is best to protect its own students."[41]

Obama's initiative was not roundly accepted. "Our No. 1 task, as a nation, is to protect our children. To achieve this, National PTA believes schools also must be completely gun-free. The administration's recommendation to expand the school resource officer program therefore comes as a disappointment," said National PTA president Betsy Landers.[42]

Former U.S. Rep. Asa Hutchinson, R-Ark., chairman of the advisory board for National School Shield, a National Rifle Association emergency-response program, says, "In today's environment, the best protection is an armed, trained security officer in every school. History has shown this is the best protection and the best response. It's regrettable that we have circumstances that call for this, but in today's society it is necessary."

After Sandy Hook, Obama appointed Vice President Joseph Biden to lead a gun control task force, which sparked national controversy when it considered funding additional police in schools as part of a larger gun-control agenda.[43] The American Federal of Teachers (AFT), which met with Biden, recommended adding police in schools on a case-by-case basis, not as stationed armed guards but as "part of the fabric of the school community."[44]

Maurice "Mo" Canady, executive director of the National Association of School Resource Officers, an organization based in Alabama that trains SROs, says having trained security guards is not about wearing a gun but working with students to prevent violence.

"There has to be some sense of safety and order and law enforcement," Canady says. "But we're not calling for more police in schools. We're calling for better trained police who are properly selected and trained to be involved in the education process and serve as informal counselors."

Kenneth S. Trump, president of National School Safety and Security Services, a Cleveland-based consulting firm, says SRO programs are often misunderstood as " 'cuff-em and stuff'em' programs." The majority of police officers in schools, he says, "build positive working relationships with students, do more counseling than arresting and perform much more preventing of problems than arresting kids."

Gun-rights advocates, however, propose countering violence from outside the schools by increasing the number of guns inside schools. "Our first preference is to have trained, armed security personnel," Hutchinson says. "Teachers should teach, and others should protect. But it should be decided by local schools. If they don't have the resources, school staff should be trained and armed."

Six national school employee organizations, joined by more than 100 education and mental health organizations, oppose arming school staff — other than trained SROs — and prefer instead to provide behavioral, mental health and social services for students and families to make schools safer.[45]

"Singular horrible events like this past week make us all upset, but if we look at the data, it doesn't make sense that that's where we need to beef up security in a very expensive way," Kenneth Dodge, director of the Center for Child and Family Policy at Duke University, said shortly after Sandy Hook. "Isn't it more straightforward to just get rid of the guns?"[46]

In the spring of 2013, a few months after Sandy Hook, 33 states proposed more than 80 bills that sought to arm teachers and staff. Seven were enacted, bringing to 18 the total number of states allowing adults, in addition to security personnel, to carry guns in school if they have permission from the school.

In Utah, school personnel have carried concealed weapons for about a decade, and in Texas four school districts allow some staff to carry concealed weapons. Tennessee passed a law to allow school employees to carry guns in school. An Arizona sheriff placed 500 armed, uniformed volunteers outside the schools in his county. This past March, Georgia lawmakers passed one of the nation's most sweeping pro-gun-rights laws, which allows school staff to carry guns at school.

A national poll conducted by CNN a month after Sandy Hook showed that 54 percent of respondents favored putting armed guards in every school in the country, while 45 percent opposed it.[47] Yet a survey conducted at the same time by the National Education Association showed almost 70 percent of teachers oppose allowing teachers and school staff to carry guns in schools.[48]

BACKGROUND

Rise of Zero Tolerance

Concerns about school safety and disparities in how discipline is meted out are not new for school administrators. As student activism grew during the 1960s, many administrators grappled with maintaining order and authority in schools while still respecting students' rights.

Race riots and rising rates of crime and violence in the 1960s and '70s also prompted school districts to adopt centralized discipline policies and use more security guards in the schools. Plagued by a tide of racial tension, drug use and murder, the Los Angeles Unified School District as early as the 1970s adopted discipline policies that resembled today's zero-tolerance policies by suspending and expelling students for having weapons and drugs.[49] Other school districts in New York and Kentucky followed suit, with mandatory expulsion for drugs, fighting and gang-related activity.[50]

As early as the 1970s, the Children's Defense Fund, a child advocacy group in Washington, was expressing concern about suspended students missing class time and about the disproportionate rate of suspensions among black students, which was two to three times higher than for white students in 1970.[51]

In the 1980s, the term "zero tolerance" was first used by a U.S. Customs Service anti-drug program, which impounded ships caught carrying illegal drugs. Under federal zero-tolerance policies adopted by some states, the number of people incarcerated for nonviolent drug offenses increased from 50,000 in 1980 to more than 400,000 by 1997.[52]

In 1986, Education Secretary William J. Bennett urged Congress to withhold federal funds from schools that did not adopt zero-tolerance expulsion for students using or selling drugs at school. Bennett's effort failed, but in 1994 Congress enacted the Gun-Free Schools Act, which required schools receiving federal money to expel for at least one year any student caught carrying a weapon on school grounds. Proponents of the law said the strict penalties would ensure safety and guarantee disciplinary equity because the uniform penalties meant that all students would be treated the same, regardless of background or circumstances.[53]

Over time, school districts began extending the tough punishments to possession of any object that might be deemed a weapon — such as nail clippers or a butter knife packed in a school lunch. Eventually, some administrators began suspending students for less serious types of misconduct, such as smoking, skipping class or ignoring dress codes.

According to critics of zero tolerance, administrators during the 2000s began relying on stiff disciplinary policies to winnow out poorly performing students because schools faced sanctions if students failed high-stakes achievement tests mandated by the sweeping No Child Left Behind school reform measure passed in 2001. Students who were disruptive in class could jeopardize classroom learning and drag down test scores.[54]

Other laws also have played a role in dictating disciplinary procedures. The Individuals with Disabilities Education Act (IDEA) of 1975 guaranteed a public school education to all disabled youth, but made it difficult to suspend or expel students if they misbehaved due to their disability, unless they committed a crime or were dangerous to themselves or others.

On the legal front, the number of school discipline cases to reach the state and federal courts expanded greatly between the 1960s and the '90s. In 1969, in the first major school discipline case to reach the U.S. Supreme Court, Des Moines, Iowa, students' First-Amendment rights were upheld after they were suspended for wearing black armbands to protest the Vietnam War.[55] In 1975, the court ruled that public schools must hold hearings before suspending students, because the suspension could potentially affect their future education and employment.[56]

After that, court rulings in student discipline cases generally were more favorable toward the schools as the court's composition and leanings changed.[57] Some researchers have said the proliferation of student lawsuits led to more states and school districts adopting uniform and inflexible discipline policies.[58] That's because students often alleged in their lawsuits that school principals applied discipline unequally based on race or other factors.[59]

Shootings and Bullying

The rise in school shootings since the early 1990s has left the nation grappling with how such crimes can occur and questioning the social causes of violence, the prevalence of gun possession and the role of bullying.

"Incidents like the shooting at [Columbine] changed the way we understood school safety and increased the

CHRONOLOGY

1960s *Vietnam War protests spark concern over student conduct; juveniles gain due-process rights.*

1967 Supreme Court rules that juveniles accused of misconduct deserve many rights given to adult defendants. . . . Students for a Democratic Society, a leftist organization started on college campuses, circulates information on how to "take over" a high school.

1969 Supreme Court rules that suspending students for wearing armbands to protest the Vietnam War violates their First Amendment rights.

1970s *Protections broadened for students; schools pour resources into security as school crime rises.*

1975 Congress passes Education for All Handicapped Children Act, requiring equal access to education for children with disabilities. . . . Supreme Court rules that suspended students are entitled to a hearing. . . . Children's Defense Fund reports disproportionate rates of suspensions for black students.

1980s *Federal push for zero-tolerance policies for illegal drug use and other crimes filters down to schools.*

1986 Education Secretary William J. Bennett unsuccessfully urges Congress to withhold money from schools rejecting zero-tolerance expulsion for students using or selling drugs at school.

1989 School districts in California, New York and Kentucky adopt zero-tolerance policies for drugs and gang activity.

1990s *Gun violence in schools spurs tough, new laws.*

1994 California and a dozen other states pass "three-strikes-and-you're-out" laws. . . . Federal crime bill includes mandatory drug sentences; Gun Free Schools Act requires expulsion for at least a year of any student caught with a firearm.

1998 More than 30 students and teachers nationally are killed in a sudden spate of school shootings.

1999 Two armed students at Columbine High School in Colorado kill 12 students and a teacher and wound 23 before committing suicide. Schools nationwide tighten security and discipline codes.

2000-Present *More student violence occurs; schools increase number of armed guards on campuses. . . . Courts and the federal government continue involvement in student-conduct issues.*

2002 President George W. Bush signs No Child Left Behind Act mandating that states identify "persistently dangerous" schools.

2006 Gunman kills five girls and then himself at a one-room Amish schoolhouse in Pennsylvania.

2007 In the deadliest shooting rampage in U.S. history, Seung-Hui Cho, a student at Virginia Tech University, kills 32 students and teachers, then commits suicide. . . . Supreme Court rules in *Morse v. Frederick* that school officials can punish student speech that can be interpreted as advocating illegal drug use.

2008 Families of Virginia Tech victims call for tighter gun control, but Virginia lawmakers defeat a bid to close a loophole on gun-show sales. . . . Rep. Linda Sanchez, D-Calif., introduces legislation to require schools to include anti-bullying policies in their conduct codes.

2012 A gunman opens fire at Sandy Hook Elementary School in Newtown, Conn., killing 26 people, including 20 children, before turning the gun on himself.

2013 A string of student suicides sparked by chronic bullying prompts all but one state to adopt laws protecting students from bullying; some include off-campus and online bullying.

2014 U.S. Departments of Education and Justice release new data on disparate rates of suspensions and expulsions, issue new guidelines for reducing racially disparate discipline and call for more extensive data collection.

responsibility to both protect and connect with all students," said Richard L. Curwin, a school discipline expert and a classroom management consultant.[60]

Although there was never conclusive evidence that the Columbine perpetrators had been victims of bullying, initial speculation about possible bullying raised the public's awareness about the problem.

The advent of the Internet, the expansion of social-networking sites and the ubiquity of cell phones has opened the way for cyberbullying, or what criminal justice professors Sameer Hinduja of Florida Atlantic University and Justin W. Patchin at the University of Wisconsin-Eau Claire have called "willful and repeated harm inflicted through the use of computers, cell phones and other electronic devices."[61] What previously had been taunts on the playground became electronic harassment that could be distributed to hundreds or thousands of people online.

Critics say some anti-cyberbullying laws violate free-speech rights, but the lower courts have issued inconsistent decisions. The U.S. Supreme Court has not yet considered the issue. In 2010, the Education Department issued new, comprehensive guidance on bullying and gave a stern warning that schools could lose federal education money unless they comply with civil rights laws protecting all students, including lesbian, gay, bisexual and transgender students.

In 2011, 28 percent of secondary students reported being bullied. Efforts to address the bullying problem were fueled in 2012 and 2013 by a string of highly visible suicides by U.S. students who had suffered chronic bullying.

School Resource Officers

The first law enforcement officer program in a school began in 1953 in Flint, Mich. It was created to foster better relationships between students and law enforcement.[62] A similar program was instituted in Fresno, Calif., in 1968 with plainclothes officers.

In the 1980s, rising juvenile crime rates spurred a greater police presence in schools. The homicide rate in schools for adolescents doubled between 1984 and 1994, and the rate of nonfatal violent incidents rose nearly 20 percent.[63] Programs putting police officers in schools also expanded quickly after the Safe Schools Act of 1994 encouraged schools and law enforcement to work together to reduce school crime.

Police presence in schools increased substantially after Columbine, mainly because of an influx of federal money. States also funded school security, and some schools hired the officers as school staff.[64] Schools also added security features such as cameras, metal detectors, staff identification badges and controlled access to buildings and grounds.

Statistics show that schools are safer today than they were in the early 1990s, and the percentage of students who said they were afraid of attack or harm at school decreased from 12 percent to 4 percent between 1995 and 2011. Yet teachers and students can attest that schools can be dangerous places. Federal crime records indicate that secondary school students were victims of theft and violent crime more often in school than out of school.[65]

The National Association of School Resource Officers' Canady partly attributes the overall decline in school violence to the greater presence of school resource officers. "The increased safety indicators coincide with the span of time of school resource officers' phenomenal growth," he says. One government study showed that students felt safer and more comfortable reporting crimes when they had a positive opinion of school resource officers, but that the relationships of officers with students varied depending on the officers' training and preparation.[66]

The increased police presence in schools coincided with adoption of more stringent discipline codes, which often mandated that serious offenses be reported immediately to the police. As a result, some students are arrested and taken directly from school to juvenile detention or issued a citation or ticket to appear before a judge.

However, Canady says, if a school has properly trained school resource officers who help school administrators educate and informally counsel students, it does not result in more arrests. The school-to-prison pipeline has been "politicized as a national phenomenon," Canady says. But, he asks, "How can all indicators of school-based crime continue to fall and juvenile arrest rates fall 17 percent since 2000 if the presence of school resource officers on campus has opened up a pipeline to the juvenile-justice system?"

However, some studies have found no evidence that police officers contribute to school safety and have found

Baltimore Seeks to Reduce Suspensions

"With trusting relationships, you have safer schools."

When a group of Baltimore middle school boys beat up students from another school and stole their cell phones, the schools didn't suspend the boys or send them to juvenile court. Instead, the boys met in the school library with the principal and the parents of the victims to talk about their actions and their punishment. The parents decided not to press criminal charges, and the boys stayed after school to participate in character development classes.[1]

This strategy is part of a larger plan in 196 Baltimore schools to improve student conduct and reduce out-of-school suspensions as a first response to misbehavior. So far, the approach has had positive results. The middle school boys said they are learning to communicate rather than fight and not jump in when others are fighting. And suspensions are down in Baltimore city schools to fewer than 9,000 from a 2004 high of 26,000. Students once sent packing for acting up are now counseled and redirected in more productive ways, unless their misdeeds threaten school safety.

"The mindset does have to change from punishment to re-inclusion and restoration," Karen Webber-Ndour, executive director of student support and safety for the district, says of the plan. "Discipline cannot be seen as separate from the entire educational process."

But the shift away from harsh punishment is controversial. Concerns linger over school safety and the effects the policies may have on teachers, staff members and well-behaved students who are trying to learn. U.S. Education Secretary Arne Duncan has praised the Baltimore strategy as a model for other schools, but he acknowledges the difficulties of working with problem students rather than kicking them out of school.[2]

And critics question whether the Baltimore model can adequately stem violence in schools and provide a safe environment for teachers and other students.

A decade ago problems were at epidemic proportions in Baltimore city schools, where the student body is roughly 85 percent African-American. Almost one-third of students were suspended each year, two-thirds of them male, and the high school graduation rate was about 50 percent, one of the worst in the nation.[3]

Out of that situation was born what Webber-Ndour calls a "crusade." With funding from school officials, local philanthropies, nonprofit organizations and the state and federal governments, the school board adopted a new discipline system in 2007 that uses zero-tolerance suspensions and expulsions only as last resorts.

When students are disrespectful to a teacher or late to class, they are sent to the principal's office, where discipline is determined on a case-by-case basis. Staff members are trained in a national model called "restorative justice" and "positive behavior intervention and support" to work with parents and students on behavior expectations and consequences. Mental health counselors work in every middle school.

Meanwhile, under a "Climate Walk" program, lay observers walk the halls and provide principals with information aimed at halting behavior problems before they

instead that, as police presence increases, more crimes involving weapons and drugs are recorded and the likelihood of students being arrested at school increase. The presence of police officers helps to define discipline as a criminal justice problem rather than a social, psychological or academic problem, says Aaron Kupchik, an associate professor of sociology and criminal justice at the University of Delaware.[67]

After the Sandy Hook shootings, school districts, including the Newtown Board of Education, hired more armed guards and installed more security devices. In 2013, 29 states introduced more than 90 bills related to school law enforcement officers, and at least 17 of those were enacted.[68]

Overall, efforts to pass gun control legislation were unsuccessful after Sandy Hook, while efforts to loosen gun laws succeeded. Every state now allows people to carry guns in some public places, and at least three states passed laws allowing teachers to carry handguns on campus. Meanwhile, no major national gun control law has been passed since 1994.[69]

happen. The school district gives principals weekly graphs and charts showing when and where suspensions occur in their schools to help them prevent future problems. A "success academy" provides an alternative means of education for students with long-term suspensions and expulsions.

Webber-Ndour says the approach reflects the realities of urban education. "In the 21st century, especially in urban settings, we must come to grips with the fact that without behavioral modifications and actually teaching and training students how to behave appropriately, we're not going to get the student achievement that we're looking for," she says. "They go hand in glove."

But critics say students inclined to push boundaries are adept at exploiting the new system. "They're not stupid; they know exactly what's going on," said Thompson Guerrier, a Baltimore elementary school teacher's aide who was injured when a student threw a desk and chair at him. "You tell them you're going to call the principal, and they laugh at you."[4]

Nevertheless, the Baltimore approach has become a model for Maryland education leaders, who this year approved sweeping changes in the state's discipline policies. The state had turned its attention to zero-tolerance policies three years earlier, when a 15-year-old football player committed suicide after a lengthy suspension from a nearby Virginia school, and two Maryland lacrosse players were suspended for carrying banned items in their gear bags they said they had brought to repair their equipment.[5]

The new regulations still allow principals to suspend students, but they encourage educators not to use zero-tolerance policies but to evaluate incidents on an individual basis. The new standards also create shorter response times for suspension appeals and call for more educational services for suspended students. Every Maryland school district has until 2015 to revise its policies.[6]

The Maryland State Education Association, the state's largest teachers union, was critical of the state changes, saying local school systems need flexibility and authority to decide discipline standards and additional state money to train school staff for handling classroom situations and provide student-behavior programs. Otherwise, the union said, school systems will bear the costs of providing such programs, and disruptive students will be returned to the classroom.

"While the ideal place for students is in their classrooms, if disciplinary action is necessary, then educators need both the autonomy to be able to make decisions that help create a safe and productive learning environment for all students, as well as resources to establish and sustain alternative educational programs and opportunities," says Adam Mendelson, a union spokesman.

But Webber-Ndour stands by the Baltimore approach. "You can never do enough to make a school safer," she says. "But if you set up an environment with trusting relationships, you have safer schools."

— *Anne Farris Rosen*

[1]Laurel Bowman, "Restorative Practices at City Springs Elementary Schools," Voice of America, http://tinyurl.com/krvnwys.

[2]Arne Duncan, "Rethinking School Discipline," Department of Education, Jan. 8, 2014, http://tinyurl.com/myt935t.

[3]Andres A. Alonzo, "State of Our High Schools 2010-2011," Baltimore City Public Schools, http://tinyurl.com/pnk6ldm.

[4]Erica L. Green, Scott Calvert and Luke Broadwater, "Painful Lessons," *The Baltimore Sun*, Feb. 16, 2014, http://tinyurl.com/obf7oo3.

[5]Donna St. George, "Maryland approves new school discipline regulations," *The Washington Post*, Jan. 28, 2014, http://tinyurl.com/nha8hmb.

[6]*Ibid.*

CURRENT SITUATION

Federal Efforts

Increased record keeping, research and media coverage of discipline policies is galvanizing a movement that seeks to replace zero-tolerance policies with alternative measures — at least for minor violations.

In January Secretary of Education Arne Duncan and Attorney General Holder, focusing on racial disparities in how zero tolerance has been administered, released the government's first legal guidelines to help schools administer school discipline under Title IV and Title VI of the Civil Rights Act of 1964, which prohibit discrimination by race, color or national origin.[70]

"Education is the civil rights of our generation," Duncan said. "The undeniable truth is that the everyday education experience for too many students of color violates the principle of equity at the heart of the American promise."[71]

Judith Browne Dianis, codirector of the Advancement Project, a civil rights organization working to reduce reliance

Students with Disabilities Face More Punishment

"Some educators just didn't want students with disabilities in their classroom."

Julie Landry's 8-year-old son suffers from autism. One day in gym class, teachers and administrators said, he ran around screaming and throwing volleyballs. He flailed his arms and resisted when administrators tried to restrain him. According to the Fairfax County, Va., school system, he punched, kicked, bit and head-butted three people. For that and other incidents, the boy was suspended for 11 days and faced expulsion hearings twice within six weeks — all during a single school year.[1]

Although students with disabilities represent only about 12 percent of the K-12 student population, they account for 25 percent of students arrested and referred to law enforcement. In an era when zero-tolerance school discipline policies can result in suspension for a range of offenses, students with disabilities are more than twice as likely as students without disabilities to receive an out-of-school suspension, according to 2011-12 data from the Office for Civil Rights at the Department of Education.[2]

Long before zero-tolerance policies, students with disabilities were treated differently from their peers, and often were denied schooling. "There were educators that just didn't want students with disabilities in their classroom," says Daniel Losen, director of the Center for Civil Rights Remedies at UCLA, a research center for civil rights and equal opportunity for minority groups in the United States. "They would say 'We think you'll be a disruption.'"

Since 1975, federal law has required that public schools provide special education services to students with disabilities, including protection from frequent suspension.[3] Zero-tolerance school discipline policies, widely implemented in the 1990s, originally required suspension and expulsion for incidents involving weapons, drugs or violence. But over time zero-tolerance policies have evolved to require the same strict punishments for a wide variety of misconduct, including

Students With Disabilities Are Disproportionately Arrested

Students with disabilities make up one-eighth of school enrollment but account for one-quarter of school-related arrests.

Percentage of Enrollment and School-Related Arrests, by Disability Status,* 2011-12

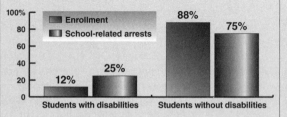

* Identified under the Individuals with Disabilities Education Act.

Source: "Civil Rights Data Collection, Data Snapshot: School Discipline," U.S. Department of Education Office of Civil Rights, March 21, 2014, p. 7, http://tinyurl.com/kls2ajo

minor infringements, such as violating the dress code. Thus, today suspensions are often given for offenses such as truancy or disobedience.[4]

"There's no question that students with disabilities are disproportionately punished" under zero tolerance, says Losen.

Students with a disability that affects their behavior usually receive behavior assessments and behavioral improvement plans, according to Losen, For instance, he says, before a student can be suspended for more than 10 days, school officials

on zero-tolerance policies, called the government's actions historic. "Disparities in school discipline have been documented since the 1970s, and we've never been able to get the federal government to step in and help stop it," she said.[72]

The guidelines are part of a multi-agency initiative to reform school discipline begun by the Obama administration

in 2011. As part of that initiative, the Education and Justice departments have overseen development of consensus recommendations, convened working sessions with researchers and educators and required some school districts to account for high rates of suspensions among minority and disabled students.[73] The initiative also has been sponsoring awareness

are required to hold a hearing to determine whether the behavior in question had to do with the student's disability or with the school not providing adequate support. For example, if a disabled student with emotional disturbances is supposed to see a counselor every Wednesday and the student "flips out" after the counselor misses an appointment, that could be considered a failure of the school system, he says.

"So the question should be asked, 'Was the failure to provide counseling contributing to the behavior?' says Losen. "Rarely are those questions addressed."

Research shows disparities between the type of disability a student has and the likelihood that a student will be suspended or expelled. A 2011 Texas study examining how school discipline relates to student success and juvenile detention found that nearly 75 percent of special education students were expelled at least once between the seventh and 12th grades. And the punishment varied significantly depending on the type of educational disability, according to the study, conducted by the Council of State Governments Justice Center, a national nonprofit organization focusing on public safety, and the Public Policy Research Institute (PPRI) at Texas A&M University.[5] For instance, students with learning disabilities and emotional disturbances were disciplined more often than those with other types of disabilities, including autism, physical disability or developmental delay.

The two major teachers' unions — the American Federation of Teachers (AFT) and the National Education Association (NEA) — are shifting away from their support of zero-tolerance policies. "It's about creating schools where our students are able to reach their full potential," said Harry Lawson, associate director of the NEA's Human and Civil Rights Department.[6]

In Virginia, Landry's son avoided expulsion because a panel of school officials and special-education experts concluded that his actions were caused by his disability.[7]

"These are children who we shouldn't expect to be capable of understanding [student rights] or being compliant like their non-disabled peers," said Elizabeth Schultz, a member of the Fairfax County School Board. "To hold them to the same standard is absurd."[8]

However, according to data from the Fairfax school system, officials ruled that a student's actions were caused by his disability in fewer than 20 percent of all cases involving students with disabilities who faced expulsion during the 2011-12 school year.

As for Landry's son, Fairfax administrators ruled that the public schools could not meet the boy's needs, so his family received state grants to cover his tuition at a private school. Landry said she hopes the new school will better help her son learn.[9]

— *Kaya Yurieff*

[1] T. Rees Shapiro, "For students with disabilities, discipline issues take toll," *The Washington Post*, July 16, 2013, http://tinyurl.com/phsj5c6.

[2] "Civil Rights Data Collection: Data Snapshot (School Discipline)," Office for Civil Rights, U.S. Department of Education, March 21 2014, http://tinyurl.com/kls2ajo.

[3] "What is IDEA?" National Center for Learning Disabilities, http://tinyurl.com/lmxhde5. For background see the following *CQ Researcher* reports: Kenneth Jost, "Learning Disabilities," Dec. 10, 1993, pp. 1081-1104; and Kathy Koch "Special Education," Nov. 10, 2000, pp. 905-928.

[4] "Zero Tolerance and Alternative Strategies: A Fact Sheet for Educators and Policymakers," National Association of School Psychologists, http://tinyurl.com/cf588nv. For background see the following *CQ Researcher* reports: Thomas J. Billitteri, "Discipline in Schools," Feb. 15, 2008, pp. 145-168; and Kathy Koch, "Zero Tolerance," March 10, 2000, pp. 185-208.

[5] Tony Fabelo, *et al.*, "Breaking Schools' Rules: A Statewide Study of How School Discipline Relates to Students' Success and Juvenile Justice Involvement," Council of State Governments Justice Center and The Public Policy Research Institute, Texas A&M University, July 2011, http://tinyurl.com/omqf2nc.

[6] Roger Glass and Virginia Myers, "Communication, relationships are keys to better discipline," American Federation of Teachers, March 25, 2014, http://tinyurl.com/kdh76dg.

[7] Shapiro, *op. cit.*

[8] *Ibid.*

[9] *Ibid.*

webinars and helped to develop curricula to train education and judicial officials in how to deal with school incidents that end up in court.

"So many of these young people need a helping hand, need assistance, but also need clear boundaries and clear guidelines," Duncan said in announcing the initiative in 2011. "What they don't need is to be pushed out the door or to start a criminal record. We need to be a lot more thoughtful in how we address this."[74]

But some question the wisdom of the federal actions. "This is fundamentally a civil rights enforcement step of the kind that is ultimately going to weaken discipline in

Getty Images/Bloomberg/Joshua Roberts

Police stand guard in the parking lot of Arapahoe High School, in Centennial, Colo., on Dec. 13, 2013, as students are bused to a nearby church after a student carried a shotgun into the school and wounded two fellow students before killing himself. Although the juvenile crime rate has dropped since peaking in 1994, and there is less violence in schools today than 20 years ago, get-tough policies coupled with added school security staffing have meant that more students face court appearances and suspensions.

our schools at a very time when things like Newtown ought to have us seeking better order in our schools, rather than discouraging school systems from enforcing discipline," said Chester Finn, president of the Fordham Institute, a conservative education-policy think tank in Washington.[75]

The federal government's new data collection now includes surveys of all of the nation's schools rather than just a sample of schools, plus information — for the first time — about the racial makeup of students referred to law enforcement and the suspension rates of preschool students.[76] Also this year, Obama endorsed a public-private initiative to help young men and boys of color reach their full potential, which builds on the federal guidance to end racial disparities in school discipline.[77]

However, the administration has not received full funding for its efforts to reform school discipline. For example, the administration asked for $50 million in grants to help train teachers in strategies to reduce behavior problems and bullying, but Congress appropriated only $30 million in fiscal year 2014, according to the Education Department.

Congress also has failed to pass any of the pending bills that would revise zero-tolerance policies, despite

holding two hearings on the subject. In 2012, a Senate subcommittee hearing entitled "Ending the School-to-Prison Pipeline" drew an overflow crowd of researchers, educators and experts who submitted 700 pages of findings and opinions about school discipline policies. It was the first congressional hearing on zero tolerance.

Several small bills have been introduced but have not moved forward. One would establish an Office for School and Discipline Policy, while another would prohibit any federal money going to schools that discipline a student for using pictures, clothing, food, body gestures or toys to resemble a weapon.

A massive bill to replace No Child Left Behind is pending in the Senate, which includes provisions for alternative discipline techniques, grievance procedures for disciplined students and the elimination of zero tolerance except for serious violent offenses.

"For the first time, the bill reauthorizing our nation's federal education policy will include provisions to address a growing crisis dubbed the 'school-to-prison pipeline,' " said Sen. Chris Murphy, D-Conn. "The bill also includes, for the first time, important support for positive, prevention-based approaches to school discipline."[78]

But experts say the measure has little chance of passage without bipartisan support. Some education groups oppose the Senate version of the legislation because they said it expands the federal role over local jurisdictions and creates an overwhelming burden for schools to collect data on nonacademic information. Sen. Richard Burr, R-N.C., called the legislation "No Child Left Behind on steroids."[79]

The Courts

Some school districts are voluntarily revamping their discipline policies, while the Justice Department has sued others referred to them by the Education Department's Office for Civil Rights, which has 152 ongoing discipline investigations in 37 states. Since 2000, the office has responded to more than 7,622 complaints involving discipline at elementary and secondary schools, says Dorie Turner Nolt, the department's press secretary.

In one case, the Oakland, Calif., school district worked with the Office for Civil Rights on a five-year voluntary plan to reduce suspensions, expulsions and disciplinary racial disparity with a variety of intervention and support programs. In Meridian, Miss., the Justice Department has sued officials for allegedly arresting students as young as

Should schools increase the number of law enforcement officers?

YES
Asa Hutchinson
Chairman, National
School Shield Advisory Board

Written for *CQ Researcher*, May 2014

The safety and security of children are fundamental to a quality education. With this principle as a foundation, it is necessary for our local schools to enhance their security because we live in a dangerous world. This increased security emphasis requires our school districts to increase the number of armed security officers.

After the tragedy at Sandy Hook Elementary School in 2012, I led a national task force funded by the National Rifle Association to examine the gaps in school security and to make recommendations. For three months I worked with security experts ranging from former Secret Service agents to nationally recognized school security experts. Our conclusions are contained in a 225-page report that recommends such solutions as increased training of armed school personnel and pilot programs to address the challenge of mental illness and bullying.

Much has been made of our finding that schools should employ trained and qualified armed security. This approach serves as a deterrent and as the fastest possible response — and many Americans agree. In fact, one-third of our nation's schools already employ some type of armed security. And a survey of more than 10,000 teachers and administrators found that 90 percent think an armed police officer in school would improve safety.

History makes it clear that a shooter does not stop until confronted by someone who is armed, usually a law enforcement officer. The shooting ends when an assailant takes his own life or surrenders. So, the response time is critical. Young lives are lost when the police must come to the school. It is essential that the school have an armed response capability on campus to minimize the time it takes to respond and disarm the assailant.

In 1997 an armed intruder killed two students and wounded seven others at Pearl High School in Pearl, Miss., before the school's assistant principal, Joel Myrick, disarmed him using a .45-caliber semi-automatic pistol he retrieved from his truck. This scenario has been repeated too often in recent years, with the attacker surrendering or taking his life after being confronted by someone who is armed.

Certainly, there is more to security than a police officer. Our report includes best practices on surveillance cameras, identification badges and many other specific challenges faced by our schools. Schools are taking action, and many choose to have an armed police officer in the school.

NO
Amanda Petteruti
Author, Education Under Arrest,
Justice Policy Institute
Jason Ziedenberg
Research and Policy Director, Justice Policy Institute

Written for *CQ Researcher*, May 2014

We all want safe schools and to give teachers and principals the tools to create a safe learning environment. While some schools require additional resources to keep them safe, we believe most schools and communities would be better off by reducing the number of school resource officers (SROs) and focusing instead on better policies to improve outcomes for all students.

In a Justice Policy Institute report, "Education Under Arrest: The Case Against Police in Schools," we found that when schools have law enforcement on site, students are more likely to be arrested rather than disciplined by school officials. This leads to more kids being funneled into the juvenile justice system, which is expensive and creates a host of negative effects on youth. Data showed that school resource officers (SROs) needlessly drive up arrests for behavior that can, and should, be dealt with at school. Data from Birmingham, Ala., for instance, found that 96 percent of student juvenile court referrals were for misdemeanors or minor violations. A study of schools with and without SROs found that those with an SRO had nearly five times the rate of arrests for disorderly conduct as schools without an SRO.

By overly relying on arrest and suspension, SROs contribute to young people starting down a path that will hurt their futures: High school students who come in contact with the courts are more likely to drop out. Police in schools also can create an environment that makes learning difficult, and sometimes SROs have caused the violence they are supposed to prevent. Additionally, SROs and harsh, zero-tolerance policies are more likely to affect youth of color and youth with disabilities.

There are other ways to improve school safety that do not overly rely on SROs. Schools are using peer-to-peer mediation and training staff so that teachers can help young people improve behavior. These result in better outcomes without unnecessary involvement in the juvenile justice system.

Research shows that police in schools are not the way to create an environment that is safe and conducive to learning. Instead, we should use evidence-based programs that create schools with high levels of structure and support by caring adults dedicated to helping meet the needs of all students. This way, we can keep kids out of the courtroom and in the classroom.

10 for rudeness and tardiness and holding them for days without a probable cause hearing. Officials named in the suit denied the allegations, and a trial is scheduled for December. In a separate action, the Meridian School District agreed to enact new disciplinary policies.

The government's legal remedies are controversial. "These 'targeted reductions' are racial quotas in all but name," said Bader, of the Competitive Enterprise Institute.[80] "Stopping school officials from disciplining black students who violate school rules just because they previously disciplined more black than white students is as crazy as ordering police to stop arresting black criminals just because they previously arrested more blacks than whites."

Bader said the Oakland agreement violates the California constitution and federal court rulings that forbid racial quotas for school discipline. "The only practical way for a school system to comply with the Education Department's demands is to adopt a de facto racial quota in discipline. But this itself puts the school system in legal jeopardy."[81]

Education Department officials said they are not trying to make discipline rates proportional by race, but to have schools evaluate whether their systems are equitable.[82]

"For years, we couldn't rely on the federal government to enforce civil rights law, so now we have an Office for Civil Rights that is finally taking up the torch," said the Advancement Project's Dianis.[83]

Reducing Suspensions

A variety of local jurisdictions are instituting new programs and laws to reduce the number of out-of-school suspensions and court appearances.

Four states recently passed legislation related to alternative education for suspended or expelled students. Of those, California is giving administrators more discretion to offer alternatives, and Indiana is calling for more research on the subject. Virginia is encouraging the establishment of regional education centers for suspended and expelled students, and Washington law says educators shall not be prevented from providing alternative education.

In Texas, officials are trying to keep minor misconduct cases from reaching the courts. The Texas legislature passed laws to prohibit school law enforcement from ticketing or fining elementary students and recommended that schools issue warnings or appoint counselors rather than issue harsh sanctions.

However, states like Massachusetts, which has a new law going into effect in July that requires schools to provide education to students even if they have been expelled or suspended, are grappling with how to pay for the services.[84] Other states provide for alternative education "when funds are available."[85]

California continues to allow suspensions for serious violations but requires schools to try alternative measures for nonviolent infractions. Los Angeles in 2013 became the nation's first school district to ban suspensions for student defiance, and school districts in Sacramento, Vallejo, Oakland and San Francisco are adopting new measures to reduce suspensions for minor violations.

In Broward County, Fla., where more students were arrested on campus than in any other district in the state, the county last November began requiring disruptive students to make reparations and receive counseling and anger-management courses. Arrests dropped 41 percent and suspensions fell 66 percent, but observers said it's probably too early to determine overall success.[86]

A variety of nonprofit organizations are working with local officials to revise discipline policies. Public Counsel, a nonprofit organization in California that provides pro bono legal services, has been helping the Los Angeles and San Francisco school districts revise policies and provides free technical support to school districts changing their policies.

Additionally, 10 school districts nationally are participating in a public-private initiative to examine discipline alternatives. Brown University's Annenberg Institute for School Reform in Providence, R.I., received a two-year $1 million grant from The Atlantic Philanthropies, an international foundation, to help schools in Chicago, Los Angeles, New York and Nashville address discipline policies. More than a dozen more cities are also revising their discipline codes.

OUTLOOK
Striking a Balance

As schools eliminate or reduce disparate zero-tolerance policies and incorporate a combination of discipline methods, the debate is expected to continue over how best to strike the right balance in school discipline.

"We are in the middle of the most recent wave of education law reform. . . . We've been through several waves since Columbine. It's going to end up as all previous waves of reform have, which is [with] a variety of different approaches to keep children safe and to educate them," said Bernard James, a professor of civil rights and education law at Pepperdine University School of Law in Los Angeles. "The goal is to let each school do what they need to do to meet kids' needs."[87]

Some educators say that without larger political, social and economic changes reforms will have a limited impact at low-performing schools struggling with racial and class-based achievement gaps.[88] Losen at UCLA'sCenter for Civil Rights Remedies says the future of education and discipline policies lies in adequate resources.

"Changing the discipline policy is not . . . the be-all and end-all of education reform, just part of it. We need [both] more resources and diversity awareness," he says. "We're making important progress but there's a lot more to do, and it's more than school discipline. In changing school discipline, leaders are thinking about how can we engage kids, and that has an effect on better learning and higher graduation rates."

The Cato Institute's Coulson says structural changes also are needed. "Unless the incentive structure changes future public school polices will look like [they do] today," he says. "There will be no real improvement except where parents can have a choice." Incentives include higher salaries for principals who incorporate more holistic alternatives, he says, and allowing education leaders to expand their changes to more campuses.

"Zero-tolerance policies were the product of political and social processes, and these same processes can be used to dismantle them," said Judith Kafka, an associate professor of educational policy and history of education at Baruch College's School of Public Affairs. Moving away from zero tolerance will require building relationships in the school communities, she said. "Without those relationships, we are likely to develop new policies that will differ from current practices in name only."[89]

New and expanded data will provide insights on how the new discipline policies are applied, said Wade Henderson, president of the Leadership Conference on Civil and Human Rights, a civil rights organization in Washington. "The new data provides a wonderful start in what I hope will be building a new movement in this anniversary of great civil rights accomplishments," Henderson said.[90]

The Council of State Governments' Thompson agrees. "The changes we're already starting to see are due, in large part, to the evidence we've been able to gather and assess regarding the effectiveness of suspension and expulsion policies," he says. "You can't fix a problem that you don't fully understand. School districts need to devote themselves to collecting more data related to students' attendance, their performance in class and their overall perception of a school's environment."

Woodland Hills School District near Pittsburgh, Pa., is one of 10 national pilot programs to use alternative discipline methods to reduce zero tolerance.[91] Superintendent Alan Johnson says new research and discipline alternatives are part of the future.

"We're going to pursue a project to really reinvent, and re-imagine and rewrite our code of conduct to incorporate some of these strategies," said Johnson. "These new practices and new learnings have only come up just in the past 10 to 15 years, and we're ready to rethink how we approach the idea of discipline."[92]

NOTES

1. Nona Willis Aronowitz, "School Spirit or Gang Signs? 'Zero Tolerance' Comes Under Fire," NBCNews.com, March 9, 2014, http://tinyurl.com/q8me6h5.

2. "Civil Rights Data Collection, Data Snapshot: School Discipline," U.S. Department of Education Office of Civil Rights, March 21, 2014, p. 2, http://tinyurl.com/kls2ajo.

3. Stacy Teicher Khadaroo, "Racial gap indiscipline found in preschool, US data show," *The Christian Science Monitor*, March 21, 2014, http://tinyurl.com/nvmljvf.

4. Arne Duncan, "Rethinking School Discipline," U.S. Secretary of Education, Jan. 8, 2014, http://tinyurl.com/omnpeyl.

5. "Civil Rights Data Collection," *op. cit.*

6. See "School suspensions: Are they helping children?" Children's Defense Fund, Sept. 1, 1975, http://tinyurl.com/le3e9ne; and Stephen Hoffman, "Estimating the Effect of Zero Tolerance Discipline Polices on Racial Disparities in School Discipline," *Education*

Policy, Sage Journals, Jan. 2, 2014, http://tinyurl .com/pdakonf.

7. Khadaroo, *op. cit.*

8. Denver Nicks and Charlotte Alter, "Report: Black Preschoolers Suspended More than Whites," *Time*, March 21, 2014, http://tinyurl.com/l5otlak.

9. Joy Resmovits, "School 'Discipline Gap' Explodes As 1 In 4 Black Students Suspended, Report Finds," *The Huffington Post*, April 8, 2013, http://tinyurl.com/ cqd2bmp.

10. "Ending the School-to-Prison Pipeline," Committee on the Judiciary, U.S. Senate, Dec. 12, 2012, p. 11, http://tinyurl.com/khyyejq.

11. "Wake Schools accused of unfair policing in federal complaint," WNCN, March 5, 2014, http://tinyurl .com/nd73tov.

12. "Breaking Schools' Rules: A Statewide Study of How School Discipline Relates to Students' Success and Juvenile Justice Involvement," Justice Center, The Council of State Governments and The Public Policy Research Institute, Texas A&M University, July 2011, http://tinyurl.com/lkdwog4.

13. Prudence Carter, Michelle Fine, and Stephen Russell, "Discipline Disparities Series: Overview," The Equity Project at Indiana University, March 2014, www.indiana.edu/~atlantic/wp-content/ uploads/2014/04/Disparity_Overview_040414.pdf.

14. Halimah Abdullah, "Minority kids disproportion- ately impacted by zero-tolerance laws," CNN, Jan. 30, 2014, http://tinyurl.com/pjljra9.

15. Susan Berry, "Obama's School Guidelines Criticized by Legal, Education Experts," Breitbart, March 31, 2013, http://tinyurl.com/kk7augr; and Stacy Teicher Khadaroo, "School suspensions: Does racial bias feed the school-to-prison pipeline?" *The Christian Science Monitor,* March 31, 2013, http://tinyurl.com/c8kdy3u.

16. Russell Skiba, *et al.*, "Are Zero Tolerance Policies Effective in the Schools? An Evidentiary Review and Recommendations," American Psychological Association Zero Tolerance Task Force, Aug. 9, 2006, http://tinyurl.com/pmyvzp8.

17. Jessica Ashley and Kimberly Burke, "Implementing restorative justice," Illinois Criminal Justice Information Authority, http://tinyurl.com/lrpdzo2.

18. Daniel Losen and Jonathan Gillespie, "Opportunities Suspended: The Disparate Impact of Disciplinary Exclusion from School," The Center for Civil Rights Remedies at the Civil Rights Project, August 2012, http://files.eric.ed.gov/fulltext/ED534178.pdf.

19. Skiba, "New Developments," *op. cit.*

20. "AASA Statement on School Climate and Discipline Guidance Release by U.S. Depts. of Justice, Education," The School Superintendents Association, Jan. 8, 2014, http://tinyurl.com/q7ckq43.

21. See for background, "The Gun-Free Schools Act of 1994," www2.ed.gov/legislation/ESEA/toc.html. Also see Thomas J. Billitteri, "Discipline in Schools," *CQ Researcher,* Feb. 15, 2008, pp. 145-168; and Kathy Koch, "Zero Tolerance," *CQ Researcher*, March 10, 2000, pp. 185-208.

22. Jacob Kang-Brown, *et al.*, "A Generation Later: What We've Learned about Zero Tolerance in Schools," Center on Youth Justice at the Vera Institute of Justice, December 2013, http://tinyurl.com/khv maqm. Simone Robers, Jana Kemp, Jennifer Truman and Thomas D. Snyder, "Indicators of School Crime and Safety: 2012," Institute of Education Sciences, National Center for Education Statistics, U.S. Department of Education, June 2013, http://nces.ed .gov/pubsearch/pubsinfo.asp?pubid=2013036.

23. "Breaking Schools' Rules," *op. cit.*

24. "State and National Grades Issued for Education Performance, Policy; U.S. Earns a C-plus, Maryland Ranks First for Fifth Straight Year," Editorial Projects in Education Research Center, *Education Week*, Jan. 10, 2013, http://tinyurl.com/abwfflb.

25. "U.S. House of Representatives Education and the Workforce Committee hearing on "Protecting Students and Teachers: A Discussion on School Safety," American Institutes for Research, Feb. 27, 2013, http://tinyurl.com/oy2e6h2.

26. Michael Leachman and Chris Mai, "Most States Funding Schools Less Than Before the Recession," Center on Budget and Policy Priorities, Sept. 12, 2013, http://tinyurl.com/odqg939.

27. Randi Weingarten, "Support staff make schools safe, welcoming places," *The PRSP Reporter*, Spring 2014, http://tinyurl.com/mjb89aj.

28. Natassia Walsh, "A Capitol Hill Briefing on States' Innovations in Juvenile Justice," The Council of State Governments Justice Center, Sept. 6, 2013, http://tinyurl.com/o55eb7x.

29. Alan Schwarz, "School Discipline Study Raises Fresh Questions," *The New York Times,* July, 19, 2011, http://tinyurl.com/o7q2qdw.

30. " 'We Like Struggle': Black Lips On The Will To Entertain," NPR, March 30, 2014, http://tinyurl.com/kowbat4.

31. *Board of Ed. of Rogers, Ark. v. McCluskey*, 458 U.S. 966, July 2, 1982, U.S. Supreme Court,

32. For background, see Thomas J. Billitteri, "Cyberbullying," *CQ Researcher*, May 2, 2008, pp. 385-408.

33. Robers, *et al.*, *op. cit.*

34. Sameer Hinduja and Justin Patchin, "Cyberbullying Fact Sheet: Identification, Prevention and Response," The Cyberbullying Research Center, 2011, http://tinyurl.com/47tmxrb.

35. Indicators of School Crime and Safety: 2012, *op. cit.*

36. Larry Magid, "When schools can discipline off-campus behavior," *The Threshold Magazine*, summer 2009, http://tinyurl.com/ybntbdl.

37. Gretchen M. Shipley, "Cyber Misconduct, Discipline and the Law," *Leadership*, September/October 2011, pp. 14-16, http://tinyurl.com/mhg65ez.

38. Sameer Hinduja and Justin W. Patchin, "State Cyberbullying Laws: A Brief Review of State Cyberbullying Laws and Policies," Cyberbullying Research Center, April 2014, http://tinyurl.com/75695nl; and "Montana Anti-Bullying Laws & Policies," Stopbullying.gov, U.S. Department of Health and Human Services, http://tinyurl.com/km6v9gq.

39. Chongmin Na and Denise C. Gottfredson, "Police Officers in Schools: Effects on School Crime and the Processing of Offending Behaviors," *The Justice Quarterly,* Vol. 30, Issue 4, 2011, http://tinyurl.com/loovp5m.

40. *Ibid.*

41. "Obama On Guns: School Police Should Be Funded By Federal Government, But Not Required," *The Huffington Post*, Jan. 16, 2013, http://tinyurl.com/b2dwutu.

42. "National PTA Praises Administration's Gun Violence Prevention Agenda," National Parent Teachers Association, Jan. 16, 2013, http://tinyurl.com/pr8ljvv.

43. Philip Rucker, "White House may consider funding for police in schools after Newton," *The Washington Post*, Jan. 10, 2013, http://tinyurl.com/a87e7kh.

44. "AFT Offers Plan for Creating Safer Schools and Communities and Reducing Gun Violence," Jan. 10, 2013, http://tinyurl.com/oojqf2k.

45. K. C. Cowan, K. Vaillancourt, E. Rossen, K. Pollitt, "A framework for safe and successful schools," National Association of School Psychologists, 2013, http://tinyurl.com/pab9jea.

46. Matt Sledge, "Arming Teachers, School Cops Could Cause More Harm Than Good," *The Huffington Post*, Dec. 20, 2012, http://tinyurl.com/pu7bq5q.

47. "Poll: CNN/Time Poll: Majority of Americans favor armed guards in schools," 2012 Election Center, CNN Politics, http://tinyurl.com/mlzp5of.

48. "Educators support stronger laws to prevent gun violence says NEA poll," National Education Association, Jan. 15, 2013, http://tinyurl.com/n767dfr.

49. Judith Kafka, *The History of "Zero Tolerance"* (2011).

50. Russell Skiba, "Zero Tolerance, Zero Evidence," Indiana Education Policy Center, Policy Research Report #SRS2, August 2000, p. 2, http://tinyurl.com/kcz6p3e.

51. Marylee Allen, Cindy Brown and Ann Rosewater, "Children Out of School In America," The Children's Defense Fund, 1974, http://tinyurl.com/q2mh9vn.

52. "A Brief History of the Drug War," Drug Policy Alliance, 2014, http://tinyurl.com/q8juwhc. Also see Kafka, *op. cit.*

53. Kafka, *op. cit.*, p. 2.

54. Deborah Gordon Klehr, "Addressing the Unintended Consequences of No Child Left Behind and Zero Tolerance: Better Strategies for Safe Schools and Successful Students," *Georgetown Journal on Poverty Law & Policy*, 2009, pp. 585-610.

55. "Tinker v. Des Moines Independent Community School District," The Oyez Project, Chicago-Kent College of Law, Illinois Institute of Technology, http://tinyurl.com/3ycpfef.

56. Richard Arum, *Judging School Discipline: The Crisis of Moral Authority* (2003), pp. 42-66.

57. *Ibid.* See also 1978 *Carey v. Piphus*, 1982 *Board of Education of Rogers, Arkansas v. McCluskey*, 1985 *New Jersey v T.L.O.*, 1986 *Bethel School District v. Fraser*.

58. *Ibid.*, and Kafka, *op. cit.*

59. "Lawyers May Oppose Zero Tolerance," The Associated Press, Feb. 14, 2001, http://tinyurl.com/lxzocsr.

60. Richard L. Curwin, Allen N. Mendler, Brian D. Mendler, *Discipline With Dignity: New Challenges, New Solutions*, 3rd edition (2008), p. 3.

61. For background see Thomas J. Billitteri, "Preventing Bullying," *CQ Researcher*, Dec. 10, 2010, pp. 1013-1036.

62. Teresa L. Sarmiento-Brooks, *The School-to-Juvenile Justice Pipeline: Factors Associated with the Use of School-based Law Enforcement Officers by Public Schools*, Fordham University, Jan. 1, 2008, p. 36.

63. Na and Gottfredson, *op. cit.*

64. "To Protect and Educate: The School Resource Officer and the Prevention of Violence in Schools," National Association of School Resource Officers, October 2012, http://tinyurl.com/p6mv5fq.

65. Indicators of School Crime and Safety: 2012, *op. cit.*

66. Peter Finn and Jack McDevitt, "National Assessment of School Resource Officer Programs Final Project Report," National Institute of Justice, February 2005, http://tinyurl.com/qzo8m8o.

67. Aaron Kupchik, *Homeroom Security: School discipline in an age of fear* (2010).

68. Justice Center, *op. cit.*

69. For background, see Barbara Mantel, "Gun Control," *CQ Researcher*, March 8, 2013, pp. 233-256.

70. "Guiding Principles: A Resource Guide for Improving School Climate and Discipline," U.S. Department of Education, January 2014, http://tinyurl.com/n2lwu44.

71. Tamar Lewin, "Black Students Face More Discipline, Data Suggests," *The New York Times*, March 6, 2012, http://tinyurl.com/7rqx8bj.

72. Donna St. George, "Holder, Duncan announce national guidelines on school discipline," *The Washington Post*, Jan. 8, 2013, http://tinyurl.com/ma8gqu4.

73. Supportive School Discipline Initiative at http://tinyurl.com/nkvh9jb and http://tinyurl .com/omq9s9c and http://tinyurl.com/3hgx46b.

74. Ben Firke, "Ending the School-to-Prison Pipeline," Home Room, The Official Blog of the U.S. Department of Education, July 22, 2011, http://tinyurl.com/msp959w.

75. "Are Some U.S. School Discipline Policies Too Punitive?" PBS Newshour, Jan. 8, 2014, http://tinyurl .com/m8mqdmh.

76. Civil Rights Data Collection, *op. cit.*

77. Valerie Jarrett and Broderick John, "My Brother's Keeper: A New White House Initiative to Empower Boys and Young Men of Color," The White House Blog, Feb. 27, 2014, http://tinyurl.com/n86kjxw.

78. "Harkin, HELP Committee Democrats Introduce Bill to Prepare All Children for Success and Fix 'No Child Left Behind,' " U.S. Committee on Health, Education, Labor and Pensions, June 4, 2013, http://tinyurl.com/nzdlxcb.

79. "The Senate Health, Education, Labor and Pensions (HELP) Committee marked up the Strengthening America's Schools Act of 2013," CSPAN, June 11, 2013, minute 58, http://tinyurl.com/omffex8.

80. Hans Bader, "Obama Administration Imposes Racial Quotas on School Discipline in Oakland," The Legal, Politics as Usual, Zeitgeist, Oct. 12, 2012, http://tinyurl.com/9cgj9e6.

81. Susan Berry, "Obama Admin's School Guidelines Criticized by Legal, Education Experts," Breitbart, Jan. 9, 2014, http://tinyurl.com/kk7augr.

82. Khadaroo, *op. cit.*, School suspensions: Does racial bias feed the school-to-prison pipeline?

83. Nadra Kareen Nittle, "U.S. Department of Education Investigating Record Number of Civil Rights Complaints in School Districts, Aims to

Improve Education for Minority Students," *America's Wire*, http://tinyurl.com/kud3b2j.

84. Alyssa Morones, "Is Massachusetts School Discipline Law an Unfunded Mandate?" *Education Week*, Feb. 13, 2014, http://tinyurl.com/ouzbm7z.

85. "School Discipline Data: A Snapshot of Legislative Action," The Justice Center, Council of State Governments, February 2014, http://tinyurl.com/m23ycfb.

86. Lizette Alvarez, "Seeing the Toll, Schools Revise Zero Tolerance," *The New York Times*, Dec. 2, 2013, http://tinyurl.com/qaj4blp.

87. "School Safety and the School Resource Officer," Oct. 12, 2012 http://tinyurl.com/9nd7prd.

88. Alan R. Sadovnik and Susan F. Semel, Introduction to Kafka, *op. cit.*

89. Judith Kafka, letters to the editor, *The New York Times*, Jan. 15, 2014, http://tinyurl.com/nxfskyb.

90. "Wade Henderson Speaks on School Discipline," The Leadership Conference Education Fund, YouTube, Jan. 16, 2013, http://tinyurl.com/oo4y8od.

91. This initiative is a product of the partnership between the American Association of Administrators, a nationwide superintendents group, and the Children's Defense Fund, which is funded for this project by the Atlantic Philanthropies.

92. Jessica Berardino, "Woodland Hills High School Sets Out To Change Their 'Zero-Tolerance' Policy," NewsRadio 1020 KDKA, Jan. 27, 2014, http://tinyurl.com/p2uohwx.

BIBLIOGRAPHY

Selected Sources

Books

Boccanfuso, Christopher and Megan Kuhfeld, *Multiple Responses, Promising Results: Evidence-based, Non-punitive Alternatives to Zero Tolerance*, Child Trends, 2011.
Education researchers review existing studies on zero-tolerance policies and highlight promising alternatives.

Kafka, Judith, *The History of "Zero Tolerance" in American Public Schooling*, Palgrave Macmillan, 2011.
An associate professor specializing in educational policy at the Baruch College School of Public Affairs reviews the historical roots of zero-tolerance policies and their intersection with race, politics and education bureaucracy.

Trump, Kenneth S., *Proactive School Security and Emergency Preparedness* Planning, Corwin, 2011.
A school safety expert provides advice and strategies for preventing violence and preparing for emergency responses.

Articles

"School Discipline Racialized," *National Review*, Jan. 16, 2014, http://tinyurl.com/ob93oj8.
Editors at the conservative magazine argue against federal guidelines on zero tolerance.

"State Highlights Reports," *Education Week*, January 2013, http://tinyurl.com/lzxs9ou.
A collection of articles and supporting multimedia data analysis spotlights school social and disciplinary climates at the state level.

"The school-to-prison pipline: By the numbers," America Tonight, Aljazeera, Jan. 23, 2014, http://tinyurl.com/puppc43.
Reporters survey zero-tolerance policies at school districts throughout the nation.

Khadaroo, Stacy Teicher, "School suspensions: Does racial bias feed the school-to-prison pipeline?" *The Christian Science Monitor*, March 31, 2013, http://tinyurl.com/c8kdy3u.
A reporter examines racial disparities in zero-tolerance suspension and expulsion rates to see whether they represent civil rights violations.

Reports and Studies

"Breaking Schools' Rules: A Statewide Study of How School Discipline Relates to Students' Success and Juvenile Justice Involvement," Council of State Governments Justice Center and the Public Policy Research Institute at Texas A&M University, July 2011, http://tinyurl.com/lkdwog4.

Researchers analyze discipline records of 1 million Texas secondary-school students over six years and find that 60 percent have been suspended or expelled at least once.

"Guiding Principles: A Resource Guide for Improving School Climate and Discipline," U.S. Department of Education, January 2014, http://tinyurl.com/n2lwu44.
The federal government issues guidelines for schools striving to reduce over-reliance on zero-tolerance disciplinary policies.

"Policy Briefing Spotlights What Works to Eliminate Disparities in School Discipline," Civil Rights Project at the University of California, Los Angeles, March 15, 2014, http://tinyurl.com/kgj7otf.
A policy briefing highlights and summarizes the work of 26 national school discipline experts.

"Report of the National School Shield Task Force," National School Shield Task Force, April 2, 2013, http://tinyurl.com/cbbshdr.
A National Rifle Association task force surveys school security standards and makes recommendations to improve security.

"A Summary of New Research Closing the School Discipline Gap: 1 Research to Policy," The Center for Civil Rights Remedies, 2013, http://tinyurl.com/bpur26a.

This summary of 16 new research studies concludes that reducing suspensions can lead to better academic outcomes and highlights successful alternatives to zero tolerance.

Kang-Brown, Jacob, Jennifer Trone, Jennifer Fratello and Tarika Daftary-Kapur, "A Generation Later: What We've Learned about Zero Tolerance in Schools," Vera Institute of Justice, December 2013, http://tinyurl.com/khvmaqm.
Juvenile-justice researchers survey empirical research to address questions on zero tolerance.

Kinsler, Joshua, "School Discipline: A Source or Salve for the Racial Achievement Gap?" *International Economic Review*, February 2013, Vol. 54, Issue 1, pp. 355-383, http://tinyurl.com/lsh7rty.
An assistant professor of economics at the University of Rochester in New York state examines the effect of reducing suspensions on overall student achievement.

Skiba, Russell J., Megan Trachok, Choong-Geun Chung, Timberly Baker, Adam Sheya and Robin Hughes, "Where Should We Intervene? Contributions of Behavior, Student, and School Characteristics to Suspension and Expulsion," Center for Civil Rights Remedies and Research-to-Practice Collaborative, April 6, 2013, http://tinyurl.com/qakexfd.
Researchers review the odds of students being suspended or expelled based on three conditions.

For More Information

Advancement Project, 1220 L St., N.W., Suite 850, Washington, DC 20005; 202-728-9557; www.advancement project.org. Civil rights organization that sponsors research and model programs on zero-tolerance policies.

Center for Evaluation and Education Policy, 509 East Third St., Bloomington, IN 47401-3654; 800-511-6575; http://ceep.indiana.edu. Conducts research on education policy, including student-discipline practices.

National School Boards Association, 1680 Duke St., Alexandria, VA 22314; 703-838-6722; www.nsba.org. Federation of state school board associations.

National School Safety Center, 141 Duesenberg Dr., Suite 7B, Westlake Village, Calif. 91362; 805-373-9977; www. schoolsafety.us. Promotes strategies and programs for safe schools.

Public Counsel, 610 S. Ardmore Ave., Los Angeles, CA 90005; 213-385-2977; www.publiccounsel.org. Pro bono law firm's project (www.fixschooldiscipline.org) provides information on how to eliminate "push-out" discipline such as suspension and expulsion.

15

Assisted Suicide

Reed Karaim

Opponents of a measure that would have legalized physician-assisted suicide for the terminally ill in Massachusetts celebrate the measure's narrow defeat on Nov. 6, 2012. Religious, medical and disability groups said the measure was open to manipulation and relied on diagnoses that could be wrong.

From *CQ Researcher*, May 17, 2013.

L ee Johnson, a retired federal worker in Portland, Ore., had started a second career as a furniture maker. When he developed terminal brain cancer, he opted for radiation treatments and chemotherapy to extend his life, even though the disease "was undeniably going to kill him," says his daughter, Heather Clish.

But as his condition deteriorated and he became bedridden, with blurred vision, sores and pain, Johnson didn't want to go on, she says. In March 2011, Johnson took advantage of Oregon's Death with Dignity Act and swallowed a lethal dose of pills prescribed by a doctor.* He was 66.

Before he ended his life, Clish says, Johnson and his family talked a lot about his values. "The essence of his being was that he was a deeply independent person who really came to believe in living by choice," she says. "What he ended up doing was very consciously going about dying with dignity and grace. If this was what he needed to have as an option to be the person he is, we understood. That was okay."

Clish felt so strongly about her father's decision that when Massachusetts, where she lives, voted on an assisted-suicide** law

---

* The fatal prescription is most often a lethal dose of barbiturates, usually Seconal or Pentobarbital.

** Supporters prefer the term "death with dignity" or "aid in dying," arguing that because the terminally ill already are dying, "assisted suicide" mischaracterizes their choice. Opponents, who view the procedure as suicide, note that the Oregon, Washington and likely to be enacted Vermont laws require only a physician's diagnosis that a patient is going to die within six months. That is too far out to know when the end will occur, and thus those who take lethal doses of medicine are choosing to end their lives prematurely, the opponents contend. Physician-assisted suicide is the term most used by the media.

Physician-Assisted Suicides Rise in Oregon Law

Oregon enacted the Death With Dignity Act in 1994, allowing terminally ill adults to self-administer lethal doses of medication prescribed by physicians. Last year 115 people received prescriptions, compared to 24 in 1998. The number of deaths involving use of the prescriptions has risen steadily since the law took effect in 1998, to 77 last year.

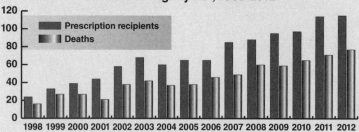

Prescription Recipients and Deaths Under Oregon Death With Dignity Act, 1998-2012

Source: "Oregon's Death With Dignity Act — 2012," Public Health Division, State of Oregon, January 2013, p. 1, public.health.oregon.gov/ ProviderPartnerResources/EvaluationResearch/DeathwithDignityAct/ Documents/year15.pdf

ALS, I had been given an easy way out with a doctor's prescription and support, I would have taken that opportunity," he said. "I would have missed the bulk of my life."

Johnson's and Norton's cases are not identical. Johnson was almost certainly in the final days of his life, whereas Norton's ALS stopped progressing before he reached that stage. But their stories testify to the deeply personal nature of the public debate surrounding physician-assisted suicide, currently legal in just three states: Oregon, Washington, Montana and soon likely in Vermont, when Gov. Peter Shumlin signs a bill enacted on May 13.

In 1997 the U.S. Supreme Court declined to recognize the right to assisted suicide but invited the states to address the issue. In his majority opinion, the late Chief Justice William Rehnquist concluded, "Americans are engaged in an earnest and profound debate about the morality, legality and practicality of physician-assisted suicide. Our holding permits this debate to continue, as it should in a democratic society."[1]

modeled on Oregon's in a ballot initiative last November, she volunteered her family's story in support.

But Clish was not the only person who felt strongly about the issue. In a written statement, John Norton, a retired bus driver from Florence, Mass., offered his own life as evidence — in opposition to the measure.

When he was 18, Norton said, he noticed a twitching in his right hand. Doctors at the University of Iowa Medical School diagnosed Norton with the usually fatal amyotrophic lateral sclerosis (ALS), commonly known as Lou Gehrig's disease. "I was told I would get progressively worse, be paralyzed and die in three to five years," he wrote.

The Mayo Clinic in Rochester, Minn., confirmed Norton's diagnosis, and for awhile his condition worsened. Twitching began in his right hand and both got weaker. Then the disease's progression stopped. That was in 1960. Today Norton is 75 with a wife and family. He enjoys singing in an amateur choir and still volunteers occasionally as a bus driver.

None of that would have happened, he wrote, if assisted suicide had been available when he was initially told he had the disease. "If, when I was diagnosed with

The debate is still going strong. Supporters cast the issue as one of individual choice, believing the terminally ill have a right to decide whether to obtain prescriptions that allow them to avoid final days stricken with pain or other debilitating conditions and choose the manner in which they meet an inevitable death. Opponents see the practice as a threat to some of the most vulnerable Americans, including the elderly and disabled, fearing some could be coerced or manipulated into making the decision to end their lives. They believe physician-assisted suicide devalues life, encourages a premature halt to medical treatment and could open the door to cutting off medical care for other patients who aren't terminally ill but may be severely disabled or incapacitated.

The Roman Catholic Church has been a leading, politically active opponent of assisted suicide. But several disability-rights groups also actively oppose it. The American Medical Association has adopted a position against the practice but does not actively lobby against it. Two public-interest groups are the leading voices supporting legalization: the Denver-based Compassion & Choices, and the Portland-based Death with Dignity National Center, which originally organized to work for the Oregon law. Some smaller religious denominations such as Unitarian Universalism also support the right of terminally ill individuals to choose assisted suicide.

Despite the passion surrounding the issue, physician-assisted suicide remains rare, even in the states where it is legal. Oregon, which passed its Death with Dignity Act through a voter referendum in 1994 and began allowing the practice in 1998, has the longest track record. The number of Oregonians who choose physician-assisted suicide has been slowly climbing; 673 cases were recorded between 1998 and 2012. In 2012, the 77 cases reported to the Public Health Division amounted to about 0.2 percent of the total deaths recorded in the state.[2] In Washington, where the law — also passed by referendum — has been in effect only since 2009, 70 people took lethal doses of prescription medicine in 2011.[3]

The number of individuals requesting the prescriptions is higher in both states, but in Oregon a little more than a third haven't used the drugs after obtaining them. "I think it's a peace-of-mind thing," says Peg Sandeen, executive director of the Death with Dignity National Center. "You're terminally ill and you're facing the possibility of some pretty tremendous suffering, and just the idea that you have this [prescription] and tomorrow you can take it if it gets really bad provides some comfort."

Montana does not spell out as clearly the requirements for assisted suicide to occur legally. The state's Supreme

Americans Slightly Divided on Assisted Suicide

Slightly more Americans say physician-assisted suicide is morally wrong than acceptable. However, in another poll, when the question about assisted suicide was worded differently — "Do you think people have the right to end their own lives?" — a strong majority approved.

Percentage Who Say Assisted Suicide is Morally Acceptable, 2011, by Age, Political Party

Overall	
Morally acceptable	45%
Morally wrong	48%
By Party	
Democrats	51%
Republicans	32%
Independents	50%
By Age Group	
18 to 34	46%
35 to 54	45%
55+	43%

Source: Lydia Saad, "Doctor-Assisted Suicide Is Moral Issue Dividing Americans Most," Gallup, May 2011, www.gallup.com/poll/147842/doctor-assisted-suicide-moral-issue-dividing-americans.aspx

Court ruled in 2009 that a physician helping a terminally ill patient die was protected by existing state law.[4] But the state has not passed a specific law regulating the practice, and it is unknown how many people have died with the assistance of their doctor.[5]

Supporters of assisted suicide point to national opinion polls and the fact that Oregon's and Washington's laws were passed by referendum in arguing that the public backs their cause.[6] "I think it's fairly clear the public believes this is a right they have," says Sandeen.

But similar laws have been defeated by referendum or failed to advance through legislatures in roughly half the states, including Massachusetts, where a ballot measure was defeated last November, 51 to 49 percent, despite leading in early polls. "It doesn't gather a lot of attention, but there's been a lot of rejection of physician-assisted suicide," says Marilyn Golden, a policy analyst with the Berkeley, Calif.-based Disability Rights Education and Defense Fund, one of several disability groups opposing assisted suicide. "Once the problems are brought out on legalization, it's very common for public opinion to shift."

However, on May 13 the Vermont House gave final approval to a bill that would make Vermont the first state to legalize physician-assisted suicide by legislation. Democratic Gov. Peter Shumlin, a supporter of the measure, is expected to sign it into law.

As advocates, physicians and the general public debate the question of whether assisted suicide should be legal, here are some of the questions they are discussing:

Do the terminally ill have a right to choose when to end their lives?

Supporters of what they call aid in dying align their cause with American values of individual liberty and freedom of choice. Barbara Coombs Lee, Compassion & Choices president, says the organization believes individuals should have options as they near the end of their lives, including expanded hospice and palliative care, which focus on relieving patients' pain and discomfort.

"We don't promote just one choice (in end-of-life decisions). We think people deserve an entire spectrum of choices," says Coombs Lee. "But people who are mentally alert and who are making a rational decision to choose — not life or death, because that decision has already been made — but when and how they will meet death, those people deserve a peaceful and gentle option in the dying process."

But Golden with the Disability Rights Education and Defense Fund believes considering the issue simply as a matter of individual rights ignores the implications for society as a whole. "Public policy is about weighing benefits and harms," she says. "Proponents of assisted suicide would want you to believe there [are] only benefits and no harms. . . . But if you look at everything, I think the risk of harms vastly overwhelm the benefits."

By supporting the idea that there is a class of people whom doctors can legally help die and by legitimizing one form of suicide, Golden and other opponents say, physician-assisted suicide potentially harms many more people than it helps both because it makes suicide more culturally acceptable and because it involves doctors in the process of ending lives, which ends a prohibition that could eventually make other forms of assisted-death acceptable, such as euthanasia.

Supporters, however, say the relatively small number of people who choose physician-assisted suicide where it is legal shows the procedure does not threaten the larger population. "Modern medicine, palliative care, pain release, hospice care can provide relief for most people," Sandeen says. "But not all people, and the Death with Dignity Act can provide relief for them."

Sandeen, who was a social worker before joining Death with Dignity, says her experience was that too many "people die badly in this country. The way modern medicine works is that they can keep people alive for a very long time past what any natural death would be, and people die badly." Individuals should have a right to escape a bad — in other words painful or lingering, debilitating — death, she says.

But opponents believe advances in palliative care including at the end of life, means a "bad death" need no longer be the case. "It is a national and international scandal that so many people do not get adequate pain control," writes Rita Marker, the founder of the Patients Rights Council, a nonprofit group in Steubenville, Ohio, that opposes assisted suicide. "But killing is not the answer to that scandal. The solution is to mandate better education of health care professionals."[7]

Some opponents say that in the most extreme cases, palliative sedation, in which a patient is drugged into unconsciousness to escape pain until he dies, provides a legal alternative. But David Mayo, a bioethicist and professor of philosophy emeritus at the University of Minnesota, Duluth, who is on the Death with Dignity board, believes such an intervention amounts to assisted dying. "The practice of terminal [palliative] sedation — which is, 'now I can't give you the drugs to kill yourself, but we can put you in a coma while you starve to death' — the idea that's somehow better is just crazy," Mayo says.

In their statement on the issue, the United States Conference of Catholic Bishops rejects the idea that assisted suicide represents an expression of freedom. "The assisted-suicide agenda promotes a narrow and distorted notion of freedom, by creating an expectation that certain people, unlike others, will be served by being helped to choose death," the statement declares. "One cannot uphold human freedom and dignity by devaluing human life. A choice to take one's life is a supreme contradiction of freedom, a choice to eliminate all choices."[8]

Orthodox Judaism, Islam and most major Protestant denominations also oppose physician-assisted suicide, although they generally have not been as active politically as the Catholic Church on the issue. Some Christian denominations, however, have not taken a position, or they support the practice as one end-of-life option.

The United Church of Christ, for instance, considers the right to choose aid in dying a legitimate decision under certain circumstances. The Unitarian Universalist Association adopted a resolution in 1988 stating, "Unitarian Universalists advocate the right to self-determination in dying, and the release from civil or criminal penalties of those who, under proper safeguards, act to honor the right of terminally ill patients to select the time of their own deaths."[9]

The Oregon and Washington laws do not require the participation of a doctor or pharmacist who, for religious or any other reason, objects to physician-assisted suicide. "The underpinning of this law is the concept of self-determination," says Sandeen. "There is no way we would want someone who believes this is wrong to have to participate. My struggle with the religious-based opposition is that they want everybody else not to be able to participate because of their [own religious] beliefs."

Does permitting assisted suicide lead to abuse?

Oregon's Death with Dignity Act and the Washington law that followed have safeguards that supporters believe clearly prevent abuses of the process. (Vermont's pending law has similar provisions.)

The laws require that a physician diagnose a terminally ill patient as having a life expectancy of six months or less. A second doctor must concur with the diagnosis. Patients must request the lethal prescription twice verbally and once in written form with a waiting period of at least two weeks between the first and last request, and the doctor who writes the prescription must believe the patient is mentally competent to make the decision. The law also requires that patients be able to take the pills on their own.

State health agencies are required to provide annual reports on how often physician-assisted suicide is used, and by whom. Outside researchers also have conducted several studies on the laws' impact. "There has never been a medical treatment that has been so closely, comprehensively and continually studied as this one," says Coombs Lee of Compassion & Choices. In all that examination, she says, there have been no substantiated cases of abuse.

But opponents question the safeguards in the laws, saying compliance is self-reported, so there is no way to be sure what's really happening. "Do we have any evidence of abuse? No, but we have a lot of circumstances that show that abuse is very possible," says Golden of the Disability Rights Education and Defense Fund.

Opponents note the laws don't require an independent witness present when a person is taking the prescription, so there is no way to be sure every dose is self-administered or taken by free will. Opponents also point out that the law does not require an outside psychological evaluation of patients who request the drugs.

"It's bad psychiatry and bad medicine," says Dr. Herbert Hendin, a professor of psychiatry at New York Medical

Getty Images/Matt Cardy

Australian physician Philip Nitschke, a supporter of voluntary euthanasia, displays a drug kit used in assisted suicides following a workshop he gave on May 5, 2009, in Bournemouth, England.

College and executive officer of Suicide Prevention Initiatives, a nonprofit group. "The weakness of the laws is that they don't enforce the practice of ordinary medical standards. They could insist on a palliative care [discussion with the patient as an alternative to assisted suicide]. They could insist on a psychiatric consult."

The idea that hundreds of people have received aid in dying without formal psychiatric evaluation or counseling undercuts the claim the law is being used solely by people making competent choices, Hendin says. "An awful lot of people who are physically ill are also depressed, and if you relieve their depression, they're no longer interested in ending their life early," he says.

Cancer Most Prevalent Malady in Oregon Cases

Of the 77 people who died last year under Oregon's Death With Dignity Act, 75 percent suffered from cancer. The median age for all deaths under the law was 69. More than 90 percent said they were concerned about losing autonomy and finding life's activities no longer enjoyable.

Characteristics of Deaths Under Oregon's Death With Dignity Act, 2012

Sex

Male	50.6%
Female	49.4%

Age

18-34	0%
35-44	1.3%
45-54	10.4%
55-64	20.8%
65-74	29.9%
75-84	23.4%
85+	14.3%

Marital status

Married	42.9%
Widowed	29.9%
Never married	7.8%
Divorced	19.5%

Underlying illness

Cancer	75.3%
Amyotrophic lateral sclerosis	6.5%
Chronic lower respiratory disease	2.6%
Heart disease	2.6%
HIV/AIDS	1.3%
Other	11.7%

End-of-life concerns

Losing autonomy	93.5%
Activities no longer enjoyable	92.2%
Loss of dignity	77.9%
Losing control of bodily functions	35.1%
Burden on loved ones and caregivers	57.1%
Inadequate pain control	29.9%
Financial implications of treatment	3.9%

Source: "Oregon's Death With Dignity Act — 2012," Public Health Division, State of Oregon, January 2013, pp. 4-5, public.health.oregon.gov/ ProviderPartnerResources/EvaluationResearch/DeathwithDignityAct/ Documents/year15.pdf

often misconstrued that way. These people are going to die. Who are we to tell them they must soldier on?"

Critics, however, believe the laws' lax definition of terminally ill invites abuse of the intent to limit assistance to those in their last weeks of their lives. "Terminal illness is a meaningless term," says Dr. Rex Greene, a longtime oncologist now semi-retired in Elida, Ohio. "The law in Oregon says a six-month prognosis. There's no physician on Earth [who] can make a six-month prognosis. The best we can do is in the last weeks of life we can be pretty close."

The issue strikes a nerve with disability groups. "Anytime I'm doing training on this issue within the disability community, I ask, 'Who of you here were first diagnosed as terminally ill and are still going strong?' " says Golden, "and every time, hands go up."

Advocates for the disabled are among the most vocal in arguing that the laws could encourage some people to end their lives to save loved ones trouble. Ben Matlin, an author born with a neuromuscular condition so debilitating that he has never been able to stand and now is unable to hold a pencil, explained his opposition to the laws. "I've lived so close to death for so long that I know how thin and porous the border between coercion and free choice is, how easy it is for someone to inadvertently influence you to feel devalued and hopeless — to pressure you ever so slightly but decidedly into being 'reasonable,' to unburdening others, to 'letting go,' " he wrote.[10]

Opponents also raise the possibility that the nature of the health care system could lead to abuse. "The frightening potential for profit-driven health care organizations to drive people toward assisted suicide for cost control is something we can't ignore," says Golden.

But Dr. Marcia Angell, a senior lecturer in social medicine at Harvard Medical School, says the terminally ill are in a different situation from other seriously ill patients. "This is not a question of life versus death," she says. "It's

But supporters respond that all these concerns have proved unfounded through years of experience with the Oregon law. "When we talk about aid in dying, a tactic of those who oppose end-of-life choice is to raise unreasonable doubt, to cast aspersions on the situation in Oregon," says Coombs Lee of Compassion & Choices.

Supporters point to a study of cases published in the *Journal of Clinical Ethics* that found no unreported cases of physician-assisted suicide in Oregon. In addition, the researchers found that terminally ill people in Oregon were no more likely to consider assisted suicide than people in states where the procedure was illegal.[11]

Supporters also cite a study led by Margaret Battin, a distinguished professor of philosophy and an adjunct professor of internal medicine in the Division of Medical Ethics, at the University of Utah in Provo. The study found no evidence that physician-assisted suicide has had a disproportionate impact on patients in vulnerable groups, including the physically disabled, the poor, individuals with low educational status or racial minorities. "Those who received physician-assisted dying in the jurisdictions studied appeared to enjoy comparative social, economic, educational, professional and other privileges," Battin and her team concluded.[12]

Does the Hippocratic Oath ethics code prevent doctors from helping patients die?

Physicians have been pledging themselves to the principles of the Hippocratic Oath, named after an ancient Greek physician, since the 4th century BC. The classical version of the oath includes this prohibition, "I will never give a deadly drug to anybody who asked for it, nor will I make a suggestion to this effect."[13]

Most graduating U.S. medical students still swear to some form of the oath, although the modern version used by most medical schools does not include that prohibition.[14]

The American Medical Association (AMA) code of ethics, however, rejects the idea of doctors providing deadly prescriptions. "Physician-assisted suicide is fundamentally incompatible with the physician's role as healer, would be difficult or impossible to control, and would pose serious societal risks," the code states.[15]

Some bioethicists, however, believe medical care must include recognizing when death is inevitable and respecting a patient's wishes at that time. "While doctors in

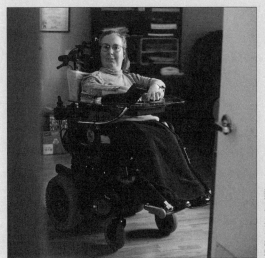

AP Photo/Jessica Hill

AP Photo/Charles Dharapak

To Assist or Not to Assist

Cathy Ludlum, a disabled-rights activist in Manchester, Conn., is concerned that physician-assisted suicide is being considered by her state's legislature. Lawmakers should focus more on "giving people a good life than giving people a good death," says Ludlum, who has spinal muscular atrophy (top). Opponents of the measure to permit assisted suicide in Connecticut succeeded in April in derailing the proposal. Supporters of Oregon's physician-assisted suicide law demonstrate in front of the U.S. Supreme Court (bottom) on Oct. 5, 2005, as the court heard Bush administration attorneys argue that the law violated the Controlled Substances Act. The court later ruled against the administration, allowing the law to stand.

general want and should work to extend life, suppose that's no longer possible?" says Angell of Harvard's medical school. "That's the case here, and if that's the case, then they must shift their objective to relieving suffering in accordance with the patients' wishes."

But many physicians believe assisting in death, even of a terminally ill patient, undermines their essential covenant with the public. "It's in the seminal code of medicine, that physicians are not to do anything to take the patient's life," says Greene, the retired oncologist, referring to the Hippocratic Oath. "One of the reasons medicine has endured all these centuries is that we have remained trustworthy in that regard. I personally don't see any way physicians can maintain that trust if they're involved [in] ending people's lives."

Greene is the current chairman of the AMA Council on Ethical and Judicial Affairs but emphasizes that he is expressing his personal opinion. He spent more than 30 years as an oncologist and now consults on palliative care.

The AMA, along with most opponents of assisted suicide, supports the removal of life-sustaining devices in the last stages of life, if patients have indicated such a preference. But Greene sees a crucial distinction between removing life-sustaining medical equipment and actively assisting patients in killing themselves.

Physician-assisted suicide supporter Jack Kevorkian talks to college students about prison reform at Detroit's Wayne State University on Nov. 29, 2007, not long after his release from prison. Nicknamed Dr. Death, the controversial pathologist spent eight years in prison following his conviction in 1999 for second-degree murder for helping in an assisted suicide. He died in 2011, at age 83, of natural causes.

By removing devices such as ventilators or respirators, in accordance with their wishes, a physician is allowing the patient to assume the natural risk of dying that is part of their condition, he says. The physician is not taking action that has the specific intent of killing the patient, he says. "That's not the intent," Greene says. "If we take on the responsibility of deciding who lives and who dies, we have so overstepped the bounds of human experience."

Other physicians, however, believe fulfilling a patient's wish to end his or her suffering at the end of life is part of the responsibility a doctor assumes when caring for the person. Dr. Eric Kress, who practices family medicine and hospice care in Missoula, Mont., says an experience with one particular patient persuaded him of that.

The patient was terminally ill with ALS; he had lost 100 pounds, couldn't walk and was being fed through a tube. "He used to be a vigorous guy, but now he was wasting away, and there was no question where he was headed," Kress recalls. His patient, whom Kress considered of sound mind, felt very strongly that he did not want to wait a few more weeks for the disease to end his life. He requested lethal medication.

Kress told him he couldn't provide it. A few weeks later the patient had stockpiled enough pain medication to kill himself anyway. But before he died, Kress says, "He called me a coward and said, 'Who are you treating here? Are you treating yourself or are you treating me?' And he got me thinking, what kind of doctor am I? Am I going to do what I want or what my patients needs?"

Kress became one of the few doctors to speak openly about providing lethal prescriptions when testifying before the Montana state legislature. He says several patients have raised the possibility of assisted suicide with him, but he has ended up providing medication to only three patients. In each case, Kress says, he obtained a written second opinion from another doctor that the patient's condition was terminal and would result in death "in a few months or less." He also says he met with the patients several times over extended periods to make sure they understood what they were doing. Moreover, he says, he sought to make sure they could self-administer the drugs.

Kress says he checked with attorneys to make sure he was in accordance with Montana law, but he says his primary concern was fulfilling his obligation to care for his patients. "This is really an issue about aiding people in

CHRONOLOGY

1960s *As medicine advances, the question of how long and under what circumstances life should be sustained by medical means gains new urgency.*

1967 After watching a friend die a slow, painful death, human-rights attorney Luis Kutner writes the first "living will," specifying under what conditions a patient should be taken off life-sustaining devices. . . . A right-to-die bill fails in Florida.

1969 The Hastings Center is founded in New York to study ethical problems in biology and medicine, including end-of-life decisions.

1970s *The idea that patients have a right to refuse treatment gains acceptance. In England, a best-selling memoir starts a debate about assisted suicide.*

1973 American Hospital Association recognizes the right of patients to refuse treatment.

1976 California Gov. Jerry Brown signs nation's first law giving terminally ill people the right to authorize withdrawal of life-sustaining medical treatment when death is imminent. Eight other states pass similar laws within a year.

1978 British journalist Derek Humphry writes a best-seller, *Jean's Way*, a memoir about helping his terminally ill wife commit suicide, kicking off international debate.

1980s *Right-to-die movement gains strength; Catholic Church issues objections.*

1980 Humphry helps form the Hemlock Society to support assisted suicide. . . . Pope John Paul II opposes "willful suicide," but supports the use of pain-relieving medicines and the right to refuse extraordinary means to sustain life.

1988 Unitarian Universalist Association becomes first religious body to support a right to die and call for those who assist in that act to be free from criminal or civil penalties.

1990s *The first state approves physician-assisted suicide; Detroit physician Jack Kevorkian further spurs debate over the procedure.*

1990 Kevorkian helps Alzheimer's patient Janet Adkins commit suicide, he will help more than 130 others die before being convicted of murder in 1999.

1991 Washington state voters reject physician-assisted suicide.

1992 California voters defeat a similar measure.

1994 American Medical Association opposes physician-assisted suicide. . . . Oregon voters approve nation's first law permitting terminally ill patients to obtain a prescription to end their life; challenged in court, the law doesn't go into effect for four years.

1997 U.S. Supreme Court rules there is no constitutional right to die, but invites states to continue debating the issue.

2000-Present *Three more states join Oregon in allowing physician-assisted suicide, but opponents win in Massachusetts.*

2005 Terri Schiavo, a Florida woman who doctors say is in a persistent vegetative state, dies after her feeding tube is removed, ending a controversial seven-year battle between her husband and parents that generates international debate on end-of-life decisions.

2008 Washington voters make the state the second to allow physician-assisted suicide.

2009 Montana Supreme Court effectively allows physicians to provide lethal prescriptions to terminally ill patients who request it.

2012 Massachusetts voters reject physician-assisted suicide.

2013 Vermont House and Senate pass differing version of a physician-assisted suicide measure (April); governor indicates willingness to sign a final bill modeled on Oregon's law. . . . Vermont House approves bill legalizing physician-assisted suicide (May 13). Democratic Gov. Peter Shumlin is expected to sign the measure into law.

Researchers Seek Advances in Pain Management

"Death isn't a medical condition."

Medicine is making advances in pain management and end-of-life care that some say may eliminate one of the reasons patients may choose assisted suicide.

Advances in the relatively new discipline of pain management known as palliative care can go a long way toward relieving unbearable pain and making people more comfortable in their last days, according to researchers.

"When we talk about palliative care, we're talking about relief of suffering," says Nancy Berlinger, who teaches ethics at the Yale School of Nursing and is co-author of *The Hastings Center Guidelines for Decisions on Life-Sustaining Treatment and Care Near the End of Life*. "The field of palliative care and hospice care has greatly taken off in the last 20 years. There are now specialized palliative care units in children's hospitals and adults' hospitals. It's still a work in progress, but it's growing."

The Center to Advance Palliative Care, based in New York City, reports that more than 1,500 hospitals now have palliative care teams — twice as many as six years ago.[1] A palliative care team includes doctors, nurses and other specialists who provide relief from the symptoms, pain and stress of serious illness.

A 2010 *New England Journal of Medicine* study found palliative care can make a significant difference in the life of patients. The study found that patients receiving early palliative care experienced less depression and survived an average of 2.7 months longer than those who did not receive the same kind of care.[2] Medical researchers also have been exploring new approaches to pain management that go beyond the typically prescribed drugs such as Oxycontin, Vicodin or morphine. Researchers at the University of Colorado in Boulder are studying the glial cells, which wrap around the neurons that transmit pain sensations and are thought to amplify chronic pain. Scientists are working on drugs that could block that effect.[3]

At Stanford University and other institutions, researchers are exploring the use of magnetic fields to cause electrical changes in the brain. The process, called "transcranial magnetic stimulation," involves putting an eight-inch electrical coil around the head. Originally developed to treat severe depression, the procedure can also reduce pain, most probably by disrupting the pain signals traveling along the neurons in the brain, early results indicate.[4]

the dying process. It's not about letting people commit suicide," Kress says. "One of the questions I asked everyone was, 'If you didn't have this [terminal] disease, would you want to die, and they all universally said no.'"

Even with all such steps, some bioethicists believe legalizing physician-assisted suicide places too much power in the hands of doctors. Daniel Callahan, president emeritus of the Hastings Center, a leading bioethics research institution in Garrison, N.Y., says he become opposed to physician-assisted suicide after studying the situation in the Netherlands, where it is legal.

An anonymous survey of doctors there revealed abuses, he says, including the euthanasia of patients without their permission. "I don't like the idea of empowering physicians to do this sort of thing," Callahan says. "They're too good at it."

BACKGROUND

'Robes of the Executioner'

Assisted suicide has been part of human culture since antiquity, and so have prohibitions against it, as Hippocrates' oath shows. A forerunner of Compassion & Choices was the Hemlock Society, named after the poison the ancient Greek philosopher Socrates drank to fulfill his death sentence.

In 1870, schoolteacher Samuel D. Williams was one of the first U.S. proponents of using an overdose of morphine, then a new pain-relieving drug, to assist death "in all cases of hopeless and painful illness."[16] Williams's euthanasia proposal was reprinted in newspapers and magazines over the years, creating enough of a stir that in 1885 the *Journal of the American Medical Association*

Less intrusive pain management techniques being studied focus on mental activity and biofeedback. A project at Stanford allows patients to see on a screen when the part of the brain that handles pain is activated. "They then use this information to learn to control their brain activation in a specific region associated with the processing and perception of pain," according to an article on a Stanford website.[5]

Dr. Ray Barfield, a pediatric oncologist who directs the Pediatric Quality of Life/Palliative Care Program at Duke University's Medical Center, says many new approaches being studied have great potential, especially those involving techniques to mentally manage one's own pain. "Some of the advances that we're making in hypnosis, biofeedback and medication that some people scoff at are tremendously effective," he says.

A major problem in managing pain, says Barfield, is the reluctance many doctors feel about prescribing pain drugs for fear of potential negative effects or of the patient becoming addicted. And patients often resist taking drugs they feel will dull their senses.

"One of the biggest advances that we need is not coming up with new medicines; we need to get people educated about the stuff we already have," Barfield says. "We have some good pain medicines and good experiences with them, and we still can't get people to use them the right way."

Barfield is a leading advocate for an end-of-life approach that focuses on medical interventions, pain management and careful attention to the physical and mental journey the patient is taking — the questions they need answered and the help they need facing what is happening to them.

Doctors, he believes, can get too focused on treatment as an end in itself and lose track of the larger needs of patients and their families. "Death isn't a medical condition," Barfield says. "Death is experiential. Your last day is still a day meaningful things can happen."

Combining careful attention to a patient and family's larger needs with proper palliative care and pain management, Barfield says, can "go a long way to reducing the need for [physician-assisted suicide] as an option." If palliative medicine continues to advance, he believes, that's where end-of-life care is headed.

— *Reed Karaim*

[1]"Palliative Care FACTS AND STATS," Center to Advance Palliative Care, www.capc.org/news-and-events/press-kit/.

[2]Jennifer S. Temel, *et al.*, "Early Palliative Care for Patients with Metastatic Non-Small-Cell Lung Cancer," *The New England Journal of Medicine*, 2010, www.nejm.org/doi/pdf/10.1056/NEJMoa1000678.

[3]Michelle Andrews, "Advances Against Chronic Pain," *U.S. News & World Report*, Sept. 5, 2012, http://health.usnews.com/health-news/articles/2012/09/05/advances-against-chronic-pain.

[4]*Ibid.*

[5]Sean Mackey, "The Strain in Pain Lies Mainly in the Brain," Stanford Systems Neuroscience and Pain Lab, http://med.stanford.edu/snapl/research/.

attacked the idea, saying it made "the physician don the robes of the executioner."

The contemporary movement in support of assisted suicide can be traced to Derek Humphry, a British journalist, who in 1978 wrote the bestselling memoir, *Jean's Way*, about assisting the suicide of his cancer-stricken wife. In 1991, Humphry published *Final Exit*, a how-to guide on assisted suicide that became a bestseller and has been translated into 12 languages.

Humphry, now 83, remains controversial. Critics charged that *Final Exit* could be used by anyone to commit suicide, not just the terminally ill. Humphry responded that many commonly known means of suicide existed and there was no evidence that the book had raised the suicide rate. The suicide of Humphry's second wife, Ann, after a bitter divorce in which she denounced him and the assisted-suicide movement she had previously supported, led to further controversy.[17]

Humphry believes assisted suicide should be available to more than just those with advanced terminal illnesses, but also for those with what he terms "hopeless illness," meaning debilitating and without cure, but not necessarily terminal. He acknowledges his position puts him on "the radical left" of the movement.[18] Many of the leading organizations, now focused on physician-assisted suicide for the terminally ill, have distanced themselves from his views.

Still, Humphry, who co-founded the Hemlock Society and is a past president of the World Federation of Right to Die Societies, continues to promote assisted suicide publicly and through the Final Exit Network, which provides counseling and support to individuals considering assisted suicide.[19]

If Humphry was the movement's inspiration, Dr. Jack Kevorkian was its first American celebrity. Kevorkian, a pathologist dubbed "Dr. Death," attracted national attention in the 1990s when he built devices that allowed the patient to self-administer lethal injections. At least 130 people used the devices, which allowed people to kill themselves by pulling a trigger that sent either a lethal dose of drugs or carbon monoxide into their blood. Early on, Kevorkian tried to advertise in Detroit newspapers for volunteers. Janet Adkins, who had been a college instructor, was the first. Adkins decided to kill herself on the day she was diagnosed with Alzheimer's disease and later did so in Dr. Kevorkian's van.[20] She was 54.

Kevorkian was brought to trial four times on various cases, but was acquitted three times and the fourth case was declared a mistrial. Eventually, he was found guilty of second-degree murder in a case in which he was shown on CBS' "60 Minutes" administering a lethal injection to a patient himself, after he had lost his license to practice medicine.[21] He served eight years in prison, and the conditions of his parole prevented him from participating in other assisted suicides. Kevorkian died of natural causes in 2011 at age 83.[22]

After-the-fact examinations of Kevorkian's patients found that many did not have terminal diseases, and five did not have any diseases at all.[23] His actions are cited by opponents of physician-assisted suicide as an example of the dangers of allowing the practice to spread. "He was just, in my opinion, a serial killer with an M.D.," says Greene, the retired oncologist, who participated in a review of Kevorkian's cases.

The next highly public battle over the life and death of a critically ill patient did not involve direct physician assistance, but it galvanized Americans about end-of-life decisions. Terri Schiavo, a young woman from St. Petersburg, Fla., originally suffered extensive brain damage in 1990 and doctors had diagnosed her condition as a "persistent vegetative state" by the time her husband sought to have her feeding tube removed in 1998.[24]

Her parents objected, believing her condition was not beyond hope, and went to court to have the feeding tube reinserted. The ensuing legal and political battle lasted seven more years and eventually involved several court rulings, the Florida legislature, the U.S. Congress and President George W. Bush, who flew back to Washington from a vacation to sign a law giving Schiavo's parents one last attempt to appeal their case.[25]

Schiavo's feeding tube was removed, then reinserted on a judge's order, removed again on another judge's order, then reinserted once again after the Florida Legislature passed "Terri's Law," which gave Gov. Jeb Bush authority to order the tube reinserted. The tube was removed a final time when the U.S. Supreme Court decided not to hear a final appeal of the case.[26] She died on March 31, 2005, but by then the battle had become a touchstone both for right-to-life and right-to-die advocates around the world.[27]

Coombs Lee of Compassion & Choices believes it also had an impact on the public view of physician-assisted suicide. "We were all privy to the very difficult battle that family was going through and how our politicians reacted, how completely tone-deaf they were to the real views and concerns of the public," she says. "And I think the public learned from that as well that this type of decision shouldn't be political; it's personal."

Battle in the States

Before the Schiavo case became public, Oregon voters had made their state the nation's first to allow physician-assisted suicide. In 1993, Oregonians organized Oregon Right to Die to lobby for an assisted-suicide law, led by Portland attorney Eli Stutsman, whom Sandeen and others cite as its principal author.

The state's Death with Dignity Act was adopted after voters approved a referendum on the issue by a 51 to 49 percent margin in 1994. Because of legal challenges, however, it did not go into effect until 1998.

In 1997, opponents placed another initiative on the ballot — one that would overturn the measure — but it failed 60 percent to 40 percent. There have been no serious repeal efforts since.

In 2001 U.S. Attorney General John Ashcroft attempted to block the law by declaring that he had the authority to prevent doctors from prescribing lethal drugs through the Controlled Substances Act. But in 2006 the U.S. Supreme Court ruled against Ashcroft's claim, allowing the Oregon law to continue.[28]

Oregon's initiative, however, was not the first attempt by supporters of physician-assisted suicide to get voters to back a law. Similar efforts in Washington and California failed in 1991 and 1992, respectively. The Hemlock Society of Oregon also backed a bill in the state legislature in 1990 that failed to get out of committee. Bills introduced in several other states also failed to gain sufficient support throughout the 1990s.

In Oregon, a key figure in helping to overcome resistance to the referendum was Dr. Peter Goodwin, a physician who spoke up on behalf of the idea at a meeting of the Oregon Medical Association.

Goodwin argued in part that doctors already were taking actions to help terminally ill patients die but were acting "often without the family knowing enough, without the patient knowing enough because it's all illegal," he told ABC News. "I wanted the patient in control, not the doctor."[29]

Goodwin later recalled that after he spoke, the medical association's incoming president met his eyes as he returned to his chair. The president-to-be then took the podium and suggested to the association that they "let the people of Oregon tell us what they want." Goodwin said, "What happened then was that the Oregon Medical Association was neutral throughout the campaign, and I think that had a huge influence on the outcome."[30]

The argument that assisted-suicide laws merely illuminate what has been going on in the shadows all along has continued to be an important one for supporters. But despite their success in Oregon, proponents of similar laws did not win in another state until Washington residents approved a law based on Oregon's in November 2008.

Supporters were optimistic that Massachusetts would provide a similar victory in 2012, and pre-election polls showed majority support for an assisted-suicide measure. After its defeat, supporters blamed heavy outspending by opponents. "I think it was four to one or even six to one," says Steve Crawford, who was a spokesman for the Massachusetts Death with Dignity Coalition during the campaign.

Public campaign-finance records indicate Catholic dioceses and organizations from around the country contributed heavily to opposition efforts, and supporters of the proposed law say they believe Catholic opposition made a crucial difference. "It's a very Catholic state," Crawford says. "I'm Roman Catholic myself, and I knew early on, based on some of the reaction we were getting from the Church, that they saw this as a red line [that could not be crossed] and they were going to put everything they could into defeating this question."

But opponents, especially disability-rights activists, believe Massachusetts voters changed their minds as they came to understand the lack of safeguards in the law. "The ballot question was defeated last year in large part

The case of Terri Schiavo, a severely brain damaged young woman in Florida, galvanized Americans about end-of-life decisions. After doctors said she was in a persistent vegetative state, her husband sought to have her feeding tube removed in 1998. Her parents went to court to have the tube reinserted, and during a seven-year court battle Florida's legislature enacted Terri's Law, which gave Florida Gov. Jeb Bush authority to have the tube reinserted. Ultimately, the state Supreme Court ruled the law unconstitutional, and the U.S. Supreme Court declined to hear a final appeal of the case. Schiavo died on March 31, 2005.

by the antidiscrimination and social justice arguments of progressives in the disability community," says Denise Karuth, a spokesperson for Second Thoughts, a group that opposed the measure. "We described — with examples from our personal experience — how misdiagnosis, inaccurate terminal diagnoses and coercion could cause people to lose years of their lives," says Karuth, a peer counselor for people with disabilities who is, herself, a blind wheelchair user. "We were adamant that no one should ever have to die to have dignity."

Global Measures

The Netherlands, Switzerland, Belgium and Luxembourg all allow assisted suicide. In all but Luxembourg, people who are not terminally ill are eligible for an assisted death if doctors agree their suffering is lasting and unbearable.

In Belgium and the Netherlands, euthanasia, in which a doctor puts a patient who requests it to death by directly administering drugs, is legal under certain conditions.[31]

The request must be made voluntarily by a patient once again suffering from a condition considered lasting and unbearable. In the Netherlands, acceptable conditions include an incurable disease or "hopeless psychological problems," according to the Radio Netherlands website.[32] A second doctor must concur in a written opinion that the patient meets the criteria.

The Netherlands law is generally considered the most liberal. U.S. opponents of assisted suicide often cite it as an example of how allowing doctors to assist in suicide can lead to more and more conditions being considered acceptable for requesting death.

The Netherlands has a series of guidelines intended to ensure that euthanasia meets the wishes and is in the best interest of patients.[33] But Callahan, the Hastings Center president emeritus, says a survey that provided doctors anonymity found the rules were widely ignored and that "somewhere near a thousand people had been euthanized without their permission."

Hendin, of Suicide Prevention Initiatives, also spent time in the Netherlands studying its system. "The more I was there, the more I saw that end-of-life care was abysmal . . . there was no interest in end-of-life care," he says. Netherlands doctors, he says, had come to see assisted suicide and euthanasia as "a quick solution" when dealing with the dying.

U.S. supporters of physician-assisted suicide respond that the situations are not comparable. "The Netherlands is a completely different culture," says Sandeen. "The 15 years of stability with Oregon's Death with Dignity Act is what we need to look at. The law has stood the test of time. It works as written."

Political leaders in several other Western nations do not seem to share the same concerns about the record in the Netherlands or other countries where assisted suicide is legal. A recent poll in the United Kingdom found strong support for legalization, and a member of Parliament is expected to introduce such a bill later in the year.[34] Other nations, including New Zealand, along with parts of Australia, are contemplating similar measures.[35]

Cultural and religious prohibitions against assisted suicide remain strong in predominantly Islamic and Catholic countries, however, and physician-assisted suicide or euthanasia remain against the law in most of the world.[36]

CURRENT SITUATION

Landmark Legislation

Vermont is set to become the first state to approve physician-assisted suicide by legislation, following action by the state House on May 13. Democratic Gov. Peter Shumlin, who supported the measure, has pledged to sign it.

"I am grateful that the legislature had such a thoughtful, respectful debate on this deeply personal issue," Shumlin said. "We will now offer Vermonters who face terminal illness at the end of life a choice to control their destiny and avoid unnecessary suffering. I believe this is the right thing to do."[37]

Several safeguards are built into the measure. Two doctors, the patient's primary physician and a second doctor, must agree the patient has a terminal illness and is able to request death-inducing drugs. The law also requires two requests for the drugs by the patient, with 15 days separating the first and second requests.

The patient must have less than six months to live, and must self-administer the drugs.

Furthermore, drugs would have to be prescribed by doctors in Vermont for state residents only, and the patient's request for drugs would have to be witnessed by two disinterested people who are not relatives or potential heirs, employees of health care facilities where the patient is being treated, nor the patient's doctor.

The Roman Catholic Diocese of Burlington fought the legislation and urged residents to press lawmakers to defeat it. "Physician-assisted suicide will forever transform the role of physician from one who preserves life to one who takes life," the diocese said in a statement earlier this year.[38]

Vermont's action would represent a landmark in the battle over physician-assisted suicide. No such law has made it through any other state legislature since the effort to legalize assisted suicide in the United States began. Vermont, however, is considered one of the nation's most liberal states, and Shumlin pledged to sign the law after it is reviewed.

Bills modeled after Oregon's law also have been introduced this year in Connecticut, Hawaii, Kansas, Montana,

> **Vermont is set to become the first state to approve physician-assisted suicide by legislation. Bills modeled after Oregon's law also have been introduced this year in Connecticut, Hawaii, Kansas, Montana, Massachussetts and New Jersey.**

Massachusetts and New Jersey. Similar bills have been introduced many times in other states in the past, however, and prospects differ widely. Massachusetts lawmakers, for example, would be unlikely to pass legislation a year after a similar measure was rejected in a referendum.

After the Vermont House voted on May 13, Coombs Lee of Compassion & Choices said "this historic legislative victory proves that the aid-in-dying issue is no longer the third rail of politics. In fact, it's a winning issue on which Gov. Shumlin campaigned."

In the Courts

Lawyers for Compassion & Choices served as co-counsel in the case that finally led the Montana Supreme Court to declare physician-assisted suicide legal under certain conditions in the state. The organization is pursuing a case in New Mexico that could similarly result in legalization. "This is a case brought by two physicians and a terminally ill patient that asks the court to clarify that an old criminal statute [applying to suicide] does not have application to the conduct of a physician providing aid in dying," says Kathryn Tucker, Compassion & Choices director of legal affairs. "The argument of the case is that the choice of a dying patient for a peaceful death is no kind of suicide." The New Mexico case is expected to get a hearing in December.

In Hawaii, the state chapter of Compassion & Choices is arguing the state's existing laws on patient rights and advance medical directives, along with the privacy clause in the state constitution, effectively mean that physician-assisted suicide already is legal in the state.[39] "We contend in Hawaii that patients can choose aid in dying there," says Tucker.

In 2011, Hawaii Attorney General David M. Louie issued an opinion to the contrary, saying that physicians who wrote lethal prescriptions with the intention of assisting in death could be charged with manslaughter. In 2012, however, several physicians in the state indicated their willingness to offer assisted suicide to patients to test the ruling.[40]

Compassion & Choices' emphasis on fighting in court to establish the legality of assisted suicide in states where the group believes existing laws make it possible reflects a different strategy than that of the Death with Dignity National Center.

Death with Dignity supports replicating the Oregon law in other states, including provisions that spell out the

Patrick the hospice dog visits a resident on Sept. 12, 2012, at the Kaplan Family Hospice House, a 20-bed facility run by the Hospice of the North Shore & Greater Boston. The facility provides end-of-life care, along with grief resources, for terminally ill patients and their families.

steps doctors must take before participating in an assisted suicide. Mayo, the Death with Dignity board member, says the organization believes this is the best way to make sure the procedure has adequate safeguards.

But Tucker says, "I don't think the provisions in the Oregon statute are a Holy Grail in any sense." The ruling in Montana established "three bright lines" that must be legally respected, she says. "The patient must be mentally competent and also terminally ill, and physician involvement is limited to providing a prescription."

But within these lines, Compassion & Choices argues that doctors should be able to work out the parameters of physician-assisted suicide within their professional standards, as they would any other procedure.

"Medicine is not typically governed by statute," says Tucker. "I think what is happening in Montana is reflecting the normalization of aid in dying, and that's the direction it's appropriate to go at this point in time. Will Montana doctors incorporate all the procedures there are in Oregon and Washington state? Probably not. There will be some organic evolution."

That evolution is one of the things that most worry opponents, who fear it will become too easy for people to receive medical assistance in killing themselves, even crossing the line to allow non-terminal cases to request and receive such help.

Getty Images/The Boston Globe/Suzanne Kreiter

Should the terminally ill have the right to assisted suicide?

YES David J. Mayo, PhD.

Professor of Philosophy Emeritus, University of Minnesota, Duluth; board member, Death with Dignity

Written for *CQ Researcher*, May 2013

NO Daniel Callahan

President emeritus, The Hastings Center; Co-director, Yale-Hastings Program in Ethics and Health Policy; Author, The Troubled Dream of Life: In Search of A Peaceful Death

Written for *CQ Researcher*, May 2013

My father, 93 and dying of colon cancer, remarked to the nurse enrolling him in hospice care that "the sooner this is over with, the better." At that point, his final life-projects were closing down. His only remaining fundamental interest and concern were the time and circumstances of his death. In Oregon or Washington state — and probably soon in Vermont — he could have ended his life peacefully, with dignity and on his own terms. As it was, he quit eating. Self-starvation struck him as his least-worst option.

Two arguments for death with dignity leap from this experience. The most intuitive derives from compassion: What possible good is served by denying escape from those final weeks of slow decline and suffering? And what horrible fear haunts many more terminal patients, not brave or determined enough to starve themselves but terrified of how their final days might play out as circumstances strip them of every shred of control? This suggests the second argument: The supreme value we place on self-determination in matters that are both private and also of fundamental concern to the individual.

Critics argue that embracing death with dignity would be a risky departure from the value we in general, and medicine in particular, place on prolonging human life — that allowing death with dignity would invite horrible abuses. But consider:

- Current law and medical practice already recognize the right of competent adults to refuse life-prolonging therapies, however trivial (for example, an antibiotic to end a life-threatening pneumonia), and even feeding tubes and hydration via IV.
- The law also recognizes a terminal patient's right to adequate palliative care, even if this requires doses of powerful analgesics high enough to hasten death by suppressing respiration. The fundamental proviso is that the earlier death must not be intended, but merely foreseen by the physician. In practice this often means the line between "optimal palliative care" and culpable homicide is drawn in terms of the invisible intentions of the physician (on which even he may not be clear). Few patients or family are informed (or ask) whether lethal doses are administered. If ever there was a situation ripe for abuse, surely this is it.
- The question of risk is always an empirical one. It's our good fortune that Oregon's 15-year experience with legalized death with dignity provides such conclusive data: The threatened abuses simply have not materialized.

As these considerations become more widely understood I expect death with dignity to gain wider acceptance.

Few of us want to die, and no one wants to die a poor death, one marked by pain and suffering. But modern medicine has brought us to a difficult place: We now live longer than earlier generations, but there are ever more clever technological ways to prolong our dying, well beyond what we may desire. One solution to that kind of end is physician-assisted suicide, giving us the power to end our life on our own terms. And it has a common-sense attraction: "It's my body, isn't it?"

I believe it is a bad solution to an unnecessary problem. We now have good home and hospital palliative care programs, effectively able to eliminate or greatly reduce pain and suffering. Making good use of those medical skills is the hospice program, now helping more than a million persons a year receive sensitive care in dying. Physician-assisted suicide is thus rarely needed, as the citizens of Oregon and Washington state, where it is legal, have demonstrated. They make use of it in exceedingly small numbers.

But what of that minority who believe they can't be helped and who even reject hospice care? By and large, research shows, they are those mainly drawn to physician-assisted suicide by a loss of autonomy and self-control in their dying — that is, not by a medical problem but by a set of values about what they consider a life worth living. Doctors should not be empowered to provide that kind of relief, which never was and is still not a valid goal of medicine. Nor is the implicit message of physician-assisted suicide one our society needs: that suicide is a good way to deal with the suffering life can bring.

We all die. Death is not an indignity. It is simply our human fate. With the help of advance directives or the appointment of a surrogate — and a final enrollment in hospice care — the odds of dying in a really bad way have been extraordinarily reduced, even if not to the vanishing point. The most important need is to greatly reduce the present aggressive medical war against death. Greater prognostic candor on the part of doctors is needed with those clearly on the way to death even if not yet clearly dying. The good doctor is one who balances the goal of saving life and seeking a patient's peaceful death.

Health Care Costs

Opponents of physician-assisted suicide argue that pressure to cut costs could make assisted-suicide more attractive to health care providers. In the Massachusetts debate, "We said, 'If private insurance companies and [health-maintenance organizations] have a choice between expensive care or a cheap lethal prescription, what do you think they will be tempted to choose?' " says Karuth of Second Thoughts.

But supporters counter that there is no evidence medical costs have played a role in encouraging assisted suicide in either Oregon or Washington. "In 15 years there's not been one incidence of coercion," says Sandeen of the Death with Dignity National Center, "for the disabled or any other vulnerable population." She adds that doctors who participated in such lobbying pressure would risk losing their license.

Analysts differ over whether cost savings would be significant enough to encourage the practice. In a 2011 study, the New York State Department of Health concluded, "Under any new system of health care delivery, as at present, it will be far less costly to give a lethal injection than to care for a patient throughout the dying process."[41]

However, in a 1998 article published in *The New England Journal of Medicine*, Ezekiel Emanuel, chair of the Department of Clinical Bioethics at the Warren G. Magnuson Clinical Center, National Institutes of Health, and the University of Utah's Battin concluded, "Physician-assisted suicide is not likely to save substantial amounts of money in absolute or relative terms, either for particular institutions or for the nation as a whole."[42]

OUTLOOK

Young Movement

Coombs Lee of Compassion & Choices thinks the aging of the baby boom generation is likely to boost support for physician-assisted suicide in coming years. As the generation has watched its parents struggle at the end of their lives, "too many of us have witnessed really horrific deaths, and from those experiences comes a vow that this will not be how I'm meeting my death," she says. "I think there's sort of a determination to make it different for ourselves."

Demonstrators in Paris lie in simulated body bags on Jan. 25, 2011, to protest a bill that would legalize euthanasia in France. The protest in front of the Luxembourg Gardens was organized by the Right to Life Alliance. The French Senate defeated the bill the next day, 170-142.

In 10 or 15 years, Coombs Lee contends, "There will be a growing acknowledgement that this is a medical treatment, just like disconnecting feeding tubes or providing palliative sedation."

But Callahan, the Hastings Center president emeritus, notes that resistance to assisted suicide based on religious beliefs remains strong in much of the United States, and he doesn't see that changing. "It's certainly not going anywhere very fast," he says. "If it has trouble in places like Massachusetts, it's not going to fly in places like Louisiana or Mississippi down in the Religious Belt."

However, Sandeen of Death with Dignity contends the effort to legalize assisted suicide nationwide is just getting started: "We are a very young social movement," she says. "We can really trace our roots back to 1990, and if you look at movements surrounding things like gay marriage or abortion, they go back way farther than that. . . . We look like we haven't had as many accomplishments, but give us 20 years, and we'll be there."

Karuth of Second Thoughts says people close to her and close to those she has counseled have asked, "If you really are this sick, why don't you just kill yourself and get it over with?" If assisted suicide becomes more widely available in coming years, Karuth says, more people who are seriously ill or living with disabilities will face those kinds of questions.

Hendin of Suicide Prevention Initiatives believes the future of the assisted-suicide movement depends on whether the nation makes further advances in pain management and palliative care. "If end-of-life care improves, I think the issue [of assisted suicide] is going to become irrelevant," he says. "If you had proper palliative care, I'm persuaded at least half of [the patients who have chosen physician-assisted suicide] would not have dreamed of going that way."

Although she found the narrow defeat in Massachusetts disappointing, Clish, the Massachusetts woman whose father chose assisted suicide in Oregon, thinks that because the referendum focused attention on the issue it will benefit the cause in the coming years. "People had to go and mark a box for something that most people don't even want to talk about," Clish says. "It definitely opened up a conversation, and I believe more will come of that conversation, now that we're finally talking about it."

NOTES

1. "Washington v. Glucksberg," 521 U.S. 702 (1997), Legal Information Institute, Cornell University School of Law, www.law.cornell.edu/supct/html/96-110.ZO.html.

2. "Oregon's Death with Dignity Act — 2012," Oregon Public Health Division, January 2013, http://public .health.oregon.gov/ProviderPartnerResources/ Evaluationresearch/deathwithdignityact/Pages/index .aspx.

3. "Washington State Department of Health 2011 Death with Dignity Act Report, Executive Summary," Washington State Department of Health, February 2012, www.doh.wa.gov/portals/1/Documents/5300/ DWDA2011.pdf.

4. Some lawyers disagree that the Montana Supreme Court decision made physician-assisted suicide legal in the state. Most prominent is Margaret Dore, an attorney in Washington state who heads Choice is an Illusion, an organization opposed to physician-assisted suicide. However, many legal analysts have characterized the ruling as allowing the practice.

5. Kirk Johnson, "Montana Ruling Bolsters Doctor-Assisted Suicide," *The New York Times*, Dec. 31, 2009, www.nytimes.com/2010/01/01/us/01suicide.html.

6. "Large Majorities Support Doctor Assisted Suicide for Terminally Ill Patients in Great Pain," Harris Interactive, Jan. 25, 2011, www.harrisinteractive.com/NewsRoom/ HarrisPolls/tabid/447/mid/1508/articleId/677/ctl/ ReadCustom%20Default/Default.aspx.

7. Rita L. Marker and Kathi Hamlon, "Isn't euthanasia or assisted suicide sometimes the only way to relieve excruciating pain?" Euthanasia and Assisted Suicide: Frequently Asked questions, the Patients Rights Council, www.patientsrightscouncil.org/site/ frequently-asked-questions/.

8. "To Live Each Day with Dignity: A Statement on Physician-Assisted Suicide," United States Conference of Catholic Bishops, adopted June 16, 2011, www.usccb.org/issues-and-action/human-life-and-dignity/assisted-suicide/to-live-each-day/ upload/bishops-statement-physician-assisted-suicide-to-live-each-day.pdf.

9. "The Right to Die with Dignity, 1988 General Resolution," Unitarian Universalist Association, www.uua.org/statements/statements/14486.shtml.

10. Ben Matlin, "Suicide by Choice? Not So fast," *The New York Times*, Oct. 31, 2012, www.nytimes .com/2012/11/01/opinion/suicide-by-choice-not-so-fast.html.

11. Susan W. Tolle, *et al.*, "Characteristics and Proportions of Dying Oregonians Who Personally Consider Physician Assisted Suicide," *The Journal of Clinical Ethics*, Summer 2004, www.ncbi.nlm.nih .gov/pubmed/15481162.

12. Margaret P. Battin, *et al.*, "Legal physician-assisted dying in Oregon and the Netherlands: evidence concerning the impact on patients in 'vulnerable' groups," *Journal of Medical Ethics*, October 2007, www.ncbi.nlm.nih.gov/pubmed/17906058.

13. Peter Tyson, "The Hippocratic Oath Today," "Nova," March 27, 2001, www.pbs.org/wgbh/nova/ body/hippocratic-oath-today.html.

14. *Ibid.*

15. "Opinion 2.211 — Physician-Assisted Suicide," American Medical Association Code of Ethics, www .ama-assn.org/ama/pub/physician-resources/medi-cal-ethics/code-medical-ethics/opinion2211.page.

16. Ezekiel J. Emanuel, "Whose Right to Die?" *The Atlantic*, March 1997, www.theatlantic.com/maga-zine/archive/1997/03/whose-right-to-die/304641/.

17. Trip Gabriel, "A Fight to the Death," *The New York Times Magazine*, Dec. 8, 1991, www.nytimes.com/1991/12/08/magazine/a-fight-to-the-death.html?pagewanted=all&src=pm.

18. Biography page, Derek Humphry, www.derekhumphry.com/derek_humphry_biography.html.

19. "Our Mission," Final Exit Network, www.finalexitnetwork.org/.

20. "Jack Kevorkian," *The Economist*, June 9, 2011, www.economist.com/node/18802492.

21. Joe Swickard, Patricia Anstett and L. L. Brasier, "Jack Kevorkian sparked a debate on death," *The Detroit Free Press*, June 4, 2011, www.freep.com/article/20110604/NEWS05/106040427/Jack-Kevorkian-sparked-debate-death. Also see "Nov. 22, 1998: Kevorkian," "60 Minutes," CBS News, www.cbsnews.com/video/watch/?id=4462047n.

22. *Ibid.*

23. "Jack Kevorkian," *op. cit.*

24. Abby Goodnough, "Schiavo Dies, Ending Bitter Case Over Feeding Tube," *The New York Times*, April 1, 2005, www.nytimes.com/2005/04/01/national/01schiavo.html.

25. *Ibid.*

26. "A Timeline in the Terri Schiavo Case," *The New York Times*, April 1, 2005, www.nytimes.com/imagepages/2005/04/01/national/20050401schiavo_graphic.html.

27. "Terri Schiavo dies, but battle continues," NBCnews.com, March 31, 2005, www.nbcnews.com/id/7293186/ns/us_news/t/terri-schiavo-dies-battle-continues/#.UYNHzHArzww.

28. "The Assisted Suicide Decision," *The New York Times*, Jan. 19, 2006, www.nytimes.com/2006/01/19/opinion/19thu1.html?_r=1&hp&oref=slogin.

29. Susan Donaldson James, "Dr. Peter Goodwin, Father of Oregon Suicide Law, Takes Own Life," ABC News, March 13, 2012, (interview in video link), http://abcnews.go.com/blogs/health/2012/03/13/dr-peter-goodwin-father-of-oregon-suicide-law-takes-own-life/.

30. *Ibid.* Years later, when he was terminally ill, Goodwin took advantage of the state's assisted suicide law.

31. "Assisted suicide: Over my dead body," *The Economist*, Oct. 20, 2012, www.economist.com/news/international/21564830-helping-terminally-ill-die-once-taboo-gaining-acceptance.

32. Belinda van Steijn, "Nine myths about euthanasia in the Netherlands," Radio Netherlands Worldwide, Feb. 29, 2012, www.rnw.nl/english/article/nine-myths-about-euthanasia-netherlands.

33. "FAQ — Euthanasia in the Netherlands," Radio Netherlands Worldwide, Sept. 29, 2009, www.rnw.nl/english/article/faq—-euthanasia-netherlands.

34. Ruth Gledhill and Francis Gibb, "Christians back change in assisted suicide law, poll finds," *The Times* (U.K.), May 1, 2013, www.thetimes.co.uk/tto/faith/article3752991.ece.

35. "Assisted Suicide: Over my dead body," *op. cit.*

36. "The legality of assisted suicide around the world," The Associated Press (*The Detroit Free Press*), June 4, 2011, www.freep.com/article/20110604/NEWS07/110604004/The-legality-assisted-suicide-around-world.

37. "Vermont Legislature Approves Assisted-Suicide Bill," NPR, May 14, 2013, www.npr.org/2013/05/14/183896062/vermont-legislature-approves-assisted-suicide-bill?sc=nd.

38. Jacob Gershman, "Vermont Lawmakers Approve Assisted Suicide Bill," *The Wall Street Journal*, Law Blog, May 14, 2013, http://blogs.wsj.com/law/2013/05/14/vermont-lawmakers-approve-assisted-suicide-bill.

39. Kevin B. O'Reilly, "5 Hawaii doctors offer assisted suicide to terminally ill patients," *American Medical News*, April 17, 2012, www.amednews.com/article/20120417/profession/304179996/8/.

40. *Ibid.*

41. "When Death is Sought," The New York State Department of Health, April 2011, http://euthanasia.procon.org/view.answers.php?questionID=000207.

42. Ezekiel Emanuel and Margaret P. Battin, "What Are the Potential Cost Savings from Legalizing Physician-Assisted Suicide?" *The New England Journal of Medicine*, July 16, 1998, www.scribd.com/doc/18428440/What-Are-the-Potential-Cost-Savings-From-Legalizing-Physician-Assisted-Suicide.

BIBLIOGRAPHY

Selected Sources
Books

Ball, Howard, *At Liberty to Die: The Battle for Death with Dignity in America*, NYU Press, 2012.
A professor of political history and law considers whether it is appropriate, legally and ethically, for a competent individual to have the liberty to decide how and when to die when faced with a terminal illness.

Berlinger, Nancy, Bruce Jennings and Susan M. Wolf, *The Hastings Center Guidelines for Decisions on Life-Sustaining Treatment and Care Near the End of Life, Revised and Expanded Second Edition*, Oxford University Press, 2013.
Three scholars connected to the Hasting Center, a bio-ethics institution in Garrison, N.Y., update a guide intended to help health care professionals navigate the ethical and medical decisions they might face in treating terminally ill patients.

Hendin, Herbert, *Seduced by Death: Doctors, Patients, and Assisted Suicide*, W. W. Norton & Co., 1998.
A psychologist and expert on suicide shares his experiences studying assisted suicide in the Netherlands and argues against legalizing the practice in the United States.

Rollin, Betty, *Last Wish*, Public Affairs, August 1998.
A veteran television correspondent writes about her struggle to come to terms with her terminally ill mother's wish to die and how she finally helped fulfill her wish.

Smith, Wesley J., *Forced Exit: Euthanasia, Assisted Suicide and the New Duty to Die*, Encounter Books, 2006.
A prolific author and journalist who writes about bioethics argues against assisted suicide and euthanasia as denigrations of the value of human life.

Wazner, Sidney, and Joseph Glenmullen, *To Die Well: Your Right to Comfort, Calm and Choice in the Last Days of Life*, De Capo Press, 2008.
The former director of Harvard Law School health services reviews the options available for making a patient's final days as comfortable as possible and defends physician-assisted suicide as one of those options.

Articles

"Over my dead body: Helping the terminally ill to die, once taboo, is gaining acceptance," *The Economist*, Oct. 20, 2012, www.economist.com/news/international/21564830-helping-terminally-ill-die-once-taboo-gaining-acceptance.
The British business magazine examines the international right-to-die movement and the effort to spread acceptance.

"Why Do Americans Balk at Euthanasia Laws?" *The New York Times*, April 10, 2012, www.nytimes.com/roomfordebate/2012/04/10/why-do-americans-balk-at-euthanasia-laws.
In a series of short opinion pieces, supporters and opponents of physician-assisted suicide and euthanasia examine why it is more controversial in the United States than in Europe.

Hafner, Katie, "In Ill Doctor, a Surprise Reflection of Who Picks Assisted Suicide," *The New York Times*, Aug. 11, 2012, www.nytimes.com/2012/08/12/health/policy/in-ill-doctor-a-surprise-reflection-of-who-picks-assisted-suicide.html?pagewanted=all.
Opponents of right-to-die laws suggest they might be used to pressure poorer people to kill themselves to save money, but a review of patients who have used the laws finds they overwhelmingly were well educated and financially comfortable.

Lloyd, Janice, "Support grows in Vermont for end-of-life bill," *USA Today*, March 22, 2013, www.usatoday.com/story/news/nation/2013/03/21/death-with-dignity-vermont-laws/2003365/.
A reporter examines the efforts of supporters of physician-assisted suicide to get a bill through the Vermont legislature.

Pickert, Kate, "A Brief History of Assisted Suicide," *Time*, March 3, 2009, www.time.com/time/nation/article/0,8599,1882684,00.html.
The writer provides an overview of some of the most significant moments in the debate over assisted suicide, including the actions of Dr. Jack Kevorkian and the decision to remove Florida's Terri Schiavo from life support.

Swickard, Joe, Patricia Anstett and L. L. Brasier, "Jack Kevorkian sparked a debate on death," *The Detroit Free*

Press, June 4, 2011, www.freep.com/article/20110604/
NEWS05/106040427/Jack-Kevorkian-sparked-debate-
death.
The controversial life of Kevorkian, known as "Dr.
Death," is reviewed by his hometown newspaper upon
his death.

Reports and Studies

"Oregon's Death With Dignity Act — 2012," Oregon
Public Health Division, January 2013, http://public
.health.oregon.gov/ProviderPartnerResources/

EvaluationResearch/DeathwithDignityAct/Documents/
year15.pdf.
The Oregon law requires the state to release an annual
report on patients who have requested lethal medication
and on how many have subsequently used the pills.

"Washington State Department of Health 2011
Death with Dignity Act Report," Washington State
Department of Health, Feb. 29, 2012, www.doh.wa
.gov/portals/1/Documents/5300/DWDA2011.pdf.
Washington provides an executive summary of its latest
report on the state's Death with Dignity Act.

For More Information

Center to Advance Palliative Care, 1255 Fifth Ave., Suite
C-2, New York, NY 10029; 212-201-2670; www.capc.org.
Works to increase the availability of quality palliative care
services for people facing serious, complex illness. Website
includes information for health care professionals and the
general public.

Compassion & Choices, P.O. Box 101810, Denver, CO
80250; 800-247-7421; www.compassionandchoices.org.
Advocates legalization of "assisted dying" and other end-of-
life options; has 60 chapters nationwide.

Death with Dignity National Center, 520 S.W. Sixth
Ave., Suite 1220, Portland, OR 97204; 503-228-4415;
www.deathwithdignity.org/. Leads the defense of Oregon's
Death with Dignity Act; promotes education about the

law and supports passage and implementation of similar
laws in other states.

Disability Rights Education and Defense Fund, 3075
Adeline St., Suite 210, Berkeley, CA 94703; 510-644-2555;
http://dredf.org. Disability-rights group opposed to legalizing
physician-assisted suicide.

The Hastings Center, 21 Malcolm Gordon Rd., Garrison,
NY 10524; 845-424-4040; www.thehastingscenter.org.
Nonpartisan research center that studies ethical issues in
health, medicine and the environment.

Patient Rights Council, P.O. Box 760, Steubenville, OH
43952; 740-282-3810; www.patientsrightscouncil.org/site/.
Provides information on end-of-life decisions and works with
other groups to oppose physician-assisted suicide.

16

Police Tactics

Peter Katel

Demonstrators block Cleveland's Public Square on Nov. 25 during a protest over the fatal shooting of 12-year-old Tamir Rice, an African-American shot by a white Cleveland police officer after waving and reportedly reaching for a toy gun at a city park. A video of the shooting shows a police car driving up next to the boy, who was shot two seconds later.

From *CQ Researcher*, December 12, 2014.

The images packed a powerful punch: men in battle dress, carrying automatic rifles, riding in armored personnel carriers and throwing noise-and-light producing "flash-bang" grenades to disperse crowds.[1]

The show of paramilitary might was happening not at a mass street demonstration in Cairo or Rio de Janeiro but the St. Louis, Mo., suburb of Ferguson. It came in response to angry, sometimes violent, protests against the death in August of Michael Brown, an unarmed 18-year-old shot to death by a city policeman.

Public and political indignation over the shooting exploded at the military appearance of the Ferguson police, helping to fuel days-long protests in the town and deepen suspicion and fear of law enforcement. "There's no question in my mind that the idea that all of this equipment . . . contributed to a mentality among the peaceful protesters that they were being treated as the enemy," Missouri Sen. Claire McClaskill, a Democrat, said in a Senate Homeland Security Committee hearing last September.[2]

The Ferguson shooting and its continuing aftermath struck a raw nerve, aggravated by a string of shootings, some fatal, arising from police-citizen encounters in several cities, including New York; Albuquerque, N.M.; Columbia, S.C., and Beavercreek, Ohio. In the Ohio case, a Walmart shopper in the Dayton suburb was seen talking on his cellphone while walking the aisles, holding a BB gun he had taken down from a shelf. Police, responding to a 911 call, shot him dead. In New York, Eric Garner died in a police choke-hold — gasping "I can't breathe" — after verbally protesting an arrest for selling single cigarettes on the street. A grand jury declined to indict the officer involved, prompting widespread protests.[3]

Vehicles, Aircraft Top List of Military Supplies

The Department of Defense has supplied local police departments with more than $1.5 billion worth of surplus equipment over the past eight years. Most of the hardware was vehicles, including armored ones, aircraft and communications and detection equipment. Only $40 million worth of the equipment was for weapons.

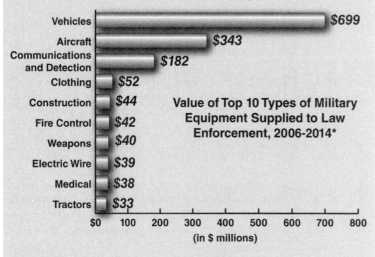

Value of Top 10 Types of Military Equipment Supplied to Law Enforcement, 2006-2014*

Vehicles	$699
Aircraft	$343
Communications and Detection	$182
Clothing	$52
Construction	$44
Fire Control	$42
Weapons	$40
Electric Wire	$39
Medical	$38
Tractors	$33

(in $ millions)

* Spending data from 2006 through April 2014

Source: Analysis by David Eads and Tyler Fisher, "MRAPs And Bayonets: What We Know About The Pentagon's 1033 Program," NPR, Sept. 2, 2014, http://tinyurl.com/p3a4fqj; original data for 1033 program expenditures located at "LESO Program data," Defense Logistics Agency, http://tinyurl.com/n7koanr

Garner was black, and the officer who choked him was white. The Walmart shopper, John Crawford III, was black, and the two officers who shot him were white. The Ferguson shooting presented the same racial pattern — as do other, but not all — of the episodes prompting current controversies over police tactics. "Ferguson laid bare . . . a simmering distrust that exists between too many police departments and too many communities of color," President Obama said at the White House. "When any part of the American family does not feel like it is being treated fairly, that's a problem for all of us."[4]

Even some police professionals say the appearance of militarization is eroding public trust in law enforcement. "Perception is reality," said Mark Lomax, executive director of the National Tactical Officers Association — a professional organization for police special weapons and tactics (SWAT) team members. "Right now, the perception is there's a militarization of policing, which becomes a reality to a lot of people."[5]

Controversy over police tactics also intersects with intensified debate over drug laws and how they are enforced. Critics, including some former law enforcement officials, say the nation's decades-long "war on drugs" — which often involves raids by helmeted, flash-bang grenade-throwing SWAT teams — has been misguided and dangerous. The military terminology associated with U.S. anti-drug policy "evokes images of friends and foes and enemies of the police and enemies of society," says former Seattle Police Chief Norm Stamper. "If you're talking about a 16-year-old nonviolent drug offender, he's not the enemy."

In Washington much of the furor over police tactics has centered on a 23-year-old program for transferring Defense Department surplus gear to police departments, a once-informal system that expanded along with the drug war. The program is now known as "1033" after the relevant section of federal law.

Since 1990, the Pentagon has shifted more than $5.1 billion worth of surplus equipment to local and federal law enforcement entities — 96 percent of it nonlethal supplies such as office furniture, tents and forklifts, but also some 90,000 pistols and assault rifles and 600 armored vehicles. (*See graphic, above.*) Data show big increases in equipment transfers in 2012 and 2013, when the wars in Iraq and Afghanistan were winding down.[6]

Critics say the gear encourages military-style tactics against civilians. "Cutting off the supply of military weaponry to our civilian police is the least we could do to begin the process of reining in police militarization and attempting to make clear the increasingly blurred distinction between the military and police," Peter Kraska, chair of criminal justice studies at Eastern Kentucky University in Richmond, Ky., told the Senate Homeland Security Committee in September. Kraska pioneered studies of police SWAT teams, first created in 1967 to deal with high-risk episodes such as hostage rescues.[7]

But police defenders call increased militarization a myth. Unlike the military, "SWAT teams do not engage the enemy with the purpose of destroying them; they are trained to protect life," says Chuck Canterbury, national president of the Fraternal Order of Police, the nation's largest law-enforcement union, and former operations chief of the county police department in Conway, S.C. "The majority of SWAT calls end with nobody injured; if the military had a record like that, they'd be losing the war."

And much of the Pentagon equipment, such as high-wheeled trucks and forklifts, are used in disaster-recovery missions, Alan Estevez, the Defense undersecretary in charge of the surplus equipment system, told a Senate committee in September.[8]

But during the early days of 1033, the Justice Department didn't cite disaster relief as a prime justification for the program. "The best examples of law enforcement and military participation in common missions are the 'wars' being waged against narcotics and terrorism," a 1997 Justice Department report on developing weapons and technology for military and police use stated.[9]

Among those tools were flash-bang grenades. They are part of SWAT team toolkits but have caused at least seven unintended deaths, including of a police officer, and burn injuries prompting a total of $2.1 million in settlements in two cases in 2010 and 2011.[10]

Last May, SWAT officers from Georgia's Habersham County and Cornelia city threw a flash-bang grenade into a house during a 3 a.m. drug raid, causing third-degree burns on a 19-month-old child and blowing a hole in his chest. The raiders were seeking a relative who wasn't home.[11]

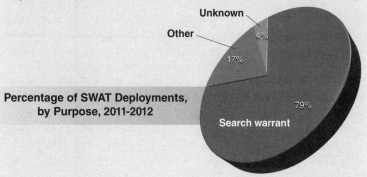

Most SWAT Deployments Are for Search Warrants

Police departments executed four out of five SWAT team deployments to serve search warrants in 2011 and 2012, according to a civil liberties organization's study of 20 law enforcement agencies. Another 17 percent of deployments were for other purposes, such as protecting visiting officials, responding to emergencies and pursuing fleeing suspects.

Percentage of SWAT Deployments, by Purpose, 2011-2012

Unknown
Other
4%
17%
79%
Search warrant

Source: "War Comes Home: The Excessive Militarization of American Policing," American Civil Liberties Union, June 2014, p. 31, http://tinyurl.com/myxzoju

County Sheriff Joey Terrell said authorities didn't know children were present but argued drug raids call for SWAT deployment. Drug dealers, he said, "are no better than a domestic terrorist, . . . and I think we should treat them as such."[12]

With many drug dealers today being heavily armed, drug raids can be extremely dangerous for cops. In 2012, a member of an Ogden, Utah, drug strike force was killed and five others were wounded during a raid on a house to serve a search warrant on a small-scale marijuana case suspect, who fired at police.[13]

SWAT teams are used predominantly to serve search warrants, mostly in drug cases. According to an American Civil Liberties Union (ACLU) survey, 79 percent of SWAT deployments in 2011-12 involved searches — 62 percent of them for drugs.[14]

Concern that SWAT teams are being wrongly assigned to duties that don't require a high-intensity approach runs through police circles. Inappropriate SWAT deployments are "more prevalent in smaller agencies," says Charles "Sid" Heal, a retired Los Angeles County Sheriff's Department officer who commanded a SWAT unit. "They may get 12 callouts a year, and they have to justify their existence." Raiding a "dime-bag dealer" does not require a tactical team, but SWAT raids against high-level drug dealers are fully justified, Heal says, given the long sentences they face if arrested. "They've got nothing to lose," he adds.

Officers face other dangerous enemies as well. Last September, a sniper killed a Pennsylvania state trooper as he ended his shift. And in Albuquerque last year, an AK-47-wielding gunman with "cop killer" tattooed on his knuckles shot and gravely wounded a sheriff's deputy before being shot to death.[15]

Part of the Albuquerque gunfight was captured on officers' body-worn cameras. Support is growing for widespread use of the devices because, supporters say, both police and citizens tend to behave better when they are being recorded.

But some experts warn against placing too much faith in cameras — or in military gear. "There is a time and place for police to . . . use military weapons and tactics to end a threat to human life," former Seattle chief Stamper says, but "there are no strings attached, no training requirements or certification that the local agency is going to use that equipment under very carefully circumscribed circumstances."

As law enforcement officials, Congress and the public weigh the use of aggressive tactics and military-style equipment by police, here are some of the questions under debate:

Do SWAT teams and military tactics and weaponry have a place in policing?

Debate over militarization was well underway before recent media reports on the 1033 program and its transfers of military guns and personnel carriers to local police departments.

Much of that early debate focused on the formation of SWAT teams.

Los Angeles formed the first SWAT team, in 1967, prompted by violent events that included a sniper attack on the University of Texas at Austin campus. By the late 1990s, about 89 percent of departments in cities with 50,000 people or more had SWAT units, a rate that experts say holds true today.[16]

An upswing in the number of heavily armed criminals, mass shootings and other emergencies prompted the spread of tactical units, concluded a 2002 California commission study of the state's SWAT operations. Most

countries would send a national police force to such emergencies, the study found, but U.S. law leaves most policing duties to cities, counties and states.

"It became clear that a new method of response to such complex, high-risk and often high-energy situations was needed," the study said. "Over the years, SWAT has evolved into the management of barricaded suspect situations, the service of high-risk warrants, dignitary protection and the actual rescue of hostages."[17]

The commission was formed after an 11-year-old boy was accidentally killed during a 2000 SWAT raid conducted with FBI and Drug Enforcement Administration (DEA) agents in Modesto, Calif. Then-state Attorney General Bill Lockyer was "concerned about the potential erosion of community confidence in local law enforcement agencies caused by such tragedies," the commission said.[18]

But SWAT teams are increasingly active, according to Kraska of Eastern Kentucky University, who found an increase of 57,000 SWAT deployments between 1980 and 2007.[19]

Moreover, Lomax, of the National Tactical Officers Association, told a Senate committee: "It is not uncommon for agencies to take receipt of such [military] equipment and receive little or no training on how to utilize it, when to deploy it and, equally as important, when not to deploy it."[20]

Critics including the ACLU and Radley Balko, a *Washington Post* blogger and one of the earliest critics of the expansion and growing use of SWAT teams, argues that many of them are being used to serve run-of-the-mill search and arrest warrants, unnecessarily using overwhelming force. "We see SWAT teams now in white-collar crimes, even regulatory crimes, [such as] barbering without a license" Balko, told an Albuquerque audience in November. He cited an 11th Circuit U.S. Court of Appeals decision in September that SWAT raids on Orlando, Fla., barbershops were unconstitutional.[21]

Police, as well as police critics, say many SWAT teams are misdirected to routine duties. A 2011 policy paper published by the Alexandria, Va.-based International Association of Chiefs of Police said serving search warrants was the "most common" task of SWAT teams — with some departments sending them to every search. That policy represented "overuse of a team created to deal with high-risk interventions," the paper said.[22]

Some specialists trace what they call an overreliance on SWAT to an eagerness to acquire military equipment. "Once you get the equipment you have to develop the military mindset to use it," says sociologist Peter Moskos, a former Baltimore police officer and professor in the Law, Police Science and Criminal Justice Administration department at John Jay College of Criminal Justice in New York. "You can have the mindset without equipment, but you can do less damage."

Weapons trainers, who teach police officers that "it's a war out there, everyone is out to get you," also foster a military mentality, says Moskos. "That is not a realistic fear."

But Canterbury, of the Fraternal Order of Police, says given the fundamental difference between military and police missions, military equipment — even attention-getting mine-resistant vehicles — have effectively been demilitarized for police use. "They don't have military weapons or computer systems on them," he says. "They're nothing but an armored vehicle once law enforcement gets them."

Richard Greenleaf, director of the criminal justice major at Elmhurst College in Elmhurst, Ill., and a former sergeant in the Albuquerque Police Department, doesn't question the view that police are militarizing. But he also says police are rightly danger-conscious because of the nation's high rate of gun ownership.[23]

"America has more guns per capita than any other country in the whole world, and many of them are very powerful," Greenleaf says. "You can't not think about that when you think about the militarization of the police."

For many policing experts, an event that confirmed the need for SWAT teams as well as heavier armament for regular patrol cops was a 44-minute shootout in North Hollywood, Calif., in 1997 in which two body-armor-wearing bank robbers with several assault rifles, plus handguns, exchanged nearly 2,000 rounds with officers, including some SWAT team members. The robbers were killed, but no police died. "Patrol officers had never before been engaged in such a protracted, high-intensity firefight," Bob Parker, a former Omaha SWAT commander, wrote in *Police* magazine.[24]

Stamper, the former Seattle police chief, was in the San Diego Police Department when a gunman killed 21 people at a McDonald's restaurant there before a police sniper killed him.[25] Stamper says military capabilities are essential, but they are being overused. He largely blames

politicians who constantly depicted drug enforcement in military terms. "It started with 'drug war,'" he says. "And there is a macho dimension to this that can't be denied. It's boys with toys."

Police departments that routinely use SWAT teams to serve drug-case warrants should return to standard procedures that would make most raids unnecessary, Stamper argues. "Why have 14 cops for one low-level offender?" he asks. "What about surveillance — watching for the suspect to come out? He comes out, goes into his car, and you conduct a routine traffic stop."

Heal, the former Los Angeles County Sheriff's Department commander, agrees that with low-level drug dealers, the best option is to determine "if you can do a door-knock and tell a guy to come out."

Nevertheless, he says, such determinations are subjective, with no easy formulas to apply. And in the case of higher-level traffickers, "Whether people want to believe it or not, drug dealers are inherently dangerous," Heal says. "I don't know of a single one anywhere I wouldn't consider them a threat."

Has police use of military-style tactics increased tensions with minority communities?

The community-police conflict that erupted in Ferguson after the shooting death of Brown illustrated, again, that controversies over police conduct often involve a racial dimension. Recent Justice Department investigations of police departments found discriminatory conduct toward African-Americans, and in some cases Latinos, in Maricopa County, Ariz.; East Haven, Conn.; New Orleans; Newark; Alamance County, N.C., and Portland, Ore.[26]

An analysis by the investigative news website ProPublica of fatal police shootings of teenagers ages 15-19 concluded that in 2010-2012, black teens were killed at a rate of 31.17 per million, compared to 1.47 per million among white teens.[27]

ProPublica acknowledged that the FBI data it used, which include victims' race — and which show 1,217 fatal police shootings overall, adults and minors, in those years — were "terribly incomplete." Indeed a *Wall Street Journal* investigation counted at least 1,800 deaths at police hands but found only 1,242 recorded in police department records. Some experts argued that though a racial disproportion exists, ProPublica's use of the data vastly overstated the trend. Moskos of John Jay College of Criminal Justice

Protesters in Los Angeles stage a sit-in on Nov. 25, one day after a grand jury decided not to indict Darren Wilson, the white Ferguson, Mo., police officer who shot and killed Michael Brown. The demonstration was one of dozens around the country since August in response to several recent cases in which unarmed African-American males have been killed by white police officers, two of whom were not indicted.

calculated, using the same data, that if ProPublica had analyzed 15 years of available statistics instead of three years, the results would show that black youths were nine times likelier — instead of 21 times likelier — to be killed by police than young white people — "a huge difference," Moskos wrote. The underlying data also showed 62 police shootings of all teenagers in 2010-2012 reported to the FBI. One of the ProPublica reporters said that the analysis focused on recent years because "the disparity is growing."[28]

In addition to the killings of Brown and Garner, other recent police-involved deaths of African-Americans include:

- John Crawford III, 22, shot dead by police in a Beavercreek, Ohio, Walmart, while talking on his cellphone and walking the aisles holding a BB gun he had taken down from a shelf;

- Akai Gurley, 28, a resident of a Brooklyn public housing project, who was shot while walking down a darkened stairway. Police called the shooting, by a rookie officer, unintentional; and

- Tamir Rice, a 12-year-old Cleveland boy who was shot after waving and then reportedly reaching for a toy pistol that resembled a real one.[29]

For many politicians and ordinary citizens, the deaths were only the latest illustrations of what they call police over-aggressiveness — if not hostility — when it comes to black men. President Obama is one of many to weigh in on the topic. "Too many young men of color feel targeted by law enforcement," Obama said in a speech to the Congressional Black Caucus in September. "We know that, statistically, in everything from enforcing drug policy to applying the death penalty to pulling people over, there are significant racial disparities."[30]

The deaths above did not arise from drug cases, but drug enforcement usually comes up in discussions of police and race. Police critics say drug-war tactics are one of the issues underlying the outcry over Brown's death. "The war on drugs and war on crime have been predominantly waged in racial and ethnic minority communities and too often against African-Americans," Hilary Shelton, the NAACP's senior vice president for advocacy, told the Senate Homeland Security Committee in September.[31]

A leading African-American political figure, the Rev. Al Sharpton of New York, connected the deaths of Brown and Garner to police action against minor offenses. Brown died after being stopped for walking in the street. The shooter, Officer Darren Wilson — who has resigned — said he believed Brown and a friend might have stolen cigarillos from a nearby store, although police initially said Wilson didn't know of that incident.

"Both of them were victims of this aggressive policing of alleged low-level crime," Sharpton said.[32]

Sharpton's role as a nationwide police critic is especially irritating to police who resent being portrayed as overly focused on African-Americans. "Al Sharpton is a race-baiter," says Canterbury of the FOP. He questioned why Sharpton hadn't visited Chicago, where 10 other black men were killed in crimes in the eight days before Brown was shot.[33]

In fact, Sharpton held a meeting in Chicago last year to address gun violence in the city's black neighborhoods. And in speaking at Brown's funeral, he said: "We've got to be straight up in our community, too. We have to be outraged at . . . our killing and shooting and running around gun-toting each other."[34]

Poverty, not race, is what focuses police attention on some communities, Canterbury says. "How about talking about poverty-stricken communities? Whether they're white, black, Hispanic, when you have a neighborhood that has high unemployment, high infant mortality, a high percentage of people who are on public assistance or have been on public assistance, when they don't see any chance of getting out of their circumstances, drugs are the only way they see to escape."

Some cities do deploy intensive patrols of poor neighborhoods, focusing on violations that affect quality of life. But whether that so-called "broken windows" strategy reduces crime is a long-running, unresolved debate among criminologists.[35]

Former Seattle police chief Stamper says police don't get orders to round up African-Americans. However, "You see wildly disproportionate numbers of young people, poor people, people of color apprehended, jailed — if not imprisoned — as a result of low-level, nonviolent drug offenses."

Race is an inescapable part of the picture, he argues. "We've ended up with a lot of young people of color on street corners doing hand-to-hand deals," he says. "They're low-hanging fruit. You get a lot of complaints about that behavior, and the police are called and do buy-and-busts and scoop up hundreds of thousands of offenders who fall into that demography."

Moskos, of the John Jay College of Criminal Justice, wrote about police and race in a memoir about a year he spent on the Baltimore police force patrolling poor African-American neighborhoods. He rebuts what he calls the "standard liberal line" that black people are shot because they're black.[36] "A cop is not shooting a black person," Moskos says. "A cop is shooting a person because he is afraid, justly or not."

Do body cameras prevent police misconduct?

Aside from race, another thread running through controversies over police tactics has been the explosive growth of documentary evidence in the form of digital imagery — still and video.

Some of this video evidence comes from police cameras, mounted on squad car dashboards or — more recently — worn on officers' bodies. Many police critics, and some officers, say the so-called "bodycams" offer a technological solution to problems that arise between police and citizens.

"We won't have to play this game of witnesses' memories and secret grand jury procedures," Benjamin Crump, the lawyer for Brown's family, said after the grand jury's decision not to indict Wilson for Brown's death, which was not recorded. "It would just be transparent, and we could see it ourselves, and we could hold people accountable when they have interactions with citizens."[37]

Obama embraced the growing movement calling for more bodycams, proposing spending $75 million over three years to provide up to 50,000 of the devices for local police departments. Technology, he said, can "enhance trust between communities and the police."[38]

Among the police-citizen encounters, some fatal, captured on video from body or dashboard cameras in recent years are:

- A Hamilton, Mont., police officer in 2010 shot and killed a fleeing driver who had fired on the officer during a routine traffic stop;
- A New Mexico State Police officer in 2013 shot at a minivan containing young children, hitting no one;
- Albuquerque Police Department officers in 2014 shot dead homeless, mentally ill James Boyd, who the video showed was preparing to surrender;
- A Salt Lake City officer this year shot and killed a man reported to have a gun, who first refused to raise his hands, then lifted his shirt and reached for his waistband; he turned out to be unarmed.[39]

Body cameras — attached to an officer's belt, lapel or helmet — were introduced in Britain in 2005.[40] In Rialto, Calif., citizen complaints against officers dropped 88 percent from the previous 12 months after some officers began wearing them two years ago. "When you put a camera on a police officer, they tend to behave a little better, follow the rules a little better," Rialto's police chief told *The New York Times*. "And if a citizen knows the officer is wearing a camera, chances are the citizen will behave a little better."[41]

Police Say 'Shoot to Wound' Is Not an Option

"If you point a gun at a police officer, you have punched your ticket."

Police veterans are of one mind when someone — a politician, a journalist, a member of the public — asks why police don't shoot to wound when they open fire, especially on an unarmed civilian.

Following the fatal shooting of Michael Brown by a Ferguson, Mo., police officer, the question came from CNN anchor Wolf Blitzer: "Why do they have to shoot to kill? . . . Why can't they shoot to injure, shall we say?"[1]

The question may seem reasonable — especially after an unarmed citizen dies in a police shooting.

In 2010, following one such death, New York state Assemblywoman Annette Robinson of Brooklyn proposed legislation that would have required a police officer to use deadly force "with the intent to stop, rather than kill." Robinson, who represents the largely African-American and low-income Bedford-Stuyvesant area, said she was responding to what she called a disproportionate number of police shootings of black men. "I do know that it happens, most often in the communities that I represent," she said, "and it happens too often."[2]

Specifically, Robinson proposed the legislation in response to the 2006 shooting death of Sean Bell, killed on his wedding day by undercover police who thought — mistakenly — that Bell and a friend, both black, were armed and about to commit a drive-by shooting.[3] But the bill died in committee amid heavy ridicule from police organizations.[4]

Police say officers in fast-moving confrontations have no time for precision shooting. "It works real well when you're shooting at a piece of paper," says Chuck Canterbury of Myrtle Beach, S.C., president of the national Fraternal Order of Police union. "We're not snipers. We're trained to point and shoot."

The objective, former police officers say, is not to kill, but to stop a threat to innocent human life. In practice, stopping a threat means shooting at the biggest target, which is the torso, what police trainers call the body's "center mass."

Former Seattle Police Chief Norm Stamper, a liberal critic of much police strategy, calls the idea that an officer can deliberately shoot to wound "a fallacy."

Police officers can be poor shots, he points out, especially in highly stressful situations. The New York Police Department reported that in 29 incidents in which officers fired their weapons, they hit at least one of their targets in only 64 percent of their shots. And in one incident, nine bystanders were injured when police fired 16 rounds at a man who had killed his ex-boss on a crowded sidewalk.[5]

Richard Greenleaf, director of the criminal justice major at Elmhurst College in Elmhurst, Ill., recalls from his days as an Albuquerque, N.M., police officer in the late 1970s and early '80s that colleagues who had been highly accurate shooters during training "in a real situation would miss 80 percent of the time."

Greenleaf says he was a bad shot on the range. But one night in 1981, he faced a man with a .22-caliber pistol who was running out of a convenience store he had just robbed. "I chased him to the back of the building," Greenleaf says. "He turned; I said, 'Oh, [no], he's going to shoot. I managed to hit him twice in three shots. He died. I do believe that if he had killed me, he would feel less remorse than I feel."

The next day, Greenleaf's girlfriend reported that a man walked into the bail bond company she ran and asked, " 'Why didn't that cop wound him?' "

Says Greenleaf: "His perception was that I should have shot the gun out of his hand."

At least one country, Israel, recognizes shooting to wound as a tactic, at least for its military (human-rights activists criticize Israeli police for shooting to kill).[6] But specially trained Israel Defense Forces (IDF) troops must go to great lengths to make such shots, which is why those tactics would be impractical for police.

"It is 10 times harder to shoot someone in the leg than to simply kill him," an ex-IDF sniper, using a pseudonym, wrote in a long account of lying in wait to wound a target

Cameras are spreading to departments bigger than Rialto's 54 patrol officers.

New York City began experimenting with bodycams in September, after U.S. District Judge Shira

at the border fence between Gaza and Israel. "The leg is narrow, easily concealed by the land and always moving."[7]

Moreover, the target must be standing. "If we shoot while he is sitting, the bullet could hit his thigh and kill him," the ex-sniper wrote. Thigh wounds can involve the femoral artery, with fatal consequences.[8]

U.S. police do have alternatives to guns, depending on the circumstances. The Taser, a device that can temporarily disable an adversary with an electric discharge, is perhaps the most widely known alternative.

But Tasers can be problematic as well. Last March, an 18-year-old Miami artist, Israel "Reefa" Hernandez, died after Miami Beach police shot him with a Taser. He had tried to run away after they saw him painting graffiti on a vacant building. The Miami-Dade medical examiner concluded that his heart failed after an "energy device discharge."[9]

In Albuquerque, a Justice Department investigation this year into improper use of force concluded that officers "frequently misused" Tasers against people who were merely ignoring orders or who posed little danger. In one case, officers fired at a man who had doused himself with gasoline. The Taser discharges set him on fire, although he survived.[10]

Donald E. Wilkes Jr., an emeritus law professor at the University of Georgia, and Athens, Ga., lawyer Lauren Farmer have compiled 618 media accounts of deaths apparently caused by police Taser discharges from 2001 through Oct. 13, 2013.[11]

Police experts are unanimous that intensive training on when to use force is essential. Former Seattle chief Stamper cited a rookie police officer's fatal shooting in November of 12-year-old Tamir Rice in Cleveland, Ohio. Rice had been waving a toy pistol. A video of the shooting — showing a police car driving up next to the boy, who was shot two seconds later — demonstrates that the shooting never had to happen, Stamper concludes, saying the officer could have taken cover behind his car and evaluated the situation more calmly.[12]

"A more mature, experienced, confident police officer would have better understood what he was facing," Stamper says.

At the same time, he says Rice's parents never should have let him outside with a replica pistol, and schools and police should ensure that children know an essential fact of life: No one seen to pose a mortal threat in the presence of police should expect to walk away, or even to survive.

"If you point a gun at a police officer, you have punched your ticket," Stamper says. "I don't care if it's a toy gun. At a minimum you are going to get two shots to the chest."

— *Peter Katel*

[1] Quoted in Ahiza Garcia, "Wolf Blitzer: Why Can't Ferguson Police Just 'Shoot To Injure?' " *Talking Points Memo*, Aug. 15, 2014, http://tinyurl.com/p8bv42l.

[2] Quoted in Brendan Scott, " 'Don't Kill' Pol in a Cop-Out — Admits: I'm No Expert," *New York Post*, May 26, 2010, http://tinyurl.com/ngaq6lx.

[3] "An act to amend the penal law, in relation to the use of deadly force by police officers," New York State Assembly, Jan. 22, 2009, http://tinyurl.com/nbclrau; Murray Weiss, "Cops furious at 'don't kill' bill," *New York Post*, May 25, 2010, http://tinyurl.com/m34xej8; Matt Flegenheimer and Al Baker, "Officer in Bell Killing Is Fired," *The New York Times*, March 23, 2012, http://tinyurl.com/oy5792m.

[4] "NY AO2952 — 2009-2010, General Assembly," http://tinyurl.com/ndc3xe5. Murray Weiss, "Cops furious at 'don't kill' bill," *New York Post*, May 25, 2010, http://tinyurl.com/m34xej8.

[5] "Annual Firearms Discharge Report," New York City Police Department, 2013, pp. 21, 27, http://tinyurl.com/mprloo3.

[6] Edo Konrad, "Intellectuals call for investigation into police shooting of Arab youth," +*972 Magazine*, Nov. 13, 2014, http://tinyurl.com/pha8ktp.

[7] Gershon Morris, "Israeli Sniper's Anguished Look Into Crosshairs," *Jewish Daily Forward*, March 21, 2014, http://tinyurl.com/mcr2vy7.

[8] *Ibid.*; Ed Nowicki, "Training for Gunshot Wound Treatment," *Law and Order*, April 2009, http://tinyurl.com/n8ashyf.

[9] Michael E. Miller, "Israel 'Reefa' Hernandez Died by Taser," *Miami New Times*, March 13, 2014, http://tinyurl.com/lz88jry; Michael E. Miller, "Teenager Israel Hernandez Dies after Miami Beach Cops Catch Him Tagging, Taser Him," *Miami New Times*, Aug. 7, 2014, http://tinyurl.com/mlwgmda.

[10] "Civil Investigation of the Albuquerque Police Department," U.S. Department of Justice, April 10, 2014, p. 3, http://tinyurl.com/n6bubpo; Patrick Lohmann, "APD guilty of Taser abuse," *Albuquerque Journal*, April 11, 2014, http://tinyurl.com/kbsgmlg.

[11] Donald E. Wilkes Jr. and Lauren Farmer, "Fatal Police Taserings, List and Annexures," December 2013, http://tinyurl.com/lnlsjh5.

[12] Emma G. Fitzsimmons, "Video Shows Cleveland Officer Shot Boy in 2 Seconds," *The New York Times*, Nov. 26, 2014, http://tinyurl.com/pajhjnl.

Scheindlin ruled that the city's police department was stopping and frisking a disproportionate number of black and Latino men, in violation of constitutional protections.[42]

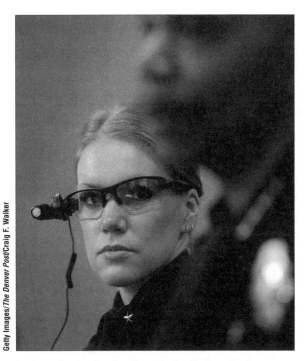

Getty Images/*The Denver Post*/Craig F. Walker

Denver police commander Magen Dodge displays a body camera during a press conference on Aug. 27. Denver Police hope to equip 800 officers, including all patrol and traffic officers, with "bodycams" by 2015. Many police critics, and some officers, say the cameras can help resolve problems between citizens and police. But some law enforcement officers worry they will have limited value, and possibly limit officers' discretion.

Experts caution that good results from cameras depend on how departments use them — including specifying what kind of encounters should not be recorded, keeping a camera on until an interaction is over and obtaining consent to record crime victims.[43]

In Albuquerque, where officers began wearing lapel or belt cameras in 2010, the Justice Department found unsystematic use. "We . . . reviewed numerous reports where offices and supervisors on the scene failed to turn on their lapel cameras or belt tapes," the department said in a highly critical assessment of the department earlier this year.[44]

Indeed, shortly after the Justice Department issued its report, an Albuquerque officer shot and killed 19-year-old Mary Hawkes, claiming the suspected truck thief had pointed a pistol at him during a foot chase. The officer, Jeremy Dear, was wearing a camera, but no video of the shooting could be found.[45]

In early December, the Albuquerque department fired Dear for "insubordination," saying he had not complied with a policy to record all interactions with citizens. Officials said Dear claimed he had turned on the camera, but the camera manufacturer said it couldn't determine if the device malfunctioned, if Dear had turned it off or had never turned it on. Dear also had failed to record two previous incidents, police said. His lawyer, Thomas Grover, said Dear hadn't been told of the recording policy.[46]

Moskos at John Jay College of Criminal Justice said in an era of ubiquitous cellphone cameras, departments need to keep up with the times. "Often on these scenes, cops are the ones without cameras," Moskos says, which argues for police having their own — perhaps more complete — record of an incident.

Nevertheless, police suspicion of cameras is understandable, Moskos says "I think it's going to limit police discretion," he says. "Sometimes you just cut a guy a break. [But] what if that guy then goes out and kills someone?"

Police union president Canterbury cites research by a private firm in Mankato, Minn., that provides expert testimony in lawsuits against officers and police departments. Cameras respond better to dim light, for instance, than the human eye. But recording speed is slower than the eye.[47] "There are things an officer may see that the camera won't," Canterbury says.

He also cautions that citizens should realize that a lot of police video, including interviews with witnesses, will be public record and available to the media. "Will they make members of the public uncomfortable?" he asks. "Absolutely." And confidential witnesses could be identified.

Former Seattle police chief Stamper, who originally opposed body cameras and now supports them, warns that they may pose serious complications for officers and, indirectly, for citizens. "Assume you're working for a hard-ass sergeant who's all about numbers, numbers, and you're a cop who's community-oriented, committed to solving landlord-tenant disputes, [and] you spend time talking with people," Stamper says. "And you've got all this on film and the sergeant says, 'You want to be social worker or a cop?' "

With greater use of cameras inevitable, citizens and police will have to adjust, experts say. "They're going to have to come to the realization that no matter how good the camera, it can't incorporate everything," Stamper says.

BACKGROUND

Troops in the Streets

Long before police militarization became a widely discussed issue, the military was used, on occasion, to enforce laws on U.S. soil.

The Posse Comitatus Act of 1878 placed limits on when the military could be used to enforce state or federal laws. It also prohibited the military from participating in emergencies, except when specifically authorized.[48] (State National Guard forces, first formally established in 1824, represented an exception, because they are under both federal and state authority; governors can deploy them to deal with natural disasters and civil disorders).[49]

Nearly 80 years after Congress passed the Posse Comitatus law, President Dwight D. Eisenhower federalized the Arkansas National Guard and ordered the 101st Airborne Division to Little Rock, to enforce a high school desegregation opposed by mobs of white segregationists. He acted under a law authorizing the military to take the place of local police if they could not protect individuals or if federal law was being violated.[50]

Although the Army in that case was sent in to do a job that police wouldn't or couldn't perform, the Defense Department and local and federal law enforcement agencies, broadly speaking, already enjoyed a cooperative relationship. The agencies had received surplus military helicopters, handheld radios and other devices from World War II and the Korean War.[51]

And in the 1960s and '70s, research funded by the Justice Department developed lightweight body armor made of Kevlar, a synthetic fiber, which became widely used by both the military and police.[52] During the same period, National Guard or Army troops were sent in to quell uprisings in black urban neighborhoods: in Los Angeles in 1965; Detroit in 1967; and Baltimore, Washington and Chicago in 1968 after the assassination of the Rev. Martin Luther King Jr.[53] In the Watts section of Los Angeles (and later in Detroit),

Blacks Rate Police Poorly for Use of Force

Seven in 10 black Americans say police do a poor job of holding other officers accountable for misconduct and treating racial and ethnic groups equally. Additionally, 57 percent of blacks say police do a poor job of using the right amount of force. By comparison, only about one-quarter of whites say police do a poor job of holding officers accountable, treating racial groups equally and using the right amount of force.

Views on Police Job Performance, by Race, 2014

How well do you think police:

Hold other officers accountable for misconduct?

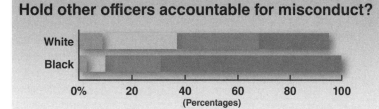

Treat racial and ethnic groups equally?

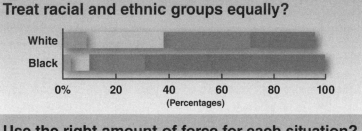

Use the right amount of force for each situation?

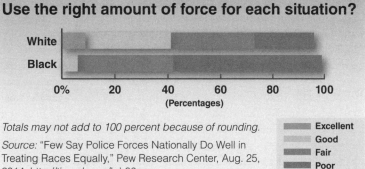

Totals may not add to 100 percent because of rounding.

Source: "Few Say Police Forces Nationally Do Well in Treating Races Equally," Pew Research Center, Aug. 25, 2014, http://tinyurl.com/lgh86qc

Looters flee with stolen shoes during widespread rioting in South-Central Los Angeles on April 30, 1992. The riots were sparked by the acquittals of three white police officers accused in the videotaped beating of black motorist Rodney King; the jury deadlocked on a fourth officer. More than 60 people died during the five days of rioting. Later that year, two of the officers were convicted of federal charges of violating King's civil rights; two were acquitted.

residents protesting police tactics shot at police, troops and firefighters.

Police thinking was also influenced by a 1966 massacre at the University of Texas, Austin, in which a student, a Marine veteran, shot 43 people from the campus clock tower, killing 13. The sniper episode, coupled with the urban unrest, prompted the Los Angeles Police Department in 1967 to form the country's first SWAT team.[54]

The team came to public attention during a search-warrant raid on a Black Panther Party headquarters in Los Angeles that resulted in a four-hour-shoot-out with armed occupants (no one was killed).[55]

War on Drugs

As the Los Angeles innovation drew growing interest from other police departments, the country was entering the early stages of what became known as the "war on drugs." (President Richard M. Nixon, widely credited as the author of the phrase, was more specific, declaring "war against heroin addiction.")[56]

Legislatively, the war began when Congress — pushed by the Nixon administration — passed the Comprehensive Drug Abuse Prevention and Control Act in 1970. Among other things, it authorized "no-knock" searches if police believed that evidence might be destroyed — which came

to be interpreted as any drug raid on a house. The measure would prove crucial to the development in smaller cities of SWAT teams as door-battering search units.[57] Four years later Congress repealed the "no-knock" authorization after a series of drug raids led to violence and abuse by police, triggering a political scandal.[58]

Nevertheless, starting in the 1980s, police conducting raids could obtain authorization not to announce they were at the door. In the 1990s, the U.S. Supreme Court upheld no-knock searches, ruling that the Fourth Amendment's protection against "unreasonable searches and seizures" did not flatly rule out unannounced searches. And, under a 1984 Supreme Court ruling, even when a search was found to be constitutionally unjustified, evidence seized can still be used against defendants.[59]

The military and police had begun cooperating in drug enforcement cases in the 1970s, a development that would reverberate decades later. From 1971 to 1981, the Army, Air Force and Navy carried out 140 joint missions with civilian law enforcement agencies and frequently provided "minor assistance," such as training, helping to transport suspected drug smugglers and lending equipment and personnel, according to the nonpartisan Government Accountability Office (GAO), then known as the General Accounting Office.[60]

During the Reagan administration, Congress brought military and police work into closer quarters. The Military Cooperation With Law Enforcement Act of 1981 ordered the armed forces to track suspected smugglers on sea and in the air and to open military intelligence files to police departments.[61]

The pace of military aid and equipment transfers to law enforcement increased in the ensuing years. In 1989, Congress authorized the Defense Department to fund state National Guard drug enforcement programs. And law enforcement agencies at all levels, including federal, could take "counterdrug" training at National Guard schools. Defense spending on such support services totaled $30 million in 1996-98.[62]

The military established a communications network for police in Alabama, Georgia, Louisiana and Mississippi to exchange and analyze counterdrug intelligence. It also provided $96 million in technology and equipment to state and local agencies; the equipment included cryptological, night-vision and chemical analysis devices and instruments.[63]

CHRONOLOGY

1957-1969 *Military forces quell civil rights conflicts and urban uprisings, under exception to law barring domestic use of armed forces.*

1957 President Dwight D. Eisenhower sends Army troops to Little Rock, Ark., to enforce school desegregation.

1966 U.S. Marine veteran shoots 43 people, killing 13, from clock tower at University of Texas at Austin, prompting early fears of mass shootings.

1967 Army sent to Detroit to quell urban uprising. . . . Los Angeles forms the first police special weapons and tactics (SWAT) team.

1970-1989 *Drug war starts; military-law enforcement cooperation grows.*

1970 Congress authorizes "no-knock" searches when police suspect evidence could be destroyed if officers announce themselves.

1971 Armed forces and civil law enforcement agencies begin cooperating in drug enforcement, including small-scale loans of military equipment and personnel.

1974 Reports of abusive police searches prompt repeal of "no-knock" provision.

1981 Congress requires that the military hunt drug smugglers.

1989 Congress authorizes Defense Department to fund National Guard drug enforcement programs.

1990-1999 *Military-police cooperation broadened.*

1990 Congress begins formal program of providing military equipment to police departments for use in drug enforcement, later known as 1033 program.

1992 Massive, deadly riots break out in South-Central Los Angeles following acquittal of four police officers charged with brutal beating of black motorist Rodney King — a beating captured on video that was widely replayed on TV.

1996 Congress removes requirement police use surplus military equipment only in drug enforcement operations.

1999 Demonstrations against World Trade Organization meeting in Seattle met by forceful police response, including mass arrests and rubber bullets. . . . In notorious school shootings, two students attack Columbine High School in Colorado, leaving 13 dead.

2001-Present *Counter-terrorism duties assigned to police departments as a result of 9/11 attacks.*

2005 State Department calls "domestic preparedness" against terrorism a "staple of law enforcement operations."

2007 At least 80 percent of police departments have SWAT teams.

2009 Outrage follows video of transit officer shooting unarmed, prone young man in Oakland, Calif., subway station.

2011 Justice Department concludes that Maricopa County, Ariz., sheriff's department practices racial profiling and other unconstitutional actions, in one of about 20 investigations of U.S. police misconduct.

2013 Bill de Blasio elected mayor of New York City after opposing "stop-and-frisk" searches that disproportionately affect young black and Latino men.

2014 After 27 fatal shootings and other violent episodes by Albuquerque, N.M., Police Department since 2010, Justice Department reports that the department has violated constitutional limits on use of force. . . . Flash-bang grenade use in SWAT raid in Cornelia, Ga., gravely injures infant. . . . Video captures police chokehold death of Eric Garner in Staten Island, N.Y. . . . Ferguson, Mo., police officer shoots unarmed 18-year-old Michael Brown, sparking violent protests there and nationwide. . . . Military gear deployed against Ferguson demonstrators prompts congressional hearing on 1033 program and police militarization. . . . St. Louis County, Mo., grand jury declines to indict police officer Darren Wilson in death of Brown, leading to widespread protests and some violence and arson. . . . Cleveland police officer fatally shoots 12-year-old boy brandishing a toy pistol.

Police Face Danger in Everyday Situations

Even routine traffic stops can suddenly turn deadly.

Eric Frein allegedly lay in wait outside the Pennsylvania State Police Troop R building in Blooming Grove, holding a .308 caliber rifle with a scope. At about 10:50 p.m. on Sept. 12, when Cpl. Bryon Dickson was leaving the building in uniform, his colleagues inside saw him suddenly drop to the ground.[1]

A 38-year-old Marine Corps veteran, Dickson was dead at the scene. Trooper Alex Douglass, one of the officers who tried to help him, was shot in the pelvis.[2]

The ambush prompted a 48-day manhunt for Frein, who was captured on Oct. 30.[3] Pennsylvania prosecutors said Frein confessed to killing Dickson, calling the act an "assassination," though seemingly not aimed at any officer in particular. In a message to his parents that police reported finding on his computer, Frein wrote: "The time seems right for a spark to ignite a fire in the hearts of men."[4]

Dickson never had a chance.

His killing underscores the risks police officers face daily, even in environments that seem completely safe — including their own headquarters, as the Pennsylvania case illustrated. Experts say constant danger is one reason many law enforcement officers see potential threats lurking even in the most routine encounters, a sense of constant peril that can lead to misjudgments.

"Officer safety does matter," says Peter Moskos, an associate professor in the Department of Law, Police Science and Criminal Justice Administration at the John Jay College of Criminal Justice in New York and a former one-year member of the Baltimore Police Department. "But the job does have risks. If you always wanted to be safe, you'd never leave the police station."

Statistically, officer fatalities have decreased since their post-World War II peak of 280 in 1974. By late November this year, 113 officers had been killed or died in the line of duty (42 of them in traffic accidents). That figure was up from 100 in 2013, according to the National Law Enforcement Officers Memorial Fund, a Washington-based group that keeps records on police deaths dating back to 1791.[5]

James Glennon, a former commander in the DuPage County, Ill., Major Crimes Task Force and now owner of Lifeline Training, a company that runs instructional programs for police, says seemingly ordinary police business can hold the most danger. "We're not getting shot at bank robberies, really," he said. "We're getting shot at during bike theft investigations, traffic stops, evictions."[6]

A video taken by a police officer's dashboard-mounted camera and widely circulated in police circles shows a 2010 traffic stop in Hamilton, Mont. "How's it going tonight?" Officer Ross Jessop asked as he stepped up to the window of an SUV. After the conversation with driver Raymond Davis took a less friendly turn, Jessop asked, "How much have you had to drink tonight?"

"Plenty," Davis replied. Seconds later he pointed a revolver out the window, fired and then drove away. Jessop, who wasn't hit, shot 14 rounds at the vehicle, one of which killed Davis. A six-person coroner's inquest jury later found the shooting justified.[7]

But in Columbia, S.C., former State Police Lance Cpl. Sean Groubert has been charged with aggravated assault and battery after shooting Levar Jones during a traffic stop in September. That encounter, also captured on Groubert's dashboard camera, made equally dramatic viewing.

As the two men stood outside Jones' SUV at a gas station, Groubert said, "Your license, please." Jones immediately turned and leaned far into his car. As soon as Jones straightened up, Groubert fired at least four shots in rapid succession.

Jones, on the ground, sounding stunned and in pain, yells, "I just got my license! You said get my license!"[8]

"Well, you dove head-first back into your car," Groubert said.

"I'm sorry," said Jones, who survived the gunshot in his hip.[9]

A year earlier, Groubert and his partner had been shot at by a man in an incident that also began as a routine traffic stop. The two officers, who returned the man's fire, wounding him, received commendations for valor for their actions during the confrontation.[10]

Referring to the September shooting of Jones, Chuck Canterbury, president of the Fraternal Order of Police union and a retired Conway, S.C., police officer, says, "The guy did make a quick turn and go into the car." Noting that

Groubert had come under fire before, he added, "If you've not been in a situation where someone pulled a gun on you . . . I will never second-guess him."

But David Klinger, a professor of criminal justice at the University of Missouri-St. Louis, said after the shooting that it could have been avoided if Groubert had not immediately demanded the license, but asked, "Do you have a driver's license?" At that point, Jones could have said he did, and it was in his car. "Then you can say, 'OK, sure, what I want you to do is slowly reach into the vehicle. . . . And then it's not a big issue."[11]

As in many other police-citizen encounters that end badly, race was part of the discussion. Groubert (who was fired and charged with aggravated assault and battery) is white and Jones is black.[12]

Gloria Browne-Marshall, a constitutional law professor at John Jay College of Criminal Justice, said, "It was almost as though the officer wanted to stop the man, anyway found a reason to stop him." (Groubert had said he stopped Jones for not wearing a seatbelt, but Jones said he removed it because he was pulling into the gas station.) "Deadly force is . . . happening when there's an African-American male."[13]

Leroy Smith, director of the South Carolina Department of Public Safety, called the shooting an "isolated incident." South Carolina State Rep. Joe Neal, former chairman of the Legislative Black Caucus, said the criminal charge against Groubert would lessen African-American anger over the shooting. "This is a good exercise in how the system can work," he said.[14]

— *Peter Katel*

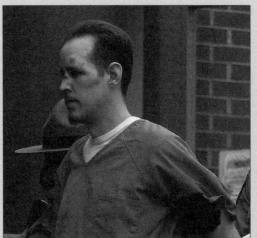

Getty Images/Kena Betancur

Eric Frein has been charged in the death of a Pennsylvania State Trooper last Sept. 12 in an ambush that underscored the daily risks faced by police. Frein was captured after a 48-day manhunt.

[1]"Affidavit of Probable Cause," Commonwealth of Pennsylvania, Pike County, Oct. 8, 2014, Docket Number CR-207-14, http://tinyurl.com/mcmmbyc.

[2]*Ibid.*

[3]"Eric Frein, Accused Killer of Pennsylvania Trooper, Arrested Using Slain Officer's Handcuffs," CNN Wire, Oct. 30, 2014, http://tinyurl.com/ltgknn2.

[4]Quoted in Pamela Lehman and Laurie Mason Schroeder, "Eric Frein in letter to mom and dad calls for 'revolution,'" *Morning Call*, Nov. 13, 2014, http://tinyurl.com/mb9n29q.

[5]"Preliminary 2014 Law Enforcement Officer Fatalities," "Officer Deaths by Year," National Law Enforcement Officers Memorial Fund, updated regularly, http://tinyurl.com/2b7co8f.

[6]Quoted in Crawford Coates, "Policing at the Level of Instinct," Calibre Press, Sept. 30, 2014, http://tinyurl.com/oa534bd.

[7]"Montana Officer Under Fire at Traffic Stop," LawOfficer, May 24, 2012, http://tinyurl.com/n5d92rn; Perry Backus, "Hamilton officer cleared in fatal shooting during January traffic stop," *Missoulian*, April 14, 2010, http://tinyurl.com/oeh75ob.

[8]John Monk, "Video Released: SC trooper charged with felony shooting at traffic stop over seat belt violation," *The Charlotte Observer*, Sept. 25, 2014, http://tinyurl.com/l5n86qd.

[9]*Ibid.*

[10]Jason Hanna, Martin Savidge and John Murgatroyd, "Video shows trooper shooting unarmed man, South Carolina police say," CNN, Sept. 26, 2014, http://tinyurl.com/k8tyvs5.

[11]"Transcript: Taking A Close Look at America's Police Force," WBUR, On Point with Tom Ashbrook, Oct. 1, 2014, http://tinyurl.com/ljmq7x7.

[12]John Monk, "Video Released: SC trooper charged with felony in shooting at traffic stop over seat belt violation," *The Charlotte Observer*, Sept. 25, 2014, http://tinyurl.com/mwberxs.

[13]"Transcript: . . .," *op. cit.*

[14]Quoted in *ibid.*; Cliff Leblanc, "Officials' silence on trooper shooting fuels anger, suspicion, demands for accounting," *The State*, Sept. 9, 2014, http://tinyurl.com/lolqp6b.

Citizen Anger

Police in Berkeley, Calif., clash with protesters on the fourth night of demonstrations sparked by recent grand jury decisions in police-involved deaths of African-American males (top). On Dec. 6, a man demands justice during the funeral service for Akai Gurley, an unarmed 28-year-old African-American man shot to death in a dark stairwell of a Brooklyn housing development by a rookie Asian-American police officer on patrol. He said his gun discharged unintentionally (bottom). Outrage spread across the political spectrum when a New York grand jury did not hand up an indictment in the death of cigarette seller Eric Garner, who was videotaped being wrestled to the ground by police officers and held in a chokehold. Calling the non-indictment "totally incomprehensible," conservative Washington Post columnist Charles Krauthammer said on Fox News, "The guy actually said, 'I can't breathe.' "

Drawing Fire

In the 1990s, military-style law enforcement operations became more controversial, particularly after two high-profile incidents — one in Ruby Ridge, Idaho, and one in Waco, Texas — involving federal agents.

The first incident involved a siege on the property of right-wing survivalist Randy Weaver, who was indicted in 1991 on a federal firearms charge after he refused to become an informant in a Bureau of Alcohol, Tobacco and Firearms (ATF) investigation of a white supremacist group.[64]

In 1992 federal agents were watching Weaver's property in a rural area of Idaho known as Ruby Ridge. After Weaver's dogs began barking a gunfight broke out in which a deputy marshal and Weaver's 14-year-old son were killed. FBI snipers wounded a friend of Weaver's and killed Weaver's wife, who was inside the cabin.[65] A Justice Department investigation later concluded that the rules of engagement guiding the snipers were unconstitutional.[66]

The following year, an ATF attempt to serve an arrest warrant on a compound near Waco, Texas, occupied by the Branch Davidian religious sect led to a gunfight in which four agents were killed, 16 were wounded and an unknown number of compound residents were wounded or killed. A subsequent 51-day siege ended after Attorney General Janet Reno authorized the FBI to fire tear gas into the compound. The Branch Davidians responded by setting fires within the property, which eventually killed most of the 75 people inside, according to the Justice Department and some fire consultants.[67]

Six years later the FBI revealed that it had fired explosive, "pyrotechnic" tear gas rounds, whose hot canisters can cause fires, into the compound during the final assault. But an independent follow-up report said those munitions did not start the fatal fires.[68]

That early instance of the use of military-style munitions followed a national lesson in the power of civilian technology. In 1991, a man with a videotape camera recorded the furious beating of a Los Angeles motorist who had tried to flee officers after being stopped for driving about 100 mph. Rodney King, the man who fled and was caught, was kicked, hit with batons and fired on with a Taser, in vivid footage replayed endlessly on television.[69]

Four officers were indicted in connection with the beating and their trial moved to the predominantly white town of Simi Valley. In 1992, three were acquitted, and the jury deadlocked on the fourth. That decision set off five days of riots and looting in South Los Angeles in which more than 60 people died, 10 of them shot by law enforcement officers, and the others victims of rioters and of riot-related events such as trying to put out a rioter-caused fire, or a traffic accident at an intersection whose lights had failed.[70]

Later that year, a federal grand jury indicted the four officers for violating King's civil rights. Two were acquitted; the other two were convicted at trial and sentenced to 30 months in prison. In a civil trial, a federal court awarded King $3.8 million in compensatory damages from the city of Los Angeles.[71]

The 1990s also saw cooperation between the military and the police become formalized, especially in counterdrug activities. In the 1990-91 Defense Authorization Act, later continued until 1996, Congress authorized transfers of excess military gear — including loaned pistols and rifles and ammunition and gifts of nonmilitary equipment — to state and federal agencies for drug enforcement.[72]

Meanwhile, the Justice and Defense departments in 1994 established a technology-sharing program.[73] The National Institute of Justice cited several reasons for the deal — one was that local law enforcement agencies needed the help to keep up with criminals and drug smugglers, who themselves were increasingly getting their hands on military gear. "Narcotics traffickers and smugglers use bulletproof vests, electro-optic devices that enable them to see at night and semiautomatic and even automatic weapons," making the transfer of military equipment to local law enforcement all the more necessary, the institute concluded.[74]

In 1997 Congress reauthorized the surplus equipment transfer system — now renamed the 1033 program — and removed the requirement that the equipment be used only in drug enforcement. However, Congress said it preferred that the gear be used for counterterrorism and antidrug activities.[75]

During the same period, the Clinton administration sent American troops on peacekeeping missions in Somalia, Haiti, Bosnia and Kosovo, with orders to limit harm to civilians and property. As a result, the armed forces developed an interest in nonlethal weapons, leading to production of the flash-bang grenades that SWAT teams now use.[76]

New Tensions

The events of Sept. 11, 2001 — the first mass-casualty terrorist strike by a foreign organization in the United States — marked an entirely new development in relations between American police and citizens. In the

SWAT team members prepare to arrest suspects believed to be armed in a house in Wichita, Kan., on Jan. 9, 2013. Critics of SWAT teams say they are overused, mostly to serve search and arrest warrants. But supporters say heavily armed SWAT teams are necessary because of the nation's widespread gun ownership.

Getty Images/The Wichita Eagle/Mike Hutmacher

Critics see the use of Pentagon equipment, such as this mine-resistant ambush protected vehicle in Sanford, Maine, as unnecessary, especially by small police departments. But supporters say the vehicles serve many purposes, including disaster relief. In the past eight years, the Defense Department has distributed more than $1.5 billion worth of surplus equipment to local police, mainly vehicles, aircraft and communications and detection equipment.

Getty Images/Portland Press Herald/Carl D. Walsh

aftermath police departments nationwide, prompted by the federal government, added counterterrorism to their responsibilities.

"The continued threat of terrorism has thrust domestic preparedness obligations to the very top of the law enforcement agenda," a 2005 State Department report concluded. "This capacity must be considered . . . a staple of law enforcement operations."[77] The Homeland Security Department began providing grants to local

Are U.S. police departments becoming dangerously militarized?

YES
Peter B. Kraska
Professor, School of Justice Studies,
University of Eastern Kentucky

From written testimony to the Senate Committee on Homeland Security and Governmental Affairs, Sept. 9, 2014

The research I've been conducting, since 1989, has documented quantitatively and qualitatively the steady and certain march of U.S. civilian policing down the militarization continuum — culturally, materially, operationally and organizationally. This is not to imply that all police — nearly 20,000 unique departments — are heading in this direction. But the . . . evidence demonstrates a troubling and highly consequential overall trend.

What we saw played out in Ferguson was the application of a very common mindset, style of uniform and appearance and weaponry, used every day in the homes of private residences during SWAT raids — some departments conducting as many as 500 of these a year.

Only 20 years ago, forced investigative searches of private residences, using the military special-operations model employed during hostage rescues, was almost unheard of and would have been considered an extreme and unacceptable police tactic. It is critical to recognize that these are not forced-reaction situations necessitating use-of-force specialists; instead they are the result of police departments choosing to use an extreme and highly dangerous tactic, not for terrorists or hostage-takers, but for small-time drug possessors and dealers.

Of course a militarized response is sometimes necessary and even unavoidable if done in self defense or to protect lives in imminent danger. The bulk of U.S. SWAT activity . . ., however, constitute a proactive approach. Numerous departments are choosing, based no doubt to an extent on political pressures, to generate on their own initiative high-risk events.

I also learned that the paramilitary culture associated with SWAT teams is highly appealing to a certain segment of civilian police. . . . As with special-operations soldiers . . ., these units' members saw themselves as the elite police, involved in real crime-fighting and danger. A large network of for-profit training, weapons and equipment suppliers heavily promotes paramilitary culture at police shows, in police magazine advertisements and in training programs sponsored by gun manufacturers. . . . The "military special operations" culture — characterized by a distinct techno-warrior garb, heavy weaponry, sophisticated technology, hyper-masculinity and dangerous function — was nothing less than intoxicating for its participants.

Military gear and garb changes and reinforces a war-fighting mentality among civilian police, where marginalized populations become the enemy and the police perceive of themselves as the thin blue line between order and chaos that can only be controlled through military-model power.

NO
Charles "Sid" Heal
Retired Commander, Special Enforcement Bureau,
Los Angeles Sheriff's Department; Retired U.S.
Marine Corps Chief Warrant Officer

Written for *CQ Researcher*, December 2014

The allegation of militarization of U.S. police departments ignores the extremely diversified and highly segmented nature of local law enforcement. Each of the nearly 18,000 local agencies is independent and governed only by the laws of the land and the communities they serve. Even the most widespread and notorious examples fail to reflect the attitudes of the law enforcement community at large.

How does equipment or training or appearance make our protectors dangerous? Weapons and equipment are inanimate objects. Complaints that they are too "militaristic" in appearance is like complaining a welder's helmet is ugly or atrocious. All workers are entitled to the tools and protective gear needed for the hazards they confront.

The so-called 1033 program for providing surplus equipment to law enforcement agencies is periodically reviewed, but the hyperbole and mischaracterizations used to challenge it obfuscate meaningful scrutiny. Lack of availability of essential equipment from military sources will require replacement through costly civilian manufacturers.

Many of the criticisms that drive the current controversy were first expressed by law enforcement. Corrective measures should be based on measurable attributes rather than biased perceptions to avoid the narrow-minded "baby and the bathwater" demands suggested by extremists.

The counter-terrorist mission thrust upon domestic law enforcement as a result of the 9/11 attacks was neither sought nor welcomed. Furthermore, this new responsibility was "in addition to" and not "instead of." The law enforcement and security resources required by the U.S. Department of Homeland Security specifies weapons, equipment and protective clothing that is basically identical to that required by military organizations. Failing to provide these because of their appearance or origin is both abhorrent and stupid. The tools used to fight the "war on crime" are inadequate to fight the "war on terrorism."

The use of SWAT teams to serve high-risk warrants is not based on race, culture or type of crime but rather dangerous criminal behaviors. Criminals and terrorists have increasingly equipped themselves with high-powered weapons, explosive devices and protective armor and enjoy the advantages provided by choosing the time, location and circumstances for their nefarious activities. The self-appointed carpers who oversimplify and ignore the perilous realities of underestimating adversaries have been bereft of viable alternatives.

police departments for antiterrorism equipment and training. By fiscal 2014, the program was totaling nearly $2 billion a year.[78]

Meanwhile, one theoretically nonlethal weapon developed under a Defense-Justice program — flash-bang grenades — was proving problematic in civilian use. Donald Wilkes Jr., a law professor emeritus at the University of Georgia, compiled — using 2003 Appellate Court decisions and media reports — a list of 39 incidents dating back to 1984 involving injuries and death from these grenades in SWAT raids.[79]

Three other developments after 9/11 have influenced the debate over police strategy and tactics:

- A large increase in the number of prison inmates since the 1980s has prompted growing criticism of mandatory sentencing laws, especially for nonviolent drug crimes.[80]
- The emergence of digital video technology, the proliferation of smartphones and security cameras and the rise of social media have led to a spate of videos posted online depicting sometimes deadly police-citizen confrontations.[81]
- A growing number of "active shooter" events in schools and public places has made police departments of all sizes aware of the need to be able to quickly respond to sudden attacks that threaten large numbers of lives.[82]

In the United States, images of police in tactical uniforms, carrying automatic rifles, became common in coverage, such as in the response to a 2012 massacre at Sandy Hook Elementary School in Newtown, Conn., and in the manhunt that followed a 2013 bombing during the Boston Marathon.

At the same time, controversy continued to grow over police conduct in minority communities. In a big-city election that received extensive coverage nationwide, liberal Bill de Blasio was elected mayor of New York, in part because he attacked the police department's controversial "stop-and-frisk" tactics, which disproportionately affect black and Latino young men, according to evidence from police data used by U.S. District Judge Scheindlin in ruling that the application of the stop-and-frisk program — though not the tactic itself — was unconstitutional.

"The city's highest officials have turned a blind eye to the evidence that officers are conducting stops in a racially discriminatory manner," she wrote in her decision.[83]

U.S. Attorney General Eric Holder embraces Missouri State Highway Patrol Capt. Ronald Johnson in Ferguson, Mo., on Aug. 20. Holder went to the troubled community to oversee the federal government's investigation into the shooting of 18-year-old Michael Brown by a police officer on Aug. 9. Johnson was widely credited with trying to defuse tensions through non-confrontational negotiations with protesters.

By the time de Blasio took office, use of the tactic had begun to fade, *The New York Times* reported in a data analysis. Police reported 33,699 stops in the second half of 2013 — less than 10 percent of the 337,410 recorded in the first half of 2012. But the videotaped death of cigarette seller Garner in an apparent police chokehold indicated to many that questionable police conduct didn't end with de Blasio's election.[84]

Police behavior is also a major factor in other cities. The Obama administration's Justice Department has opened more than two dozen investigations into possible civil rights violations by police departments in recent years after questions arose about whether police resort to force unnecessarily.[85]

The crucial event touching off the recent national debate over police tactics occurred Aug. 9 in Ferguson, Mo., when then-Officer Wilson shot Brown during a violent street confrontation.[86] By all accounts, the conflict began inside Wilson's patrol vehicle and continued with both men outside the car. According to conflicting accounts, Brown was either charging the officer or raising his arms in surrender.[87]

The latter account gave rise to the widely adopted slogan and arm gesture of protesters in Ferguson and elsewhere: "Hands up — don't shoot."[88]

Brown's death set off weeks of street protests in Ferguson, including looting and vandalism by a minority of demonstrators, as well as tear gas and rubber bullets from police. As conflict worsened between police outfitted with military garb and equipment and increasingly bitter and angry demonstrators, Missouri Gov. Jay Nixon put Highway Patrol Capt. Ronald S. Johnson in charge of the law enforcement response in Ferguson. Johnson, an African-American, set a new tone by marching with demonstrators, dressed in his standard uniform — no combat fatigues or helmet.

"We are going to have a different approach and have the approach that we're in this together," he said.[89]

CURRENT SITUATION

Stemming the Flow

As Congress rushes to finish its year-end work before the Christmas recess, efforts in both chambers to restrict — though not end — the flow of military equipment to police departments remain on the table.

Obama entered the fray in early December, announcing that he would issue an executive order designed to ensure that the 1033 program is "transparent." The order will also be designed "to make sure that we're not building a militarized culture inside our local law enforcement."[90]

In Congress, even in a highly polarized political environment, bipartisan efforts are emerging to put more controls on the program. In the House, Democrat Hank Johnson of Georgia and Republican Raul Labrador of Idaho are pushing their Stop Militarizing Law Enforcement Act of 2014, which would limit the kinds of equipment the Pentagon can give or lend to law enforcement agencies. Labrador said the 1033 program was "introducing a military model of overwhelming force in our cities and towns."[91]

In case the legislation doesn't survive the lame-duck congressional session, Johnson asked the heads of the Armed Services committees in both chambers for a moratorium on transfers of some Pentagon equipment, saying Congress needs to "press pause . . . and revisit the merits of a militarized America."[92]

The bill would block transfer of what the sponsors called high-caliber weapons, grenade launchers, armed drones, armored vehicles and grenades or other explosives. Some of this material may already be blocked for police

use. Current law, for instance, restricts weapons of more than 7.62 mm caliber, such as the AK-47 assault rifle.[93]

And the bill would end a requirement that police departments use Defense Department equipment within one year of receiving it. In the legislators' view, that encourages departments to use the gear inappropriately.

In the Senate, which will turn to Republican control next year, the sponsor of an identically titled bill on 1033 is Sen. Tom Coburn, an Oklahoma Republican. In a September hearing on the 1033 program he said: "Our Founders saw no role for the federal government in state and local police forces. We're on dangerous ground of undermining the very principles that built the country."[94]

Troubled Cities

A New York grand jury's decision on Dec. 3 not to indict the police officer whose chokehold led to cigarette seller Garner's death set off the second wave of autumn protests over police conduct.

"I can't breathe," marchers chanted in New York, echoing Garner's final words, captured on cellphone video. Demonstrators also took to the streets in Oakland and Los Angeles, Calif., following the grand jury's no-indictment of Officer Daniel Pantaleo.[95]

In response, Attorney General Eric Holder announced a Justice Department investigation of the Garner case. And Mayor de Blasio announced a police retraining program, including steps to de-escalate street confrontations.[96]

Patrick J. Lynch, president of the Patrolmen's Benevolent Association union said officers felt that the mayor had thrown them "under the bus." The mayor didn't say, Lynch added, "that you cannot resist arrest."[97] In the video Garner is seen loudly complaining to police about harassment, but never actively resists arrest.

However, the facts of Garner's death as shown on video brought some law-and-order conservatives to side — unlike in the Ferguson case — with police critics. Charles Krauthammer, a conservative *Washington Post* columnist, called Pantaleo's non-indictment "totally incomprehensible." Speaking on Fox News, Krauthammer said, "The guy actually said, 'I can't breathe.' "[98]

But not all conservatives agreed. Republican Rep. Peter King of New York, who represents Long Island, said that Garner died because he was obese and asthmatic. "The police had no reason to know he was in serious condition."[99]

In a reminder that growing tension over police actions isn't limited to one or two places, Holder on the day following the Garner non-indictment announced that an 18-month investigation of the Cleveland police department found a pattern of "unnecessary and excessive use of deadly force" as well as African-Americans' repeated claims that police were "verbally and physically aggressive toward them because of their race."[100]

Cleveland — the city where a policeman had shot and killed 12-year-old Rice in late November after the boy was seen in a park waving a toy replica of a gun — agreed to formulate a consent decree with Justice under which police would be supervised by an independent monitor. Albuquerque reached that kind of agreement earlier this year; and 14 other cities have signed consent decrees in recent years.[101]

> **"We are going to have a different approach and have the approach that we're in this together."**
>
> — *Missouri Highway Patrol Capt. Ronald S. Johnson, on how he would direct the law enforcement response to the protests in Ferguson, Mo.*

Developments in New York and Cleveland came the week after the St. Louis County grand jury's decision not to indict Wilson (now resigned from the police department) for Brown's death in Ferguson.

Immediately after county Prosecuting Attorney Robert P. McCulloch announced the decision in an evening press conference three days before Thanksgiving, protests broke out in downtown Ferguson. Although many were peaceful, violence-inclined groups torched about 12 businesses and burned some police cars, and gunfire could be heard during the disturbances.[102]

Street protests over the grand jury's decision spread beyond Ferguson and St. Louis to Oakland and San Francisco, Calif.; Chicago; New York; Washington, D.C.; and Seattle. Protesters demonstrated in shopping areas on "Black Friday," with protesters chanting, "If we don't get no justice, they don't get no profits."[103]

OUTLOOK
Re-engineering Police Culture

The debate over 21st-century police tactics should not be confused with a debate over police brutality, say critics of police adoption of military equipment, tactics and mentality.

"In the '60s and '70s cops were more brutal," says former officer Moskos of the John Jay College of Criminal Justice. "Cops are not allowed to beat people up like they used to. They may still have the attitude that 'you've got to do this or else,' but the 'else' is more limited. The rest of society has evolved; you would say it has progressed — if you're on that side — to the point where cops are not supposed to do that."

Former Seattle Police Chief Stamper characterizes old-school brutality as "punitive force" and says that today, "much of what we see as excessive force or police brutality is a perversion of officer safety tactics."

The idea that police live in constant danger reflects a drug war-spawned militarization that intensified after 9/11, Stamper says. "Many departments have treated low-level drug offenders as the enemy for so long that re-engineering the culture and structure of American policing is going to take generations."

Indeed, some police say, issues that give rise to protests and debates over police conduct are rooted in generations-old problems — not police tactics. "It's decades of racial disparity and economic disparity," Jeff Roorda, business manager of the St. Louis Police Officers Association, told CBS News. "It's not a problem with the police."[104]

Whether Justice Department investigations and police retraining programs will lead to rapid changes in interactions between police and minority group members, particularly black men, is far from clear. In angry and despairing tones that were echoed in remarks from protesters, Ta-Nehisi Coates, an influential essayist at *The Atlantic* magazine, wrote after the Ferguson non-indictment, "America does not really believe in nonviolence, so much as it believes in order. . . . The death of all our Michael Browns at the hands of people who are supposed to protect them originates in a force more powerful than any president: American society itself."[105]

Nevertheless, in Los Angeles, whose police department was once considered heavy-handed with minority communities, civil rights lawyer Constance Rice, who worked with the department in a reportedly successful reform program, argues that change is possible. Like other experts, she points to fear — rather than outright racism — as the key element in many police-citizen encounters that turn violent. "I have known cops who haven't had a racist bone in their bodies," Rice told NPR. "They weren't overtly racist. They weren't consciously racist. But you know what they had in their minds that made them act out and beat a black suspect unwarrantedly? They had fear. They were afraid of black men."[106]

On Dec. 9 the National Urban League, the 103-year-old African-American civil rights organization, issued a 10-point plan it said would help ease tensions between police and citizens, which included "comprehensive retraining" of all police, appointment of special prosecutors to investigate police misconduct and "widespread use" of dashboard and body cameras.[107]

Apart from conflicts reflecting race and class divides, "active shooter" mass-killing incidents — some of the most dangerous and stressful incidents that police encounter — have been increasing in number since 2000, the FBI reported in September. And these are not likely to lessen officers' sense of ever-present peril.[108]

Former Los Angeles Sheriff's Department commander Heal notes that ordinary patrol officers may be rushed into highly dangerous "active shooter" incidents that were once reserved for SWAT teams because the new police tactical doctrine is that waiting costs too many lives. "More than 90 percent of victims are killed in the first eight minutes," Heal says.

And Fraternal Order of Police President Canterbury and other experts say military equipment, such as rifles and armored cars, are essential in dealing with mass shootings. The debate over the appropriateness of this gear for police raises the danger, Canterbury says, of "not having the equipment because of the perception that that's militarized policing."

On the nonmilitary equipment side, as a consensus forms that all police should wear body cameras, other technological approaches to policing issues are in the pipeline. In Santa Cruz, Calif., police are testing a pistol-borne sensor designed to immediately send out an alert when an officer unholsters or fires his gun.[109]

Data on how a weapon was used would help in post-incident investigations. "If we know the gun was holstered, that could resolve a critical element in the courtroom," Robert Stewart, CEO of Yardarm Technologies, a Capitola, Calif., start-up that is developing the sensor, told *PCWorld* magazine.[110]

Technology may be moving more quickly than social changes that could lessen police-citizen tensions. But, wherever the debate over militarization takes policing, experts agree the spotlight that mobile digital recording has focused on police practices is permanent and growing.

"In the age of social media," says Charles Wexler, executive director of the Police Executive Research Forum, "your actions get translated out there a thousandfold."

NOTES

1. John Eligon, "Anger, Hurt and Moments of Hope in Ferguson," *The New York Times*, Aug. 20, 2014, http://tinyurl.com/l8ps8qz.

2. "Police militarization," Google images, http://tinyurl.com/ppaqytz; "Sen. Thomas R. Carper Holds a Hearing on State and Local Law Enforcement Oversight, Panel 2," Senate Committee on Homeland Security and Governmental Affairs, Sept. 9, 2014, CQ Transcriptions LLC.

3. "Tracking the Events in the Wake of Michael Brown's Shooting," *The New York Times*, Aug. 9, 2014, http://tinyurl.com/q3rwm5j; "Beavercreek Wal-Mart police shooting: Does video tell whole story?" The Associated Press (via Cleveland.com), Sept. 30, 2014, http://tinyurl.com/pqhj2fu; J. David Goodman and Al Baker, "Wave of Protests After Grand Jury Doesn't Indict Officer in Eric Garner Chokehold Case," *The New York Times*, Dec. 3, 2014, http://tinyurl.com/nlx3dax; Dan McKay, "Video: Camper turning from officers when shot," *Albuquerque Journal*, March 22, 2014, http://tinyurl.com/ltuzozq; Coleen Heild, "Policing the police across the USA," *Albuquerque Journal*, Nov. 9, 2014, http://tinyurl.com/kp3h6h2.

4. "Remarks by the President After Meeting with Elected Officials, Community and Faith Leaders, and Law Enforcement Officials on How Communities and Law Enforcement Can Work Together to Build Trust to Strengthen Neighborhoods Across the Country," The White House, Dec. 1, 2014, http://tinyurl.com/nj7t6yh.

5. "Sen. Thomas R. Carper . . . ," *op. cit.*

6. Written Testimony, Alan Estevez, Principal Deputy Under Secretary of Defense for Acquisition Logistics and Technology, Senate Committee on Homeland Security and Governmental Affairs, Sept. 9, 2014, http://tinyurl.com/n9flmo8; Daniel H. Else, "The '1033 Program,' Department of Defense Support to Law Enforcement," Congressional Research Service, Aug. 28, 2014, pp. 1-2, http://tinyurl.com/l79spln; Arezou Rezvani, Jessica Pupovac, David Eads and Tyler Fisher, "MRAPs and Bayonets: What We Know About the Pentagon's 1033 Program," NPR, Sept. 2, 2014, http://tinyurl.com/p3a4fqj; Alicia Parlapiano, "The Flow of Money and Equipment to Local Police," *The New York Times*, updated Dec. 1, 2014, http://tinyurl.com/oeswx3y.

7. *Ibid.*; "Sen. Thomas R. Carper . . . ," *op. cit.*

8. Written Testimony, Alan Estevez, *op. cit.*

9. "Department of Justice and Department of Defense Joint Technology Program: Second Anniversary Report," National Institute of Justice, February 1997, http://tinyurl.com/m6vgdwe.

10. Corey Mitchell, "Disquiet builds nationwide over police flash-bang use," *Minneapolis Star-Tribune*, Dec. 31, 2011, http://tinyurl.com/kpgcjax.

11. "War Comes Home: The Excessive Militarization of American Policing," American Civil Liberties Union, June 2014, p. 15, http://tinyurl.com/lakqla6.

12. Quoted in Rob Moore, "Child burned by distraction device during raid," AccessNorthGa.com, May 29, 2014, http://tinyurl.com/mc3ac4j; David Beasley, "Georgia deputies cleared after stun grenade injured toddler," Reuters, Oct. 6, 2014, http://tinyurl.com/p7padk2.

13. Nate Carlisle, *et. al.*, "Ogden officer killed in firefight 'doing exactly what he wanted to do,' " *The Salt Lake Tribune*, Jan. 6, 2012, http://tinyurl.com/mznsutg; Jessica Miller, "Police detail what went wrong in fatal shootout with Matthew David Stewart," *The Salt Lake Tribune*, July 17, 2014, http://tinyurl.com/mloq29u.

14. "War Comes Home . . . ," *op. cit.*, pp. 27, 31.

15. John Bacon, "Pa. schools close in manhunt for accused cop killer," *USA Today*, Oct. 21, 2014, http://tinyurl.com/kjmvgrv; Leslie Linthicum, "A bullet, a rescue and a long road home," *Albuquerque Journal*, Dec. 22, 2013, http://tinyurl.com/nuz9g6x; "10/26/13: Officer Luke McPeek and Others Shoot Christopher Chase," *Albuquerque Journal*, 2014, http://tinyurl.com/p5z334c.

16. Peter B. Kraska, "Militarization and Policing — Its Relevance to 21st Century Police," *Policing*, 2007, http://tinyurl.com/nc3aazu.

17. "Commission on Special Weapons and Tactics (S.W.A.T.), Final Report," Attorney General's Commission on Special Weapons and Tactics, Sept. 10, 2002, p. 3, http://tinyurl.com/pvbzm9z.

18. *Ibid.*, p. 1; Radley Balko, *Rise of the Warrior Cop: The Militarization of America's Police Forces* (2014), pp. 248-249.

19. *Ibid.*, pp. 4, 7. Michael Rubinkam, "Trooper ambush suspect caught, death penalty eyed," The Associated Press, Oct. 31, 2014, http://tinyurl.com/of3cfps; Andrew Ba Tran and Luke Knox, "Map of school shootings from 2013-14," *The Boston Globe*, June 10, 2014, http://tinyurl.com/pywyqmr; "Boston Marathon Terror Attack Fast Facts," CNN, Nov. 1, 2014, http://tinyurl.com/q7ldwbc; Kraska testimony, *op. cit.*

20. "Sen. Thomas R. Carper . . . ," *op. cit.*

21. Debra Cassens Weiss, "SWAT-like raids for barber's license checks violated Constitution, 11th Circuit says," *ABA Journal*, Sept. 22, 2014, http://tinyurl.com/mozr9nb.

22. "Special Weapons and Tactics (SWAT), Concepts and Issues Paper," International Association of Chiefs of Police, March 2011, http://tinyurl.com/njfmadw.

23. "Gun Ownership Trends and Demographics," Pew Research Center, March 12, 2013, http://tinyurl.com/q822p6y; "Gun homicides and gun ownership by country," *The Washington Post*, Dec. 17, 2012, http://tinyurl.com/c53hytw.

24. Bob Parker, "How the North Hollywood Shootout Changed Patrol Arsenals," *Police Magazine*, Feb. 28, 2012, http://tinyurl.com/mppn9w2; Rick Orlov,

"North Hollywood shootout, 15 years later," *Los Angeles Daily News*, Feb. 26, 2012, http://tinyurl .com/o9f2tg7.

25. Steve Bosh, "Survivors recount San Ysidro McDonald's massacre after 30 years," KUSI News, July 18, 2014, http://tinyurl.com/produ87.

26. "Special Litigation Section Cases and Matters, Law Enforcement Agencies," U.S. Justice Department, Civil Rights Division, http://tinyurl.com/lu76yt8.

27. Ryan Gabrielson, Ryann Grochowski Jones, Eric Sagara, "Deadly Force, in Black and White," *ProPublica*, October 2014, http://tinyurl.com/ qfx6qmr.

28. "Quoted in William H. Freivogel, "How Many Police Kill Black Men? Without Database, We Can't Know," St. Louis Public Radio, Dec. 10, 2014, http://tinyurl.com/k3c85bb; *Ibid.*; Rob Barry and Coulter Jones, "Hundreds of Police Killings Are Uncounted in Federal Stats," *The Wall Street Journal*, Dec. 3, 2014, http://tinyurl.com/kra7pqj.

29. "Tracking the Events in the Wake of Michael Brown's Shooting," *op. cit.*; Paddock, Parascandola and Siemaszko, *op. cit.*; J. David Goodman, "In Brooklyn, 2 Young Men, a Dark Stairwell and a Gunshot," *The New York Times*, Nov. 23, 2014, http://tinyurl.com/opw75w9; Emma G. Fitzsimmons, "12-Year-Old Boy Dies After Police in Cleveland Shoot Him," *The New York Times*, Nov. 23, 2014, http://tinyurl.com/opw75w9; "Beavercreek Wal-Mart police shooting: Does video tell whole story?" The Associated Press (via Cleveland .com), Sept. 30, 2014, http://tinyurl.com/pqhj2fu.

30. "Remarks by the President at Congressional Black Caucus Awards Dinner," The White House, Sept. 28, 2014, http://tinyurl.com/occq8f5.

31. "Sen. Thomas R. Carper . . . ," *op. cit.*

32. Quoted in Erik Badia and Corky Siemaszko, "Rev. Al Sharpton accuses Ferguson, Mo., police chief of 'smear campaign' against Michael Brown," *New York Daily News*, Aug. 16, 2014, http://tinyurl.com/ pqatdn8; Erik Eckholm, "Witness Told Grand Jury That Michael Brown Charged at Darren Wilson, Prosecutor Says," *The New York Times*, Nov. 24, 2014, http://tinyurl.com/ntyezrm; Trymaine Lee and Michele Richinick, "Police: Michael Brown stopped because he blocked traffic," MSNBC, Aug. 15, 2014, http://tinyurl.com/leltynp.

33. "Homicide Watch Chicago," *Chicago Sun-Times*, regularly updated, http://tinyurl.com/nlsfr2z; Amy Sherman, "A look at statistics on black-on-black murders," *PolitiFact Florida*, July 17, 2013, http:// tinyurl.com/mhfw7f4.

34. Quoted in Steve Chapman, "Sharpton on black-on-black crime," *Chicago Tribune*, Aug. 28, 2014, http://tinyurl.com/k8sbp64; Jamelle Bouie, "Actually Blacks Do Care About Black Crime," *Slate*, Dec. 1, 2014, http://tinyurl.com/k7brpue.

35. "Broken Windows Policing," Center for Evidence-Based Crime Policy, George Mason University, undated, http://tinyurl.com/koravg6.

36. Peter Moskos, *Cop in the Hood: My Year Policing Baltimore's Eastern District* (2008).

37. Quoted in Michael B. Marois, "Body-Worn Cameras for Police Get Renewed Attention After Ferguson," Bloomberg News, Nov. 25, 2014, http:// tinyurl.com/n4on8lv.

38. "Remarks by the President . . . ," *op. cit.*; Mark Landler, "Obama Offers New Standards on Police Gear," *The New York Times*, Dec. 1, 2014, http:// tinyurl.com/lyde4wh.

39. Katti Gray and Dean Schabner, "UC Davis Pepper Spraying: Cops Suspended," ABC News, Nov. 20, 2011, http://tinyurl.com/7r9kk76; Matthew B. Stannard and Demian Bulwa, "BART shooting captured on video," *San Francisco Chronicle*, Jan. 7, 2009, http://tinyurl.com/bv89orh; Ryan Owens, "Cop's 'Heart Sank' on Realizing Shots Fired at Minivan Full of Kids," ABC News, Jan. 17, 2014, http://tinyurl.com/qe4wnct; Ryan Boetel, "APD detective who shot homeless camper James Boyd planning to retire," *Albuquerque Journal*, Nov. 18, 2014, http://tinyurl.com/lb9mtjn; Josh Sanburn, "Behind the Video of Eric Garner's Deadly Confrontation With New York Police," *Time*, July 22, 2014, http://tinyurl.com/oh94f6v; Pat Reavy, "Body cam helps justify fatal South Salt Lake police shooting," KSL.com, Sept. 30, 2014, http://tinyurl .com/q8z8pqn.

40. Michael D. White, "Police Officer Body-Worn Cameras: Assessing the Evidence," Office of Justice Programs, U.S. Justice Department, 2014, p. 16, http://tinyurl.com/q87pdtu.

41. Quoted in Ian Lovett, "In California, a Champion for Police Cameras," *The New York Times*, Aug. 21, 2013, http://tinyurl.com/k5mxafg.

42. Rocco Parascandola, "60 NYPD cops set to begin wearing body cameras in pilot program," *New York Daily News*, Sept. 4, 2014, http://tinyurl.com/qgqohaf.

43. "Implementing a Body-Worn Camera Program: Recommendations and Lessons Learned," Police Executive Research Forum, U.S. Justice Department, 2014, pp. 54-56, http://tinyurl.com/lxdg7ej.

44. "Findings of civil investigation," U.S. Justice Department, April 10, 2014, http://tinyurl.com/n6bubpo; Gwyneth Doland, "Police body cameras didn't provide accountability in New Mexico," Al Jazeera America, April 16, 2014, http://tinyurl.com/l8gowe9.

45. Patrick Lohmann, "No video of Mary Hawkes shooting, APD says," *Albuquerque Journal*, May 22, 2014, http://tinyurl.com/qzlorxz.

46. Quoted in Nicole Perez, "Officer who shot Mary Hawkes fired for insubordination," *Albuquerque Journal*, Dec. 1, 2014, http://tinyurl.com/paatg2a.

47. "10 limitations of body cams you need to know for your protection," Force Science Institute Ltd., undated, http://tinyurl.com/m94y3vw.

48. *Ibid.*, pp. 5-6.

49. Maj. Gen. Timothy J. Lowenberg, "The Role of the National Guard in National Defense and Homeland Security," National Guard Association of the United States, undated, http://tinyurl.com/qbmsnbd.

50. *Ibid.*, p. 40.

51. "Department of Justice and Department of Defense Joint Technology Program: Second Anniversary Report," National Institute of Justice, Department of Justice," February 1977, p. 2, http://tinyurl.com/qyemysa.

52. *Ibid.*; Jeremy Peace, "Stephanie L. Kwolek, Inventor of Kevlar, Is Dead at 90," *The New York Times*, June 20, 2014, http://tinyurl.com/nlhzb3l.

53. Charles Doyle and Jennifer K. Elsea, "The Posse Comitatus Act and Related Matters: The Use of the Military to Execute Civilian Law," Congressional Research Service, Aug. 16, 2012, pp. 35-36, http://tinyurl.com/l29a4ea.

54. *Ibid.*, Balko, p. 62; "The UT Tower Shooting," *Texas Monthly*, undated, http://tinyurl.com/kaybz73.

55. Paul Clinton, "Daryl Gates and the origins of LAPD SWAT," *Police Magazine*, April 16, 2010, http://tinyurl.com/q2d95ql; Radley Balko, *Rise of the Warrior Cop: The Militarization of America's Police Forces* (2013), pp. 76-80; and "144 Hours in August 1965," Governor's Commission on the Los Angeles Riots, 1965, http://tinyurl.com/3zab8bg.

56. Richard Nixon, "Special Message to the Congress on Drug Abuse Prevention and Control, June 17, 1971," The American Presidency Project, University of California, Santa Barbara, http://tinyurl.com/l56dh26.

57. *Ibid.* Also see Radley Balko, *Rise of the Warrior Cop: The Militarization of America's Police Forces* (2014), pp. 81-134.

58. *Ibid.*, Balko; Clinton, *op. cit.*, p. 2.

59. Balko, *op. cit.*, pp. 116-125; "War Comes Home: The Excessive Militarization of American Policing," ACLU, June 2014, http://tinyurl.com/lx56xmg; *U.S. v. Leon*, 488 U.S. 897 (1984), http://tinyurl.com/238nbgx.

60. Ronald F. Lauve, "Statement Before the Subcommittee on Crime, House Committee on the Judiciary on Military Cooperation With Civilian Law Enforcement Agencies," General Accounting Office, July 28, 1983, http://tinyurl.com/ouckbgl.

61. Balko, *op. cit.*, pp. 96-97, 145-146.

62. "Crime Technology: Department of Defense Assistance to State and Local Law Enforcement Agencies," U.S. General Accounting Office, (now Government Accountability Office), October 1999, pp. 3-5, http://tinyurl.com/o5tfgev.

63. *Ibid.*, pp. 7-9.

64. "Department of Justice Report on Internal Review Regarding the Ruby Ridge Hostage Situation and Shootings by Law Enforcement Personnel," U.S. Justice Department, 1994, Executive Summary, http://tinyurl.com/p8q988z; Balko, *op. cit.*, pp. 200-201.

65. *Ibid.,* Balko.

66. *Ibid.*, "Department of Justice."

67. "Report to the Deputy Attorney General on the Events at Waco, Texas, February 28 to April 19, 1993, Executive Summary, http://tinyurl.com/o3yaxp7; Jim Hoft, "Author: Hillary Clinton Ordered Attack on David Koresh's Compound in Waco, Texas," *Free Republic*, March 4, 2014, http://tinyurl.com/ouqak4k.

68. "Final Report to the Deputy Attorney General Concerning the 1993 Confrontation at the Mt. Carmel Complex, Waco, Texas," Special Counsel John C. Danforth, Nov. 8, 2000, p. 29, http://tiny-url.com/nm59o2h; Matt Alsdorf, "Waco Twofer: Pyrotechnic Tear Gas and Delta Force," *Slate*, Sept. 2, 1999, http://tinyurl.com/ceduvf8.

69. Jennifer Medina, "Rodney King Dies a 47," *The New York Times*, June 17, 2012, http://tinyurl.com/8xdbzgc.

70. *Ibid.*, "Los Angeles riots: Remember the 63 people who died," *Los Angeles Times*, April 26, 2012, http://tinyurl.com/ljb86rg; Linda Deutsch, "Rodney King's Death: Reporter Remembers Trial That Sparked Riots," The Associated Press, Aug. 18, 2012, http://tinyurl.com/n7a9fhl.

71. "Los Angeles Riots Fast Facts," CNN, May 3, 2014, http://tinyurl.com/njj82eh.

72. Daniel H. Else, "The '1033 Program,' " *op. cit.*, pp. 1-2.

73. "Department of Justice and Department of Defense Joint Technology," *op. cit.*, p. 1.

74. *Ibid.*, pp. 5-6.

75. Else, *op. cit.*

76. "Department of Justice and Department of Defense Joint Technology," *op. cit.*, pp. 5, 11; "War Comes Home," *op. cit.*, pp. 2-3.

77. Lois M. Davis, *et al.*, "Long-Term Effects of Law Enforcement's Post-9/11 Focus on Counterterrorism

and Homeland Security," RAND Corp., 2010, p. xv, http://tinyurl.com/k3a2tas.

78. "DHS Announces Grant Allocations for Fiscal Year 2014 Preparedness Grants," U.S. Department of Homeland Security, July 25, 2014, http://tinyurl.com/lphyxtd; Alicia Parlapiano, "The Flow of Money and Equipment to Local Police," *The New York Times*, updated Dec. 1, 2014, http://tinyurl.com/oeswx3y.

79. Donald E. Wilkes Jr., "Explosive Dynamic Entry," *Flagpole*, July 20, 2003, http://tinyurl.com/qeqzxoq.

80. Lisa D. Moore and Amy Elkavich, "Who's Using and Who's Doing Time: Incarceration, the War on Drugs, and Public Health," *American Journal of Public Health*, May, 2008, http://tinyurl.com/mnu-7awa; John Schmitt, Kris Warner, Sarika Gupta, "The High Budgetary Cost of Incarceration," Center for Economic and Policy Research, June 2010, http://tinyurl.com/27yos76.

81. "Social Media and Tactical Considerations for Law Enforcement," Community Oriented Policing Services, U.S. Justice Department and Police Executive Research Forum, 2013, http://tinyurl.com/karmhqx.

82. Tracy L. Frazzano and G. Matthew Snyder, "Hybrid Targeted Violence: Challenging Conventional 'Active Shooter' Response Strategies," Homeland Security Affairs, Naval Postgraduate School Center for Homeland Defense and Security, 2014, http://tinyurl.com/oeoj7rj.

83. Quoted in Joseph Goldstein, "Judge Rejects New York's Stop-and-Frisk Policy," *The New York Times*, Aug. 12, 2013, http://tinyurl.com/m826bvo; Michael Barbaro and David W. Chen, "De Blasio Is Elected New York City Mayor in Landslide," *The New York Times*, Nov. 5, 2013, http://tinyurl.com/ozbnwsu.

84. Mike Bostock and Ford Fessenden, " 'Stop-and-Frisk' Is All but Gone From New York," *The New York Times*, Sept. 19, 2014, http://tinyurl.com/p7qma2a.

85. "Police Reform and Accountability Accomplishments Under Attorney General Eric

Holder," U.S. Justice Department, Dec. 4, 2014, http://tinyurl.com/ocf4w5a.

86. Rachel Clarke and Christopher Lett, "What happened when Michael Brown met Officer Darren Wilson," CNN, Nov. 11, 2014, http://tinyurl.com/opdowzu.

87. *Ibid.*

88. Matt Pearce, "Protesters use hands-up gesture defiantly after Michael Brown shooting," *Los Angeles Times*, Aug. 12, 2014, http://tinyurl.com/ku56bs6.

89. Quoted in Elahe Izadi and Wesley Lowery, "Meet the Missouri Highway State Patrol captain who has taken over in Ferguson," *The Washington Post*, Aug. 15, 2014, http://tinyurl.com/nvscevv.

90. "Remarks by the President," *op. cit.*

91. Press release, "Reps. Johnson, Labrador introduce bill to de-militarize police," Website of Rep. Hank Johnson, Sept. 16, 2014, http://tinyurl.com/myz4s4p.

92. *Ibid.*

93. "M14 7.62mm Rifle," Federation of American Scientists, Military Analysis Network, updated Feb. 22, 2000, http://tinyurl.com/pghfqdm; Written Testimony, Alan Estevez, *op. cit.*, pp. 3-4.

94. "Sen. Thomas R. Carper Holds a Hearing," *op. cit.*

95. Vivian Yee, " 'I Can't Breathe,' Is Echoed in Voices of Fury and Despair," *The New York Times*, Dec. 3, 2014, http://tinyurl.com/ndm9c3k; Bill Chapell, "Protests Spread in New York and Beyond Over Eric Garner Case," NPR, Dec. 3, 2014, http://tinyurl.com/pqj72rs.

96. Mollie Reilly, "Justice Department to Investigate Eric Garner's Death," *The Huffington Post*, Dec. 3, 2014, http://tinyurl.com/lngbeqn; Marc Santora, "Mayor de Blasio Calls for Retraining of New York Police Dept.," *The New York Times*, Dec. 4, 2014, http://tinyurl.com/o7uywau.

97. Quoted in Santora, *ibid.*

98. Quoted in Karen Tumulty, "Ferguson, Staten Island: Similar events bring very different reaction," *The Washington Post*, Dec. 4, 2014, http://tinyurl.com/mw9uykk.

99. Quoted in Nia-Malika Henderson, "Peter King blames asthma and obesity for Eric Garner's death. That's a problem for the GOP," *The Washington Post*, Dec. 4, 2014, http://tinyurl.com/mf6qcc9.

100. "Investigation of the Cleveland Division of Police," U.S. Department of Justice, Dec. 4, 2014, pp. 3, 49, http://tinyurl.com/keuaqgz.

101. Richard A. Oppel Jr., "Cleveland Police Abuse Pattern Cited by Justice Department," *The New York Times*, Dec. 4, 2014, http://tinyurl.com/mm97l4h; "Police Reform and Accountability Accomplishments Under Attorney General Eric Holder," U.S. Justice Department, Dec. 4, 2014, http://tinyurl.com/ocf4w5a.

102. Ellen Wulfhorst, Daniel Wallis and Edward McAllister, "More troops deployed in Ferguson to guard against fresh riots," Reuters, Nov. 25, 2014, http://tinyurl.com/k5drrwa.

103. Quoted in John Eligon, "Protesters United Against Ferguson Decision, but Challenged in Unity," *The New York Times*, Nov. 28, 2014, http://tinyurl.com/m7sag4f.

104. Quoted in Matt Apuzzo, "Past Remarks by Loretta Lynch, Attorney General Nominee, Offer Insight on Race Issues," *The New York Times*, Dec. 2, 2014, http://tinyurl.com/mykozju.

105. Ta-Nehisi Coates, "Barack Obama, Ferguson, and the Evidence of Things Unsaid," *The Atlantic*, Nov. 26, 2014, http://tinyurl.com/mtjyjqz.

106. Quoted in "Civil Rights Attorney On How She Built Trust With Police," NPR, Dec. 5, 2014, http://tinyurl.com/l3s86oc.

107. "10-Point Justice Plan: National urban League Police Reform and Accountability Recommendations," National Urban League, December 2014, http://tinyurl.com/m2j2k7u.

108. "FBI Releases Study on Active Shooter Incidents," FBI, Sept. 24, 2014, http://tinyurl.com/nfm5pww.

109. Zach Miners, "Startup arms cops with Internet-connected 'smart' guns," *PCWorld*, Oct. 27, 2014, http://tinyurl.com/lmwmbht.

110. Quoted in *ibid.*

BIBLIOGRAPHY
Selected Sources
Books

Balko, Radley, *Rise of the Warrior Cop: The Militarization of America's Police Forces*, PublicAffairs, 2014.
A longtime critic of police tactics traces hardening of police methods to the spread of SWAT teams.

McCoy, Candace, ed., *Holding Police Accountable*, Urban Institute Press, 2010.
A group of academics, including two former police officers, examine changes in laws and procedures guiding police conduct.

Moskos, Peter, *Cop in the Hood: My Year Policing Baltimore's Eastern District*, Princeton University Press, 2008.
A former police officer who was trained as a sociologist examines his own and colleagues' actions and attitudes in policing poor, African-American neighborhoods.

Stamper, Norm, *Breaking Ranks: A Top Cop's Exposé of the Dark Side of American Policing*, Nation Books, 2005.
A career police officer who rose to Seattle police chief criticizes drug laws and drug enforcement.

Articles

Barrett, Devlin, "Attorney General Eric Holder Urges Broad Review of Police Tactics," *The Wall Street Journal*, Oct. 8, 2014, http://tinyurl.com/nunrumb.
The outgoing Justice Department chief calls for a thorough examination of police departments' policies and actions.

Devaney, Tim, "Senators blast DOD program that 'militarized police,'" *The Hill*, Sept. 9, 2014, http://tinyurl.com/lxns2q6.
Bipartisan criticism erupted at a Senate committee hearing on transfers to police departments of military gear.

Heal, Charles "Sid," "Swarming," *The Tactical Edge*, Spring 2011, http://tinyurl.com/pke2bjb.
A former Los Angeles Sheriff's Department commander analyzes a tactic in which police in a sudden emergency rush a shooter from several directions — a method Heal calls a departure from the military approach.

Lind, Dara, "How do police departments train cops to use force?," *Vox*, Sept. 5, 2014, http://tinyurl.com/ncfnjjn.
A justice system specialist details how officers are taught when and when not to shoot.

McKay, Dan, "Video: Camper turning from officers when shot," *Albuquerque Journal*, March 22, 2014, http://tinyurl.com/ltuzozq.
A video of police shooting to death a mentally disturbed man intensified criticism of an already troubled Albuquerque, N.M., police department.

Moore, Rob, "Child burned by distraction device during raid," Access North Georgia, May 29, 2014, http://tinyurl.com/mc3ac4j.
A county sheriff in charge of a disastrous SWAT raid in which an infant was gravely wounded by a flash-bang grenade says his men had had no information a child was in the house but defends the operation as based on available intelligence.

Nehring, Abbie, " 'Less Lethal' Flash-Bangs Used in Ferguson Leave Some Feeling the Burn," *ProPublica*, Aug. 22, 2014, http://tinyurl.com/olovoph.
A journalist reports being burned by a flash-bang grenade used against demonstrators in Ferguson, Mo., and experts debate their use as crowd-control devices.

Proctor, Jeff, "Boyd shooter: 'Welcome to ROP; mistakes now cease to exist,' " KRQE News, Oct. 7, 2014, http://tinyurl.com/pqmhewu.
An investigative reporter recounts the little-known story of a specialized Albuquerque, N.M., Police Department unit — now disbanded — whose logo was a hangman's noose.

Swaine, Jon, "Doubts cast on witness's account of black man killed by police in Walmart," *The Guardian*, Sept. 7, 2014, http://tinyurl.com/k4g3gvg.
A U.S. correspondent for a London-based newspaper probes the evidence in a police shooting that left an unarmed man dead in a Walmart store in Beavercreek, Ohio, after picking up a BB rifle from a shelf and walking around the store with it.

Reports and Studies

Else, Daniel H., "The '1033 Program,' Department of Defense Support to Law Enforcement," Congressional Research Service, Aug. 28, 2014, http://tinyurl.com/l79spln.
A CRS specialist examines the requirements governing military equipment transfers to police.

"Police Under Attack: A Police Foundation Review of the Christopher Dorner Incident," Police Foundation, 2013, http://tinyurl.com/letwcga.
A team of career police officers working for a think tank analyzes and draws lessons from the 2013 manhunt for an ex-Los Angeles Police Department officer and U.S. Navy veteran who killed the daughter of a former superior, a police officer and a sheriff's deputy. Police shot at, but didn't kill, three civilians during the search.

"War Comes Home: The Excessive Militarization of American Policing," American Civil Liberties Union (ACLU), June 2014, http://tinyurl.com/nneqyrk.
The ACLU analyzes data from a small sample of police departments to conclude that U.S. police tactics and equipment are overly militarized.

For More Information

American Civil Liberties Union, 125 Broad St., New York, NY 10004; 212-549-2500; http://tinyurl.com/kghjobr. The rights-advocacy organization has published a series of detailed reports alleging police misconduct nationally and in several states and cities.

Law Enforcement Against Prohibition, 8730 Georgia Ave., Silver Spring, MD 20910; 301-565-0807; http://tinyurl.com/3ndoyw. The U.S.-based international organization of retired police officers, prosecutors and judges advocates legalizing and regulating drug use.

National Fraternal Order of Police, 701 Marriott Dr., Nashville, TN 37214; 615-399-0900; http://tinyurl.com/omy84xb. The nation's major police union advocates for its members on all issues affecting police safety and benefits.

National Tactical Officers Association, http://tinyurl.com/lrognsr. The main organization for SWAT team members offers training in crisis negotiation, hostage rescue, sniper shooting and other situations in which SWAT teams are mobilized.

Police Executive Research Forum, 1120 Connecticut Ave., N.W., Washington, DC 20036; 202-466-7820; http://tinyurl.com/kytrfy9. The think tank and consultancy recommends policies designed to improve police-community relations.

Police Foundation, 1201 Connecticut Ave., N.W., Washington, DC 20036; 202-833-1460; http://tinyurl.com/q85srua. Affiliated with three universities in the United States and United Kingdom, the foundation researches new developments affecting police departments and proposes strategies to deal with them.

U.S. Department of Justice, Civil Rights Division, 950 Pennsylvania Ave., N.W., Washington, DC 20530; 202-514-6255; http://tinyurl.com/lu76yt8. The division's Special Litigation Section has conducted detailed investigations and negotiated settlements — all available on the section's website — on police misconduct in numerous cities.